THE
FAMILY ATLAS
OF THE
WORLD

THE
FAMILY ATLAS
OF THE
WORLD

GALLERY BOOKS
An Imprint of W. H. Smith Publishers Inc.
112 Madison Avenue
New York City 10016

This edition first published in the United States in 1989 by Gallery Books
An imprint of W. H. Smith Publishers Inc.
112 Madison Avenue
New York City 10016

By arrangement with Octopus Books Limited

ISBN 0-8317-3174-5

Printed in Hong Kong by Mandarin Offset

CONTENTS

GENERAL REFERENCE

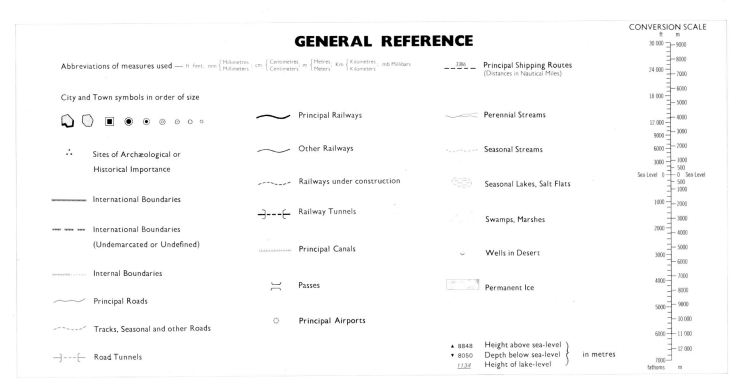

Abbreviations of measures used — ft Feet, mm {Millimetres / Millimeters} cm {Centimetres / Centimeters} m {Metres / Meters} Km {Kilometres / Kilometers} mb Millibars

City and Town symbols in order of size

∴ Sites of Archæological or Historical Importance

International Boundaries

International Boundaries (Undemarcated or Undefined)

Internal Boundaries

Principal Roads

Tracks, Seasonal and other Roads

Road Tunnels

Principal Railways

Other Railways

Railways under construction

Railway Tunnels

Principal Canals

Passes

Principal Airports

3386 Principal Shipping Routes (Distances in Nautical Miles)

Perennial Streams

Seasonal Streams

Seasonal Lakes, Salt Flats

Swamps, Marshes

Wells in Desert

Permanent Ice

▲ 8848 Height above sea-level
▼ 8050 Depth below sea-level } in metres
1134 Height of lake-level

CONVERSION SCALE
ft   m
30 000 — 9000
— 8000
24 000 — 7000
— 6000
18 000 — 5000
— 4000
12 000 — 3000
9000 — 2000
6000 — 1000
3000 — 500
Sea-Level 0 — 0 Sea-Level
— 500
1000 — 1000
— 2000
2000 — 3000
3000 — 5000
— 6000
4000 — 7000
— 8000
5000 — 9000
— 10 000
6000 — 11 000
— 12 000
7000
fathoms   m

THE WORLD
Physical
1:150 000 000

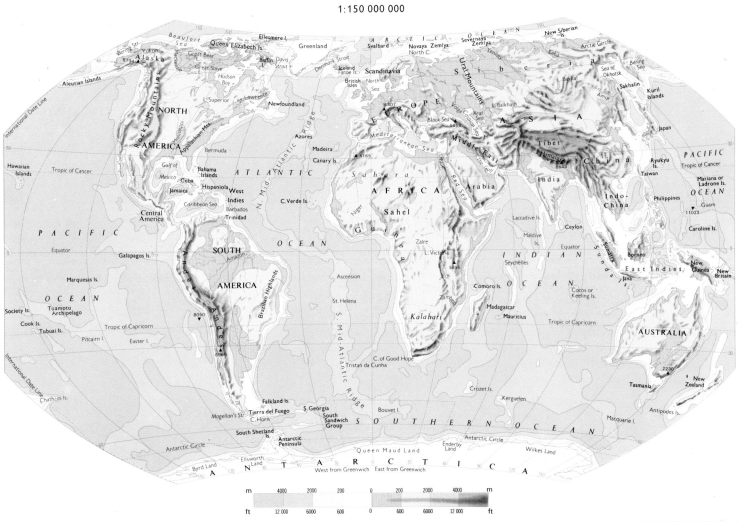

m 4000 2000 200 0 200 2000 4000 m
ft 12 000 6000 600 0 600 6000 12 000 ft

Projection: Hammer Equal Area

COPYRIGHT. GEORGE PHILIP & SON. LTD.

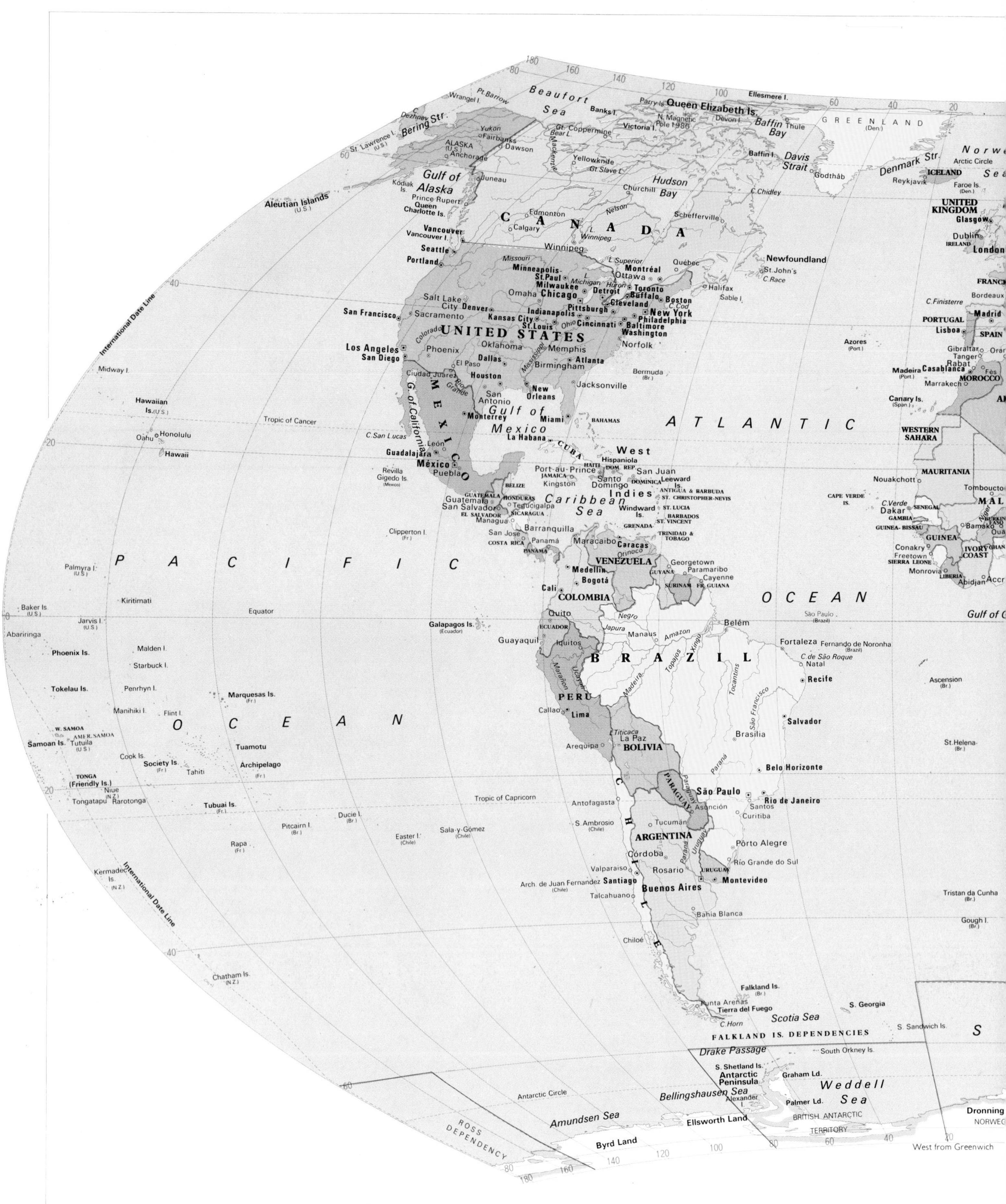

Beaufort Sea
Wrangel I.
Pt. Barrow
Dezhnev C.
Bering Str.
St. Lawrence I. (U.S.)
Yukon
Fairbanks
ALASKA (U.S.)
Anchorage
Dawson
Banks I.
Gt. Bear L.
Coppermine
Mackenzie
Victoria I.
Parry Is.
Queen Elizabeth Is.
N. Magnetic Pole 1980
Devon I.
Ellesmere I.
Baffin Bay
Thule
GREENLAND (Den.)
Baffin I.
Davis Strait
Godthåb
Denmark Str.
ICELAND
Reykjavik
Arctic Circle
Faroe Is. (Den.)
Yellowknife
Gt. Slave L.
Hudson Bay
Churchill
C. Chidley
Gulf of Alaska
Juneau
Kodiak Is.
Prince Rupert
Queen Charlotte Is.
Aleutian Islands (U.S.)
Edmonton
Calgary
Nelson
Schefferville
CANADA
L. Winnipeg
Winnipeg
Vancouver
Vancouver I.
Seattle
Portland
UNITED KINGDOM
Glasgow
Dublin
IRELAND
London
Newfoundland
St. John's
C. Race
Missouri
L. Superior
Montréal
Québec
Ottawa
Minneapolis-St. Paul
Milwaukee
Michigan
Huron
Toronto
Detroit
Buffalo
Omaha
Chicago
Boston
C. Cod
Halifax
Sable I.
Salt Lake City
Denver
Cleveland
Pittsburgh
New York
Philadelphia
Baltimore
Washington
San Francisco
Sacramento
Kansas City
Indianapolis
St. Louis
Ohio
Cincinnati
Colorado
UNITED STATES
Oklahoma
Memphis
Norfolk
Los Angeles
San Diego
Phoenix
Dallas
Atlanta
Birmingham
Mississippi
El Paso
Ciudad Juárez
Rio Grande
Houston
New Orleans
Jacksonville
Bermuda (Br.)
San Antonio
Gulf of Mexico
Miami
BAHAMAS
Monterrey
MEXICO
G. of California
C. San Lucas
La Habana
CUBA
León
Guadalajara
México
Puebla
West Indies
Hispaniola
HAITI
DOM. REP.
San Juan
Port-au-Prince
JAMAICA
Kingston
Santo Domingo
DOMINICA
Leeward Is.
ANTIGUA & BARBUDA
ST. CHRISTOPHER-NEVIS
BELIZE
Revilla Gigedo Is. (Mexico)
GUATEMALA
HONDURAS
Guatemala
Tegucigalpa
San Salvador
EL SALVADOR
NICARAGUA
Managua
Caribbean Sea
Windward Is.
ST. LUCIA
BARBADOS
ST. VINCENT
GRENADA
TRINIDAD & TOBAGO
Barranquilla
San José
COSTA RICA
Panamá
PANAMA
Maracaibo
Caracas
Orinoco
VENEZUELA
Georgetown
Paramaribo
Cayenne
GUYANA
SURINAM
FR. GUIANA
Clipperton I. (Fr.)
Medellín
Bogotá
Cali
COLOMBIA
Quito
ECUADOR
Galapagos Is. (Ecuador)
Guayaquil
Iquitos
Negro
Japura
Manaus
Amazon
Belém
Xingu
Tapajós
Fortaleza
Fernando de Noronha (Brazil)
C. de São Roque
Natal
Recife
BRAZIL
Madeira
Tocantins
São Francisco
Marañón
Ucayali
PERU
Callao
Lima
Salvador
Brasília
L. Titicaca
La Paz
BOLIVIA
Arequipa
Paraná
Belo Horizonte
PARAGUAY
Paraguay
São Paulo
Rio de Janeiro
Santos
Asunción
Curitiba
Antofagasta
Tucumán
S. Ambrosio (Chile)
ARGENTINA
Uruguay
Pôrto Alegre
Córdoba
Rio Grande do Sul
Valparaíso
Rosario
URUGUAY
Montevideo
Arch. de Juan Fernandez (Chile)
Santiago
Buenos Aires
Talcahuano
Bahía Blanca
CHILE
Chiloé
Falkland Is. (Br.)
Punta Arenas
Tierra del Fuego
C. Horn
Scotia Sea
S. Georgia
FALKLAND IS. DEPENDENCIES
S. Sandwich Is.
Drake Passage
South Orkney Is.
S. Shetland Is.
Antarctic Peninsula
Graham Ld.
Weddell Sea
Bellingshausen Sea
Alexander I.
Palmer Ld.
BRITISH ANTARCTIC TERRITORY
Amundsen Sea
Ellsworth Land
Byrd Land
Antarctic Circle
ROSS DEPENDENCY
Dronning
NORWEG
West from Greenwich
International Date Line
Midway I.
Hawaiian Is. (U.S.)
Tropic of Cancer
Oahu
Honolulu
Hawaii
PACIFIC OCEAN
Palmyra I. (U.S.)
Kiritimati
Baker Is. (U.S.)
Jarvis I. (U.S.)
Equator
Abariringa
Phoenix Is.
Malden I.
Starbuck I.
Tokelau Is.
Penrhyn I.
Marquesas Is. (Fr.)
Manihiki I.
Flint I.
W. SAMOA
AMER. SAMOA
Samoan Is.
Tutuila (U.S.)
Cook Is.
Society Is. (Fr.)
Tahiti
Tuamotu Archipelago (Fr.)
TONGA (Friendly Is.)
Niue (N.Z.)
Tongatapu
Rarotonga
Tubuai Is. (Fr.)
Tropic of Capricorn
Pitcairn I. (Br.)
Ducie I. (Br.)
Easter I. (Chile)
Sala-y-Gómez (Chile)
Rapa (Fr.)
Kermadec Is. (N.Z.)
Chatham Is. (N.Z.)
ATLANTIC OCEAN
Azores (Port.)
Madeira (Port.)
Canary Is. (Span.)
Norwegian Sea
FRANCE
Bordeaux
C. Finisterre
PORTUGAL
Lisboa
Madrid
SPAIN
Gibraltar
Tanger
Rabat
Casablanca
Fès
MOROCCO
Marrakech
WESTERN SAHARA
MAURITANIA
Nouakchott
Tombouctou
CAPE VERDE IS.
C. Verde
Dakar
SENEGAL
GAMBIA
GUINEA-BISSAU
GUINEA
Bamako
Conakry
Freetown
SIERRA LEONE
IVORY COAST
Monrovia
LIBERIA
Abidjan
Gulf of Guinea
São Paulo (Brazil)
Ascension (Br.)
St. Helena (Br.)
Tristan da Cunha (Br.)
Gough I. (Br.)

Projection: *Hammer Equal Area*

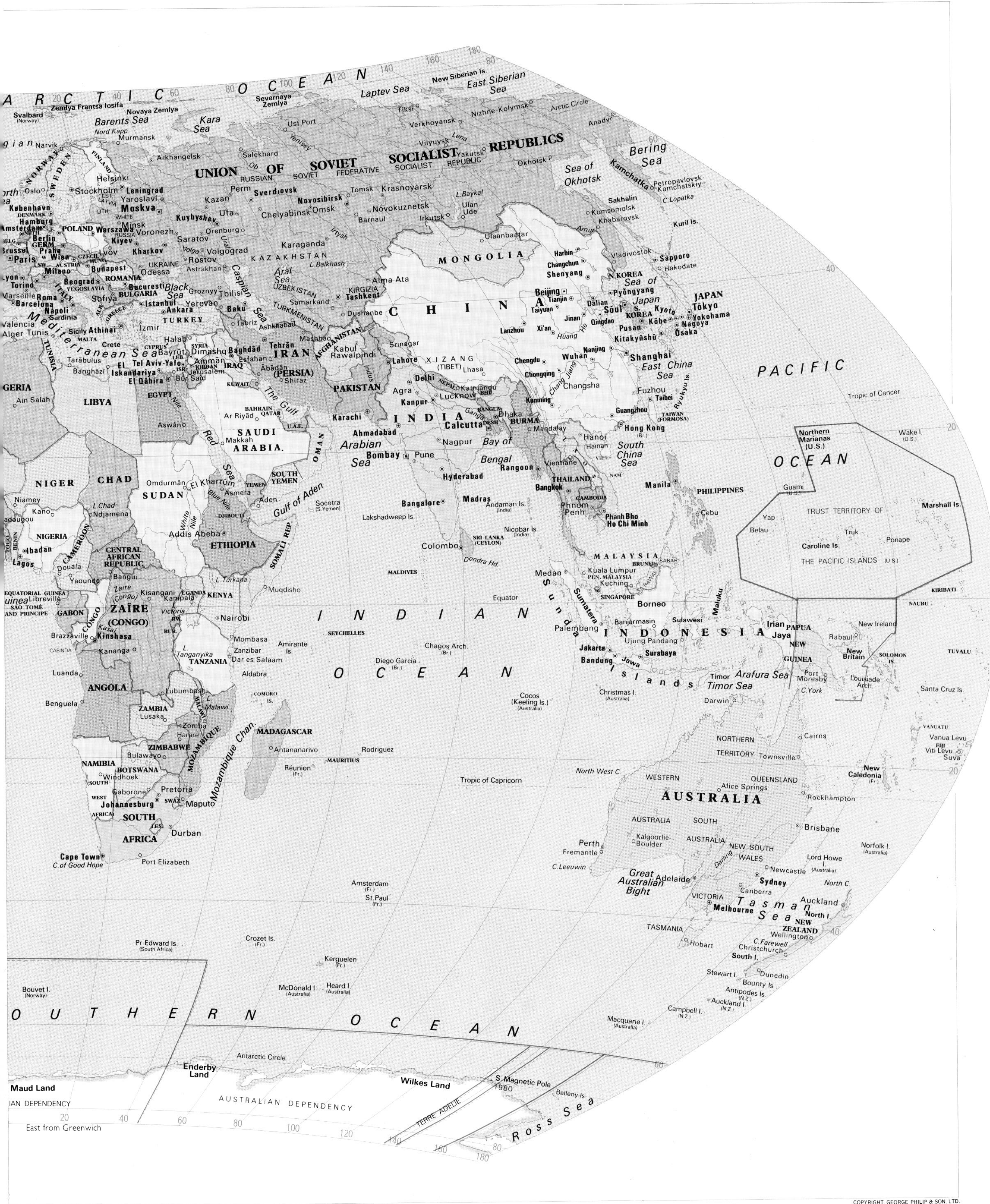

A R C T I C   O C E A N

Svalbard
(Norway)
Zemlya Frantsa Iosifa   Novaya Zemlya
Barents Sea   Kara Sea   Severnaya Zemlya   New Siberian Is.   East Siberian Sea   *Laptev Sea*
Nord Kapp   Ust Port   Tiksi   Verkhoyansk   Nizhne-Kolymsk   Arctic Circle   Anadyr
Narvik   Murmansk   Yenisey   Lena   Yakutsk

UNION   OF   SOVIET   SOCIALIST   FEDERATIVE   SOCIALIST   REPUBLICS
Arkhangelsk   Salekhard   RUSSIAN   SOVIET   REPUBLIC   Yakutsk   Okhotsk   *Bering Sea*   Kamchatka
NORWAY   SWEDEN   FINLAND   Helsinki   Vilyuysk   *Sea of Okhotsk*   Petropavlovsk-Kamchatskiy
Oslo   Stockholm   Leningrad   Perm   Sverdlovsk   Tomsk   Krasnoyarsk   Ulan Ude   S. L.Lopatka
Kobenhavn   DENMARK   Moskva   Kazan   Yaroslavl   Novosibirsk   Barnaul   L.Baykal   Irkutsk   Komsomolsk   Sakhalin   Kuril Is.
Hamburg   POLAND   Warszawa   Minsk   Kuybyshev   Ufa   Chelyabinsk Omsk   Novokuznetsk   Irtysh   Ulaanbaatar   Amur   Khabarovsk
Amsterdam   GERM.   Berlin   Praha   Voronezh   Saratov   KAZAKHSTAN   Karaganda   MONGOLIA   Harbin   Vladivostok   Sapporo
Brussel   Paris   Wien   Budapest   UKRAINE   Rostov   Volgograd   L.Balkhash   Alma Ata   Changchun   N.KOREA   Hakodate
Lyon   Torino   Milano   AUSTRIA   Beograd   Bucuresti   Odessa   Astrakhan   Aral Sea   KIRGIZIA   Shenyang   Pyongyang   *Sea of Japan*
Marseille   Roma   ITALY   YUGOSLAVIA   ROMANIA   *Black Sea*   Groznyy   UZBEKISTAN   Tashkent   Samarkand   Beijing   Tianjin   SEOUL   S.KOREA   Tokyo
Barcelona   Napoli   Sardinia   BULGARIA   Istanbul   Yerevan   Baku   TURKMENISTAN   Dushanbe   Taiyuan   Jinan   Qingdao   Pusan   Kobe   Yokohama
Valencia   Sicily Athinai   GREECE   Sofiya   Ankara   Tbilisi   Ashkhabad   CHINA   Lanzhou   Xi'an   Huang   Kitakyushu   Osaka
Alger Tunis   Mediterranean Sea   TURKEY   Izmir   Tabriz   Mashhad   AFGHANISTAN   XIZANG   Chengdu   JAPAN
MALTA   Crete   CYPRUS   Halab   Tehran   Kabul   Srinagar   (TIBET)   Lhasa   Chongqing   Wuhan   Nanjing   PACIFIC
TUNISIA   Tarabulus   SYRIA   Dimashq   Baghdad   Esfahan   Rawalpindi   Lahore   Changsha   Shanghai
Banghazi   Bayrut   Tel Aviv-Yafo   IRAQ   IRAN   Delhi   NEPAL Kathmandu   *Chang Jiang*   *East China Sea*
LIBYA   El Iskandariya   Jerusalem   Abadan   (PERSIA)   Agra   BHU.   Kanpur   Lucknow   BANGLA.   Fuzhou   OCEAN
EGYPT   El Qahira   JORDAN   Shiraz   PAKISTAN   Ganga   Dhaka   Kunming   Taibei   *Tropic of Cancer*
ALGERIA   Ain Salah   Nile   KUWAIT   Karachi   Ahmadabad   INDIA   Calcutta   BURMA   Guangzhou   TAIWAN   (FORMOSA)
Aswan   BAHRAIN   QATAR   Nagpur   Bombay   Pune   Mandalay   Hanoi   Hong Kong   Northern   Wake I.
NIGER   CHAD   Omdurman   El Khartum   U.A.E.   SAUDI   Red   Hyderabad   *Bay of*   Rangoon   Hainan   *South*   Marianas   (U.S.)
Niamey   Kano   Ndjamena   SUDAN   Makkah   ARABIA   Sea   OMAN   *Arabian*   Madras   *Bengal*   THAILAND   *China Sea*   20
Ouagadougou   NIGERIA   Bangalore   Andaman Is.   Bangkok   Manila   PHILIPPINES   Guam (U.S.)   OCEAN
BENIN   Ibadan   CENTRAL   Asmera   YEMEN   Aden   *Gulf of Aden*   Socotra   (Indian)   CAMBODIA   Cebu   TRUST TERRITORY OF
Lagos   CAMEROON   AFRICAN   Addis Abeba   (S.Yemen)   DJIBOUTI   Lakshadweep Is.   SRI LANKA   Nicobar Is.   Phnom Penh   Yap
EQUATORIAL GUINEA   REPUBLIC   ETHIOPIA   SOMALI REP.   Colombo   (CEYLON)   (India)   Phanh Bho   Belau   THE PACIFIC ISLANDS (U.S.)
SAO TOME   GABON   Bangui   UGANDA   KENYA   MALDIVES   *Dondra Hd.*   Ho Chi Minh   MALAYSIA   Caroline Is.   Truk   Ponape   KIRIBATI
AND PRINCIPE   Kisangani   Kampala   L.Turkana   Medan   Kuala Lumpur   SABAH   NAURU
ZAIRE   Victoria   Nairobi   Equator   PEN. MALAYSIA   BRUNEI   Borneo
Libreville   (CONGO)   RW.   BUR.   Kuching   SINGAPORE   Sulawesi   Maluku   PAPUA
Brazzaville   CABINDA   Kinshasa   Kananga   Mombasa   SEYCHELLES   Sumatera   Banjarmasin   Irian   NEW   New Ireland
CONGO   Kasai   Zanzibar   Amirante   Chagos Arch.   INDONESIA   Jaya   GUINEA   Rabaul
Luanda   Kisangani   TANZANIA   Dar es Salaam   Is.   (Br.)   Palembang   Jakarta   Surabaya   Ujung Pandang   Port   New   Louisiade
ANGOLA   L.Tanganyika   Aldabra   Diego Garcia   (Br.)   Bandung   Jawa   Moresby   Britain   Arch.   TUVALU
Benguela   COMORO   *Islands*   C.York   SOLOMON Is.
ZAMBIA   Lilongwe   Timor   *Arafura Sea*   Santa Cruz Is.
NAMIBIA   Lubumbashi   L.Malawi   MADAGASCAR   Antananarivo   Rodriguez   Christmas I.   *Timor Sea*   Darwin   VANUATU
Lusaka   Zomba   Cocos   (Australia)   Vanua Levu
ZIMBABWE   MOZAMBIQUE   MAURITIUS   (Keeling) Is.   NORTHERN   Cairns   FIJI   Viti Levu
BOTSWANA   Harare   Reunion   (Australia)   TERRITORY   Townsville   New   Suva
Windhoek   Bulawayo   (Fr.)   *Tropic of Capricorn*   North West C.   WESTERN   QUEENSLAND   Caledonia   20
SOUTH   Gaborone   SWAZI.   Pretoria   Alice Springs   Rockhampton   (Fr.)
Johannesburg   AFRICA   Maputo   AUSTRALIA   AUSTRALIA   SOUTH   Brisbane   Norfolk I.
WEST   SOUTH   LES.   Durban   Amsterdam   St.Paul   Perth   Kalgoorlie-Boulder   AUSTRALIA   NEW SOUTH   (Australia)
Cape Town   AFRICA   (Fr.)   (Fr.)   Fremantle   *Great*   Adelaide   WALES   Lord Howe
C.of Good Hope   Port Elizabeth   *Australian*   C.Leeuwin   Canberra   Newcastle   (Australia)
Pr.Edward Is.   Crozet Is.   *Bight*   VICTORIA   Sydney   North C.
(South Africa)   (Fr.)   Kerguelen   TASMAN   Melbourne   *Tasman*   Auckland   40
McDonald I.   (Fr.)   SEA   NEW   North I.
Bouvet I.   Heard I.   Wellington   ZEALAND
(Norway)   (Australia)   TASMANIA   C.Farewell
S O U T H E R N   O C E A N   Hobart   Christchurch
South I.   Dunedin
Antarctic Circle   Stewart I.   Bounty Is.
Enderby   Antipodes Is.   (N.Z.)
Land   Macquarie I.   Campbell I.   Auckland Is.   (N.Z.)
Maud Land   *Wilkes Land*   S.Magnetic Pole   (Australia)   (N.Z.)
IAN DEPENDENCY   AUSTRALIAN DEPENDENCY   1980   Balleny Is.
East from Greenwich   20   40   60   80   100   120   TERRE ADELIE   140   160   180   *Ross Sea*   80

1:20 000 000

100 0 100 200 300 400 500 miles
100 0 200 400 600 800 km

CASPIAN SEA
−28

Ural Mountains
Obshchsi
Volga Uplands
Caucasus
5663
5165

BLACK SEA
2211
Sea of Azov
Crimea
Anatolia
3770
Cyprus 1951

Central Russian Uplands
Ukraine
Danube
Don

White Sea
Kola Peninsula
Kanin Peninsula

Russian Plain

Finland
Pripyat (Pripet) Marshes
Carpathians
2655
Balkans
Rhodope
Peninsula
7766
Aegean Sea

North Cape
Lapland
Scandinavia
Gulf of Bothnia

Gulf of Finland
Gulf of Riga
Gotland

BALTIC SEA
NORTH

Transylvanian Alps
Wallachia
Plain of Hungary
Tisza
Balkan Peninsula
Pindus
Morea
5121
C. Matapan
Crete

2123
2469

Vesterålen
Lofoten

NORWEGIAN SEA
3734

Öland

Sudetes
Bohemian For.
Erz Geb.
Harz 1142

Kattegat
Skagerrak
Jutland

Elbe
Weser

Dinaric Alps
ADRIATIC SEA
Str. of Otranto
Ionian Is.
Ionian Sea

Apennines
Gran Sasso
2914
Tyrrhenian Sea
Sicily
Etna 3263
Str. of Messina
C. Bon
Malta

Dogger Bank
DOGGER BANK
Heligoland
GERMAN BIGHT
Netherlands
Rhine

Black For.
Vosges
Jura
Alps
4807
Po
Ligurian Sea
Corsica
Str. of Bonifacio
Sardinia
C. Blanco

MEDITERRANEAN SEA

Iceland
2119
ICELAND

British Isles
Great Britain
1085
Ireland

Irish Sea
English Channel
Brittany
Loire

Central Massif
1886
Cévennes
Rhône
G. of Lions
Maritime Alps
Plateau of the Shotts

Bay of Biscay
Pyrenees
3404
Cantabrian Mts.
Old Castile
New Castile
Iberian Peninsula
Sierra Morena
Andalusia
Sa. Nevada
3478
Str. of Gibraltar
Rif
Maritime Atlas

ATLANTIC OCEAN

Finisterre
C. Finisterre
C. St. Vincent
C. Trafalgar
C. Spartel

m ft
12 000 4000
6000 2000
3000 1000
1200 400
600 200
0
200 600
2000 6000
4000 12 000
ft m

Projection : Bonne   West from Greenwich 0 East from Greenwich

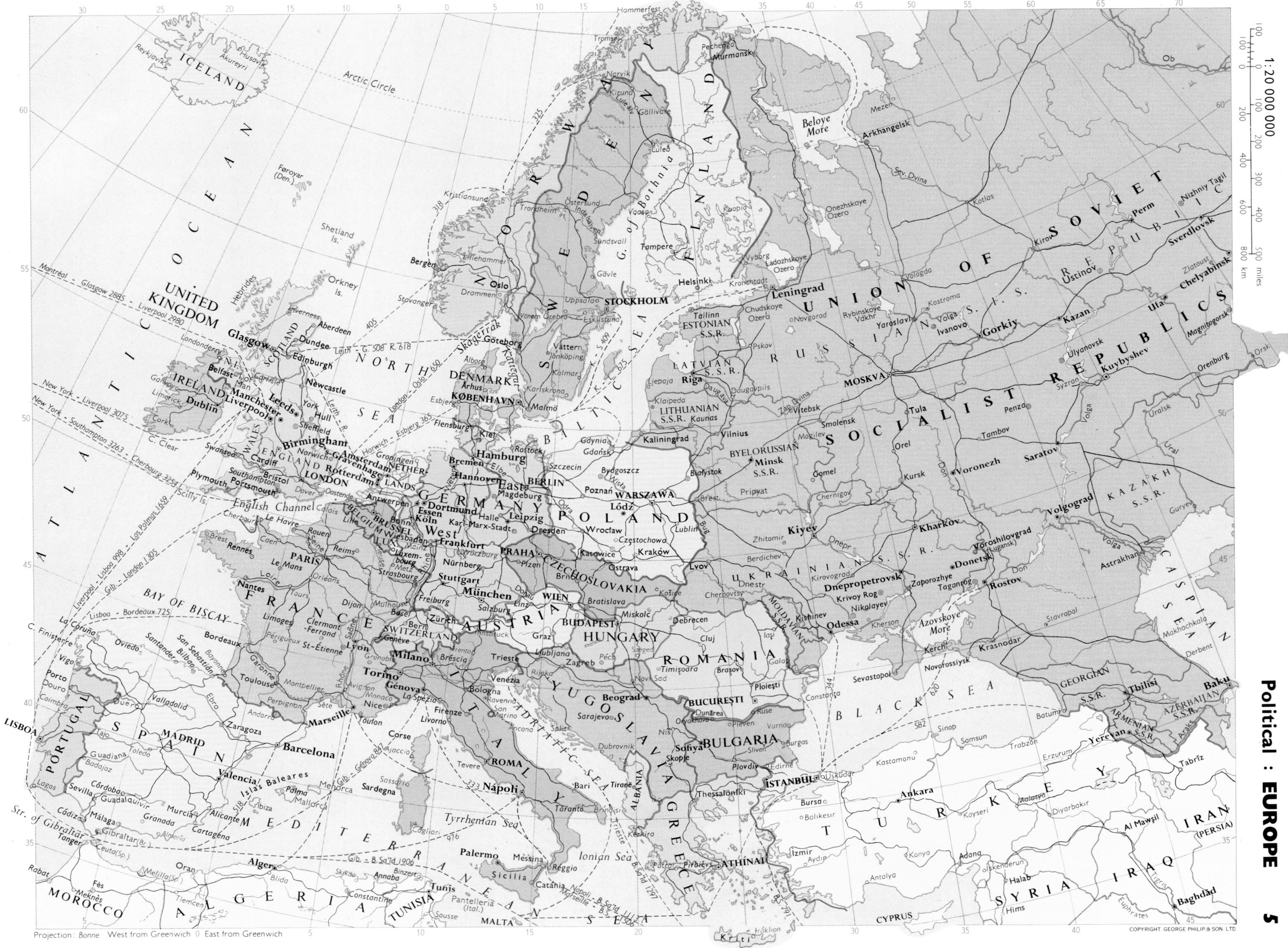
1:20 000 000
miles
km
UNION OF SOVIET SOCIALIST REPUBLICS
RUSSIAN S.F.S.R.
UKRAINIAN S.S.R.
BYELORUSSIAN S.S.R.
ESTONIAN S.S.R.
LATVIAN S.S.R.
LITHUANIAN S.S.R.
MOLDAVIAN S.S.R.
GEORGIAN S.S.R.
ARMENIAN S.S.R.
AZERBAIJAN S.S.R.
KAZAKH S.S.R.
FINLAND
SWEDEN
NORWAY
DENMARK
UNITED KINGDOM
IRELAND
ICELAND
FRANCE
SPAIN
PORTUGAL
ITALY
GERMANY
POLAND
CZECHOSLOVAKIA
AUSTRIA
SWITZERLAND
HUNGARY
ROMANIA
BULGARIA
YUGOSLAVIA
GREECE
ALBANIA
TURKEY
SYRIA
IRAQ
IRAN (PERSIA)
CYPRUS
ALGERIA
TUNISIA
MOROCCO
ATLANTIC OCEAN
NORTH SEA
BALTIC SEA
BLACK SEA
CASPIAN SEA
MEDITERRANEAN SEA
ADRIATIC SEA
BAY OF BISCAY
English Channel
Tyrrhenian Sea
Ionian Sea
Arctic Circle
Projection: Bonne West from Greenwich 0 East from Greenwich

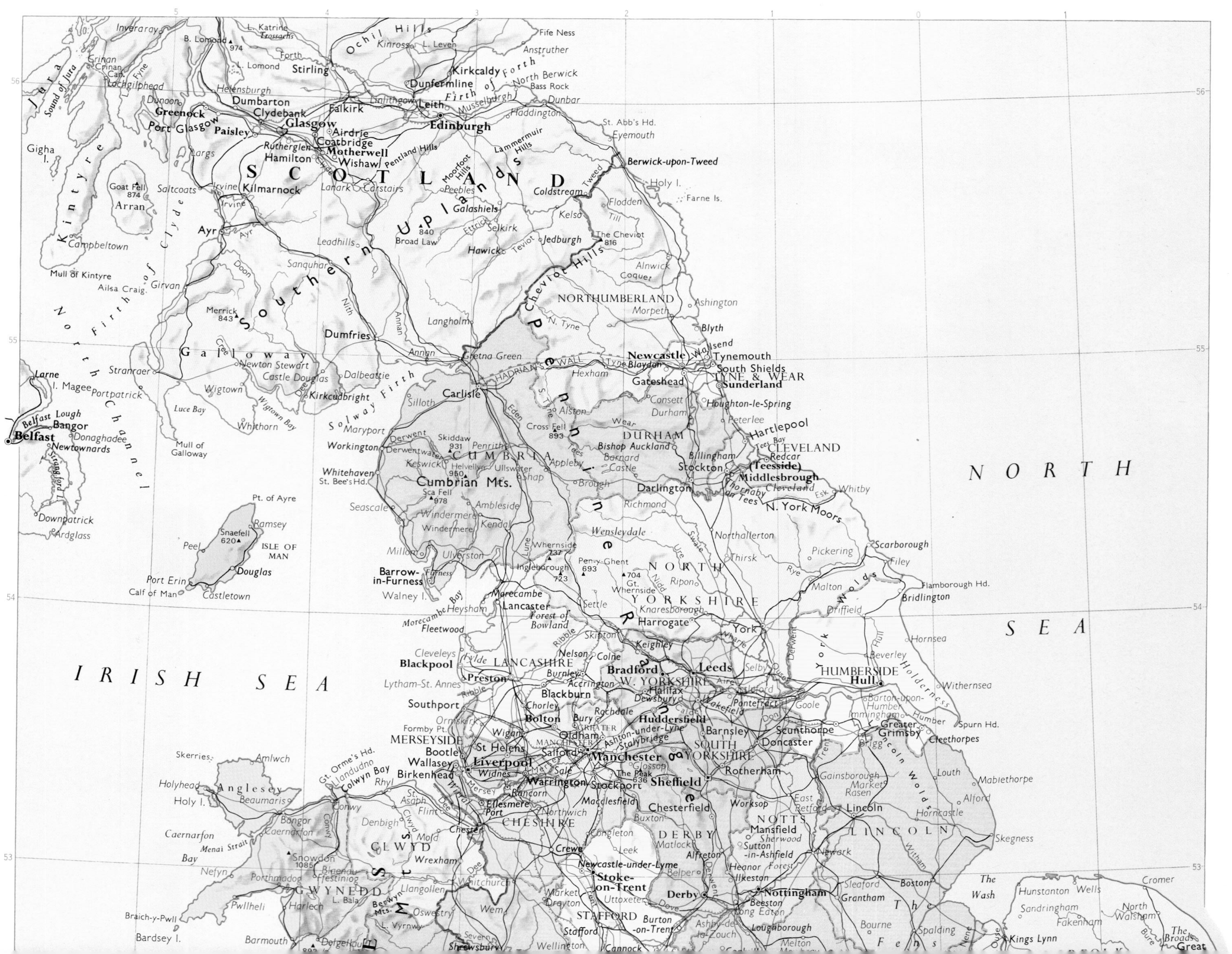
NORTH SEA
IRISH SEA
North Channel
SCOTLAND
Southern Uplands
NORTHUMBERLAND
DURHAM
CLEVELAND
TYNE & WEAR
CUMBRIA
Cumbrian Mts.
Pennines
NORTH YORKSHIRE
W. YORKSHIRE
SOUTH YORKSHIRE
HUMBERSIDE
LANCASHIRE
MERSEYSIDE
CHESHIRE
DERBY
NOTTS
LINCOLN
STAFFORD
CLWYD
GWYNEDD
ISLE OF MAN
Cheviot Hills
N. York Moors
York Wolds
Lincoln Wolds
The Wash
Solway Firth
Firth of Forth
Firth of Clyde
Galloway
Kintyre
Arran
Anglesey
Edinburgh
Glasgow
Paisley
Greenock
Dumbarton
Stirling
Falkirk
Kirkcaldy
Dunfermline
Motherwell
Hamilton
Kilmarnock
Ayr
Dumfries
Berwick-upon-Tweed
Carlisle
Newcastle
Gateshead
Tynemouth
South Shields
Sunderland
Hartlepool
Middlesbrough (Teesside)
Stockton
Darlington
Whitby
Scarborough
Bridlington
York
Harrogate
Leeds
Bradford
Halifax
Huddersfield
Hull
Grimsby
Scunthorpe
Doncaster
Barnsley
Sheffield
Rotherham
Manchester
Oldham
Bolton
Wigan
Stockport
Liverpool
Birkenhead
Wallasey
Bootle
St Helens
Warrington
Preston
Blackpool
Blackburn
Lancaster
Barrow-in-Furness
Whitehaven
Workington
Chester
Crewe
Wrexham
Stoke-on-Trent
Derby
Nottingham
Mansfield
Chesterfield
Lincoln
Boston
Douglas
Belfast
Bangor
Larne
Holyhead
Snowdon 1085
Scafell 978
Helvellyn 950
Cross Fell 893
The Cheviot 816
Snaefell 620

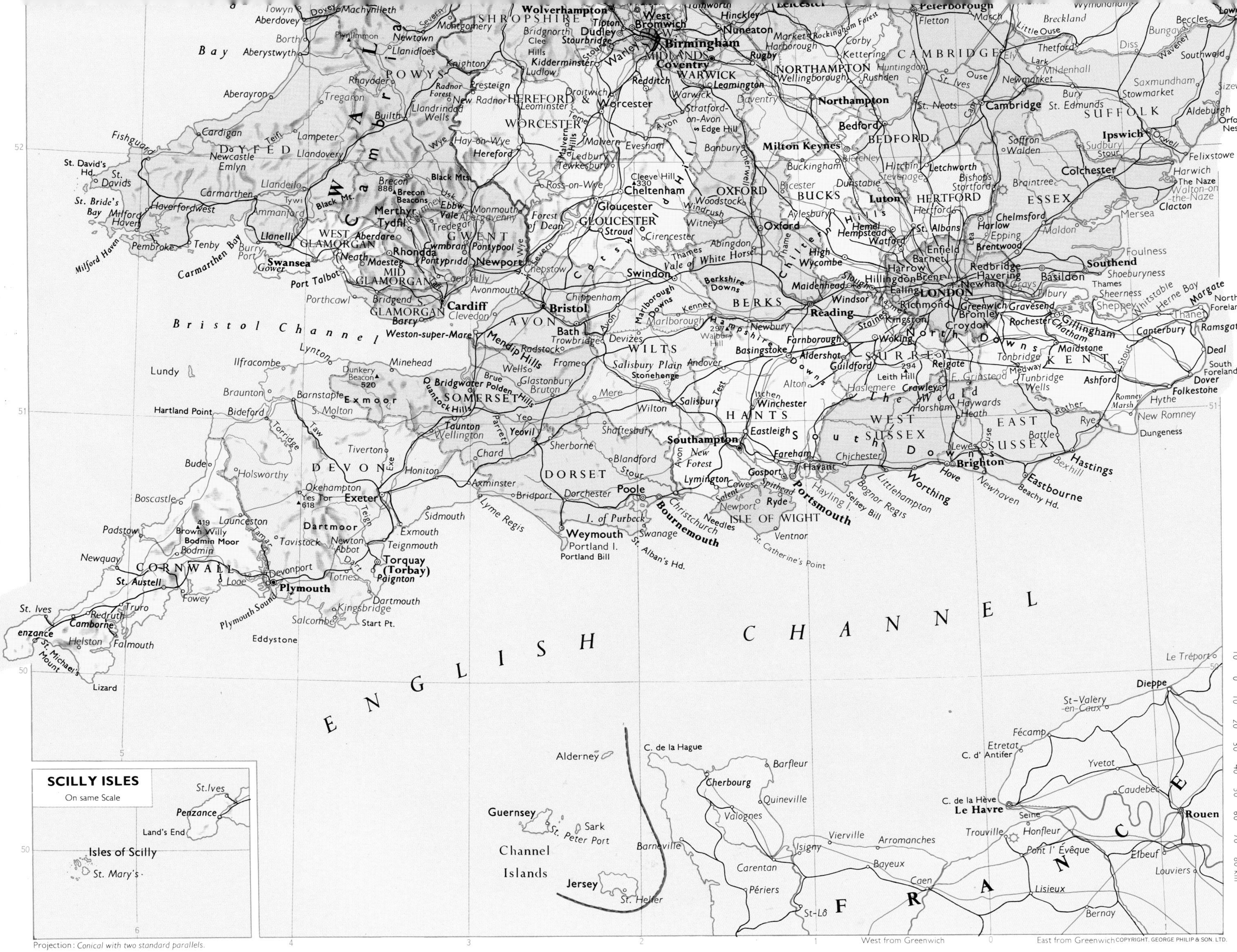

1 : 2 000 000

10 0 10 20 30 40 50 miles
10 0 10 20 30 40 50 60 70 80 km

Projection: Conical with two standard parallels.

East from Greenwich   COPYRIGHT GEORGE PHILIP & SON, LTD.

West from Greenwich

E N G L I S H   C H A N N E L

F R A N C E

SCILLY ISLES
On same Scale

Isles of Scilly
St. Mary's

SUFFOLK
ESSEX
KENT
EAST SUSSEX
WEST SUSSEX
CAMBRIDGE
BEDFORD
HERTFORD
BUCKS
OXFORD
BERKS
HANTS
WILTS
DORSET
SOMERSET
DEVON
CORNWALL
AVON
GWENT
GLAMORGAN
MID GLAMORGAN
WEST GLAMORGAN
SOUTH GLAMORGAN
DYFED
POWYS
SHROPSHIRE
WORCESTER
HEREFORD
WARWICK
NORTHAMPTON
ISLE OF WIGHT

Lowestoft
Ipswich
Colchester
Southend
Cambridge
Bedford
Northampton
Milton Keynes
Luton
Reading
LONDON
Oxford
Birmingham
Coventry
West Bromwich
Wolverhampton
Dudley
Worcester
Gloucester
Cheltenham
Bristol
Bath
Cardiff
Newport
Swansea
Llanelli
Merthyr Tydfil
Rhondda
Brighton
Worthing
Hove
Eastbourne
Hastings
Portsmouth
Southampton
Winchester
Bournemouth
Poole
Weymouth
Dorchester
Exeter
Plymouth
Torquay (Torbay)
Paignton
Penzance
Camborne
Redruth
Truro
St. Austell
Falmouth

Dieppe
Rouen
Le Havre
Cherbourg
Guernsey
Jersey
Channel Islands
Alderney
Sark
St. Peter Port
St. Helier

Bristol Channel
Cardigan Bay
Lundy
Hartland Point
Land's End
St. Ives

1:2 000 000

10 0 10 20 30 40 50 miles
10 0 10 20 30 40 50 60 70 80 km

ORKNEY IS.
On same scale

SHETLAND IS.
On same scale

Projection: Conical with two standard parallels.

West from Greenwich

COPYRIGHT, GEORGE PHILIP & SON, LTD.

1:2 000 000

Towns underlined in Northern Ireland give their
names to the Districts in which they stand
The remaining Districts are:—

1	Fermanagh	5	Castlereagh
2	Moyle	6	Ards
3	Newtownabbey	7	Down
4	North Down	8	Newry & Mourne

Projection: Conical with two standard parallels.   West from Greenwich   COPYRIGHT. GEORGE PHILIP & SON. LTD.

1 : 4 000 000

The DISTRICTS of Northern Ireland have been numbered and can be identified by reference to this table.

1	Londonderry	14	Craigavon
2	Limavady	15	Armagh
3	Coleraine	16	Newry & Mourne
4	Ballymoney	17	Banbridge
5	Moyle	18	Down
6	Larne	19	Lisburn
7	Ballymena	20	Antrim
8	Magherafelt	21	Newtownabbey
9	Cookstown	22	Carrickfergus
10	Strabane	23	North Down
11	Omagh	24	Ards
12	Fermanagh	25	Castlereagh
13	Dungannon	26	Belfast

ORKNEY — Kirkwall — HIGHLAND

SHETLAND — Lerwick

Metropolitan Counties :- On 1st April 1986 the administrative functions of the six metropolitan counties such as planning, education, transportation, libraries and social services were transferred to the city and town boroughs and various non-elected residuary bodies.

WESTERN ISLES · Stornoway

HIGHLAND · Inverness · GRAMPIAN · Aberdeen

SCOTLAND

TAYSIDE · Dundee

FIFE · Glenrothes

CENTRAL · Stirling · Edinburgh · LOTHIAN · Glasgow

STRATHCLYDE

BORDERS · Newtown St. Boswells

DUMFRIES AND GALLOWAY · Dumfries · Carlisle · NORTHUMBERLAND · Newcastle · TYNE AND WEAR · Durham

CUMBRIA · DURHAM · CLEVELAND · Middlesbrough · Northallerton

ATLANTIC OCEAN

NORTH SEA

ISLE OF MAN · Douglas

NORTH YORKSHIRE

DONEGAL · Lifford · Londonderry · Antrim · NORTHERN IRELAND · Tyrone · Fermanagh · Belfast · Down · Armagh

Sligo · SLIGO · LEITRIM · Carrick-on-Shannon · MONAGHAN · Monaghan · Cavan · CAVAN · Dundalk · LOUTH

MAYO · Castlebar · ROSCOMMON · Roscommon · LONGFORD · Longford · An Uaimh (Navan) · MEATH · WESTMEATH · Mullingar

IRISH SEA

LANCASHIRE · Preston · WEST YORKSHIRE · Wakefield · Barnsley · SOUTH YORKSHIRE

HUMBERSIDE · Hull

GREATER MANCHESTER · Manchester · MERSEYSIDE · Liverpool · Chester · CHESHIRE · DERBYSHIRE · NOTTINGHAMSHIRE · Nottingham · Matlock · Lincoln · LINCOLNSHIRE · ENGLAND

GALWAY · Galway · OFFALY · Tullamore · DUBLIN · Dublin · KILDARE · Naas

IRELAND · Port Laoise · LAOIS · Carlow · CARLOW · WICKLOW · Wicklow

CLARE · Ennis · TIPPERARY · Kilkenny · KILKENNY · Clonmel · WEXFORD · Wexford

Caernarfon · Mold · CLWYD · GWYNEDD · Stafford · STAFFORDSHIRE · Shrewsbury · SHROPSHIRE · WEST MIDLANDS · Birmingham · Warwick · WARWICKSHIRE · Leicester · LEICESTERSHIRE · NORTHAMPTONSHIRE · Northampton · CAMBRIDGESHIRE · Cambridge · NORFOLK · Norwich · SUFFOLK · Ipswich

Limerick · LIMERICK · Tralee · KERRY

WALES · POWYS · Llandrindod Wells · HEREFORD AND WORCESTER · Worcester · Gloucester · GLOUCESTERSHIRE · Oxford · OXFORDSHIRE · Bedford · BEDFORDSHIRE · BUCKINGHAMSHIRE · Aylesbury · Hertford · HERTFORDSHIRE · ESSEX · Chelmsford

CORK · Cork · DYFED · Carmarthen · WEST GLAMORGAN · Swansea · MID GLAMORGAN · GWENT · Cwmbran · Cardiff · SOUTH GLAMORGAN · Bristol · AVON · WILTSHIRE · Trowbridge · BERKSHIRE · Reading · GREATER LONDON · Kingston · Maidstone · SURREY · KENT

St. George's Channel · WATERFORD · Waterford

CELTIC SEA

SOMERSET · Taunton · HAMPSHIRE · Winchester · WEST SUSSEX · EAST SUSSEX · Lewes · Chichester

DEVON · Exeter · DORSET · Dorchester · Newport · ISLE OF WIGHT

CORNWALL · Truro

ENGLISH CHANNEL · FRANCE

○ Norwich — Administrative headquarters
MERSEYSIDE — Metropolitan counties
Antrim — Former Northern Ireland counties

Projection: Conical with two standard parallels

West from Greenwich 0 East from Greenwich
COPYRIGHT. GEORGE. PHILIP & SON. LTD.

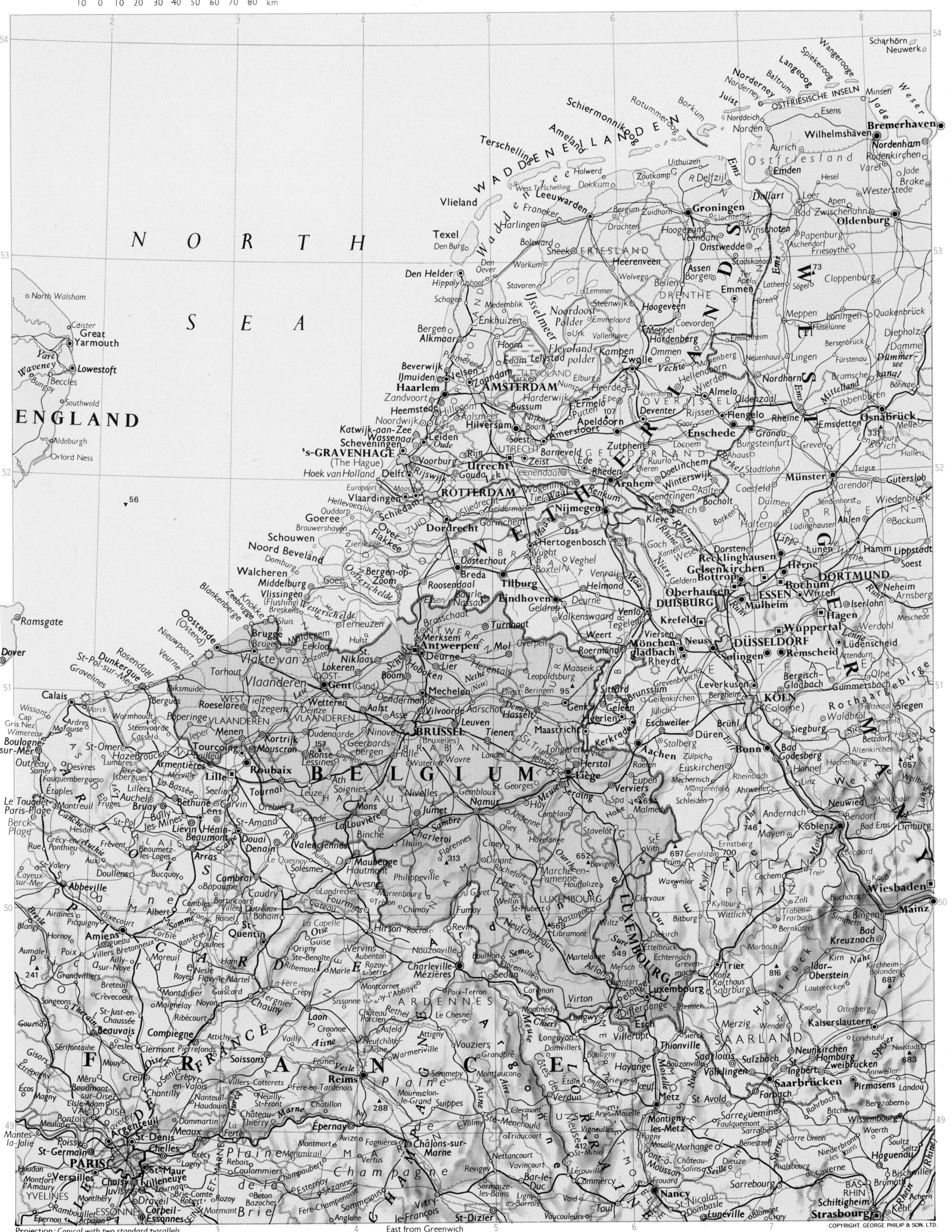
1:2 500 000
10 0 10 20 30 40 50 miles
10 0 10 20 30 40 50 60 70 80 km
NORTH SEA
ENGLAND
NETHERLANDS
BELGIUM
LUXEMBOURG
FRANCE
GERMANY
Projection: Conical with two standard parallels
East from Greenwich

1 : 5 000 000

Scale: 50 — 0 — 50 — 100 miles
50 — 0 — 50 — 100 — 150 km

FRENCH DEPARTMENTS

Abbr.	No.	Department
A.	01	Ain
Ai.	02	Aisne
Al.	03	Allier
A.H.P.	04	Alpes-de-Haute-Provence
H.A.	05	Hautes-Alpes
A.M.	06	Alpes-Maritimes
Ard.	07	Ardèche
Ar.	08	Ardennes
Ari.	09	Ariège
Aud.	10	Aube
Aud.	11	Aude
Av.	12	Aveyron
B.Rh.	13	Bouches-du-Rhône
C.	14	Calvados
Ca.	15	Cantal
Che.	16	Charente
Ch.M.	17	Charente-Maritime
Che.	18	Cher
Co.	19	Corrèze
C.(i)	20	Corse (i) Haute-Corse
C.(ii)	20	Corse (ii) Corse du Sud
C.O.	21	Côte-d'Or
C.N.	22	Côtes-du-Nord
Cr.	23	Creuse
D.	24	Dordogne
Do.	25	Doubs
Dr.	26	Drôme
E.	27	Eure
E.L.	28	Eure-et-Loir
F.	29	Finistère
G.	30	Gard
H.G.	31	Haute-Garonne
Ge.	32	Gers
Gi.	33	Gironde
H.	34	Hérault
I.V.	35	Ille-et-Vilaine
I.	36	Indre
I.L.	37	Indre-et-Loire
Is.	38	Isère
J.	39	Jura
L.	40	Landes
L.C.	41	Loir-et-Cher
Loi.	42	Loire
H.Loi.	43	Haute-Loire
L.A.	44	Loire-Atlantique
Loi.	45	Loiret
L.C.	46	Lot
L.G.	47	Lot-et-Garonne
Lo.	48	Lozère
M.L.	49	Maine-et-Loire
Ma.	50	Manche
M.	51	Marne
H.M.	52	Haute-Marne
May.	53	Mayenne
M.M.	54	Meurthe-et-Moselle
Me.	55	Meuse
Mo.	56	Morbihan
Mos.	57	Moselle
N.	58	Nièvre
N.	59	Nord
O.	60	Oise
Or.	61	Orne
P.C.	62	Pas-de-Calais
P.D.	63	Puy-de-Dôme
B.P.	64	Pyrénées-Atlantiques
H.P.	65	Hautes-Pyrénées
P.O.	66	Pyrénées-Orientales
B.Rh.	67	Bas-Rhin
H.Rh.	68	Haut-Rhin
Rh.	69	Rhône
H.S.	70	Haute-Saône
S.L.	71	Saône-et-Loire
Sa.	72	Sarthe
Sa.	73	Savoie
H.Sa.	74	Haute-Savoie
Pa.	75	Paris
S.Me.	76	Seine-Maritime
S.M.	77	Seine-et-Marne
Yv.	78	Yvelines
D.S.	79	Deux-Sèvres
So.	80	Somme
T.	81	Tarn
T.G.	82	Tarn-et-Garonne
Va.	83	Var
Va.	84	Vaucluse
Ve.	85	Vendée
Vi.	86	Vienne
H.V.	87	Haute-Vienne
Vo.	88	Vosges
Y.	89	Yonne
B.	90	Belfort
E.	91	Essonne
H.Se.	92	Hauts-de-Seine
S.S.D.	93	Seine-St-Denis
V.M.	94	Val-de-Marne
V.O.	95	Val-d'Oise

CORSICA
On same scale

Corse — Calvi — Bastia — Mte. Cinto 2710 — Haute-Corse — Mte. Rotondo 2625 — Corte — Ajaccio — Corse du Sud — Porto Vecchio — Bonifacio

Projection: Conical with two standard parallels

West from Greenwich — East from Greenwich

MEDITERRANEAN SEA

BAY OF BISCAY

ENGLISH CHANNEL

1:5 000 000

50   0   50   100 miles

50   0   50   100   150   km

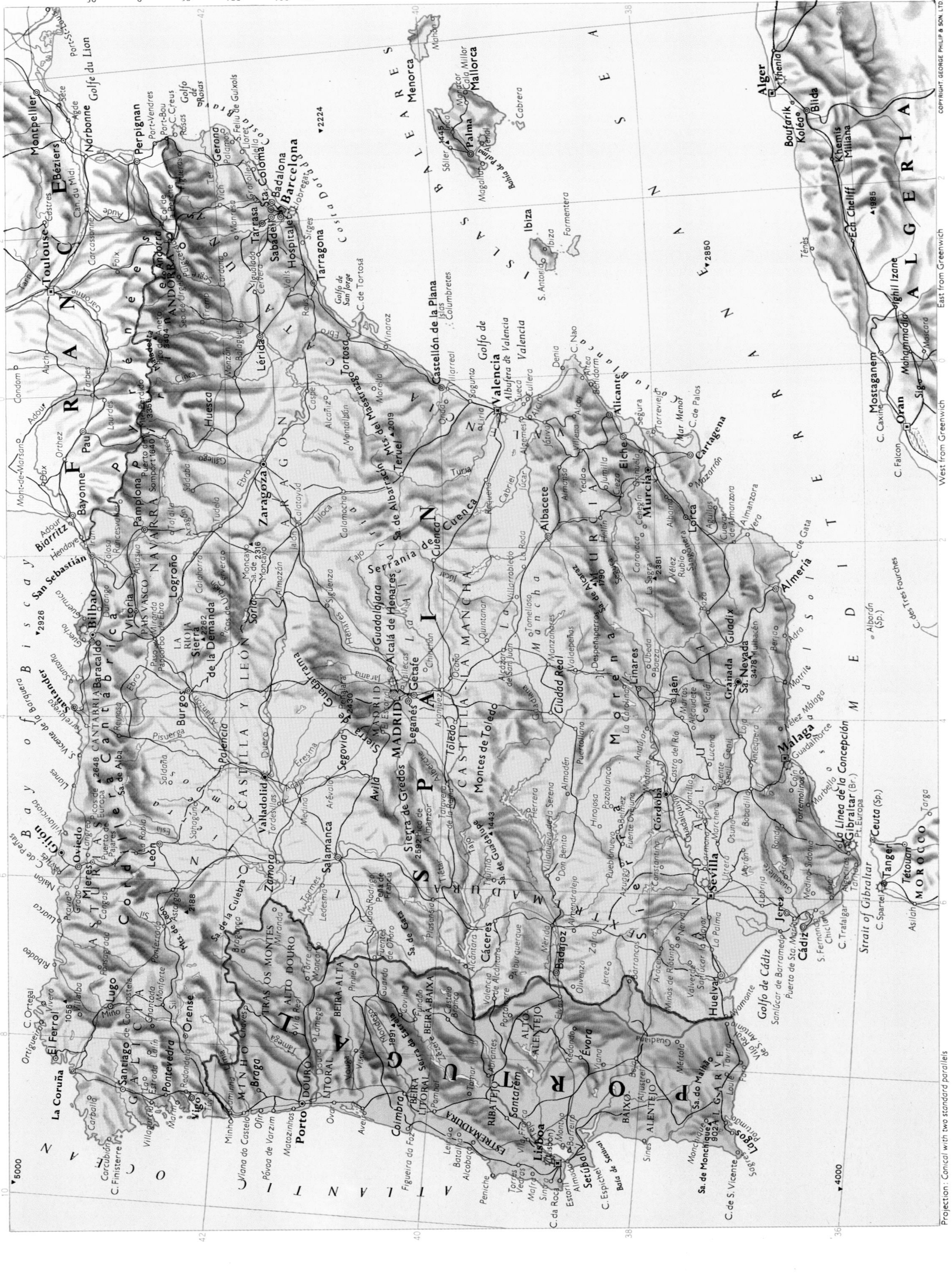

East from Greenwich

West from Greenwich

Projection: Conical with two standard parallels

5000

4000

Major labels:

FRANCE

SPAIN

PORTUGAL

ALGERIA

MOROCCO

ATLANTIC OCEAN

MEDITERRANEAN SEA

ISLAS BALEARES

Bay of Biscay

GALICIA · ASTURIAS · CANTABRIA · PAIS VASCO · NAVARRA · LA RIOJA · ARAGON · CATALUÑA · CASTILLA Y LEON · CASTILLA-LA MANCHA · MADRID · EXTREMADURA · VALENCIA · MURCIA · ANDALUCIA · Sierra Morena

MINHO · DOURO LITORAL · TRAS OS MONTES · ALTO DOURO · BEIRA ALTA · BEIRA LITORAL · BEIRA BAIXA · ESTREMADURA · RIBATEJO · ALTO ALENTEJO · BAIXO ALENTEJO · ALGARVE

Cities and towns:

Montpellier · Béziers · Narbonne · Toulouse · Perpignan · Bayonne · Biarritz · Pau · San Sebastián · Pamplona · Bilbao · Vitoria · Logroño · Zaragoza · Huesca · Lérida · Gerona · Barcelona · Badalona · Sabadell · Tarrasa · Sta. Coloma · Hospitalet · Tarragona · Tortosa · Castellón de la Plana · Valencia · Alicante · Elche · Murcia · Cartagena · Lorca · Almería · Guadix · Granada · Jaén · Linares · Córdoba · Sevilla · Cádiz · Jerez · Huelva · Badajoz · Cáceres · Mérida · Málaga · Algeciras · Gibraltar · Ceuta · Tanger · Tetouan

Soria · Burgos · Valladolid · Palencia · León · Zamora · Salamanca · Avila · Segovia · Madrid · Getafe · Leganés · Alcalá de Henares · Guadalajara · Cuenca · Albacete · Ciudad Real · Toledo

La Coruña · Santiago de Compostela · Lugo · Orense · Pontevedra · Vigo · Oviedo · Gijón · Mieres · Santander

Porto · Braga · Coimbra · Aveiro · Viseu · Lisboa · Setúbal · Santarém · Évora · Lagos

Palma · Mallorca · Menorca · Ibiza · Formentera · Cabrera · Cabrera

Alger · Blida · Boufarik · Koléa · Oran · Mostaganem

Physical features / heights:

Pyrénées · Sierra de Gredos · Sierra de Guadarrama · Sierra Nevada · Sierra de la Demanda · Cordillera Cantábrica · Montes de Toledo · Serranía de Cuenca · Mts. del Maestrazgo

Mulhacén 3478 · Aneto 3404 · Maladeta 3355 · 2924 · Almanzor 2592 · Moncayo 2316 · 2262 · 2648 · 2926 · 2188 · 2224 · 2850 · 1986 · 1056 · 891

Ebro · Duero · Tajo · Guadiana · Guadalquivir · Miño · Júcar · Segura · Genil

Golfo de Valencia · Golfo de San Jorge · Golfo de Cádiz · Golfo de Rosas · Strait of Gibraltar · Cabo de Gata · C. de Palos · C. de la Nao · C. de Creus · C. Finisterre · C. Ortegal

ANDORRA

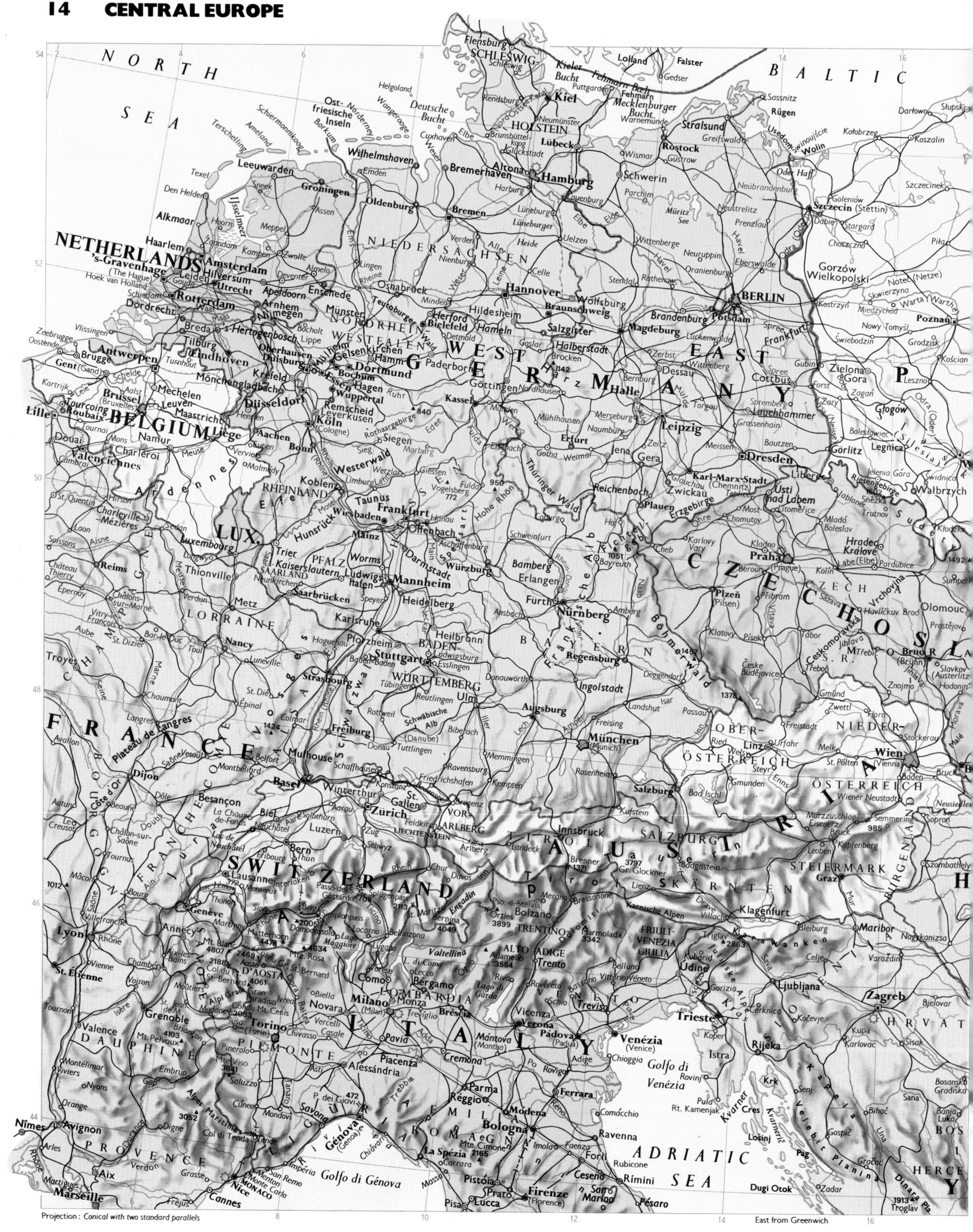
NORTH SEA
BALTIC
NETHERLANDS
BELGIUM
LUX.
WEST GERMANY
EAST GERMANY
CZECHOSLOVAKIA
FRANCE
SWITZERLAND
AUSTRIA
ITALY
ADRIATIC SEA
Golfo di Génova
Golfo di Venézia
Flensburg
SCHLESWIG
Kiel
Lolland
Falster
Gedser
Kieler Bucht
Fehmarn Belt
Mecklenburger Bucht
Sassnitz
Rügen
Stralsund
Greifswald
Usedom
Swinoujście
Wolin
Kołobrzeg
Koszalin
Darłowo
Słupsk
Helgoland
Wangerooge
Norderney
Ost-friesische Inseln
Borkum
Schiermonnikoog
Ameland
Terschelling
Texel
Deutsche Bucht
Cuxhaven
Neumünster
HOLSTEIN
Lübeck
Wismar
Rostock
Güstrow
Wilhelmshaven
Emden
Bremerhaven
Altona
Hamburg
Schwerin
Oder Haff
Szczecin (Stettin)
Szczecinek
Goleniów
Stargard
Leeuwarden
Den Helder
Groningen
Oldenburg
Bremen
Lauenburg
Parchim
Neubrandenburg
Alkmaar
IJsselmeer
Hoorn
Assen
Meppel
Lüneburg
Lüneburger Heide
Müritz See
Neustrelitz
Prenzlau
Choszczno
Piła
Haarlem
Zaandam
Kampen
Zwolle
NIEDERSACHSEN
Verden
Nienburg
Uelzen
Celle
Wittenberge
Neuruppin
Oranienburg
Eberswalde
Gorzów Wielkopolski
Noteć (Netze)
Amsterdam
's-Gravenhage (The Hague)
Hoek van Holland
Leiden
Hilversum
Gouda
Utrecht
Apeldoorn
Deventer
Almelo
Enschede
Lingen
Osnabrück
Hannover
Wolfsburg
Stendal
Rathenow
BERLIN
Potsdam
Kostrzyn
Skwierzyna
Warta (Warthe)
Poznań
Schiedam
Rotterdam
Dordrecht
Arnhem
Nijmegen
Münster
Minden
Herford
Bielefeld
Hildesheim
Braunschweig
Brandenburg
Frankfurt
Międzychód
Nowy Tomyśl
Świebodzin
Grodzisk
Vlissingen
Zeebrugge
Oostende
Brugge
Antwerpen
Breda
Tilburg
's-Hertogenbosch
Eindhoven
Bocholt
NORDRHEIN WESTFALEN
Detmold
Hameln
Salzgitter
Magdeburg
Goslar
Halberstadt
Zerbst
Luckenwalde
Gent (Gand)
Turnhout
Oberhausen
Duisburg
Mülheim
Gelsenkirchen
Hamm
Dortmund
Bochum
Essen
Paderborn
Brocken
Harz
Dessau
Wittenberg
Cottbus
Gubin
Zielona Góra
Leszno
Kortrijk
Aalst
Mönchengladbach
Krefeld
Hagen
Wuppertal
Ruhr
Göttingen
Nordhausen
Bernburg
Halle
Torgau
Forst
Żary
Żagań
Kościan
Tourcoing
Roubaix
Lille
Brussel (Bruxelles)
Mechelen
Leuven
Maastricht
Düsseldorf
Remscheid
Leverkusen
Köln (Cologne)
Rothaargebirge
Kassel
Münden
Mühlhausen
Merseburg
Leipzig
Spremberg
Lauchhammer
Grossenhain
Głogów
Odra (Oder)
Douai
Tournai
Mons
Namur
Liège
Aachen
Eupen
Bonn
Siegen
Eder
Fulda
Werra
Naumburg
Erfurt
Eisenach
Gotha
Weimar
Jena
Gera
Zeitz
Meissen
Dresden
Bautzen
Görlitz
Legnica
Bolesławiec
Silesia
Valenciennes
Charleroi
Meuse
Verviers
Malmédy
Westerwald
Marburg
Wetzlar
Giessen
Limburg
Vogelsberg
Thüringer Wald
Reichenbach
Karl-Marx-Stadt (Chemnitz)
Glauchau
Zwickau
Plauen
Erzgebirge
Teplice
Ústí nad Labem
Liberec
Jelenia Góra
Riesengebirge
Śnieżka
Wałbrzych
Świdnica
Cambrai
St. Quentin
Hirson
Ardennes
RHEINLAND
Eifel
Koblenz
Taunus
Wiesbaden
Frankfurt
Hanau
Offenbach
Hohe Rhön
Coburg
Hof
Most
Chomutov
Litoměřice
Mladá Boleslav
Trutnov
Sudety
Kłodzko
Charleville-Mézières
Sedan
Luxembourg
Hunsrück
Mainz
Aschaffenburg
Schweinfurt
Bamberg
Bayreuth
Fichtelgebirge
Cheb
Karlovy Vary
Kladno
Praha (Prague)
Hradec Králové
Labe (Elbe)
Pardubice
Kolín
Laon
Soissons
Aisne
Reims
Longwy
Thionville
Trier
PFALZ
SAARLAND
Kaiserslautern
Worms
Ludwigshafen
Mannheim
Darmstadt
Würzburg
Erlangen
Fränkische Alb
Naab
Plzeň (Pilsen)
Příbram
Vltava
Sázava
Vrchovina
Olomouc
Prostějov
Château Thierry
Épernay
Neunkirchen
Saarbrücken
Speyer
Heidelberg
Fürth
Nürnberg
Amberg
Böhmerwald
Havlíčkův Brod
Jihlava
Châlons-sur-Marne
Verdun
Metz
LORRAINE
Karlsruhe
Pforzheim
Heilbronn
BADEN
Ansbach
Regensburg
Klatovy
Písek
Tábor
Českomoravská
Vitry-le-François
Aube
Bar-le-Duc
St. Dizier
Nancy
Toul
Haguenau
Stuttgart
Ludwigsburg
Esslingen
Baden-Baden
WÜRTTEMBERG
Troyes
CHAMPAGNE
Marne
Lunéville
Strasbourg
Tübingen
Reutlingen
Donauwörth
Ingolstadt
Deggendorf
České Budějovice
Třeboň
Brno (Brünn)
Třebíč
Slavkov (Austerlitz)
Hodonín
Znojmo
Seine
Chaumont
St. Dié
Épinal
Vosges
ALSACE
Schwarzwald
Ulm
Schwäbische Alb
Augsburg
Landshut
Isar
Passau
Gmünd
Zwettl
Horn
Langres
Plateau de Langres
Colmar
Freiburg
Rottweil
Biberach
Iller
Lech
Freising
Ammer
München (Munich)
Inn
OBER-ÖSTERREICH
Ried
Wels
Linz
Urfahr
Freistadt
NIEDER-ÖSTERREICH
Stockerau
Melk
St. Pölten
Wien (Vienna)
Morava
Avallon
Dijon
Saône
Vesoul
Belfort
Montbéliard
Mulhouse
Donau (Danube)
Tuttlingen
Schaffhausen
Memmingen
Ravensburg
Friedrichshafen
Kempten
Rosenheim
Salzburg
Steyr
Gmunden
Enns
Bad Ischl
Baden
Wiener Neustadt
Bruck
Neusiedler See
Sopron
Autun
Côte d'Or
Beaune
Dôle
Besançon
Doubs
La Chaux-de-Fonds
Biel
Aare
Solothurn
Neuchâtel
Basel
Konstanz
Winterthur
Zürich
St. Gallen
Bregenz
Feldkirch
LIECHTENSTEIN
VORARLBERG
Arlberg
Landeck
Innsbruck
TIROL
Kufstein
SALZBURG
Mürzzuschlag
Semmering
Eisenerz
Leoben
Kapfenberg
STEIERMARK
BURGENLAND
Szombathely
Le Creusot
Chalon-sur-Saône
Tournus
Lac de Neuchâtel
Fribourg
Bern
Thun
Luzern
Zug
Schwyz
Rhein
Chur
Davos
Brenner
Gr. Glockner
Badgastein
KÄRNTEN
Graz
Mur
Mâcon
Lausanne
Montreux
Interlaken
Passo del S. Gottardo
Splügenpass
Engadin
St. Moritz
Bernina
Lac Léman
Thonon
Genève
Bourg
Ain
JURA
Martigny
Rhône
Simplonpass
Domodossola
Ticino
Locarno
Bellinzona
Stelvio
Ortles
Merano
Bressanone
Lienz
Karnische Alpen
Drava
Villach
Klagenfurt
Maribor
Nagykanizsa
Bleiburg
Karawanken
Lyon
Villefranche
Annecy
SAVOIE
Matterhorn
Mt. Blanc
Mte. Rosa
Lago Maggiore
Lugano
Valtellina
Adamello
ALTO ADIGE
TRENTINO
Bolzano
Dolomiti
Marmolada
FRIULI-VENEZIA GIULIA
Triglav
Kobarid
Julijske Alpe
Celje
Varaždin
St. Étienne
Vienne
Chambéry
Aix-les-Bains
Aosta
Gr. St. Bernard
Col du Pt. St. Bernard
VALLE D'AOSTA
Gran Paradiso
Biella
Ivrea
Varese
Como
L. di Como
Lecco
Bergamo
Oglio
Lago di Garda
Riva
Trento
Belluno
Vittorio Veneto
Udine
Gorizia
Ljubljana
Sava
Zagreb
Voiron
Moûtiers
Mt. Cenis
Col du Mt. Cenis
Alpi Graie
Novara
Milano (Milan)
Monza
Treviglio
LOMBARDIA
Brescia
Rovereto
Bassano
Schio
Treviso
Piave
VENETO
Trieste
Koper
Cerknica
Kočevje
Bjelovar
HRVATSKA
Tournon
Valence
Grenoble
Isère
Briançon
Mt. Pelvoux
DAUPHINÉ
Susa
Torino (Turin)
Chivasso
Vercelli
Casale
Pavia
Adda
Vicenza
Verona
Mántova (Mantua)
Pádova (Padua)
Venézia (Venice)
Chioggia
Adige
Istra
Rijeka
Kupa
Karlovac
Sisak
Montélimar
Viviers
Pinerolo
PIEMONTE
Mt. Viso
Embrun
Gap
Asti
Alessándria
Po
Piacenza
Cremona
Rovigo
Rovinj
Krk
Senj
Kapela
Nyons
Saluzzo
Cúneo
Tanaro
P. dei Giovi
Trebbia
Parma
Réggio
Módena
Ferrara
Reno
Pula
Rt. Kamenjak
Kvarner
Cres
Kvarnerić
Bosanska Gradiška
Orange
Alpes Maritimes
Mondovì
Savona
LIGURIA
Génova (Genoa)
EMILIA-ROMAGNA
Bologna
Comácchio
Bihać
Una
Banja Luka
BOSNIA I HERCEGOVINA
Nîmes
Avignon
Durance
Digne
Col di Tenda
Chiávari
La Spézia
Mte. Cimone
Imola
Faenza
Ravenna
Lošinj
Gospić
Velebit Planina
Gračac
Arles
PROVENCE
Verdon
Aix
Grasse
San Remo
Impéria
Menton
Monte Carlo
MONACO
Nice
Carrara
Massa
Pistóia
Prato
Forlì
Cesena
Rubicone
Rímini
Pag
Dugi Otok
Zadar
Dinara Pla.
Marseille
Martigues
Fréjus
Cannes
Pisa
Lucca
Firenze (Florence)
San Marino
Pésaro
Troglav
Projection: Conical with two standard parallels
East from Greenwich

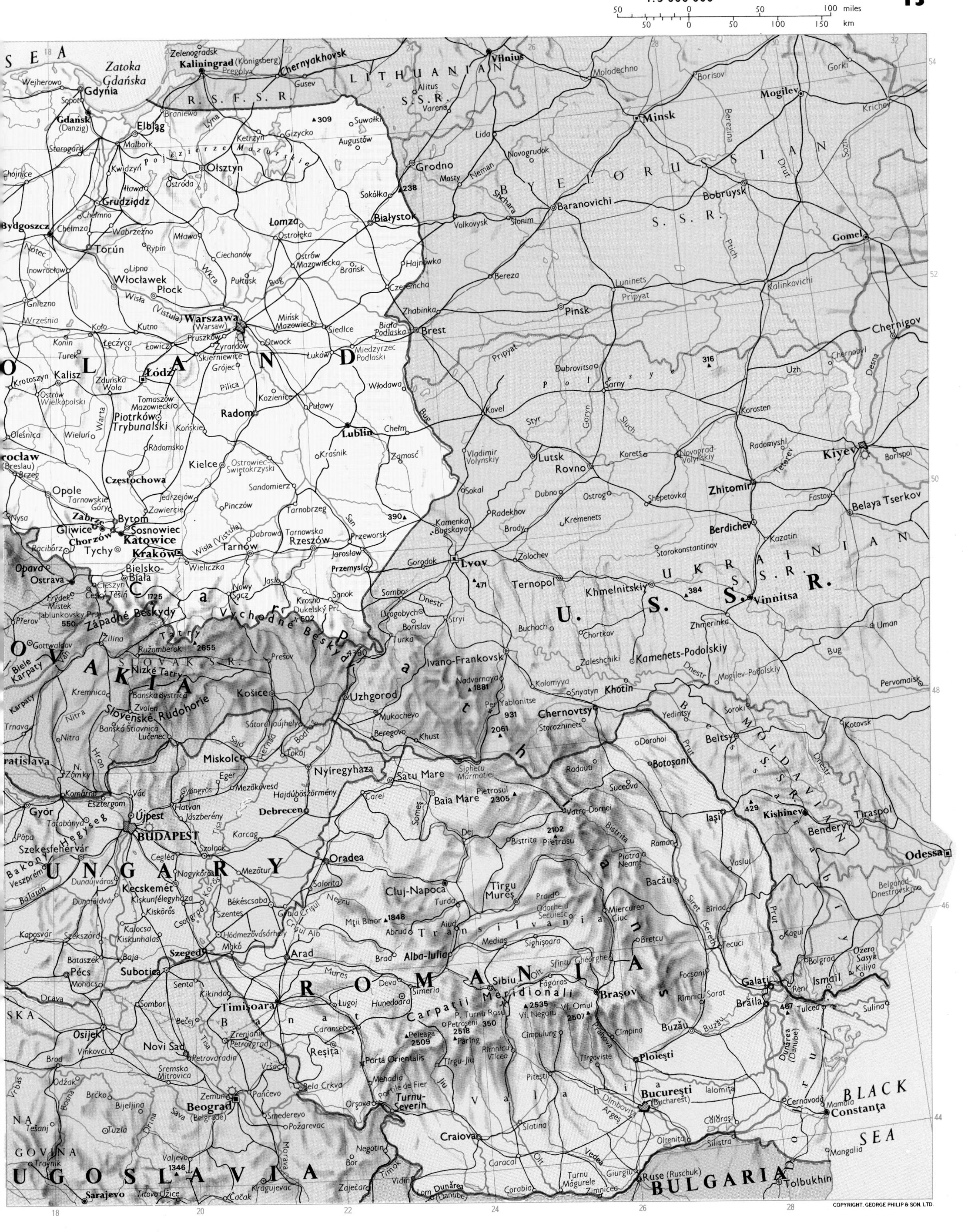

1:5 000 000
50 0 50 100 miles
50 0 50 100 150 km
SEA
Zatoka Gdańska
Zelenogradsk
Kaliningrad (Königsberg)
Pregolya
Chernyakhovsk
Gusev
R. S. F. S. R.
LITHUANIAN S.S.R.
Vilnius
Alitus
Varena
Molodechno
Borisov
Gorki
Mogilev
Krichev
Minsk
Wejherowo
Gdynia
Sopot
Gdańsk (Danzig)
Elbląg
Braniewo
Starogard
Malbork
Ketrzyn
Gizycko
309
Suwałki
Augustów
Pojezierze Mazurskie
Chojnice
Kwidzyń
Olsztyn
Ostróda
Iława
Grudziądz
Chełmno
Chełmza
Bydgoszcz
Noteć
Toruń
Wąbrzeźno
Rypin
Mława
Łomża
Ostrołęka
Białystok
Sokółka
238
Grodno
Mosty
Neman
Lida
Novogrudok
Berezina
Drut
Sozh
BYELORUSSIAN S.S.R.
Baranovichi
Shchara
Slonim
Volkovysk
Bobruysk
Gomel
Ptich
Inowrocław
Lipno
Włocławek
Płock
Ciechanów
Pułtusk
Wkra
Bug
Ostrów Mazowiecka
Brańsk
Hajnówka
Bereza
Luninets
Pripyat
Kalinkovichi
Gniezno
Września
Wisła (Vistula)
Warszawa (Warsaw)
Mińsk Mazowiecki
Siedlce
Czeremcha
Zhabinka
Biała Podlaska
Brest
Pinsk
Chernigov
Koło
Kutno
Konin
Łęczyca
Łowicz
Pruszków
Żyrardów
Skierniewice
Grójec
Otwock
Łuków
Międzyrzec Podlaski
Turek
Krotoszyn
Kalisz
Zduńska Wola
Łódź
Pilica
Kozienice
Puławy
Włodawa
Pripyat
Dubrovitsa
Polesye
Sarny
316
Chernobyl
Uzh
Desna
POLAND
Ostrów Wielkopolski
Tomaszów Mazowiecki
Piotrków Trybunalski
Warta
Radom
Lublin
Chełm
Kovel
Styr
Goryn
Sluch
Korosten
Oleśnica
Wieluń
Końskie
Radomsko
Kraśnik
Zamość
Vladimir Volynskiy
Lutsk
Rovno
Korets
Novograd-Volynskiy
Radomyshl
Teterev
Kiyev
Borispol
Wrocław (Breslau)
Brzeg
Kielce
Ostrowiec Świętokrzyski
Częstochowa
Sandomierz
Sokal
Dubno
Ostrog
Shepetovka
Zhitomir
Fastov
Belaya Tserkov
Opole
Tarnowskie Góry
Jędrzejów
Zawiercie
Pińczów
Tarnobrzeg
San
390
Radekhov
Kremenets
Brody
Berdichev
Kazatin
Nysa
Zabrze
Bytom
Sosnowiec
Gliwice
Chorzów
Katowice
Racibórz
Tychy
Kraków
Wisła (Vistula)
Dąbrowa Tarnowska
Tarnów
Rzeszów
Przeworsk
Kamenka Bugskaya
Starokonstantinov
UKRAINIAN S.S.R.
Opava
Ostrava
Bielsko-Biała
Wieliczka
Jarosław
Przemyśl
Gorodok
Lvov
Zolochev
Ternopol
Khmelnitskiy
384
Vinnitsa
U. S. S. R.
Cieszyn
Český Těšín
1725
Nowy Sącz
Jasło
Krosno
Dukelský Pr.
502
Sanok
Sambor
Dnestr
471
Frýdek Místek
Jablunkovský Pr.
550
Přerov
Západné Beskydy
Carpathians
Východné Beskydy
Drogobych
Borislav
Stryi
Buchach
Chortkov
Zhmerinka
Uman
Gottwaldov
Váh
Žilina
Tatry
Ružomberok
2655
Prešov
SLOVAK S.R.
1380
Turka
Ivano-Frankovsk
Zaleshchiki
Kamenets-Podolskiy
Bug
Biele Karpaty
CZECHOSLOVAKIA
Nízké Tatry
Banská Bystrica
Košice
Nadvornaya
1881
Kolomyya
Snyatyn
Khotin
Dnestr
Mogilev-Podolskiy
Pervomaisk
Kremnica
Zvolen
Slovenské Rudohorie
Uzhgorod
Per Yablonitse
931
Chernovtsy
Yedintsy
Soroki
Kotovsk
Karpaty
Nitra
Trnava
Banská Štiavnica
Lučenec
Sátoraljaújhely
Mukachevo
Beregovo
Khust
2061
Storozhinets
Dorohoi
Beltsy
MOLDAVIAN S.S.R.
Bratislava
Hron
Sajó
Hernád
Bodrog
Tokaj
Miskolc
Nyíregyháza
Satu Mare
Sighetu Marmaţiei
Radauti
Botoşani
Prut
Dnestr
N. Zámky
Komárno
Eger
Mezőkövesd
Gyöngyös
Hajdúböszörmény
Carei
Baia Mare
Pietrosul
2305
Suceava
Győr
Esztergom
Vác
Hatvan
Jászberény
Debrecen
Someş
Vatra Dornei
Iaşi
429
Kishinev
Tiraspol
Pápa
Tatabánya
Újpest
BUDAPEST
Tisza
Karcag
Dej
Bistrita
2102
Pietrosu
Bistrita
Roman
Bendery
Odessa
Székesfehérvár
Bakony
Veszprém
Szolnok
Cegléd
Mezőtúr
Oradea
Piatra Neamţ
Vaslui
HUNGARY
Dunaújváros
Nagykőrös
Kecskemét
Kiskunfélegyháza
Salonta
Cluj-Napoca
Tirgu Mureş
Bacău
Belgorod-Dnestrovskiy
Balaton
Dunaföldvár
Kiskőrös
Békéscsaba
Szentes
Gyula
Crişul Negru
Turda
Praid
Odorheiu Secuiesc
Miercurea Ciuc
Siret (Sereth)
Bîrlad
Kaposvár
Szekszárd
Kalocsa
Kiskunhalas
Csongrád
Hódmezővásárhely
Mţii Bihor
1848
Abrud
Aiud
Transilvania
Mediaş
Sighişoara
Breţcu
Tecuci
Kagul
Bataszék
Baja
Szeged
Makó
Arad
Brad
Alba-Iulia
Sfintu Gheorghe
Ozero Sasyk
Bolgrad
Kiliya
Pécs
Mohács
Subotica
Senta
Mureş
Deva
Simeria
ROMANIA
Sibiu
Olt
Făgăraş
Focşani
Galaţi
Reni
Ismail
Drava
Kikinda
Timişoara
Lugoj
Hunedoara
Carpaţii Meridionali
Braşov
Rîmnicu Sarat
Brăila
467
Tulcea
Sulina
Sombor
Banat
P. Turnu Roşu
2535
Vf. Negoiu
Vf. Omul
2507
Prahova
Buzău
Osijek
Bečej
Zrenjanin (Petrovgrad)
Caransebeş
Peleaga 2509
Petroşeni
2518
Paring
350
Rîmnicu Vîlcea
Cîmpulung
Cîmpina
Dunărea (Danube)
Dobrogea
Vinkovci
Novi Sad
Tisa
Petrovaradin
Reşiţa
Porta Orientalis
Tîrgu-Jiu
Tîrgoviste
Ploieşti
Brod
Sremska Mitrovica
Vršac
Mehadia
Portile de Fier
Jiu
Piteşti
Vrbas
Odžak
Brčko
Bosna
Bijeljina
Zemun
Pančevo
Beograd (Belgrade)
Bela Crkva
Orşova
Turnu-Severin
Walachia
Dîmboviţa
Argeş
Bucureşti (Bucharest)
Ialomiţa
Cernavodă
BLACK SEA
Mamaia
Constanţa
Tešanj
Tuzla
Drina
Sava
Smederevo
Požarevac
Craiova
Slatina
Olteniţa
Călăraşi
Silistra
Mangalia
Travnik
Morava
Negotin
Bor
Caracal
Olt
Vedea
Giurgiu
Valjevo
1346
YUGOSLAVIA
Timok
Vidin
Turnu Măgurele
Zimnicea
Ruse (Ruschuk)
BULGARIA
Tolbukhin
Sarajevo
Titovo Užice
Čačak
Kragujevac
Zaječar
Lom
Dunărea (Danube)
Corabia
18
20
22
24
26
28
30
32
54
52
50
48
46
44
COPYRIGHT, GEORGE PHILIP & SON, LTD.

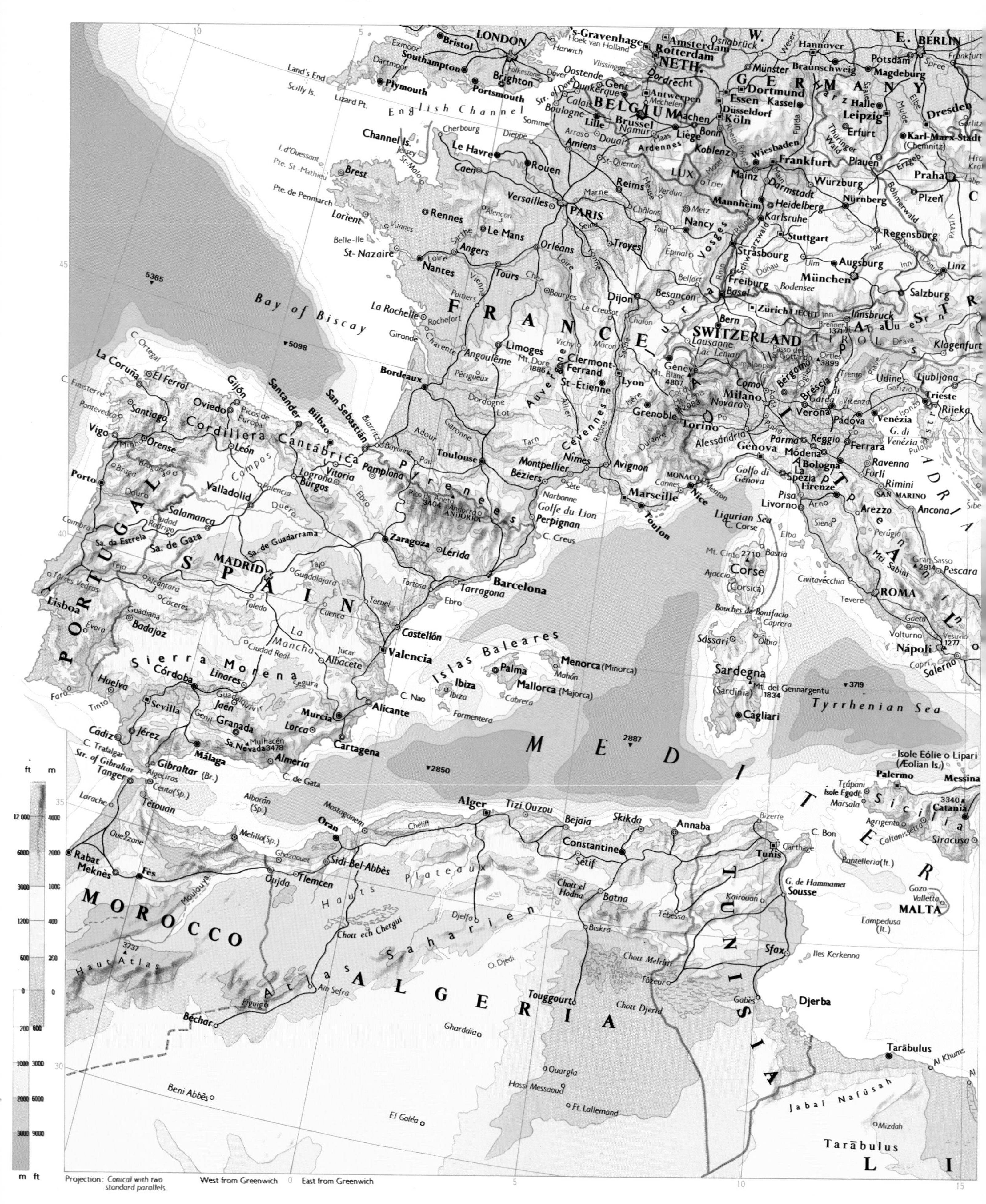

LONDON
Bristol
Southampton
Brighton
Portsmouth
Plymouth
Land's End
Scilly Is.
Lizard Pt.
English Channel
Channel Is.
Cherbourg
Le Havre
Rouen
Caen
Brest
Lorient
Rennes
Le Mans
Angers
Nantes
St-Nazaire
Tours
Orléans
PARIS
Versailles
Reims
Amiens
Lille
Dunkerque
Calais
Boulogne
Str. of Dover
Oostende
Gent
Antwerpen
BELGIUM
Brussel
Liège
Aachen
Köln
Bonn
Koblenz
Düsseldorf
Essen
Dortmund
Kassel
Münster
Amsterdam
Rotterdam
's-Gravenhage
Hoek van Holland
Harwich
NETH.
Dordrecht
Osnabrück
Hannover
Braunschweig
Magdeburg
Potsdam
E. BERLIN
W. GERMANY
Halle
Leipzig
Dresden
Erfurt
Karl-Marx-Stadt (Chemnitz)
Plauen
Praha
Plzeň
Frankfurt
Wiesbaden
Mainz
Darmstadt
Mannheim
Heidelberg
Karlsruhe
Würzburg
Nürnberg
Regensburg
Stuttgart
Augsburg
München
Ulm
Linz
Salzburg
Innsbruck
Klagenfurt
LUX
Metz
Nancy
Strasbourg
Vosges
Troyes
Dijon
Besançon
Freiburg
Basel
Zürich
Bern
SWITZERLAND
Lausanne
Genève
Mt. Blanc 4807
Lyon
Grenoble
Torino
Milano
Como
Bergamo
Brescia
Verona
Padova
Venézia
Trieste
Rijeka
Ljubljana
Udine
Novara
Alessándria
Génova
Parma
Réggio
Bologna
Ferrara
Ravenna
Forlì
Rimini
SAN MARINO
Firenze
La Spezia
Pisa
Livorno
Arezzo
Ancona
Perúgia
Gran Sasso 2914
Pescara
ROMA
Civitavécchia
Nápoli
Salerno
Capri
Vesuvio 1277
Golfo di Génova
Ligurian Sea
Corse (Corsica)
Mt. Cinto 2710
Bastia
Ajaccio
Bouches de Bonifacio
Sardegna (Sardinia)
Sassari
Mt. del Gennargentu 1834
Cagliari
Tyrrhenian Sea
Isole Eólie o Lipari (Æolian Is.)
Palermo
Messina
Trápani
Marsala
Sicilia
Catania 3340
Agrigento
Caltanissetta
Siracusa
Pantelleria (It.)
MALTA
Gozo
Valletta
Lampedusa (It.)
Marseille
Toulon
Nice
MONACO
Cannes
Avignon
Nîmes
Montpellier
Béziers
Sète
Narbonne
Golfe du Lion
Perpignan
C. Creus
Toulouse
Bordeaux
Limoges
Angoulême
Clermont-Ferrand
St-Étienne
Cévennes
Auvergne
La Rochelle
Rochefort
Poitiers
Bay of Biscay
5365
5098
FRANCE
Pyrenees
Pico de Aneto 3404
ANDORRA
Bayonne
Biarritz
Pau
San Sebastián
Bilbao
Santander
Gijón
Oviedo
Cordillera Cantábrica
La Coruña
El Ferrol
Santiago
Vigo
Orense
León
Burgos
Vitoria
Pamplona
Logroño
Valladolid
Salamanca
Sa. de Gata
Sa. de Guadarrama
Sa. da Estrela
Porto
Coimbra
PORTUGAL
Lisboa
Évora
Badajoz
MADRID
SPAIN
Toledo
Guadalajara
Zaragoza
Lérida
Barcelona
Tarragona
Tortosa
Teruel
Cuenca
Castellón
Valencia
Albacete
La Mancha
Ciudad Real
Sierra Morena
Córdoba
Linares
Jaén
Sevilla
Granada
Sa. Nevada
Mulhacén 3478
Málaga
Almería
Murcia
Lorca
Cartagena
Alicante
C. Nao
Huelva
Cádiz
Jérez
Faro
C. Trafalgar
Str. of Gibraltar
Gibraltar (Br.)
Algeciras
Islas Baleares
Ibiza
Formentera
Mallorca (Majorca)
Palma
Cabrera
Menorca (Minorca)
Mahón
MEDITERRANEAN
2887
2850
3719
C. de Gata
Alborán (Sp.)
Tanger
Ceuta (Sp.)
Tétouan
Larache
Melilla (Sp.)
Rabat
Meknès
Fès
MOROCCO
Haut Atlas
3737
Oujda
Tlemcen
Oran
Mostaganem
Sidi-Bel-Abbès
Alger
Tizi Ouzou
Bejaia
Skikda
Annaba
Constantine
Sétif
Batna
Biskra
Chott el Hodna
Hauts Plateaux
Atlas Saharien
Djelfa
Chott ech Chergui
Ain Sefra
Figuig
Béchar
ALGERIA
Touggourt
Ghardaïa
Ouargla
Hassi Messaoud
Ft. Lallemand
El Goléa
Beni Abbès
Chott Melrhir
Chott Djerid
Tozeur
Tunis
Bizerte
Carthage
C. Bon
G. de Hammamet
Sousse
Kairouan
Tébessa
Sfax
Iles Kerkenna
Gabès
Djerba
TUNISIA
Tarābulus
Al Khums
Jabal Nafūsah
Mizdah
LIBYA
Projection: Conical with two standard parallels.
West from Greenwich
East from Greenwich

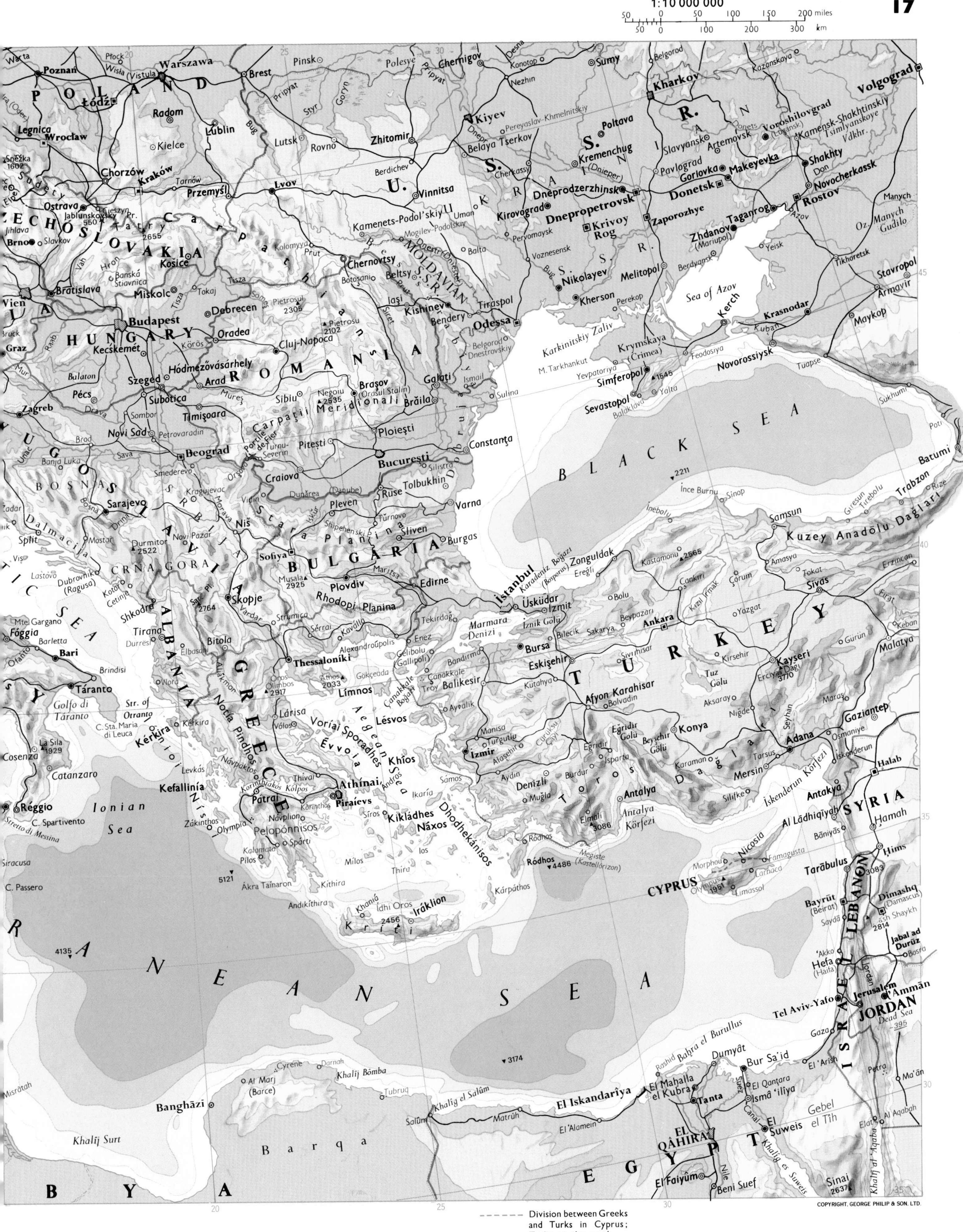

1:10 000 000

BLACK SEA

MEDITERRANEAN SEA

Division between Greeks
and Turks in Cyprus;
Turks to the north.

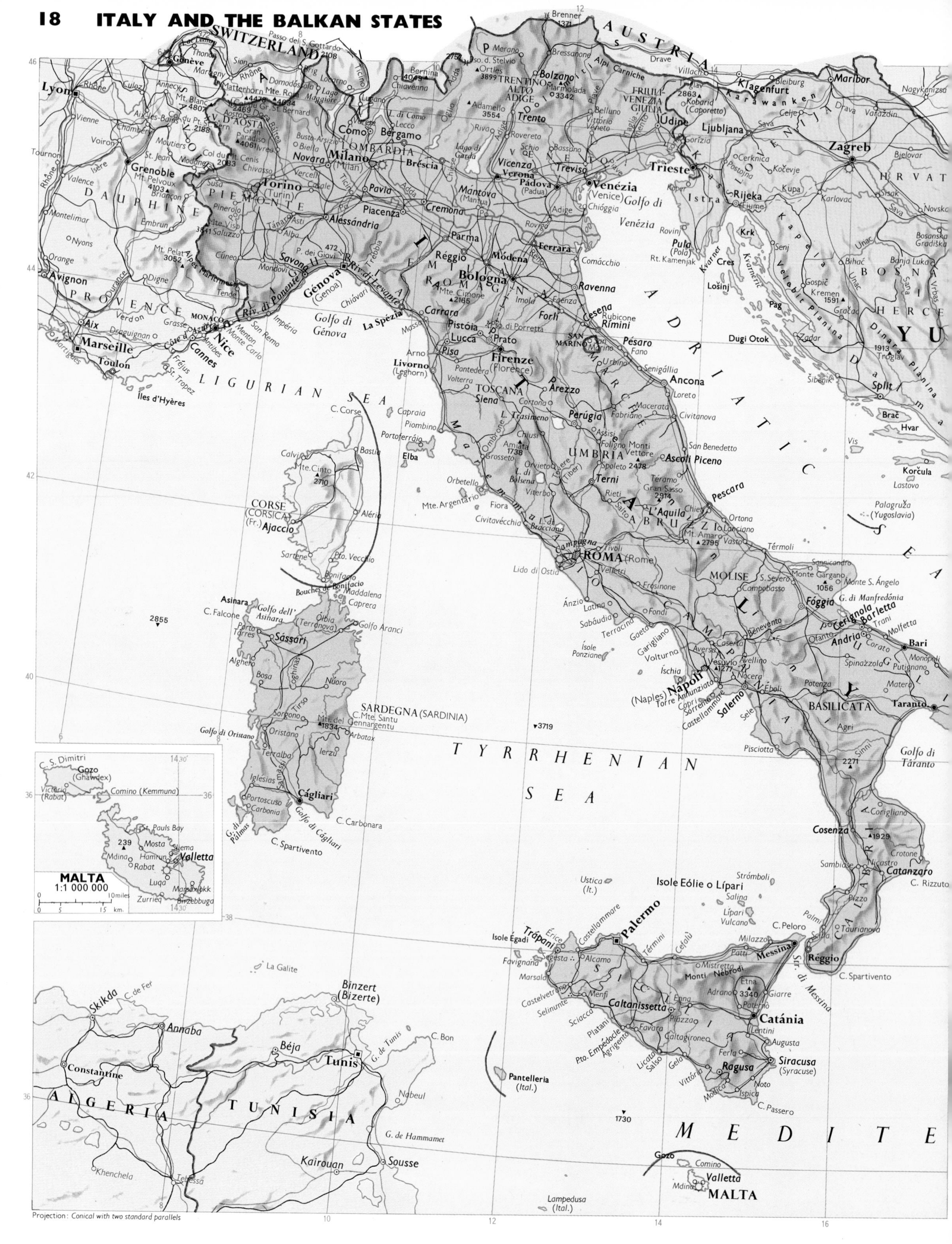

Projection: Conical with two standard parallels

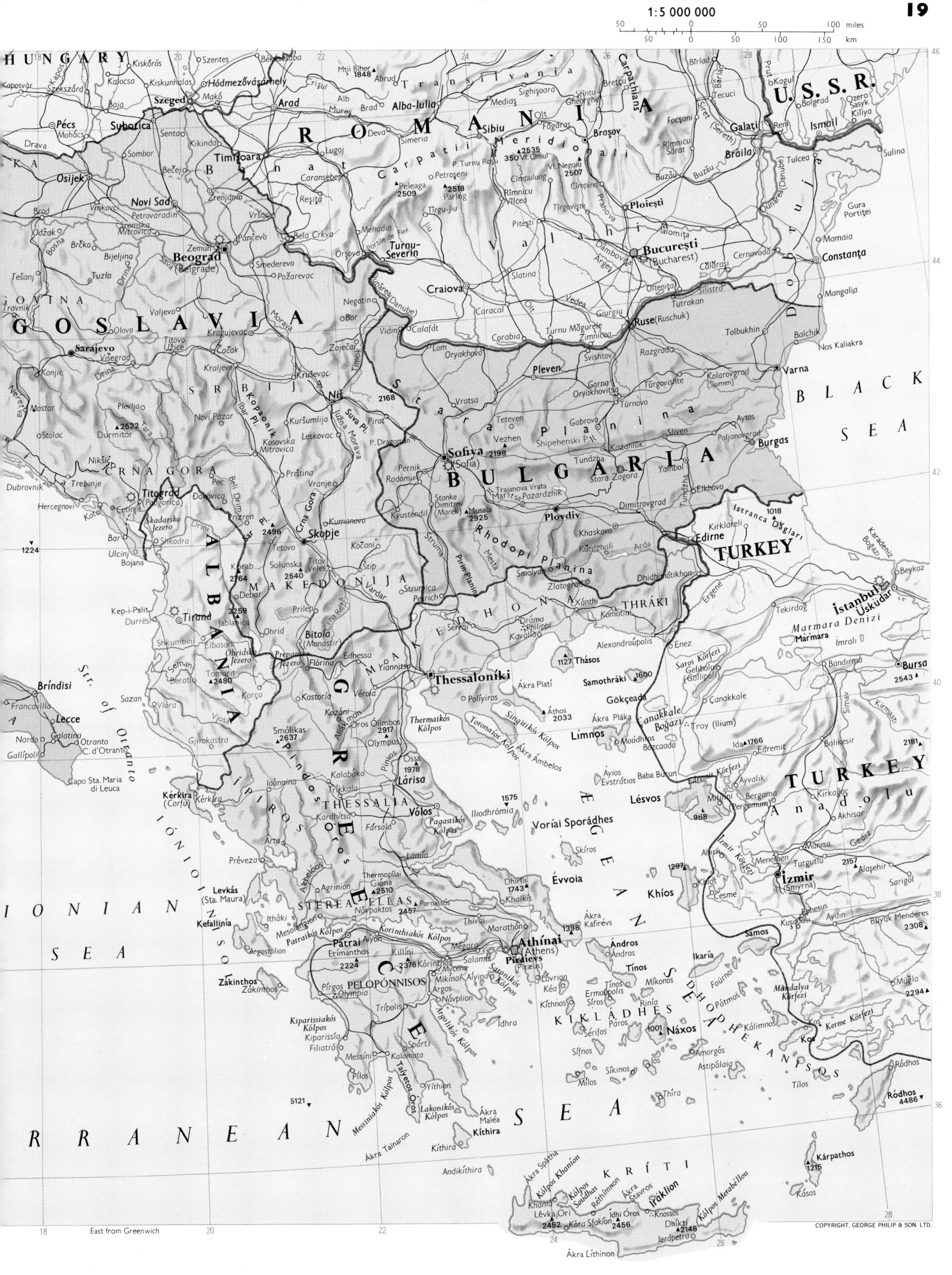
1:5 000 000
50 0 50 100 miles
50 0 50 100 150 km
HUNGARY
ROMANIA
U.S.S.R.
YUGOSLAVIA
BULGARIA
ALBANIA
GREECE
TURKEY
BLACK SEA
IONIAN SEA
AEGEAN SEA
MEDITERRANEAN SEA
Str. of Otranto
Transilvania
Carpathians
Carpatii Meridionali
Banat
Valahia
Dobruja
Stara Planina
Rhodopi Planina
Makedonija
Makedhonia
Thráki
Crna Gora
Srbija
Thessalia
Stereá Ellas
Pelopónnisos
Ipiros
Kiklådhes
Dhodhekanisos
Kríti
Anadolu
Voríai Sporádhes
Marmara Denizi
Szeged
Subotica
Pécs
Timișoara
Arad
Alba-Iulia
Sibiu
Brașov
Galați
Brăila
Ploiești
București (Bucharest)
Constanța
Craiova
Turnu-Severin
Ruse (Ruschuk)
Osijek
Novi Sad
Beograd (Belgrade)
Sarajevo
Niš
Skopje
Titograd (Podgorica)
Tiranë
Sofiya (Sofia)
Plovdiv
Pleven
Varna
Burgas
Edirne
İstanbul
Üsküdar
Bursa
İzmir (Smyrna)
Thessaloníki
Lárisa
Vólos
Athínai (Athens)
Piraiévs (Piraeus)
Pátrai
Brindisi
Lecce
Kérkira (Corfu)
Kefallinía
Zákinthos
Lésvos
Khíos
Límnos
Évvoia
Náxos
Ródhos
Kárpathos
Kíthira
Iráklion
Akra Líthinon
East from Greenwich

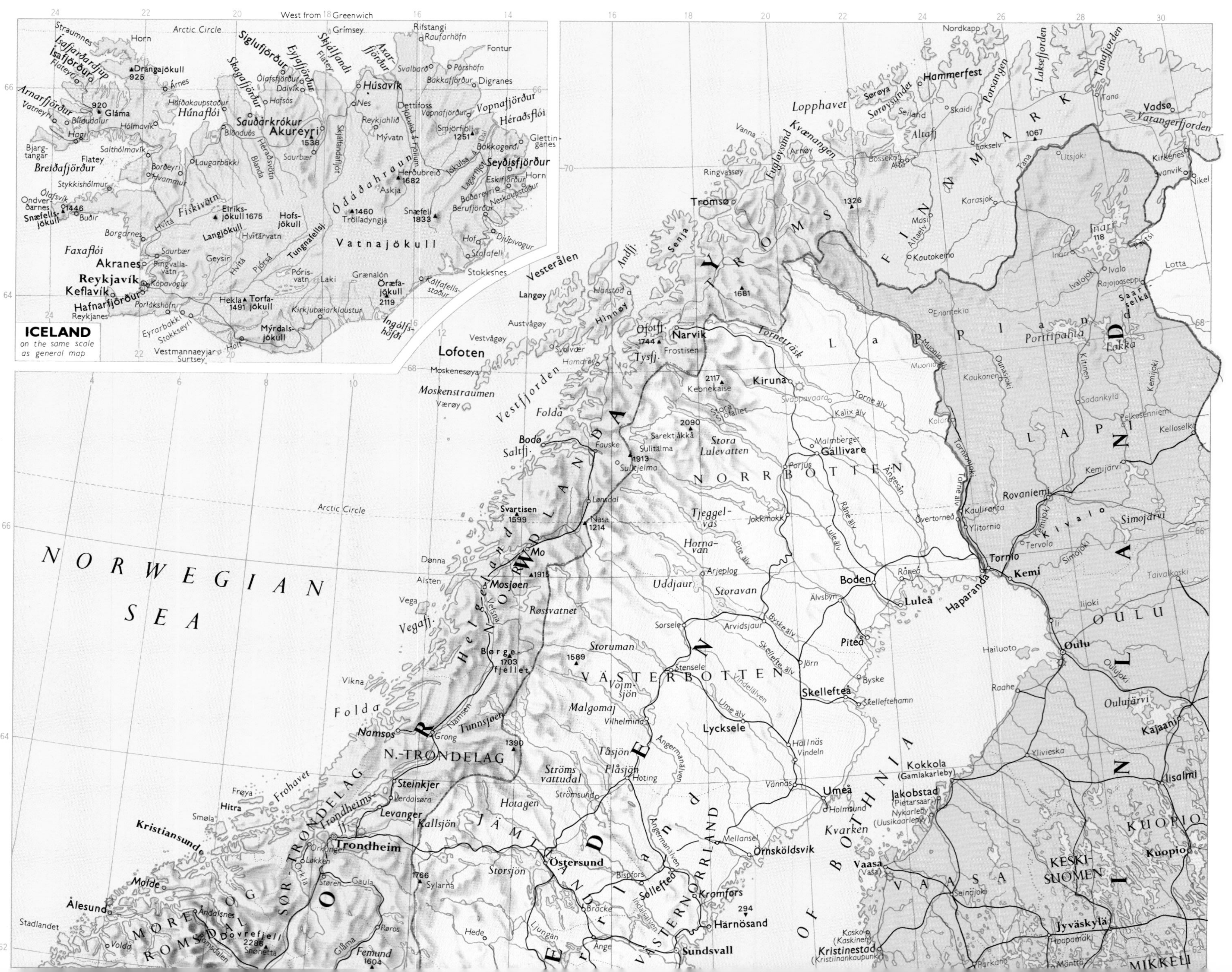
ICELAND
on the same scale as general map
West from Greenwich
Arctic Circle
Grímsey
Siglufjörður
Eyjafjörður
Skjálfandi
Axarfjörður
Húsavík
Akureyri
Sauðárkrókur
Húnaflói
Ísafjörður
Ísafjarðardjúp
Breiðafjörður
Faxaflói
Akranes
Reykjavík
Keflavík
Hafnarfjörður
Reykjanes
Vatnajökull
Ódáðahraun
Hofsjökull
Langjökull
Mýrdalsjökull
Hekla 1491
Öræfajökull 2119
Seyðisfjörður
Vopnafjörður
Héraðsflói
Vestmannaeyjar
Surtsey
Ingólfshöfði
Lofoten
Vesterålen
Vestfjorden
Moskenstraumen
Narvik
Tromsø
Hammerfest
Lopphavet
Vadsø
Varangerfjorden
Tanafjorden
Laksefjorden
Porsangen
Nordkapp
FINNMARK
TROMS
NORDLAND
Bodø
Mo
Mosjøen
Svartisen 1599
Arctic Circle
NORWEGIAN SEA
N.-TRØNDELAG
SØR-TRØNDELAG
MØRE OG ROMSDAL
Namsos
Steinkjer
Levanger
Trondheim
Trondheimsfj.
Kristiansund
Molde
Ålesund
Stadlandet
Dovrefjell
Snøhetta 2286
Femund 1604
Røros
Hitra
Frøya
Smøla
Folda
Vikna
Vega
Dønna
Alsten
Børgefjellet 1703
Kiruna
Kebnekaise 2117
Sarektjåkkå 2090
Gällivare
Stora Lulevatten
Tornetråsk
Torne älv
Kalix älv
Lule älv
Pite älv
Skellefte älv
Ume älv
Ångermanälven
Indalsälven
Ljungan
NORRBOTTEN
VÄSTERBOTTEN
VÄSTERNORRLAND
JÄMTLAND
Lappland
Norrland
Jokkmokk
Arvidsjaur
Arjeplog
Boden
Luleå
Piteå
Skellefteå
Lycksele
Umeå
Örnsköldsvik
Härnösand
Sundsvall
Östersund
Storsjön
Storuman
Uddjaur
Storavan
Hornavan
Malgomaj
Vilhelmina
Sorsele
Kramfors
Sollefteå
Haparanda
GULF OF BOTHNIA
Kvarken
FINLAND
LAPPI
OULU
VAASA
KESKI-SUOMEN
KUOPIO
MIKKELI
Rovaniemi
Tornio
Kemi
Oulu
Kajaani
Iisalmi
Kuopio
Jyväskylä
Vaasa (Vasa)
Kokkola (Gamlakarleby)
Jakobstad (Pietarsaari)
Kristinestad (Kristiinankaupunki)
Inari
Inari 118
Ivalo
Porttipahta
Lokka
Saariselkä
Kemijärvi
Kittilä
Enontekiö
Pasvik
Kirkenes
Nikel
Lotta
Hailuoto
Oulujärvi
Raahe

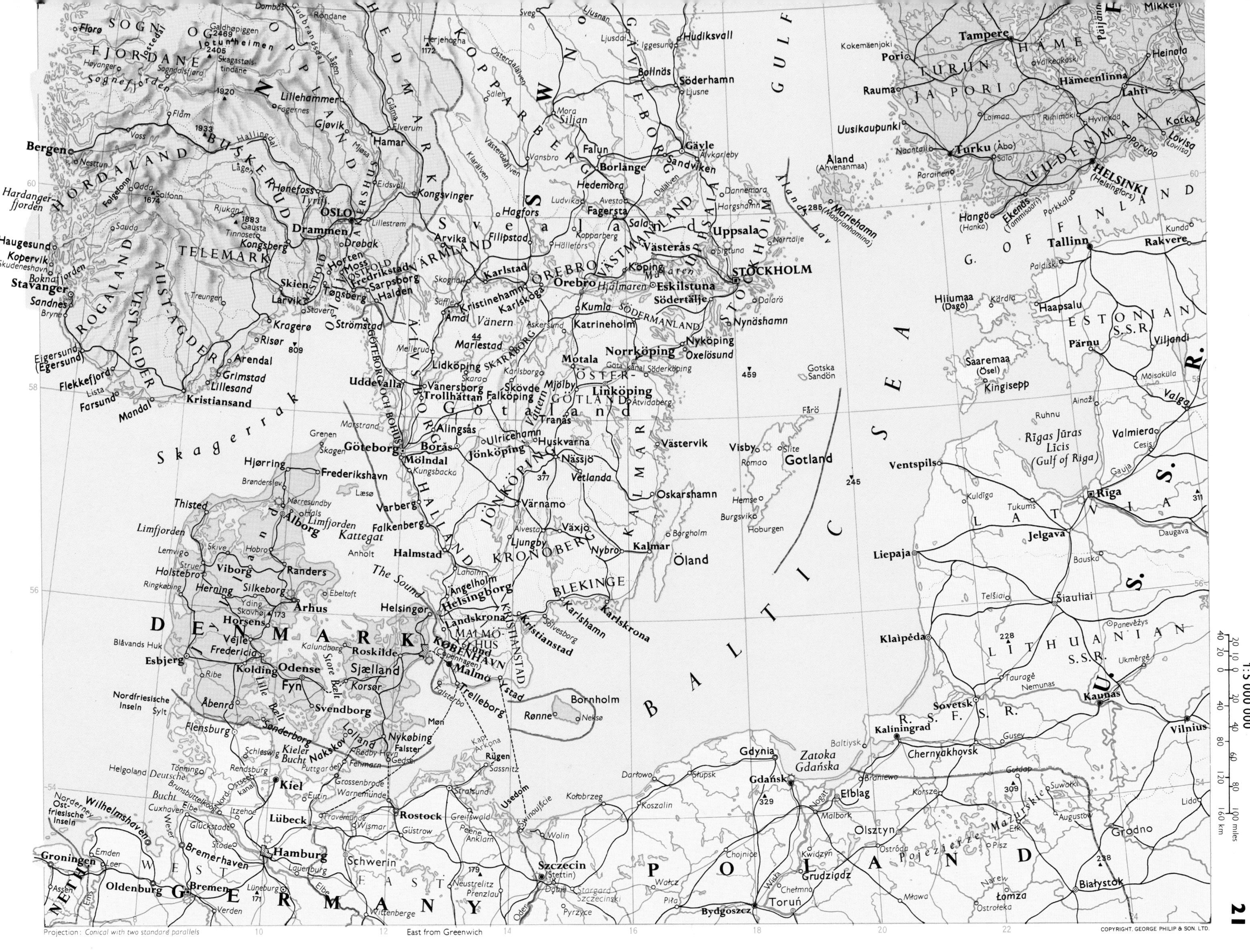

GULF OF FINLAND
BALTIC SEA
Skagerrak
Kattegat
The Sound
Rīgas Jūras Līcis (Gulf of Riga)
Zatoka Gdańska
Ålands hav
SVEALAND
GÖTALAND
DENMARK
POLAND
EAST GERMANY
WEST GERMANY
ESTONIAN S.S.R.
LATVIAN S.S.R.
LITHUANIAN S.S.R.
R.S.F.S.R.
U.S.S.R.
STOCKHOLM
HELSINKI (Helsingfors)
OSLO
KØBENHAVN (Copenhagen)
Riga
Tallinn
Vilnius
Kaunas
Kaliningrad
Gdańsk
Gdynia
Szczecin (Stettin)
Hamburg
Kiel
Lübeck
Rostock
Bremen
Bremerhaven
Göteborg
Malmö
Uppsala
Västerås
Örebro
Norrköping
Linköping
Jönköping
Karlstad
Gävle
Turku (Åbo)
Tampere
Bergen
Stavanger
Kristiansand
Drammen
Århus
Odense
Ålborg
Esbjerg
Gotland
Öland
Bornholm
Saaremaa (Ösel)
Hiiumaa (Dagö)
Åland (Ahvenanmaa)
Mariehamn (Maarianhamina)
Visby
Kalmar
Karlskrona
Sjælland
Fyn
Lolland
Falster
Rügen
Usedom
Projection: Conical with two standard parallels
East from Greenwich
COPYRIGHT, GEORGE PHILIP & SON, LTD.
1:5 000 000
20 10 0 20 40 60 80 100 miles
40 20 0 40 80 120 160 km

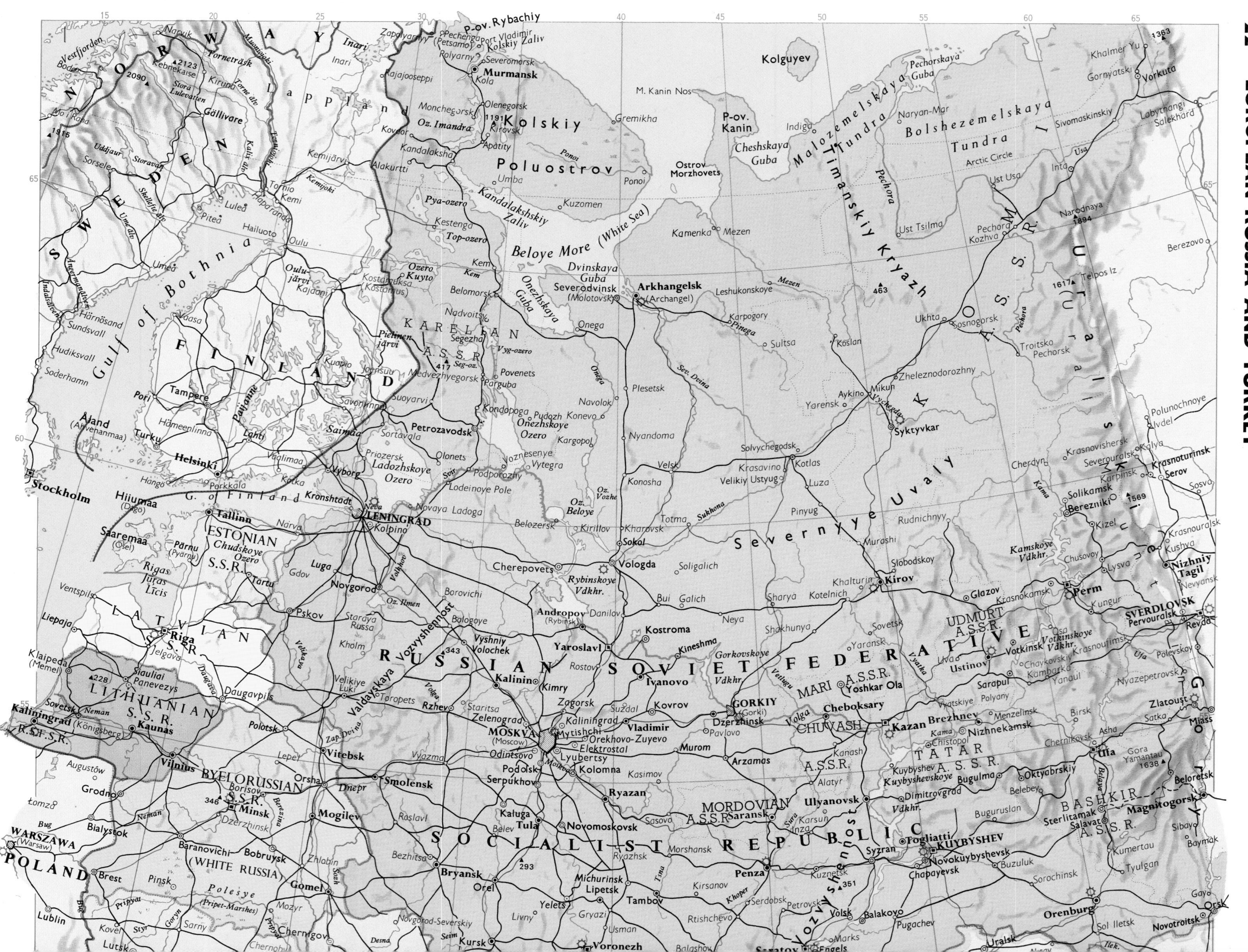

RUSSIAN SOVIET FEDERATIVE SOCIALIST REPUBLIC
FINLAND
SWEDEN
NORWAY
POLAND
Lappland
Kolskiy Poluostrov
Beloye More (White Sea)
Gulf of Bothnia
G. of Finland
Timanskiy Kryazh
Bolshezemelskaya Tundra
Malozemelskaya Tundra
Severnyye Uvaly
Urals
KARELIAN A.S.S.R.
KOMI A.S.S.R.
ESTONIAN S.S.R.
LATVIAN S.S.R.
LITHUANIAN S.S.R.
BYELORUSSIAN S.S.R.
(WHITE RUSSIA)
UDMURT A.S.S.R.
TATAR A.S.S.R.
BASHKIR A.S.S.R.
MARI A.S.S.R.
CHUVASH A.S.S.R.
MORDOVIAN A.S.S.R.
MOSKVA
(Moscow)
LENINGRAD
GORKIY
KUYBYSHEV
SVERDLOVSK
Helsinki
Stockholm
Tallinn
Riga
Vilnius
Minsk
Kazan
Perm
Arkhangelsk
Murmansk
Kolguyev
Valdayskaya Vozvyshennost
Polesye
(Pripet-Marshes)

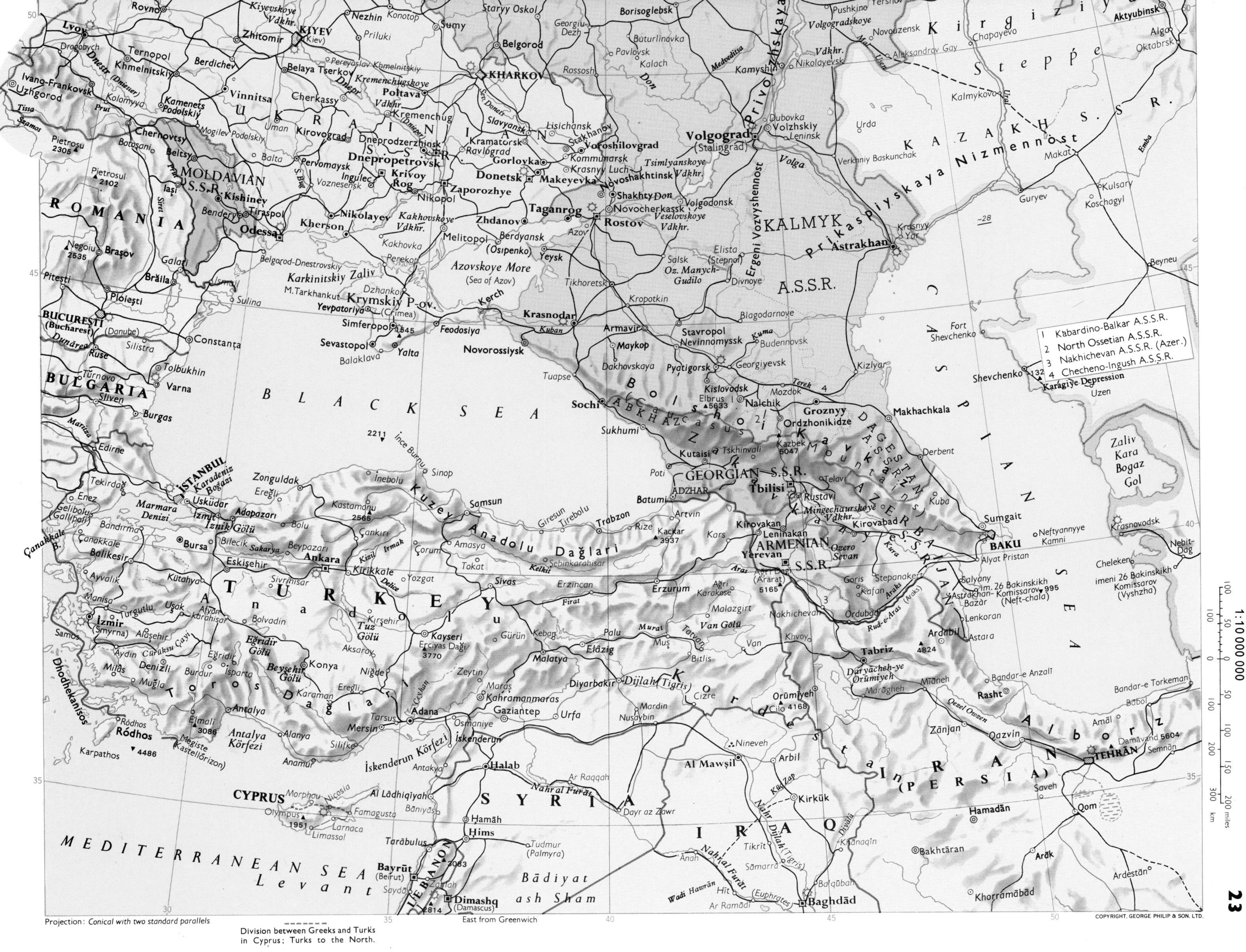

1:10 000 000

100   50   0   50   100   150   200 miles
100   0   100   200   300 km

COPYRIGHT. GEORGE PHILIP & SON. LTD.

1 Kabardino-Balkar A.S.S.R.
2 North Ossetian A.S.S.R. (Azer.)
3 Nakhichevan A.S.S.R. (Azer.)
4 Checheno-Ingush A.S.S.R.

Karagiye Depression

East from Greenwich

Division between Greeks and Turks
in Cyprus; Turks to the North.

Projection: Conical with two standard parallels

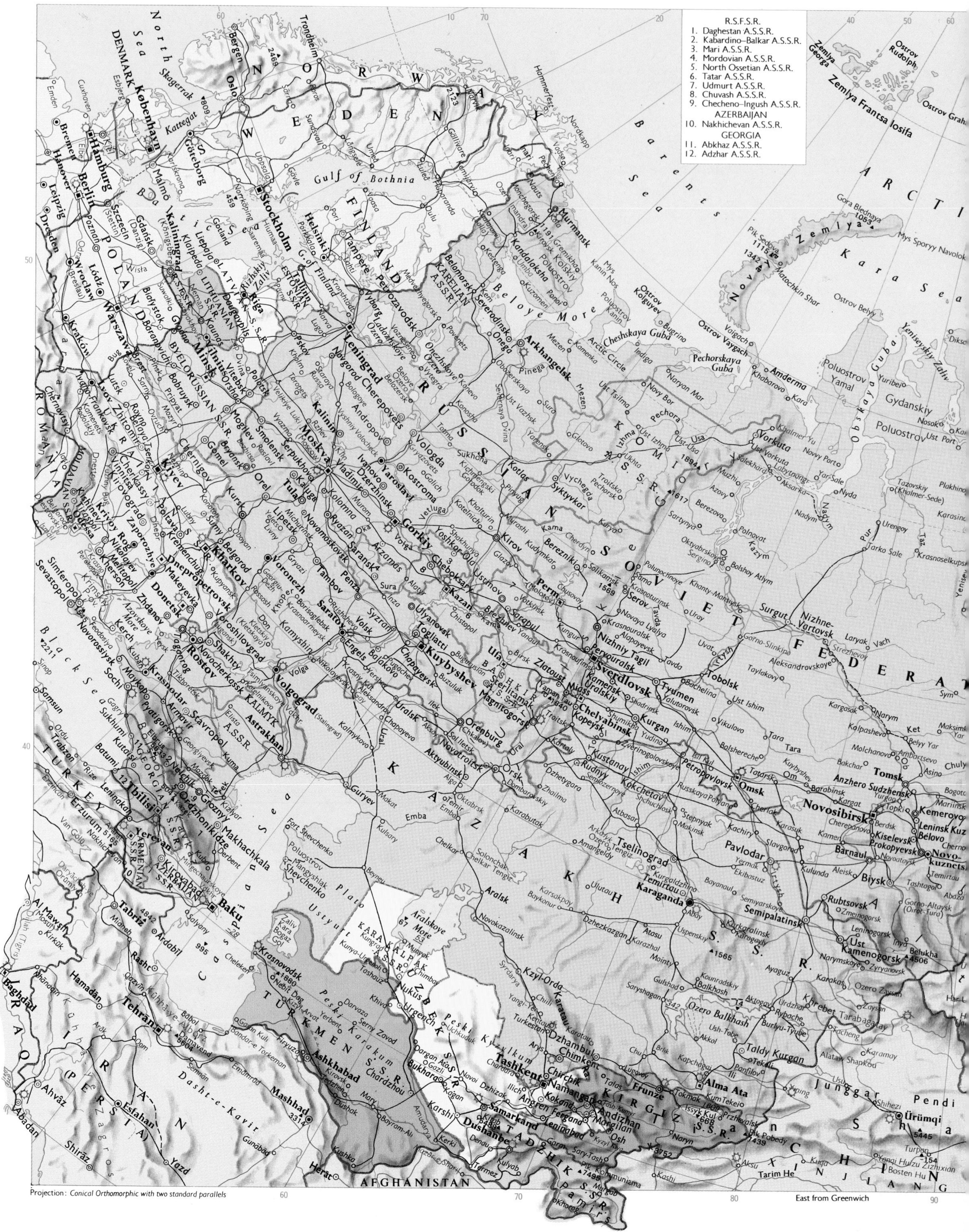

R.S.F.S.R.
1. Daghestan A.S.S.R.
2. Kabardino–Balkar A.S.S.R.
3. Mari A.S.S.R.
4. Mordovian A.S.S.R.
5. North Ossetian A.S.S.R.
6. Tatar A.S.S.R.
7. Udmurt A.S.S.R.
8. Chuvash A.S.S.R.
9. Checheno-Ingush A.S.S.R.
AZERBAIJAN
10. Nakhichevan A.S.S.R.
GEORGIA
11. Abkhaz A.S.S.R.
12. Adzhar A.S.S.R.

Projection: Conical Orthomorphic with two standard parallels

East from Greenwich

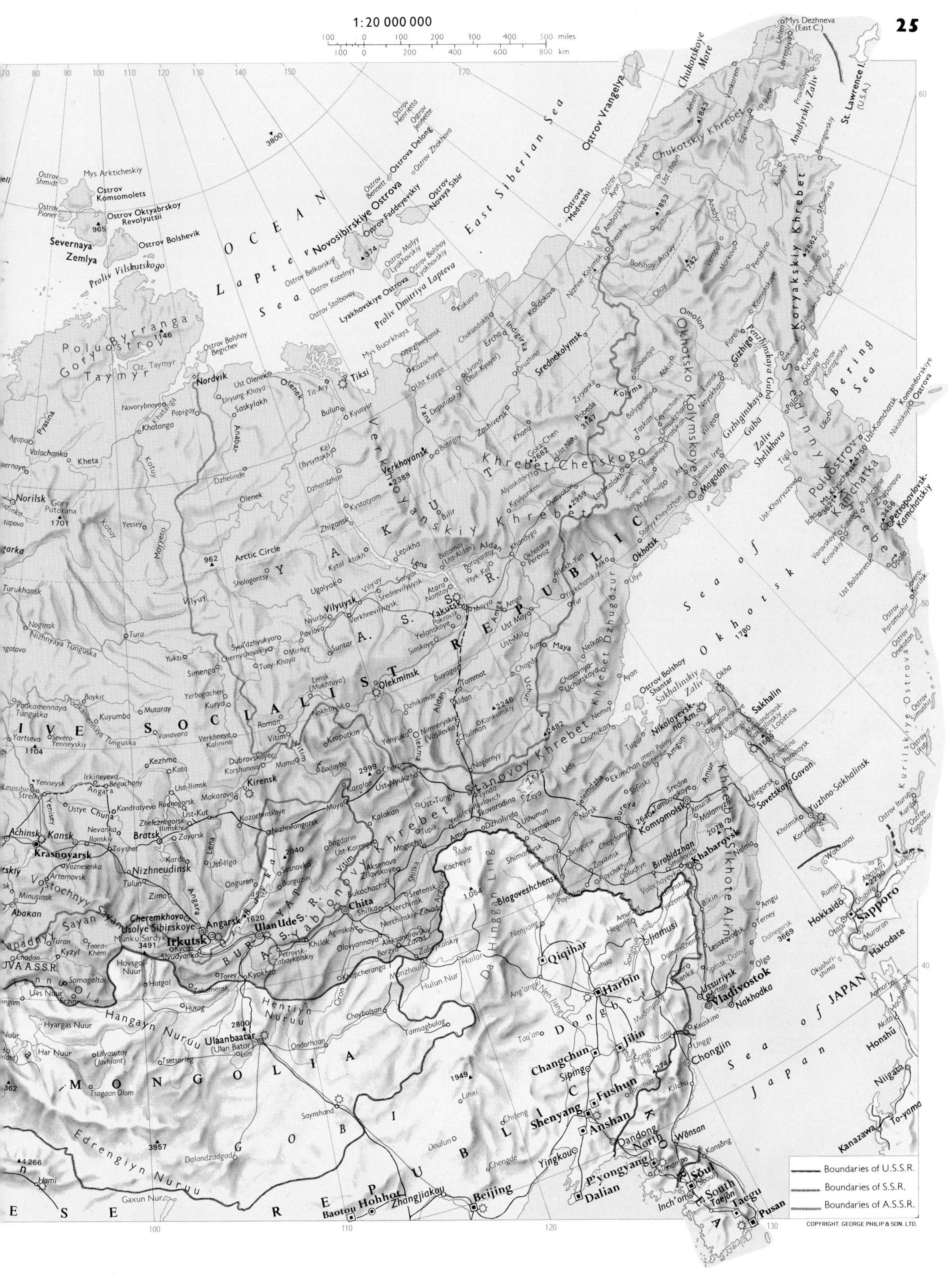
1:20 000 000
100 0 100 200 300 400 500 miles
100 0 200 400 600 800 km
Boundaries of U.S.S.R.
Boundaries of S.S.R.
Boundaries of A.S.S.R.
Mys Dezhneva (East C.)
Chukotskoye More
St. Lawrence I. (U.S.A.)
Anadyrskiy Zaliv
Chukotskiy Khrebet
Ostrov Vrangelya
East Siberian Sea
Ostrova De Long
Ostrov Henrietta
Ostrov Jeannette
Ostrov Bennett
Ostrov Zhokhova
Novosibirskiye Ostrova
Ostrov Faddeyevskiy
Ostrov Novaya Sibir
Ostrov Kotelnyy
Ostrov Belkovskiy
Ostrov Stolbovoy
Lyakhovskiye Ostrova
Ostrov Malyy Lyakhovskiy
Ostrov Bolshoy Lyakhovskiy
Proliv Dmitriya Lapteva
Laptev Sea
OCEAN
Mys Arkticheskiy
Ostrov Shmidt
Ostrov Komsomolets
Ostrov Pioner
Ostrov Oktyabrskoy Revolyutsii
Ostrov Bolshevik
Severnaya Zemlya
Proliv Vilkitskogo
Gory Byrranga
Poluostrov Taymyr
Ostrov Bolshoy Begichev
Oz. Taymyr
Ostrova Medvezhi
Ostrov Ayon
Koryakskiy Khrebet
Sredinnyy Khrebet
Bering Sea
Komandorskiye Ostrova
Poluostrov Kamchatka
Petropavlovsk-Kamchatskiy
Penzhinskaya Guba
Gizhiginskaya Guba
Zaliv Shelikhova
Okhotsko Kolymskoye
Khrebet Cherskogo
Verkhoyanskiy Khrebet
YAKUT A.S.S.R.
Sea of Okhotsk
Khrebet Dzhugdzur
Stanovoy Khrebet
Sakhalinskiy Zaliv
Ostrov Bolshoy Shantar
Sakhalin
Kurilskiye Ostrova
Yablonovyy Khrebet
BURYAT A.S.S.R.
Vostochnyy Sayan
TUVA A.S.S.R.
Khrebet Sikhote Alin
Sea of JAPAN
Hokkaido
Sapporo
Hakodate
Honshū
Niigata
Kanazawa
To-yama
Akita
Aomori
Vladivostok
Nakhodka
Khabarovsk
Komsomolsk
Birobidzhan
Blagoveshchensk
Harbin
Qiqihar
Jilin
Changchun
Shenyang
Fushun
Anshan
Dalian
Dandong
Beijing
Hohhot
Baotou
Zhangjiakou
Chongjin
P'yongyang
Wŏnsan
Sŏul
Inch'on
Taejŏn
Taegu
Pusan
NORTH KOREA
SOUTH KOREA
Dongbei
Da Hinggan Ling
Hulun Nur
MONGOLIA
Ulaanbaatar (Ulan Bator)
Hangayn Nuruu
Hentiyn Nuruu
GOBI
Edrengiyn Nuruu
Gaxun Nur
Hami
Hovsgol Nuur
Irkutsk
Angarsk
Ulan Ude
Chita
Bratsk
Krasnoyarsk
Kansk
Achinsk
Abakan
Norilsk
Igarka
Yakutsk
Verkhoyansk
Magadan
Okhotsk
Tiksi
Nordvik
Olekminsk
Vilyuysk
Kirensk
Nizhneudinsk
Tayshet
Cheremkhovo
Usolye Sibirskoye
Arctic Circle
Lena
Aldan
Vilyuy
Kolyma
Indigirka
Yana
Olenek
Anabar
Amur
Zeya
Angara
Yenisey
Podkamennaya Tunguska
Nizhnyaya Tunguska
Vitim
Olekma
Uchur
Omolon
Anadyr
Kamchatka
Ussuri
Songhua Jiang
Nen Jiang
Ostrov Paramushir
Ostrov Onekotan
Ostrov Simushir
Ostrov Urup
Ostrov Iturup
Ostrov Kunashir
Kurilsk
Korsakov
Yuzhno-Sakhalinsk
Kholmsk
Sovetskaya Gavan
Nikolayevsk-na-Amure
Ostrov Karaginskiy
Ust-Kamchatsk
Klyuchevskaya 4750
Ust Bolsheretsk
Sea of Japan
Yellow Sea
CHINA
REPUBLIC
UNION OF SOVIET SOCIALIST REPUBLICS

1:50 000 000

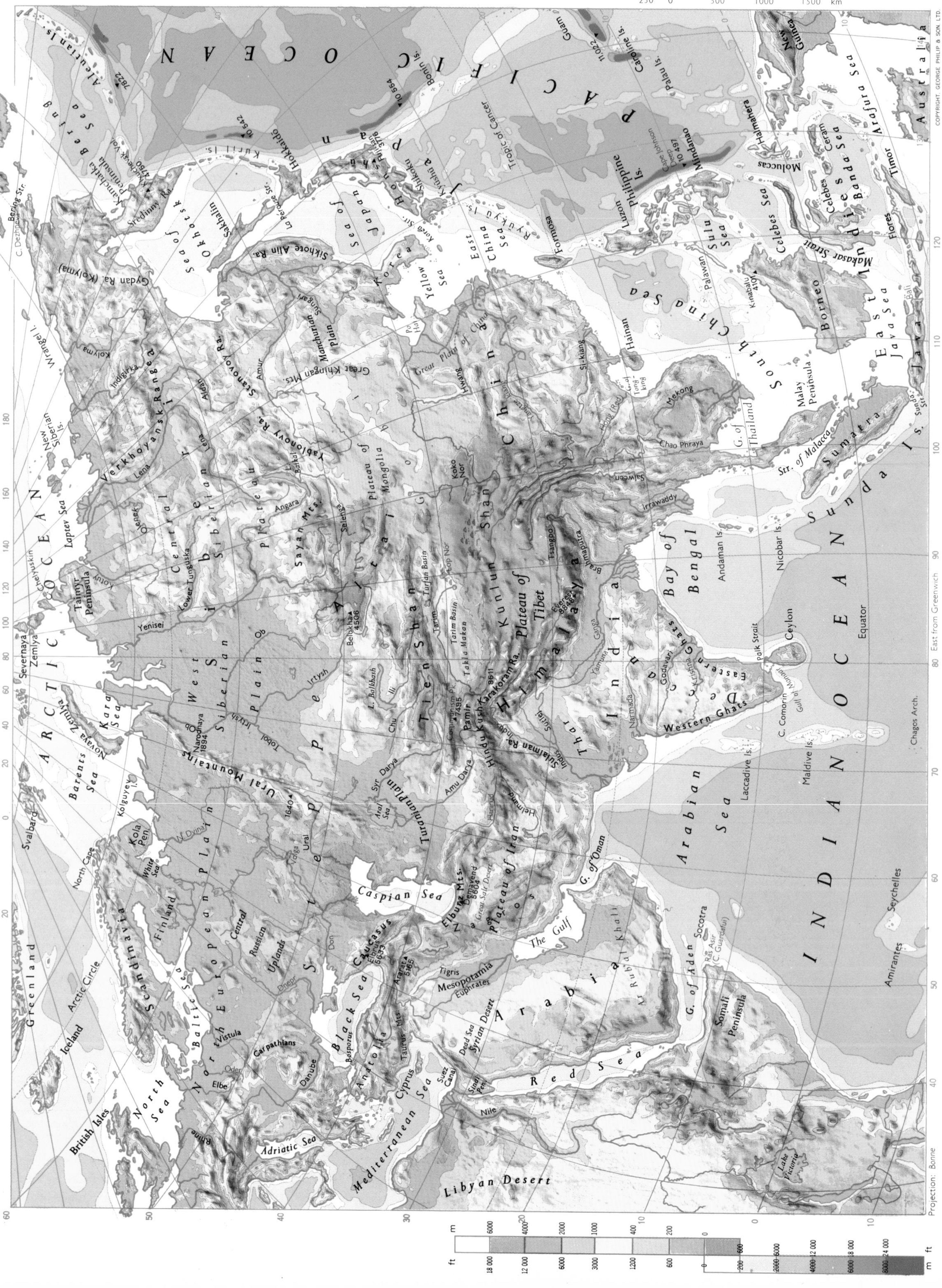

250   0   250   500   750   1000 miles
250   0   500   1000   1500 km

PACIFIC OCEAN

Aleutian Is.
Bering Sea
Kamchatka Peninsula
Bonin Is.
Guam
Caroline Is.
Palau Is.
New Guinea
Australia
Arafura Sea
Banda Sea
Ceram
Halmahera
Moluccas
Celebes Sea
Celebes
Timor
Flores
Bali
Java Sea
East Indies
Borneo
Macassar Strait
Kinabalu 4101
Sulu Sea
Palawan
Philippine Is.
Luzon
Mindanao
Cape Johnson No. 497
Formosa
Hainan
South China Sea
G. of Thailand
Malay Peninsula
Str. of Malacca
Sumatra
Sunda Is.
Sunda Str.

Tropic of Cancer

Kurile Is.
Sakhalin
Hokkaido
Sea of Japan
Japan
Korea Str.
North Str.
Ryukyu Is.
East China Sea
Yellow Sea
Si-Kiang
Mekong
Chao Phraya
Salween
Irrawaddy
Andaman Is.
Nicobar Is.
Bay of Bengal
Ceylon
Polk Strait
Chagos Arch.

Sikhote Alin Ra.
Manchurian Plain
Great Khingan Mts.
Great Plain of China
Hwang-ho
Yangtse
Tsangpo
Brahmaputra
Ganges
Eastern Ghats
Godavari
Krishna
Western Ghats
Narmada
Jumna
Sutlej
Indus
Maldive Is.
Laccadive Is.

INDIAN OCEAN
Equator
Seychelles
Amirantes
Socotra
G. of Aden
Somali Peninsula
Ras Asir (C. Guardafui)
Arabian Sea
C. Comorin
Gulf of Manaar

ARCTIC OCEAN
Svalbard
Greenland
Iceland
Arctic Circle
Barents Sea
Kara Sea
Novaya Zemlya
Severnaya Zemlya
Laptev Sea
Taimyr Peninsula
C. Chelyuskin
New Siberian Is.
Wrangel I.
Bering Str.
C. Dezhnev
Kola Pen.
White Sea
North Cape
Kolguyev I.
Ob
Irtysh
Yenisei
Lena
Angara
Lower Tunguska
Aldan
Amur
Kolyma
Indigirka
Gydan Ra. (Kolyma)
Verkhoyansk Range
Stanovoy Ra.
Yablonovy Ra.
Central Siberian Plateau
Sayan Mts.
Plateau of Mongolia
Koko Nor
Altai
Tien Shan
Tarim Basin
Takla Makan
Turfan Basin
Lop Nor
Kunlun Shan
Plateau of Tibet
Himalaya
Karakoram 8611
Pamir 7495
Hindu Kush
Sulaiman Ra.
Thar Desert
Deccan

West Siberian Plain
Ob
Tobol
Irtysh
Ural Mountains 1640
Narodnaya 1894
Belukha 4506
Steppe
Aral Sea
L. Balkhash
Ili
Chu
Syr Darya
Amu Darya
Turan Plain
Helmand
Zagend
Mt Demavend
Great Salt Desert
Plateau of Iran
G. of Oman
The Gulf

North European Plain
Scandinavia
Finland
Baltic Sea
North Sea
British Isles
W. Dvina
Central Russian Uplands
Volga
Don
Dnepr
Caspian Sea
Ural
Caucasus Elbruz 5633
Ararat 5165
Black Sea
Bosporus
Anatolia
Taurus Mts.
Cyprus
Elburz Mts.
Tigris
Euphrates
Mesopotamia
Dead Sea
Syrian Desert
Arabia
Rub' al Khali

Rhine
Elbe
Oder
Vistula
Danube
Carpathians
Adriatic Sea
Mediterranean Sea
Suez Canal
Red Sea
Nile
Libyan Desert
Lake Victoria

East from Greenwich

Projection: Bonne

m   ft
18 000   6000
12 000   4000
6000   2000
3000   1000
1200   400
600   200
0   0
200   600
2000   6000
4000   12 000
6000   18 000
8000   24 000
ft   m

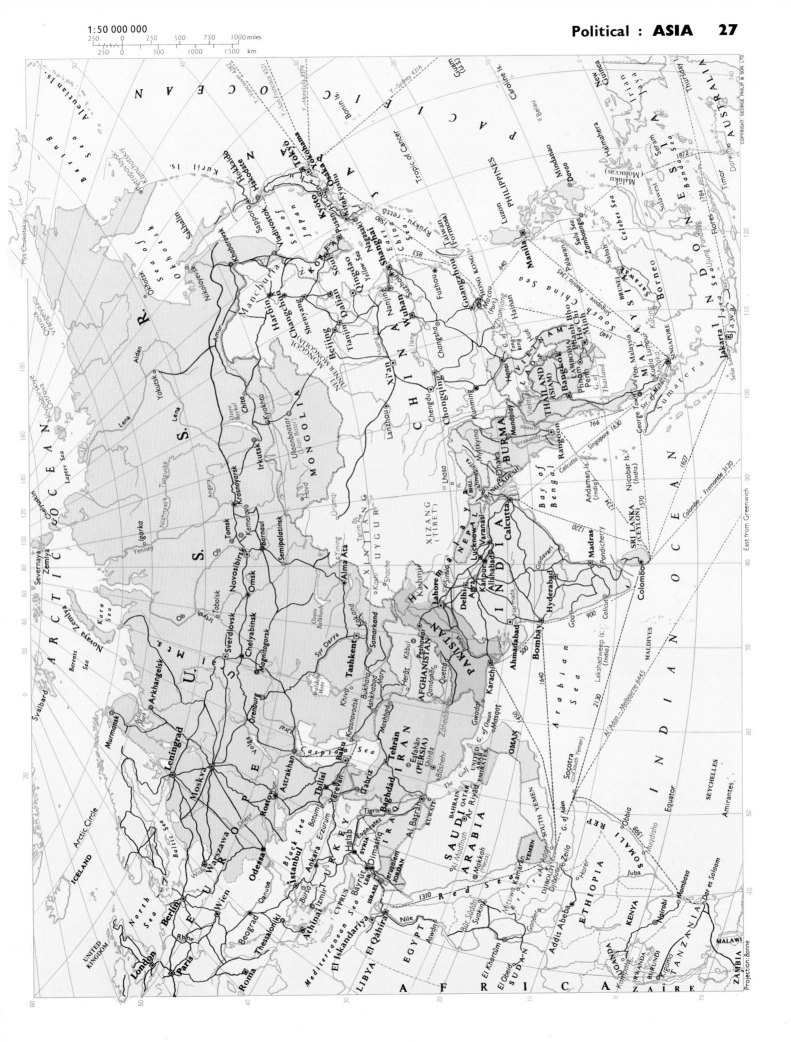

1:50 000 000

COPYRIGHT: GEORGE PHILIP & SON, LTD.

Projection: Bonne

1:1 000 000

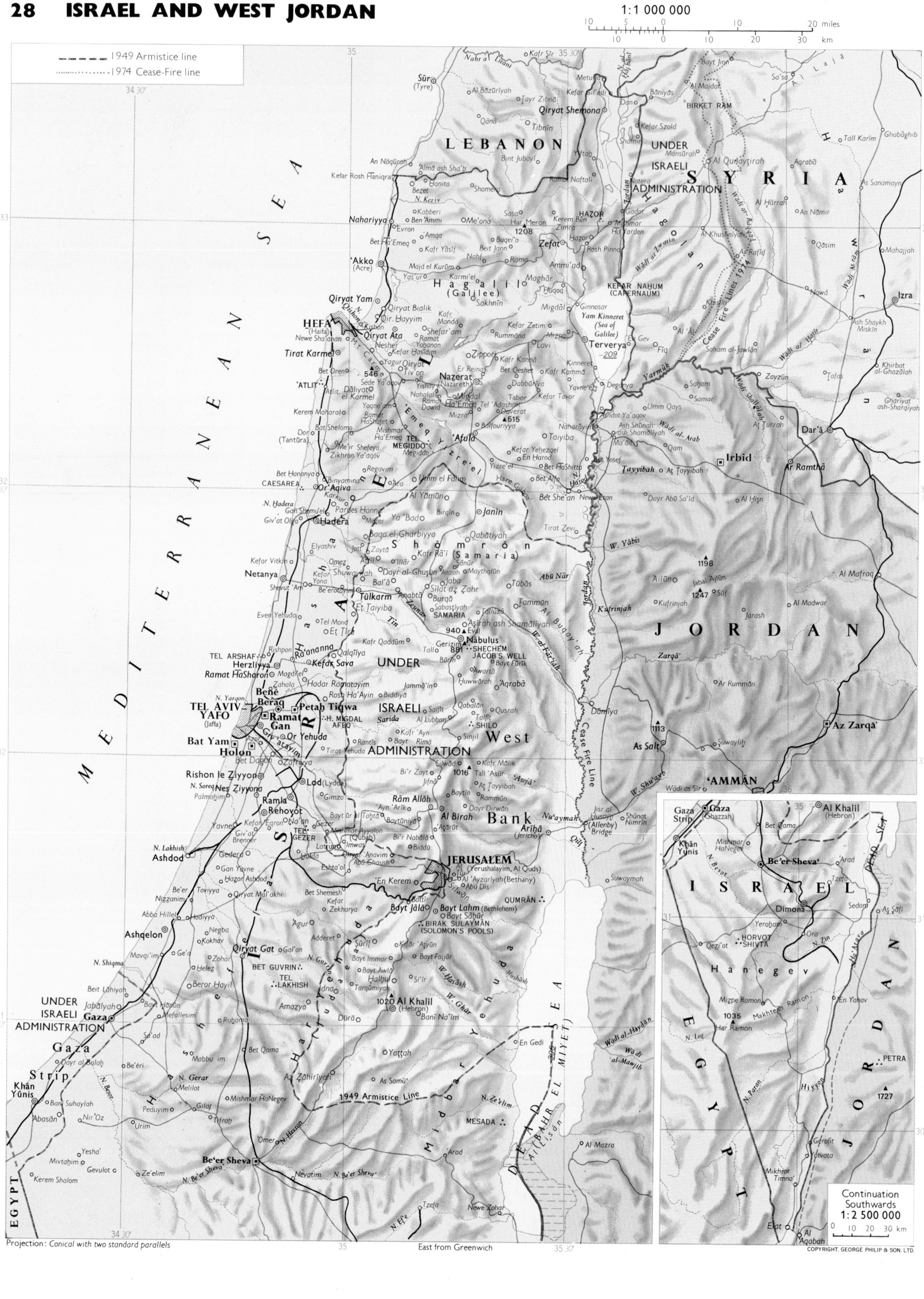

10   0   10   20 miles
10   0   10   20   30 km

─ ─ ─ 1949 Armistice line
········· 1974 Cease-Fire line

MEDITERRANEAN SEA

LEBANON

SYRIA

UNDER ISRAELI ADMINISTRATION

Qiryat Shemona
BIRKET RAM

Sūr (Tyre)
An Nāqūrah
Kefar Rosh Haniqra
Nahariyya
'Akko (Acre)
Qiryat Yam
Qir. Bialik
Qiryat Ata
HEFA (Haifa)
Newe Sha'anan
Tirat Karmel
'ATLIT
Atlit
Daliyat el Karmel
Kerem Maharal
Dor (Tantūra)
CAESAREA
Or 'Aqiva
Hadera
Netanya
Kefar Vitkin
TEL ARSHAF
Herzliyya
Ra'anana
Kefar Sava
Ramat HaSharon
Beñe Beraq
TEL AVIV-YAFO (Jaffa)
Ramat Gan
Bat Yam
Holon
Rishon le Ziyyon
Nes Ziyyona
Ramla
Rehovot
Lod (Lydda)
Ashdod
Gan Yavne
Qiryat Mal'akhi
Ashqelon
Qiryat Gat
BET GUVRIN
TEL LAKHISH
Gaza
Khān Yūnis
UNDER ISRAELI ADMINISTRATION
Gaza Strip

Hagalil (Galilee)
Har Meron 1208
ZEFAT
Rosh Pinna
KEFAR NAHUM (CAPERNAUM)
Yam Kinneret (Sea of Galilee)
Terverya -209
Nazerat (Nazareth)
Tabor
Tel 'Adashim
TEL MEGIDDO
'Afula
Bet She'an
Janin
Shomron (Samaria)
Tūlkarm
SAMARIA
Nābulus
SHECHEM
JACOB'S WELL
UNDER ISRAELI ADMINISTRATION
West Bank
SHILO
Rām Allāh
Al Birah
Ariha (Jericho)
JERUSALEM (Yerushalayim, Al Quds)
Al 'Ayzariya (Bethany)
QUMRĀN
Bayt Jālā
Bayt Lahm (Bethlehem)
BIRAK SULAYMĀN (SOLOMON'S POOLS)
Al Khalil (Hebron)

JORDAN
Irbid
Ar Ramthā
Dar'ā
Jabal 'Ajlūn 1247
Jarash
As Salt
Az Zarqā'
'AMMĀN
Zarqā'

DEAD SEA (BAHR EL MIYET)
En Gedi
MESADA

1949 Armistice Line

Be'er Sheva

EGYPT

Projection: Conical with two standard parallels
East from Greenwich

Inset
Continuation Southwards
1:2 500 000
0 10 20 30 km

Gaza
Al Khalil (Hebron)
Gaza Strip
Khān Yūnis
Be'er Sheva'
ISRAEL
Dimona
HORVOT SHIVTA
Hanegev
Mizpe Ramon
Makhtesh Ramon
EGYPT
JORDAN
PETRA
1727
Elat
Al 'Aqaba

COPYRIGHT GEORGE PHILIP & SON, LTD.

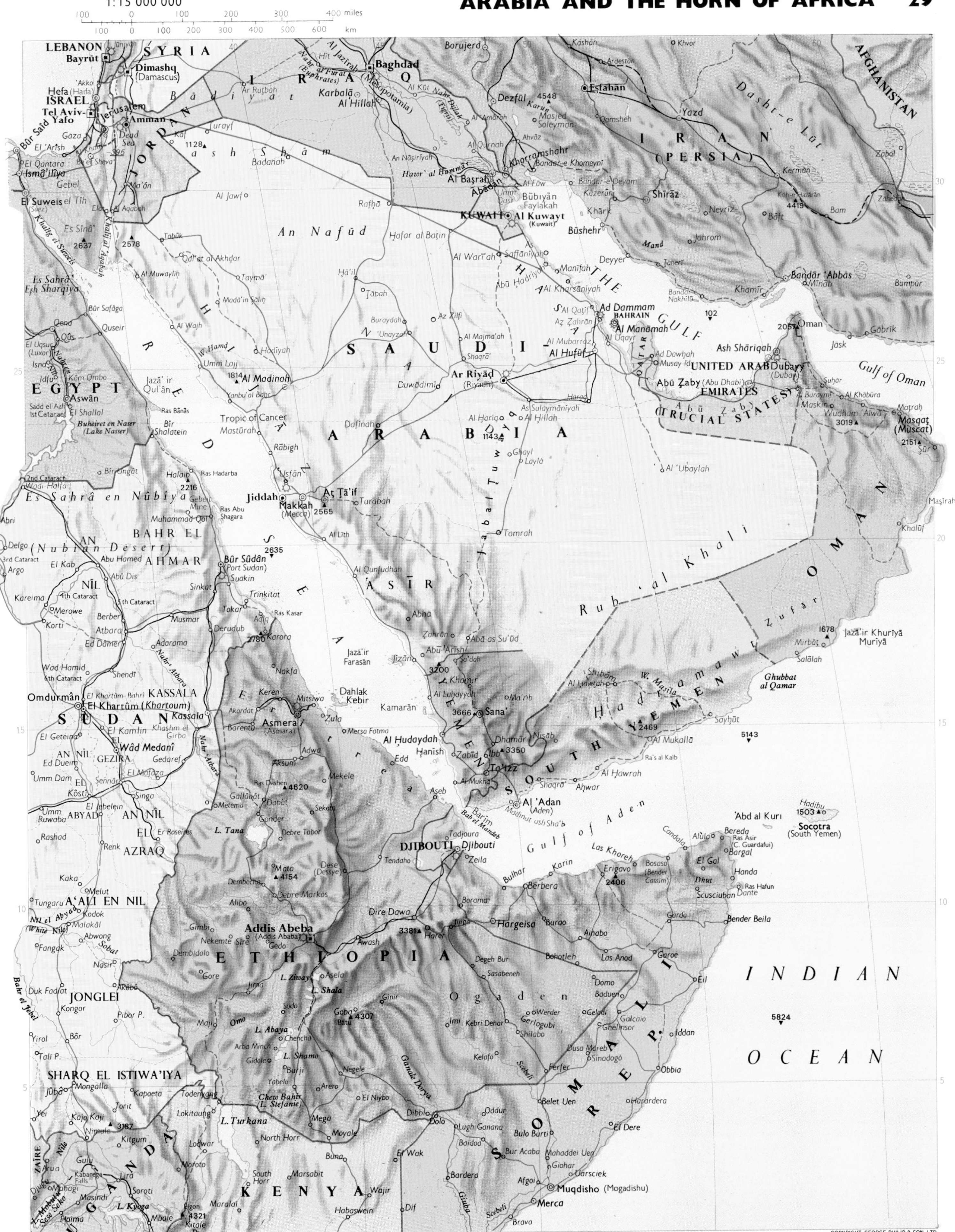

1:15 000 000

100   0   100   200   300   400 miles
100   0   100   200   300   400   500   600 km

SYRIA
LEBANON
Bayrût
Dimashq
(Damascus)
Hefa (Haifa)
ISRAEL
Tel Aviv-Yafo
Jerusalem
Amman
Gaza
El 'Arîsh
El Qantara
Ismâ'îlîya
El Suweis (Suez)
Gebel
Es Sîna'
2637
2578

IRAQ
Baghdad
Karbalā'
Al Hillah
Al Başrah
KUWAIT
Al Kuwayt (Kuwait)

IRAN (PERSIA)
Eşfahān
Yazd
Shīrāz
Kermān
BandarʿAbbās

SAUDI ARABIA
Ar Riyāḍ (Riyadh)
Al Madīnah
Makkah (Mecca)
Jiddah
Aţ Ţāʾif

EGYPT
Aswân
Buheiret en Naser (Lake Nasser)

SŪDAN
El Khartûm (Khartoum)
Omdurmân

ETHIOPIA
Addis Abeba (Addis Ababa)

YEMEN
Sana'
SOUTH YEMEN
Al ʿAdan (Aden)

OMAN
Masqaṭ (Muscat)

UNITED ARAB EMIRATES

Rubʿ al Khali

Gulf of Aden

INDIAN OCEAN

SOMALI REP.

KENYA

UGANDA

Socotra (South Yemen)

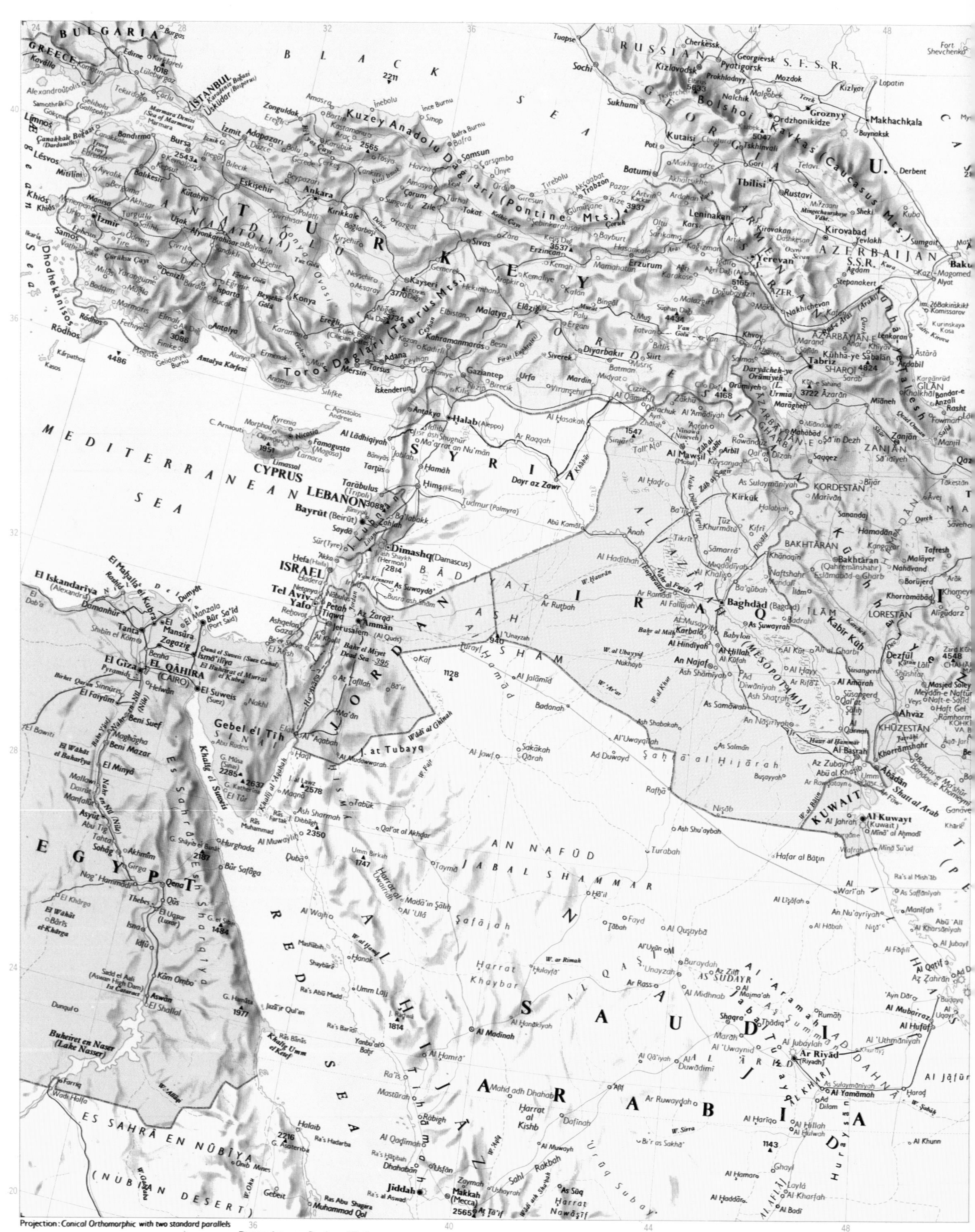

Projection: Conical Orthomorphic with two standard parallels

Division between Greeks and Turks
in Cyprus; Turks to the North.

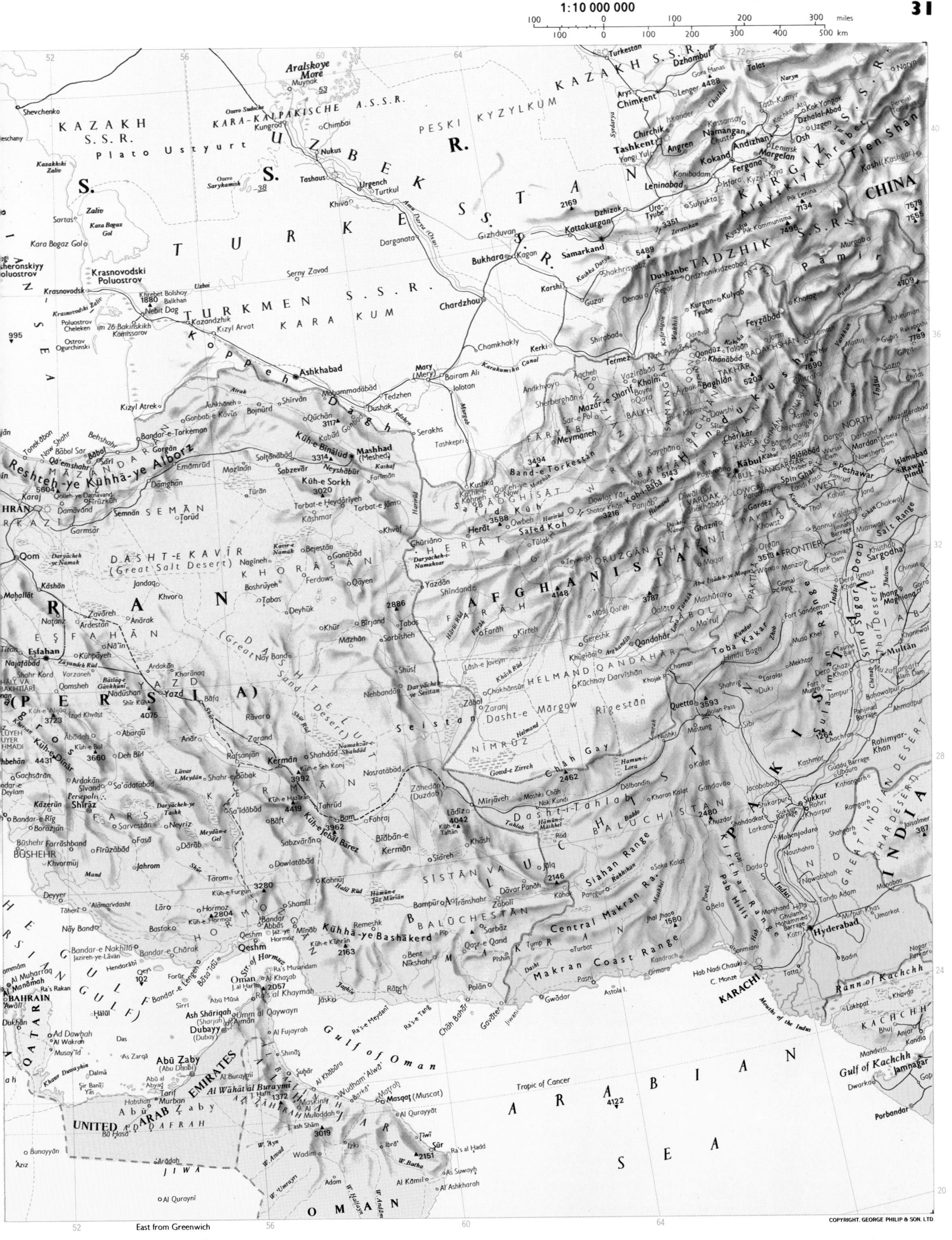

U.S.S.R.

AFGHANISTAN

HERAT   GHOWR   BĀMIĀN   HINDU KUSH   BADAKHSHAN   TAKHĀR

FARĀH   GHAZNĪ   PAKTIĀ   NORTH WEST FRONTIER

HELMAND   QANDAHĀR   PAKTIKA   JAMMU AND KASHMIR

NIMRŪZ   BALUCHISTAN   Peshawar   Srinagar   KARAKORAM

I R A N (PERSIA)

Kabul   Rawalpindi   Islamabad   HIMACHAL PRADESH

Quetta   Lahore   Faisalabad   Amritsar   Ludhiana   Simla   Dehra Dun

PUNJAB   Chandigarh   Ambala   Saharanpur

Karachi   Hyderabad   Sukkur   Multan   Bahawalpur   DELHI   Meerut   Moradabad   Rampur   Bareilly

ARABIAN SEA

Tropic of Cancer

R A J A S T H A N   Bikaner   Jaipur   Agra   Gwalior   Kanpur

Jodhpur   Ajmer   Jhansi

Thar (Great Indian) Desert   Rann of Kachchh   Gulf of Kachchh

G U J A R A T   Ahmadabad   Rajkot   Vadodara (Baroda)   Indore   Bhopal   M A D H Y A   P R A D E S H

Jamnagar   Junagadh   Surat   Bombay   Nagpur

Kathiawar   Gulf of Khambhat   Daman   DADRA & NAGAR HAVELI

M A H A R A S H T R A   Nasik   Aurangabad   Nanded

Pune (Poona)   Solapur   Gulbarga   A N D H R A   P R A D E S H   Hyderabad   Warangal

Kolhapur   Belgaum   GOA   Dharwad   Karnataka

Inset (Continuation Southwards):

GOA   KARNATAKA   Dharwad   Bellary   Kurnool   Adoni

Mangalore   Bangalore   Madras   Vellore   Pulicat Lake

Mysore   TAMIL NADU   Salem   Pondicherry   Cuddalore

Calicut (Kozhikode)   Coimbatore   Tiruchchirappalli   Thanjavur   Nagappattinam

Cochin   Ernakulam   Madurai   Palk Strait   Jaffna

KERALA   Quilon   Trivandrum   Nagercoil   Cape Comorin   Gulf of Mannar (Manaar)   Adam's Bridge

SRI LANKA (CEYLON)   Colombo   Kandy   Trincomalee   Moratuwa   Galle   Dondra Head

Cardamon Hills   Coromandel Coast   Malabar Coast

Continuation Southwards on same scale

Projection: Conical with two standard parallels

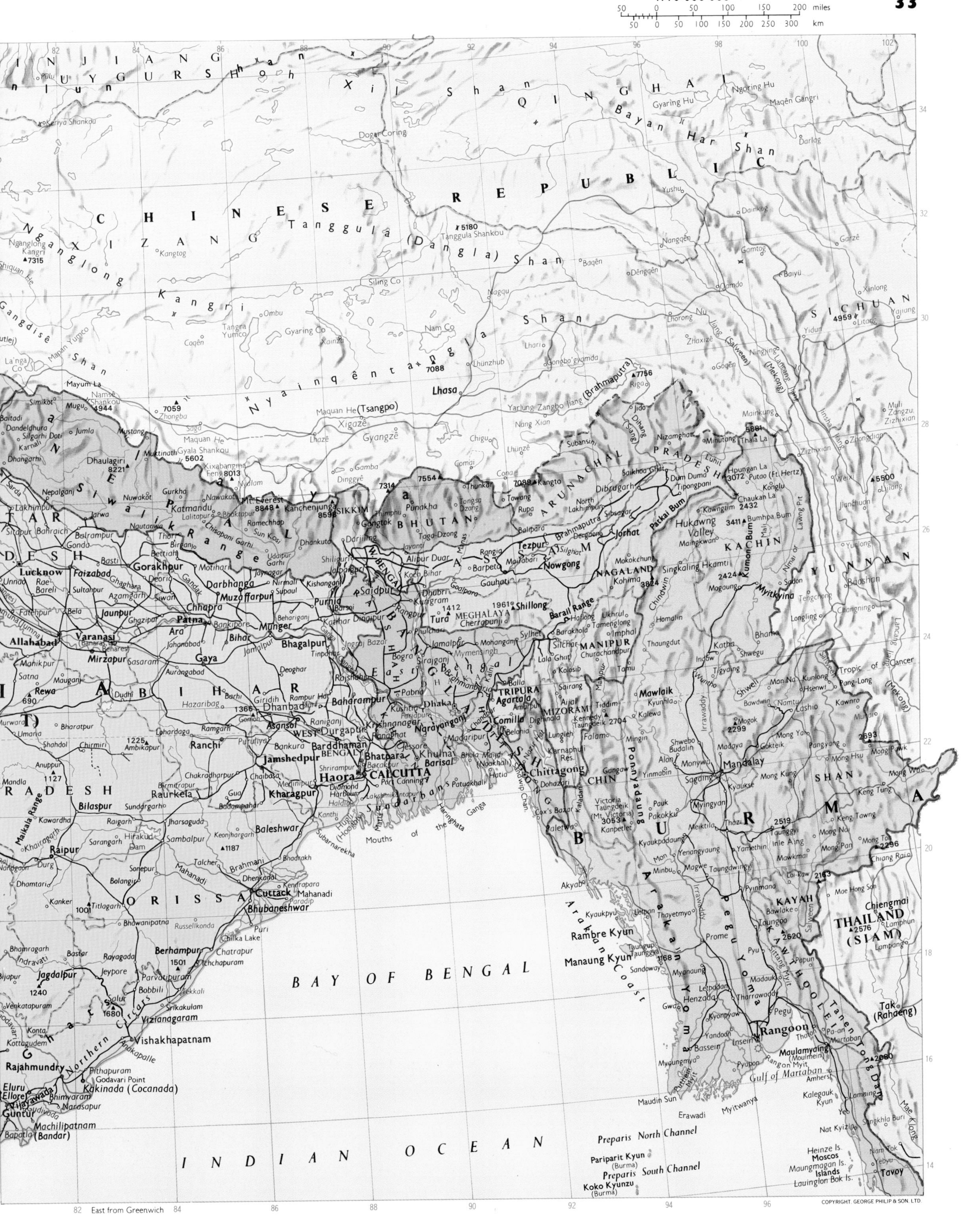

1:10 000 000
miles
km
CHINESE REPUBLIC
QINGHAI
XIZANG
SICHUAN
YUNNAN
Tanggula (Dangla) Shan
Bayan Har Shan
Xil Shan
Nyainqêntanglha Shan
Nganglong Kangri
Gangdisê Shan
Lhasa
NEPAL
Katmandu
Mt. Everest
8848
Kanchenjunga
SIKKIM
Gangtok
BHUTAN
Thimphu
ARUNACHAL PRADESH
ASSAM
NAGALAND
MANIPUR
MIZORAM
TRIPURA
MEGHALAYA
Shillong
BANGLADESH
Dhaka
Chittagong
Khulna
Barisal
Sundarbans
CALCUTTA
Haora
WEST BENGAL
BIHAR
Patna
Ranchi
Jamshedpur
Gaya
Varanasi
Allahabad
Lucknow
Gorakhpur
ORISSA
Cuttack
Bhubaneshwar
Raipur
Bilaspur
Vishakhapatnam
Vizianagaram
Rajahmundry
Kakinada (Cocanada)
Machilipatnam (Bandar)
Northern Circars
BURMA
KACHIN
CHIN
SHAN
KAYAH
KAWTHOOLEI
Mandalay
Rangoon
Myitkyina
Akyab
Bassein
Moulmein
Tavoy
Pegu Yoma
Arakan Yoma
Arakan Coast
Gulf of Martaban
THAILAND (SIAM)
Chiengmai
Tropic of Cancer
BAY OF BENGAL
Mouths of the Ganga
INDIAN OCEAN
Preparis North Channel
Preparis South Channel
East from Greenwich

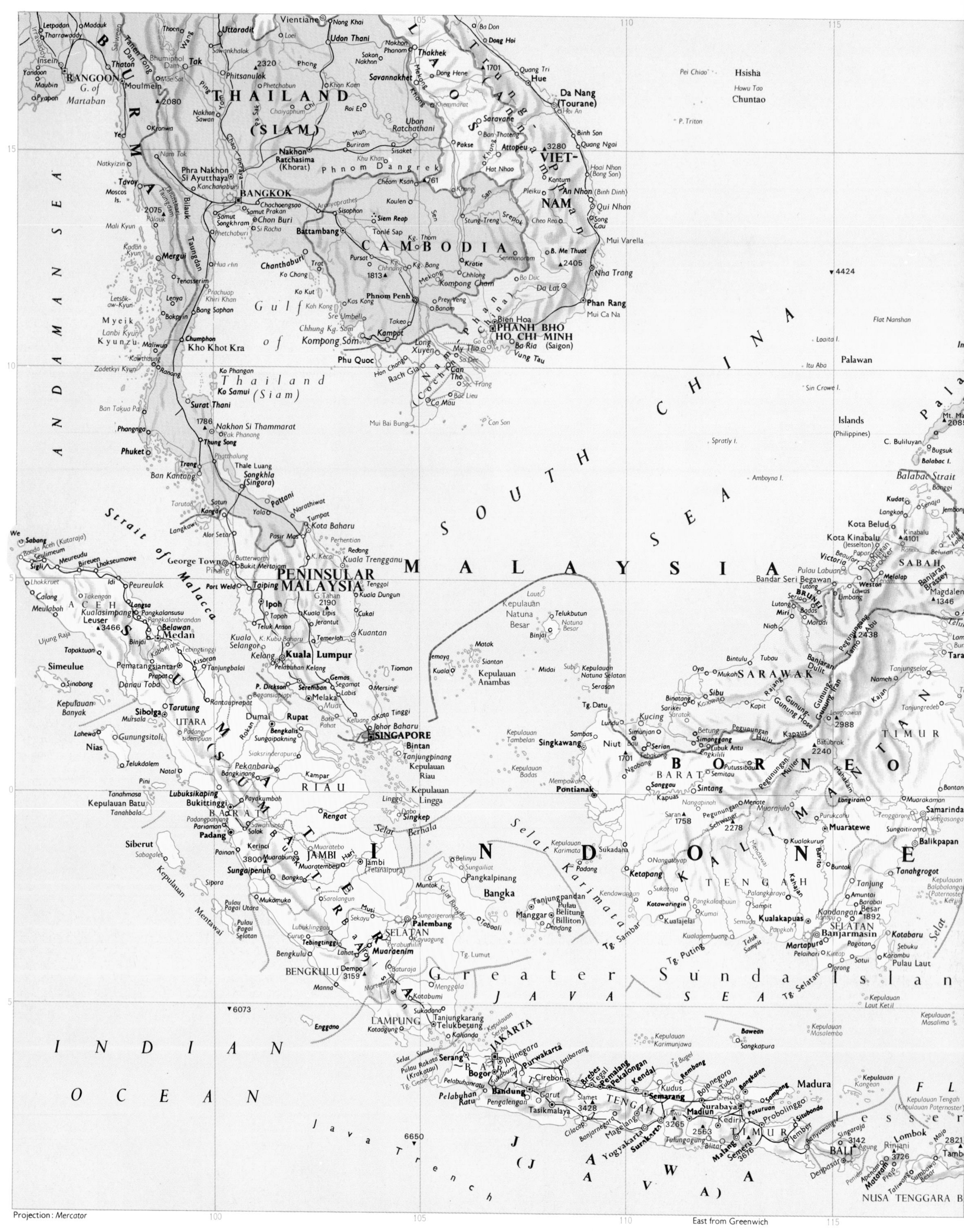

BURMA
RANGOON
G. of Martaban
Moulmein
Tavoy
Mergui
Victoria Point
ANDAMAN SEA
THAILAND (SIAM)
BANGKOK
Phra Nakhon Si Ayutthaya
Nakhon Ratchasima (Khorat)
Phnom Dangrek
Chiang Mai
Uttaradit
Phitsanulok
Tak
Nakhon Sawan
Ubon Ratchathani
Udon Thani
Vientiane
Nong Khai
LAOS
Thakhek
Savannakhet
Pakse
Saravane
Attopeu
Hue
Quang Tri
Dong Hoi
Da Nang (Tourane)
Quang Ngai
Qui Nhon
Kontum
Pleiku
An Nhon
VIET-NAM
Nha Trang
Phan Rang
Da Lat
B. Me Thuot
CAMBODIA
Battambang
Siem Reap
Tonlé Sap
Kompong Cham
Kratie
Phnom Penh
Kampot
Kompong Som
Takeo
Chanthaburi
Trat
PHANH BHO HO CHI MINH (Saigon)
Bien Hoa
Vung Tau
My Tho
Can Tho
Long Xuyen
Rach Gia
Soc Trang
Bac Lieu
Ca Mau
Phu Quoc
Con Son
Gulf of Thailand (Siam)
Chumphon
Kho Khot Kra
Ranong
Surat Thani
Ko Samui
Ko Phangan
Nakhon Si Thammarat
Thung Song
Phuket
Phangnga
Trang
Songkhla (Singora)
Pattani
Narathiwat
Kota Baharu
Alor Setar
George Town Pinang
Butterworth
Taiping
Ipoh
Kuala Trengganu
Kuantan
PENINSULAR MALAYSIA
Kuala Lumpur
Kelang
Seremban
Melaka
Muar
Johor Baharu
SINGAPORE
Bintan
Tanjungpinang
Kepulauan Riau
RIAU
Lingga
Singkep
Strait of Malacca
SOUTH CHINA SEA
MALAYSIA
Hsisha
Chuntao
Spratly I.
Amboyna I.
Palawan
Islands (Philippines)
Balabac Strait
Kudat
Kota Belud
Kota Kinabalu (Jesselton)
Kinabalu 4101
SABAH
Pulau Labuan
BRUNEI
Bandar Seri Begawan
Miri
Bintulu
SARAWAK
Sibu
Kucing
Kepulauan Natuna Besar
Kepulauan Anambas
Kepulauan Natuna Selatan
Singkawang
Pontianak
BORNEO
KALIMANTAN
BARAT
TIMUR
TENGAH
SELATAN
Sintang
Ketapang
Samarinda
Balikpapan
Banjarmasin
Kotabaru
Pulau Laut
Selat Karimata
Sabang
Banda Aceh (Kutaraja)
ACEH
Lhokseumawe
Medan
Belawan
Binjai
Tebingtinggi
Pematangsiantar
Danau Toba
Tarutung
Sibolga
Simeulue
Nias
Gunungsitoli
Kepulauan Banyak
UTARA
SUMATERA
Padang
Bukittinggi
Payakumbuh
Pekanbaru
Dumai
Bengkalis
Jambi
JAMBI
Rengat
Siberut
Kepulauan Mentawai
Sipora
Pulau Pagai Utara
Pulau Pagai Selatan
Bengkulu
BENGKULU
Lahat
Palembang
Muaraenim
Bangka
Pangkalpinang
Belitung
Tanjungpandan
Manggar
Kotabumi
LAMPUNG
Tanjungkarang-Telukbetung
Enggano
INDONESIA
Greater Sunda Islands
JAVA SEA
Kepulauan Karimunjawa
Bawean
Madura
JAKARTA
Bogor
Serang
Bandung
Cirebon
Tegal
Pekalongan
Semarang
Kudus
Surakarta
Yogyakarta
Madiun
Kediri
Surabaya
Malang
Semeru 3676
Probolinggo
Jember
BALI
Lombok
Rinjani 3726
Mataram
JAWA (JAVA)
TIMUR
TENGAH
BARAT
INDIAN OCEAN
Java Trench
NUSA TENGGARA B

Projection: *Mercator*

East from Greenwich

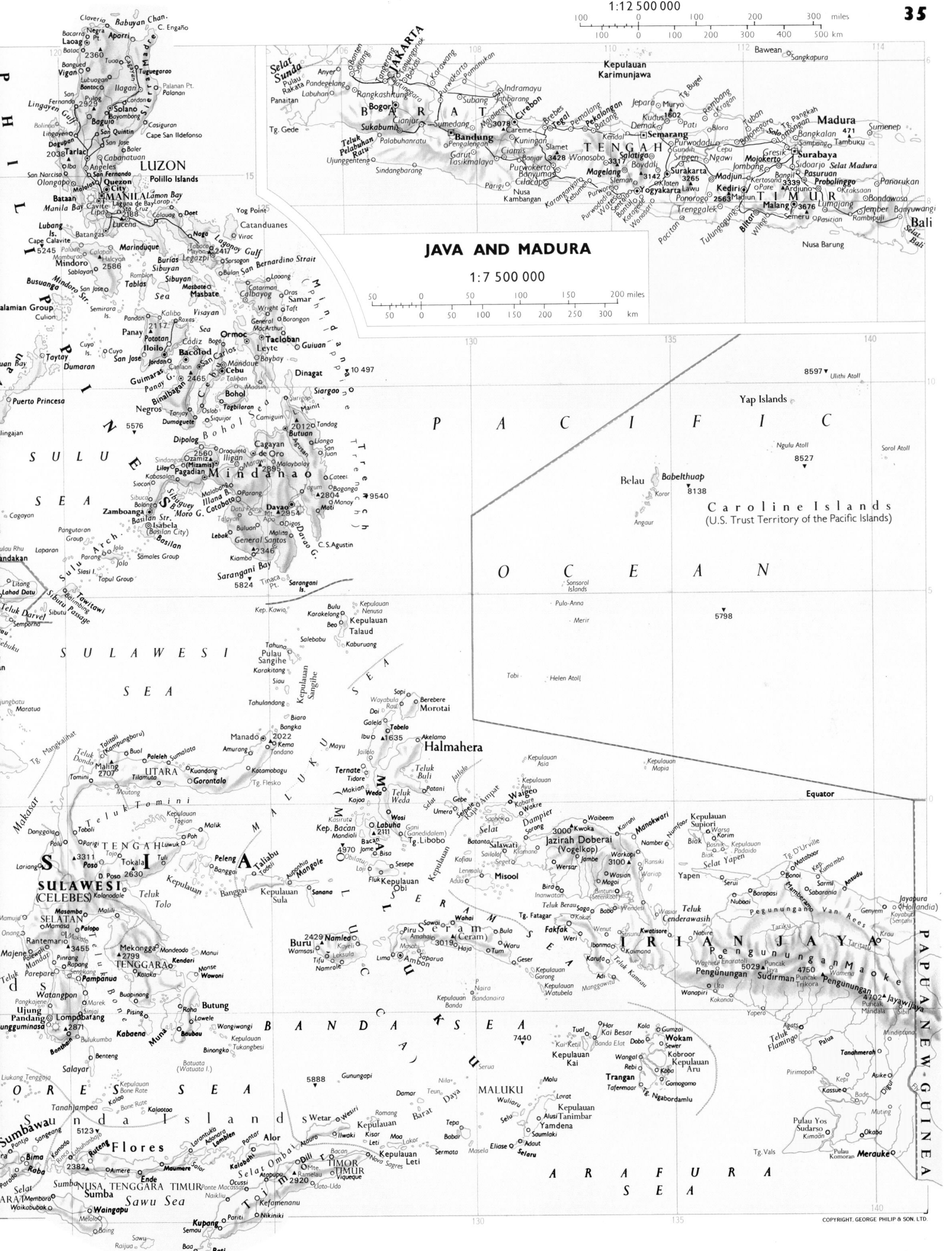

1:12 500 000

100   0   100   200   300 miles
100   0   100   200   300   400   500 km

JAVA AND MADURA

1:7 500 000

50   0   50   100   150   200 miles
50   0   50   100   150   200   250   300 km

PACIFIC

OCEAN

Caroline Islands
(U.S. Trust Territory of the Pacific Islands)

Yap Islands

Equator

LUZON

MANILA

PHILIPPINE

Mindoro

SULU
SEA

Mindanao

Zamboanga
Davao

SULAWESI
SEA

SULAWESI
(CELEBES)

MALUKU
SEA

Halmahera

Ternate

SERAM SEA

BANDA SEA

FLORES SEA

MALUKU

Flores

NUSA TENGGARA TIMUR

TIMOR

ARAFURA
SEA

IRIAN JAYA

PAPUA NEW GUINEA

Jayapura
(Hollandia)

Merauke

JAKARTA
Bogor
Bandung
Semarang
Surakarta
Yogyakarta
Surabaya
Madura
Malang
Bali

BARAT   TENGAH   TIMUR

SEA OF JAPAN

PACIFIC OCEAN

Sea of Okhotsk

SEA OF JAPAN

PACIFIC OCEAN

SOUTH KOREA

CHŪGOKU
KINKI
SHIKOKU
KYŪSHŪ
HOKKAIDO
TOHOKU
CHŪBU
KANTŌ

1:5 000 000
East from Greenwich
25 0 25 50 75 100 miles
25 0 50 100 150 km
Projection: Conical with two standard parallels

1:10 000 000
East from Greenwich
100 50 0 50 100 150 200 miles
100 0 100 200 300 km
Projection: Bonne

Ōsumi-Shotō 1935
Tane-ga-Shima
Yaku-Shima
Tokara-Kaikyō
Tokara-Shima
Suwanose-Jima
Nansei-Shoto
Amami-Ō-Shima
Toku-no-Shima
Continuation Southwards on same scale

REFERENCE TO PREFECTURES		
HOKKAIDO DISTRICT		**KINKI DISTRICT**
1 Hokkaidō		24 Hyogo
TŌHOKU DISTRICT		25 Kyōto
2 Aomori		26 Shiga
3 Akita		27 Ōsaka
4 Iwate		28 Nara
5 Yamagata		29 Mie
6 Miyagi		30 Wakayama
7 Fukushima		**CHŪGOKU DISTRICT**
CHŪBU DISTRICT		31 Tottori
8 Niigata		32 Okayama
9 Ishikawa		33 Shimane
10 Toyama		34 Hiroshima
11 Fukui		35 Yamaguchi
12 Gifu		**SHIKOKU DISTRICT**
13 Nagano		36 Kagawa
14 Yamanashi		37 Tokushima
15 Aichi		38 Ehime
16 Shizuoka		39 Kōchi
KANTŌ DISTRICT		**KYŪSHŪ DISTRICT**
17 Gumma		40 Fukuoka
18 Tochigi		41 Saga
19 Saitama		42 Nagasaki
20 Ibaraki		43 Kumamoto
21 Tōkyō		44 Ōita
22 Chiba		45 Miyazaki
23 Kanagawa		46 Kagoshima

1:20 000 000

100   0   100   200   300   400 miles
100   0   100   200   300   400   500   600 km

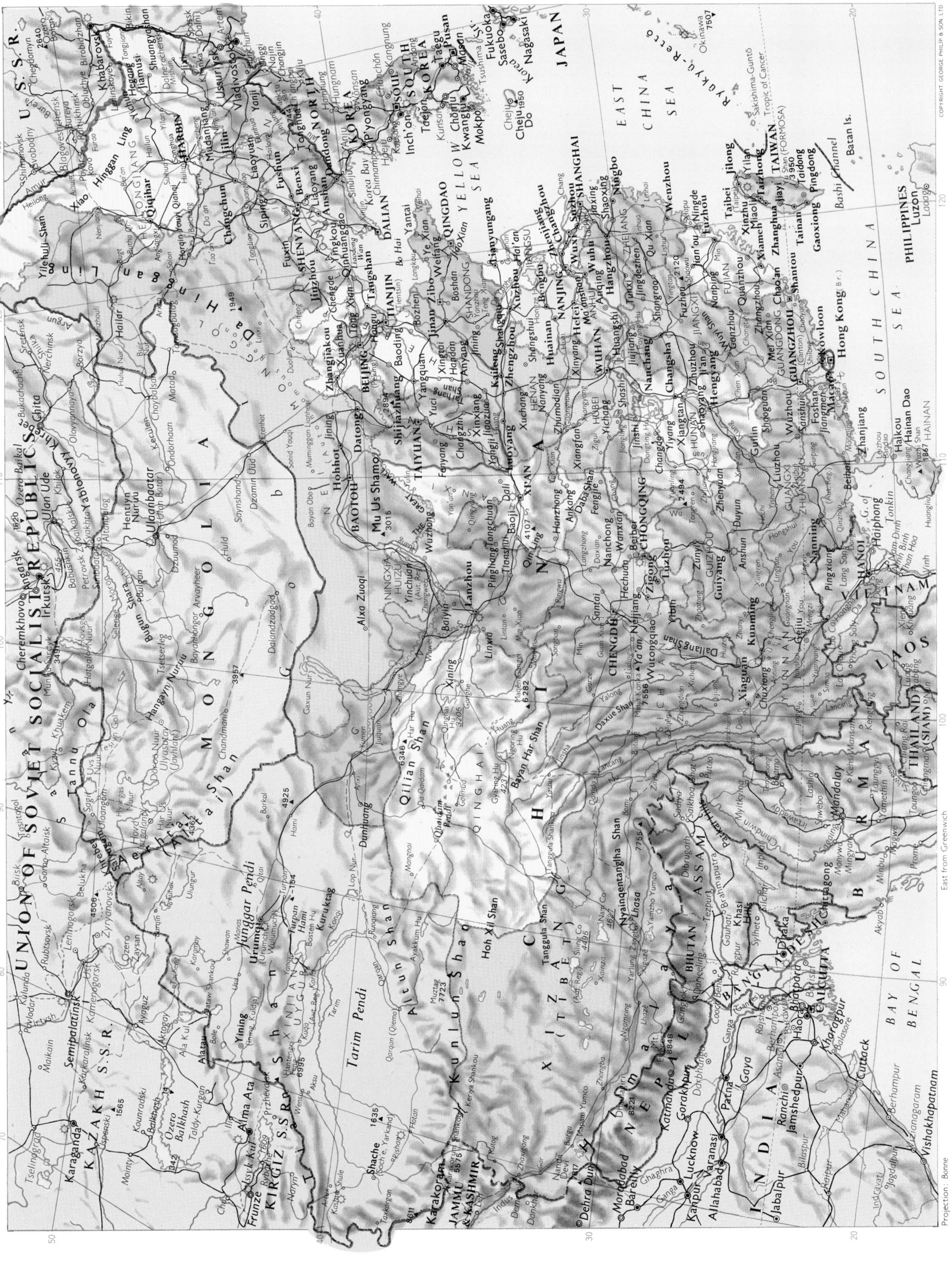

UNION OF SOVIET SOCIALIST REPUBLICS

MONGOLIA

C H I N A

JAPAN

SOUTH KOREA

NORTH KOREA

YELLOW SEA

EAST CHINA SEA

SOUTH CHINA SEA

BAY OF BENGAL

INDIA

NEPAL

BHUTAN

BANGLADESH

BURMA

THAILAND (SIAM)

LAOS

VIETNAM

PHILIPPINES

TAIWAN (FORMOSA)

KAZAKH S.S.R.

KIRGIZ S.S.R.

JAMMU & KASHMIR

XIZANG (TIBET)

QINGHAI

XINJIANG UYGUR

GANSU

SICHUAN

YUNNAN

GUIZHOU

GUANGXI

GUANGDONG

HUNAN

HUBEI

JIANGXI

FUJIAN

ZHEJIANG

JIANGSU

ANHUI

HENAN

SHANDONG

SHANXI

SHAANXI

HEBEI

NINGXIA HUIZU

NEI MONGOL

LIAONING

JILIN

HEILONGJIANG

BEIJING

SHANGHAI

TIANJIN

SHENYANG

HARBIN

DALIAN

QINGDAO

NANJING

WUHAN

CHONGQING

CHENGDU

XI'AN

TAIYUAN

BAOTOU

LANZHOU

KUNMING

GUANGZHOU

HONG KONG (B.C.)

Macao

Kowloon

HANOI

CALCUTTA

Dhaka

Kathmandu

Lhasa

Ulaanbaatar

Ulan Ude

Irkutsk

Khabarovsk

Vladivostok

Pusan

Taegu

Pyongyang

Seoul

Inch'ŏn

Fukuoka

Nagasaki

Taibei

Gaoxiong

Luzon

Hainan Dao

HAINAN

Tropic of Cancer

East from Greenwich

Projection: Bonne

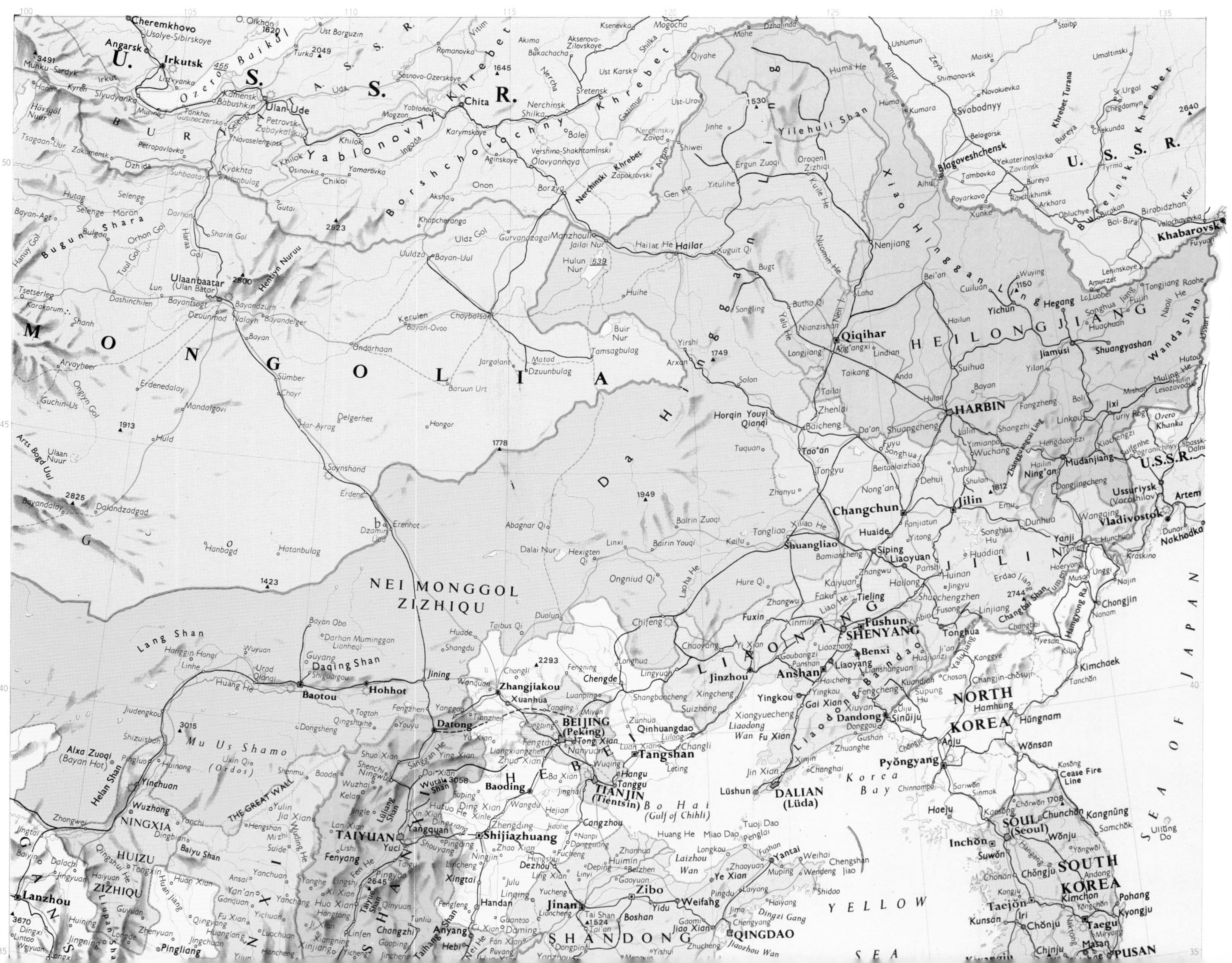
U. S. S. R.
MONGOLIA
HEILONGJIANG
JILIN
LIAONING
NEI MONGGOL ZIZHIQU
HEBEI
SHANXI
SHANDONG
NINGXIA HUIZU ZIZHIQU
NORTH KOREA
SOUTH KOREA
SEA OF JAPAN
YELLOW SEA
Korea Bay
Bo Hai (Gulf of Chihli)
Liaodong Bandao
Ozero Baykal
Hulun Nur
Buir Nur
Xiao Hinggan Ling
Da Hinggan Ling
Yablonovyy Khrebet
Borshchovochny Khrebet
Yilehuli Shan
Wanda Shan
Changbai Shan
Hentiyn Nuruu
Lang Shan
Daqing Shan
Helan Shan
Mu Us Shamo (Ordos)
THE GREAT WALL
Huang He
Irkutsk
Angarsk
Cheremkhovo
Ulan-Ude
Chita
Blagoveshchensk
Svobodnyy
Khabarovsk
Ussuriysk (Voroshilov)
Vladivostok
Nakhodka
Artem
Ulaanbaatar (Ulan Bator)
Choybalsan
Hailar
Qiqihar
HARBIN
Jiamusi
Hegang
Yichun
Mudanjiang
Jixi
Changchun
Jilin
Siping
Liaoyuan
Fushun
SHENYANG
Benxi
Anshan
Liaoyang
Jinzhou
Yingkou
Dandong
DALIAN (Lüda)
Lüshun
Zhangjiakou
BEIJING (Peking)
TIANJIN (Tientsin)
Tangshan
Qinhuangdao
Chengde
Datong
Hohhot
Baotou
Baoding
Shijiazhuang
TAIYUAN
Handan
Jinan
Zibo
Weifang
Yantai
QINGDAO
Yinchuan
Lanzhou
Pyŏngyang
Hŭngnam
Chongjin
Kimchaek
SOUL (Seoul)
Inchŏn
Taejŏn
Taegu
PUSAN
Cease Fire Line

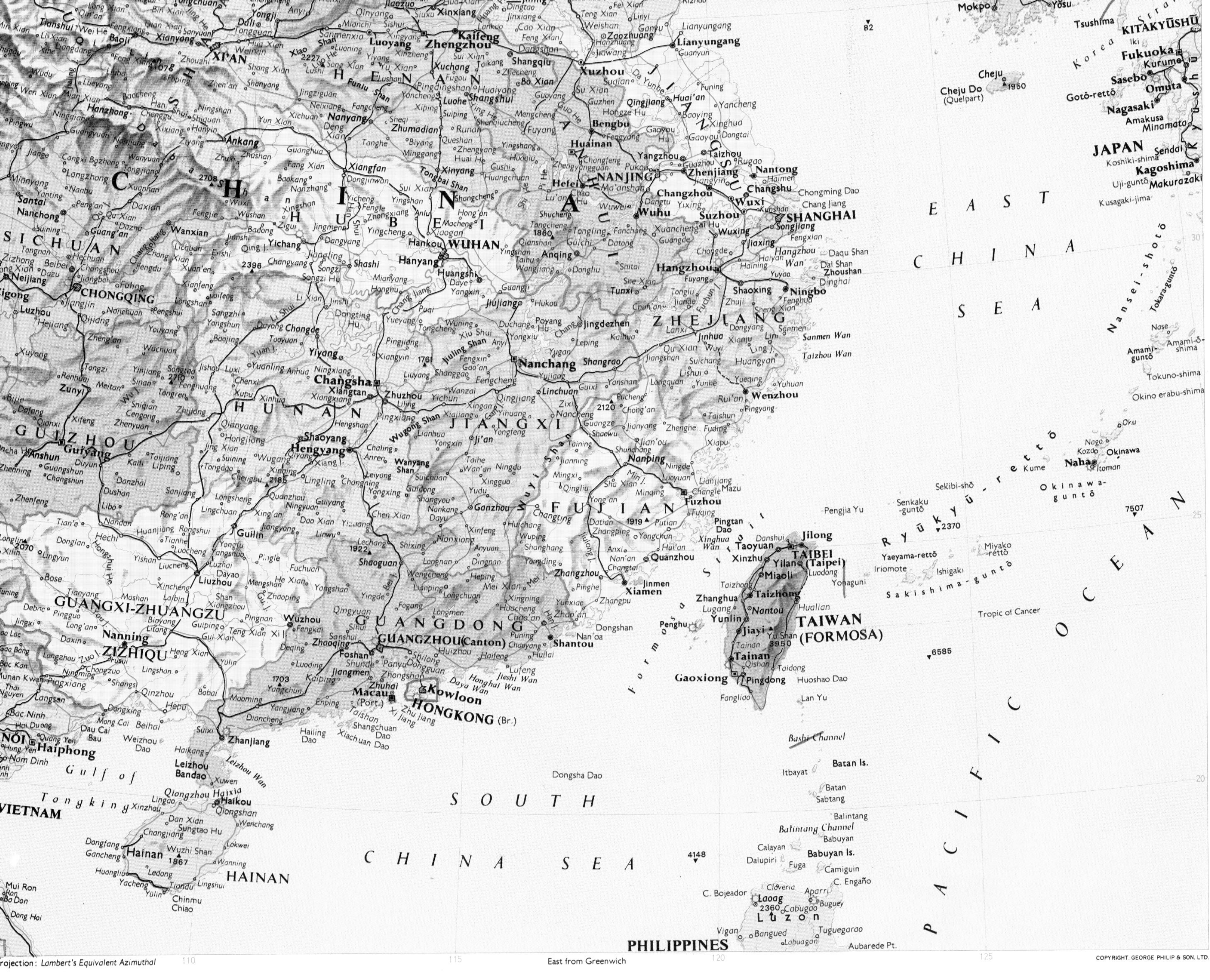

1:10 000 000

50   0   50   100   150   200   250 miles
50   0   50 100 150 200 250 300 350 400 km

KITAKYŪSHŪ
Fukuoka
Kurume
Sasebo Senddi
Nagasaki Kagoshima Makurazaki
Amakusa Minamata
JAPAN
Goto-retto Uji-guntō Koshiki-shima
Tsushima Iki

Koshiki-shima
Kōzu-guntō
Tokara-guntō
Nose
Amami-ō-shima
Amami guntō
Tokuno erabu-jima

MOKPO

Cheju
Cheju Do
(Quelpart)

Nansei-shotō

Oku
Oshima
Kozu Okinawa
Naha Okinawa
gunto
Kume

Okino

N
A
N
S
E
I

EAST

CHINA

SEA

Miyako
Miyako-rettō
Kume

Senkaku
guntō
Sekibi-shō
2370
Iriomote Ishigaki
Yaeyama-rettō
Yonaguni
Sakishima-guntō

7607

Tropic of Cancer

R
Y
U
K
Y
U

O
C
E
A
N

6585

Pengjia Yu

Jilong
TAIBEI (Taipei)
Danshui Yilan
Taoyuan Yilan
Xinzhu Miaoli
Taizhong
Zhanghua Nantou
Yunlin
Jiayi A Shan
Tainan 3950
Gaoxiong Pingdong
Penghu Luodong
Hualian

TAIWAN
(FORMOSA)

Huoshao Dao
Lan Yu

Fangliao

Batan Is.
Batan
Sabtang

Balintang Channel
Balintang
Babuyan Is.
Camiguin
Fuga
Dalupiri
Calayan

Itbayat

C. Engaño
Aparri
Cabugao
Tuguegarao
Lubugan

Laoag 2360
Vigan Bangued

L u z o n

C. Bojeador

PHILIPPINES

PACIFIC

SHANGHAI
Nantong Changshu
Changzhou Haimen
Wuxi Changjiang Dao
Suzhou Jiaxing
Songjiang
Hangzhou Wan
Daqu Shan
Zhoushan

Chongming Dao

Shaoxing
Ningbo
Yuyao

Sanmen Wan
Taizhou Wan

Wenzhou

Z H E J I A N G

Lianyungang
Guanyun

J I A N G S U

Yancheng
Xinghua
Dongtai

Yangzhou
Zhenjiang
NANJING
Wuhu

Hefei
A N H U I

Huainan
Bengbu

Nanchang

WUHAN
Hankou
Hanyang

H U B E I

Nanchang

J I A N G X I

FUJIAN

W
u
y
i
S
h
a
n

Fuzhou

Nanping

Quanzhou
Xiamen
Jinmen

Shantou

GUANGDONG

GUANGZHOU
(Canton)
Macau (Port.)
HONGKONG (Br.)
Kowloon

Zhuhai

Changsha
H U N A N
Hengyang
Shaoyang

Guilin

Liuzhou

GUANGXI-ZHUANGZU
Nanning

ZIZHIQU

HAINAN
Haikou
Hainan

VIETNAM
HANOI
Haiphong

GUIZHOU
Guiyang

Zunyi

CHONGQING

SICHUAN

Chengdu

XI'AN

S H A N X I

HENAN
Zhengzhou
Luoyang
Kaifeng
Xinxiang

Xuzhou

Nanyang

Xiangfan

Yichang

SOUTH

CHINA

SEA

Dongsha Dao

East from Greenwich

Projection: Lambert's Equivalent Azimuthal

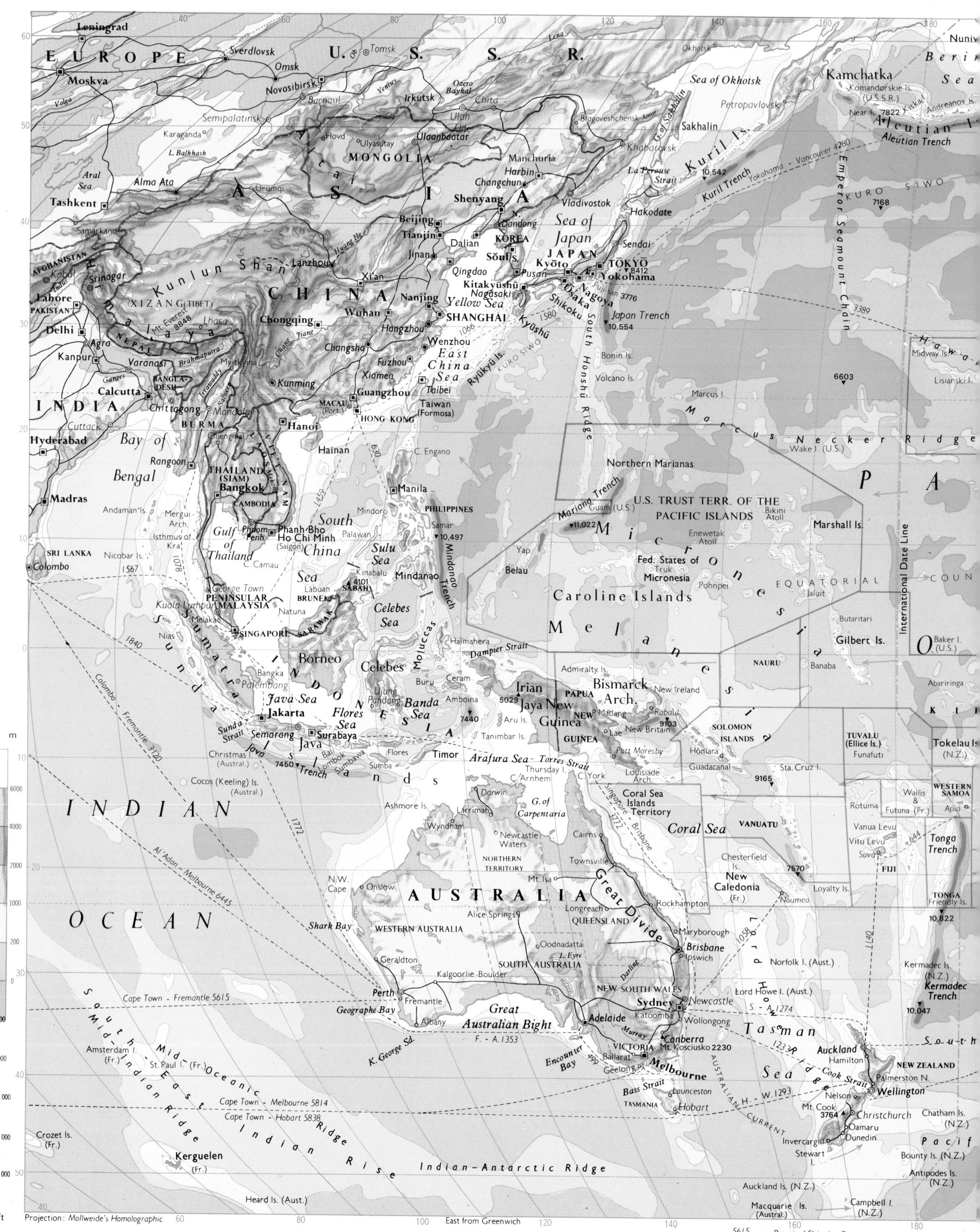

Projection: Mollweide's Homolographic

East from Greenwich

___ ___ 5615 ___ Principal Shipping Routes
(Distances in Nautical Miles)

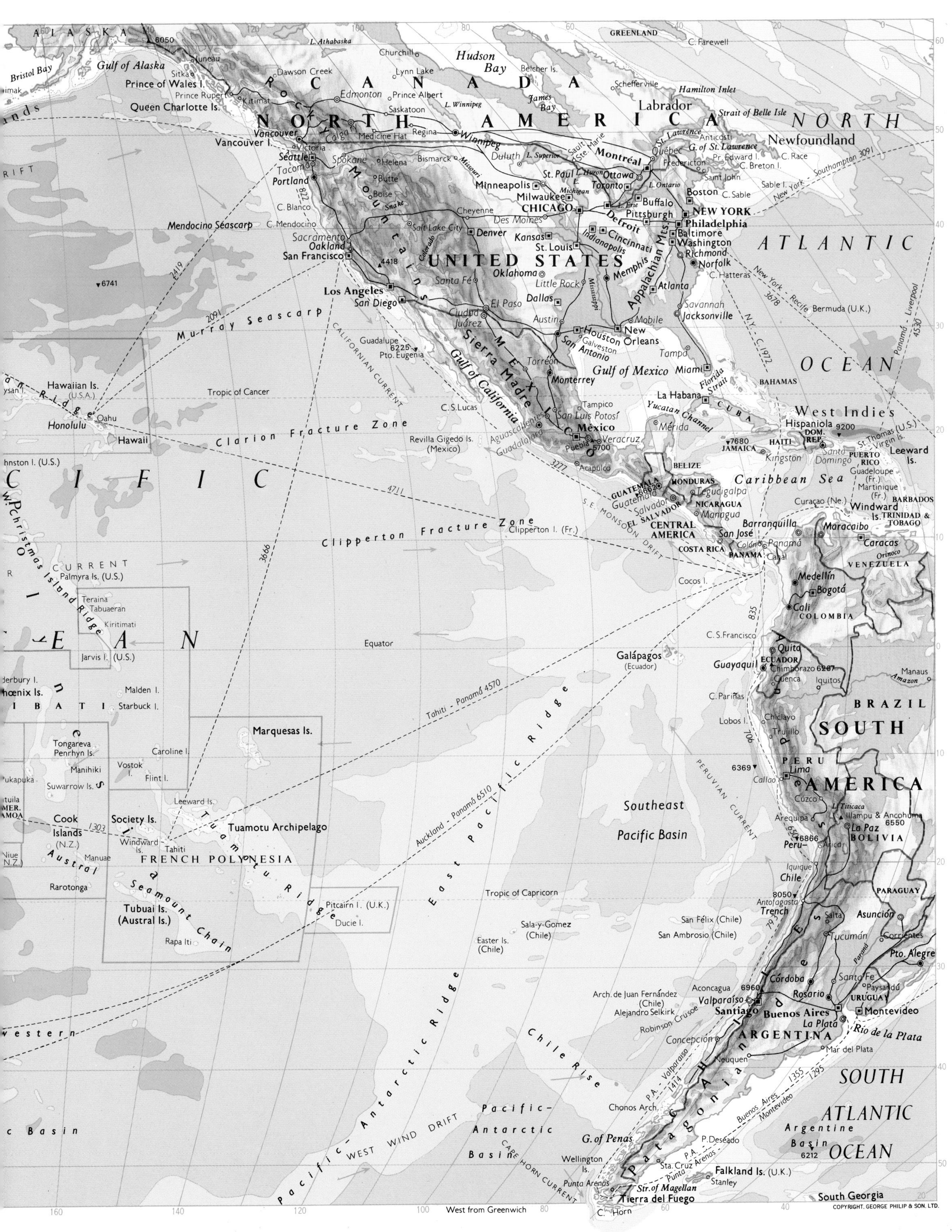

ALASKA
6050
Bristol Bay
Gulf of Alaska
Imak
Juneau
Sitka
Prince of Wales I.
Prince Rupert
Queen Charlotte Is.
Kitimat
DRIFT
ROCKY
Dawson Creek
CANADA
Churchill
Lynn Lake
Hudson Bay
Betcher Is.
GREENLAND
C. Farewell
NORTH
L. Athabaska
Edmonton
Prince Albert
James Bay
Scheffer ville
Labrador
Hamilton Inlet
Strait of Belle Isle
Newfoundland
C. Race

NORTH AMERICA
Vancouver
Vancouver I.
Victoria
Seattle
Tacoma
Portland
Calg.
Medicine Hat
Regina
Winnipeg
L. Winnipeg
Saskatoon
MOUNTAINS
Spokane
Helena
Butte
Boise
Snake
882
Bismarck
Missouri
Cheyenne
Duluth
L. Superior
Sault Ste. Marie
St. Paul
Minneapolis
Milwaukee
L. Huron
Michigan
CHICAGO
Montréal
Ottawa
Toronto
L. Ontario
Québec
St. Lawrence
G. of St. Lawrence
Anticosti
Pr. Edward I.
Fredericton
Saint John
C. Breton I.
Sable I.
C. Sable
Strait
50
Southampton 3091
NORTH
60

Mendocino Seascarp
C. Blanco
C. Mendocino
Sacramento
Oakland
San Francisco
6741
4418
Colorado
Salt Lake City
Denver
Kansas
St. Louis
Des Moines
UNITED STATES
Santa Fé
Oklahoma
Little Rock
Memphis
Cincinnati
Indianapolis
Detroit
Erie
Buffalo
Pittsburgh
Appalachian Mts.
NEW YORK
Philadelphia
Baltimore
Washington
Richmond
Norfolk
C. Hatteras
ATLANTIC
New York - Recife
3678
Bermuda (U.K.)
40

2419
Murray Seascarp
2091
Los Angeles
San Diego
Ciudad Juárez
El Paso
Dallas
Austin
San Antonio
Houston
Galveston
New Orleans
Mississippi
Atlanta
Savannah
Jacksonville
Mobile
Tampa
Miami
Florida Strait
BAHAMAS
OCEAN
NY-C 1972
Panamá - Liverpool
4530
30

CALIFORNIAN CURRENT
Hawaiian Is. (U.S.A.)
ysan I.
Oahu
Honolulu
Hawaii
Tropic of Cancer
Guadalupe
6225
Pto. Eugenia
C. S. Lucas
Gulf of California
SIERRA MADRE
MEXICO
Torreón
Monterrey
Tampico
San Luis Potosí
Aguascalientes
Guadalajara
MÉXICO
Veracruz
Mérida
Yucatan Channel
La Habana
CUBA
West Indies
Hispaniola
DOM. REP.
9200
HAITI
JAMAICA
7680
St. Thomas (U.S.)
Virgin Is.
Santo Domingo
PUERTO RICO
Kingston
Guadeloupe (Fr.)
Leeward Is.
Martinique (Fr.)

PACIFIC
Clarion Fracture Zone
Revilla Gigedo Is. (Mexico)
3277
4711
Clipperton Fracture Zone
Clipperton I. (Fr.)
Puebla
6700
Acapulco
GUATEMALA
Guatemala
6662
BELIZE
HONDURAS
Tegucigalpa
Salvador
NICARAGUA
Managua
S. E. MONSOON DRIFT
Caribbean Sea
Barranquilla
Curaçao (Ne.)
BARBADOS
Windward Is.
TRINIDAD & TOBAGO

CHRISTMAS ISLAND RIDGE
hnston I. (U.S.)
CURRENT
Palmyra Is. (U.S.)
Teraina
Tabuaeran
Kiritimati
Jarvis I. (U.S.)
3666
3636
Equator
Galápagos (Ecuador)
CENTRAL AMERICA
COSTA RICA
San José
Colón
Panamá
PANAMA
Canal
Cocos I.
Medellín
Bogotá
Cali
COLOMBIA
VENEZUELA
Caracas
Maracaibo
Orinoco
C. S. Francisco
835
Quito
ECUADOR
Guayaquil
Chimborazo
6287
Cuenca
Iquitos
Amazon
Manaus
10

Malden I.
IBATI
Starbuck I.
OCEAN
derbury Is.
hoenix Is.
Tongareva
Penrhyn Is.
Manihiki
Suwarrow Is.
Vostok I.
Flint I.
Caroline I.
Marquesas Is.
Leeward Is.
C. Pariñas
Lobos I.
Chiclayo
Trujillo
706
BRAZIL
SOUTH
PERU
6369
Lima
Callao
10

kapuka
ula
MER.
AMOA
Cook Islands (N.Z.)
1303
Society Is.
Manuae
Tahiti
Windward Is.
Tuamotu Archipelago
Tahiti - Panamá 4570
Auckland - Panamá 6510
EAST PACIFIC RIDGE
PERUVIAN CURRENT
Cuzco
L. Titicaca
Arequipa
Illampu & Ancohuma
6550
6866
La Paz
Peru-
Arica
AMERICA
BOLIVIA
20

Niue
N.Z.
FRENCH POLYNESIA
Rarotonga
Tubuai Is. (Austral Is.)
Rapa Iti
AUSTRAL
SEAMOUNT CHAIN
Pitcairn I. (U.K.)
Ducie I.
Sala-y-Gomez (Chile)
San Félix (Chile)
San Ambrosio (Chile)
Easter I. (Chile)
Tropic of Capricorn
Southeast Pacific Basin
8050
Antofagasta
Trench
Iquique
Chile
Salta
Tucumán
Corrientes
PARAGUAY
Asunción
ANDES
30

ANTARCTIC RIDGE
Western
c Basin
PACIFIC
WEST WIND DRIFT
Pacific- Antarctic Basin
Chile Rise
CAPE HORN CURRENT
Arch. de Juan Fernández (Chile)
Alejandro Selkirk
Robinson Crusoe
Concepción
Chonos Arch.
G. of Penas
P. Deseado
Wellington
Sta. Cruz Arenas
Punta Arenas
Str. of Magellan
Tierra del Fuego
C. Horn
Aconcagua
6960
Valparaíso
Santiago
ARGENTINA
Córdoba
Rosario
Buenos Aires
La Plata
Santa Fe
URUGUAY
Montevideo
Paysandú
Río de la Plata
Mar del Plata
P.A. - Valparaíso
1414
Neuquén
PATAGONIA
1355
1295
6212
Falkland Is. (U.K.)
Stanley
South Georgia
SOUTH ATLANTIC OCEAN
Argentine Basin
40
50

West from Greenwich
COPYRIGHT. GEORGE PHILIP & SON. LTD.

AUSTRALIA AND
NEW ZEALAND : Physical and Political

1:40 000 000

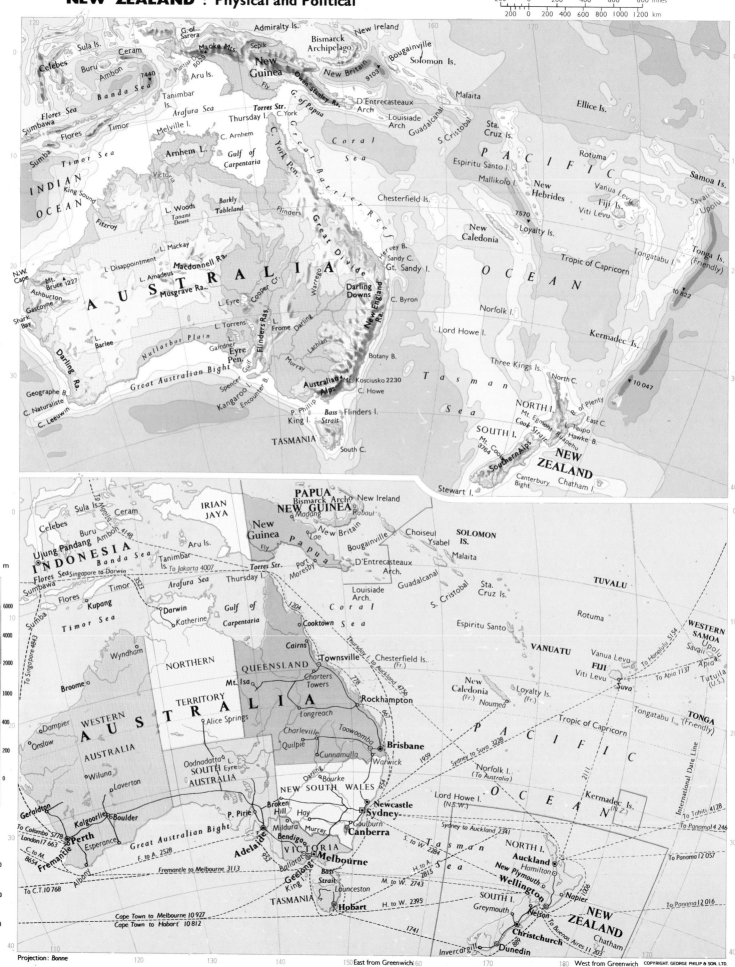

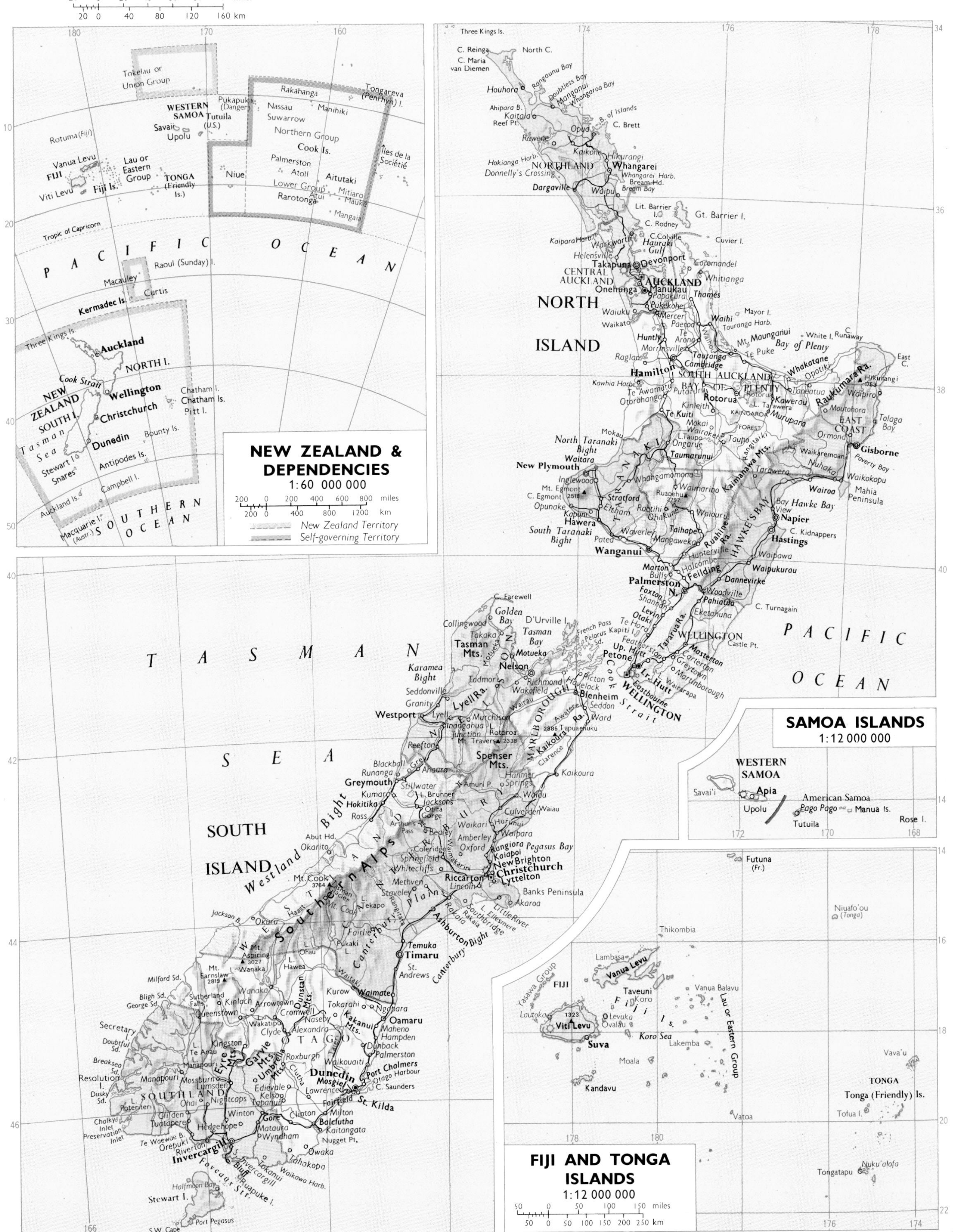

1:6 000 000

20   0   20   40   60   80   100 miles
20   0   40   80   120   160 km

180   170   160

Tokelau or
Union Group

WESTERN
SAMOA   Pukapuka
(Dangers)   Rakahanga   Tongareva
Savaii   Tutuila   Nassau   Manihiki   (Penrhyn) I.
Upolu   (U.S.)   Suwarrow
Northern Group
TONGA   Cook Is.   Îles de la
(Friendly   Palmerston   Société
Rotuma (Fiji)   Is.)   Atoll   Aitutaki
Vanua Levu   Niue   Lower Group   Mitiaro
Lau or   Atiu   Mauke
Eastern   Rarotonga
FIJI   Group   Mangaia
Viti Levu   Fiji Is.

Tropic of Capricorn

P A C I F I C   O C E A N

Raoul (Sunday) I.
Macauley
Kermadec Is.   Curtis

Three Kings Is.
Auckland
NORTH I.
Cook Strait   Chatham I.
NEW   Wellington   Chatham Is.
ZEALAND   Christchurch   Pitt I.
SOUTH I.
Tasman   Dunedin   Bounty Is.
Sea
Stewart I.   Antipodes Is.
Snares
Campbell I.
Auckland Is.
Macquarie I.   S O U T H E R N
(Austr.)   O C E A N

**NEW ZEALAND &
DEPENDENCIES**
1:60 000 000

200   0   200   400   600   800 miles
200   0   400   800   1200 km

New Zealand Territory
Self-governing Territory

SAMOA ISLANDS
1:12 000 000

WESTERN
SAMOA   Apia
Savai'i   American Samoa
Upolu   Pago Pago   Manua Is.
Tutuila   Rose I.

172   170   168

**FIJI AND TONGA
ISLANDS**
1:12 000 000

50   0   50   100   150 miles
50   0   50   100   150   200   250 km

Projection: Conical with two standard parallels

COPYRIGHT. GEORGE PHILIP & SON. L.TD.

Bass Strait
Flinders Island
Furneaux Group
Cape Barren I.
King Island
Launceston
Hobart
TASMANIA
Kent Group
Port Davey
S.W. Cape
S.E. Cape

CORAL SEA
Great Barrier Reef
Gulf of Carpentaria
Cape York Peninsula
Great Dividing Range
QUEENSLAND
GREAT ARTESIAN BASIN
NORTHERN TERRITORY
Arnhem Land
Barkly Tableland
Simpson Desert
Gregory Range
Selwyn Range
Macdonnell Ranges
Toko Range
Davenport Range
Wellesley Is.
Mornington I.
Groote Eylandt
Sir Edward Pellew Group
Wessel Is.
Torres Strait
Thursday I.
Prince of Wales I.
Endeavour Strait
Cairns
Townsville
Mackay
Rockhampton
Gladstone
Mount Isa
Cloncurry
Charters Towers
Hughenden
Winton
Longreach
Alice Springs
Tennant Creek
Bowen
Ayr
Ingham
Innisfail
Mareeba
Cooktown
Yeppoon
Hinchinbrook I.
Whitsunday I.
Northumberland Islands
Cumberland Islands
Tropic of Capricorn
Mt. Bartle Frere 1612
Mt. Bray
Mt. Norma 418
Mt. Tableton 823
Macdonnell Ranges 1128

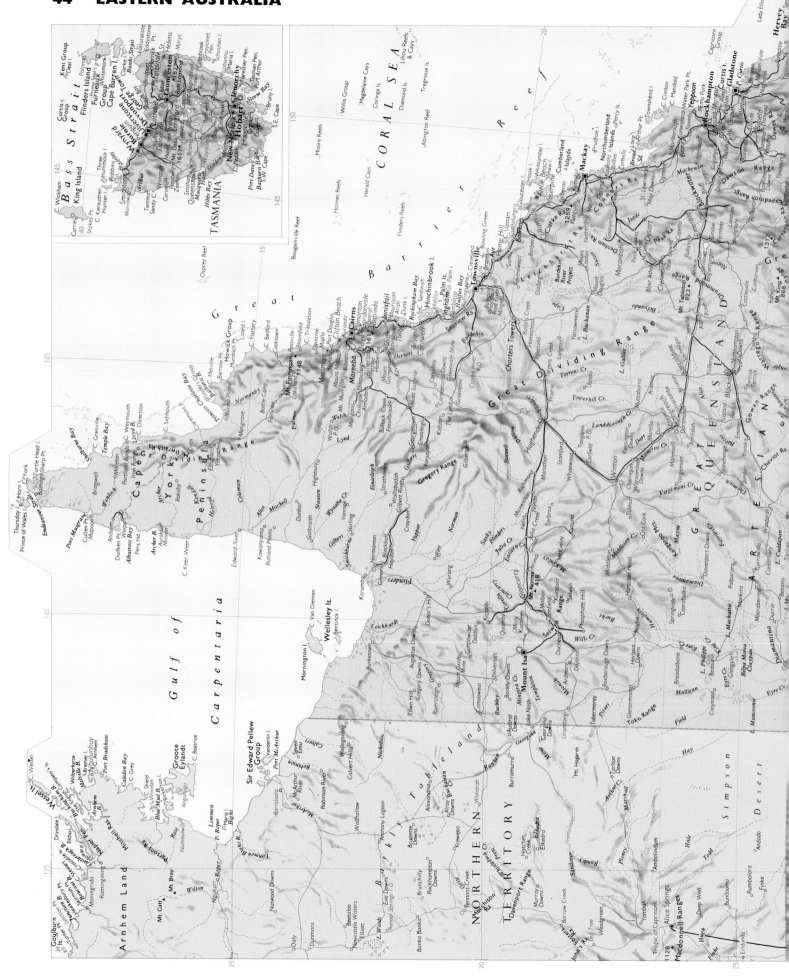

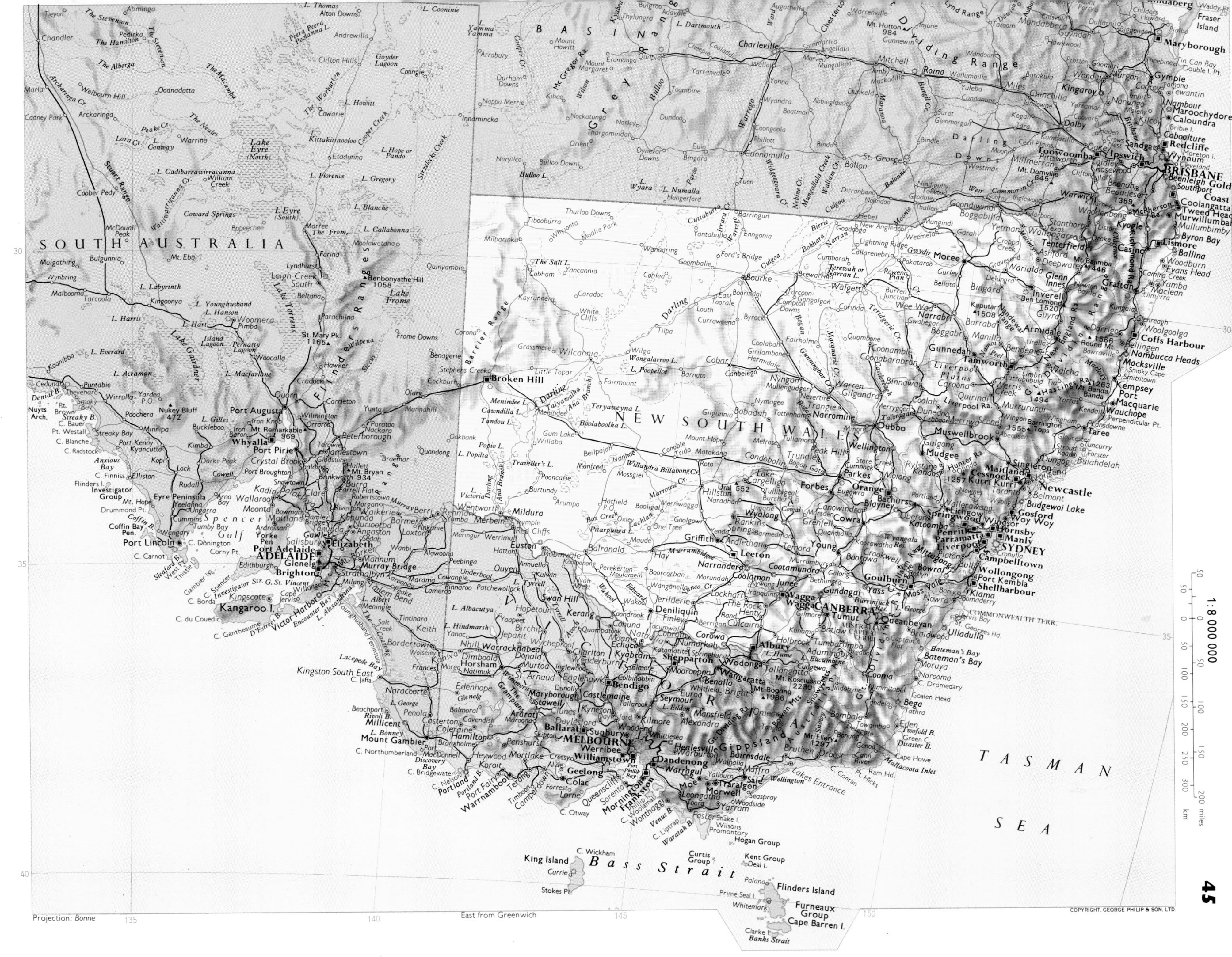
1:8 000 000
50 0 50 100 150 200 miles
50 0 50 100 150 200 250 300 km
SOUTH AUSTRALIA
NEW SOUTH WALES
TASMAN SEA
Bass Strait
Spencer Gulf
Lake Eyre (North)
Lake Torrens
Lake Gairdner
Lake Frome
Flinders Ranges
Great Dividing Range
Grey Range
Darling Downs
Kangaroo I.
King Island
Flinders Island
Furneaux Group
Cape Barren I.
BRISBANE
SYDNEY
MELBOURNE
ADELAIDE
CANBERRA
Newcastle
Wollongong
Geelong
Ballarat
Bendigo
Broken Hill
Mildura
Port Augusta
Port Pirie
Whyalla
Port Lincoln
Mount Gambier
Wagga Wagga
Albury
Dubbo
Orange
Bathurst
Tamworth
Armidale
Toowoomba
Warrnambool
Coffs Harbour
COPYRIGHT. GEORGE PHILIP & SON. LTD
Projection: Bonne
East from Greenwich

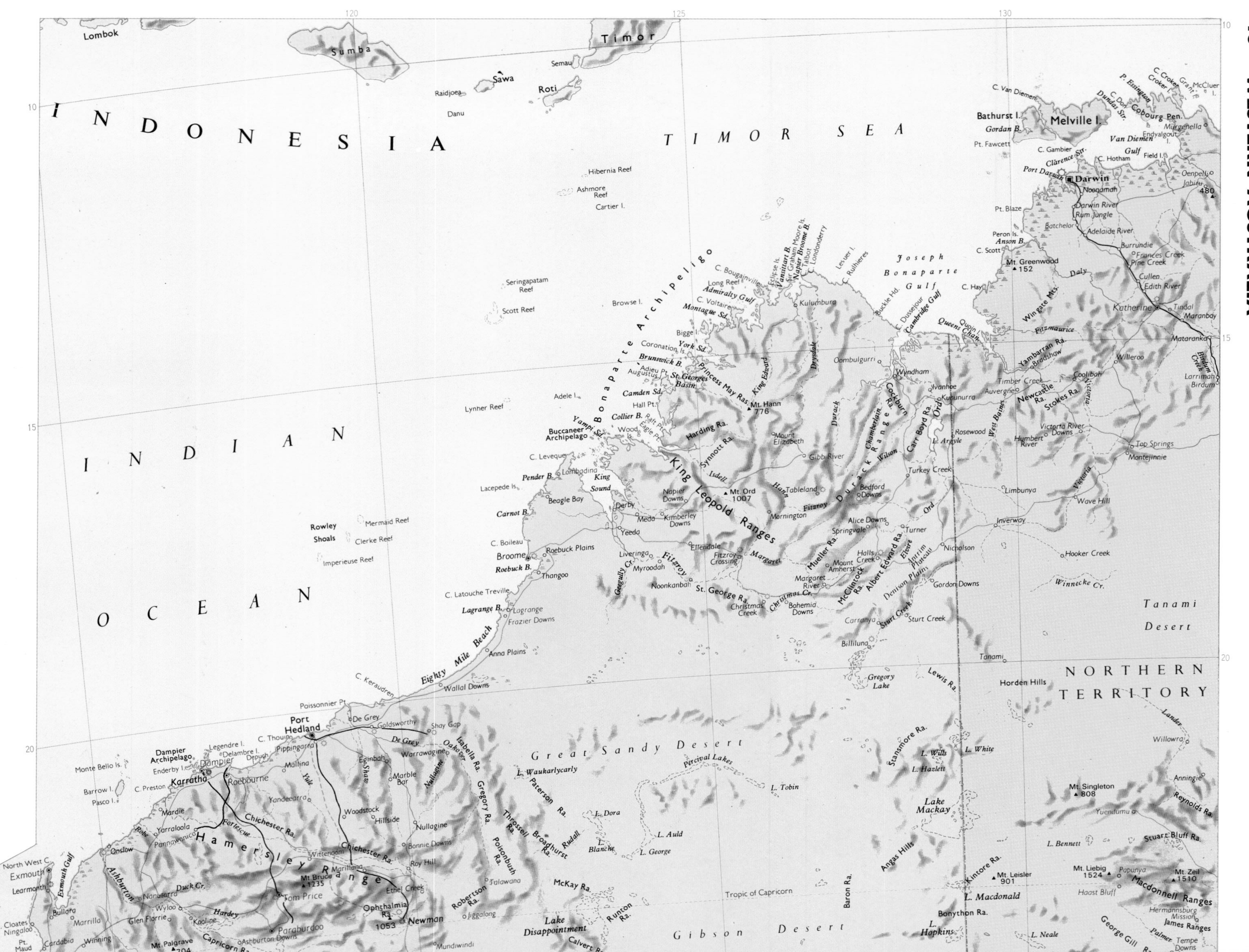

INDONESIA
TIMOR SEA
INDIAN OCEAN
NORTHERN TERRITORY
Tanami Desert
Great Sandy Desert
Gibson Desert
Tropic of Capricorn
Timor
Sumba
Lombok
Roti
Sawa
Melville I.
Bathurst I.
Darwin
Katherine
Joseph Bonaparte Gulf
Bonaparte Archipelago
Wyndham
Kununurra
King Leopold Ranges
Derby
Broome
Eighty Mile Beach
Port Hedland
Karratha
Dampier
Hamersley Range
Newman
Exmouth
Exmouth Gulf
Rowley Shoals
Lake Mackay
Lake Disappointment
Macdonnell Ranges

1:8 000 000

50   0   50   100   150   200 miles
50 0 50 100 150 200 250 300 km

Projection. Bonne

East from Greenwich

SOUTHERN OCEAN

WESTERN AUSTRALIA

SOUTH AUSTRALIA

Great Australian Bight

Nullarbor Plain

Hampton Tableland

Great Victoria Desert

PERTH

Ayers Rock 868
Mt. Woodroffe 1549
Mt. Morris 1387
Musgrave Ranges
Mt. Olga 1069
Everard Ranges
The Officer
Mann Ra.
1174
Everard Park
Dingas Downs

L. Meramangye
Wilkinson Lakes
L. Dey-Dey
L. Maurice
Narrari Lakes
Serpentine Lakes
Ooldea
Watson
Fisher
Barton
Cook
Hughes
Moralana
Nullarbor
Head of Bight
Coorabie
C. Nuyts
Fowlers B.
Eucla
Coombana
Pintumba
Eucla Motel
Wilson Bluff
Low Pt.
Mundrabilla
Madura
Madura Motel
Red Rocks Pt.

Mt. Aloysius 1058
Mt. Blackstone
Rawlinson Ra.
Cavenagh Ra.
Mt. Forrest
Christopher I.
Mt. Davies
Mt. Buttfield
Rawlinson Ra. 1126

Barrow Ra.
Warburton
Mt. Squires 705
Warburton Ra.
Pt. Lilian 466
Macintosh Ra. 466
Saunders Pt. 466

Deakin
Reid
Forrest
Loongana
Nurina
Haig
Rawlinna
Naretha
Kitchener
Zanthus
Cundeelee
Karonie
Balladonia
Pt. Culver
C. Pasley
Israelite B.
Eastern Group
Pt. Malcolm

L. Ell
Shell Lakes
Jubilee L.
L. Yeo
L. Throssel
L. Rebecca

L. Breaden
Baker L.
L. Gillen
Ernest Giles 712
Rason L.
Cosmo Newberry
Laverton
Mt. Morgans
L. Wells
L. Carey
Yundamindera
L. Raeside
Edjudina
L. Yindarlgooda
Broad Arrow
Kanowna
Yerilla
Menzies

Brassey Ra.
Mt. Normanhurst
L. Buchanan
L. Carnegie
Earaheedy
Granite Peak
L. Eureka
Mt. Eureka 499
Bandya
Wongawol
Bates Ra.
Mt. Keith
Mt. Alexander
Leonora
Gwalia
Ida Valley
Kookynie
Malcolm
Niagara
Leinster
Randall
L. Darlot
Melrose
L. Ballard
Mt. Redcliffe 576
Pinnacles
Yilgangi
Goongarrie
Ora Banda
Riverina
Mt. Burges 354
Kalgoorlie-Boulder
East Coolgardie
Coolgardie
Widgiemooltha
Higginsville
Norseman
L. Cowan
L. Dundas
Mt. Ridley
Salmon Gums
Mondrain I.
Esperance
Esperance B.
Archipelago of the Recherche
Middle I.
Sandy Bight
South East Is.
Mt. Ragged 585
C. Arid
Mt. Burges
Mt. Coman
L. Lefroy
L. Johnston
Kurnalpi
Mt. Monger
Kambalda
Marvel Loch
L. Cronin
Woolgangie
Bulla Bulling
Kwoolyin
L. King
L. Cronin
Mt. Gilmore 503
Peak Eleanora 503
L. Tay
Mt. Hope
Lake King
Newdegate
Ravensthorpe
Hopetoun

Kennedy Ra.
Mt. Essendon 906
Godfrey Ra.
Glenburgh
Mount Augustus 1105
Collier Ra.
Three Rivers
Mt. Fraser 799
Robinson Ra.
Peak Hill
L. Gregory
Murchison Downs
New Springs
Cashmere Downs
Wiluna
Barr Smith Ra.
Nabberu
Montague Ra.
Sandstone
Youanmi Downs
Maynard Hills
Mt. Elvire
Mt. Manifold
Mt. Jackson
Bullfinch
L. Deborah
Bonnie Rock
Mukinbudin
Mt. Marshall
Beacon
Southern Cross
Koolyanobbing
Yellowdine
Bullabulling

Kenneth Ra.
Minnie Creek
Williambury
Lyons
Mt. Clere
Mt. Phillips
Lyons R.
Mt. Augustus
Waldburg Ra.
Meekatharra
Mount Gould
Belele
Murgoo
Mileura
Mt. Magnet
Boolardy
Meka
Yalgoo
Tallering Peak 439
Morawa
Perenjori
Canna
Nicholson Ra.
Coodardy
Mooloogool
Mt. Vernon
Ashburton
Kenya
Errabiddy
Carnarvon Ra.
Nimbing
Mungiwongaloo

C. Ronsard
C. Cuvier
Bernier I.
Dorre I.
Shark Bay
Denham
Dirk Hartog
Steep Pt.
Peron
Geographe Channel
C. Farquhar
C. St. Cricq
Inscription Pt.
Hamelin Pool
Yaringa
Ajana
Kalbarri
Murchison
Ajana
Northampton
Geraldton
Greenough
Houtman Abrolhos
Dongara
Mingenew
Three Springs
Arrino
Coorow
Carnamah
Eneabba
Yarra Yarra Lakes
Jurien B.
Lancelin
Moora
Dandaragan
Gingin
Bolgart
Toodyay
Northam
York
Beverley
Brookton
Pingelly
Cuballing
Narrogin
Wagin
Dumbleyung
Katanning
Broomehill
Tambellup
Kojonup
Gnowangerup
Cranbrook
Mt. Barker
Stirling Ra. 1073
Bluff Knoll
Albany
King George Sound
Bald Hd.
C. Riche
Cheyne B.
Hood Pt.

FREMANTLE
Rottnest
Kwinana
Rockingham
New Town
Pinjarra
Mandurah
Yunderup
Waroona
Harvey
Brunswick Junction
Collie
Bunbury
Geographe B.
Busselton
C. Naturaliste
Dunsborough
Margaret River
Augusta
C. Leeuwin
Nannup
Bridgetown
Manjimup
Pemberton
Northcliffe
Windy Harbour
Pt. D'Entrecasteaux
Denmark
Wilson Inlet
West C. Howe

1:40 000 000

200   0   200   400   600   800   1000 miles
200   0   200   400   600   800   1000   1200   1400   1600 km

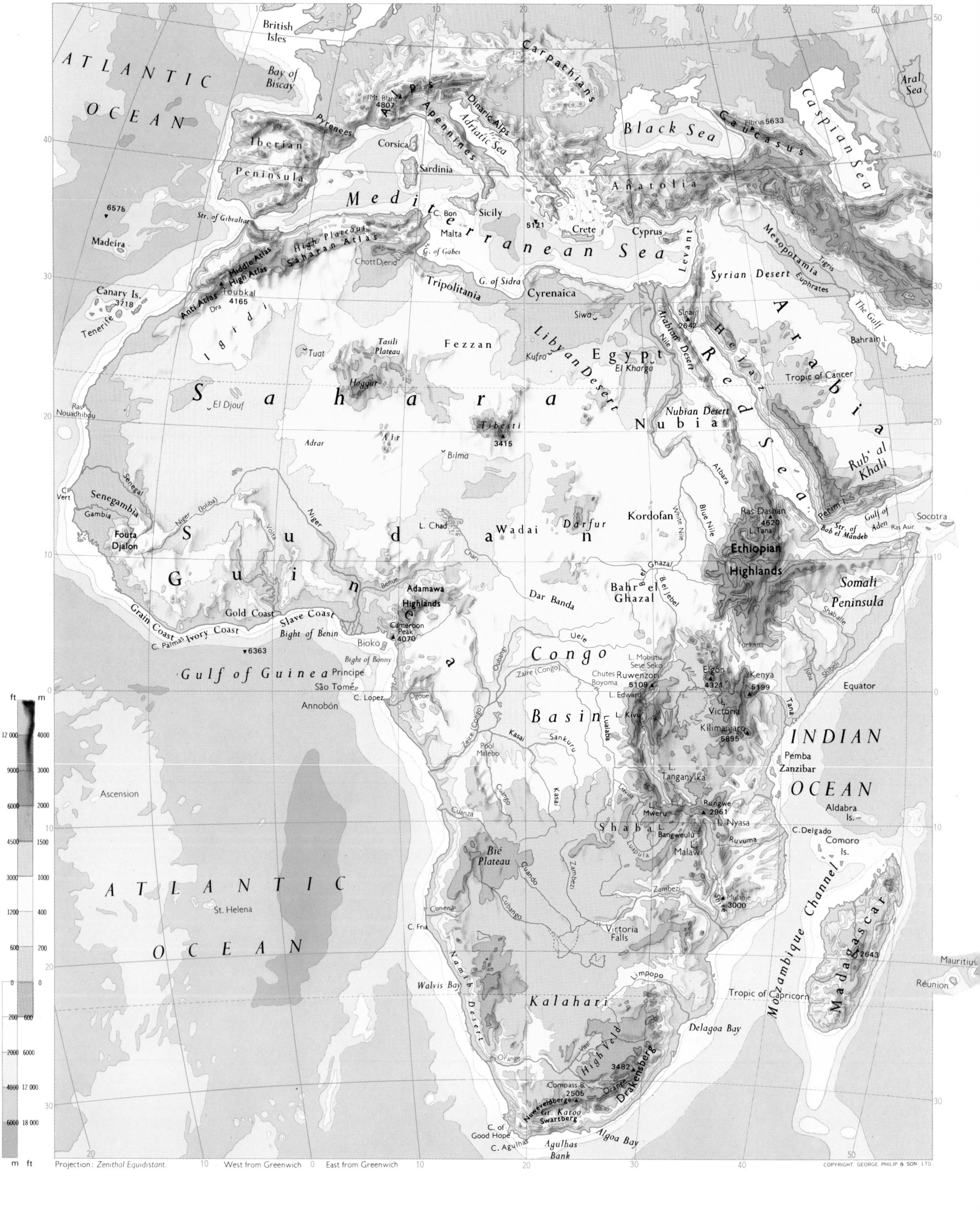

British Isles

ATLANTIC OCEAN

Bay of Biscay

Carpathians

Aral Sea

Mt. Blanc 4807   Alps   Dinaric Alps   Black Sea   Elbrus 5633   Caucasus   Caspian Sea

Pyrenees   Apennines   Adriatic Sea

Iberian Peninsula   Corsica   Anatolia

6576   Sardinia

Madeira   Str. of Gibraltar   Mediterranean Sea   Sicily   5121   Crete   Cyprus   Levant   Mesopotamia   Tigris   Euphrates

Malta   G. of Gabes

High Plateaus   C. Bon   The Gulf

Middle Atlas   High Atlas   Saharan Atlas   G. of Sidra   Cyrenaica   Libyan Desert   Syrian Desert   Bahrain I.

Canary Is.   Anti Atlas   Toubkal   Chott Djerid   Tripolitania   Siwa   Sinai 2642   Arabian Desert   Hejaz

3718   Tenerife   4165   Dra   Igidi   Fezzan   Kufra   Egypt   El Kharga   Nile   Tropic of Cancer

Ras Nouadhibou   Tasili Plateau   Nubia   Nubian Desert   Rub' al Khali

Sahara   Hoggar   Tibesti   Atbara   Ras Dashan 4620   L. Tana   Str. of Bab el Mandeb   Socotra

El Djouf   Air   3415   Ras Asir

Adrar   Bilma   Kordofan   Ethiopian Highlands   Somali Peninsula

C. Vert   Senegal   Senegambia   Niger (Joliba)   Wadai   Darfur   White Nile   Blue Nile   Elgon 4321

Gambia   Fouta Djalon   Voltа   Niger   L. Chad   Sudan   Perim I.   Gulf of Aden

Sou   Guin   Benue   Chari   Dar Banda   Bahr el Ghazal   Shebelle

Grain Coast   Gold Coast   Slave Coast   Adamawa Highlands   Uele   Congo   L. Mobutu Sese Seko   Turkana   Kenya 5199

C. Palmas   Ivory Coast   Bight of Benin   Cameroon Peak 4070   Oubangui   Zaire (Congo)   Chutes Boyoma   Ruwenzori 5109   Equator

Bioko   6363   Bight of Bonny   Dar Banda   L. Edward   Victoria   Kilimanjaro 5895

Gulf of Guinea   Principe   São Tomé   C. Lopez   Ogoué   Zaire (Congo)   Basin   L. Kivu   Pemba   Zanzibar

Annobón   Kasai   Sankuru   Lualaba   L. Tanganyika   INDIAN OCEAN

Ascension   Pool Malebo   Kasai   Aldabra Is.

Cuanza   Rungwe 2961   Mweru   L. Nyasa   C. Delgado   Comoro Is.

Shaba   L. Bangweulu   Malawi   Ruvuma

St. Helena   Bié Plateau   Cuango   Zambezi   Muh18 3000

ATLANTIC OCEAN   Cubango   Cunene   Zambezi   Victoria Falls   Mozambique Channel   Madagascar   2643   Mauritius

C. Frio   Namib Desert   Kalahari   Limpopo   Tropic of Capricorn   Réunion

Walvis Bay   Delagoa Bay

Orange   High Veld   3482   Drakensberg

Compass B. 2505   Orange   Algoa Bay

Nieuveldberge   Gr. Karoo   Swartberg

C. of Good Hope   Agulhas Bank   C. Agulhas

ft   m
12 000   4000
9000   3000
6000   2000
4500   1500
3000   1000
1200   400
600   200
0   0
200   600
2000   6000
4000   12 000
6000   18 000
m   ft

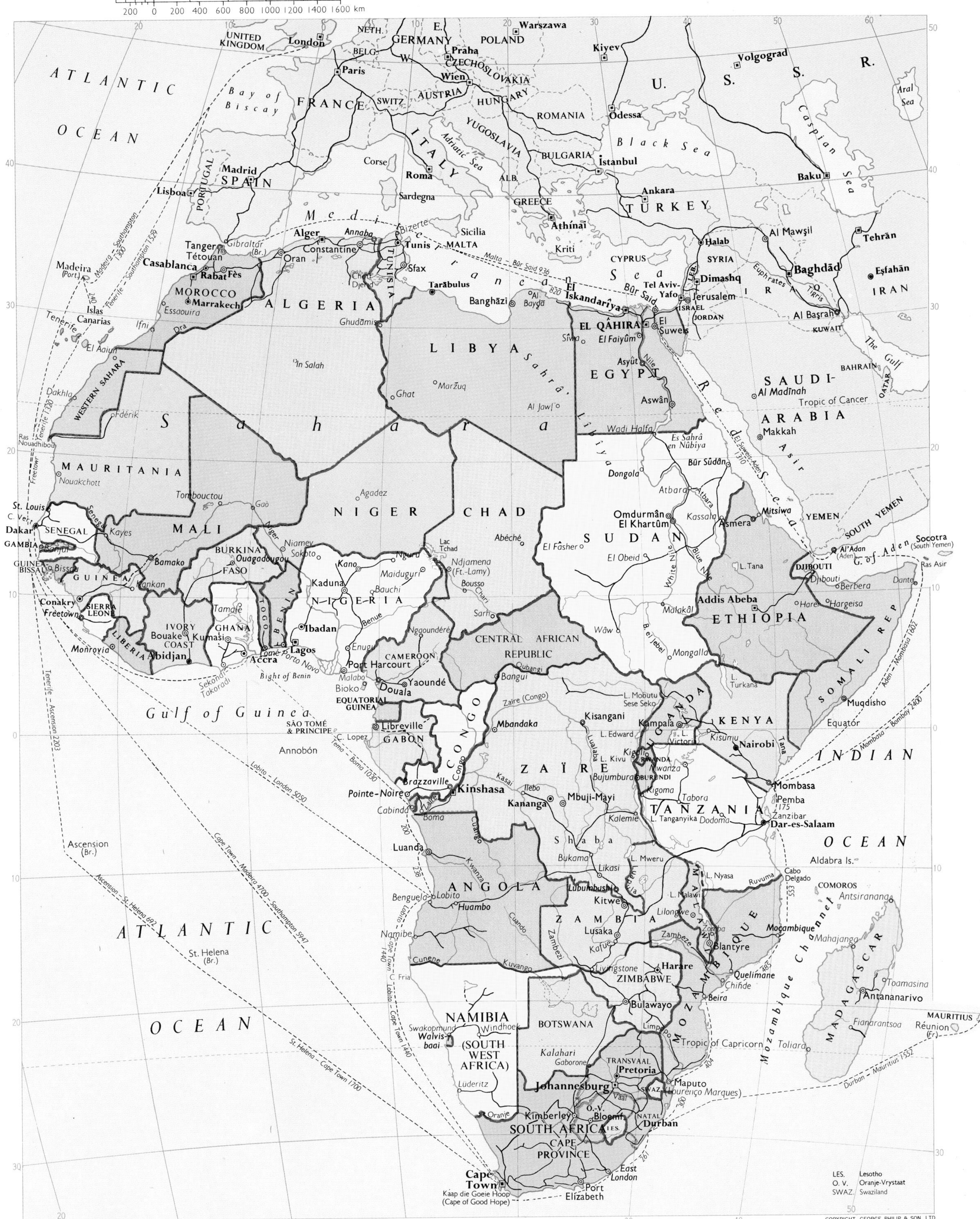

1 : 40 000 000

200   0   200   400   600   800   1000 miles
200   0   200 400 600 800 1000 1200 1400 1600 km

ATLANTIC OCEAN

UNITED KINGDOM
London
NETH.
GERMANY
BELG.
W.
E.
POLAND
Warszawa
Kiyev
Volgograd
Paris
FRANCE
Praha
CZECHOSLOVAKIA
Wien
SWITZ.
AUSTRIA
HUNGARY
ROMANIA
Odessa
Bay of Biscay
ITALY
YUGOSLAVIA
Corse
Roma
Adriatic Sea
BULGARIA
İstanbul
Black Sea
Baku
Caspian Sea
Aral Sea
U. S. S. R.

Madrid
SPAIN
PORTUGAL
Lisboa
Sardegna
Sicilia
ALB.
GREECE
Athínai
Kriti
Ankara
TURKEY
Tehrān
Esfahān

ATLANTIC OCEAN

Madeira (Port.)
Islas Canarias
Tenerife
El Aaiun
WESTERN SAHARA
Dakhla
Fdérik

Tanger
Tétouan
Casablanca
Rabat Fès
MOROCCO
Marrakech
Essaouira
Ifni
Oran
Alger
Constantine
Annaba
Bizerte
Tunis
TUNISIA
Sfax
MALTA
Tarābulus
Banghāzi
Al Bayda
Mediterranean Sea
El Iskandarīya
Tel Aviv-Yafo
Jerusalem
El Qāhira
El Suweis
Dimashq
Halab
SYRIA
Baghdād
IRAN
Al Başrah
KUWAIT
The Gulf
BAHRAIN
QATAR

ALGERIA
Ghudāmis
In Salah
LIBYA
Marzūq
Ghat
Al Jawf
Sahrā' Libya
EGYPT
El Faiyûm
Asyût
Aswân
Tropic of Cancer
SAUDI-ARABIA
Al Madīnah
Makkah
Asir

Sahara
MAURITANIA
Nouakchott
Tombouctou
Gao
Agadez
NIGER
CHAD
Wadi Halfa
Es Sahra en Nūbiya
Dongola
Atbara
Bûr Sûdân
SUDAN
Omdurmân
El Khartûm
Kassala
Asmera
Mitsiwa
YEMEN
Al 'Adan
SOUTH YEMEN (South Yemen)
Socotra
Ras Asir

St. Louis
C. Vert
Dakar
SENEGAL
GAMBIA
GUINEA-BISSAU
Bissau
Conakry
Freetown
SIERRA LEONE
Kayes
Bamako
MALI
Kankan
GUINEA
BURKINA FASO
Ouagadougou
Niamey
Sokoto
Kano
Maiduguri
Nguru
Bauchi
Kaduna
NIGERIA
Lac Tchad
Ndjamena (Ft.-Lamy)
Bousso
Chari
Abéché
El Fâsher
El Obeid
Waw
B. el Jebel
Malakâl
Mongalla
ETHIOPIA
Addis Abeba
Harer
Hargeisa
Berbera
DJIBOUTI
Djibouti
G. of Aden
Dante
SOMALI REP

IVORY COAST
Bouaké
Kumasi
GHANA
Tamale
BENIN
TOGO
Accra
Porto Novo
Lagos
Ibadan
Enugu
Benue
Port Harcourt
CAMEROON
Yaoundé
Douala
Ngaoundéré
Bangui
CENTRAL AFRICAN REPUBLIC
Oubangui
Zaire (Congo)
Kisangani
L. Mobutu Sese Seko
UGANDA
Kampala
KENYA
L. Turkana
Nairobi
Equator
INDIAN OCEAN

LIBERIA
Monrovia
Abidjan
São Tomé
SÃO TOMÉ & PRINCIPE
Bioko
EQUATORIAL GUINEA
Malabo
Gulf of Guinea
Bight of Benin
Sekondi-Takoradi
C. Lopez
Annobón
Libreville
GABON
CONGO
Brazzaville
Kinshasa
Mbandaka
ZAÏRE
Kananga
Mbuji-Mayi
L. Edward
L. Kivu
RWANDA
BURUNDI
Bujumbura
Kigali
Kigoma
Mwanza
L. Victoria
Kisumu
L. Tana
Mombasa
Pemba
Zanzibar
TANZANIA
Dodoma
Tabora
Dar-es-Salaam
OCEAN

Ascension (Br.)
Annobón
Pointe-Noire
Boma
Cabinda
Luanda
Kasai
Ilebo
Kalemie
L. Tanganyika
Shaba
Bukama
Likasi
L. Mweru
Lubumbashi
Kitwe
Kalemie

ATLANTIC OCEAN

St. Helena (Br.)
Benguela
Lobito
Huambo
ANGOLA
Namibe
Cunene
Kwando
Kwanza
ZAMBIA
Lusaka
Lilongwe
MALAWI
L. Malawi (L. Nyasa)
COMOROS
Antsiranana
Ruvuma
Cabo Delgado
MOZAMBIQUE
Mahajanga
MADAGASCAR

NAMIBIA (SOUTH WEST AFRICA)
Windhoek
Swakopmund
Walvis baai
Lüderitz
Kalahari
BOTSWANA
Gaborone
Livingstone
Victoria Falls
ZIMBABWE
Harare
Bulawayo
Zambezi
Beira
Quelimane
Chinde
Blantyre
Moçambique
Mozambique Channel
Toamasina
Antananarivo
MAURITIUS
Réunion (Fr.)
Fianarantsoa
Toliara
Tropic of Capricorn

Oranje
Kimberley
TRANSVAAL
Pretoria
Johannesburg
Maputo
Lourenço Marques
SWAZ.
Vaal
O.V.
Bloemf.
L.E.S.
NATAL
Durban
SOUTH AFRICA
CAPE PROVINCE
Cape Town
Kaap die Goeie Hoop (Cape of Good Hope)
Port Elizabeth
East London

LES. Lesotho
O.V. Oranje-Vrystaat
SWAZ. Swaziland

Projection: Zenithal Equidistant.
West from Greenwich East from Greenwich
COPYRIGHT. GEORGE PHILIP & SON, LTD.

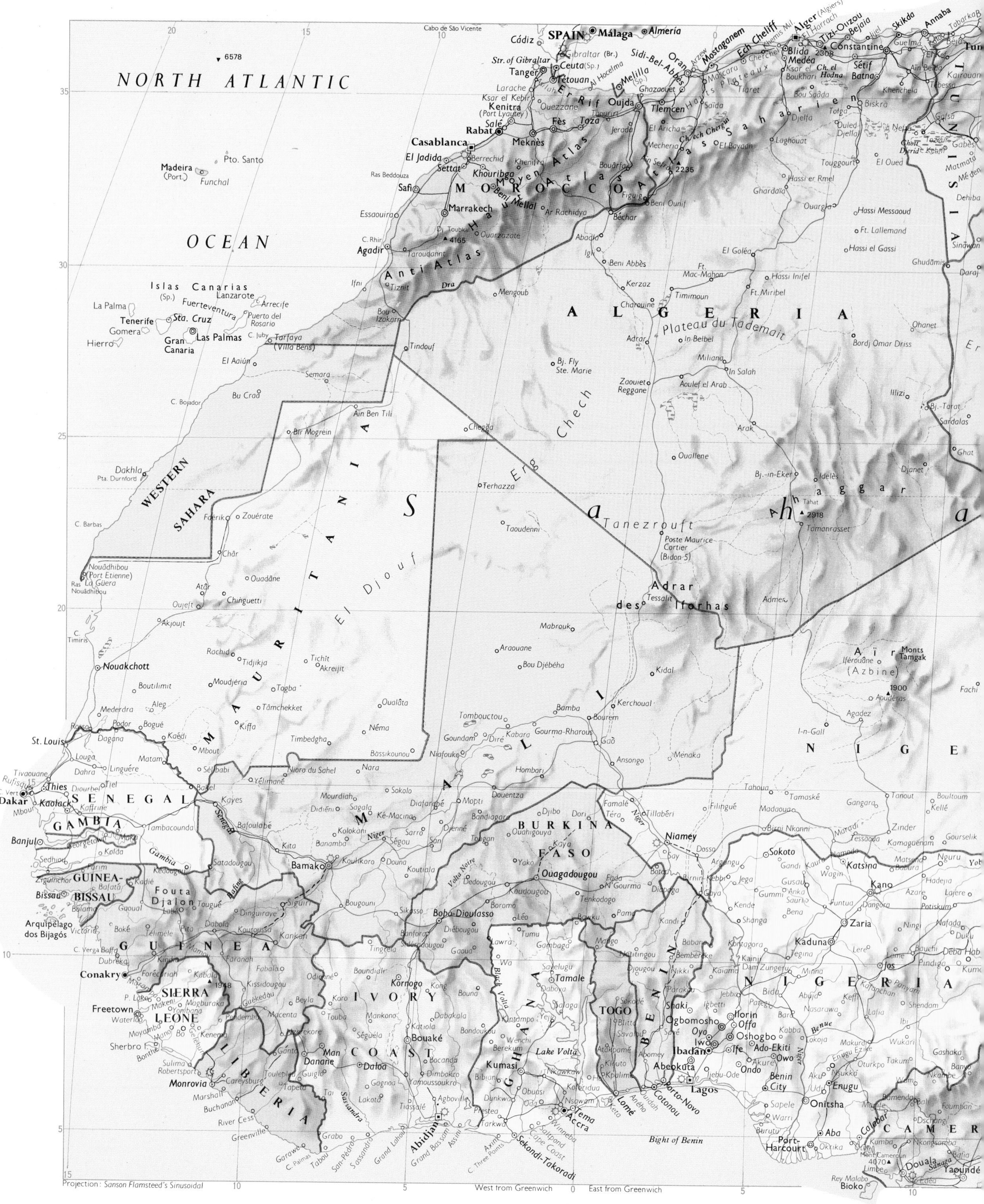

NORTH ATLANTIC

OCEAN

SPAIN

MOROCCO

WESTERN SAHARA

M A U R I T A N I A

A L G E R I A

M A L I

SENEGAL

GAMBIA

GUINEA-BISSAU

GUINEA

SIERRA LEONE

LIBERIA

IVORY COAST

BURKINA FASO

GHANA

TOGO

BENIN

NIGER

NIGERIA

1:15 000 000

100   0   100   200   300   400 miles
100   0   100 200 300 400 500 600 km

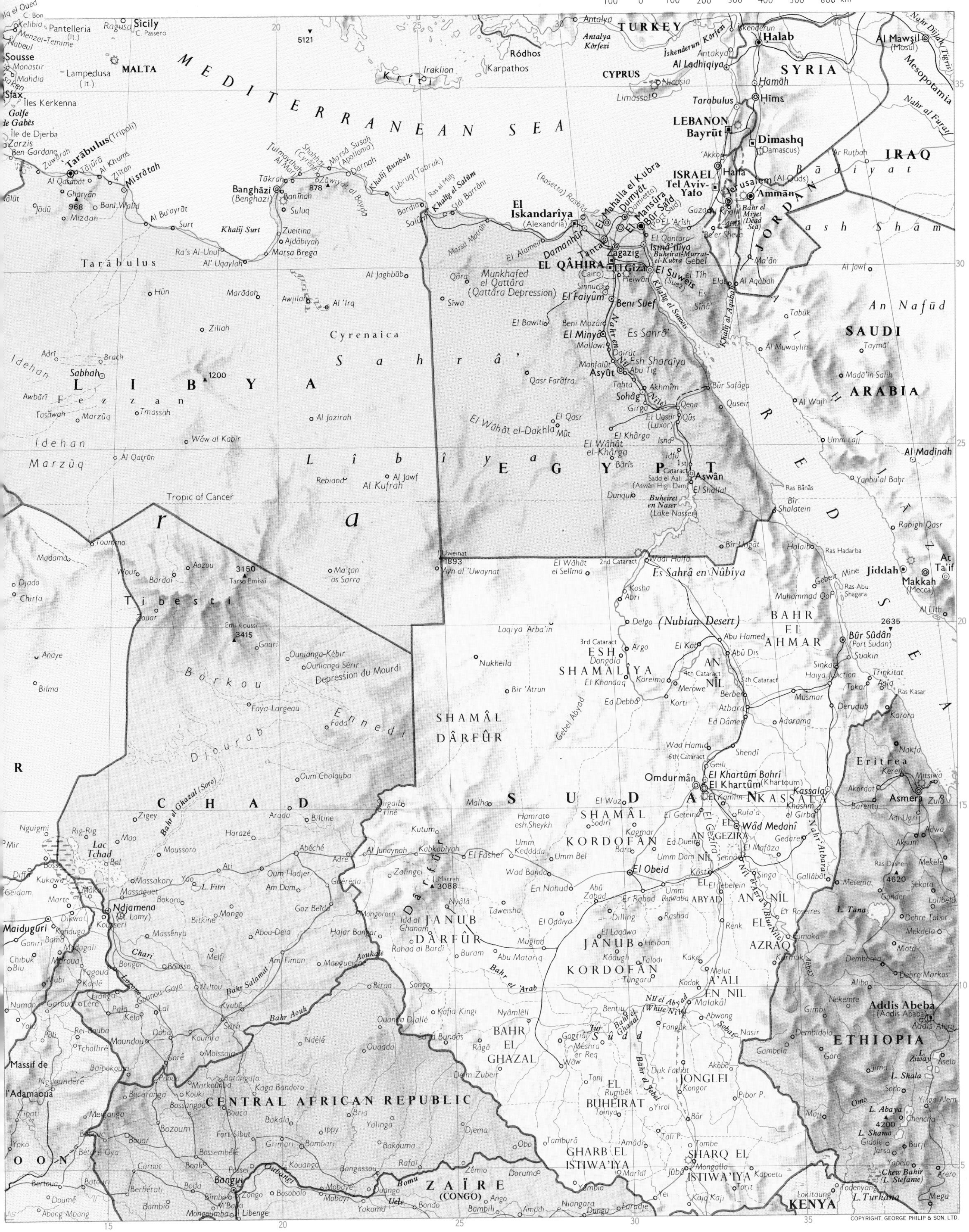

MEDITERRANEAN SEA

Sicily
C. Passero
MALTA
Pantelleria (It.)
Ragusa
Lampedusa (It.)
Kelibia
C. Bon
Menzel-Temime
Nabeul
Sousse
Monastir
Mahdia
Sfax
Iles Kerkenna
Golfe de Gabès
Île de Djerba
Zarzis
Ben Gardane
Zuwârah
Tarâbulus (Tripoli)
Al Khums
Zlîtan
Misrâtah
Jâdû
Gharyân
968
Banî Walîd
Mizdah
Al Bu'ayrât
Al Qabât
Surt
Khalîj Surt
Zueitina
Ajdâbiyah
Ra's Al-Unuf
Marsa Brega
Al' Uqaylah
Marâdah
Hûn
Zillah
Sabhah
1200
Brach
Adrî
Idehan Fezzan
Awbârî
Tasâwah
Marzûq
Tmassah
Idehan Marzûq
Wâw al Kabîr
Al Qatrûn

Banghâzî (Benghazi)
Banî nah
878
Suluq
Al Jaghbûb
Qâra
Sîwa

Tûkrah
Shahhât (Cyrene)
Marsa Susah
Apollonia
Darnah
Khalîj Bunbah
Tulmaythah (Ptolemais)
Tubruq (Tobruk)
Bardia
Sîdî Barrânî
Salûm
Ras al Milh
Khalîg el Salûm
Marsa Matrûh
El Alamein

TURKEY
Antalya
Antalya Körfezi
Rôdhos
Karpathos
Iraklion
Kriti
CYPRUS
Nicosia
Limassol
İskenderun
İskenderun Körfezi
Al Ladhiqîya
Hamâh
Tarabulus
Hims
SYRIA
Halab
Al Mawsil (Mosul)
Nahr Dijlah (Tigris)
Mesopotamia
Nahr al Furat
Ar Rutbah
IRAQ
LEBANON
Bayrût
Dimashq (Damascus)
Akko
Haifa
ISRAEL
Tel Aviv-Yafo
Jerusalem (Al Quds)
'Ammân
JORDAN
Gazza
Be'er Sheva
Bahr el Miyet (Dead Sea)
Ma'ân
Al Jawf
Bâdiyat ash Sham

El Iskandarîya (Alexandria)
Damanhûr
El Mahalla el Kubra
Tanta
El Mansûra
Dumyât
(Rosetta) Rashîd
Dumyât (Damietta)
Pôr Sa'îd
El 'Arîsh
El Qantara
Isma'îlîya
El Suweis (Suez)
Zagazig
EL QÂHIRA (Cairo)
El Gîza
Helwân
El Faiyûm
Beni Suef
Buheirat-Murrat-el-Kubra
Gebel
Khalîg el Suweis
El Tîh
Sînâ
Elat
Al 'Aqabah
Tabûk
Al Muwaylih
Al Jawf
An Nafûd
SAUDI
ARABIA
Tayma'
Mada'in Salih
El Bawiti
El Minya
Mallawi
Manfalût
Asyût
Qasr Farâfra
El Wâhât el-Dakhla
Mût
El Qasr
El Kharga
El Wâhât el-Khârga
Bârîs
Dairût
Abu Tig
Tahta
Sohâg
Girga
Akhmîm
Bûr Safâga
El Qasr
Qena
El Uqsur (Luxor)
Qûs
Isnâ
Edfu
Qusier
Al Wajh
Yanbu' al Bahr
Al Madînah
Sadd el Aali (Aswân High Dam)
Aswân
El Shallal
1st Cataract
Buheiret en Naser (Lake Nasser)
Ras Bânâs
Dunqul
Bîr
Shalatein
Bîr Ungât
Halaïb
Ras Hadarba
Rabigh Qasr
At Ta'if
El Wâhât el Selîma
Wadi Halfa
2nd Cataract
Es Sahrâ en Nûbîya
Mine
Gebeit
Jiddah
Makkah (Mecca)
Al Lith
Ras Abu Shagara
Muhammad Qol
Kosha
Abri
Delgo
(Nubian Desert)
Laqiya Arba'in
Nukheila
3rd Cataract
Argo
Dongola
ESH SHAMALÎYA
El Kab
Abu Hamed
BAHR EL AHMAR
Bûr Sûdân (Port Sudan)
2635
Suakin
Sinkat
El Khandaq
Kareima
4th Cataract
Merowe
Korti
Berber
Atbara
Ed Debba
El Dâmer
Adarama
Derudeb
Karora
Nakfa
Eritrea
Kerera
Mitsiwa
Zula
Asmera
Akordat
Barentu
Adr Ugri
Aksum
Adwa
Mekele
4620
Gonder
Sekota
Lalibela
L. Tana
Debre Tabor
Mota
Dembecha
Debre Markos
Bahr el Ghazal (Soro)
Laqiya Arba'in
Bir 'Atrun
Gebel Abyad
Ed Debba
Malha
SHAMÂL DÂRFÛR
SHAMÂL KORDOFAN
AN NÎL
6th Cataract
Gerli
Shendi
Wad Hamid
Omdurmân
El Khartûm Bahrî
El Khartûm (Khartoum)
El Kamlin
El Gezîra
Wâd Medanî
Kassala
KASSALA
Khashm el Girba
En Nahud
Bara
El Obeid
Ed Dueim
Umm Ruwaba
Rufa'a
El Hasaheisa
El Managil
Sennar
Singa
El Dilling
Talodi
Kaka
JANUB KORDOFAN
Tungaru
Renk
Melut
Kodok
A'ALI EN NIL
Malakal
Nasir
Abwong
Nekemte
Gore
Gambela
Gimbi
Dembidolo
ETHIOPIA
Addis Abeba (Addis Ababa)
Jima
L. Shala
Asela
Soddo
Ziway
L. Zwai
Yirga Alem
L. Abaya
4200
L. Shamo
Chencha
Gidole
Burji
Mega
Arero
L. Turkana
KENYA
Lokichokio
Kapoeta
Torit
Juba
ISTIWÂ'IYA
SHARQ EL ISTIWÂ'IYA
GHARB EL ISTIWÂ'IYA
Yambio
Tombe
Tombura
Amâdi
Maridi
ZAÏRE (CONGO)
Faradje
Dungu
Niangara
Bondo
Aba
Yakoma
Mobaye
Bangassou
Zémio
Obo

LIBYA
EGYPT
Cyrenaica
Sahrâ'
Lîbîyeg
Tropic of Cancer
Sahrâ'
Munkhafed el Qattâra (Qattâra Depression)
Es Sahrâ
Esh Sharqîya
1893
'Uweinat
Ayn al 'Uwaynat
5121

CHAD
Tournno
Madama
Djado
Chirfa
Andye
Bilma
Aozou
Bardai
3150
Tarso Emissi
Emi Koussi
3415
Zouar
Tibesti
Gouri
Ounianga-Kébir
Ounianga Sérir
Fada
Ennedi
Borkou
Faya-Largeau
Djourab
Depression du Mourdi
Oum Chalouba
Kalaït
Arada
Biltine
Iriba
Kutum
Tiné
Guéréda
Abéché
Adré
Am Dam
Goz Beïda
Abou-Deïa
Mongo
Bitkine
Massenya
Hajar Bongar
Mongororo
Am Timan
Aouk
Haraze
Moussoro
Yao
L. Fitri
Bokoro
Massaguet
Massakory
Ndjamena (Ft. Lamy)
Dikwa
Kousséri
Maroua
Mora
Mokolo
Bama
Maiduguri
Ngala
Marte
Kukawa
Rig-Rig
Zigey
Mao
Lac Tchad
Nguigmi
Diffa
Geidam
Damaturu
Potiskum
Gombe

SUDAN
SHAMÂL DÂRFÛR
Kabkabîya
El Fasher
El Junaynah
Zalingei
Melli
3088
Jebel Marra
Idd el Ghanam
JANUB DÂRFÛR
Nyâlâ
Rahad el Bardi
Buram
Mugtar
Ed Da'ein
Abu Matariq
Adilla
Tûmât
Daîn Zubeir
Raqa
Bahr el 'Arab
Bahr el 'Arab
BAHR EL GHAZAL
Aweil
Nyâmlêll
Gogrial
Warab
Tonj
Rumbêk
EL BUHEIRAT
Yirol
JONGLEI
Bor
Kongor
Pibor P.
Akobo
Duk Faiwil
Fangak
Fashoda
Tawisha
Wad Banda
En Nahud
El Odaiya
El Laqâwa
El Fula
Heiban
Kadugli
Abu Zabad
Wad Bandag

CENTRAL AFRICAN REPUBLIC
Ndélé
Ouadda
Ouanda Djallé
Kafia Kingi
Raga
Birao
Songo
Aoukalé
Goré
Bozoum
Bossangoa
Bouca
Batangafo
Kaga Bandoro
Bambari
Bria
Yalinga
Ippy
Grimari
Bakala
Alindao
Bakouma
Mbrès
Damara
Boali
Bangui
Bimbo
Mbaïki
Mobaye
Bangassou
Rafaï
Bambari
Kouango
Sibut
Fort-Sibut
Kaga Bandoro

CAMEROON
Ngaoundéré
Massif de l'Adamaoua
Tibati
Meiganga
Bétaré-Oya
Garoua-Boulaï
Baïbokoum
Moundou
Doba
Kélo
Pala
Léré
Figuil
Guider
Maroua
Rei-Bouba
Tcholliré
Poli
Ngaoundéré
Bertoua
Abong-Mbang
Doumé
Batouri
Nola
Berbérati
Gamboula
Carnot
Boda
Boual

CHARI
Bahr Salamat
Chari
Logone
Bousso
Laï
Kélo
Bongor
Gounou-Gaya
Kyabé
Miltou
Maïngana
Maro
Koumra
Sarh
Kouanga
Moïssala
Ndélé

Kawkaw
Mao
Moussoro
Massakory
Massaguet
Bokoro
Djedaa

TARÂBULUS

1 : 7 500 000

50   50   0   50   100   150   miles
50   0   50   100   150   200   250 km

SUDAN   **ETHIOPIA**

SOMALI REP.

KENYA

UGANDA

ZAIRE

RWANDA

BURUNDI

TANZANIA

ZAMBIA

MOZAMBIQUE

INDIAN OCEAN

LAKE VICTORIA 1134

LAKE TANGANYIKA

LAKE MALAWI

Lake Turkana (Lake Rudolf)

High Lava Plateau

Serengeti National Park

Serengeti Plain

Masai Steppe

Selous Game Reserve

Nairobi
Kampala
Entebbe
Jinja
Kisumu
Eldoret
Kitale
Mbale
Tororo
Nakuru
Nyeri
Nanyuki
Meru
Isiolo
Marsabit
Moyale
Mega
Wajir
El Wak
Mandera
Garissa
Malindi
Mombasa and Kilindini
Lamu
Mtwara
Lindi
Kilwa Kivinje
Kilwa Kisiwani
Dar-es-Salaam
Zanzibar
Tanga
Pangani
Bagamoyo
Morogoro
Dodoma
Iringa
Mbeya
Tukuyu
Njombe
Songea
Tabora
Kigoma-Ujiji
Mwanza
Bukoba
Musoma
Shinyanga
Singida
Kondoa
Arusha
Moshi
Voi
Kitui
Machakos
Thika
Embu
Murang'a
Naivasha
Gilgil
Kigali
Bujumbura (Usumbura)
Gitega
Bukavu
Kabale
Mbarara
Masaka
Fort Portal
Masindi
Gulu
Arua
Soroti
Lira
Kampala
Kasama
Mpika
Mansa
Mbala
Sumbawanga
Kalemie
Moba

Kilimanjaro 5895
Mt. Kenya 5199
Mt. Elgon 4321
Ruwenzori Margherita 5109
Meru 4565

East from Greenwich

Projection: Modified Polyconic

1:8 000 000

50 0 50 100 150 200 miles
50 0 50 100 150 200 250 300 km

NIGER

NIGERIA

CHAD

CAMEROON

MALI

BURKINA

BENIN

TOGO

GHANA

IVORY COAST

EQUATORIAL GUINEA

GULF OF GUINEA

Bight of Benin

Slave Coast

Gold Coast

Niger Delta

Lac Tchad

LAGOS

IBADAN

ACCRA

DOUALA

Yaoundé

Port-Harcourt

Benin City

Kumasi

Kano

Kaduna

Zaria

Maiduguri

Niamey

Ouagadougou

Cotonou

Porto-Novo

Lomé

Tema

Sekondi-Takoradi

Cape Coast

Projection: Lambert's Equivalent Azimuthal

East from Greenwich

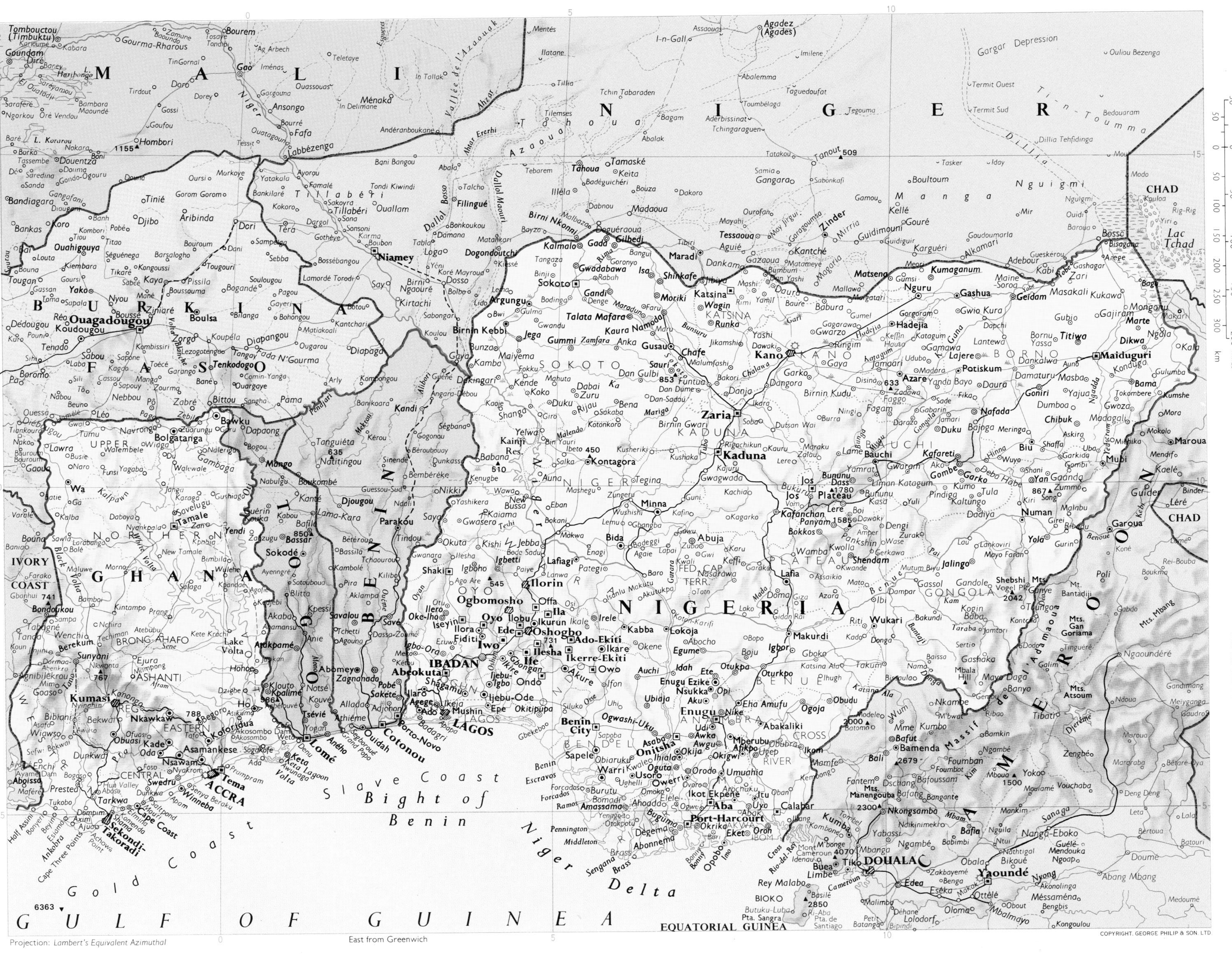

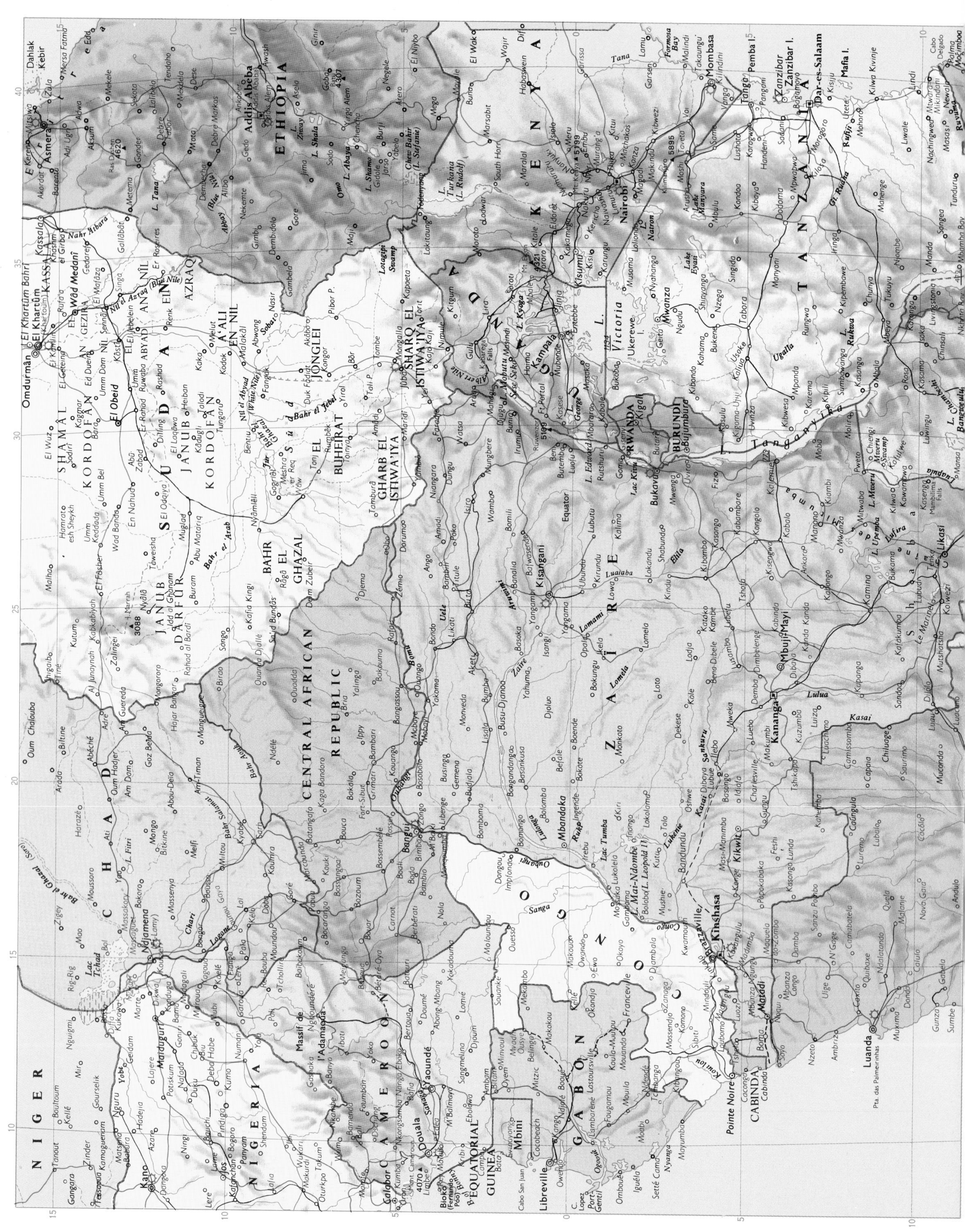
NIGER
CHAD
NIGERIA
CAMEROON
CENTRAL AFRICAN REPUBLIC
EQUATORIAL GUINEA
GABON
CONGO
CABINDA
ZAÏRE
RWANDA
BURUNDI
ETHIOPIA
KENYA
TANZANIA
BAHR EL GHAZAL
JANUB DARFUR
SHAMAL KORDOFAN
JANUB KORDOFAN
EL BUHEIRAT
JONGLEI
Addis Abeba
Asmera
El Khartûm
Omdurmân
Kassala
Wad Medanî
El Obeid
Nairobi
Mombasa
Kampala
Kigali
Bujumbura
Dar-es-Salaam
Zanzibar
Kinshasa
Brazzaville
Bangui
Ndjamena
Yaoundé
Douala
Libreville
Pointe Noire
Luanda
Kisangani
Mbandaka
Kananga
Mbuji-Mayi
Likasi
Kano
Maiduguri
L. Victoria
L. Tanganyika
L. Tana
Lac Tchad
Zanzibar I.
Pemba I.
Mafia I.

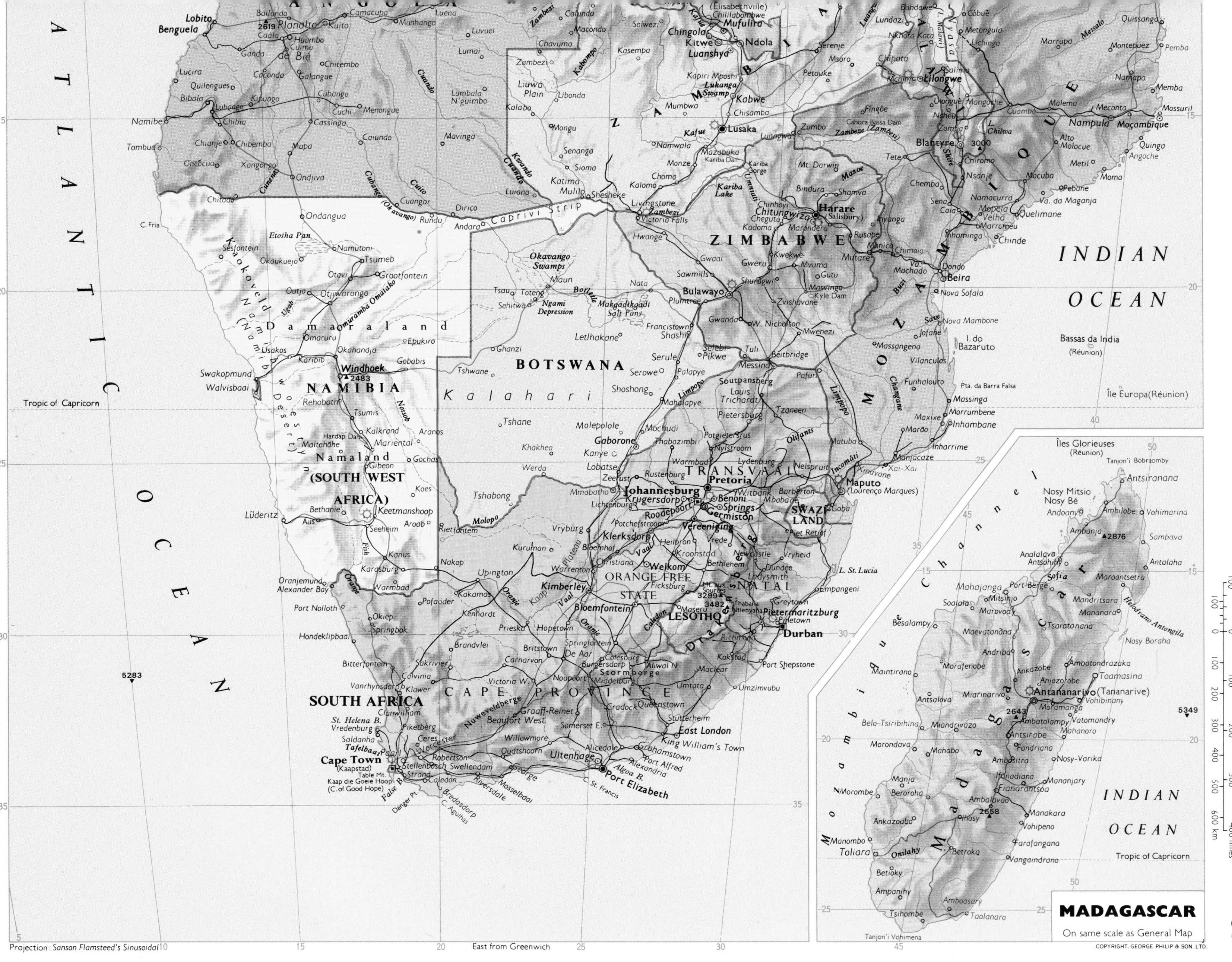

1:15 000 000

100   0   100   200   300   400 miles

100   0   100   200   300   400   500   600 km

MADAGASCAR
On same scale as General Map

COPYRIGHT GEORGE PHILIP & SON. LTD.

INDIAN OCEAN

INDIAN OCEAN

Tropic of Capricorn

ATLANTIC OCEAN

Tropic of Capricorn

ANGOLA

ZAMBIA

ZIMBABWE

BOTSWANA

Kalahari

NAMIBIA (SOUTH WEST AFRICA)

Namaqualand

Damaraland

SOUTH AFRICA

CAPE PROVINCE

ORANGE FREE STATE

TRANSVAAL

SWAZILAND

LESOTHO

NATAL

Caprivi Strip

Okavango Swamps

Ngami Depression

Windhoek

Cape Town (Kaapstad)

Port Elizabeth

East London

Durban

Pietermaritzburg

Pretoria

Johannesburg

Kimberley

Bloemfontein

Harare

Bulawayo

Lusaka

Gaborone

Maputo (Lourenço Marques)

Beira

Blantyre

Nyasa (L. Malawi)

Lilongwe

East from Greenwich

Projection: Sanson Flamsteed's Sinusoidal 10

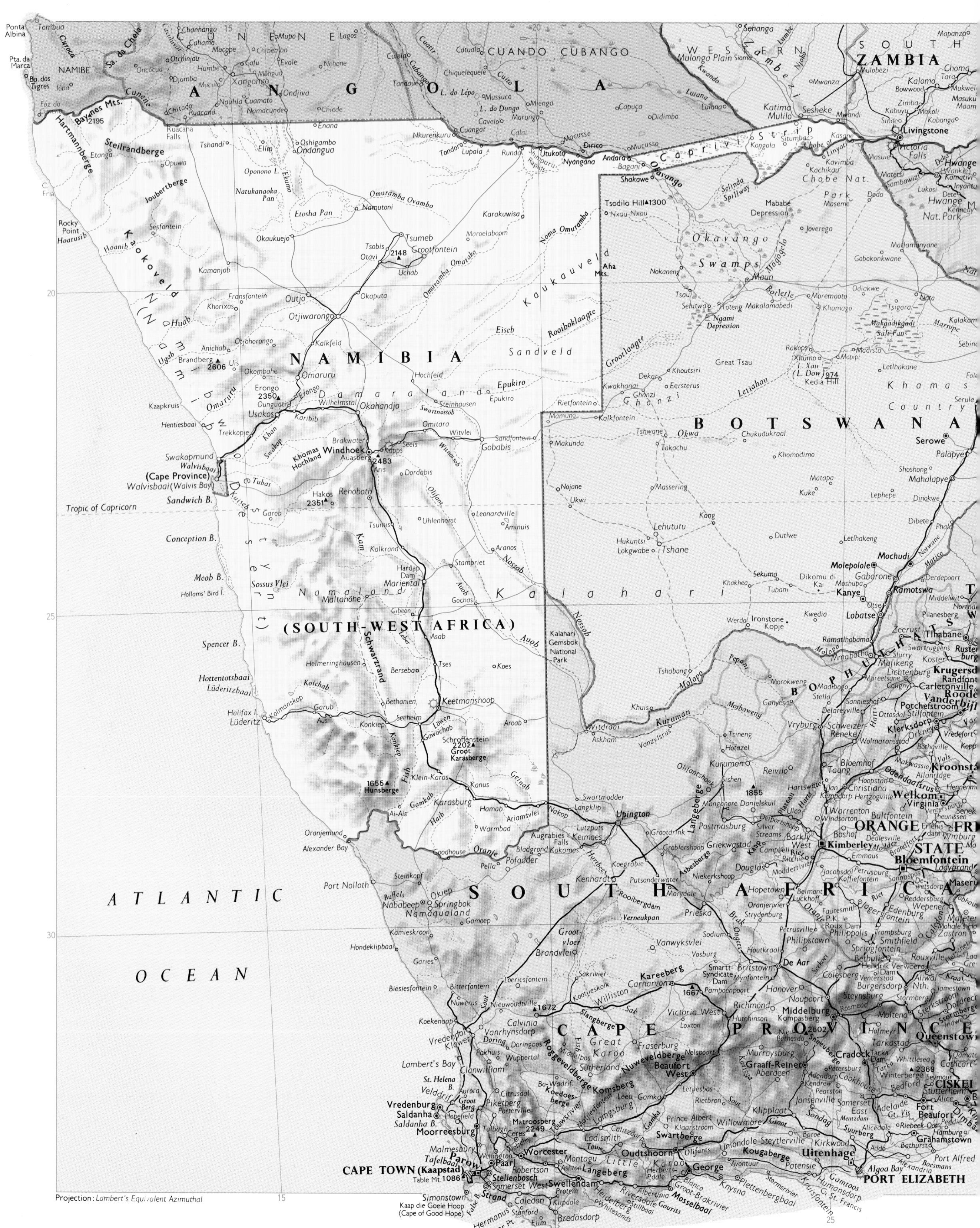
ANGOLA
CUANDO CUBANGO
NAMIBE
ZAMBIA
Livingstone
Victoria Falls
Caprivi Strip
Okavango Swamps
Ngami Depression
Makgadikgadi Salt Pans
BOTSWANA
Khamas Country
Serowe
Mahalapye
Mochudi
Molepolole
Gaborone
Kanye
Lobatse
Kalahari
Kalahari Gemsbok National Park
Tsodilo Hill 1300
Maun
Ghanzi
Tshane
Lehututu
Kaukauveld
Sandveld
NAMIBIA
(SOUTH-WEST AFRICA)
Damaraland
Namaland
Namib Desert
Kaokoveld
Tsumeb
Grootfontein
Otavi
Outjo
Otjiwarongo
Omaruru
Okahandja
Windhoek
Khomas Hochland
Swakopmund
Walvisbaai
(Cape Province)
Walvisbaai (Walvis Bay)
Sandwich B.
Tropic of Capricorn
Rehoboth
Gobabis
Mariental
Maltahöhe
Keetmanshoop
Lüderitz
Lüderitzbaai
Karasburg
Oranjemund
Alexander Bay
Etosha Pan
Brandberg 2606
Hartmannberge
Baynes Mts. 2195
Steilrandberge
Conception B.
Meob B.
Spencer B.
Hottentotsbaai
Schwarzrand
Hunsberge
Groot Karasberge
ATLANTIC
OCEAN
SOUTH AFRICA
BOPHUTHATSWANA
ORANGE FREE STATE
Bloemfontein
Kimberley
Welkom
Kroonstad
Vryburg
Mafikeng
Upington
Oranje
Port Nolloth
Springbok
Namaqualand
Calvinia
CAPE PROVINCE
Great Karoo
Little Karoo
Beaufort West
Nuweveldberge
Roggeveldberge
Middelburg
Graaff-Reinet
Cradock
Queenstown
De Aar
Colesberg
Prieska
Carnarvon
Vredenburg
Saldanha
Saldanha B.
St. Helena B.
Lambert's Bay
Moorreesburg
Malmesbury
Paarl
Worcester
Stellenbosch
Swellendam
Oudtshoorn
George
Knysna
Mosselbaai
Uitenhage
PORT ELIZABETH
Algoa Bay
Grahamstown
Port Alfred
CISKEI
CAPE TOWN (Kaapstad)
Table Mt. 1086
Tafelbaai
Simonstown
Kaap die Goeie Hoop
(Cape of Good Hope)
Hermanus
Danger Pt.
Quoin Pt.
C. Agulhas
Projection: Lambert's Equivalent Azimuthal

1:8 000 000

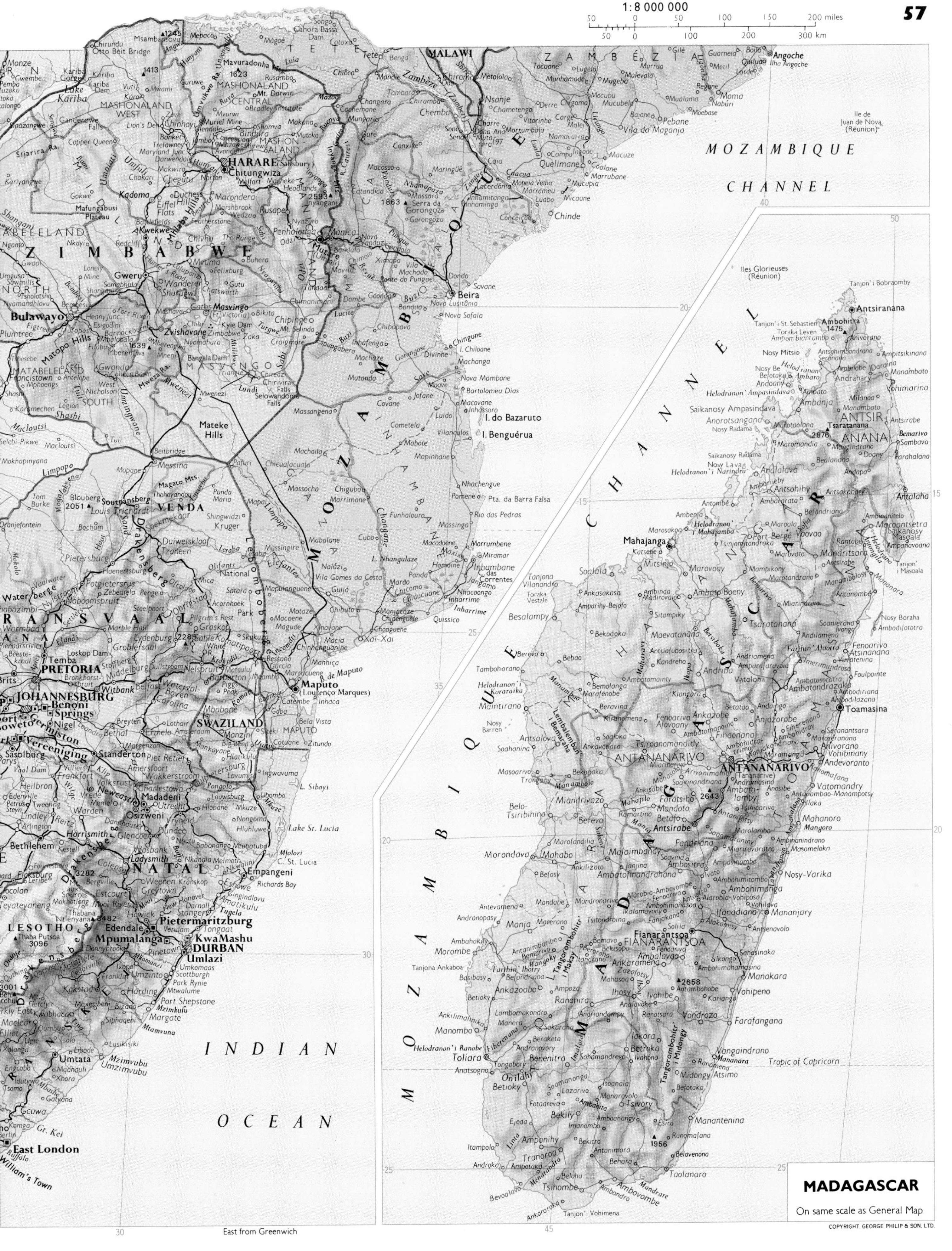
50 0 50 100 150 200 miles
50 0 100 200 300 km
MADAGASCAR
On same scale as General Map
MOZAMBIQUE CHANNEL
INDIAN OCEAN
ZIMBABWE
MOZAMBIQUE
MADAGASCAR
SWAZILAND
LESOTHO
NATAL
TRANSVAAL
MALAWI
ZAMBÉZIA
TETE
MANICA
SOFALA
GAZA
INHAMBANE
MAPUTO
MASHONALAND CENTRAL
MASHONALAND WEST
MASHONALAND EAST
MATABELELAND NORTH
MATABELELAND SOUTH
MASVINGO
MIDLANDS
VENDA
ANTSIRANANA
MAHAJANGA
ANTANANARIVO
FIANARANTSOA
TOAMASINA
TOLIARA
HARARE
Chitungwiza
Bulawayo
Gweru
Mutare
Beira
Maputo
(Lourenço Marques)
Quelimane
Chinde
Angoche
PRETORIA
JOHANNESBURG
Pietermaritzburg
DURBAN
Umlazi
KwaMashu
East London
Umtata
Ladysmith
Empangeni
Newcastle
Antsiranana
Mahajanga
Toamasina
Antsirabe
Fianarantsoa
Toliara
Morondava
Taolanaro
Manakara
Ile de Juan de Nova (Réunion)
Iles Glorieuses (Réunion)
I. do Bazaruto
I. Benguérua
Tropic of Capricorn
East from Greenwich

1:35 000 000

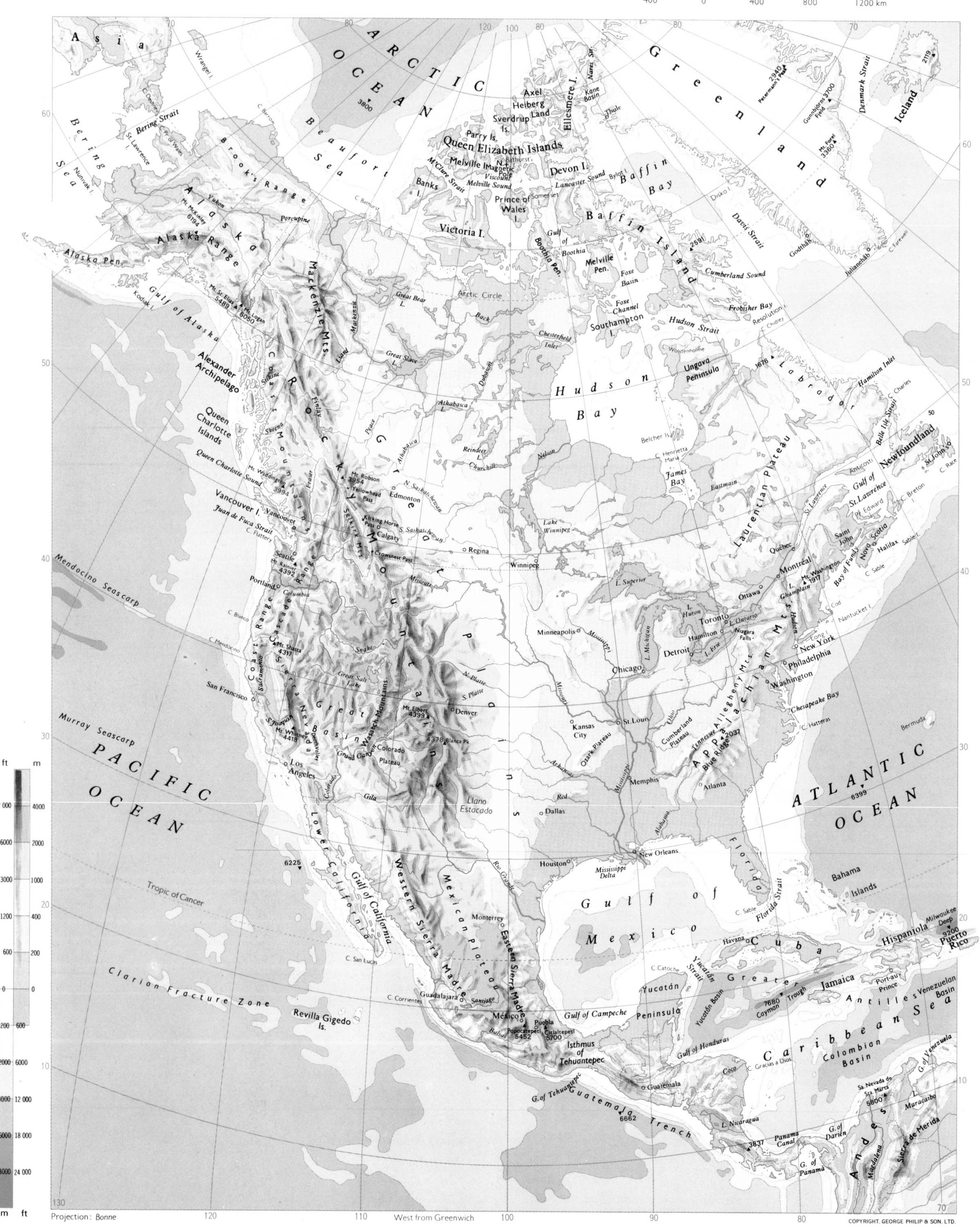

Projection: Bonne   West from Greenwich

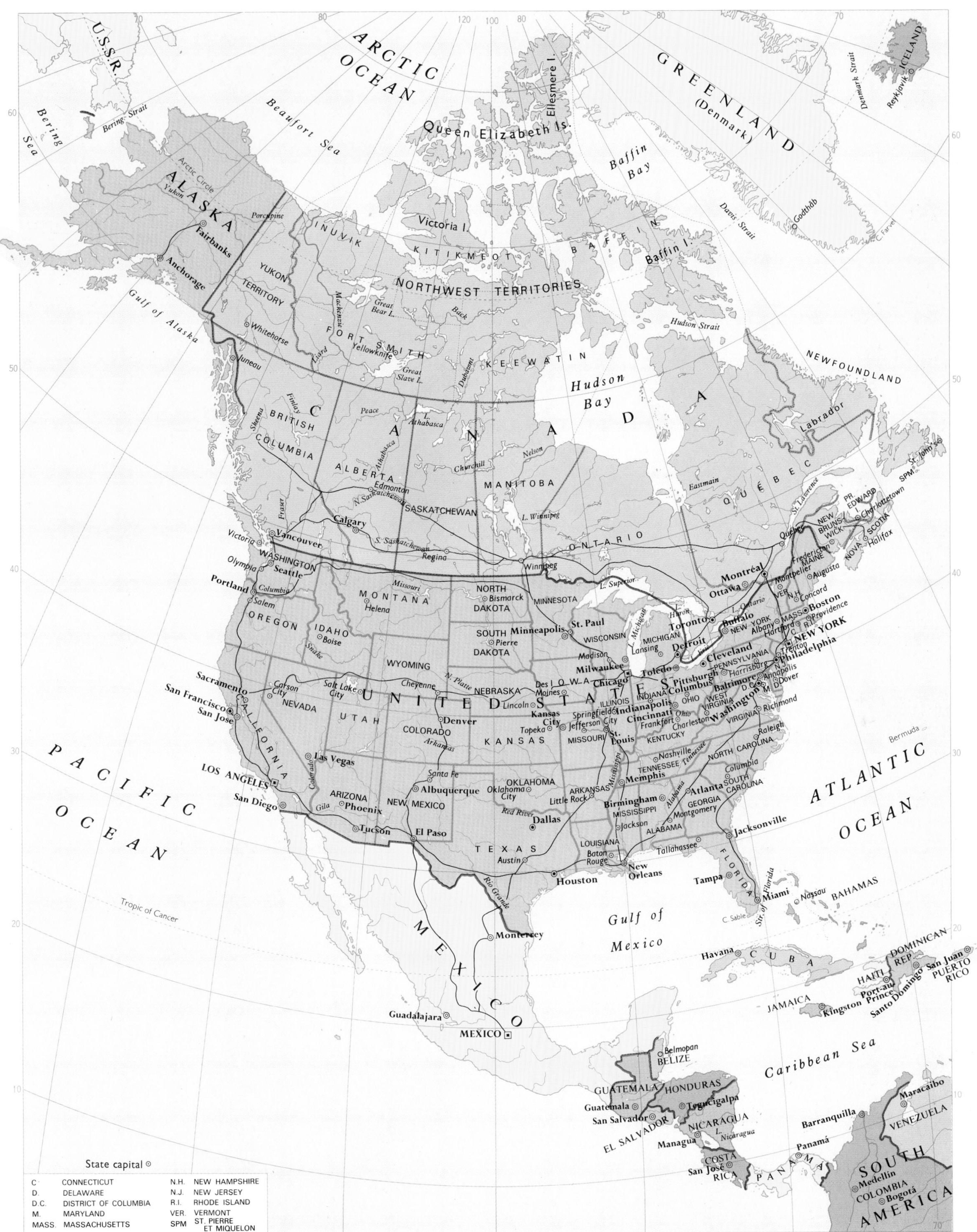

1:35 000 000

200   0   200   400   600   800 miles
400   0   400   800   1200 km

ARCTIC OCEAN

GREENLAND (Denmark)

U.S.S.R.

Bering Strait

Beaufort Sea

Queen Elizabeth Is.

Ellesmere I.

Baffin Bay

Denmark Strait

ICELAND

Reykjavik

Bering Sea

ALASKA

Arctic Circle

Yukon

Fairbanks

Anchorage

Gulf of Alaska

Porcupine

Victoria I.

INUVIK

KITIKMEOT

BAFFIN

Baffin I.

Davis Strait

Godthåb

C. Farvel

YUKON TERRITORY

Whitehorse

Juneau

Liard

Mackenzie

Great Bear L.

NORTHWEST TERRITORIES

FORT SMITH

Yellowknife

Great Slave L.

Back

Dubawnt

KEEWATIN

Hudson Bay

NEWFOUNDLAND

BRITISH COLUMBIA

Skeena

Finlay

Peace

Athabasca

CANADA

Churchill

Nelson

Eastmain

Labrador

QUÉBEC

St. John's

SPM

Fraser

Victoria

Vancouver

Calgary

ALBERTA

Edmonton

N. Saskatchewan

SASKATCHEWAN

S. Saskatchewan

Regina

MANITOBA

L. Winnipeg

Winnipeg

ONTARIO

St. Lawrence

Québec

PR. EDWARD I.

Charlottetown

NEW BRUNS- WICK

NOVA SCOTIA

Halifax

Fredericton

MAINE

Montréal

Ottawa

Montpelier

Augusta

WASHINGTON

Olympia

Seattle

Portland

Salem

Columbia

OREGON

MONTANA

Helena

Missouri

NORTH DAKOTA

Bismarck

MINNESOTA

St. Paul

Minneapolis

L. Superior

WISCONSIN

L. Michigan

Madison

Lansing

MICHIGAN

L. Huron

Toronto

L. Ontario

Buffalo

NEW YORK

Albany

Detroit

VER.

N.H.

MASS.

Boston

Concord

Hartford

Providence

R.I.

NEW YORK

IDAHO

Boise

Snake

WYOMING

Cheyenne

N. Platte

NEBRASKA

Lincoln

IOWA

Des Moines

Chicago

Milwaukee

ILLINOIS

INDIANA

OHIO

Toledo

Cleveland

Pittsburgh

PENNSYLVANIA

Philadelphia

Harrisburg

N.J.

Sacramento

San Francisco

San Jose

Carson City

NEVADA

Salt Lake City

UTAH

COLORADO

Denver

Topeka

KANSAS

Arkansas

Kansas City

MISSOURI

Jefferson City

St. Louis

Springfield

Indianapolis

Cincinnati

Columbus

Frankfort

WEST VIRGINIA

Charleston

Baltimore

Annapolis

M.

D.C.

Washington

Dover

VIRGINIA

Richmond

UNITED STATES

KENTUCKY

Las Vegas

CALIFORNIA

Los Angeles

San Diego

Santa Fe

ARIZONA

Phoenix

Tucson

Gila

Colorado

NEW MEXICO

Albuquerque

El Paso

Oklahoma City

OKLAHOMA

Red River

ARKANSAS

Little Rock

Memphis

TENNESSEE

Nashville

Tennessee

NORTH CAROLINA

Raleigh

Columbia

SOUTH CAROLINA

Atlanta

GEORGIA

Birmingham

MISSISSIPPI

ALABAMA

Jackson

Montgomery

Jacksonville

FLORIDA

Tallahassee

TEXAS

Austin

Dallas

Houston

LOUISIANA

Baton Rouge

New Orleans

Rio Grande

Tampa

Miami

C. Sable

Str. of Florida

Bermuda

ATLANTIC OCEAN

PACIFIC OCEAN

Tropic of Cancer

MEXICO

Monterrey

Gulf of Mexico

Havana

CUBA

BAHAMAS

Nassau

HAITI

Port-au-Prince

DOMINICAN REP.

Santo Domingo

PUERTO RICO

San Juan

JAMAICA

Kingston

Guadalajara

MEXICO

BELIZE

Belmopan

Caribbean Sea

Maracaibo

VENEZUELA

GUATEMALA

Guatemala

San Salvador

EL SALVADOR

HONDURAS

Tegucigalpa

NICARAGUA

Managua

L. Nicaragua

COSTA RICA

San José

PANAMA

Panamá

Barranquilla

Medellín

COLOMBIA

Bogotá

SOUTH AMERICA

State capital ⊙

C.	CONNECTICUT	N.H.	NEW HAMPSHIRE
D.	DELAWARE	N.J.	NEW JERSEY
D.C.	DISTRICT OF COLUMBIA	R.I.	RHODE ISLAND
M.	MARYLAND	VER.	VERMONT
MASS.	MASSACHUSETTS	SPM	ST. PIERRE ET MIQUELON

Projection: Bonne

West from Greenwich

COPYRIGHT. GEORGE PHILIP & SON. LTD.

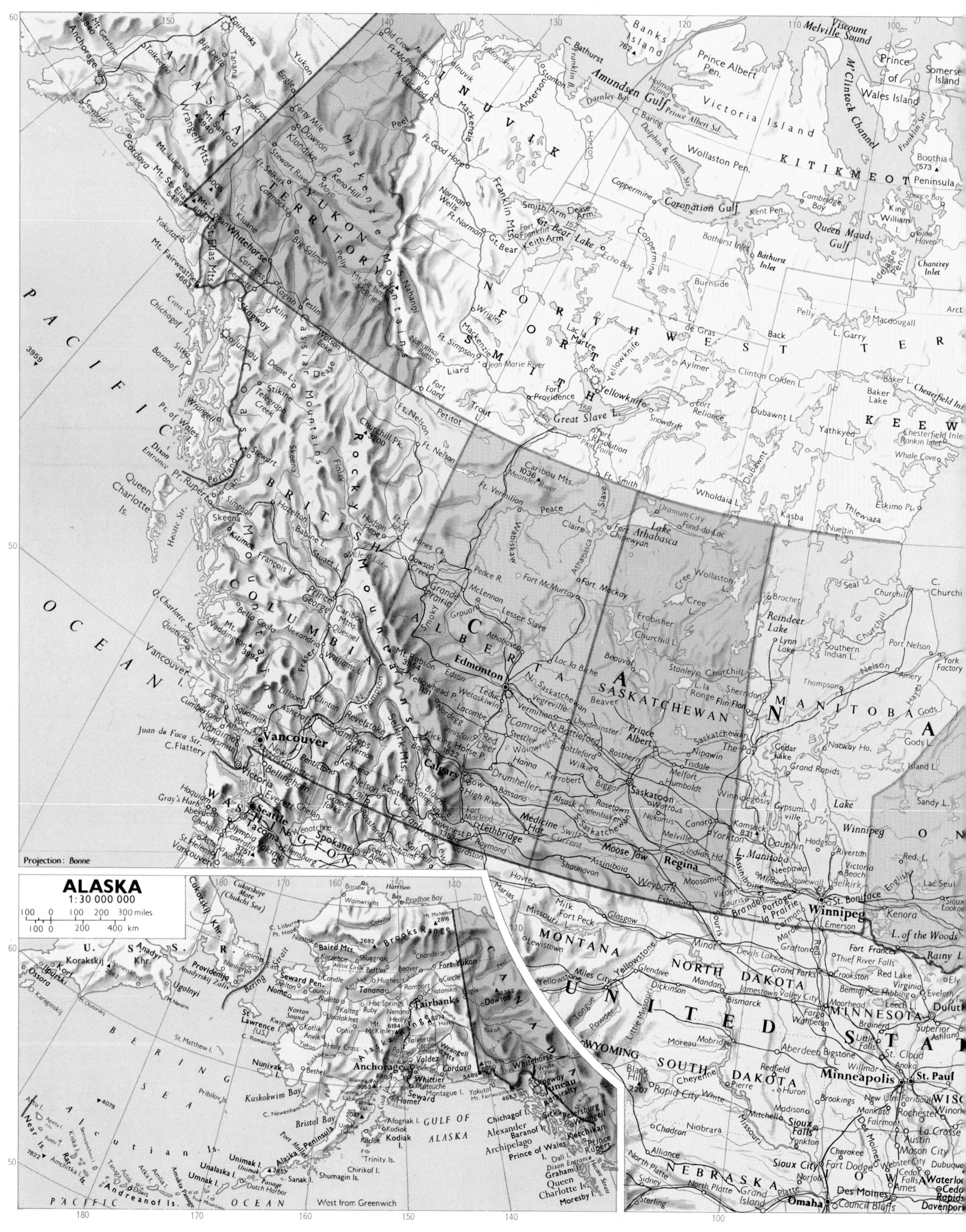

Projection: Bonne

ALASKA
1:30 000 000
100 0 100 200 300 miles
100 0 200 400 km

1:15 000 000

100 50 0 100 200 300 400 miles

100 0 100 200 300 400 500 600 km

Baffin Bay
Davis Strait
GREENLAND
ATLANTIC OCEAN
BAFFIN I.
Hudson Strait
Ungava Bay
Ungava Peninsula
Hudson Bay
James Bay
Foxe Basin
Foxe Channel
Cumberland Sd.
Frobisher Bay
COAST OF LABRADOR
NEWFOUNDLAND
QUEBEC
ONTARIO
Gulf of St. Lawrence
NEW BRUNSWICK
NOVA SCOTIA
PR. EDWARD I.
MAINE
NEW HAMPSHIRE
VERMONT
NEW YORK
MASS.
CONN.
NEW JERSEY
PENNSYLVANIA
OHIO
INDIANA
ILLINOIS
WISCONSIN
MONTREAL
Québec
Ottawa
TORONTO
Boston
Halifax
St. John's
DETROIT
CHICAGO
Lake Superior
Lake Huron
L. Ontario
Lake Erie
L. Michigan

West from Greenwich

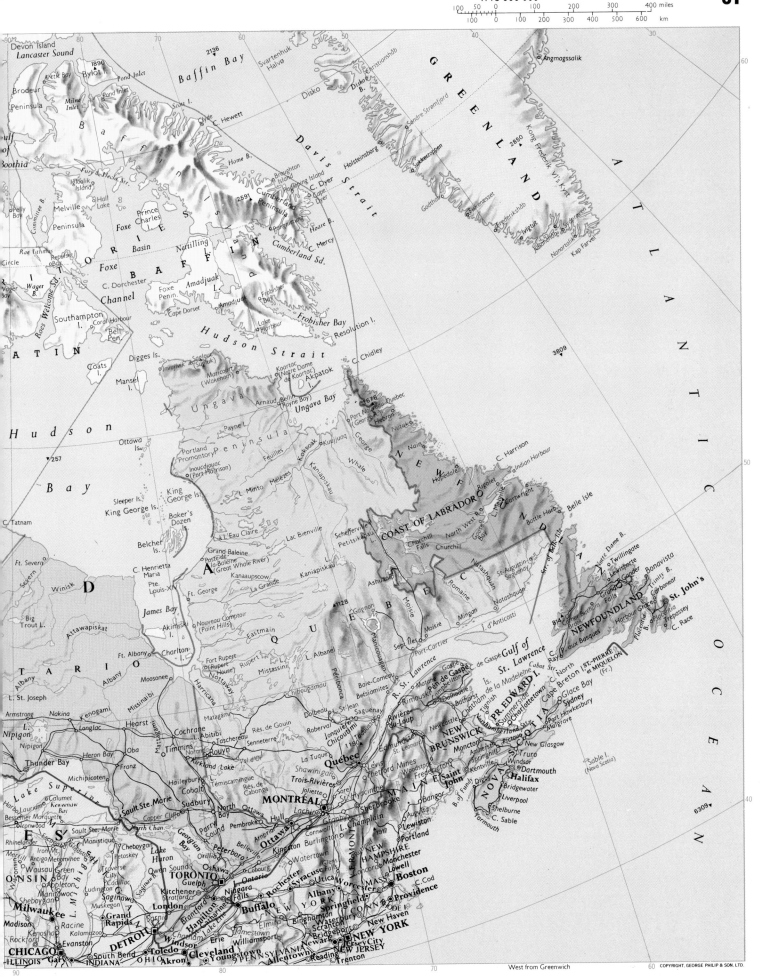

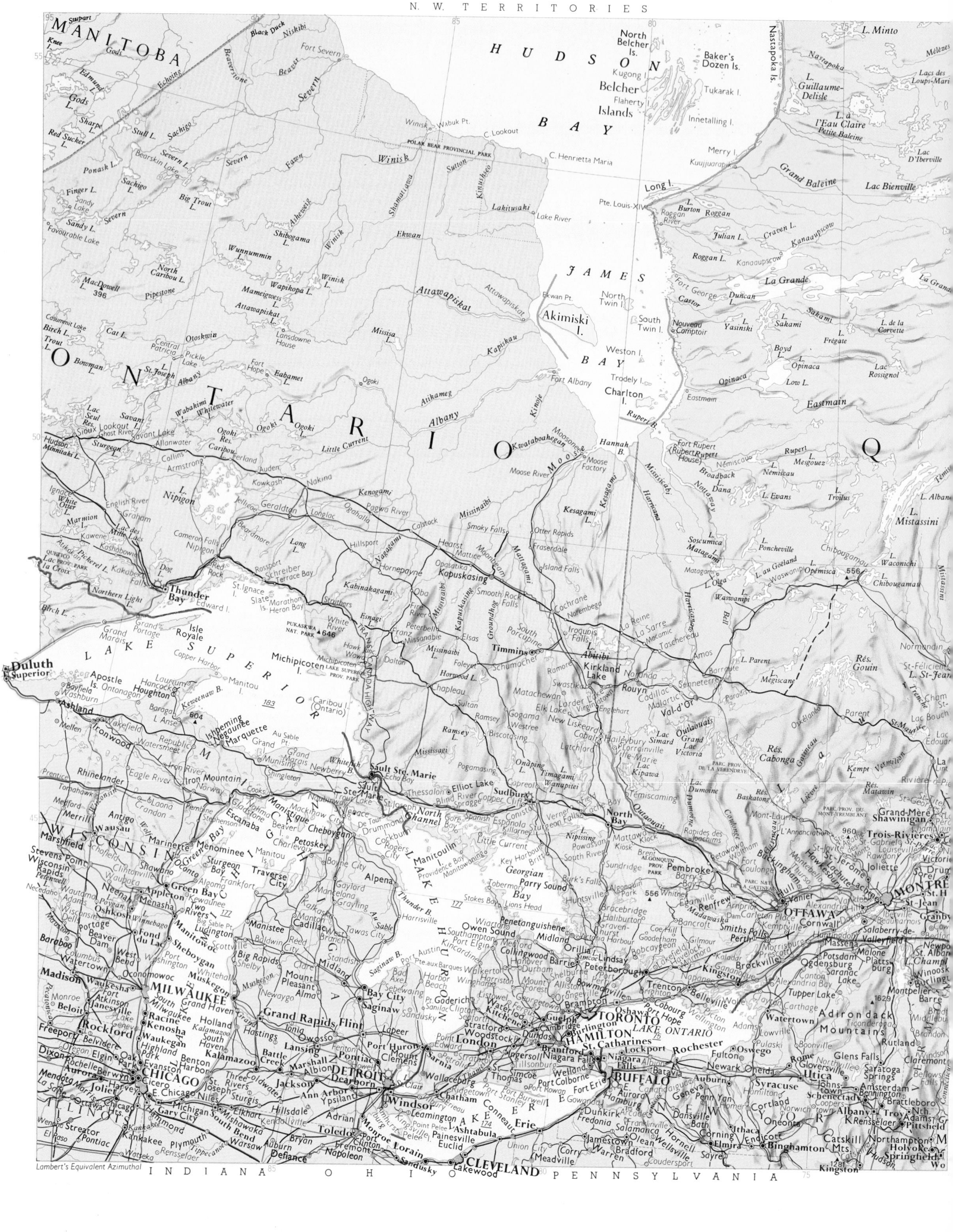

N. W. TERRITORIES

MANITOBA

HUDSON BAY

North Belcher Is.
Baker's Dozen Is.
Kugong I.
Belcher Islands
Flaherty I.
Tukarak I.
Innetalling I.

L. Minto
Nastapoka Is.
Lacs des Loups-Mari
Mélèzes
Lac à l'Eau Claire
Petite Baleine
Lac Guillaume-Delisle
Lacs des Loups-Marins

POLAR BEAR PROVINCIAL PARK
C. Henrietta Maria
Merry I.
Kuujjuarapik
Grand Baleine
Lac D'Iberville
Lac Bienville

Winisk
C. Lookout
Long I.
Pte. Louis-XIV
Burton Roggan
Roggan River
Roggan L.
Lac à la Grande

JAMES BAY
Ekwan Pt.
North Twin I.
South Twin I.
Akimiski I.
Weston I.
Trodely I.
Charlton
Eastmain
Fort George
Duncan
Castor
Nouveau Comptoir
Sakami L.
Yasinski
Opinaca L.
Boyd L.
Lac Rossignol
Eastmain

ONTARIO

QUEBEC
Fort Rupert
(Rupert House)
Rupert R.
Némiscau
Broadback
Dana
L. Evans
Chibougamau
Matagami
Opémisca
Chibougamau
L. Mistassini

Thunder Bay
LAKE SUPERIOR
Isle Royale
Duluth
Superior
Apostle Is.
Houghton
Marquette
Michipicoten
PUKASKWA NAT. PARK
LAKE SUPERIOR PROV. PARK
Sault Ste. Marie

Timmins
Kirkland Lake
Rouyn
Val-d'Or
Noranda

MICHIGAN
WISCONSIN
Milwaukee
Madison
Green Bay
Appleton
Oshkosh
Fond du Lac
Sheboygan
Manitowoc

Sudbury
North Bay
ALGONQUIN PROV. PARK
Pembroke
Ottawa
Hull
MONTREAL
St-Jean
Trois-Rivières
Shawinigan
Grand-Mère

LAKE HURON
Georgian Bay
Parry Sound
Owen Sound
Barrie
Orillia
Lake Simcoe
Peterborough
Kingston
Belleville
Brockville
Cornwall

Traverse City
Cadillac
Saginaw
Bay City
Flint
Grand Rapids
Lansing
Detroit
Dearborn
Windsor
Ann Arbor

TORONTO
HAMILTON
St. Catharines
Niagara Falls
BUFFALO
Rochester
London
Brantford
Kitchener
Guelph
LAKE ONTARIO

Chicago
Rockford
CHICAGO
Gary
ILLINOIS
INDIANA
South Bend
Toledo
CLEVELAND
LAKE ERIE
Erie
OHIO
PENNSYLVANIA

Adirondack Mountains
Watertown
Syracuse
Utica
Binghamton
Elmira
NEW YORK

Lambert's Equivalent Azimuthal

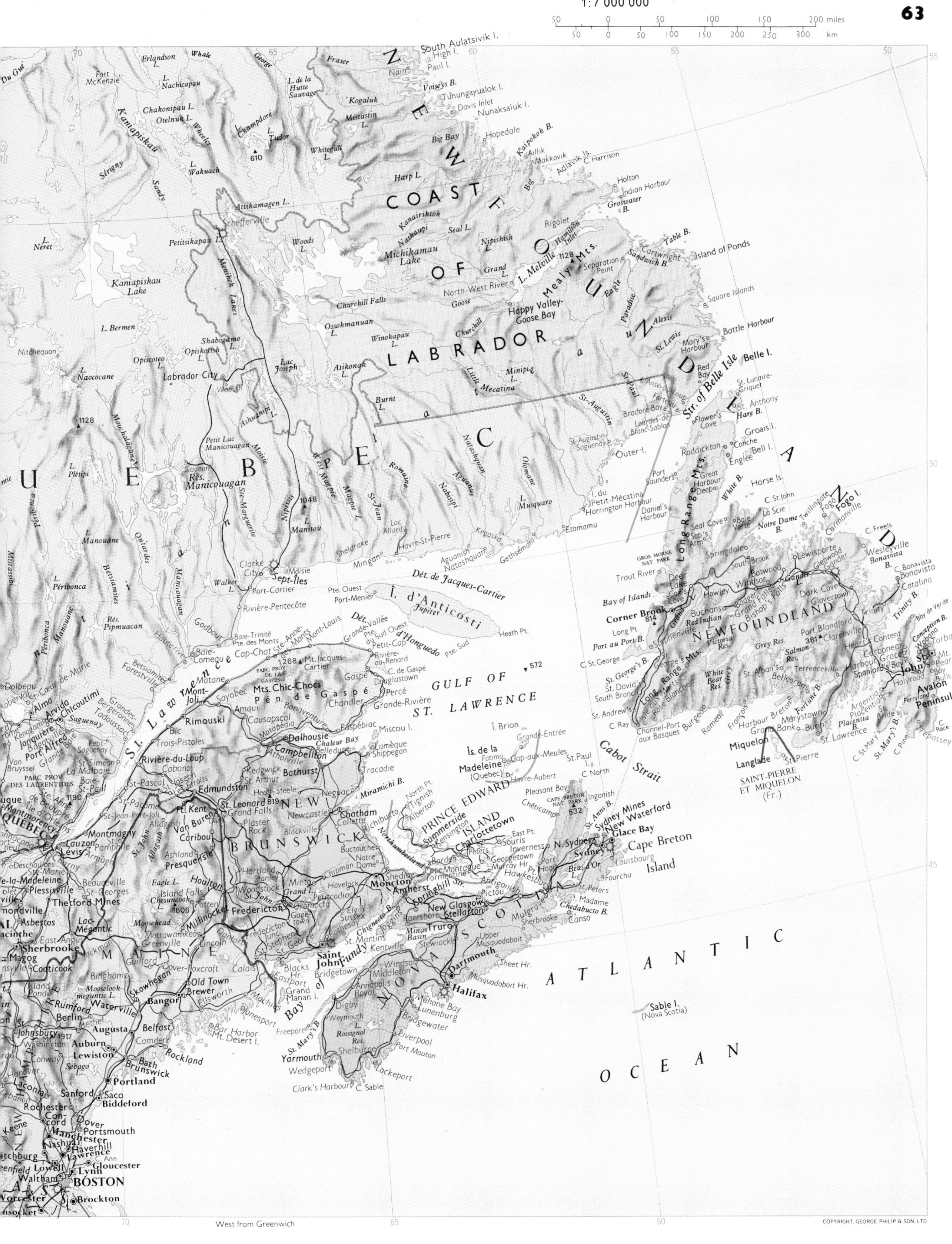

1:7 000 000

50   50   100   150   200 miles
50   0   50   100   150   200   250   300   km

West from Greenwich

COPYRIGHT. GEORGE PHILIP & SON. LTD.

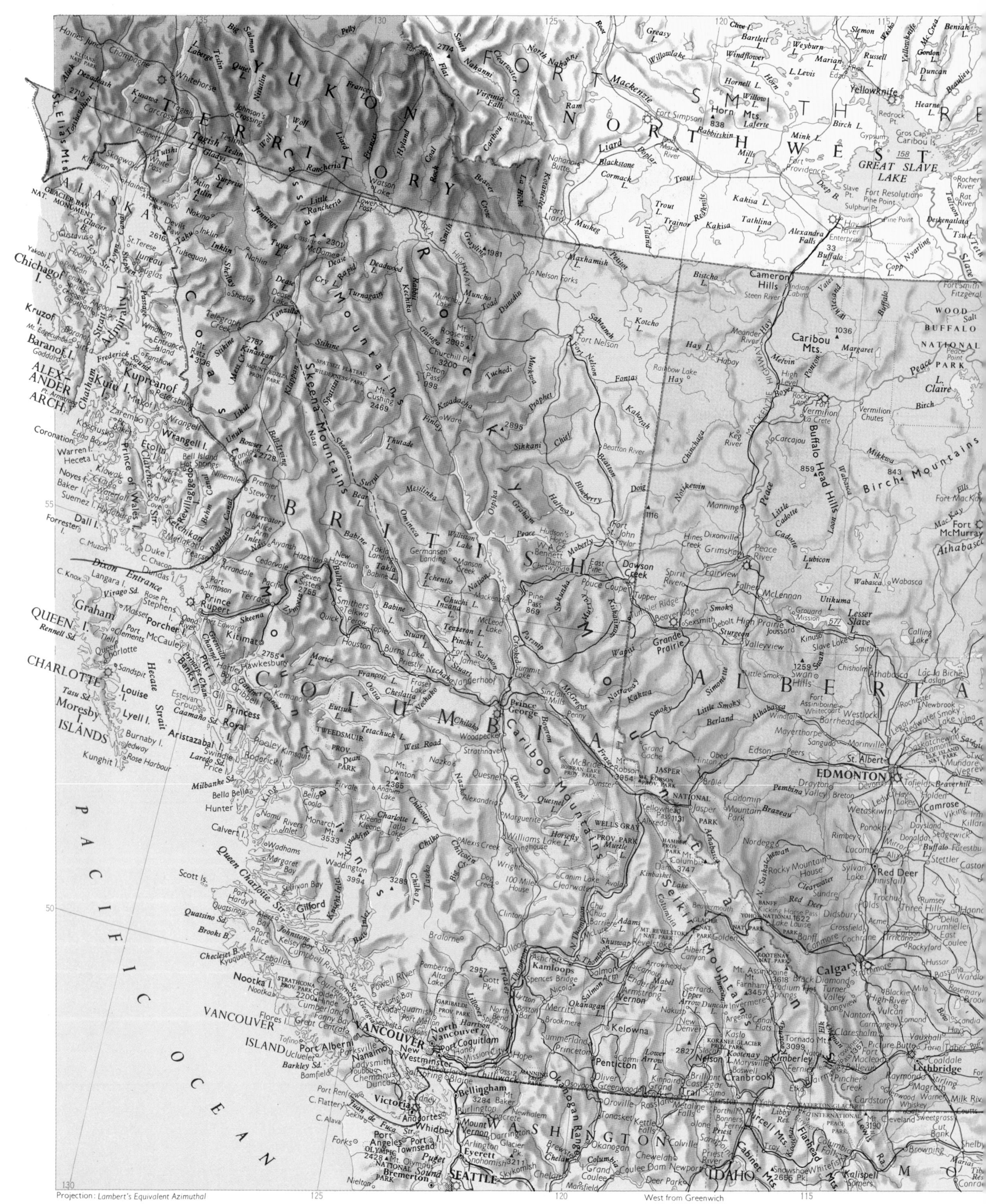
YUKON TERRITORY
NORTHWEST TERRITORIES
FORT SMITH
BRITISH COLUMBIA
ALBERTA
ALASKA
WASHINGTON
IDAHO
PACIFIC OCEAN
GREAT SLAVE LAKE
Whitehorse
Yellowknife
Fort Simpson
Fort Nelson
Prince Rupert
Prince George
Dawson Creek
Grande Prairie
EDMONTON
Calgary
Red Deer
Lethbridge
Kamloops
Kelowna
Penticton
Nelson
VANCOUVER
Victoria
Nanaimo
Bellingham
SEATTLE
QUEEN CHARLOTTE ISLANDS
VANCOUVER ISLAND
Coast Mountains
Rocky Mountains
Cassiar Mountains
Skeena Mountains
Cariboo Mountains
Selkirk Mountains
Purcell Mts.
Cabinet Mts.
Birch Mountains
Caribou Mts.
Buffalo Head Hills
Cameron Hills
Horn Mts.
Dixon Entrance
Hecate Strait
Queen Charlotte Str.
Juan de Fuca Str.
Str. of Georgia
WOOD BUFFALO NATIONAL PARK
JASPER NATIONAL PARK
BANFF NATIONAL PARK
WELLS GRAY PROV. PARK
TWEEDSMUIR PROV. PARK
Mackenzie
Liard
Peace
Athabasca
Fraser
Columbia
Skeena
Stikine
Finlay
Parsnip
Smoky
Thompson
Okanagan
Williston Lake
Lesser Slave L.
Kootenay L.
Mt. Robson 3954
Mt. Waddington 3994
Mt. Columbia 3747
Mt. Assiniboine 3618
Projection: Lambert's Equivalent Azimuthal
West from Greenwich

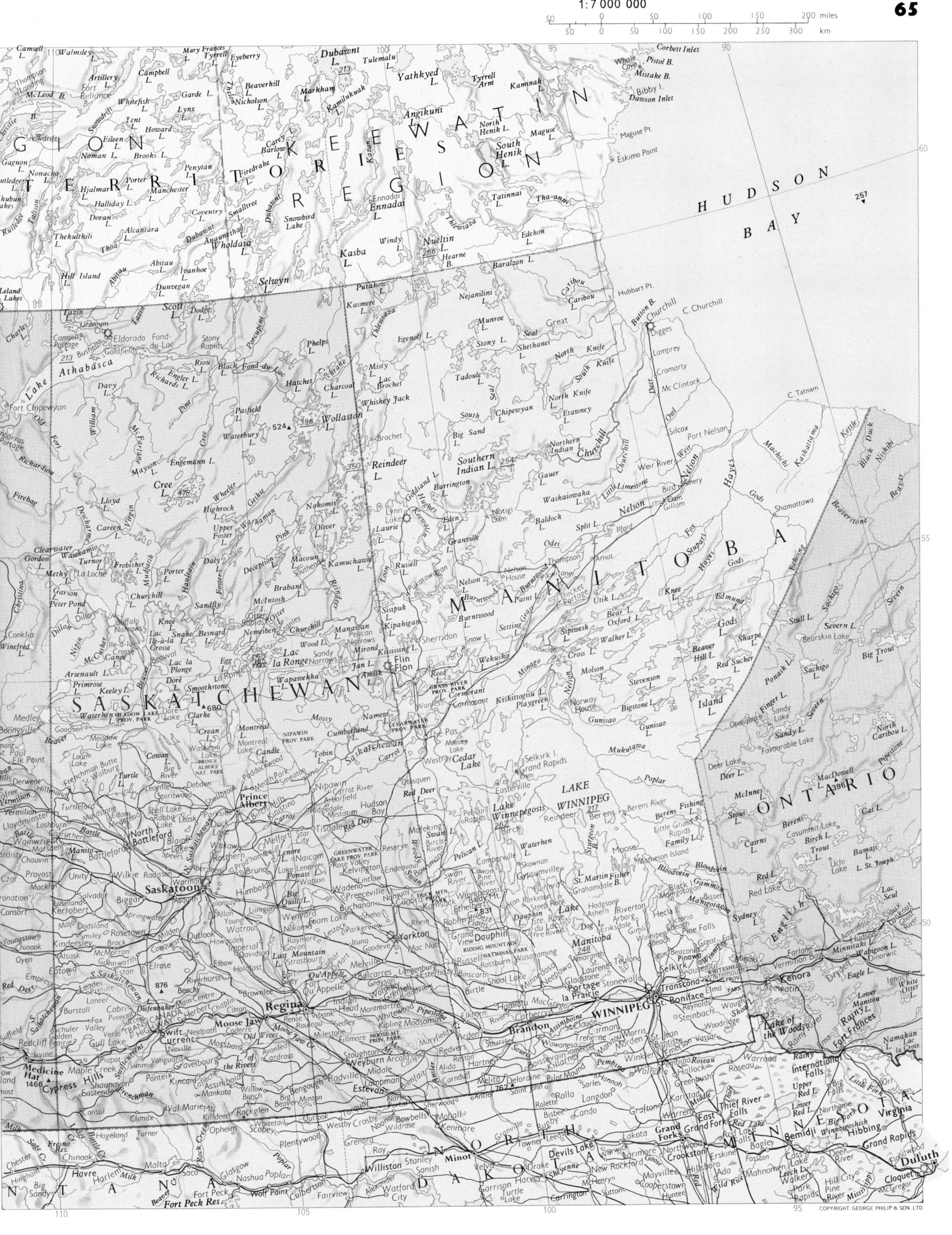

1:7 000 000
50 0 50 100 150 200 miles
50 0 50 100 150 200 250 300 km
KEEWATIN REGION
HUDSON BAY
SASKATCHEWAN
MANITOBA
ONTARIO
NORTH DAKOTA
MINNESOTA
Lake Athabasca
Wollaston L.
Reindeer L.
Southern Indian L.
Nueltin L.
Kasba L.
Selwyn L.
Churchill
C. Churchill
Port Nelson
Nelson
Hayes
Flin Flon
The Pas
Cedar Lake
Lake Winnipegosis
LAKE WINNIPEG
Lake Manitoba
Prince Albert
North Battleford
Saskatoon
Regina
Moose Jaw
Swift Current
Medicine Hat
Cypress Hills
Yorkton
Dauphin
Brandon
WINNIPEG
St. Boniface
Portage la Prairie
Estevan
Weyburn
Minot
Williston
Devils Lake
Grand Forks
Crookston
Bemidji
Hibbing
Duluth
Kenora
Lake of the Woods
Fort Frances
International Falls
Lac la Ronge
Fort Peck Res.
Havre
COPYRIGHT, GEORGE PHILIP & SON, LTD.

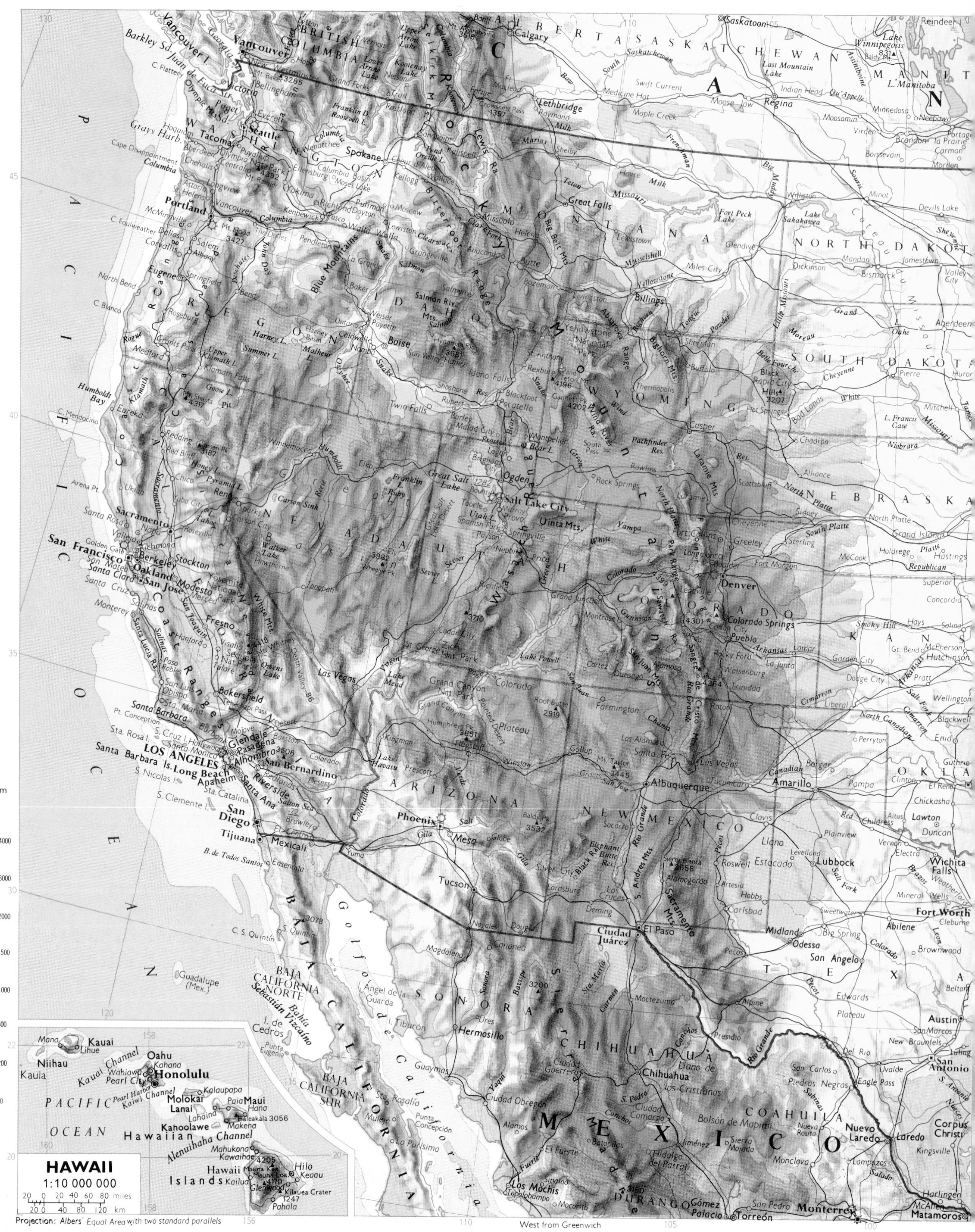

HAWAII
1:10 000 000

Projection: Albers' Equal Area with two standard parallels

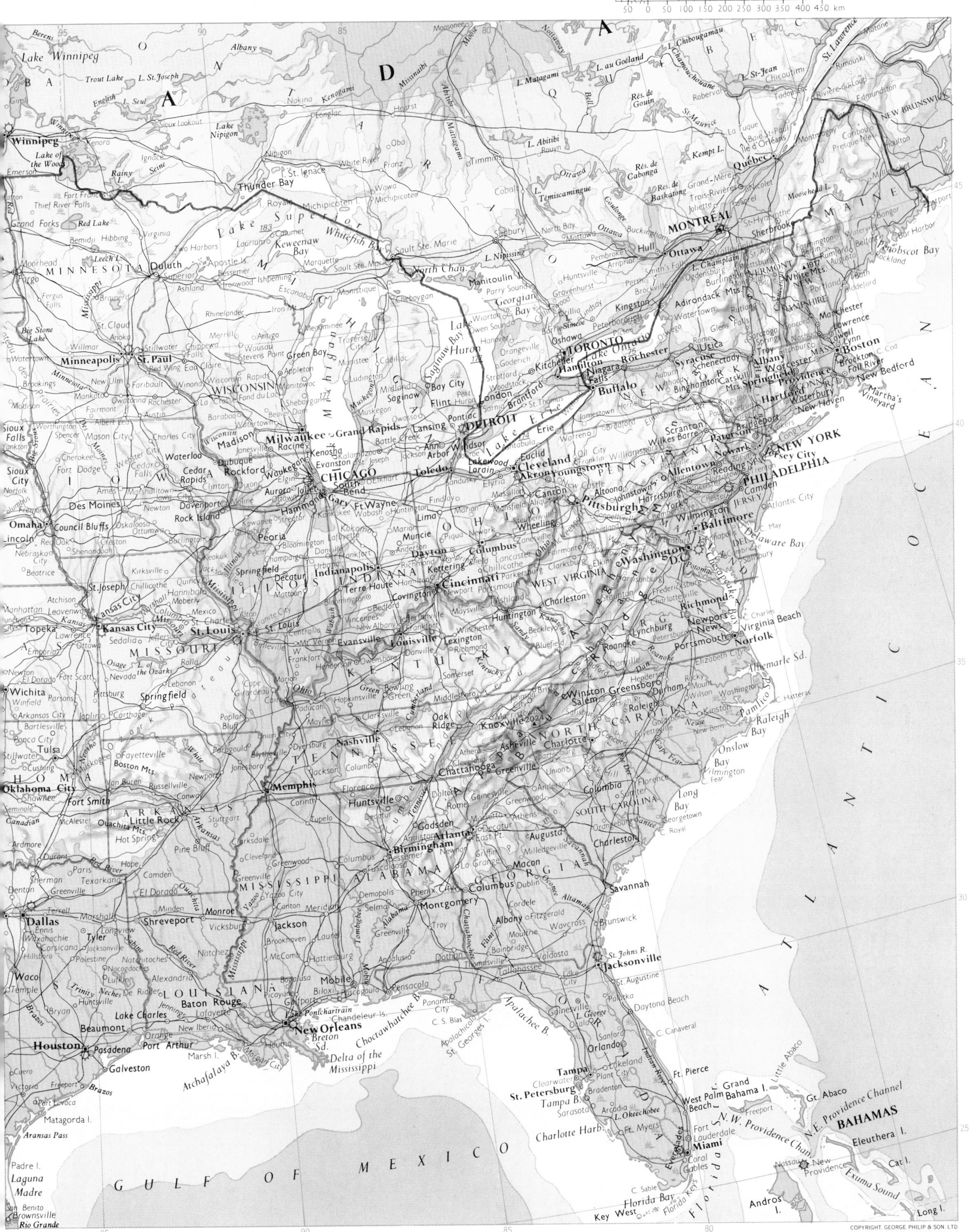

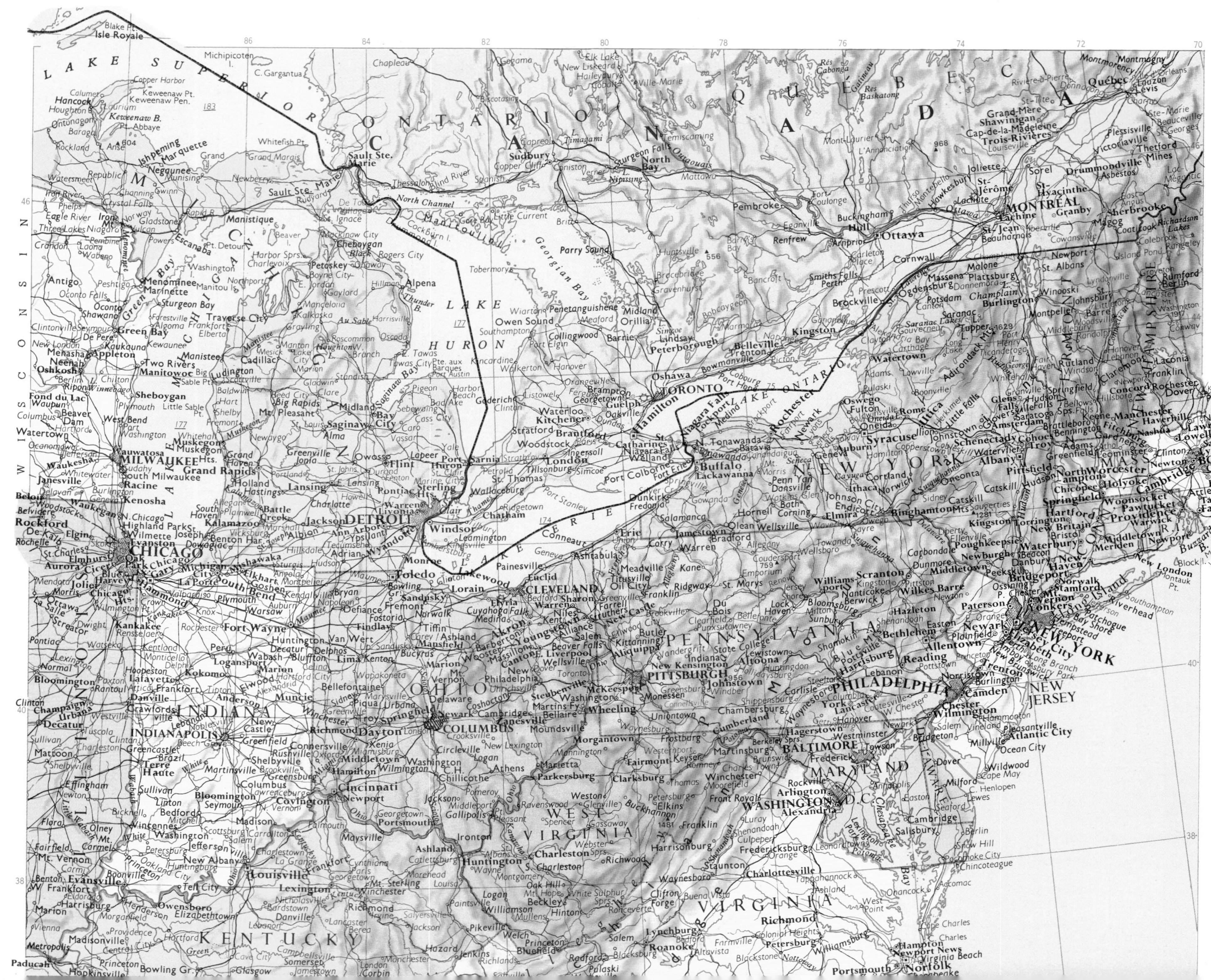

QUEBEC

MONTREAL

VERMONT

NEW HAMPSHIRE

MAINE

BOSTON

ONTARIO

NEW YORK

TORONTO

LAKE ONTARIO

LAKE ERIE

LAKE HURON

LAKE MICHIGAN

LAKE SUPERIOR

Georgian Bay

Parry Sound

MICHIGAN

WISCONSIN

CHICAGO

MILWAUKEE

DETROIT

CLEVELAND

OHIO

COLUMBUS

INDIANA

INDIANAPOLIS

KENTUCKY

PENNSYLVANIA

PITTSBURGH

WEST VIRGINIA

VIRGINIA

RICHMOND

MARYLAND

WASHINGTON, D.C.

BALTIMORE

PHILADELPHIA

NEW JERSEY

NEW YORK

DELAWARE

Chesapeake Bay

Chesapeake Bay

NEW YORK

Isle Royale

Sault Ste. Marie

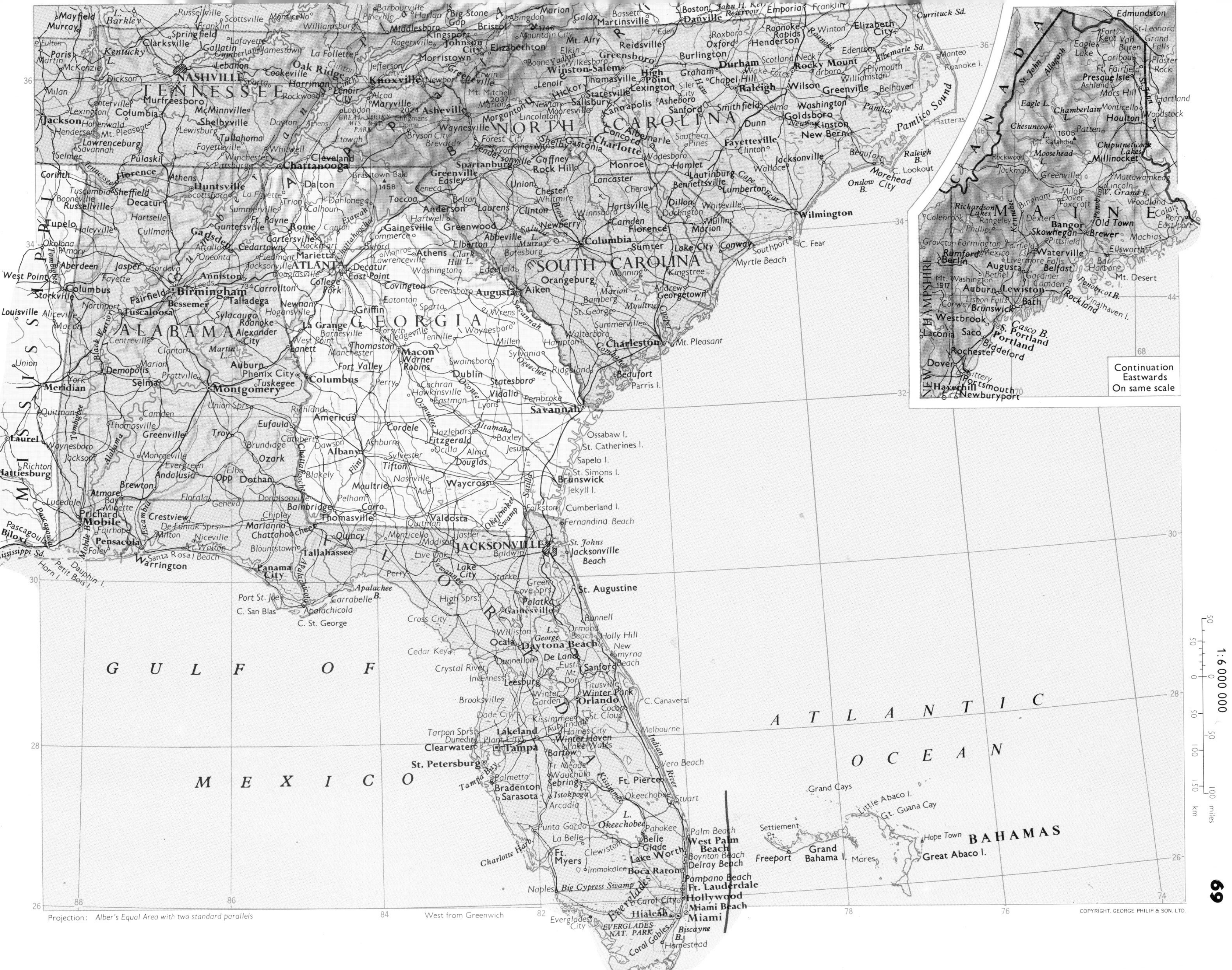

1 : 6 000 000

50   0   50   100 miles
50   0   50   100   150 km

Continuation
Eastwards
On same scale

BAHAMAS

ATLANTIC

OCEAN

Great Abaco I.

Hope Town

Little Abaco I.

Gt. Guana Cay

Grand Bahama I.

Freeport

Settlement Pt.

Grand Cays

West from Greenwich

Projection: Alber's Equal Area with two standard parallels

CANADA

MAINE

NEW HAMPSHIRE

Bangor
Portland
Augusta
Lewiston
Brunswick
Bath
Biddeford
Portsmouth

Portland

Casco B.

GULF OF MEXICO

VIRGINIA

NORTH CAROLINA

SOUTH CAROLINA

GEORGIA

FLORIDA

ALABAMA

TENNESSEE

MISSISSIPPI

Nashville

Memphis

Chattanooga

Knoxville

Atlanta

Birmingham

Montgomery

Mobile

Pensacola

Tallahassee

Jacksonville

St. Augustine

Daytona Beach

Orlando

Tampa

St. Petersburg

Miami

Miami Beach

Ft. Lauderdale

West Palm Beach

EVERGLADES NAT. PARK

Charleston

Columbia

Savannah

Wilmington

Raleigh

Durham

Greensboro

Charlotte

Raleigh

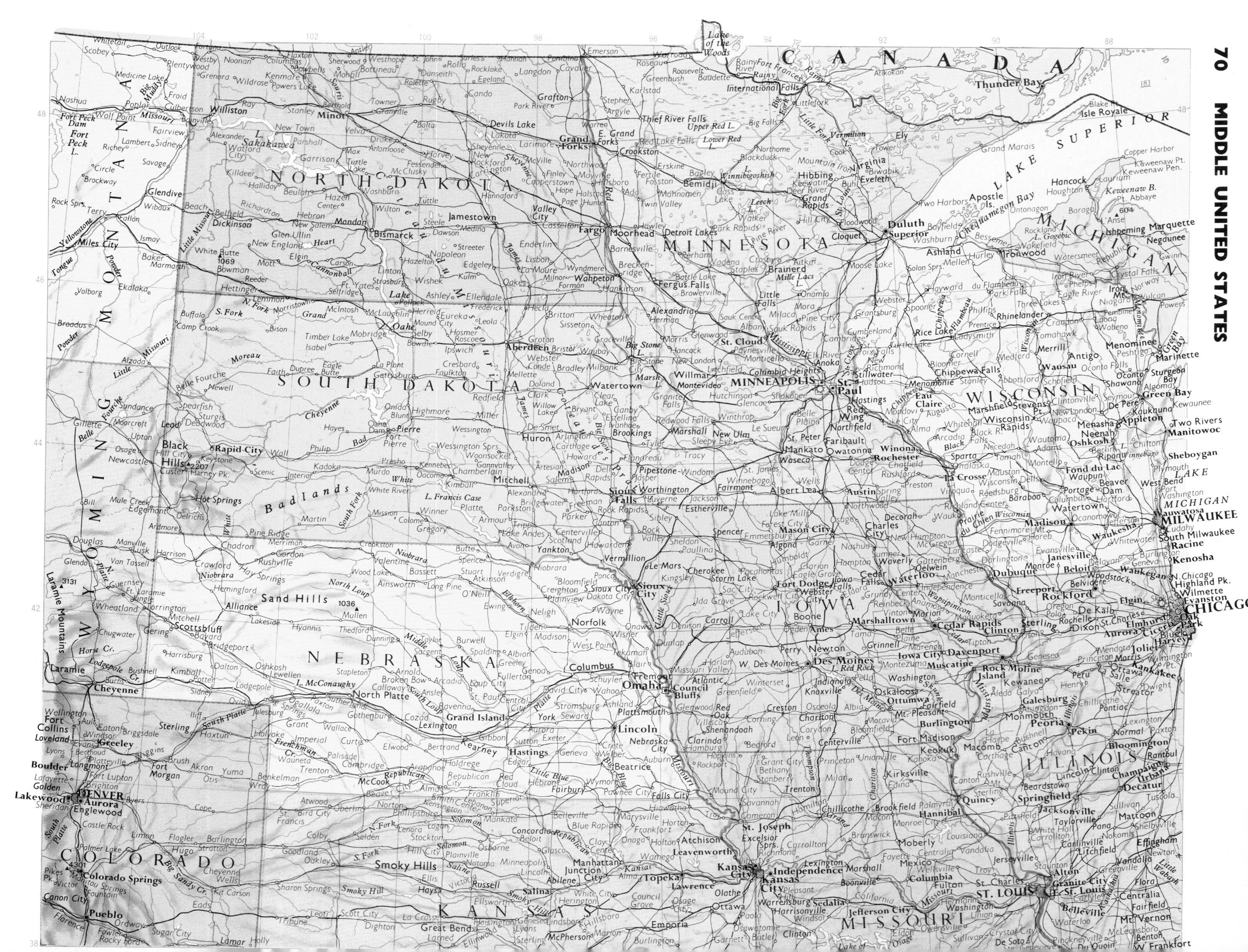
CANADA
LAKE SUPERIOR
LAKE MICHIGAN
MICHIGAN
MINNESOTA
WISCONSIN
IOWA
ILLINOIS
MISSOURI
NORTH DAKOTA
SOUTH DAKOTA
NEBRASKA
KANSAS
COLORADO
WYOMING
MONTANA
CHICAGO
MILWAUKEE
MINNEAPOLIS
St. Paul
ST. LOUIS
Kansas City
Omaha
Des Moines
Duluth
Thunder Bay
DENVER
Cheyenne
Lincoln
Sand Hills
Badlands
Black Hills
Laramie Mountains
Smoky Hills

1 : 6 000 000

50   0   50   100 miles

50   0   50   100   150 km

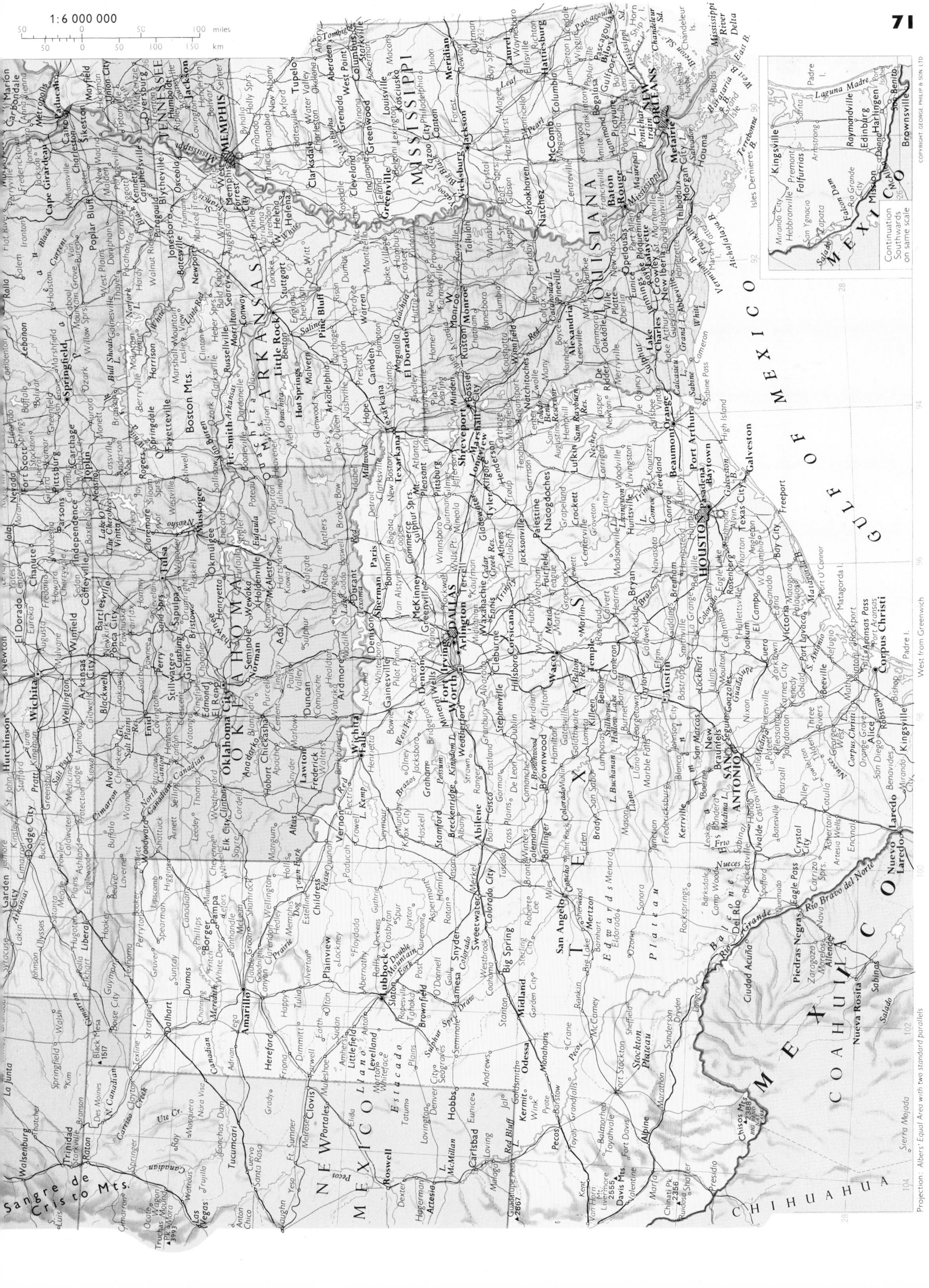

TENNESSEE

MISSISSIPPI

LOUISIANA

ARKANSAS

OKLAHOMA

TEXAS

NEW MEXICO

NEW ORLEANS

MEMPHIS

Baton Rouge

Little Rock

Shreveport

DALLAS

Fort Worth

Arlington   Irving

HOUSTON

SAN ANTONIO

Austin

Waco

Wichita Falls

Amarillo

Lubbock

Odessa   Midland

San Angelo

Corpus Christi

Laredo   Nuevo Laredo

Wichita

Hutchinson

Tulsa

Oklahoma City

Springfield

Fayetteville

El Dorado

Garden City

Dodge City

Edwards   Plateau

Stockton Plateau

Llano   Estacado

Boston Mts.

Ouachita Mts.

Sangre de Cristo Mts.

Chisos Mts. 2388

Davis Mts. 2555

Guadalupe Pk. 2667

Black Mesa 1517

GULF OF MEXICO

Laguna Madre

Padre I.

Mississippi River Delta

Chandeleur Is.

Rio Bravo del Norte / Rio Grande

MEXICO

COAHUILA

CHIHUAHUA

Nueva Rosita

Piedras Negras

Ciudad Acuña

Eagle Pass

Del Rio

Brownsville

Kingsville

McAllen   Harlingen

Edinburg

Continuation Southwards on same scale

COPYRIGHT GEORGE PHILIP & SON, LTD.

West from Greenwich

Projection : Albers' Equal Area with two standard parallels

1 : 6 000 000

50   0   50   100 miles

50   0   50   100   150 km

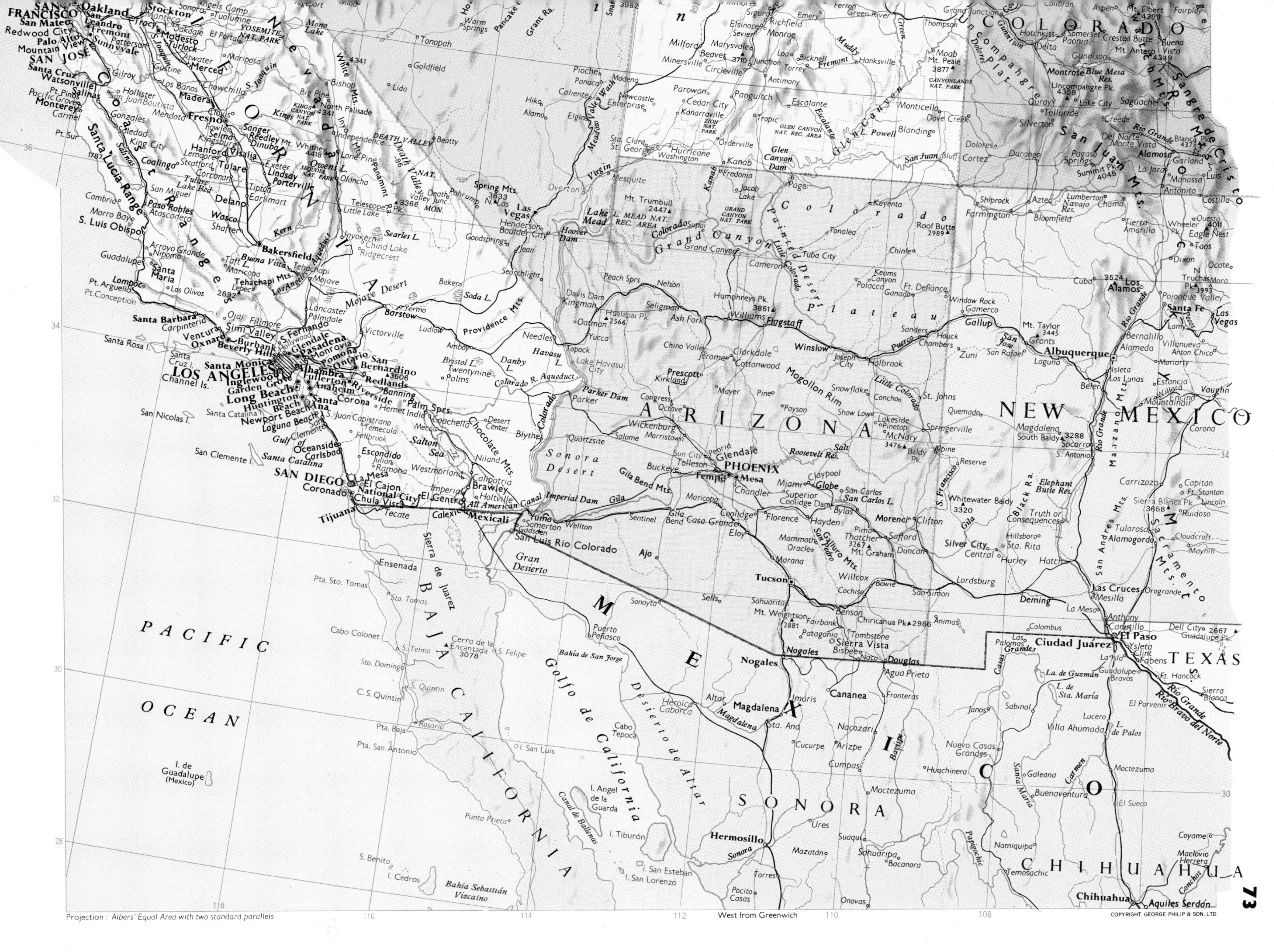

Projection: Albers' Equal Area with two standard parallels

West from Greenwich

PACIFIC OCEAN

BAJA CALIFORNIA

Golfo de California

SONORA

CHIHUAHUA

MEXICO

TEXAS

NEW MEXICO

ARIZONA

COLORADO

CALIFORNIA

Nevada

LOS ANGELES

SAN DIEGO

PHOENIX

Tucson

Albuquerque

El Paso

Ciudad Juarez

Santa Fe

Las Vegas

SAN FRANCISCO

SAN JOSE

Fresno

Bakersfield

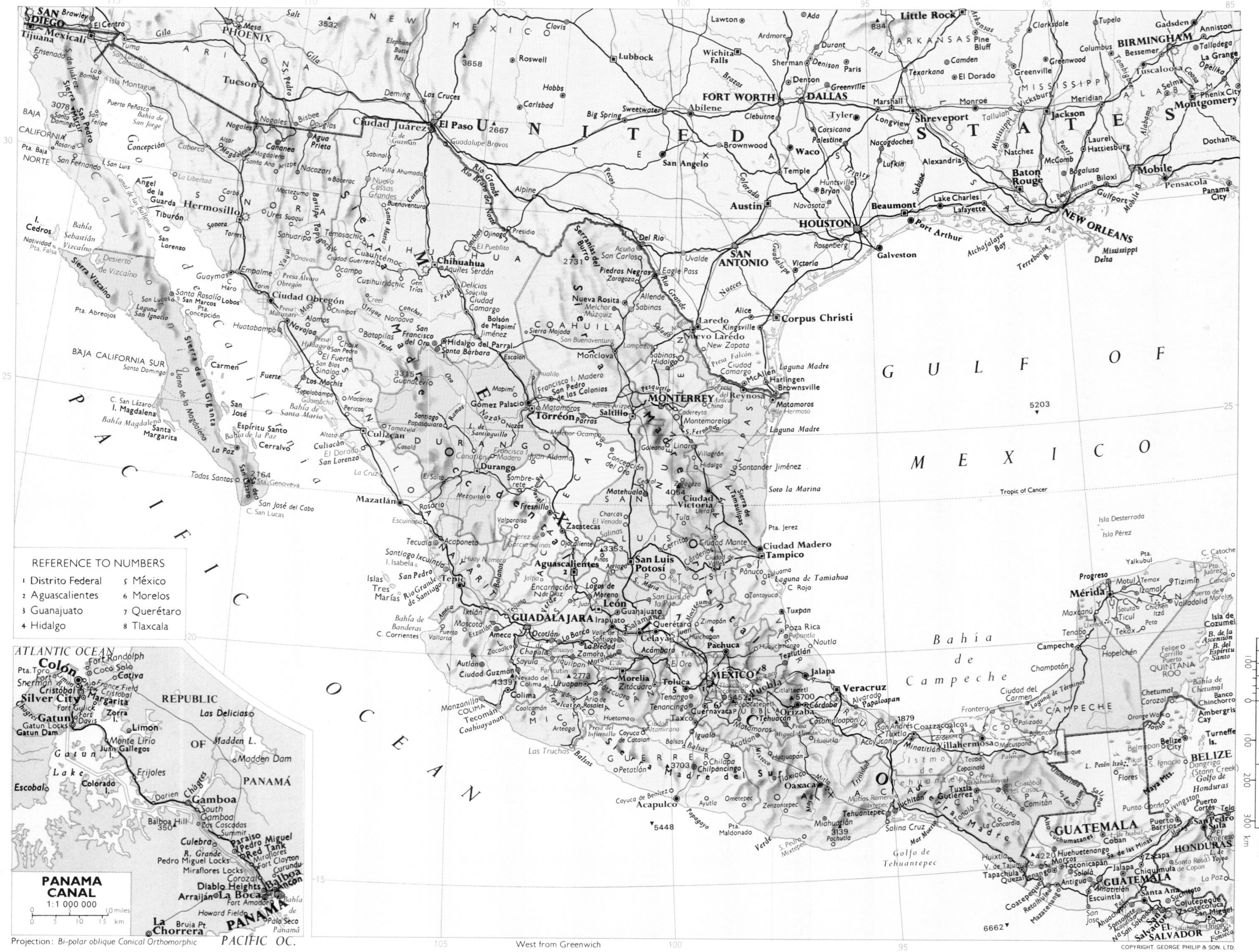

1:12 000 000

West from Greenwich

Projection: Bi-polar oblique Conical Orthomorphic

REFERENCE TO NUMBERS

1 Distrito Federal	5 México
2 Aguascalientes	6 Morelos
3 Guanajuato	7 Querétaro
4 Hidalgo	8 Tlaxcala

PANAMA CANAL
1:1 000 000

1:12 000 000

100   200 miles
100   0   100   200   300 km

WINDWARD ISLANDS 1:8 000 000

TRINIDAD & TOBAGO 1:8 000 000

JAMAICA 1:8 000 000

LEEWARD ISLANDS 1:8 000 000

BERMUDA 1:1 000 000

ATLANTIC OCEAN

CARIBBEAN SEA

GULF OF MEXICO

PACIFIC OCEAN

GREATER ANTILLES

LESSER ANTILLES

WINDWARD ISLANDS

LEEWARD ISLANDS

HISPANIOLA

BAHAMAS

GREAT BAHAMA BANK

CUBA

JAMAICA

HAITI

DOMINICAN REP.

PUERTO RICO

NETH. ANTILLES

Countries and places:
FLORIDA, MIAMI, Fort Lauderdale, West Palm Beach, Fort Pierce, Key West, Fort Myers, Sarasota

MEXICO, Pinar del Río, C. Catoche, Isla de Cozumel

CUBA, LA HABANA, Matanzas, Cárdenas, Cienfuegos, Santa Clara, Sancti Spíritus, Camagüey, Ciego de Ávila, Holguín, Bayamo, Santiago de Cuba, Guantánamo, Manzanillo, Nuevitas

BAHAMAS, Nassau, New Providence, Andros Town, Cat I., San Salvador (Watling I., Guanahani), Long I., Crooked I., Acklins I., Great Inagua I., Mayaguana I., Turks I., Caicos Islands

JAMAICA, KINGSTON, Spanish Town, Montego Bay

HAITI, Port-au-Prince, Cap-Haïtien, Gonaïves

DOMINICAN REP., Santo Domingo, Santiago, San Pedro de Macorís, Barahona, Puerto Plata

PUERTO RICO, San Juan, Ponce, Mayagüez, Arecibo, Caguas

Cayman Islands, Grand Cayman 7680

Swan Islands (U.S.A.)

HONDURAS, Tegucigalpa, La Ceiba, Islas de la Bahía

NICARAGUA, Managua, León, Granada, Corn Is., Puerto Cabezas, Bluefields, Cayos Miskitos, C. Gracias a Dios

COSTA RICA, San José, Limón, Puntarenas

PANAMA, PANAMA CANAL, Colón, Archipiélago de San Blas, Golfo de Panamá, I. de Coiba, Archipiélago de las Perlas, I. del Rey

COLOMBIA, BARRANQUILLA, Cartagena, Santa Marta, Montería, Sincelejo, Magangué, Ocaña, Cúcuta, I. de San Andrés, I. de Providencia

VENEZUELA, CARACAS, MARACAIBO, Valencia, Barquisimeto, Maracay, Barcelona, Cumaná, Ciudad Bolívar, Ciudad Guayana, Maturín, Punto Fijo, Coro, Trujillo, Mérida, San Cristóbal, Barinas, La Guaira, Golfo de Venezuela, Lago de Maracaibo, Isla de Margarita, La Asunción, Los Roques, La Orchila, La Blanquilla, Los Testigos, Bonaire, Curaçao, Aruba, Willemstad

TRINIDAD & TOBAGO, Port of Spain, San Fernando, Tobago, Golfo de Paria

GRENADA, St. George's, The Grenadines

ST. VINCENT, Kingstown

ST. LUCIA, Castries

BARBADOS, Bridgetown, Speightstown

MARTINIQUE (Fr.), Fort-de-France, St. Pierre

DOMINICA, Roseau

GUADELOUPE (Fr.), Basse Terre, Pointe-à-Pitre, Marie-Galante, Grand Bourg

ANTIGUA, St. John's, BARBUDA

ST. CHRISTOPHER NEVIS, Basseterre, Charlestown

MONTSERRAT, Plymouth

ANGUILLA (Br.), ST. MARTIN (Fr.), St. Maarten (Neth.), ST. BARTHÉLEMY (Fr.), SABA, ST. EUSTATIUS

VIRGIN ISLANDS, St. Croix, St. Thomas

GUIANA

West from Greenwich

Projection: Bi-polar oblique Conical Orthomorphic

COPYRIGHT GEORGE PHILIP & SON LTD.

1:30 000 000

100 0 100 200 300 400 500 miles
100 0 200 400 600 800 km

5994 ▼

PACIFIC OCEAN

Panama Canal
Gulf of Panama
Sa. Nevada de Santa Marta
Barranquilla
▲5800
Maracaibo
G. of Darien
Maracaibo
L. Maracaibo
Cord. de Mérida
Caracas
Margarita
Tobago I.
Trinidad

Medellín
Cali
Bogotá
Cordillera Occidental
Cordillera Central
Cordillera Oriental
Magdalena

Llanos
Meta
Orinoco
Guaviare
Caquetá
Caquetá

Guiana Highlands
Georgetown
2810 Roraima
Sierra Pacaraima
Serra de Tumucumaque
C. Orange

ATLANTIC OCEAN

C. de San Francisco
Quito Cotopaxi 5897
Chimborazo 6267▲
Putumayo
Napo
Japurá
Negro
Amazon
Manaus
Pará
Marajó I.
Equator
Belém

Guayaquil
G. of Guayaquil
Marañón
Juruá
Purus
Madeira
Amazon
Tocantins
Fortaleza
C. São Roque

Pta. Pariñas
Pta. Aguja
Lobos Is.
Ucayali
Juruá
Purus
Madeira
Aripuanã
Roosevelt
Tapajos
Xingu
Araguaia
Parnaiba
Plateau of Borborema
Recife
C. Branco

Huascarán 6768
Madre de Dios
Guaporé
Mamoré
Teles Pires
Arinos
Plateau of Mato Grosso
Brazilian Highlands
São Francisco
Salvador

Lima
Chincha Is.
L. Titicaca
Ancohuma & Illampu 6550
La Paz
Bolivian Plateau
L. Poopó
Plateau of Mato Grosso
Brasília
Belo Horizonte
Abrolhos Bank

Peru Trench
Chile
Guaporé
Paraguay
Paraná
Serra da Mantiqueira
2890 Pico da Bandeira
São Paulo
Rio de Janeiro
C. Frio

Tropic of Capricorn
S. Félix
S. Ambrosio
8050
Atacama Desert
Gran Chaco
Pilcomayo
Asunción
Iguaçu Falls
Uruguay
Serra do Mar
Pôrto Alegre
Lagoa dos Patos

Ojos del Salado 6863
Tucumán
Salado
Salinas Grandes
Córdoba
Sierra de Córdoba
L. Mar Chiquita
Entre Ríos
Paraná

Aconcagua 6960
Uspallata Pass
Valparaíso
Santiago
Rosario
Buenos Aires
La Plata
Montevideo
Río de la Plata

Arch. de Juan Fernández
Pampas
Colorado
Negro
Bahía Blanca
Pta. Mogotes

SOUTH ATLANTIC OCEAN

Chile Rise
G. of San Matias
Valdés Peninsula
G. of San Jorge
Argentine Basin
6212 ▼

Chiloé I.
Chonos Archipelago
Taitao Peninsula
G. of Peñas
Patagonia
▲4058 S. Valentin
Chubut

Wellington
Madre de Dios I.
Magellan's Strait
Santa Inés I.
Cockburn Chan.
Beagle Chan.
C. Horn
Tierra del Fuego
Staten I.

West Falkland
Falkland Islands
East Falkland
Magellan's Strait

ft	m
18 000	6000
12 000	4000
9000	3000
6000	2000
3000	1000
1200	400
600	200
	0
200	600
2000	6000
4000	12 000
6000	18 000
8000	24 000
m	ft

Projection: Lambert's Equivalent Azimuthal

West from Greenwich

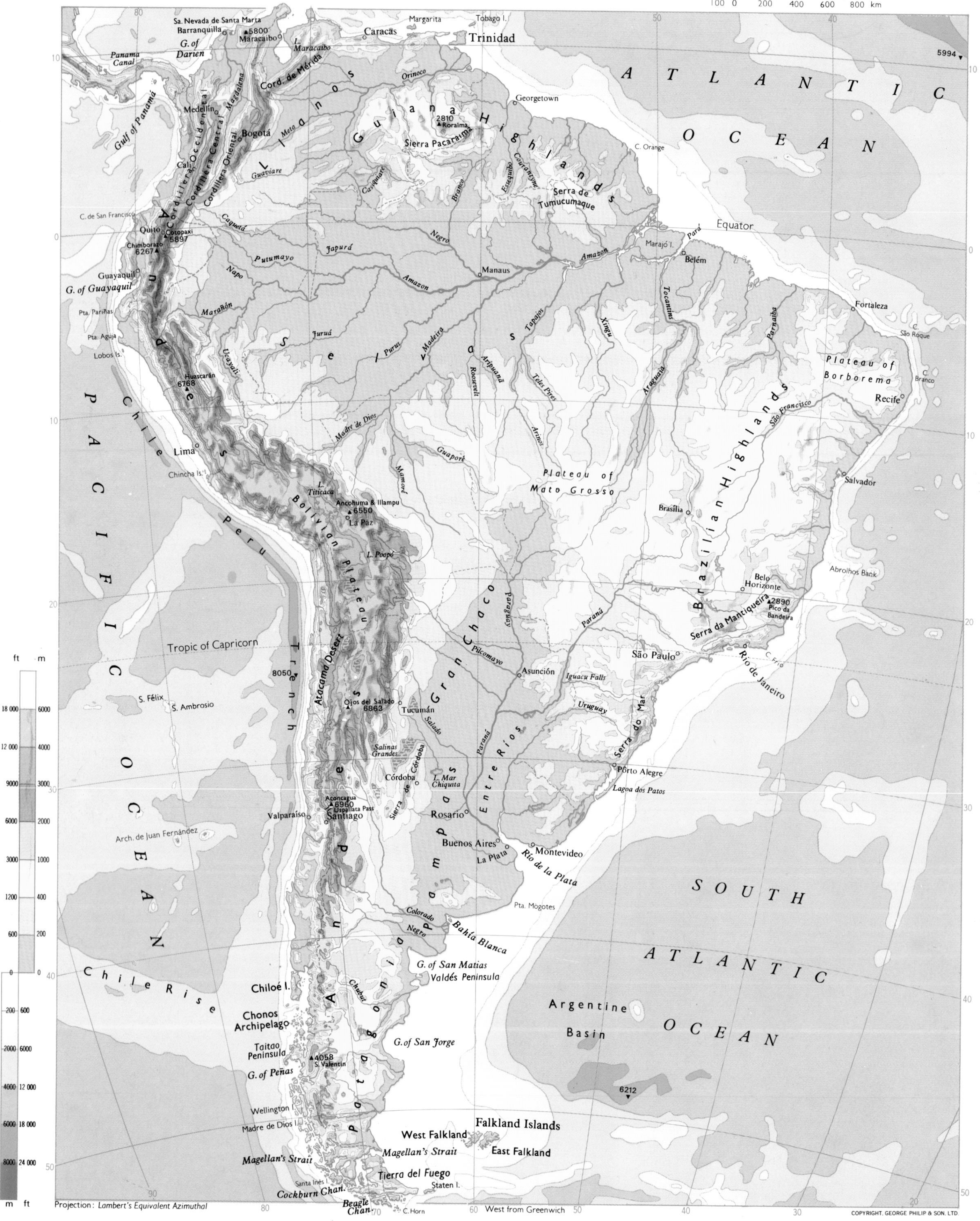

1 : 30 000 000

100   200   300   400   500 miles
100 0   200   400   600   800 km

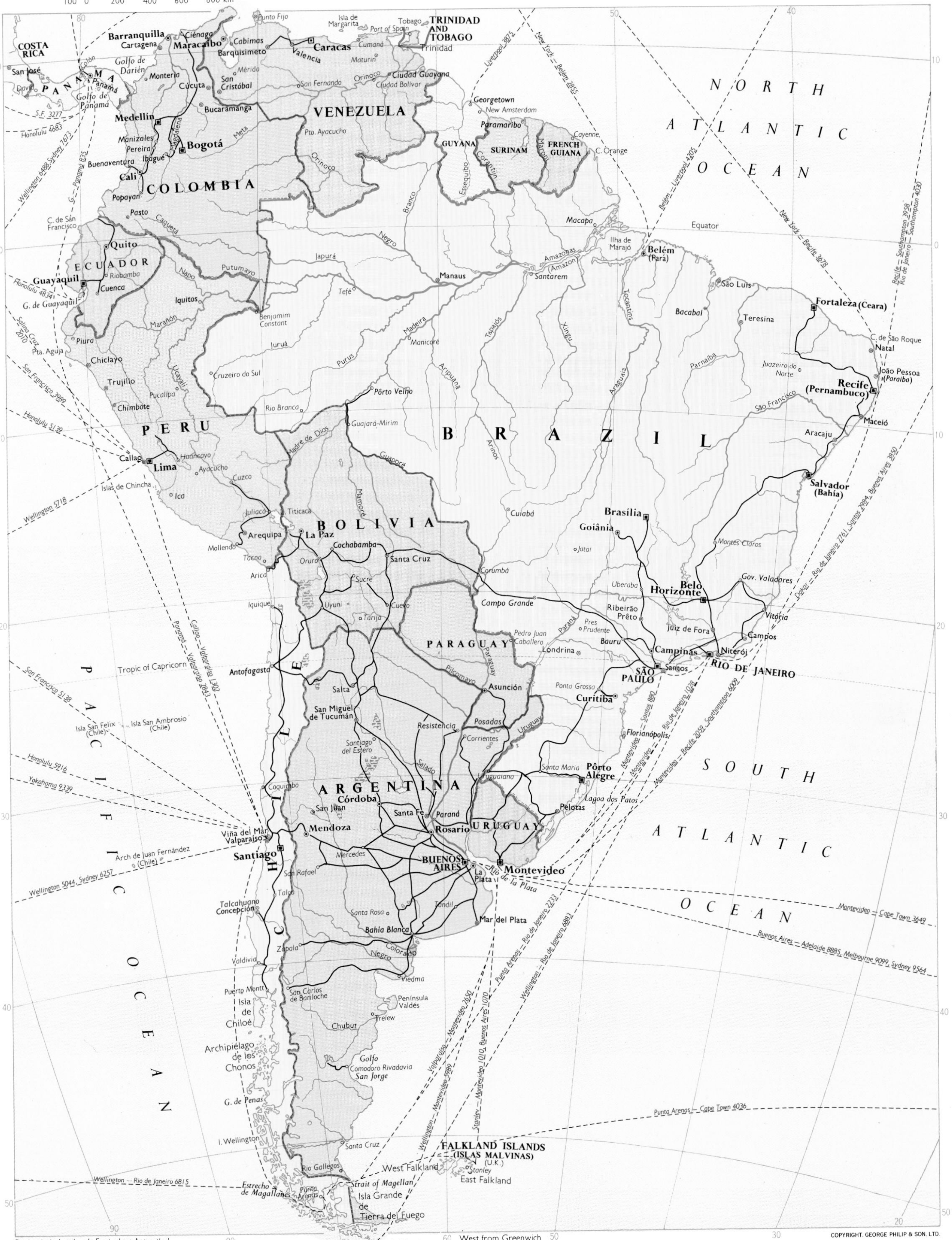

COSTA RICA

PANAMA

San José

S.F. 3277

Honolulu 4883 Sydney 7613

Barranquilla
Cartagena
Maracaibo
Cabimas
Barquisimeto
Cúcuta
Valencia
Caracas
Cumaná
Maturín

Isla de Margarita
Port of Spain
Tobago

TRINIDAD AND TOBAGO
Trinidad

NORTH

ATLANTIC

OCEAN

Golfo de Darién
Monteria
San Cristóbal
Mérida

Orinoco
Ciudad Guayana
Ciudad Bolívar
San Fernando

VENEZUELA

Pto. Ayacucho

Georgetown
New Amsterdam
Paramaribo
Cayenne
C. Orange

GUYANA
SURINAM
FRENCH GUIANA

Medellín
Manizales
Pereira
Ibagué
Bogotá

COLOMBIA

Buenaventura
Cali
Popayán
Pasto

Meta

Orinoco

Caquetá

Napo

C. de San Francisco

ECUADOR

Quito
Guayaquil
Riobamba
Cuenca

G. de Guayaquil

Putumayo

Negro

Japurá

Branco

Macapá

Ilha de Marajó

Belém (Pará)

Equator

Honolulu 4834

Sta. Cruz 2010
Pta. Aguja

Piura
Chiclayo
Trujillo
Chimbote

San Francisco 3090

Marañón

Iquitos

Benjamim Constant

Juruá

Manaus

Tefé

Amazonas

Amazon

Santarem

São Luís

Bacabal

Teresina

Fortaleza (Ceará)

Natal

C. de São Roque

Honolulu 5139

Callao
Lima

PERU

Huancayo
Ayacucho
Cuzco

Islas de Chincha

Pucallpa

Cruzeiro do Sul

Rio Branco

Pôrto Velho

Guajará-Mirim

Madre de Dios

Guaporé

B R A Z I L

Madeira

Aripuanã

Tapajós

Xingu

Araguaia

Tocantins

Arinos

Manicoré

Parnaíba

Juazeiro do Norte

João Pessoa (Paraíba)

Recife (Pernambuco)

Maceió

Aracaju

São Francisco

Wellington 5718

Ica

Juliaca
Titicaca

Arequipa
La Paz

BOLIVIA

Cochabamba
Oruro
Sucre
Santa Cruz

Mamoré

Corumbá

Cuiabá

Brasília
Goiânia

Jataí

Montes Claros

Salvador (Bahia)

Mollendo
Tacna
Arica
Iquique

Uyuni

Tarija

Cueto

Campo Grande

PARAGUAY

Paraguay

Pedro Juan Caballero

Uberaba

Ribeirão Prêto

Belo Horizonte

Gov. Valadares

Vitória

Campos

Tropic of Capricorn

Antofagasta

Salta

San Miguel de Tucumán

Resistencia

Posadas
Corrientes

Asunción

Pilcomayo

Paraná

Londrina

Pres. Prudente

Bauru

Campinas

São Paulo
Santos

Juiz de Fora

Niterói
RIO DE JANEIRO

Salado

Santiago del Estero

Ponta Grossa

Curitiba

Florianópolis

SOUTH

Collico–Valparaíso 1290

Paraná–Valparaíso 2043

San Francisco 5138

Isla San Félix (Chile)
Isla San Ambrosio (Chile)

Honolulu 5916

Yokohama 9339

Coquimbo

San Juan

Córdoba

Santa Fe
Paraná
Rosario

Mercedes

Uruguay

Uruguaiana

Santa Maria

Pôrto Alegre

Pelotas

Lagoa dos Patos

ATLANTIC

Viña del Mar
Valparaíso
Santiago

ARGENTINA

Mendoza

San Rafael

URUGUAY

Montevideo

Buenos Aires
La Plata

Rio de la Plata

Montevideo – Cape Town 3649

Wellington 5044 Sydney 6257

Talcahuano
Concepción

Talca

Santa Rosa

Tandil

Mar del Plata

Buenos Aires – Adelaide 8885, Melbourne 9099, Sydney 9564

OCEAN

Bahía Blanca

Zapala

Colorado

Valdivia

Negro

Viedma

Puerto Montt

San Carlos de Bariloche

Chubut

Península Valdés

Trelew

OCEAN

Isla de Chiloé

Archipiélago de los Chonos

Golfo Comodoro Rivadavia
San Jorge

G. de Penas

Volparaíso 2650
Montevideo – Montevideo 1990

Buenos Aires 1070

Wellington 7305

Buenos Aires 2233

Punta Arenas – Rio de Janeiro 4861

Rio de Janeiro 4951

Buenos Aires – Rio de Janeiro

Southampton

I. Wellington

Santa Cruz

Punta Arenas – Cape Town 4036

FALKLAND ISLANDS (ISLAS MALVINAS) (U.K.)

Stanley
West Falkland
East Falkland

Rio Gallegos

Estrecho de Magallanes

West Falkland

Strait of Magellan

Wellington – Rio de Janeiro 6815

Punta Arenas

Isla Grande de Tierra del Fuego

West from Greenwich

Cabo de Hornos (Cape Horn)

Projection: Lambert's Equivalent Azimuthal

COPYRIGHT. GEORGE PHILIP & SON. LTD.

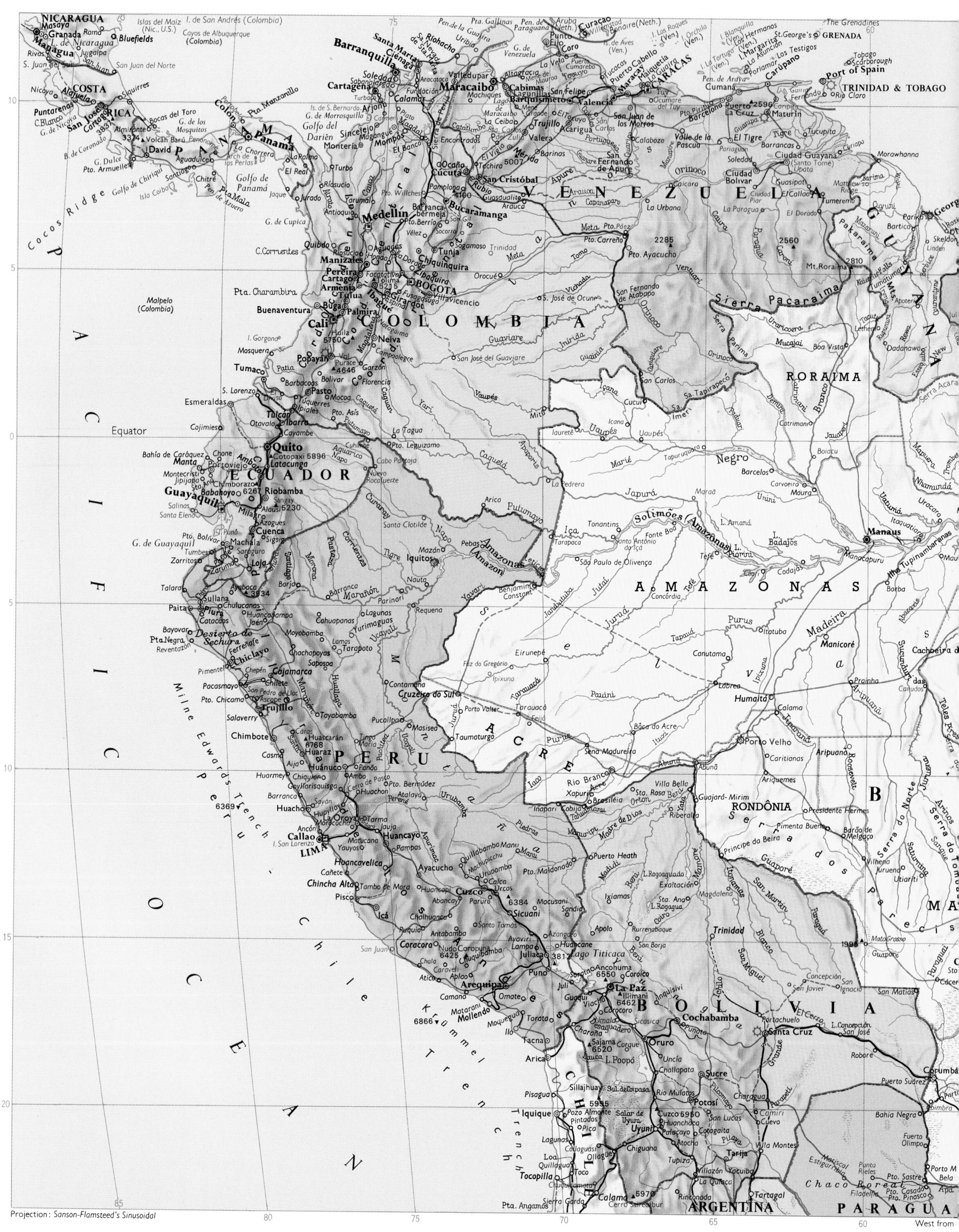
NICARAGUA
Managua
Granada
L. de Nicaragua
Bluefields
Islas del Maíz (Nic., U.S.)
I. de San Andrés (Colombia)
Cayos de Albuquerque (Colombia)
San Juan del Norte
COSTA RICA
San José
Puntarenas
Bocas del Toro
Volcán Barú
David
PANAMA
Panamá
Colón
Golfo de Panamá
Pta. Mala
Cocos Ridge
Pta. Gallinas
Aruba
Curaçao
Bonaire (Neth.)
Barranquilla
Cartagena
Santa Marta
Riohacha
Maracaibo
Cabimas
Barquisimeto
Valencia
Maracay
CARACAS
Puerto Cabello
Barcelona
Cumaná
Carúpano
Port of Spain
TRINIDAD & TOBAGO
GRENADA
The Grenadines
St. George's
Tobago
Scarborough
Maturín
Ciudad Bolívar
Ciudad Guayana
Orinoco
VENEZUELA
Mérida
San Cristóbal
Cúcuta
Bucaramanga
Medellín
Manizales
Pereira
Armenia
Ibagué
BOGOTA
Tunja
Villavicencio
Cali
Buenaventura
Popayán
Neiva
Pasto
Tumaco
COLOMBIA
Malpelo (Colombia)
Golfo del Darién
G. de Cupica
C. Corrientes
Pta. Charambira
Meta
Guaviare
Vaupés
Caquetá
Putumayo
Esmeraldas
Equator
Quito
Cotopaxi 5896
ECUADOR
Chimborazo 6267
Riobamba
Sangay 6230
Guayaquil
Cuenca
Machala
G. de Guayaquil
Loja
Tumbes
Talara
Sullana
Piura
Paita
Desierto de Sechura
Chiclayo
Cajamarca
Trujillo
Chimbote
Huascarán 6768
Huaraz
Huánuco
Cerro de Pasco
Huacho
Callao
LIMA
Huancayo
Huancavelica
Ayacucho
Cuzco
Pisco
Ica
PERU
Iquitos
Amazonas
Marañón
Ucayali
Huallaga
Pucallpa
Cruzeiro do Sul
Arequipa
Mollendo
Moquegua
Tacna
Arica
Lago Titicaca
Puno
Juliaca
La Paz
Illimani 6462
Ancohuma 6550
Cochabamba
Oruro
L. Poopó
Sucre
Potosí
Uyuni
Salar de Uyuni
Tarija
Santa Cruz
Trinidad
BOLIVIA
Iquique
Tocopilla
Calama
CHILE
ARGENTINA
PARAGUAY
Chaco Boreal
Corumbá
Puerto Suárez
Pisagua
Pta. Angamos
Milne Edwards Trench
Peru Chile Trench
Krümmel Trench
PACIFIC OCEAN
GUYANA
Georgetown
Mt. Roraima 2810
Sierra Pacaraima
RORAIMA
Boa Vista
Negro
Manaus
Solimões (Amazonas)
AMAZONAS
Japurá
Tefé
Juruá
Purus
Madeira
Manicoré
Humaitá
Porto Velho
Lábrea
ACRE
Rio Branco
RONDÔNIA
Guajará-Mirim
Serra dos Parecis
Guaporé
Beni
Mamoré
Manu
Madre de Dios
Puerto Maldonado
Cobija
Projection: Sanson-Flamsteed's Sinusoidal
West from
85
80
75
70
65
60
10
5
0
5
10
15
20

1:16 000 000

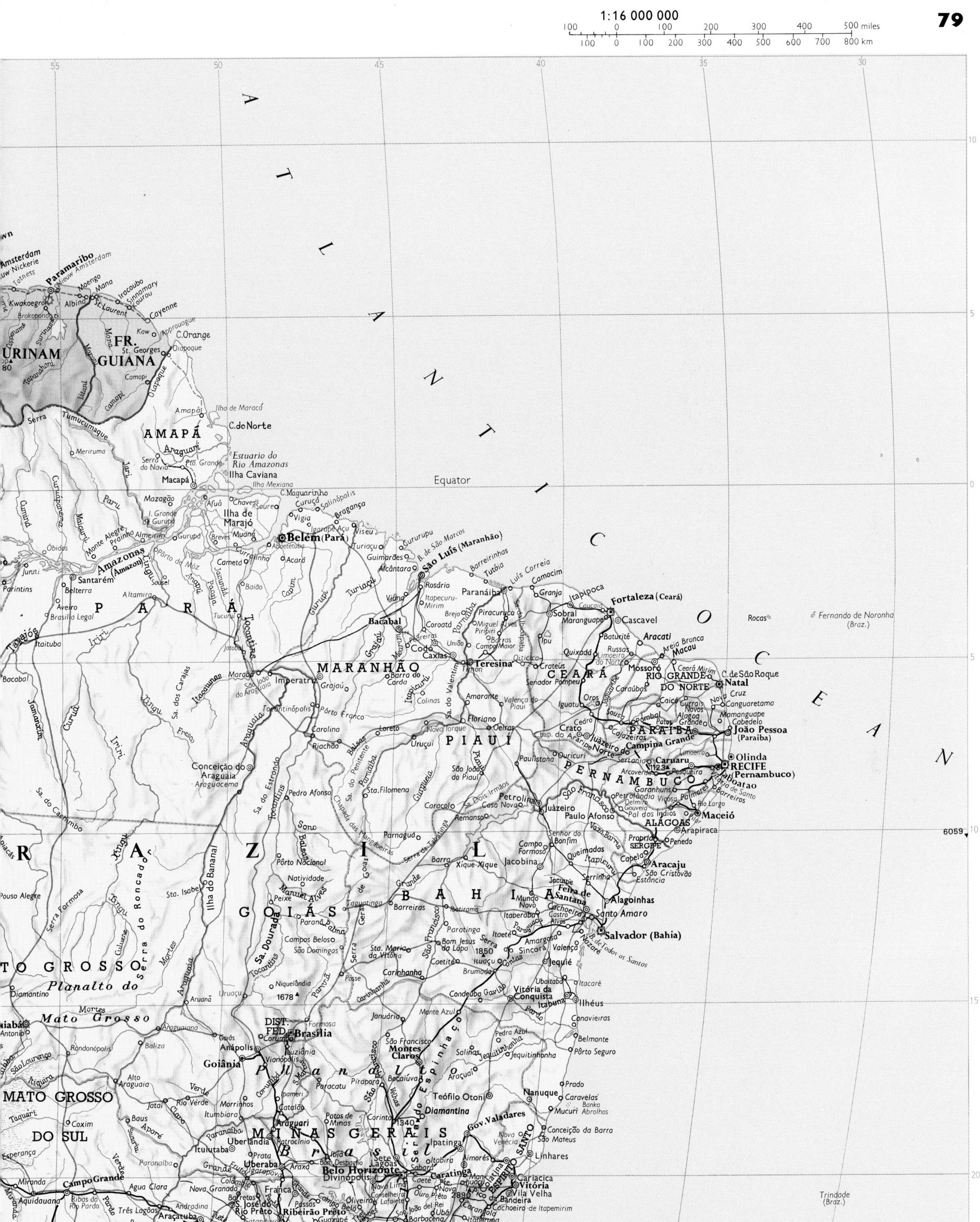
ATLANTIC OCEAN
BRAZIL
MARANHÃO
PIAUÍ
CEARÁ
PERNAMBUCO
BAHIA
GOIÁS
MINAS GERAIS
AMAPÁ
PARÁ
FR. GUIANA
Equator
Belém (Pará)
São Luís (Maranhão)
Fortaleza (Ceará)
Teresina
Natal
João Pessoa
RECIFE (Pernambuco)
Maceió
Aracaju
Salvador (Bahia)
Brasília
Belo Horizonte
RIO DE JANEIRO
Fernando de Noronha (Braz.)
Trindade (Braz.)

1:16 000 000

100 50 0 100 200 300 miles
100 0 100 200 300 400 km

MATO GROSSO DO SUL

PARAGUAY

PARANÁ

RIO DE JANEIRO

SÃO PAULO

São Paulo
Santos
Curitiba
Paranaguá

Asunción

Formosa

SANTA CATARINA

Florianópolis

RIO GRANDE DO SUL

Pôrto Alegre

Lagoa dos Patos

Pelotas
Rio Grande

URUGUAY

MONTEVIDEO

Antofagasta

Tropic of Capricorn

Salta
San Miguel de Tucumán

Catamarca

La Rioja

Córdoba

San Juan

Mendoza

Santa Fe
Paraná
Rosario

BUENOS AIRES

La Plata

Mar del Plata

Bahía Blanca

Neuquén

Valdivia

Puerto Montt

I. de Chiloé

Archipiélago de los Chonos

SANTIAGO
Valparaíso
Viña del Mar

Concepción
Talcahuano

Comodoro Rivadavia
Golfo San Jorge

Península Valdés
Golfo San Matías

Trelew
Puerto Madryn

Río Gallegos

Tierra del Fuego

Estrecho de Magallanes (Magellan's Str.)

Punta Arenas

Cabo de Hornos (C. Horn)

SOUTH ATLANTIC OCEAN

FALKLAND ISLANDS (ISLAS MALVINAS) (Br.)
West Falkland
East Falkland
Stanley

South Georgia (Br.)

Projection: Sanson-Flamsteed's Sinusoidal

West from Greenwich

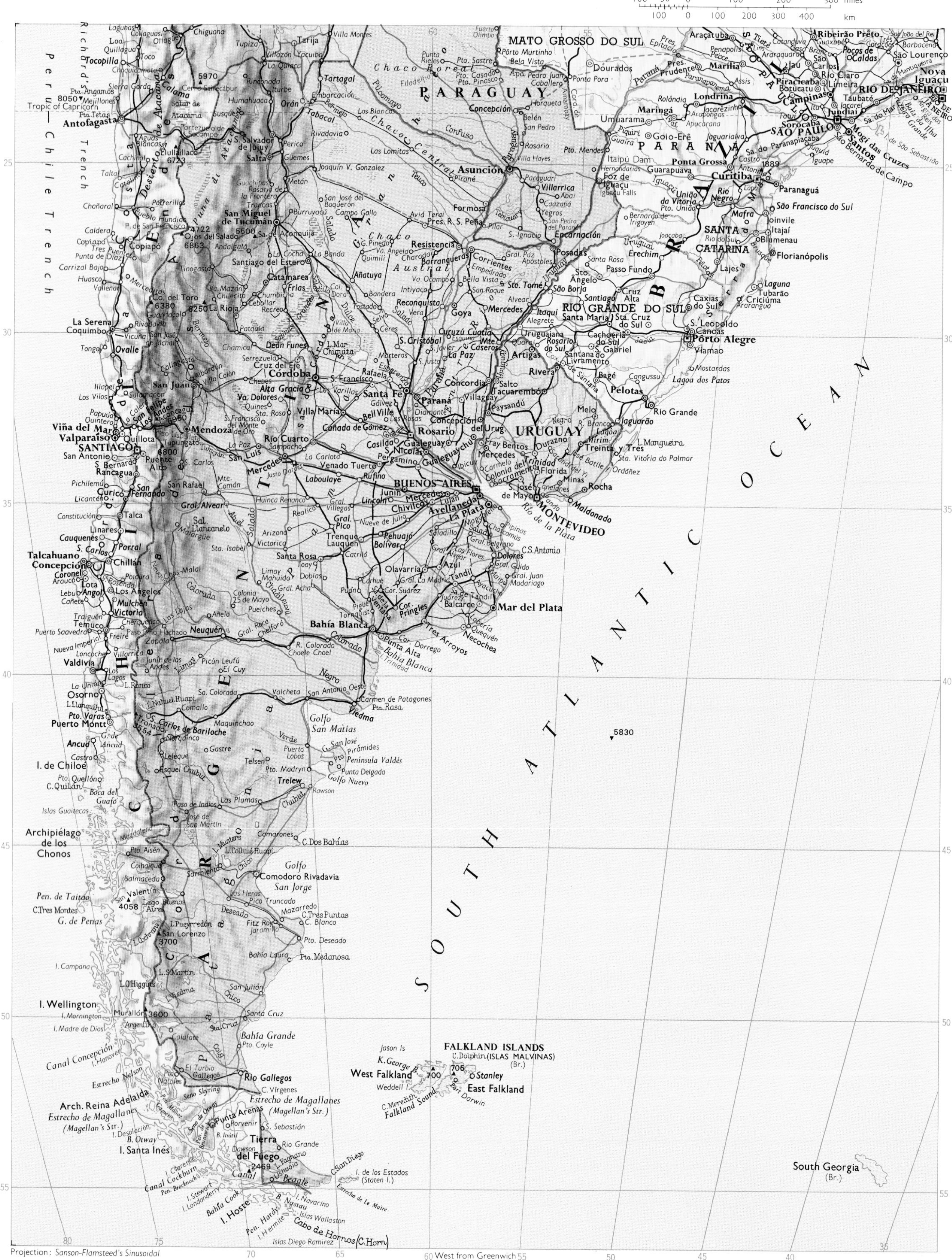

INDEX

The number in dark type which follows each name in the index refers to the page number where that feature or place will be found.

The geographical co-ordinates which follow the place name are sometimes only approximate but are close enough for the place name to be located.

An open square □ signifies that the name refers to an administrative division of a country while a solid square ■ follows the name of a country.

Rivers have been indexed to their mouth or to where they join another river. All rivers are followed by the symbol →.

The alphabetic order of names composed of two or more words is governed primarily by the first word and then by the second. This is an example of the rule:

> East Tawas
> Eastbourne
> Easter Is.
> Eastern Ghats
> Eastleigh

Names composed of a proper name (*Mexico*) and a description (*Gulf of*) are positioned alphabetically by the proper name. If the same word occurs in the name of a town and a geographical feature, the town name is listed first followed by the name or names of the geographical features.

Names beginning with M', Mc are all indexed as if they were spelled Mac.

Names composed of the definite article (Le, La, Les, L') and a proper name are usually alphabetized by the proper name:

> Havre, Le
> Spezia, La

If the same place name occurs twice or more in the index and the places are in different countries, they will be followed by the country and be in the latter's alphabetical order:

> Boston, U.K.
> Boston, U.S.A.

If the same place name occurs two or more times in the index and all are in the same country, each is followed by the name of the administrative subdivision in which it is located. The names are placed in the alphabetical order of the subdivisions. For example:

> Columbus, Ga., U.S.A.
> Columbus, Miss., U.S.A.
> Columbus, Ohio, U.S.A.

If there is a mixture of these situations, the primary order is fixed by the alphabetical sequence of the countries and the secondary order by that of the country subdivisions:

> Rochester, U.K.
> Rochester, Minn., U.S.A.
> Rochester, N.Y., U.S.A.

Below is a list of abbreviations used in the index.

A.S.S.R. – Autonomous Soviet Socialist Republic
Ala. – Alabama
Arch. – Archipelago
Ariz. – Arizona
Ark. – Arkansas
B. – Baie, Bahia, Bay, Boca, Bucht, Bugt
B.C. – British Columbia
Br. – British
C. – Cabo, Cap, Cape
Calif. – California
Chan. – Channel
Col. – Colombia
Colo. – Colorado
Conn. – Connecticut
Cord. – Cordillera
D.C. – District of Columbia
Del. – Delaware
Dep. – Dependency
Des. – Desert
Dist. – District
Dom. Rep. – Dominican Republic
E. – East
Fd. – Fjord

Fed. – Federal, Federation
Fla. – Florida
Fr. – France, French
G. – Golfe, Golfo, Gulf, Guba
Ga. – Georgia
Gt. – Great
Hts. – Heights
I.(s) – Ile, Ilha, Insel, Isla, Island(s)
Ill. – Illinois
Ind. – Indiana
K. – Kap, Kapp
Kans. – Kansas
Ky. – Kentucky
L. – Lac, Lacul, Lago, Lagoa, Lake, Limni, Loch, Lough
La. – Louisiana
Ld. – Land
Mad. P. – Madhya Pradesh
Man. – Manitoba
Mass. – Massachusetts
Md. – Maryland
Mich. – Michigan
Minn. – Minnesota
Miss. – Mississippi
Mo. – Missouri

Mont. – Montana
Mt.(s) – Mont, Monta, Monti, Muntii, Montaña, Mount, Mountain(s)
N. – North, Northern
N.B. – New Brunswick
N.C. – North Carolina
N. Dak. – North Dakota
N.H. – New Hampshire
N.J. – New Jersey
N. Mex. – New Mexico
N.S. – Nova Scotia
N.S.W. – New South Wales
N.Y. – New York
N.Z. – New Zealand
Nat. Park – National Park
Nebr. – Nebraska
Neth. – Netherlands
Nev. – Nevada
Nfld. – Newfoundland
Nic. – Nicaragua
Nig. – Nigeria
Okla. – Oklahoma
Ont. – Ontario
Oreg. – Oregon
P. – Pass, Paso, Pasul

Pa. – Pennsylvania
Pak. – Pakistan
Pass. – Passage
Pen. – Peninsula
Pk. – Peak
Plat. – Plateau
Prov. – Province, Provincial
Pt. – Point
Pta. – Ponta, Punta
Pte. – Pointe
Qué. – Québec
R. – Rio, River
R.S.F.S.R. – Russian Soviet Federative Socialist Republic
Ra.(s) – Range(s)
Rep. – Republic
Res. – Reserve, Reservoir
S. – South
S. Africa – South Africa
S.C. – South Carolina
S. Dak. – South Dakota
S.S.R. – Soviet Socialist Republic
Sa. – Serra, Sierra
Sask. – Saskatchewan

Scot. – Scotland
Sd. – Sound
Sp. – Spain, Spanish
St. – Saint
Str. – Strait, Stretto
Tenn. – Tennessee
Terr. – Territory
Tex. – Texas
U.K. – United Kingdom
U.S.A. – United States of America
U.S.S.R. – Union of Soviet Socialist Republics
Ut. P. – Uttar Pradesh
Va. – Virginia
Vic. – Victoria
Vt. – Vermont
Wash. – Washington
W. – West
W. Va. – West Virginia
Wis. – Wisconsin
Wyo. – Wyoming
Yug. – Yugoslavia

Aachen

A

Aachen 14 50 47N 6 4 E
Aalborg = Ålborg 21 57 2N 9 54 E
A'âli en Nîl □ 51 9 30N 31 30 E
Aalsmeer 11 52 17N 4 43 E
Aalst 11 50 56N 4 2 E
Aalten 11 51 56N 6 35 E
Aarau 14 47 23N 8 4 E
Aare → 14 47 33N 8 14 E
Aarhus = Århus 21 56 8N 10 11 E
Aarschot 11 50 59N 4 49 E
Aba 53 5 10N 7 19 E
Âbâdân 30 30 22N 48 20 E
Âbâdeh 31 31 8N 52 40 E
Abadla 50 31 2N 2 45W
Abaetetuba 79 1 40S 48 50W
Abagnar Qi 38 43 52N 116 2 E
Abakan 25 53 40N 91 10 E
Abariringa 40 2 50S 171 40W
Abarqū 31 31 10N 53 20 E
'Abasân 28 31 19N 34 21 E
Abashiri 36 44 0N 144 15 E
Abashiri-Wan 36 44 0N 144 30 E
Abay 24 49 38N 72 53 E
Abaya, L. 51 6 30N 37 50 E
Abaza 24 52 39N 90 6 E
Abbay = Nîl el Azraq → 51 15 38N 32 31 E
Abbaye, Pt. 68 46 58N 88 4W
Abbeville, France 12 50 6N 1 49 E
Abbeville, La., U.S.A. 71 30 0N 92 7W
Abbeville, S.C., U.S.A. 69 34 12N 82 21W
Abbieglassie 45 27 15S 147 28 E
Abbotsford, Canada 64 49 5N 122 20W
Abbotsford, U.S.A. 70 44 55N 90 20W
Abbottabad 32 34 10N 73 15 E
Abd al Kūrī 29 12 5N 52 20 E
Abéché 51 13 50N 20 35 E
Åbenrå 21 55 3N 9 25 E
Abeokuta 53 7 3N 3 19 E
Aberaeron 7 52 15N 4 16W
Aberayron = Aberaeron 7 52 15N 4 16W
Abercorn = Mbala 54 8 46S 31 24 E
Abercorn 45 25 12S 151 5 E
Aberdare 7 51 43N 3 27W
Aberdeen, Australia 45 32 9S 150 56 E
Aberdeen, Canada 65 52 20N 106 8W
Aberdeen, S. Africa 56 32 28S 24 2 E
Aberdeen, U.K. 8 57 9N 2 6W
Aberdeen, Ala., U.S.A. 69 33 49N 88 33W
Aberdeen, Idaho, U.S.A. 72 42 57N 112 50W
Aberdeen, S. Dak., U.S.A. 70 45 30N 98 30W
Aberdeen, Wash., U.S.A. 72 47 0N 123 50W
Aberdovey 7 52 33N 4 3W
Aberfeldy 8 56 37N 3 50W
Abergavenny 7 51 49N 3 1W
Abernathy 71 33 49N 101 49W
Abert, L. 72 42 40N 120 8W
Aberystwyth 7 52 25N 4 6W
Abidjan 50 5 26N 3 58W
Abilene, Kans., U.S.A. 70 39 0N 97 16W
Abilene, Tex., U.S.A. 71 32 22N 99 40W
Abingdon, U.K. 7 51 40N 1 17W
Abingdon, Ill., U.S.A. 70 40 53N 90 23W
Abingdon, Va., U.S.A. 69 36 46N 81 56W
Abington Reef 44 18 0S 149 35 E
Abitau → 65 59 53N 109 3W
Abitau L. 65 60 27N 107 15W
Abitibi L. 62 48 40N 79 40W
Abkhaz A.S.S.R. □ 23 43 0N 41 0 E
Abkit 25 64 10N 157 10 E
Abminga 45 26 8S 134 51 E
Abohar 32 30 10N 74 10 E
Abomey 53 7 10N 2 5 E
Abong-Mbang 54 4 0N 13 8 E
Abonnema 53 4 41N 6 49 E
Abou-Deïa 51 11 20N 19 20 E
Aboyne 8 57 4N 2 48W
Abrantes 13 39 24N 8 7W
Abreojos, Pta. 74 26 50N 113 40W
Abri 51 20 50N 30 27 E
Abrolhos, Banka 79 18 0S 38 0W
Abrud 15 46 19N 23 5 E
Abruzzi □ 18 42 15N 14 0 E
Absaroka Ra. 72 44 40N 110 0W
Abū al Khaşīb 30 30 25N 48 0 E
Abū 'Alī 30 27 20N 49 27 E
Abu 'Arīsh 29 16 53N 42 48 E
Abu Dhabi = Abū Ẓāby 31 24 28N 54 22 E
Abū Dīs, Jordan 28 31 47N 35 16 E
Abū Dis, Sudan 51 19 12N 33 38 E
Abū Ghaush 28 31 48N 35 6 E
Abu Hamed 51 19 32N 33 13 E
Abū Kamāl 30 34 30N 41 0 E
Abū Madd, Ra's 30 24 50N 37 7 E
Abu Matariq 51 10 59N 26 9 E
Abu Rudeis 30 28 54N 33 11 E
Abu Tig 51 27 4N 31 15 E
Abū Zabad 51 12 25N 29 10 E
Abū Ẓāby 31 24 28N 54 22 E
Abuja 53 9 16N 7 2 E
Abukuma-Gawa → 36 38 6N 140 52 E
Abunã 78 9 40S 65 20W
Abunã → 78 9 41S 65 20W
Abut Hd. 43 43 7S 170 15 E
Abwong 51 9 2N 32 14 E
Acámbaro 74 20 0N 100 40W
Acaponeta 74 22 30N 105 20W
Acapulco 74 16 51N 99 56W
Acarigua 78 9 33N 69 12W
Acatlán 74 18 10N 98 3W
Acayucan 74 17 59N 94 58W
Accomac 68 37 43N 75 40W
Accra 53 5 35N 0 6W
Accrington 6 53 46N 2 22W
Aceh □ 34 4 15N 97 30 E
Achalpur 32 21 22N 77 32 E
Achill 9 53 56N 9 55W
Achill Hd. 9 53 59N 10 15W
Achill I. 9 53 58N 10 5W
Achill Sound 9 53 53N 9 55W
Achinsk 25 56 20N 90 20 E
Ackerman 71 33 20N 89 8W
Acklins I. 75 22 30N 74 0W
Acme 64 51 33N 113 30W
Aconcagua, Cerro 80 32 39S 70 0W
Aconquija, Mt. 80 27 0S 66 0W
Açores, Is. dos = Azores 2 38 44N 29 0W
Acre = 'Akko 28 32 55N 35 4 E
Acre □ 78 9 1S 71 0W
Acre → 78 8 45S 67 22W
Ad Dahnā 30 24 30N 48 10 E
Ad Dammām 30 26 20N 50 5 E
Ad Dawhah 31 25 15N 51 35 E
Ad Dilam 30 23 55N 47 10 E
Ad Dīwānīyah 30 32 0N 45 0 E
Ada, Minn., U.S.A. 70 47 20N 96 30W
Ada, Okla., U.S.A. 71 34 50N 96 45W
Adaja → 13 41 32N 4 52W
Adam 31 22 15N 57 28 E
Adamaoua, Massif de l' 51 7 20N 12 20 E
Adamawa Highlands = Adamaoua, Massif de l' 51 7 20N 12 20 E
Adamello, Mt. 18 46 10N 10 34 E
Adaminaby 45 36 0S 148 45 E
Adams, N.Y., U.S.A. 68 43 50N 76 3W
Adams, Wis., U.S.A. 70 43 59N 89 50W
Adams, Mt. 72 46 10N 121 28W
Adam's Bridge 32 9 15N 79 40 E
Adams L. 64 51 10N 119 40W
Adam's Peak 32 6 48N 80 30 E
Adana 30 37 0N 35 16 E
Adapazarı 30 40 48N 30 25 E
Adarama 51 17 10N 34 52 E
Adaut 35 8 8S 131 7 E
Adavale 45 25 52S 144 32 E
Adda → 18 45 8N 9 53 E
Addis Ababa = Addis Abeba 51 9 2N 38 42 E
Addis Abeba 51 9 2N 38 42 E
Addis Alem 51 9 0N 38 17 E
Addo 56 33 32S 25 45 E
Adel 69 31 10N 83 28W
Adelaide, Australia 45 34 52S 138 30 E
Adelaide, S. Africa 57 32 42S 26 20 E
Adelaide Pen. 60 68 15N 97 30W
Adelaide River 46 13 15S 131 7 E
Adele, I. 46 15 32S 123 9 E
Aden = Al 'Adan 29 12 45N 45 0 E
Aden, G. of 29 12 30N 47 30 E
Adendorp 56 32 15S 24 30 E
Adi 35 4 15S 133 30 E
Adi Ugri 51 14 58N 38 48 E
Adieu, C. 47 32 0S 132 10 E
Adieu Pt. 46 15 14S 124 35 E
Adige → 18 45 9N 12 20 E
Adilabad 32 19 33N 78 20 E
Adin 72 41 10N 121 0W
Adin Khel 31 32 45N 68 5 E
Adirondack Mts. 68 44 0N 74 15W
Adlavik Is. 63 55 2N 57 45W
Admer 50 20 21N 5 27 E
Admiralty G. 46 14 20S 125 55 E
Admiralty I. 60 57 40N 134 35W
Admiralty Inlet 72 48 0N 122 40W
Admiralty Is. 40 2 0S 147 0 E
Ado 53 6 36N 2 56 E
Ado Ekiti 53 7 38N 5 12 E
Adonara 35 8 15S 123 5 E
Adoni 32 15 33N 77 18W
Adour → 12 43 32N 1 32W
Adra 13 36 43N 3 3W
Adrano 18 37 40N 14 49 E
Adrar 50 27 51N 0 11W
Adré 51 13 40N 22 20 E
Adrī 51 27 32N 13 2 E
Adrian, Mich., U.S.A. 68 41 55N 84 0W
Adrian, Tex., U.S.A. 71 35 19N 102 37W
Adriatic Sea 16 43 0N 16 0 E
Adua 35 1 45S 129 50 E
Adwa 51 14 15N 38 52 E
Adzhar A.S.S.R. □ 23 42 0N 42 0 E
Ægean Sea 17 37 0N 25 0 E
Æolian Is. = Eólie, Is. 18 38 30N 14 50 E
Aerht'ai Shan 37 46 40N 92 45 E
Afars & Issas, Terr. of = Djibouti ■ 29 12 0N 43 0 E
Afghanistan ■ 31 33 0N 65 0 E
Afgoi 29 2 7N 44 59 E
'Afif 30 23 53N 42 56 E
Afognak I. 60 58 10N 152 50W
Africa 48 10 0N 20 0 E
Afuá 79 0 15S 50 20W
Afula 28 32 37N 35 17 E
Afyonkarahisar 30 38 45N 30 33 E
Agadès = Agadez 53 16 58N 7 59 E
Agadez 53 16 58N 7 59 E
Agadir 50 30 28N 9 55W
Agano → 36 37 57N 139 8 E
Agapa 25 71 27N 89 15 E
Agartala 33 23 50N 91 23 E
Agassiz 64 49 14N 121 46W
Agats 35 5 33S 138 0 E
Agattu I. 60 52 25N 172 30 E
Agboville 50 5 55N 4 15W
Agde 12 43 19N 3 28 E
Agen 12 44 12N 0 38 E
Aghil Mts. 32 36 0N 77 0 E
Aginskoye 25 51 6N 114 32 E
Agra 32 27 17N 77 58 E
Agri → 18 40 13N 16 44 E
Ağri Daği 30 39 50N 44 15 E
Ağri Karakose 30 39 44N 43 3 E
Agrigento 18 37 19N 13 33 E
Agrinion 19 38 37N 21 27 E
Água Clara 79 20 25S 52 45W
Agua Prieta 74 31 20N 109 32W
Aguadas 78 5 40N 75 38W
Aguadilla 75 18 27N 67 10W
Aguanish 63 50 14N 62 2W
Aguanus → 63 50 13N 62 5W
Aguarico → 78 0 59S 75 11W
Aguas Blancas 80 24 15S 69 55W
Aguascalientes 74 21 53N 102 12W
Aguascalientes □ 74 22 0N 102 20W
Aguilas 13 37 23N 1 35W
Agulhas, C. 56 34 52S 20 0 E
Agung 34 8 20S 115 28 E
'Agur 28 31 42N 34 55 E
Agusan → 35 9 0N 125 30 E
Aha Mts. 56 19 45S 21 0 E
Ahaggar 50 23 0N 6 30 E
Ahar 30 38 35N 47 0 E
Ahipara B. 43 35 5S 173 5 E
Ahiri 32 19 30N 80 0 E
Ahmadabad 32 23 0N 72 40 E
Ahmadnagar 32 19 7N 74 46 E
Ahmadpur 32 29 12N 71 10 E
Ahmedabad = Ahmadabad 32 23 0N 72 40 E
Ahmednagar = Ahmadnagar 32 19 7N 74 46 E
Ahuachapán 75 13 54N 89 52W
Ahvāz 30 31 20N 48 40 E
Ahvenanmaa = Åland 21 60 15N 20 0 E
Aḩwar 29 13 30N 46 40 E
Aichi □ 36 35 0N 137 15 E
Aigues-Mortes 12 43 35N 4 12 E
Aihui 38 50 10N 127 30 E
Aija 78 9 50S 77 45W
Aiken 69 33 34N 81 50W
Aillik 63 55 11N 59 18W
Ailsa Craig 8 55 15N 5 7W
'Ailūn 28 32 18N 35 47 E
Aim 25 59 0N 133 55 E
Aimere 35 8 45S 121 3 E
Aimorés 79 19 30S 41 4W
Ain □ 12 46 5N 5 20 E
Ain Banaiyan 31 23 0N 51 0 E
Aïn Beïda 50 35 50N 7 29 E
Ain Ben Tili 50 25 59N 9 27W
Aïn-Sefra 50 32 47N 0 37W
Ainabo 29 9 0N 46 25 E
Ainsworth 70 42 33N 99 52W
Aïr 50 18 30N 8 0 E
Airdrie 8 55 53N 3 57W
Aire → 6 53 42N 0 55W
Airlie Beach 44 20 16S 148 43 E
Aisne □ 12 49 42N 3 40 E
Aisne → 12 49 26N 2 50 E
Aitkin 70 46 32N 93 43W
Aiud 15 46 19N 23 44 E
Aix-en-Provence 12 43 32N 5 27 E
Aix-la-Chapelle = Aachen 14 50 47N 6 4 E
Aiyansh 64 55 17N 129 2W
Áiyina 19 37 45N 23 26 E
Aiyion 19 38 15N 22 5 E
Aizawl 33 23 40N 92 44 E
Aizuwakamatsu 36 37 30N 139 56 E
Ajaccio 12 41 55N 8 40 E
Ajanta Ra. 32 20 28N 75 50 E
Ajdâbiyah 51 30 54N 20 4 E
'Ajmān 31 25 25N 55 30 E
Ajmer 32 26 28N 74 37 E
Ajo 73 32 18N 112 54W
Ak Dağ 30 36 30N 30 0 E
Akaroa 43 43 49S 172 59 E
Akashi 36 34 45N 135 0 E
Akelamo 35 1 35N 129 40 E
Akershus fylke □ 21 60 0N 11 10 E
Aketi 54 2 38N 23 47 E
Akhelóös → 19 38 36N 21 14 E
Akhisar 30 38 56N 27 48 E
Akhmîm 51 26 31N 31 47 E
Akimiski I. 62 52 50N 81 30W
Akita 36 39 45N 140 7 E
Akita □ 36 39 40N 140 30 E
Akjoujt 50 19 45N 14 15W
'Akko 28 32 55N 35 4 E
Akkol 24 45 0N 75 39 E
Aklavik 60 68 12N 135 0W
Akobo → 51 7 48N 33 3 E
Akola 32 20 42N 77 2 E
Akordat 51 15 30N 37 40 E
Akosombo Dam 53 6 20N 0 5 E
Akpatok I. 61 60 25N 68 8W
Akranes 20 64 19N 21 58W
Akreïjit 50 18 19N 9 11W
Akron, Colo., U.S.A. 70 40 13N 103 15W
Akron, Ohio, U.S.A. 68 41 7N 81 31W
Aksai Chih 32 35 15N 79 55 E
Aksaray 30 38 25N 34 2 E
Aksarka 24 66 31N 67 50 E
Aksay 24 51 11N 53 0 E
Akşehir 30 38 18N 31 30 E
Aksenovo Zilovskoye 25 53 20N 117 40 E
Aksu 37 41 5N 80 10 E
Aksum 51 14 5N 38 40 E
Aktogay 24 46 57N 79 40 E
Aktyubinsk 23 50 17N 57 10 E
Aku 53 6 40N 7 18 E
Akure 53 7 15N 5 5 E
Akureyri 20 65 40N 18 6W
Akyab = Sittwe 33 20 18N 92 45 E
Al 'Adan 29 12 45N 45 0 E
Al Aḩsā 30 25 50N 49 0 E
Al Amādīyah 30 37 5N 43 30 E
Al Amārah 30 31 55N 47 15 E
Al 'Aqabah 28 29 31N 35 0 E
Al 'Aramah 30 25 30N 46 0 E
Al Ashkhara 31 21 50N 59 30 E
Al 'Ayzarīyah 28 31 47N 35 15 E
Al Badī' 30 22 0N 46 35 E
Al Başrah 30 30 30N 47 50 E
Al Bāzūrīyah 28 33 15N 35 16 E
Al Bīrah 28 31 55N 35 12 E
Al Bu'ayrāt 51 31 24N 15 44 E
Al Buqay'ah 28 32 15N 35 30 E
Al Fallūjah 30 33 20N 43 55 E
Al Fāw 30 30 0N 48 30 E
Al Fujayrah 31 25 7N 56 18 E
Al Hābah 30 27 10N 47 0 E
Al Haddār 30 21 58N 45 57 E
Al Ḩadīthah 30 34 0N 41 13 E
Al Ḩāmad 30 31 30N 39 30 E
Al Ḩamar 30 22 23N 46 6 E
Al Ḩamrā' 30 24 2N 38 55 E
Al Ḩarīq 30 23 29N 46 27 E
Al Ḩarīr, W. → 28 32 44N 35 59 E
Al Ḩasakah 30 36 35N 40 45 E
Al Ḩawrah 29 13 50N 47 35 E
Al Ḩayy 30 32 5N 46 5 E
Al Ḩijāz 29 26 0N 37 30 E
Al Ḩillah, Iraq 30 32 30N 44 25 E
Al Ḩillah, Si. Arabia 30 23 35N 46 50 E
Al Hindīyah 30 32 30N 44 10 E
Al Ḩişnn 28 32 29N 35 52 E
Al Hoceïma 50 35 8N 3 58W
Al Ḩudaydah 29 14 50N 43 0 E
Al Hufūf 30 25 25N 49 45 E
Al Ḩulwah 30 23 24N 46 48 E
Al Irq 51 29 5N 21 35 E
Al Ittihad = Madīnat ash Sha'b 29 12 50N 45 0 E
Al Jāfūrah 30 25 0N 50 15 E
Al Jaghbūb 51 29 42N 24 38 E
Al Jahrah 30 29 25N 47 40 E
Al Jalāmīd 30 31 20N 39 45 E
Al Jawf, Libya 51 24 10N 23 24 E
Al Jawf, Si. Arabia 30 29 55N 39 40 E
Al Jazirah, Asia 30 33 30N 44 0 E
Al Jazirah, Libya 51 26 10N 21 20 E
Al Jubayl 30 27 0N 49 50 E
Al Jubaylah 30 24 55N 46 25 E
Al Junaynah 51 13 27N 22 45 E
Al Khābūra 31 23 57N 57 5 E
Al Khalīl 28 31 32N 35 6 E
Al Khalūf 29 20 30N 58 13 E
Al Kharfah 30 22 0N 46 35 E
Al Kharj 30 24 0N 47 0 E
Al Kufrah 51 24 17N 23 15 E
Al Kūt 30 32 30N 46 0 E
Al Kuwayt 30 29 30N 48 0 E
Al Lādhiqīyah 30 35 30N 35 45 E
Al Lubban 28 32 9N 35 14 E
Al Luḩayyah 29 15 45N 42 40 E
Al Madīnah 29 24 35N 39 52 E
Al-Mafraq 28 32 17N 36 14 E
Al Majma'ah 30 25 57N 45 22 E
Al Manāmah 31 26 10N 50 30 E
Al Marj 51 32 25N 20 30 E
Al Mawşil 30 36 15N 43 5 E
Al Mazra 28 31 16N 35 31 E
Al Midhnab 30 25 50N 44 18 E
Al Miqdādīyah 30 34 0N 45 0 E
Al Mish'āb 30 28 12N 48 36 E
Al Mubarraz 30 25 30N 49 40 E
Al Muḩarraq 31 26 15N 50 40 E
Al Mukallā 29 14 33N 49 2 E
Al Mukhā 29 13 18N 43 15 E
Al Musayyib 30 32 40N 44 25 E
Al Muwaylih 30 27 40N 35 30 E
Al Owuho = Otukpa 53 7 9N 7 41 E
Al Qadīmah 30 22 20N 39 13 E
Al Qā'iyah 30 24 33N 43 15 E
Al Qāmishli 30 37 10N 41 10 E
Al Qaşabát 51 32 39N 14 1 E
Al Qaşīm 30 26 0N 43 0 E
Al Qaţīf 30 26 35N 50 0 E
Al Qaţrūn 51 24 56N 15 3 E
Al Quaisūmah 30 28 10N 46 20 E
Al Quds = Jerusalem 28 31 47N 35 10 E
Al Qurayyāt 31 23 17N 58 53 E
Al Qurnah 30 31 1N 47 25 E
Al 'Ulā 30 26 35N 38 0 E
Al Uqaylah ash Sharqīgah 51 30 12N 19 10 E
Al Uqayr 30 25 40N 50 15 E
Al 'Uthmānīyah 30 25 5N 49 22 E
Al 'Uwaynid 30 24 50N 46 0 E
Al' 'Uwayqīlah 30 30 30N 42 10 E
Al 'Uyūn 30 26 30N 43 50 E
Al Wakrah 31 25 10N 51 40 E
Al Wari'āh 30 27 51N 47 25 E
Al Yamāmah 30 24 5N 47 30 E
Al Yāmūn 28 32 29N 35 14 E
Alabama □ 69 33 0N 87 0W
Alabama → 69 31 8N 87 57W
Alagoa Grande 79 7 3S 35 35W
Alagoas □ 79 9 0S 36 0W
Alagoinhas 79 12 7S 38 20W
Alajuela 75 10 2N 84 8W
Alakamisy 57 21 19S 47 14 E
Alakurtti 22 67 0N 30 30 E
Alameda 73 35 10N 106 43W
Alamo 73 36 21N 115 10W
Alamogordo 73 32 59N 106 0W
Alamos 74 27 0N 109 0W
Alamosa 73 37 30N 106 0W
Åland 21 60 15N 20 0 E
Ålands hav 21 60 0N 19 30 E
Alandur 32 13 0N 80 15 E
Alanya 30 36 38N 32 0 E
Alaotra, Farihin' 57 17 30S 48 30 E
Alapayevsk 24 57 52N 61 42 E
Alaşehir 23 38 23N 28 30 E
Alaska □ 60 65 0N 150 0W
Alaska, G. of 60 58 0N 145 0W
Alaska Highway 64 60 0N 130 0W
Alaska Pen. 60 56 0N 160 0W
Alaska Range 60 62 50N 151 0W
Alataw Shankou 37 45 5N 81 57 E
Alatyr 22 54 45N 46 35 E
Alausi 78 2 0S 78 50W
Alava, C. 72 48 10N 124 40W
Alawoona 45 34 45S 140 30 E
Alba 18 44 41N 8 1 E
Alba Iulia 15 46 8N 23 39 E
Albacete 13 39 0N 1 50W
Albacutya, L. 45 35 45S 141 58 E
Albania ■ 19 41 0N 20 0 E
Albany, Australia 47 35 1S 117 58 E
Albany, Ga., U.S.A. 69 31 40N 84 10W
Albany, Minn., U.S.A. 70 45 37N 94 38W
Albany, N.Y., U.S.A. 68 42 35N 73 47W
Albany, Oreg., U.S.A. 72 44 41N 123 0W
Albany, Tex., U.S.A. 71 32 45N 99 20W
Albany → 62 52 17N 81 31W
Albardón 80 31 20S 68 30W
Albarracín, Sierra de 13 40 30N 1 30W
Albatross B. 44 12 45S 141 30 E
Albemarle 69 35 27N 80 15W
Albemarle Sd. 69 36 0N 76 30W
Alberche → 13 39 58N 4 46W

Bettiah

Bay City, Oreg., U.S.A. 72 45 45N 123 58W
Bay City, Tex., U.S.A. 71 28 59N 95 55W
Bay de Verde 63 48 5N 52 54W
Bay Minette 69 30 54N 87 43W
Bay St. Louis 71 30 18N 89 22W
Bay Springs 71 31 58N 89 18W
Bay View 43 39 25S 176 50 E
Bayamo 75 20 20N 76 40W
Bayamón 75 18 24N 66 10W
Bayan 38 46 5N 127 24 E
Bayan Har Shan 37 34 0N 98 0 E
Bayan Hot = Alxa Zuoqi 38 38 50N 105 40 E
Bayan Obo 38 41 52N 109 59 E
Bayanaul 24 50 45N 75 45 E
Bayanhongor 37 46 8N 102 43 E
Bayard 70 41 48N 103 17W
Bayázeh 31 33 30N 54 40 E
Baybay 35 10 40N 124 55 E
Bayburt 30 40 15N 40 20 E
Bayern □ 14 49 7N 11 30 E
Bayeux 12 49 17N 0 42W
Bayfield 70 46 50N 90 48W
Baykal, Oz. 25 53 0N 108 0 E
Baykit 25 61 50N 95 50 E
Baykonur 24 47 48N 65 50 E
Baymak 22 52 36N 58 19 E
Baynes Mts. 56 17 15S 13 0 E
Bayombong 35 16 30N 121 10 E
Bayonne 12 43 30N 1 28W
Bayovar 78 5 50S 81 0W
Bayram-Ali 24 37 37N 62 10 E
Bayreuth 14 49 56N 11 35 E
Bayrūt 30 33 53N 35 31 E
Bayt Awlá 28 31 37N 35 2 E
Bayt Fajjār 28 31 38N 35 9 E
Bayt Fūrīk 28 32 11N 35 20 E
Bayt Ḥānūn 28 31 32N 34 32 E
Bayt Jālā 28 31 43N 35 11 E
Bayt Lahm 28 31 43N 35 12 E
Bayt Rīma 28 32 2N 35 6 E
Bayt Sāḥūr 28 31 42N 35 13 E
Bayt Ummar 28 31 38N 35 7 E
Bayt 'ūr al Taḥtā 28 31 54N 35 5 E
Baytīn 28 31 56N 35 14 E
Baytown 71 29 42N 94 57W
Baytūniyā 28 31 54N 35 10 E
Baza 13 37 30N 2 47W
Bazaruto, I. do 57 21 40S 35 28 E
Bazhong 39 31 52N 106 46 E
Beach 70 46 57N 103 58W
Beachport 45 37 29S 140 0 E
Beachy Head 7 50 44N 0 16 E
Beacon, Australia 47 30 26S 117 52 E
Beacon, U.S.A. 68 41 32N 73 58W
Beaconia 65 50 25N 96 31W
Beagle, Canal 80 55 0S 68 30W
Beagle Bay 46 16 58S 122 40 E
Bealanana 57 14 33N 48 44 E
Bear I. 9 51 38N 9 50W
Bear L., B.C., Canada 64 56 10N 126 52W
Bear L., Man., Canada 65 55 8N 96 0W
Bear L., U.S.A. 72 42 0N 111 20W
Bearcreek 72 45 11N 109 6W
Beardmore 62 49 36N 87 57W
Beardstown 70 40 0N 90 25W
Béarn 12 43 20N 0 30W
Bearpaw Mts. 72 48 15N 109 30W
Bearskin Lake 62 53 58N 91 2W
Beata, C. 75 17 40N 71 30W
Beatrice 70 40 20N 96 40W
Beatrice, C. 44 14 20S 136 55 E
Beatton → 64 56 15N 120 45W
Beatton River 64 57 26N 121 20W
Beatty 73 36 58N 116 46W
Beauce, Plaine de la 12 48 10N 1 45 E
Beauceville 63 46 13N 70 46W
Beaudesert 45 27 59S 153 0 E
Beaufort, Malaysia 34 5 30N 115 40 E
Beaufort, N.C., U.S.A. 69 34 45N 76 40W
Beaufort, S.C., U.S.A. 69 32 25N 80 40W
Beaufort Sea 58 72 0N 140 0W
Beaufort West 56 32 18S 22 36 E
Beauharnois 62 45 20N 73 52W
Beaulieu → 64 62 3N 113 11W
Beauly 8 57 29N 4 27W
Beauly → 8 57 26N 4 28W
Beaumaris 6 53 16N 4 7W
Beaumont 71 30 5N 94 8W
Beaune 12 47 2N 4 50 E
Beauséjour 65 50 5N 96 35W
Beauvais 12 49 25N 2 8 E
Beauval 65 55 9N 107 37W
Beaver, Alaska, U.S.A. 60 66 20N 147 30W
Beaver, Okla., U.S.A. 71 36 52N 100 31W
Beaver, Utah, U.S.A. 73 38 20N 112 45W
Beaver →, B.C., Canada 64 59 52N 124 20W
Beaver →, Ont., Canada 62 55 55N 87 48W
Beaver →, Sask., Canada 65 55 26N 107 45W
Beaver City 70 40 13N 99 50W
Beaver Dam 70 43 28N 88 50W
Beaver Falls 68 40 44N 80 20W
Beaver Hill L. 65 54 5N 94 50W
Beaver I. 68 45 40N 85 31W
Beaverhill L., Alta., Canada 64 53 27N 112 32W
Beaverhill L., N.W.T., Canada 65 63 2N 104 22W
Beaverlodge 64 55 11N 119 29W
Beavermouth 64 51 32N 117 23W
Beaverstone → 62 54 59N 89 25W
Beawar 32 26 3N 74 18 E
Beboa 57 17 22S 44 33 E
Beccles 7 52 27N 1 33 E
Bečej 19 45 36N 20 3 E
Béchar 50 31 38N 2 18W
Beckley 68 37 50N 81 8W
Bedford, Canada 62 45 7N 72 59W
Bedford, S. Africa 56 32 40S 26 10 E
Bedford, U.K. 7 52 8N 0 29W
Bedford, Ind., U.S.A. 68 38 50N 86 30W
Bedford, Iowa, U.S.A. 70 40 40N 94 41W
Bedford, Ohio, U.S.A. 68 41 23N 81 32W
Bedford, Va., U.S.A. 68 37 25N 79 30W
Bedford □ 7 52 4N 0 28W
Bedford, C. 44 15 14S 145 21 E
Bedford Downs 46 17 19S 127 20 E
Bedourie 44 24 30S 139 30 E
Beech Grove 68 39 40N 86 2W
Beechworth 45 36 22S 146 43 E
Beechy 65 50 53N 107 24W
Beenleigh 45 27 43S 153 10 E
Be'er Sheva' 28 31 15N 34 48 E
Be'er Sheva' → 28 31 12N 34 40 E
Be'er Toviyya 28 31 44N 34 42 E
Be'eri 28 31 25N 34 30 E
Be'erotayim 28 32 19N 34 59 E
Beersheba = Be'er Sheva' 28 31 15N 34 48 E
Beeston 6 52 55N 1 11W
Beetaloo 44 17 15S 133 50 E
Beeville 71 28 27N 97 44W
Befale 54 0 25N 20 45 E
Befandriana 57 21 55S 44 0 E
Befotaka 57 23 49S 47 0 E
Bega 45 36 41S 149 51 E
Behara 57 24 55S 46 20 E
Behbehān 30 30 30N 50 15 E
Behshahr 31 36 45N 53 35 E
Bei Jiang → 39 23 2N 112 58 E
Bei'an 38 48 10N 126 20 E
Beibei 39 29 47N 106 22 E
Beihai 39 21 28N 109 6 E
Beijing 38 39 55N 116 20 E
Beijing □ 38 39 55N 116 20 E
Beilen 11 52 52N 6 27 E
Beilpajah 45 32 54S 143 52 E
Beira 55 19 50S 34 52 E
Beira-Alta 13 40 35N 7 35W
Beira-Baixa 13 40 2N 7 30W
Beira-Litoral 13 40 5N 8 30W
Beirut = Bayrūt 30 33 53N 35 31 E
Beit Lāhiyah 28 31 32N 34 30 E
Beitaolaizhao 38 44 58N 125 58 E
Beitbridge 55 22 12S 30 0 E
Beizhen 38 37 20N 118 2 E
Beja, Portugal 13 38 2N 7 53W
Béja, Tunisia 50 36 43N 9 12 E
Bejaia 50 36 42N 5 2 E
Bejestān 31 34 30N 58 5 E
Bekasi 35 6 14S 106 59 E
Békéscsaba 15 46 40N 21 5 E
Bekily 57 24 13S 45 19 E
Bela, India 33 25 50N 82 0 E
Bela, Pakistan 32 26 12N 66 20 E
Bela Crkva 19 44 55N 21 27 E
Bela Vista, Brazil 80 22 12S 56 20W
Bela Vista, Mozam. 57 26 10S 32 44 E
Belau Is. 40 7 30N 134 30 E
Belavenona 57 24 50S 47 4 E
Belawan 34 3 33N 98 32 E
Belaya → 22 56 0N 54 32 E
Belaya Tserkov 23 49 45N 30 10 E
Belcher Is. 62 56 15N 78 45W
Belebey 22 54 7N 54 7 E
Belém 79 1 20S 48 30W
Belén, Paraguay 80 23 30S 57 6W
Belen, U.S.A. 73 34 40N 106 50W
Belet Uen 29 4 30N 45 5 E
Belev 22 53 50N 36 5 E
Belfast, S. Africa 57 25 42S 30 2 E
Belfast, U.K. 9 54 35N 5 56W
Belfast, U.S.A. 63 44 30N 69 0W
Belfast □ 9 54 35N 5 56W
Belfast, L. 9 54 40N 5 50W
Belfield 70 46 54N 103 11W
Belfort 12 47 38N 6 50 E
Belfry 72 45 10N 109 2W
Belgaum 32 15 55N 74 35 E
Belgium ■ 11 50 30N 5 0 E
Belgorod 23 50 35N 36 35 E
Belgorod-Dnestrovskiy 23 46 11N 30 23 E
Belgrade = Beograd 19 44 50N 20 37 E
Belgrade 72 45 50N 111 10W
Belhaven 69 35 34N 76 35W
Beli Drim → 19 42 6N 20 25 E
Belinga 54 1 10N 13 2 E
Belinyu 34 1 35S 105 50 E
Belitung 34 3 10S 107 50 E
Belize ■ 74 17 0N 88 30W
Belize City 74 17 25N 88 0W
Belkovskiy, Ostrov 25 75 32N 135 44 E
Bell → 62 49 48N 77 38W
Bell Bay 44 41 6S 146 53 E
Bell I. 63 50 46N 55 35W
Bell-Irving → 64 56 12N 129 5W
Bell Peninsula 61 63 50N 82 0W
Bell Ville 80 32 40S 62 40W
Bella Bella 64 52 10N 128 10W
Bella Coola 64 52 25N 126 40W
Bella Unión 80 30 15S 57 40W
Bella Vista 80 28 33S 59 0W
Bellaire 68 40 1N 80 46W
Bellary 32 15 10N 76 56 E
Bellata 45 29 53S 149 46 E
Belle, La 69 26 45N 81 22W
Belle Fourche 70 44 43N 103 52W
Belle Fourche → 70 44 25N 102 19W
Belle Glade 69 26 43N 80 38W
Belle-Ile 12 47 20N 3 10W
Belle Isle 63 51 57N 55 25W
Belle Isle, Str. of 63 51 30N 56 30W
Belle Plaine, Iowa, U.S.A. 70 41 51N 92 18W
Belle Plaine, Minn., U.S.A. 70 44 35N 93 48W
Belledune 63 47 55N 65 50W
Bellefontaine 68 40 20N 83 45W
Bellefonte 68 40 56N 77 45W
Belleoram 63 47 31N 55 25W
Belleville, Canada 62 44 10N 77 23W
Belleville, Ill., U.S.A. 70 38 30N 90 0W
Belleville, Kans., U.S.A. 70 39 51N 97 38W
Bellevue, Canada 64 49 35N 114 22W
Bellevue, U.S.A. 72 43 25N 114 23W
Bellin 61 60 0N 70 0W
Bellingen 45 30 25S 152 50 E
Bellingham 72 48 45N 122 27W
Bellinzona 14 46 11N 9 1 E
Bello 78 6 20N 75 33W
Bellows Falls 68 43 10N 72 30W
Belluno 18 46 8N 12 13 E
Bellville 71 29 58N 96 18W
Bélmez 13 38 17N 5 17W
Belmont, Australia 45 33 4S 151 42 E
Belmont, S. Africa 56 29 28S 24 22 E
Belmonte 79 16 0S 39 0W
Belmopan 74 17 18N 88 30W
Belmullet 9 54 13N 9 58W
Belo Horizonte 79 19 55S 43 56W
Belo-sur-Mer 57 20 42S 44 0 E
Belo-Tsiribihina 57 19 40S 44 30 E
Belogorsk 25 51 0N 128 20 E
Beloha 57 25 10S 45 3 E
Beloit, Kans., U.S.A. 70 39 32N 98 9W
Beloit, Wis., U.S.A. 70 42 35N 89 0W
Belomorsk 22 64 35N 34 30 E
Belonia 33 23 15N 91 30 E
Beloretsk 22 53 58N 58 24 E
Belovo 24 54 30N 86 0 E
Beloye, Oz. 22 60 10N 37 35 E
Beloye More 22 66 30N 38 0 E
Belozersk 22 60 0N 37 30 E
Beltana 45 30 48S 138 25 E
Belterra 79 2 45S 55 0W
Belton, S.C., U.S.A. 69 34 31N 82 39W
Belton, Tex., U.S.A. 71 31 4N 97 30W
Belton Res. 71 31 8N 97 32W
Beltsy 23 47 48N 28 0 E
Belturbet 9 54 6N 7 28W
Belukha 24 49 50N 86 50 E
Beluran 34 5 48N 117 35 E
Belvidere 70 42 15N 88 55W
Belyando → 44 21 38S 146 50 E
Belyy, Ostrov 24 73 30N 71 0 E
Belyy Yar 24 58 26N 84 39 E
Belzoni 71 33 12N 90 30W
Bemaraha, Lembalemban' i 57 18 40S 44 45 E
Bemarivo 57 21 45S 44 45 E
Bemarivo → 57 15 27S 47 40 E
Bemavo 57 21 33S 45 25 E
Bembéréke 53 10 11N 2 43 E
Bemidji 70 47 30N 94 50W
Ben 'Ammi 28 33 0N 35 7 E
Ben Cruachan 8 56 26N 5 8W
Ben Dearg 8 57 47N 4 58W
Ben Gardane 51 33 11N 11 11 E
Ben Hope 8 58 24N 4 36W
Ben Lawers 8 56 33N 4 13W
Ben Lomond, N.S.W., Australia 45 30 1S 151 43 E
Ben Lomond, Tas., Australia 44 41 38S 147 42 E
Ben Lomond, U.K. 8 56 12N 4 39W
Ben Macdhui 8 57 4N 3 40W
Ben Mhor 8 57 16N 7 21W
Ben More, Central, U.K. 8 56 23N 4 31W
Ben More, Strathclyde, U.K. 8 56 26N 6 2W
Ben More Assynt 8 58 7N 4 51W
Ben Nevis 8 56 48N 5 0W
Ben Vorlich 8 56 22N 4 15W
Ben Wyvis 8 57 40N 4 35W
Bena 53 11 20N 5 50 E
Bena Dibele 54 4 4S 22 50 E
Benagerie 45 31 25S 140 22 E
Benalla 45 36 30S 146 0 E
Benares = Varanasi 33 25 22N 83 0 E
Benavides 71 27 35N 98 28W
Benbecula 8 57 26N 7 21W
Benbonyathe, Mt. 45 30 25S 139 11 E
Bencubbin 47 30 48S 117 52 E
Bend 72 44 2N 121 15W
Bendel □ 53 6 0N 6 0 E
Bender Beila 29 9 30N 50 48 E
Bendering 47 32 23S 118 18 E
Bendery 23 46 50N 29 30 E
Bendigo 45 36 40S 144 15 E
Benē Beraq 28 32 6N 34 51 E
Benenitra 57 23 27S 45 5 E
Benevento 18 41 7N 14 45 E
Bengal, Bay of 33 15 0N 90 0 E
Bengbu 39 32 58N 117 20 E
Benghazi = Banghāzī 51 32 11N 20 3 E
Bengkalis 34 1 30N 102 10 E
Bengkulu 34 3 50S 102 12 E
Bengkulu □ 34 3 48S 102 16 E
Bengough 65 49 25N 105 10W
Benguela 55 12 37S 13 25 E
Benguérua, I. 57 21 58S 35 28 E
Beni 54 0 30N 29 27 E
Beni → 78 10 23S 65 24W
Beni Abbès 50 30 5N 2 5W
Beni Mazâr 51 28 32N 30 44 E
Beni Mellal 50 32 21N 6 21W
Beni Ounif 50 32 0N 1 10W
Beni Suef 51 29 5N 31 6 E
Beniah L. 64 63 23N 112 17W
Benidorm 13 38 33N 0 9W
Benin ■ 53 10 0N 2 0 E
Benin, Bight of 53 5 0N 3 0 E
Benin City 53 6 20N 5 31 E
Benjamin Constant 78 4 40S 70 15W
Benkelman 70 40 7N 101 32W
Benlidi 44 24 35S 144 50 E
Bennett 64 59 56N 134 53W
Bennett, Ostrov 25 76 21N 148 56 E
Bennettsville 69 34 38N 79 39W
Bennington 68 42 52N 73 12W
Benoni 57 26 11S 28 18 E
Benson 73 31 59N 110 19W
Bent 31 26 20N 59 31 E
Benteng 35 6 10S 120 30 E
Bentinck I. 44 17 3S 139 35 E
Benton, Ark., U.S.A. 71 34 30N 92 35W
Benton, Ill., U.S.A. 70 38 0N 88 55W
Benton Harbor 68 42 10N 86 28W
Benue □ 53 7 30N 7 30 E
Benue → 53 7 48N 6 46 E
Benxi 38 41 20N 123 48 E
Beo 35 4 25N 126 50 E
Beograd 19 44 50N 20 37 E
Beowawe 72 40 35N 116 30W
Beppu 36 33 15N 131 30 E
Berau, Teluk 35 2 30S 132 30 E
Berber 51 18 0N 34 0 E
Berbera 29 10 30N 45 2 E
Berbérati 54 4 15N 15 40 E
Berbice → 78 6 20N 57 32W
Berdichev 23 49 57N 28 30 E
Berdsk 24 54 47N 83 2 E
Berdyansk 23 46 45N 36 50 E
Berea 68 37 35N 84 18W
Berebere 35 2 25N 128 45 E
Bereda 29 11 45N 51 0 E
Berekum 50 7 29N 2 34W
Berens → 65 52 25N 97 2W
Berens I. 65 52 18N 97 18W
Berens River 65 52 25N 97 0W
Berevo, Mahajanga, Madag. 57 17 14S 44 17 E
Berevo, Toliara, Madag. 57 19 44S 44 58 E
Berezina → 22 52 33N 30 14 E
Berezniki 24 59 24N 56 46 E
Berezovo 22 64 0N 65 0 E
Bergama 30 39 8N 27 15 E
Bérgamo 18 45 42N 9 40 E
Bergen, Neth. 11 52 40N 4 43 E
Bergen, Norway 21 60 23N 5 20 E
Bergen-op-Zoom 11 51 30N 4 18 E
Bergerac 12 44 51N 0 30 E
Bergum 11 53 13N 5 59 E
Bergville 57 28 52S 29 18 E
Berhala, Selat 34 1 0S 104 15 E
Berhampore = Baharampur 33 24 2N 88 27 E
Berhampur 33 19 15N 84 54 E
Bering Sea 60 58 0N 167 0 E
Bering Str. 60 66 0N 170 0W
Beringen 11 51 3N 5 14 E
Beringovskiy 25 63 3N 179 19 E
Berja 13 36 50N 2 56W
Berkeley, U.K. 7 51 41N 2 28W
Berkeley, U.S.A. 72 37 52N 122 20W
Berkeley Springs 68 39 38N 78 12W
Berkshire □ 7 51 30N 1 20W
Berland → 64 54 0N 116 50W
Berlin, Germany 14 52 32N 13 24 E
Berlin, Md., U.S.A. 68 38 19N 75 12W
Berlin, N.H., U.S.A. 68 44 29N 71 10W
Berlin, Wis., U.S.A. 68 43 58N 88 55W
Bermejo →, Formosa, Argentina 80 26 51S 58 23W
Bermejo →, San Juan, Argentina 80 32 30S 67 30W
Bermuda ■ 2 32 45N 65 0W
Bern 14 46 57N 7 28 E
Bernado 73 34 30N 106 53W
Bernalillo 73 35 17N 106 37W
Bernardo de Irigoyen 80 26 15S 53 40W
Bernburg 14 51 40N 11 42 E
Berne = Bern 14 46 57N 7 28 E
Bernier I. 47 24 50S 113 12 E
Beror Hayil 28 31 34N 34 38 E
Beroroha 57 21 40S 45 10 E
Beroun 14 49 57N 14 5 E
Berrechid 50 33 18N 7 36W
Berri 45 34 14S 140 35 E
Berry, Australia 45 34 46S 150 43 E
Berry, France 12 46 50N 2 0 E
Berry Is. 75 25 40N 77 50W
Berryville 71 36 23N 93 35W
Berthold 70 48 19N 101 45W
Berthoud 70 40 21N 105 5W
Bertoua 54 4 30N 13 45 E
Bertrand 70 40 35N 99 38W
Berufjörður 20 64 48N 14 29W
Berwick 68 41 4N 76 17W
Berwick-upon-Tweed 6 55 47N 2 0W
Berwyn Mts. 6 52 54N 3 26W
Besalampy 57 16 43S 44 29 E
Besançon 12 47 15N 6 0 E
Besar 34 2 40S 116 0 E
Besnard L. 65 55 25N 106 0W
Besni 30 37 41N 37 52 E
Besor, N. → 28 31 28N 34 22 E
Bessemer, Ala., U.S.A. 69 33 25N 86 57W
Bessemer, Mich., U.S.A. 70 46 27N 90 0W
Bet Alfa 28 32 31N 35 25 E
Bet Dagan 28 32 1N 34 49 E
Bet Guvrin 28 31 37N 34 54 E
Bet Ha'Emeq 28 32 58N 35 8 E
Bet Hashitta 28 32 31N 35 27 E
Bet Qeshet 28 32 41N 35 21 E
Bet She'an 28 32 30N 35 30 E
Bet Shemesh 28 31 44N 35 0 E
Bet Yosef 28 32 34N 35 33 E
Betafo 57 19 50S 46 51 E
Bétaré Oya 54 5 40N 14 5 E
Bethal 57 26 27S 29 28 E
Bethanien 56 26 31S 17 8 E
Bethany = Al 'Ayzarīyah 28 31 47N 35 15 E
Bethany, S. Africa 56 29 34S 25 59 E
Bethany, U.S.A. 70 40 18N 94 0W
Bethel 60 60 50N 161 50W
Bethlehem = Bayt Lahm 28 31 43N 35 12 E
Bethlehem, S. Africa 57 28 14S 28 18 E
Bethlehem, U.S.A. 68 40 39N 75 24W
Bethulie 56 30 30S 25 59 E
Béthune 12 50 30N 2 38 E
Bethungra 45 34 45S 147 51 E
Betioky 57 23 48S 44 20 E
Betoota 44 25 45S 140 42 E
Betroka 57 23 16S 46 0 E
Betsiamites 63 48 56N 68 40W
Betsiamites → 63 48 56N 68 38W
Betsiboka → 57 16 3S 46 36 E
Betsjoeanaland 56 26 30S 22 30 E
Bettiah 33 26 48N 84 33 E

Betul

Betul 32 21 58N 77 59 E
Betung 34 1 24N 111 31 E
Beulah 70 47 18N 101 47W
Beverley, Australia 47 32 9S 116 56 E
Beverley, U.K. 6 53 52N 0 26W
Beverly 72 46 55N 119 59W
Beverly Hills 73 34 4N 118 29W
Beverwijk 11 52 28N 4 38 E
Beyla 50 8 30N 8 38W
Beyneu 23 45 10N 55 3 E
Beypazarı 30 40 10N 31 56 E
Beyşehir Gölü 30 37 40N 31 45 E
Bezet 28 33 4N 35 8 E
Bezhitsa 22 53 19N 34 17 E
Béziers 12 43 20N 3 12 E
Bezwada = Vijayawada 33 16 31N 80 39 E
Bhachau 32 23 20N 70 16 E
Bhadrakh 33 21 10N 86 30 E
Bhadravati 32 13 49N 75 40 E
Bhagalpur 33 25 10N 87 0 E
Bhakra Dam 32 31 30N 76 45 E
Bhamo 33 24 15N 97 15 E
Bhandara 32 21 5N 79 42 E
Bhanrer Ra. 32 23 40N 79 45 E
Bharat = India ■ 32 20 0N 78 0 E
Bharatpur 32 27 15N 77 30 E
Bhatpara 33 22 50N 88 25 E
Bhaunagar = Bhavnagar 32 21 45N 72 10 E
Bhavnagar 32 21 45N 72 10 E
Bhawanipatna 33 19 55N 80 10 E
Bhilsa = Vidisha 32 23 28N 77 53 E
Bhilwara 32 25 25N 74 38 E
Bhima → 32 16 25N 77 17 E
Bhimavaram 33 16 30N 81 30 E
Bhind 32 26 30N 78 46 E
Bhiwandi 32 19 20N 73 0 E
Bhiwani 32 28 50N 76 9 E
Bhola 33 22 45N 90 35 E
Bhopal 32 23 20N 77 30 E
Bhubaneshwar 33 20 15N 85 50 E
Bhuj 32 23 15N 69 49 E
Bhumibol Dam 34 17 15N 98 58 E
Bhusaval 32 21 3N 75 46 E
Bhutan ■ 33 27 25N 90 30 E
Biafra, B. of = Bonny, Bight of 54 3 30N 9 20 E
Biak 35 1 10S 136 6 E
Biała Podlaska 15 52 4N 23 6 E
Białystok 15 53 10N 23 10 E
Biaro 35 2 5N 125 26 E
Biarritz 12 43 29N 1 33W
Bibai 36 43 19N 141 52 E
Bibala 55 14 44S 13 24 E
Bibby I. 65 61 55N 93 0W
Biberach 14 48 5N 9 49 E
Bibiani 50 6 30N 2 8W
Biboohra 44 16 56S 145 25 E
Bic 63 48 20N 68 41W
Biche, La → 64 59 57N 123 50W
Bickerton I. 44 13 45S 136 10 E
Bicknell, Ind., U.S.A. 68 38 50N 87 20W
Bicknell, Utah, U.S.A. 73 38 16N 111 35W
Bida 53 9 3N 5 58 E
Bidar 32 17 55N 77 35 E
Biddeford 63 43 30N 70 28W
Biddiyā 28 32 7N 35 4 E
Biddū 28 31 50N 35 8 E
Bideford 7 51 1N 4 13W
Bidon 5 = Poste Maurice Cortier 50 22 14N 1 2 E
Bié, Planalto de 55 12 0S 16 0 E
Bieber 72 41 4N 121 6W
Biel 14 47 8N 7 14 E
Bielé Karpaty 15 49 5N 18 0 E
Bielefeld 14 52 2N 8 31 E
Biella 18 45 33N 8 3 E
Bielsko-Biała 15 49 50N 19 2 E
Bien Hoa 34 10 57N 106 49 E
Bienfait 65 49 10N 102 50W
Bienne = Biel 14 47 8N 7 14 E
Bienville, L. 62 55 5N 72 40W
Biesiesfontein 56 30 57S 17 58 E
Big → 63 54 50N 58 55W
Big B. 63 55 43N 60 35W
Big Beaver 65 49 10N 105 10W
Big Belt Mts. 72 46 50N 111 30W
Big Bend 57 26 50S 31 58 E
Big Bend Nat. Park 71 29 15N 103 15W
Big Black → 71 32 0N 91 5W
Big Blue → 70 39 11N 96 40W
Big Cr. → 64 51 42N 122 41W
Big Cypress Swamp 69 26 12N 81 10W
Big Falls 70 48 11N 93 48W
Big Fork → 70 48 31N 93 43W
Big Horn Mts. = Bighorn Mts. 72 44 30N 107 30W
Big Lake 71 31 12N 101 25W
Big Muddy → 70 48 8N 104 36W
Big Pine 73 37 12N 118 17W
Big Piney 72 42 32N 110 3W
Big Quill L. 65 51 55N 104 50W
Big Rapids 68 43 42N 85 27W
Big River 65 53 50N 107 0W
Big Sable Pt. 68 44 5N 86 30W
Big Sand L. 65 57 45N 99 45W
Big Sandy 72 48 12N 110 9W
Big Sandy Cr. → 70 38 6N 102 29W
Big Sioux → 70 42 30N 96 25W
Big Spring 71 32 10N 101 25W
Big Springs 70 41 4N 102 3W
Big Stone City 70 45 20N 96 30W
Big Stone Gap 69 36 52N 82 45W
Big Stone L. 70 45 30N 96 35W
Big Timber 72 45 53N 110 0W
Big Trout L. 62 53 40N 90 0W
Bigfork 72 48 3N 114 2W
Biggar, Canada 65 52 4N 108 0W
Biggar, U.K. 8 55 38N 3 31W
Bigge I. 46 14 35S 125 10 E
Biggenden 45 25 31S 152 4 E
Bighorn 72 46 11N 107 25W
Bighorn → 72 46 9N 107 28W
Bighorn Mts. 72 44 30N 107 30W
Bigorre 12 43 10N 0 5 E
Bigstone L. 65 53 42N 95 44W
Bihać 18 44 49N 15 57 E
Bihar 33 25 5N 85 40 E
Bihar □ 33 25 0N 86 0 E
Bijagós, Arquipélago dos 50 11 15N 16 10W
Bijapur, Karnataka, India 32 16 50N 75 55 E
Bijapur, Mad. P., India 33 18 50N 80 50 E
Bijār 30 35 52N 47 35 E
Bijeljina 19 44 46N 19 17 E
Bijie 39 27 20N 105 16 E
Bijnor 32 29 27N 78 11 E
Bikaner 32 28 2N 73 18 E
Bikin 25 46 50N 134 20 E
Bikini Atoll 40 12 0N 167 30 E
Bilara 32 26 14N 73 53 E
Bilaspur 33 22 2N 82 15 E
Bilauk Taungdan 34 13 0N 99 0 E
Bilbao 13 43 16N 2 56W
Bildudalur 20 65 41N 23 36W
Bilecik 30 40 5N 30 5 E
Bilibino 25 68 3N 166 20 E
Bilir 25 65 40N 131 20 E
Bill 70 43 18N 105 18W
Billabalong 47 27 25S 115 49 E
Billiluna 46 19 37S 127 41 E
Billingham 6 54 36N 1 18W
Billings 72 45 43N 108 29W
Billiton Is. = Belitung 34 3 10S 107 50 E
Bilma 51 18 50N 13 30 E
Biloela 44 24 24S 150 31 E
Biloxi 71 30 24N 88 53W
Bilpa Morea Claypan 44 25 0S 140 0 E
Biltine 51 14 40N 20 50 E
Bilyana 44 18 5S 145 50 E
Bima 35 8 22S 118 49 E
Bimbo 54 4 15N 18 33 E
Bimini Is. 75 25 42N 79 25W
Bin Xian 39 35 2N 108 4 E
Bina-Etawah 32 24 13N 78 14 E
Binalbagan 35 10 12N 122 50 E
Bīnālūd, Kūh-e 31 36 30N 58 30 E
Binatang 34 2 10N 111 40 E
Binbee 44 20 19S 147 56 E
Binche 11 50 26N 4 10 E
Binda 45 27 52S 147 21 E
Bindi Bindi 47 30 37S 116 22 E
Bindle 45 27 40S 148 45 E
Bindura 55 17 18S 31 18 E
Bingara, N.S.W., Australia 45 29 52S 150 36 E
Bingara, Queens., Australia 45 28 10S 144 37 E
Bingham 63 45 5N 69 50W
Bingham Canyon 72 40 31N 112 10W
Binghamton 68 42 9N 75 54W
Bingöl 30 38 53N 40 29 E
Binh Dinh = An Nhon 34 13 55N 109 7 E
Binh Son 34 15 20N 108 40 E
Binjai 34 3 20N 98 30 E
Binnaway 45 31 28S 149 24 E
Binongko 35 5 55S 123 55 E
Binscarth 65 50 37N 101 17W
Bint Jubayl 28 33 8N 35 25 E
Bintan 34 1 0N 104 0 E
Bintulu 34 3 10N 113 0 E
Bintuni 35 2 7S 133 32 E
Binyamina 28 32 32N 34 56 E
Binyang 39 23 12N 108 47 E
Binzert = Bizerte 50 37 15N 9 50 E
Bioko 53 3 30N 8 40 E
Biq'at Bet Netofa 28 32 49N 35 22 E
Bir 32 19 0N 75 54 E
Bir Autrun 51 18 15N 26 40 E
Bir Mogrein 50 25 10N 11 25W
Bi'r Nabālā 28 31 52N 35 12 E
Bîr Ungât 51 22 8N 33 48 E
Bi'r Zayt 28 31 59N 35 11 E
Bira 35 2 3S 132 2 E
Birak Sulaymān 28 31 42N 35 7 E
Birao 51 10 20N 22 47 E
Birch Hills 65 52 59N 105 25W
Birch I. 65 52 26N 99 54W
Birch L., N.W.T., Canada 64 62 4N 116 33W
Birch L., Ont., Canada 62 51 23N 92 18W
Birch L., U.S.A. 62 47 48N 91 43W
Birch Mts. 64 57 30N 113 10W
Birch River 65 52 24N 101 6W
Birchip 45 35 56S 142 55 E
Bird 65 56 30N 94 13W
Bird City 70 39 48N 101 33W
Bird I. = Aves, I. de 75 15 45N 63 55W
Bird I. 56 32 3S 18 17 E
Birdlip 7 51 50N 2 7W
Birdsville 44 25 51S 139 20 E
Birdum 46 15 39S 133 13 E
Birecik 30 37 0N 38 0 E
Bireuen 34 5 14N 96 39 E
Birkenhead 6 53 24N 3 1W
Birlad 15 46 15N 27 38 E
Birmingham, U.K. 7 52 30N 1 55W
Birmingham, U.S.A. 69 33 31N 86 50W
Birmitrapur 33 22 24N 84 46 E
Birni Nkonni 50 13 55N 5 15 E
Birnin Kebbi 53 12 32N 4 12 E
Birnin Kudu 53 11 30N 9 29 E
Birobidzhan 25 48 50N 132 50 E
Birqīn 28 32 27N 35 15 E
Birr 9 53 7N 7 55W
Birrie → 45 29 43S 146 37 E
Birsk 22 55 25N 55 30 E
Birtle 65 50 30N 101 5W
Birur 32 13 30N 75 55 E
Bisa 35 1 15S 127 28 E
Bisbee 73 31 30N 110 0W
Biscay, B. of 16 45 0N 2 0W
Biscayne B. 69 25 40N 80 12W
Biscostasing 62 47 18N 82 9W
Bisho 57 32 50S 27 23 E
Bishop, Calif., U.S.A. 73 37 20N 118 26W
Bishop, Tex., U.S.A. 71 27 35N 97 49W
Bishop Auckland 6 54 40N 1 40W
Bishop's Falls 63 49 2N 55 30W
Bishop's Stortford 7 51 52N 0 11 E
Biskra 50 34 50N 5 44 E
Bislig 35 8 15N 126 27 E
Bismarck 70 46 49N 100 49W
Bismarck Arch. 40 2 30S 150 0 E
Bison 70 45 34N 102 28W
Bispfors 20 63 1N 16 37 E
Bissagos = Bijagós, Arquipélago dos 50 11 15N 16 10W
Bissau 50 11 45N 15 45W
Bissett 65 51 2N 95 41W
Bistcho L. 64 59 45N 118 50W
Bistrița 15 47 9N 24 35 E
Bistrița → 15 46 30N 26 57 E
Bitam 54 2 5N 11 25 E
Bitkine 51 11 59N 18 13 E
Bitlis 30 38 20N 42 3 E
Bitola 19 41 5N 21 10 E
Bitolj = Bitola 19 41 5N 21 10 E
Bitter Creek 72 41 39N 108 36W
Bitter L. = Buheirat-Murrat-el-Kubra 51 30 15N 32 40 E
Bitterfontein 56 31 1S 18 32 E
Bitterroot → 72 46 52N 114 6W
Bitterroot Range 72 46 0N 114 20W
Biu 51 10 40N 12 3 E
Biwa-Ko 36 35 15N 136 10 E
Biwabik 70 47 33N 92 19W
Biyang 39 32 38N 113 21 E
Biysk 24 52 40N 85 0 E
Bizana 57 30 50S 29 52 E
Bizerte 50 37 15N 9 50 E
Bjargtangar 20 65 30N 24 30W
Bjelovar 18 45 56N 16 49 E
Black →, Ark., U.S.A. 71 35 38N 91 19W
Black →, Wis., U.S.A. 70 43 52N 91 22W
Black Diamond 64 50 45N 114 14W
Black Forest = Schwarzwald 14 48 0N 8 0 E
Black Hills 70 44 0N 103 50W
Black I. 65 51 12N 96 30W
Black L., Canada 65 59 12N 105 15W
Black L., U.S.A. 68 45 28N 84 15W
Black Mesa, Mt. 71 36 57N 102 55W
Black Mt. = Mynydd Du 7 51 45N 3 45W
Black Mts. 7 51 52N 3 5W
Black Range 73 33 30N 107 55W
Black River 75 18 0N 77 50W
Black River Falls 70 44 23N 90 52W
Black Sea 17 43 30N 35 0 E
Black Volta → 50 8 41N 1 33W
Black Warrior → 69 32 32N 87 51W
Blackall 44 24 25S 145 45 E
Blackball 43 42 22S 171 26 E
Blackbull 44 17 55S 141 45 E
Blackburn 6 53 44N 2 30W
Blackduck 70 47 43N 94 32W
Blackfoot 72 43 13N 112 12W
Blackfoot → 72 46 52N 113 53W
Blackfoot Res. 72 43 0N 111 35W
Blackie 64 50 36N 113 37W
Blackpool 6 53 48N 3 3W
Blacks Harbour 63 45 3N 66 49W
Blacksburg 68 37 17N 80 23W
Blacksod B. 9 54 6N 10 0W
Blackstone 68 37 6N 78 0W
Blackstone → 64 61 5N 122 55W
Blackstone Ra. 47 26 0S 128 30 E
Blackville 63 46 44N 65 50W
Blackwater 44 23 35S 148 53 E
Blackwater →, Ireland 9 51 55N 7 50W
Blackwater →, U.K. 9 54 31N 6 35W
Blackwater Cr. → 45 25 56S 144 30 E
Blackwell 71 36 55N 97 20W
Blaenau Ffestiniog 6 53 0N 3 57W
Blagodarnoye 23 45 7N 43 37 E
Blagoveshchensk 25 50 20N 127 30 E
Blaine 72 48 59N 122 43W
Blaine Lake 65 52 51N 106 52W
Blair 70 41 38N 96 10W
Blair Athol 44 22 42S 147 31 E
Blair Atholl 8 56 46N 3 50W
Blairgowrie 8 56 36N 3 20W
Blairmore 64 49 40N 114 25W
Blake Pt. 70 48 12N 88 27W
Blakely 69 31 22N 85 0W
Blanc, Mont 12 45 48N 6 50 E
Blanca, B. 80 39 10S 61 30W
Blanca Peak 73 37 35N 105 29W
Blanchard 71 35 8N 97 40W
Blanche, C. 45 33 1S 134 9 E
Blanche L., S. Austral., Australia 45 29 15S 139 40 E
Blanche L., W. Austral., Australia 46 22 25S 123 17 E
Blanco, S. Africa 56 33 55S 22 23 E
Blanco, U.S.A. 71 30 7N 98 30W
Blanco, C., C. Rica 75 9 34N 85 8W
Blanco, C., U.S.A. 72 42 50N 124 40W
Blanda → 20 65 20N 19 40W
Blandford Forum 7 50 52N 2 10W
Blanding 73 37 35N 109 30W
Blankenberge 11 51 20N 3 9 E
Blantyre 55 15 45S 35 0 E
Blarney 9 51 57N 8 35W
Blåvands Huk 21 55 33N 8 4 E
Blaydon 6 54 56N 1 47W
Blayney 45 33 32S 149 14 E
Blaze, Pt. 46 12 56S 130 11 E
Blednaya, Gora 24 76 20N 65 0 E
Bleiburg 14 46 35N 14 49 E
Blekinge län □ 21 56 20N 15 20 E
Blenheim 43 41 38S 173 57 E
Bletchley 7 51 59N 0 44W
Blida 50 36 30N 2 49 E
Bligh Sound 43 44 47S 167 32 E
Blind River 62 46 10N 82 58W
Blitar 35 8 5S 112 11 E
Blitta 53 8 23N 1 6 E
Block I. 68 41 11N 71 35W
Bloemfontein 56 29 6S 26 7 E
Bloemhof 56 27 38S 25 32 E
Blois 12 47 35N 1 20 E
Blönduós 20 65 40N 20 12W
Bloodvein → 65 51 47N 96 43W
Bloody Foreland 9 55 10N 8 18W
Bloomer 70 45 8N 91 30W
Bloomfield, Australia 44 15 56S 145 22 E
Bloomfield, Iowa, U.S.A. 70 40 44N 92 26W
Bloomfield, N. Mex., U.S.A. 73 36 46N 107 59W
Bloomfield, Nebr., U.S.A. 70 42 38N 97 40W
Bloomington, Ill., U.S.A. 70 40 27N 89 0W
Bloomington, Ind., U.S.A. 68 39 10N 86 30W
Bloomsburg 68 41 0N 76 30W
Blora 35 6 57S 111 25 E
Blouberg 57 23 8S 28 59 E
Blountstown 69 30 28N 85 5W
Blue Island 68 41 40N 87 40W
Blue Lake 72 40 53N 124 0W
Blue Mesa Res. 73 38 30N 107 15W
Blue Mts., Oreg., U.S.A. 72 45 15N 119 0W
Blue Mts., Pa., U.S.A. 68 40 30N 76 30W
Blue Mud B. 44 13 30S 136 0 E
Blue Nile = An Nîl el Azraq □ 51 12 30N 34 30 E
Blue Nile = Nîl el Azraq → 51 15 38N 32 31 E
Blue Rapids 70 39 41N 96 39W
Blue Ridge Mts. 69 36 30N 80 15W
Blue Stack Mts. 9 54 46N 8 5W
Blueberry → 64 56 45N 120 49W
Bluefield 68 37 18N 81 14W
Bluefields 75 12 20N 83 50W
Bluff, Australia 44 23 35S 149 4 E
Bluff, N.Z. 43 46 37S 168 20 E
Bluff, U.S.A. 73 37 17N 109 33W
Bluff Knoll 47 34 24S 118 15 E
Bluff Pt. 47 27 50S 114 5 E
Bluffton 68 40 43N 85 9W
Blumenau 80 27 0S 49 0W
Blunt 70 44 32N 100 0W
Bly 72 42 23N 121 0W
Blyth 6 55 8N 1 32W
Blythe 73 33 40N 114 33W
Bo 50 7 55N 11 50W
Bo Duc 34 11 58N 106 50 E
Bo Hai 38 39 0N 120 0 E
Bo Xian 39 33 50N 115 45 E
Boa Vista 78 2 48N 60 30W
Boaco 75 12 29N 85 35W
Boatman 45 27 16S 146 55 E
Bobadah 45 32 19S 146 41 E
Bobai 39 22 17N 109 59 E
Bobbili 33 18 35N 83 30 E
Bobcaygeon 62 44 33N 78 33W
Bobo-Dioulasso 50 11 8N 4 13W
Bóbr → 14 52 4N 15 4 E
Bobraomby, Tanjon' i 57 12 40S 49 10 E
Bobruysk 22 53 10N 29 15 E
Boca, La 74 8 56N 79 30W
Bôca do Acre 78 8 50S 67 27W
Boca Raton 69 26 21N 80 5W
Bocaiúva 79 17 7S 43 49W
Bocanda 50 7 5N 4 31W
Bocaranga 51 7 0N 15 35 E
Bocas del Toro 75 9 15N 82 20W
Bocholt 14 51 50N 6 35 E
Bochum 14 51 28N 7 12 E
Boda 54 4 19N 17 26 E
Bodaybo 25 57 50N 114 0 E
Boddington 47 32 50S 116 30 E
Boden 20 65 50N 21 42 E
Bodensee 14 47 35N 9 25 E
Bodhan 32 18 40N 77 44 E
Bodmin 7 50 28N 4 44W
Bodmin Moor 7 50 33N 4 36W
Bodrog → 15 48 15N 21 35 E
Bodrum 30 37 5N 27 30 E
Boegoebergdam 56 29 7S 22 9 E
Boende 54 0 24S 21 12 E
Boerne 71 29 48N 98 41W
Boffa 50 10 16N 14 3W
Bogalusa 71 30 50N 89 55W
Bogan → 45 29 59S 146 17 E
Bogan Gate 45 33 7S 147 49 E
Bogantungan 44 23 41S 147 17 E
Bogata 71 33 26N 95 10W
Boggabilla 45 28 36S 150 24 E
Boggabri 45 30 45S 150 0 E
Boggeragh Mts. 9 52 2N 8 55W
Bognor Regis 7 50 47N 0 40W
Bogo 35 11 3N 124 0 E
Bogong, Mt. 45 36 47S 147 17 E
Bogor 35 6 36S 106 48 E
Bogorodskoye 25 52 22N 140 30 E
Bogotá 78 4 34N 74 0W
Bogotol 24 56 15N 89 50 E
Bogra 33 24 51N 89 22 E
Boguchany 25 58 40N 97 30 E
Bogué 50 16 45N 14 10W
Bohemia Downs 46 18 53S 126 14 E
Bohemian Forest = Böhmerwald 14 49 30N 12 40 E
Bohena Cr. → 45 30 17S 149 42 E
Böhmerwald 14 49 30N 12 40 E
Bohol 35 9 50N 124 10 E
Bohol Sea 35 9 0N 124 0 E
Bohotleh 29 8 20N 46 25 E
Boileau, C. 46 17 40S 122 7 E
Boise 72 43 43N 116 9W
Boise City 71 36 45N 102 30W
Boissevain 65 49 15N 100 5W
Bojador C. 50 26 0N 14 30W
Bojana → 19 41 52N 19 22 E
Bojnūrd 31 37 30N 57 20 E
Bojonegoro 35 7 11S 111 54 E
Boju 53 7 22N 7 55 E
Boké 50 10 56N 14 17W
Bokhara → 45 29 55S 146 42 E
Bokkos 53 9 17N 9 1 E
Boknafjorden 21 59 14N 5 40 E
Bokoro 51 12 25N 17 14 E
Bokote 54 0 12S 21 8 E
Bokungu 54 0 35S 22 50 E

Bronte Park

Bol .... 51 13 30N 15 0 E
Bolama 50 11 30N 15 30W
Bolan Pass .... 31 29 50N 67 20 E
Bolaños → 74 21 14N 104 8W
Bolbec .... 12 49 30N 0 30 E
Bole .... 37 45 11N 81 37 E
Bolesławiec ...... 14 51 17N 15 37 E
Bolgatanga 53 10 44N 0 53W
Boli .... 38 45 46N 130 31 E
Bolinao C. .... 35 16 23N 119 55 E
Bolívar, Argentina . 80 36 15S 60 53W
Bolívar, Colombia . 78 2 0N 77 0W
Bolivar, Mo., U.S.A. 71 37 38N 93 22W
Bolivar, Tenn.,
U.S.A. 71 35 14N 89 0W
Bolivia ■ 78 17 6S 64 0W
Bolivian Plateau ... 76 20 0S 67 30W
Bollnäs .... 21 61 21N 16 24 E
Bollon .... 45 28 2S 147 29 E
Bolobo .... 54 2 6S 16 20 E
Bologna .... 18 44 30N 11 20 E
Bologoye .... 22 57 55N 34 0 E
Bolomba .... 54 0 35N 19 0 E
Bolong .... 35 7 6N 122 14 E
Bolsena, L. di ..... 18 42 35N 11 55 E
Bolshereche ...... 24 56 4N 74 45 E
Bolshevik, Ostrov . 25 78 30N 102 0 E
Bolshezemelskaya
Tundra .... 22 67 0N 56 0 E
Bolshoi Kavkas ... 23 42 50N 44 0 E
Bolshoy Anyuy → 25 68 30N 160 49 E
Bolshoy Atlym .... 24 62 25N 66 50 E
Bolshoy Begichev,
Ostrov .... 25 74 20N 112 30 E
Bolshoy
Lyakhovskiy,
Ostrov .... 25 73 35N 142 0 E
Bolsward .... 11 53 3N 5 32 E
Bolton 6 53 35N 2 26W
Bolu .... 30 40 45N 31 35 E
Bolvadin .... 30 38 45N 31 4 E
Bolzano .... 18 46 30N 11 20 E
Bom Despacho ... 79 19 43S 45 15W
Bom Jesus da Lapa 79 13 15S 43 25W
Boma .... 54 5 50S 13 4 E
Bomaderry .... 45 34 52S 150 37 E
Bombala .... 45 36 56S 149 15 E
Bombay .... 32 18 55N 72 50 E
Bomboma .... 54 2 25N 18 55 E
Bomili .... 54 1 45N 27 5 E
Bomongo .... 54 1 27N 18 21 E
Bomu → .... 54 4 40N 22 30 E
Bon, C. .... 51 37 1N 11 2 E
Bonaire 75 12 10N 68 15W
Bonang .... 45 37 11S 148 41 E
Bonanza 75 13 54N 84 35W
Bonaparte
Archipelago .... 46 14 0S 124 30 E
Bonaventure 63 48 5N 65 32W
Bonavista 63 48 40N 53 5W
Bonavista, C. 63 48 42N 53 5W
Bondo .... 54 3 55N 23 53 E
Bondoukou 50 8 2N 2 47W
Bondowoso ...... 35 7 55S 113 49 E
Bone, Teluk ...... 35 4 10S 120 50 E
Bone Rate .... 35 7 25S 121 5 E
Bone Rate,
Kepulauan ..... 35 6 30S 121 10 E
Bo'ness 8 56 0N 3 38W
Bong Son = Hoai
Nhon .... 34 14 28N 109 1 E
Bongandanga .... 54 1 24N 21 3 E
Bongor .... 51 10 35N 15 20 E
Bonham 71 33 30N 96 10W
Bonifacio .... 12 41 24N 9 10 E
Bonifacio, Bouches
de .... 18 41 12N 9 15 E
Bonin Is. .... 40 27 0N 142 0 E
Bonn .... 14 50 43N 7 6 E
Bonne Terre 71 37 57N 90 33W
Bonners Ferry 72 48 38N 116 21W
Bonney, L. .... 45 37 50S 140 20 E
Bonnie Downs .... 44 22 7S 143 50 E
Bonnie Rock ..... 47 30 29S 118 22 E
Bonny, Bight of ... 54 3 30N 9 20 E
Bonnyville 65 54 20N 110 45W
Bonoi .... 35 1 45S 137 41 E
Bontang .... 34 0 10N 117 30 E
Bonthain .... 35 5 34S 119 56 E
Bonthe 50 7 30N 12 33W
Bontoc .... 35 17 7N 120 58 E
Bonython Ra. ..... 46 23 40S 128 45 E
Boogardie .... 47 28 2S 117 45 E
Bookabie .... 47 31 50S 132 41 E
Booker 71 36 29N 100 30W
Boolaboolka, L. ... 45 32 38S 143 10 E
Booligal .... 45 33 58S 144 53 E
Boom .... 11 51 6N 4 20 E
Boonah .... 45 27 58S 152 41 E
Boone, Iowa, U.S.A. 70 42 5N 93 53W
Boone, N.C., U.S.A. 69 36 14N 81 43W
Booneville, Ark.,
U.S.A. 71 35 10N 93 54W
Booneville, Miss.,
U.S.A. 69 34 39N 88 34W
Boonville, Ind.,
U.S.A. 68 38 3N 87 13W
Boonville, Mo.,
U.S.A. 70 38 57N 92 45W
Boonville, N.Y.,
U.S.A. 68 43 31N 75 20W
Boorindal .... 45 30 22S 146 11 E
Boorowa .... 45 34 28S 148 44 E
Boothia, Gulf of ... 61 71 0N 90 0W
Boothia Pen. 60 71 0N 94 0W
Bootle, Cumbria,
U.K. 6 54 17N 3 24W
Bootle, Merseyside,
U.K. 6 53 28N 3 1W
Booué .... 54 0 5S 11 55 E
Bophuthatswana □ 56 25 49S 25 30 E
Boquilla, Presa de la 74 27 40N 105 30W
Bôr, Sudan .... 51 6 10N 31 40 E
Bor, Yugoslavia ... 19 44 8N 22 7 E
Borah, Pk. 72 44 19N 113 46W
Borama .... 29 9 55N 43 7 E
Borås .... 21 57 43N 12 56 E
Borāzjān .... 31 29 22N 51 10 E
Borba 78 4 12S 59 34W
Borda, C. .... 45 35 45S 136 34 E
Bordeaux 12 44 50N 0 36W
Borden, Australia .. 47 34 3S 118 12 E
Borden, Canada .. 63 46 18N 63 47W
Borders □ 8 55 35N 2 50W
Bordertown ...... 45 36 19S 140 45 E
Borðeyri 20 65 12N 21 6W
Bordj Fly Ste. Marie 50 27 19N 2 32W
Bordj-in-Eker ..... 50 24 9N 5 3 E
Bordj Omar Driss .. 50 28 10N 6 40 E
Bordj-Tarat .... 50 25 55N 9 3 E
Borgarnes 20 64 32N 21 55W
Børgefjellet .... 20 65 20N 13 45 E
Borger, Neth. ..... 11 52 54N 6 44 E
Borger, U.S.A. 71 35 40N 101 20W
Borgholm .... 21 56 52N 16 39 E
Borisoglebsk ..... 23 51 27N 42 5 E
Borisov .... 22 54 17N 28 28 E
Borja 78 4 20S 77 40W
Borkou .... 51 18 15N 18 50 E
Borkum .... 14 53 36N 6 42 E
Borlänge .... 21 60 29N 15 26 E
Borneo .... 34 1 0N 115 0 E
Bornholm .... 21 55 10N 15 0 E
Borno □ .... 53 12 30N 12 30 E
Borobudur .... 35 7 36S 110 13 E
Borogontsy ...... 25 62 42N 131 8 E
Boromo 50 11 45N 2 58W
Borongan .... 35 11 37N 125 26 E
Bororen .... 44 24 13S 151 33 E
Borovichi .... 22 58 25N 33 55 E
Borroloola .... 44 16 4S 136 17 E
Borth 7 52 29N 4 3W
Borujerd .... 30 33 55N 48 50 E
Borzya .... 25 50 24N 116 31 E
Bosa .... 18 40 17N 8 32 E
Bosanska Gradiška 18 45 10N 17 15 E
Bosaso .... 29 11 12N 49 18 E
Boscastle 7 50 42N 4 42W
Bose .... 39 23 53N 106 35 E
Boshan .... 38 36 28N 117 49 E
Boshoek .... 56 25 30S 27 9 E
Boshof .... 56 28 31S 25 13 E
Boshrūyeh .... 31 33 50N 57 30 E
Bosna → .... 19 45 4N 18 29 E
Bosna i
Hercegovina □ .. 18 44 0N 18 0 E
Bosnia = Bosna i
Hercegovina □ .. 18 44 0N 18 0 E
Bosnik .... 35 1 5S 136 10 E
Bōsō-Hantō ...... 36 35 20N 140 20 E
Bosobolo .... 54 4 15N 19 50 E
Bosporus =
Karadeniz Boğazı 30 41 10N 29 10 E
Bossangoa .... 51 6 35N 17 30 E
Bossekop .... 20 69 57N 23 15 E
Bossembélé ...... 51 5 25N 17 40 E
Bossier City 71 32 28N 93 48W
Bosso .... 51 13 43N 13 19 E
Bosten Hu .... 37 41 55N 87 40 E
Boston, U.K. 6 52 59N 0 2W
Boston, U.S.A. 68 42 20N 71 0W
Boston Bar 64 49 52N 121 30W
Boswell, Canada .. 64 49 28N 116 45W
Boswell, U.S.A. 71 34 1N 95 50W
Botany Bay ...... 45 34 0S 151 14 E
Bothaville .... 56 27 23S 26 34 E
Bothnia, G. of .... 20 63 0N 20 0 E
Bothwell .... 44 42 20S 147 1 E
Botletle → ...... 56 20 10S 23 15 E
Botoşani .... 15 47 42N 26 41 E
Botswana ■ ...... 56 22 0S 24 0 E
Bottineau 70 48 49N 100 25W
Bottrop .... 11 51 34N 6 59 E
Botucatu 80 22 55S 48 30W
Botwood 63 49 6N 55 23W
Bou Djébéha 50 18 25N 2 45W
Bou Izakarn 50 29 12N 9 46W
Bouaké 50 7 40N 5 2W
Bouar .... 54 6 0N 15 40 E
Bouârfa .... 50 32 32N 1 58 E
Bouca .... 51 6 45N 18 25 E
Boucaut B. .... 44 12 0S 134 25 E
Bouches-du-
Rhône □ .... 12 43 37N 5 2 E
Bougainville C. .... 46 13 57S 126 4 E
Bougainville Reef .. 44 15 30S 147 5 E
Bougie = Bejaia .. 50 36 42N 5 2 E
Bougouni 50 11 30N 7 20W
Bouillon .... 11 49 44N 5 3 E
Boulder, Colo.,
U.S.A. 70 40 3N 105 10W
Boulder, Mont.,
U.S.A. 72 46 14N 112 4W
Boulder City 73 35 58N 114 50W
Boulder Dam =
Hoover Dam 73 36 0N 114 45W
Boulia .... 44 22 52S 139 51 E
Boulogne-sur-Mer . 12 50 42N 1 36 E
Boultoum .... 53 14 45N 10 25 E
Bouna 50 9 10N 3 0W
Boundiali 50 9 30N 6 20W
Bountiful 72 40 57N 111 58W
Bounty I. .... 40 48 0S 178 30 E
Bourbonnais ..... 12 46 28N 3 0 E
Bourem 53 17 0N 0 24W
Bourg-en-Bresse .. 12 46 13N 5 12 E
Bourges .... 12 47 9N 2 25 E
Bourgogne .... 12 47 0N 4 50 E
Bourke .... 45 30 8S 145 55 E
Bournemouth 7 50 43N 1 53W
Bousso .... 51 10 34N 16 52 E
Boutilimit 50 17 45N 14 40W
Bouvet I. =
Bouvetøya ..... 3 54 26S 3 24 E
Bouvetøya .... 3 54 26S 3 24 E
Bovigny .... 11 50 12N 5 55 E
Bovill 72 46 58N 116 27W
Bow Island 64 49 50N 111 23W
Bowbells 70 48 47N 102 19W
Bowdle 70 45 30N 99 40W
Bowelling .... 47 33 25S 116 30 E
Bowen .... 44 20 0S 148 16 E
Bowen Mts. ...... 45 37 0S 148 0 E
Bowie, Ariz., U.S.A. 73 32 15N 109 30W
Bowie, Tex., U.S.A. 71 33 33N 97 50W
Bowland, Forest of 6 54 0N 2 30W
Bowling Green, Ky.,
U.S.A. 68 37 0N 86 25W
Bowling Green,
Ohio, U.S.A. 68 41 22N 83 40W
Bowling Green, C. . 44 19 19S 147 25 E
Bowman 70 46 12N 103 21W
Bowmans .... 45 34 10S 138 17 E
Bowmanville 62 43 55N 78 41W
Bowmore 8 55 45N 6 18W
Bowral .... 45 34 26S 150 27 E
Bowraville .... 45 30 37S 152 52 E
Bowron → 64 54 3N 121 50W
Bowser L. 64 56 30N 129 30W
Bowsman 65 52 14N 101 12W
Boxtel .... 11 51 36N 5 20 E
Boyce 71 31 25N 92 39W
Boyer → 64 58 27N 115 57W
Boyle 9 53 58N 8 19W
Boyne → 9 53 43N 6 15W
Boyne City 68 45 13N 85 1W
Boyni Qara ...... 31 36 20N 67 0 E
Boynton Beach ... 69 26 31N 80 3W
Boyoma, Chutes .. 48 0 35N 25 23 E
Boyup Brook ..... 47 33 50S 116 23 E
Bozeman 72 45 40N 111 0W
Bozen = Bolzano . 18 46 30N 11 20 E
Bozoum .... 51 6 25N 16 35 E
Brabant □ .... 11 50 46N 4 30 E
Brabant L. 65 55 58N 103 43W
Brač .... 18 43 20N 16 40 E
Bracadale, L. 8 57 20N 6 30W
Bracciano, L. di ... 18 42 8N 12 11 E
Bracebridge 62 45 2N 79 19W
Brach .... 51 27 31N 14 20 E
Bräcke .... 20 62 45N 15 26 E
Brackettville 71 29 21N 100 20W
Brad .... 15 46 10N 22 50 E
Bradenton 69 27 25N 82 35W
Bradford, U.K. 6 53 47N 1 45W
Bradford, U.S.A. .. 68 41 58N 78 41W
Bradley, Ark., U.S.A. 71 33 7N 93 39W
Bradley, S. Dak.,
U.S.A. 70 45 10N 97 40W
Bradore Bay 63 51 27N 57 18W
Bradshaw .... 46 15 21S 130 16 E
Brady 71 31 8N 99 25W
Braemar .... 45 33 12S 139 35 E
Braga 13 41 35N 8 25W
Bragança, Brazil .. 79 1 0S 47 2W
Bragança, Portugal 13 41 48N 6 50W
Brahmanbaria .... 33 23 58N 91 15 E
Brahmani → .... 33 20 39N 86 46 E
Brahmaputra → . 33 24 2N 90 59 E
Braich-y-pwll 6 52 47N 4 46W
Braidwood .... 45 35 27S 149 49 E
Brăila .... 15 45 19N 27 59 E
Brainerd 70 46 20N 94 10W
Braintree .... 7 51 53N 0 34 E
Brak → .... 56 29 35S 22 55 E
Brakwater .... 56 22 28S 17 3 E
Bralorne 64 50 50N 122 50W
Brampton 62 43 45N 79 45W
Bramwell .... 44 12 8S 142 37 E
Branco → 78 1 20S 61 50W
Brandenburg ..... 14 52 24N 12 33 E
Brandfort .... 56 28 40S 26 30 E
Brandon 65 49 50N 99 57W
Brandon, Mt. 9 52 15N 10 15W
Brandon B. 9 52 17N 10 8W
Brandvlei .... 56 30 25S 20 30 E
Braniewo .... 15 54 25N 19 50 E
Brańsk .... 15 52 45N 22 50 E
Branson, Colo.,
U.S.A. 71 37 4N 103 53W
Branson, Mo., U.S.A. 71 36 40N 93 18W
Brantford 62 43 10N 80 15W
Branxholme ...... 45 37 52S 141 49 E
Bras d'Or, L. 63 45 50N 60 50W
Brasil, Planalto 76 18 0S 46 30W
Brasiléia 78 11 0S 68 45W
Brasília 79 15 47S 47 55W
Braşov .... 15 45 38N 25 35 E
Brasschaat .... 11 51 19N 4 27 E
Brassey, Banjaran . 34 5 0N 117 15 E
Brassey Ra. ...... 47 25 8S 122 15 E
Brasstown Bald, Mt. 69 34 54N 83 45W
Bratislava .... 14 48 10N 17 7 E
Bratsk .... 25 56 10N 101 30 E
Brattleboro 68 42 53N 72 37W
Braunschweig .... 14 52 17N 10 28 E
Braunton 7 51 6N 4 9W
Brava .... 29 1 20N 44 8 E
Bravo del Norte → 74 25 57N 97 9W
Brawley 73 32 58N 115 30W
Bray 9 53 12N 6 6W
Bray, Mt. .... 44 14 0S 134 30 E
Bray-sur-Seine .... 12 48 25N 3 14 E
Brazeau → 64 52 55N 115 14W
Brazil 68 39 32N 87 8W
Brazil ■ 79 12 0S 50 0W
Brazilian Highlands
= Brasil, Planalto 76 18 0S 46 30W
Brazos → 71 28 53N 95 23W
Brazzaville ...... 54 4 9S 15 12 E
Brčko .... 19 44 54N 18 46 E
Breadalbane,
Australia .... 44 23 50S 139 35 E
Breadalbane, U.K. . 8 56 30N 4 15W
Breaden, L. ...... 47 25 51S 125 28 E
Breaksea Sd. ..... 43 45 35S 166 35 E
Bream Bay .... 43 35 56S 174 28 E
Bream Head ..... 43 35 51S 174 36 E
Brebes .... 35 6 52S 109 3 E
Brechin 8 56 44N 2 40W
Breckenridge, Colo.,
U.S.A. 72 39 30N 106 2W
Breckenridge, Minn.,
U.S.A. 70 46 20N 96 36W
Breckenridge, Tex.,
U.S.A. 71 32 48N 98 55W
Brecon 7 51 57N 3 23W
Brecon Beacons .. 7 51 53N 3 27W
Breda .... 11 51 35N 4 45 E
Bredasdorp ...... 56 34 33S 20 2 E
Bredbo .... 45 35 58S 149 10 E
Bregenz .... 14 47 30N 9 45 E
Breiðafjörður 20 65 15N 23 15W
Brejo 79 3 41S 42 47W
Bremen .... 14 53 4N 8 47 E
Bremer I. .... 44 12 5S 136 45 E
Bremerhaven ..... 14 53 34N 8 35 E
Bremerton 72 47 30N 122 38W
Brenham 71 30 5N 96 27W
Brenner Pass ..... 14 47 0N 11 30 E
Brent, Canada 62 46 2N 78 29W
Brent, U.K. 7 51 33N 0 18W
Brentwood .... 7 51 37N 0 19 E
Bréscia .... 18 45 33N 10 13 E
Breskens .... 11 51 23N 3 33 E
Breslau = Wrocław 14 51 5N 17 5 E
Bressanone ...... 18 46 43N 11 40 E
Bressay I. 8 60 10N 1 5W
Bresse .... 12 46 50N 5 10 E
Brest, France 12 48 24N 4 31W
Brest, U.S.S.R. .... 22 52 10N 23 40 E
Bretagne 12 48 0N 3 0W
Bretçu .... 15 46 7N 26 18 E
Breton 64 53 7N 114 28W
Breton Sd. 71 29 40N 89 12W
Brett, C. .... 43 35 10S 174 20 E
Brevard 69 35 19N 82 42W
Brewarrina .... 45 30 0S 146 51 E
Brewer 63 44 43N 68 50W
Brewster 72 48 10N 119 51W
Brewton 69 31 9N 87 2W
Breyten .... 57 26 16S 30 0 E
Brezhnev .... 24 55 42N 52 19 E
Bria .... 51 6 30N 21 58 E
Briançon .... 12 44 54N 6 39 E
Bribie I. .... 45 27 0S 152 58 E
Bridgend 7 51 30N 3 35W
Bridgeport, Calif.,
U.S.A. 73 38 14N 119 15W
Bridgeport, Conn.,
U.S.A. 68 41 12N 73 12W
Bridgeport, Nebr.,
U.S.A. 70 41 42N 103 10W
Bridgeport, Tex.,
U.S.A. 71 33 15N 97 45W
Bridger 72 45 20N 108 58W
Bridgeton 68 39 29N 75 10W
Bridgetown,
Australia .... 47 33 58S 116 7 E
Bridgetown,
Barbados 75 13 0N 59 30W
Bridgetown, Canada 63 44 55N 65 18W
Bridgewater,
Canada 63 44 25N 64 31W
Bridgewater, U.S.A. 70 43 34N 97 29W
Bridgewater, C. ... 45 38 23S 141 23 E
Bridgnorth 7 52 33N 2 25W
Bridgwater 7 51 7N 3 0W
Bridlington 6 54 6N 0 11W
Bridport, Australia . 44 40 59S 147 23 E
Bridport, U.K. 7 50 43N 2 45W
Brie, Plaine de la .. 12 48 35N 3 10 E
Brig .... 14 46 18N 7 59 E
Brigg 6 53 33N 0 30W
Briggsdale 70 40 40N 104 20W
Brigham City 72 41 30N 112 1W
Bright .... 45 36 42S 146 56 E
Brighton, Australia . 45 35 5S 138 30 E
Brighton, Canada . 62 44 2N 77 44W
Brighton, U.K. 7 50 50N 0 9W
Brighton, U.S.A. ... 70 39 59N 104 50W
Brilliant 64 49 19N 117 38W
Bríndisi .... 19 40 39N 17 55 E
Brinkley 71 34 55N 91 15W
Brinkworth .... 45 33 42S 138 26 E
Brion, I. 63 47 46N 61 26W
Brisbane .... 45 27 25S 153 2 E
Brisbane → ..... 45 27 24S 153 9 E
Bristol, U.K. 7 51 26N 2 35W
Bristol, Conn.,
U.S.A. 68 41 44N 72 57W
Bristol, S. Dak.,
U.S.A. 70 45 25N 97 43W
Bristol, Tenn., U.S.A. 69 36 36N 82 11W
Bristol B. 60 58 0N 160 0W
Bristol Channel ... 7 51 18N 4 30W
Bristol L. 73 34 23N 116 50W
Bristow 71 35 55N 96 28W
British Columbia □ 64 55 0N 125 15W
British Guiana =
Guyana ■ 78 5 0N 59 0W
British Honduras =
Belize ■ 74 17 0N 88 30W
British Isles 4 55 0N 4 0W
Brits .... 57 25 37S 27 48 E
Britstown .... 56 30 37S 23 30 E
Britt 62 45 46N 80 34W
Brittany = Bretagne 12 48 0N 3 0W
Britton 70 45 50N 97 47W
Brixton .... 44 23 32S 144 57 E
Brlik .... 24 43 40N 73 49 E
Brno .... 14 49 10N 16 35 E
Broad → 69 33 59N 82 39W
Broad Arrow ..... 47 30 23S 121 15 E
Broad B. 8 58 14N 6 16W
Broad Haven 9 54 20N 9 55W
Broad Law 8 55 30N 3 22W
Broad Sd. .... 44 22 0S 149 45 E
Broadhurst Ra. ... 46 22 30S 122 30 E
Broads, The ...... 6 52 45N 1 30 E
Broadus 70 45 28N 105 27W
Broadview 65 50 22N 102 35W
Brochet 65 57 53N 101 40W
Brochet, L. 65 58 36N 101 35W
Brock 65 51 26N 108 43W
Brocken .... 14 51 48N 10 40 E
Brockport 68 43 12N 77 56W
Brockville 62 44 35N 75 41W
Brockway 70 47 18N 105 46W
Brodeur Pen. 61 72 30N 88 10W
Brodick 8 55 34N 5 9W
Brogan 72 44 14N 117 32W
Broken Bow, Nebr.,
U.S.A. 70 41 25N 99 35W
Broken Bow, Okla.,
U.S.A. 71 34 2N 94 43W
Broken Hill =
Kabwe .... 55 14 30S 28 29 E
Broken Hill .... 45 31 58S 141 29 E
Bromfield 7 52 25N 2 45W
Bromley .... 7 51 20N 0 5 E
Brønderslev ...... 21 57 16N 9 57 E
Bronkhorstspruit .. 57 25 46S 28 45 E
Bronte 71 31 54N 100 18W
Bronte Park ...... 44 42 8S 146 30 E

Brookfield

Brookfield 70 39 50N 93 4W
Brookhaven 71 31 40N 90 25W
Brookings, Oreg., U.S.A. 72 42 4N 124 10W
Brookings, S. Dak., U.S.A. 70 44 20N 96 45W
Brookmere 64 49 52N 120 53W
Brooks 64 50 35N 111 55W
Brooks B. 64 50 15N 127 55W
Brooks L. 65 61 55N 106 35W
Brooks Ra. 60 68 40N 147 0W
Brooksville 69 28 32N 82 21W
Brookville 68 39 25N 85 0W
Brooloo 45 26 30S 152 43 E
Broom, L. 8 57 55N 5 15W
Broome 46 18 0S 122 15 E
Broomehill 47 33 51S 117 39 E
Brora 8 58 0N 3 50W
Brora → 8 58 4N 3 52W
Brosna → 9 53 8N 8 0W
Brothers 72 43 56N 120 39W
Broughton Island 61 67 33N 63 0W
Broughty Ferry 8 56 29N 2 50W
Brouwershaven 11 51 45N 3 55 E
Browerville 70 46 3N 94 50W
Brown, Pt. 45 32 32S 133 50 E
Brown Willy 7 50 35N 4 34W
Brownfield 71 33 10N 102 15W
Browning 72 48 35N 113 0W
Brownlee 65 50 43N 106 1W
Brownsville, Oreg., U.S.A. 72 44 29N 123 0W
Brownsville, Tenn., U.S.A. 71 35 35N 89 15W
Brownsville, Tex., U.S.A. 71 25 56N 97 25W
Brownwood 71 31 45N 99 0W
Brownwood, L. 71 31 51N 98 35W
Browse I. 46 14 7S 123 33 E
Bruay-en-Artois 12 50 29N 2 33 E
Bruce, Mt. 46 22 37S 118 8 E
Bruce Rock 47 31 52S 118 8 E
Bruck an der Leitha 14 48 1N 16 47 E
Brue → 7 51 10N 2 59W
Bruges = Brugge 11 51 13N 3 13 E
Brugge 11 51 13N 3 13 E
Brûlé 64 53 15N 117 58W
Brumado 79 14 14S 41 40W
Brunchilly 44 18 50S 134 30 E
Brundidge 69 31 43N 85 45W
Bruneau 72 42 57N 115 55W
Bruneau → 72 42 57N 115 58W
Brunei = Bandar Seri Begawan 34 4 52N 115 0 E
Brunei ■ 34 4 50N 115 0 E
Brunette Downs 44 18 40S 135 55 E
Brunner, L. 43 42 37S 171 27 E
Bruno 65 52 20N 105 30W
Brunsbüttelkoog 14 53 52N 9 13 E
Brunswick = Braunschweig 14 52 17N 10 28 E
Brunswick, Ga., U.S.A. 69 31 10N 81 30W
Brunswick, Maine, U.S.A. 63 43 53N 69 50W
Brunswick, Md., U.S.A. 68 39 20N 77 38W
Brunswick, Mo., U.S.A. 70 39 26N 93 10W
Brunswick, Pen. de 80 53 30S 71 30W
Brunswick B. 46 15 15S 124 50 E
Brunswick Junction 47 33 15S 115 50 E
Bruny I. 44 43 20S 147 15 E
Brush 70 40 17N 103 33W
Brusque 80 27 5S 49 0W
Brussel 11 50 51N 4 21 E
Brussels = Brussel 11 50 51N 4 21 E
Bruthen 45 37 42S 147 50 E
Bruxelles = Brussel 11 50 51N 4 21 E
Bryan, Ohio, U.S.A. 68 41 30N 84 30W
Bryan, Tex., U.S.A. 71 30 40N 96 27W
Bryan, Mt. 45 33 30S 139 0 E
Bryansk 22 53 13N 34 25 E
Bryant 70 44 35N 97 28W
Bryne 21 58 44N 5 38 E
Bryson City 69 35 28N 83 25W
Bu Craa 50 26 45N 12 50W
Buapinang 35 4 40S 121 30 E
Buayan 35 6 3N 125 6 E
Bucak 30 37 28N 30 36 E
Bucaramanga 78 7 0N 73 0W
Buccaneer Arch. 46 16 7S 123 20 E
Buchan 8 57 32N 2 8W
Buchan Ness 8 57 29N 1 48W
Buchanan, Canada 65 51 40N 102 45W
Buchanan, Liberia 50 5 57N 10 2W
Buchanan, L., Queens., Australia 44 21 35S 145 52 E
Buchanan, L., W. Austral., Australia 47 25 33S 123 2 E
Buchanan, L., U.S.A. 71 30 50N 98 25W
Buchans 63 48 50N 56 52W
Bucharest = Bucureşti 15 44 27N 26 10 E
Buckeye 73 33 28N 112 40W
Buckhannon 68 39 2N 80 10W
Buckhaven 8 56 10N 3 2W
Buckie 8 57 40N 2 58W
Buckingham, Canada 62 45 37N 75 24W
Buckingham, U.K. 7 52 0N 0 59W
Buckingham □ 7 51 50N 0 55W
Buckingham B. 44 12 10S 135 40 E
Buckland Newton 7 50 45N 2 25W
Buckle Hd. 46 14 26S 127 52 E
Buckleboo 45 32 54S 136 12 E
Buckley 72 47 10N 122 2W
Bucklin 71 37 37N 99 40W
Buctouche 63 46 30N 64 45W
Bucureşti 15 44 27N 26 10 E
Bucyrus 68 40 48N 83 0W
Budalin 33 22 20N 95 10 E
Budapest 15 47 29N 19 5 E
Bude 7 50 49N 4 33W
Budennovsk 23 44 50N 44 10 E
Budgewoi Lake 45 33 13S 151 34 E
Búðareyri 20 65 2N 14 13W
Búðir 20 64 49N 23 23W
Budjala 54 2 50N 19 40 E
Buea 53 4 10N 9 9 E
Buena Vista, Colo., U.S.A. 73 38 56N 106 6W
Buena Vista, Va., U.S.A. 68 37 47N 79 23W
Buena Vista L. 73 35 15N 119 21W
Buenaventura, Colombia 78 3 53N 77 4W
Buenaventura, Mexico 74 29 50N 107 30W
Buenos Aires 80 34 30S 58 20W
Buenos Aires, L. 80 46 35S 72 30W
Buffalo, Mo., U.S.A. 71 37 40N 93 5W
Buffalo, N.Y., U.S.A. 68 42 55N 78 50W
Buffalo, Okla., U.S.A. 71 36 55N 99 42W
Buffalo, S. Dak., U.S.A. 70 45 39N 103 31W
Buffalo, Wyo., U.S.A. 72 44 25N 106 50W
Buffalo → 64 60 5N 115 5W
Buffalo Head Hills 64 57 25N 115 55W
Buffalo L. 64 52 27N 112 54W
Buffalo Narrows 65 55 51N 108 29W
Buffels → 56 29 36S 17 3 E
Buford 69 34 5N 84 0W
Bug →, Poland 15 52 31N 21 5 E
Bug →, U.S.S.R. 23 46 59N 31 58 E
Buga 78 4 0N 76 15W
Bugel, Tanjung 34 6 26S 111 3 E
Bugsuk 34 8 15N 117 15 E
Bugt 38 48 47N 121 56 E
Bugulma 22 54 33N 52 48 E
Buguma 53 4 42N 6 55 E
Buguruslan 22 53 39N 52 26 E
Buheirat-Murrat-el-Kubra 51 30 15N 32 40 E
Buhl, Idaho, U.S.A. 72 42 35N 114 54W
Buhl, Minn., U.S.A. 70 47 30N 92 46W
Buick 71 37 38N 91 2W
Builth Wells 7 52 10N 3 26W
Buir Nur 37 47 50N 117 42 E
Bujumbura 54 3 16S 29 18 E
Bukachacha 25 52 55N 116 50 E
Bukama 54 9 10S 25 50 E
Bukavu 54 2 20S 28 52 E
Bukene 54 4 15S 32 48 E
Bukhara 24 39 48N 64 25 E
Bukittinggi 34 0 20S 100 20 E
Bukoba 54 1 20S 31 49 E
Bukombe 52 3 31S 32 4 E
Bula 35 3 6S 130 30 E
Bulahdelah 45 32 23S 152 13 E
Bulan 35 12 40N 123 52 E
Bulandshahr 32 28 28N 77 51 E
Bulawayo 55 20 7S 28 32 E
Bulgan 37 48 45N 103 34 E
Bulgaria ■ 19 42 35N 25 30 E
Bulgroo 45 25 47S 143 58 E
Bulgunnia 45 30 10S 134 53 E
Bulhar 29 10 25N 44 30 E
Buli, Teluk 35 1 5N 128 25 E
Buliluyan, C. 34 8 20N 117 15 E
Bulkley → 64 55 15N 127 40W
Bull Shoals L. 71 36 40N 93 5W
Bullara 46 22 40S 114 3 E
Bullaring 47 32 30S 117 45 E
Buller → 43 41 44S 171 36 E
Bulli 45 34 15S 150 57 E
Bullock Creek 44 17 43S 144 31 E
Bulloo → 45 28 43S 142 30 E
Bulloo Downs, Queens., Australia 45 28 31S 142 57 E
Bulloo Downs, W. Austral., Australia 47 24 0S 119 32 E
Bulloo L. 45 28 43S 142 25 E
Bulls 43 40 10S 175 24 E
Bulo Burti 29 3 50N 45 33 E
Bulsar = Valsad 32 20 40N 72 58 E
Bultfontein 56 28 18S 26 10 E
Bulu Karakelong 35 4 35N 126 50 E
Bulukumba 35 5 33S 120 11 E
Bulun 25 70 37N 127 30 E
Bumba 54 2 13N 22 30 E
Bumhpa Bum 33 26 51N 97 14 E
Buna 54 2 58N 39 30 E
Bunbah, Khalīj 51 32 20N 23 15 E
Bunbury 47 33 20S 115 35 E
Buncrana 9 55 8N 7 28W
Bundaberg 45 24 54S 152 22 E
Bundey → 44 21 46S 135 37 E
Bundi 32 25 30N 75 35 E
Bundooma 44 24 54S 134 16 E
Bundoran 9 54 24N 8 17W
Bungil Cr. → 45 27 5S 149 5 E
Bungo-Suidō 36 33 0N 132 15 E
Bungun Shara 37 49 0N 104 0 E
Bunia 54 1 35N 30 20 E
Bunji 32 35 45N 74 40 E
Bunkie 71 31 1N 92 12W
Bunnell 69 29 28N 81 12W
Buntok 34 1 40S 114 58 E
Bununu Dass 53 10 0N 9 31 E
Bunyu 34 3 35N 117 50 E
Buol 35 1 15N 121 32 E
Buon Me Thuot 34 12 40N 108 3 E
Buorkhaya, Mys 25 71 50N 132 40 E
Buqayq 30 26 0N 49 45 E
Buqei'a 28 32 58N 35 20 E
Bur Acaba 29 3 12N 44 20 E
Bûr Safâga 51 26 43N 33 57 E
Bûr Sa'îd 51 31 16N 32 18 E
Bûr Sûdân 51 19 32N 37 9 E
Bura 52 1 4S 39 58 E
Burao 29 9 32N 45 32 E
Buras 71 29 20N 89 33W
Buraydah 30 26 20N 44 8 E
Buraymī, Al Wāhāt al 31 24 10N 55 43 E
Burbank 73 34 9N 118 23W
Burcher 45 33 30S 147 16 E
Burdekin → 44 19 38S 147 25 E
Burdett 64 49 50N 111 32W
Burdur 30 37 45N 30 22 E
Burdwan = Barddhaman 33 23 14N 87 39 E
Bure → 6 52 38N 1 45 E
Bureya → 25 49 27N 129 30 E
Burgas 19 42 33N 27 29 E
Burgenland □ 14 47 20N 16 20 E
Burgeo 63 47 37N 57 38W
Burgersdorp 56 31 0S 26 20 E
Burges, Mt. 47 30 50S 121 5 E
Burgos 13 42 21N 3 41W
Burgsvik 21 57 3N 18 19 E
Burgundy = Bourgogne 12 47 0N 4 50 E
Burias 35 12 55N 123 5 E
Burica, Pta. 75 8 3N 82 51W
Burin, Canada 63 47 1N 55 14W
Būrīn, Jordan 28 32 11N 35 15 E
Buriram 34 15 0N 103 0 E
Burji 51 5 29N 37 51 E
Burkburnett 71 34 7N 98 35W
Burke 72 47 31N 115 56W
Burke → 44 23 12S 139 33 E
Burketown 44 17 45S 139 33 E
Burkina Faso ■ 50 12 0N 1 0W
Burk's Falls 62 45 37N 79 24W
Burley 72 42 37N 113 55W
Burlington, Colo., U.S.A. 70 39 21N 102 18W
Burlington, Iowa, U.S.A. 70 40 50N 91 5W
Burlington, Kans., U.S.A. 70 38 15N 95 47W
Burlington, N.C., U.S.A. 69 36 7N 79 27W
Burlington, N.J., U.S.A. 68 40 5N 74 50W
Burlington, Vt., U.S.A. 68 44 27N 73 14W
Burlington, Wash., U.S.A. 72 48 29N 122 19W
Burlington, Wis., U.S.A. 68 42 41N 88 18W
Burlyu-Tyube 24 46 30N 79 10 E
Burma ■ 33 21 0N 96 30 E
Burnaby I. 64 52 25N 131 19W
Burnet 71 30 45N 98 11W
Burney 72 40 56N 121 41W
Burngup 47 33 2S 118 42 E
Burnie 44 41 4S 145 56 E
Burnley 6 53 47N 2 15W
Burns, Oreg., U.S.A. 72 43 40N 119 4W
Burns, Wyo., U.S.A. 70 41 13N 104 18W
Burns Lake 64 54 20N 125 45W
Burnside → 60 66 51N 108 4W
Burnside, L. 47 25 22S 123 0 E
Burntwood → 65 56 8N 96 34W
Burntwood L. 65 55 22N 100 26W
Burqā 28 32 18N 35 11 E
Burqān 30 29 0N 47 57 E
Burqin 37 47 43N 87 0 E
Burra 45 33 40S 138 55 E
Burramurra 44 20 25S 137 15 E
Burren Junction 45 30 7S 148 59 E
Burrendong Dam 45 32 39S 149 6 E
Burrinjuck Res. 45 35 0S 148 36 E
Burro, Serranías del 74 29 0N 102 0W
Burrundie 46 13 32S 131 42 E
Burruyacú 80 26 30S 64 40W
Burry Port 7 51 41N 4 17W
Bursa 30 40 15N 29 5 E
Burstall 65 50 39N 109 54W
Burton L. 62 54 45N 78 20W
Burton-upon-Trent 6 52 48N 1 39W
Burtundy 45 33 45S 142 15 E
Buru 35 3 30S 126 30 E
Burundi ■ 54 3 15S 30 0 E
Burutu 53 5 20N 5 29 E
Burwell 70 41 49N 99 8W
Bury 6 53 36N 2 19W
Bury St. Edmunds 7 52 15N 0 42 E
Buryat A.S.S.R. □ 25 53 0N 110 0 E
Buşayyah 30 30 0N 46 10 E
Būshehr 31 28 55N 50 55 E
Būshehr □ 31 28 20N 51 45 E
Bushell 65 59 31N 108 45W
Bushire = Būshehr 31 28 55N 50 55 E
Bushnell, Ill., U.S.A. 70 40 32N 90 30W
Bushnell, Nebr., U.S.A. 70 41 18N 103 50W
Businga 54 3 16N 20 59 E
Buskerud fylke □ 21 60 13N 9 0 E
Busra ash Shām 30 32 30N 36 25 E
Busselton 47 33 42S 115 15 E
Bussum 11 52 16N 5 10 E
Busto Arsizio 18 45 40N 8 50 E
Busu-Djanoa 54 1 43N 21 23 E
Busuanga 35 12 10N 120 0 E
Buta 54 2 50N 24 53 E
Butare 54 2 31S 29 52 E
Butaritari 40 3 30N 174 0 E
Bute 8 55 48N 5 2W
Bute Inlet 64 50 40N 124 53W
Butembo 54 0 9N 29 18 E
Butha Qi 38 48 0N 122 32 E
Butler, Mo., U.S.A. 70 38 17N 94 18W
Butler, Pa., U.S.A. 68 40 52N 79 52W
Butte, Mont., U.S.A. 72 46 0N 112 31W
Butte, Nebr., U.S.A. 70 42 56N 98 54W
Butterworth = Gcuwa 57 32 20S 28 11 E
Butterworth 34 5 24N 100 23 E
Buttfield, Mt. 47 24 45S 128 9 E
Button B. 65 58 45N 94 23W
Butty Hd. 47 33 54S 121 39 E
Butuan 35 8 57N 125 33 E
Butung 35 5 0S 122 45 E
Buturlinovka 23 50 50N 40 35 E
Buxton, S. Africa 56 27 38S 24 42 E
Buxton, U.K. 6 53 16N 1 54W
Buy 22 58 28N 41 28 E
Buyaga 25 59 50N 127 0 E
Buzău 15 45 10N 26 50 E
Buzău → 15 45 26N 27 44 E
Buzen 36 33 35N 131 5 E
Buzi → 55 19 50S 34 43 E
Buzuluk 22 52 48N 52 12 E
Buzzards Bay 68 41 45N 70 38W
Bydgoszcz 15 53 10N 18 0 E
Byelorussian S.S.R. □ 22 53 30N 27 0 E
Byers 70 39 46N 104 13W
Byhalia 71 34 53N 89 41W
Bylas 73 33 11N 110 9W
Bylot I. 61 73 13N 78 34W
Byro 47 26 5S 116 11 E
Byrock 45 30 40S 146 27 E
Byron Bay 45 28 43S 153 37 E
Byrranga, Gory 25 75 0N 100 0 E
Byske 20 64 57N 21 11 E
Byske älv → 20 64 57N 21 13 E
Bytom 15 50 25N 18 54 E

C

Ca Mau = Quan Long 34 9 7N 105 8 E
Caála 55 12 46S 15 30 E
Caamano Sd. 64 52 55N 129 25W
Cabanatuan 35 15 30N 120 58 E
Cabano 63 47 40N 68 56W
Cabedelo 79 7 0S 34 50W
Cabimas 78 10 23N 71 25W
Cabinda 54 5 33S 12 11 E
Cabinda □ 54 5 0S 12 30 E
Cabinet Mts. 72 48 0N 115 30W
Cabo Blanco 80 47 15S 65 47W
Cabo Frio 79 22 51S 42 3W
Cabo Pantoja 78 1 0S 75 10W
Cabonga, Réservoir 62 47 20N 76 40W
Cabool 71 37 10N 92 8W
Caboolture 45 27 5S 152 58 E
Cabora Bassa Dam 55 15 20S 32 50 E
Caborca 74 30 40N 112 10W
Cabot Strait 63 47 15N 59 40W
Cabrera, I. 13 39 8N 2 57 E
Cabri 65 50 35N 108 25W
Cabriel → 13 39 14N 1 3W
Čačak 19 43 54N 20 20 E
Cáceres, Brazil 78 16 5S 57 40W
Cáceres, Spain 13 39 26N 6 23W
Cache Bay 62 46 22N 80 0W
Cachimbo, Serra do 79 9 30S 55 0W
Cachoeira 79 12 30S 39 0W
Cachoeira de Itapemirim 79 20 51S 41 7W
Cachoeira do Sul 80 30 3S 52 53W
Cacólo 54 10 9S 19 21 E
Caconda 55 13 48S 15 8 E
Cacongo 54 5 11S 12 5 E
Caddo 71 34 8N 96 18W
Cadell Cr. → 44 22 35S 141 51 E
Cader Idris 6 52 43N 3 56W
Cadibarrawirracanna, L. 45 28 52S 135 27 E
Cadillac, Canada 62 48 14N 78 23W
Cadillac, U.S.A. 68 44 16N 85 25W
Cadiz, Phil. 35 10 57N 123 15 E
Cádiz, Spain 13 36 30N 6 20W
Cádiz, G. de 13 36 40N 7 0W
Cadney Park 45 27 55S 134 3 E
Cadomin 64 53 2N 117 20W
Cadotte → 64 56 43N 117 10W
Cadoux 47 30 46S 117 7 E
Caen 12 49 10N 0 22W
Caernarfon 6 53 8N 4 17W
Caernarfon B. 6 53 4N 4 40W
Caernarvon = Caernarfon 6 53 8N 4 17W
Caerphilly 7 51 34N 3 13W
Caesarea 28 32 30N 34 53 E
Caeté 79 19 55S 43 40W
Caetité 79 13 50S 42 32W
Cafu 56 16 30S 15 8 E
Cagayan → 35 18 25N 121 42 E
Cagayan de Oro 35 8 30N 124 40 E
Cágliari 18 39 15N 9 6 E
Cágliari, G. di 18 39 8N 9 10 E
Caguas 75 18 14N 66 4W
Caha Mts. 9 51 45N 9 40W
Cahama 56 16 17S 14 19 E
Caher 9 52 23N 7 56W
Cahersiveen 9 51 57N 10 13W
Cahore Pt. 9 52 34N 6 11W
Cahors 12 44 27N 1 27 E
Cahuapanas 78 5 15S 77 0W
Caia 55 17 51S 35 24 E
Caibarién 75 22 30N 79 30W
Caicara 78 7 38N 66 10W
Caicó 79 6 20S 37 0W
Caicos Is. 75 21 40N 71 40W
Caicos Passage 75 22 45N 72 45W
Cairn Gorm 8 57 7N 3 40W
Cairn Toul 8 57 3N 3 44W
Cairngorm Mts. 8 57 6N 3 42W
Cairns 44 16 57S 145 45 E
Cairo = El Qâhira 51 30 1N 31 14 E
Cairo, Ga., U.S.A. 69 30 52N 84 12W
Cairo, Ill., U.S.A. 71 37 0N 89 10W
Caithness, Ord of 8 58 9N 3 37W
Caiundo 55 15 50S 17 28 E
Caiza 78 20 2S 65 40W
Cajamarca 78 7 5S 78 28W
Cajàzeiras 79 6 52S 38 30W
Calabar 53 4 57N 8 20 E
Calábria □ 18 39 24N 16 30 E
Calafate 80 50 19S 72 15W
Calahorra 13 42 18N 1 59W
Calais, France 12 50 57N 1 56 E
Calais, U.S.A. 63 45 11N 67 20W
Calama, Brazil 78 8 0S 62 50W
Calama, Chile 80 22 30S 68 55W
Calamar, Bolívar, Colombia 78 10 15N 74 55W
Calamar, Vaupés, Colombia 78 1 58N 72 32W
Calamian Group 35 11 50N 119 55 E
Calamocha 13 40 50N 1 17W
Calang 34 4 37N 95 37 E
Calapan 35 13 25N 121 7 E
Calatayud 13 41 20N 1 40W
Calauag 35 13 55N 122 15 E
Calavite, Cape 35 13 26N 120 20 E
Calbayog 35 12 4N 124 38 E
Calca 78 13 22S 72 0W
Calcasieu L. 71 30 0N 93 17W
Calcutta 33 22 36N 88 24 E
Calder → 6 53 44N 1 21W
Caldera 80 27 5S 70 55W
Caldwell, Idaho, U.S.A. 72 43 45N 116 42W

Clipperton, I.

Cherryvale 71 37 20N 95 33W
Cherskiy 25 68 45N 161 18 E
Cherskogo Khrebet 25 65 0N 143 0 E
Cherwell → 7 51 46N 1 18W
Chesapeake 68 36 43N 76 15W
Chesapeake Bay 68 38 0N 76 12W
Cheshire □ 6 53 14N 2 30W
Cheshskaya Guba 22 67 20N 47 0 E
Cheslatta L. 64 53 49N 125 20W
Chester, U.K. 6 53 12N 2 53W
Chester, Calif., U.S.A. 72 40 22N 121 14W
Chester, Ill., U.S.A. 71 37 58N 89 50W
Chester, Mont., U.S.A. 72 48 31N 111 0W
Chester, Pa., U.S.A. 68 39 54N 75 20W
Chester, S.C., U.S.A. 69 34 44N 81 13W
Chesterfield 6 53 14N 1 26W
Chesterfield, Îles 40 19 52S 158 15 E
Chesterfield Inlet 60 63 30N 90 45W
Chesterton Range 45 25 30S 147 27 E
Chesuncook L. 63 46 0N 69 10W
Chéticamp 63 46 37N 60 59W
Chetumal 74 18 30N 88 20W
Chetumal, B. de 74 18 40N 88 10W
Chetwynd 64 55 45N 121 36W
Cheviot, The 6 55 29N 2 8W
Cheviot Hills 6 55 20N 2 30W
Cheviot Ra. 44 25 20S 143 45 E
Chew Bahir 51 4 40N 36 50 E
Chewelah 72 48 17N 117 43W
Cheyenne, Okla., U.S.A. 71 35 35N 99 40W
Cheyenne, Wyo., U.S.A. 70 41 9N 104 49W
Cheyenne → 70 44 40N 101 15W
Cheyenne Wells 70 38 51N 102 10W
Cheyne B. 47 34 35S 118 50 E
Chhapra 33 25 48N 84 44 E
Chhatarpur 32 24 55N 79 35 E
Chhindwara 32 22 2N 78 59 E
Chhlong 34 12 15N 105 58 E
Chi → 34 15 11N 104 43 E
Chiamis 35 7 20S 108 21 E
Chiamussu = Jiamusi 38 46 40N 130 26 E
Chiange 55 15 35S 13 40 E
Chiapa → 74 16 42N 93 0W
Chiapas □ 74 17 0N 92 45W
Chiba 36 35 30N 140 7 E
Chiba □ 36 35 30N 140 20 E
Chibabava 57 20 17S 33 35 E
Chibatu 35 7 6S 107 59 E
Chibemba, Cunene, Angola 55 15 48S 14 8 E
Chibemba, Huila, Angola 56 16 20S 15 20 E
Chibia 55 15 10S 13 42 E
Chibougamau 62 49 56N 74 24W
Chibougamau L. 62 49 50N 74 20W
Chibuk 53 10 52N 12 50 E
Chic-Chocs, Mts. 63 48 55N 66 0W
Chicacole = Srikakulam 33 18 14N 83 58 E
Chicago 68 41 53N 87 40W
Chicago Heights 68 41 29N 87 37W
Chichagof I. 64 58 0N 136 0W
Chichester 7 50 50N 0 47W
Chichibu 36 36 5N 139 10 E
Ch'ich'ihaerh = Qiqihar 38 47 26N 124 0 E
Chickasha 71 35 0N 98 0W
Chiclana de la Frontera 13 36 26N 6 9W
Chiclayo 78 6 42S 79 50W
Chico 72 39 45N 121 54W
Chico →, Chubut, Argentina 80 44 0S 67 0W
Chico →, Santa Cruz, Argentina 80 50 0S 68 30W
Chicomo 57 24 31S 34 6 E
Chicopee 68 42 6N 72 37W
Chicoutimi 63 48 28N 71 5W
Chicualacuala 57 22 6S 31 42 E
Chidambaram 32 11 20N 79 45 E
Chidenguele 57 24 55S 34 11 E
Chidley, C. 61 60 23N 64 26W
Chiede 56 17 15S 16 22 E
Chiengi 54 8 45S 29 10 E
Chiese → 18 45 8N 10 25 E
Chieti 18 42 22N 14 10 E
Chifeng 38 42 18N 118 58 E
Chignecto B. 63 45 30N 64 40W
Chiguana 78 21 0S 67 58W
Chihli, G. of = Bo Hai 38 39 0N 120 0 E
Chihuahua 74 28 40N 106 3W
Chihuahua □ 74 28 40N 106 3W
Chiili 24 44 20N 66 15 E
Chik Bollapur 32 13 25N 77 45 E
Chikmagalur 32 13 15N 75 45 E
Chilako → 64 53 53N 122 57W
Chilapa 74 17 40N 99 11W
Chilas 32 35 25N 74 5 E
Chilaw 32 7 30N 79 50 E
Chilcotin → 64 51 44N 122 23W
Childers 45 25 15S 152 17 E
Childress 71 34 30N 100 15W
Chile ■ 80 35 0S 72 0W
Chile Rise 41 38 0S 92 0W
Chilete 78 7 10S 78 50W
Chililabombwe 55 12 18S 27 43 E
Chilin = Jilin 38 43 44N 126 30 E
Chilka L. 33 19 40N 85 25 E
Chilko → 64 52 0N 123 40W
Chilko, L. 64 51 20N 124 10W
Chillagoe 44 17 7S 144 33 E
Chillán 80 36 40S 72 10W
Chillicothe, Ill., U.S.A. 70 40 55N 89 32W
Chillicothe, Mo., U.S.A. 70 39 45N 93 30W
Chillicothe, Ohio, U.S.A. 68 39 20N 82 58W
Chilliwack 64 49 10N 121 54W
Chiloane, I. 57 20 40S 34 55 E
Chiloé, I. de 80 42 30S 73 50W
Chilpancingo 74 17 30N 99 30W
Chiltern Hills 7 51 44N 0 42W
Chilton 68 44 1N 88 12W
Chiluage 54 9 30S 21 50 E
Chilumba 52 10 28S 34 12 E
Chilwa, L. 55 15 15S 35 40 E
Chimay 11 50 3N 4 20 E
Chimbay 24 42 57N 59 47 E
Chimborazo 78 1 29S 78 55W
Chimbote 78 9 0S 78 35W
Chimkent 24 42 18N 69 36 E
Chimoio 55 19 4S 33 30 E
Chin □ 33 22 0N 93 0 E
Chin Ling Shan = Qinling Shandi 39 33 50N 108 10 E
China 74 25 40N 99 20W
China ■ 37 30 0N 110 0 E
Chinan = Jinan 38 36 38N 117 1 E
Chinandega 75 12 35N 87 12W
Chinati Pk. 71 30 0N 104 25W
Chincha Alta 78 13 25S 76 7W
Chinchilla 45 26 45S 150 38 E
Chinchón 13 40 9N 3 26W
Chinchorro, Banco 74 18 35N 87 20W
Chinchou = Jinzhou 38 41 5N 121 3 E
Chincoteague 68 37 58N 75 21W
Chinde 55 18 35S 36 30 E
Chindwin → 33 21 26N 95 15 E
Chingola 55 12 31S 27 53 E
Ch'ingtao = Qingdao 38 36 5N 120 20 E
Chinguetti 50 20 25N 12 24W
Chingune 57 20 33S 35 0 E
Chinhae 38 35 9N 128 47 E
Chinhanguanine 57 25 21S 32 30 E
Chinhoyi 55 17 20S 30 8 E
Chiniot 32 31 45N 73 0 E
Chinju 38 35 12N 128 2 E
Chinle 73 36 14N 109 38W
Chinnampo 38 38 52N 125 10 E
Chino Valley 73 34 54N 112 28W
Chinon 12 47 10N 0 15 E
Chinook, Canada 65 51 28N 110 59W
Chinook, U.S.A. 72 48 35N 109 19W
Chinsali 54 10 30S 32 2 E
Chinteche 52 11 50S 34 5 E
Chióggia 18 45 13N 12 15 E
Chíos = Khíos 19 38 27N 26 9 E
Chipata 55 13 38S 32 28 E
Chipatujah 35 7 45S 108 0 E
Chipewyan L. 65 58 0N 98 27W
Chipley 69 30 45N 85 32W
Chipman 63 46 6N 65 53W
Chippenham 7 51 27N 2 7W
Chippewa → 70 44 25N 92 10W
Chippewa Falls 70 44 55N 91 22W
Chiquián 78 10 10S 77 0W
Chiquimula 75 14 51N 89 37W
Chiquinquira 78 5 37N 73 50W
Chirala 32 15 50N 80 26 E
Chirchik 24 41 29N 69 35 E
Chiricahua Pk. 73 31 53N 109 14W
Chirikof I. 60 55 50N 155 40W
Chiriquí, G. de 75 8 0N 82 10W
Chiriquí, L. de 75 9 10N 82 0W
Chirmiri 33 23 15N 82 20 E
Chiromo 55 16 30S 35 7 E
Chirripó Grande, Cerro 75 9 29N 83 29W
Chisamba 55 14 55S 28 20 E
Chisapani Garhi 33 27 30N 84 2 E
Chisholm 64 54 55N 114 10W
Chisos Mts. 71 29 20N 103 15W
Chistopol 22 55 25N 50 38 E
Chita 25 52 0N 113 35 E
Chitado 55 17 10S 14 8 E
Chitembo 55 13 30S 16 50 E
Chitral 31 35 50N 71 56 E
Chitré 75 7 59N 80 27W
Chittagong 33 22 19N 91 48 E
Chittagong □ 33 24 5N 91 0 E
Chittaurgarh 32 24 52N 74 38 E
Chittoor 32 13 15N 79 5 E
Chiusi 18 43 1N 11 58 E
Chivasso 18 45 10N 7 52 E
Chivilcoy 80 34 55S 60 0W
Chkalov = Orenburg 22 51 45N 55 6 E
Chobe National Park 56 18 0S 25 0 E
Choele Choel 80 39 11S 65 40W
Choix 74 26 40N 108 23W
Chojnice 15 53 42N 17 32 E
Chokurdakh 25 70 38N 147 55 E
Cholet 12 47 4N 0 52W
Choluteca 75 13 20N 87 14W
Choma 55 16 48S 26 59 E
Chomutov 14 50 28N 13 23 E
Chon Buri 34 13 21N 101 1 E
Chonan 38 36 48N 127 9 E
Chone 78 0 40S 80 0W
Chong'an 39 27 45N 118 0 E
Chongde 39 30 32N 120 26 E
Chongjin 38 41 47N 129 50 E
Chŏngju, N. Korea 38 39 40N 125 5 E
Chŏngju, S. Korea 38 36 39N 127 27 E
Chongli 38 40 58N 115 15 E
Chongming Dao 39 31 40N 121 30 E
Chongqing 39 29 35N 106 25 E
Chongzuo 39 22 23N 107 20 E
Chŏnju 38 35 50N 127 4 E
Chonos, Arch. de los 80 45 0S 75 0W
Chorley 6 53 39N 2 39W
Chorregon 44 22 40S 143 32 E
Chorrera, La 74 8 50N 79 50W
Chŏrwŏn 38 38 15N 127 10 E
Chorzów 15 50 18N 18 57 E
Chos-Malal 80 37 20S 70 15W
Chosan 38 40 50N 125 47 E
Chōshi 36 35 45N 140 51 E
Choszczno 14 53 7N 15 25 E
Choteau 72 47 50N 112 10W
Chotila 32 22 23N 71 15 E
Chowchilla 73 37 11N 120 12W
Choybalsan 37 48 4N 114 30 E
Christchurch, N.Z. 43 43 33S 172 47 E
Christchurch, U.K. 7 50 44N 1 33W
Christiana 56 27 52S 25 8 E
Christie B. 65 62 32N 111 10W
Christina → 65 56 40N 111 3W
Christmas Cr. → 46 18 29S 125 23 E
Christmas Creek 46 18 29S 125 23 E
Christmas I. = Kiritimati 2 1 58N 157 27W
Christmas I. 3 10 30S 105 40 E
Christopher L. 47 24 49S 127 42 E
Chu 24 43 36N 73 42 E
Chu Chua 64 51 22N 120 10W
Ch'uanchou = Quanzhou 39 24 55N 118 34 E
Chūbu □ 36 36 45N 137 30 E
Chubut → 80 43 20S 65 5W
Chuchi L. 64 55 12N 124 30W
Chudskoye, Oz. 22 58 13N 27 30 E
Chūgoku □ 36 35 0N 133 0 E
Chūgoku-Sanchi 36 35 0N 133 0 E
Chugwater 70 41 48N 104 47W
Chuka 52 0 23S 37 38 E
Chukotskiy Khrebet 25 68 0N 175 0 E
Chukotskoye More 25 68 0N 175 0W
Chula Vista 73 32 39N 117 8W
Chulman 25 56 52N 124 52 E
Chulucanas 78 5 8S 80 10W
Chulym → 24 57 43N 83 51 E
Chumbicha 80 29 0S 66 10W
Chumikan 25 54 40N 135 10 E
Chumphon 34 10 35N 99 14 E
Chuna → 25 57 47N 94 37 E
Chun'an 39 29 35N 119 3 E
Chunchŏn 38 37 58N 127 44 E
Chungking = Chongqing 39 29 35N 106 25 E
Chunya 54 8 30S 33 27 E
Chuquibamba 78 15 47S 72 44W
Chuquicamata 80 22 15S 69 0W
Chuquisaca □ 78 23 30S 63 30W
Chur 14 46 52N 9 32 E
Churachandpur 33 24 20N 93 40 E
Churchill 65 58 47N 94 11W
Churchill →, Man., Canada 65 58 47N 94 12W
Churchill →, Nfld., Canada 63 53 19N 60 10W
Churchill, C. 65 58 46N 93 12W
Churchill Falls 63 53 36N 64 19W
Churchill L. 65 55 55N 108 20W
Churchill Pk. 64 58 10N 125 10W
Churu 32 28 20N 74 50 E
Chushal 32 33 40N 78 40 E
Chusovoy 22 58 15N 57 40 E
Chuvash A.S.S.R.□ 22 55 30N 47 0 E
Ci Xian 38 36 20N 114 25 E
Cianjur 35 6 49S 107 8 E
Cibadok 35 6 53S 106 47 E
Cibatu 35 7 8S 107 59 E
Cicero 68 41 48N 87 48W
Ciechanów 15 52 52N 20 38 E
Ciego de Avila 75 21 50N 78 50W
Ciénaga 78 11 1N 74 15W
Cienfuegos 75 22 10N 80 30W
Cieszyn 15 49 45N 18 35 E
Cieza 13 38 17N 1 23W
Cijulang 35 7 42S 108 27 E
Cikajang 35 7 25S 107 48 E
Cikampek 35 6 23S 107 28 E
Cilacap 35 7 43S 109 0 E
Cilician Gates P. 30 37 20N 34 52 E
Cimahi 35 6 53S 107 33 E
Cimarron, Kans., U.S.A. 71 37 50N 100 20W
Cimarron, N. Mex., U.S.A. 71 36 30N 104 52W
Cimarron → 71 36 10N 96 17W
Cimone, Mte. 18 44 10N 10 40 E
Cîmpina 15 45 10N 25 45 E
Cîmpulung 15 45 17N 25 3 E
Cinca → 13 41 26N 0 21 E
Cincinnati 68 39 10N 84 26W
Ciney 11 50 18N 5 5 E
Cinto, Mte. 12 42 24N 8 54 E
Circle, Alaska, U.S.A. 60 65 50N 144 10W
Circle, Mont., U.S.A. 70 47 26N 105 35W
Circleville, Ohio, U.S.A. 68 39 35N 82 57W
Circleville, Utah, U.S.A. 73 38 12N 112 24W
Cirebon 35 6 45S 108 32 E
Cirencester 7 51 43N 1 59W
Cisco 71 32 25N 99 0W
Ciskei □ 57 33 0S 27 0 E
Citlaltépetl 74 19 0N 97 20W
Citrusdal 56 32 35S 19 0 E
Ciudad Altamirano 74 18 20N 100 40W
Ciudad Bolívar 78 8 5N 63 36W
Ciudad Camargo 74 27 41N 105 10W
Ciudad de Valles 74 22 0N 99 0W
Ciudad del Carmen 74 18 38N 91 50W
Ciudad Delicias = Delicias 74 28 10N 105 30W
Ciudad Guayana 78 8 0N 62 30W
Ciudad Guerrero 74 28 33N 107 28W
Ciudad Guzmán 74 19 40N 103 30W
Ciudad Juárez 74 31 40N 106 28W
Ciudad Madero 74 22 19N 97 50W
Ciudad Mante 74 22 50N 99 0W
Ciudad Obregón 74 27 28N 109 59W
Ciudad Real 13 38 59N 3 55W
Ciudad Rodrigo 13 40 35N 6 32W
Ciudad Trujillo = Santo Domingo 75 18 30N 69 59W
Ciudad Victoria 74 23 41N 99 9W
Civitanova Marche 18 43 18N 13 41 E
Civitavécchia 18 42 6N 11 46 E
Çivril 30 38 20N 29 43 E
Cizre 30 37 19N 42 10 E
Clackline 47 31 40S 116 32 E
Clacton-on-Sea 7 51 47N 1 10 E
Claire, L. 64 58 35N 112 5W
Clairemont 71 33 9N 100 44W
Clanton 69 32 48N 86 36W
Clanwilliam 56 32 11S 18 52 E
Clara 9 53 20N 7 38W
Clara → 44 19 8S 142 30 E
Clare, Australia 45 33 50S 138 37 E
Clare, U.S.A. 68 43 47N 84 45W
Clare □ 9 52 20N 9 0W
Clare → 9 53 22N 9 5W
Clare I. 9 53 48N 10 0W
Claremont 68 43 23N 72 20W
Claremont Pt. 44 14 1S 143 41 E
Claremore 71 36 40N 95 37W
Claremorris 9 53 45N 9 0W
Clarence →, Australia 45 29 25S 153 22 E
Clarence →, N.Z. 43 42 10S 173 56 E
Clarence, I. 80 54 0S 72 0W
Clarence Str., Australia 46 12 0S 131 0 E
Clarence Str., U.S.A. 64 55 40N 132 10W
Clarendon, Ark., U.S.A. 71 34 41N 91 20W
Clarendon, Tex., U.S.A. 71 34 58N 100 54W
Clarenville 63 48 10N 54 1W
Claresholm 64 50 0N 113 33W
Clarinda 70 40 45N 95 0W
Clarion 70 42 41N 93 46W
Clarion Fracture Zone 41 20 0N 120 0W
Clark 70 44 55N 97 45W
Clark Fork 72 48 9N 116 9W
Clark Fork → 72 48 9N 116 15W
Clark Hill Res. 69 33 45N 82 20W
Clarkdale 73 34 53N 112 3W
Clarke City 63 50 12N 66 38W
Clarke I. 44 40 32S 148 10 E
Clarke L. 65 54 24N 106 54W
Clarke Ra. 44 20 45S 148 20 E
Clark's Fork → 72 45 39N 108 43W
Clark's Harbour 63 43 25N 65 38W
Clarksburg 68 39 18N 80 21W
Clarksdale 71 34 12N 90 33W
Clarkston 72 46 28N 117 2W
Clarksville, Ark., U.S.A. 71 35 29N 93 27W
Clarksville, Tenn., U.S.A. 69 36 32N 87 20W
Clarksville, Tex., U.S.A. 71 33 37N 94 59W
Clatskanie 72 46 9N 123 12W
Claude 71 35 8N 101 22W
Claveria 35 18 37N 121 4 E
Clay Center 70 39 27N 97 9W
Claypool 73 33 27N 110 55W
Clayton, Idaho, U.S.A. 72 44 12N 114 31W
Clayton, N. Mex., U.S.A. 71 36 30N 103 10W
Cle Elum 72 47 15N 120 57W
Clear, C. 9 51 26N 9 30W
Clear I. 9 51 26N 9 30W
Clear L. 72 39 5N 122 47W
Clear Lake, S. Dak., U.S.A. 70 44 48N 96 41W
Clear Lake, Wash., U.S.A. 72 48 27N 122 15W
Clear Lake Res. 72 41 55N 121 10W
Clearfield, Pa., U.S.A. 68 41 0N 78 27W
Clearfield, Utah, U.S.A. 72 41 10N 112 0W
Clearmont 72 44 43N 106 29W
Clearwater, Canada 64 51 38N 120 2W
Clearwater, U.S.A. 69 27 58N 82 45W
Clearwater →, Alta., Canada 64 52 22N 114 57W
Clearwater →, Alta., Canada 65 56 44N 111 23W
Clearwater Cr. → 64 61 36N 125 30W
Clearwater Mts. 72 46 20N 115 30W
Clearwater Prov. Park 65 54 0N 101 0W
Cleburne 71 32 18N 97 25W
Cleethorpes 6 53 33N 0 2W
Cleeve Cloud 7 51 56N 2 0W
Clerke Reef 46 17 22S 119 20 E
Clermont 44 22 49S 147 39 E
Clermont-Ferrand 12 45 46N 3 4 E
Clervaux 11 50 4N 6 2 E
Cleveland, Australia 45 27 30S 153 15 E
Cleveland, Miss., U.S.A. 71 33 43N 90 43W
Cleveland, Ohio, U.S.A. 68 41 28N 81 43W
Cleveland, Okla., U.S.A. 71 36 21N 96 33W
Cleveland, Tenn., U.S.A. 69 35 9N 84 52W
Cleveland, Tex., U.S.A. 71 30 18N 95 0W
Cleveland □ 6 54 35N 1 8 E
Cleveland, C. 44 19 11S 147 1 E
Clew B. 9 53 54N 9 50W
Clewiston 69 26 44N 80 50W
Clifden, Ireland 9 53 30N 10 2W
Clifden, N.Z. 43 46 1S 167 42 E
Clifton, Australia 45 27 59S 151 53 E
Clifton, Ariz., U.S.A. 73 33 8N 109 23W
Clifton, Tex., U.S.A. 71 31 46N 97 35W
Clifton Beach 44 16 46S 145 39 E
Clifton Forge 68 37 49N 79 51W
Clifton Hills 45 27 1S 138 54 E
Climax 65 49 10N 108 20W
Clinch → 69 36 0N 84 29W
Clingmans Dome 69 35 35N 83 30W
Clint 73 31 37N 106 11W
Clinton, B.C., Canada 64 51 6N 121 35W
Clinton, Ont., Canada 62 43 37N 81 32W
Clinton, N.Z. 43 46 12S 169 23 E
Clinton, Ark., U.S.A. 71 35 37N 92 30W
Clinton, Ill., U.S.A. 70 40 8N 89 0W
Clinton, Ind., U.S.A. 68 39 40N 87 22W
Clinton, Iowa, U.S.A. 70 41 50N 90 12W
Clinton, Mass., U.S.A. 68 42 26N 71 40W
Clinton, Mo., U.S.A. 70 38 20N 93 46W
Clinton, N.C., U.S.A. 69 35 5N 78 15W
Clinton, Okla., U.S.A. 71 35 30N 99 0W
Clinton, S.C., U.S.A. 69 34 30N 81 54W
Clinton, Tenn., U.S.A. 69 36 6N 84 10W
Clinton C. 44 22 30S 150 45 E
Clinton Colden L. 60 63 58N 107 27W
Clintonville 70 44 35N 88 46W
Clipperton, I. 41 10 18N 109 13W

Clipperton Fracture Zone

Clipperton Fracture Zone 41 19 0N 122 0W
Clive L. 64 63 13N 118 54W
Cloates, Pt. 46 22 43S 113 40 E
Clocolan 57 28 55S 27 34 E
Clonakilty 9 51 37N 8 53W
Clonakilty B. 9 51 33N 8 50W
Cloncurry 44 20 40S 140 28 E
Cloncurry → 44 18 37S 140 40 E
Clones 9 54 10N 7 13W
Clonmel 9 52 22N 7 42W
Cloquet 70 46 40N 92 30W
Cloud Peak 72 44 23N 107 10W
Cloudcroft 73 33 0N 105 48W
Cloverdale 72 38 49N 123 0W
Clovis, Calif., U.S.A. 73 36 47N 119 45W
Clovis, N. Mex., U.S.A. 71 34 20N 103 10W
Cluj-Napoca 17 46 47N 23 38 E
Clunes 45 37 20S 143 45 E
Cluny 12 46 26N 4 38 E
Clutha → 43 46 20S 169 49 E
Clwyd □ 6 53 5N 3 20W
Clwyd → 6 53 20N 3 30W
Clyde 43 45 12S 169 20 E
Clyde → 8 55 56N 4 29W
Clyde, Firth of 8 55 20N 5 0W
Clyde River 61 70 30N 68 30W
Clydebank 8 55 54N 4 25W
Coachella 73 33 44N 116 13W
Coahoma 71 32 17N 101 20W
Coahuayana → 74 18 41N 103 45W
Coahuila □ 74 27 0N 103 0W
Coal → 64 59 39N 126 57W
Coalcomán 74 18 40N 103 10W
Coaldale 64 49 45N 112 35W
Coalgate 71 34 35N 96 13W
Coalinga 73 36 10N 120 21W
Coalville, U.K. 6 52 43N 1 21W
Coalville, U.S.A. 72 40 58N 111 24W
Coari 78 4 8S 63 7W
Coast Mts. 64 40 0N 123 0W
Coast Ranges 72 41 0N 123 0W
Coastal Plains Basin 47 30 10S 115 30 E
Coatbridge 8 55 52N 4 2W
Coatepeque 75 14 46N 91 55W
Coatesville 68 39 59N 75 55W
Coaticook 63 45 10N 71 46W
Coats I. 61 62 30N 83 0W
Coatzacoalcos 74 18 7N 94 25W
Cobalt 62 47 25N 79 42W
Cobán 75 15 30N 90 21W
Cobar 45 31 27S 145 48 E
Cóbh 9 51 50N 8 18W
Cobham 45 30 18S 142 7 E
Cobija 78 11 0S 68 50W
Cobleskill 68 42 40N 74 30W
Cobourg 62 43 58N 78 10W
Cobourg Pen. 46 11 20S 132 15 E
Cobram 45 35 54S 145 40 E
Cobre 72 41 6N 114 25W
Cóbué 55 12 0S 34 58 E
Coburg 14 50 15N 10 58 E
Cocanada = Kakinada 33 16 57N 82 11 E
Cocha, La 80 27 50S 65 40W
Cochabamba 78 17 26S 66 10W
Cochin 32 9 59N 76 22 E
Cochin China = Nam-Phan 34 10 30N 106 0 E
Cochise 73 32 6N 109 58W
Cochran 69 32 25N 83 23W
Cochrane, Alta., Canada 64 51 11N 114 30W
Cochrane, Ont., Canada 62 49 0N 81 0W
Cochrane → 65 59 0N 103 40W
Cochrane, L. 80 47 10S 72 0W
Cockburn 45 32 5S 141 0 E
Cockburn, Canal 80 54 30S 72 0W
Cockburn I. 62 45 55N 83 22W
Cockburn Ra. 46 15 46S 128 0 E
Cocklebiddy Motel 47 32 0S 126 3 E
Coco → 75 15 0N 83 8W
Coco Solo 74 9 22N 79 53W
Cocoa 69 28 22N 80 40W
Cocobeach 54 0 59N 9 34 E
Cocos I. 41 5 25N 87 55W
Cocos Is. 3 12 10S 96 55 E
Cod, C. 67 42 8N 70 10W
Codajás 78 3 55S 62 0W
Coderre 65 50 11N 106 31W
Codó 79 4 30S 43 55W
Cody 72 44 35N 109 0W
Coe Hill 62 44 52N 77 50W
Coen 44 13 52S 143 12 E
Coetivy Is. 3 7 8S 56 16 E
Cœur d'Alene 72 47 45N 116 51W
Cœur d'Alene L. 72 47 32N 116 48W
Coevorden 11 52 40N 6 44 E
Coffeyville 71 37 0N 95 40W
Coffs Harbour 45 30 16S 153 5 E
Coghinas → 18 40 55N 8 48 E
Cognac 12 45 41N 0 20W
Cohagen 72 47 2N 106 36W
Cohoes 68 42 47N 73 42W
Cohuna 45 35 45S 144 15 E
Coiba, I. 75 7 30N 81 40W
Coig → 80 51 0S 69 10W
Coihaique 80 45 30S 71 45W
Coimbatore 32 11 2N 76 59 E
Coimbra, Brazil 78 19 55S 57 48W
Coimbra, Portugal 13 40 15N 8 27W
Coín 13 36 40N 4 48W
Cojimies 78 0 20N 80 0W
Cojutepequé 75 13 41N 88 54W
Cokeville 72 42 4N 111 0W
Colac 45 38 21S 143 35 E
Colatina 79 19 32S 40 37W
Colbinabbin 45 36 38S 144 48 E
Colby 70 39 27N 101 2W
Colchester 7 51 54N 0 55 E
Coldstream 8 55 39N 2 14W
Coldwater 71 37 18N 99 24W
Colebrook, Australia 44 42 31S 147 21 E
Colebrook, U.S.A. 68 44 54N 71 29W
Coleman, Canada 64 49 40N 114 30W
Coleman, U.S.A. 71 31 52N 99 30W
Coleman → 44 15 6S 141 38 E
Colenso 57 28 44S 29 50 E
Coleraine, Australia 45 37 36S 141 40 E
Coleraine, U.K. 9 55 8N 6 40W
Coleraine □ 9 55 8N 6 40 E
Coleridge, L. 43 43 17S 171 30 E
Colesberg 56 30 45S 25 5 E
Colfax, La., U.S.A. 71 31 35N 92 39W
Colfax, Wash., U.S.A. 72 46 57N 117 28W
Colhué Huapi, L. 80 45 30S 69 0W
Coligny 57 26 17S 26 15 E
Colima 74 19 10N 103 40W
Colima □ 74 19 10N 103 40W
Colima, Nevado de 74 19 35N 103 45W
Colinas 79 6 0S 44 10W
Coll 8 56 40N 6 35W
Collaguasi 78 21 5S 68 45W
Collarenebri 45 29 33S 148 34 E
Collbran 73 39 16N 107 58W
College Park 69 33 42N 84 27W
Collette 63 46 40N 65 30W
Collie 47 33 22S 116 8 E
Collier B. 46 16 10S 124 15 E
Collier Ra. 47 24 45S 119 10 E
Collingwood, Canada 62 44 29N 80 13W
Collingwood, N.Z. 43 40 41S 172 40 E
Collins 62 50 17N 89 27W
Collinsville 44 20 30S 147 56 E
Collooney 9 54 11N 8 28W
Colmar 12 48 5N 7 20 E
Colne 6 53 51N 2 11W
Colo → 45 33 25S 150 52 E
Cologne = Köln 14 50 56N 6 58 E
Colomb-Béchar = Béchar 50 31 38N 2 18W
Colômbia 79 20 10S 48 40W
Colombia ■ 78 3 45N 73 0W
Colombo 32 6 56N 79 58 E
Colombus 73 31 54N 107 43W
Colome 70 43 20N 99 44W
Colón, Cuba 75 22 42N 80 54W
Colón, Panama 75 9 20N 79 54W
Colonia 80 34 25S 57 50W
Colonia Dora 80 28 34S 62 59W
Colonial Hts. 68 37 19N 77 25W
Colonsay, Canada 65 51 59N 105 52W
Colonsay, U.K. 8 56 4N 6 12W
Colorado □ 66 37 40N 106 0W
Colorado →, Argentina 80 39 50S 62 8W
Colorado →, Calif., U.S.A. 73 31 45N 114 40W
Colorado →, Tex., U.S.A. 71 28 36N 95 58W
Colorado, I. 74 9 12N 79 50W
Colorado City 71 32 25N 100 50W
Colorado Desert 66 34 20N 116 0W
Colorado Plateau 73 36 40N 110 30W
Colorado R. Aqueduct 73 34 17N 114 10W
Colorado Springs 70 38 55N 104 50W
Colton 72 46 41N 117 6W
Columbia, La., U.S.A. 71 32 7N 92 5W
Columbia, Miss., U.S.A. 71 31 16N 89 50W
Columbia, Mo., U.S.A. 70 38 58N 92 20W
Columbia, Pa., U.S.A. 68 40 2N 76 30W
Columbia, S.C., U.S.A. 69 34 0N 81 0W
Columbia, Tenn., U.S.A. 69 35 40N 87 0W
Columbia → 72 46 15N 124 5W
Columbia, District of □ 68 38 55N 77 0W
Columbia, Mt. 64 52 8N 117 20W
Columbia Basin 72 47 30N 118 30W
Columbia Falls 72 48 25N 114 16W
Columbia Heights 70 45 5N 93 10W
Columbretes, Is. 13 39 50N 0 50 E
Columbus, Ga., U.S.A. 69 32 30N 84 58W
Columbus, Ind., U.S.A. 68 39 14N 85 55W
Columbus, Kans., U.S.A. 71 37 15N 94 30W
Columbus, Miss., U.S.A. 69 33 30N 88 26W
Columbus, Mont., U.S.A. 72 45 38N 109 14W
Columbus, N. Dak., U.S.A. 70 48 52N 102 48W
Columbus, Nebr., U.S.A. 70 41 30N 97 25W
Columbus, Ohio, U.S.A. 68 39 57N 83 1W
Columbus, Tex., U.S.A. 71 29 42N 96 33W
Columbus, Wis., U.S.A. 70 43 20N 89 2W
Colusa 72 39 15N 122 1W
Colville 72 48 33N 117 54W
Colville → 60 70 25N 151 0W
Colville, C. 43 36 29S 175 21 E
Colwyn Bay 6 53 17N 3 44W
Comácchio 18 44 41N 12 10 E
Comallo 80 41 0S 70 5W
Comanche, Okla., U.S.A. 71 34 27N 97 58W
Comanche, Tex., U.S.A. 71 31 55N 98 35W
Combahee → 69 32 30N 80 31W
Comblain-au-Pont 11 50 29N 5 35 E
Comeragh Mts. 9 52 17N 7 35W
Comet 44 23 36S 148 38 E
Comet Vale 47 29 55S 121 4 E
Comilla 33 23 28N 91 10 E
Comino 18 36 0N 14 20 E
Comitán 74 16 18N 92 9W
Commerce, Ga., U.S.A. 69 34 10N 83 25W
Commerce, Tex., U.S.A. 71 33 15N 95 50W
Committee B. 61 68 30N 86 30W
Commoron Cr. → 45 28 22S 150 8 E
Communism Pk. = Kommunizma, Pik 31 39 0N 72 2 E
Como 18 45 48N 9 5 E
Como, L. di 18 46 5N 9 17 E
Comodoro Rivadavia 80 45 50S 67 40W
Comorin, C. 32 8 3N 77 40 E
Comoro Is. ■ 3 12 10S 44 15 E
Comox 64 49 42N 124 55W
Compiègne 12 49 24N 2 50 E
Compton Downs 45 30 28S 146 30 E
Conakry 50 9 29N 13 49W
Conara Junction 44 41 50S 147 26 E
Concarneau 12 47 52N 3 56W
Conceição da Barra 79 18 35S 39 45W
Conceição do Araguaia 79 8 0S 49 2W
Concepción, Bolivia 78 16 15S 62 8W
Concepción, Chile 80 36 50S 73 0W
Concepción, Paraguay 80 23 22S 57 26W
Concepción → 74 30 32N 113 2W
Concepción, L. 78 17 20S 61 20W
Concepción, Punta 74 26 55N 111 59W
Concepción del Oro 74 24 40N 101 30W
Concepción del Uruguay 80 32 35S 58 20W
Conception, Pt. 73 34 30N 120 34W
Conception B. 56 23 55S 14 22 E
Conception I. 75 23 52N 75 9W
Conchas Dam 71 35 25N 104 10W
Conche 63 50 55N 55 58W
Concho 73 34 32N 109 43W
Concho → 71 31 30N 99 45W
Conchos → 74 29 32N 104 25W
Concord, Calif., U.S.A. 72 37 59N 122 2W
Concord, N.C., U.S.A. 69 35 28N 80 35W
Concord, N.H., U.S.A. 68 43 12N 71 30W
Concordia, Argentina 80 31 20S 58 2W
Concórdia, Brazil 78 4 36S 66 36W
Concordia, U.S.A. 70 39 35N 97 40W
Concordia, La 74 16 8N 92 38W
Concrete 72 48 35N 121 49W
Condamine 45 26 56S 150 9 E
Conde 70 45 13N 98 5W
Condeúba 79 14 52S 42 0W
Condobolin 45 33 4S 147 6 E
Condon 72 45 15N 120 8W
Confuso → 80 25 9S 57 34W
Congleton 6 53 10N 2 12W
Congo = Zaïre → 54 6 4S 12 24 E
Congo (Kinshasa) = Zaïre ■ 54 3 0S 23 0 E
Congo ■ 54 1 0S 16 0 E
Congo Basin 48 0 10S 24 30 E
Congress 73 34 11N 112 56W
Coniston 62 46 29N 80 51W
Conjeeveram = Kanchipuram 32 12 52N 79 45 E
Conjuboy 44 18 35S 144 35 E
Conklin 65 55 38N 111 5W
Conlea 45 30 7S 144 35 E
Conn, L. 9 54 3N 9 15W
Connacht 9 53 23N 8 40W
Conneaut 68 41 55N 80 32W
Connecticut □ 68 41 40N 72 40W
Connecticut → 68 41 17N 72 21W
Connell 72 46 36N 118 51W
Connellsville 68 40 3N 79 32W
Connemara 9 53 29N 9 45W
Conner, La 72 48 22N 122 27W
Connersville 68 39 40N 85 10W
Connors Ra. 44 21 40S 149 10 E
Conoble 45 32 55S 144 33 E
Conon → 8 57 33N 4 28W
Cononaco → 78 1 32S 75 35W
Cononbridge 8 57 32N 4 30W
Conquest 65 51 32N 107 14W
Conrad 72 48 11N 112 0W
Conran, C. 45 37 49S 148 44 E
Conroe 71 30 15N 95 28W
Conselheiro Lafaiete 79 20 40S 43 48W
Consort 65 52 1N 110 46W
Constance = Konstanz 14 47 39N 9 10 E
Constance, L. = Bodensee 14 47 35N 9 25 E
Constanța 15 44 14N 28 38 E
Constantina 13 37 51N 5 40W
Constantine 50 36 25N 6 42 E
Constitución 80 35 20S 72 30W
Consul 65 49 20N 109 30W
Contact 72 41 50N 114 56W
Contai 33 21 54N 87 46 E
Contamana 78 7 19S 74 55W
Contas → 79 14 17S 39 1W
Contra Costa 57 25 9S 33 30 E
Conway = Conwy 6 53 17N 3 50W
Conway = Conwy → 6 53 18N 3 50W
Conway, Ark., U.S.A. 71 35 5N 92 30W
Conway, N.H., U.S.A. 68 43 58N 71 8W
Conway, S.C., U.S.A. 69 33 49N 79 2W
Conway, L. 45 28 17S 135 35 E
Conwy 6 53 17N 3 50W
Conwy → 6 53 18N 3 50W
Cooch Behar = Koch Bihar 33 26 22N 89 29 E
Coodardy 47 27 15S 117 39 E
Cook, Australia 47 30 37S 130 25 E
Cook, U.S.A. 70 47 49N 92 39W
Cook, B. 80 55 10S 70 0W
Cook, Mt. 43 43 36S 170 9 E
Cook Inlet 60 59 0N 151 0W
Cook Is. 2 17 0S 160 0W
Cook Strait 43 41 15S 174 29 E
Cookeville 69 36 12N 85 30W
Cookhouse 56 32 44S 25 47 E
Cookstown 9 54 40N 6 43W
Cookstown □ 9 54 40N 6 43W
Cooktown 44 15 30S 145 16 E
Coolabah 45 31 1S 146 43 E
Cooladdi 45 26 37S 145 23 E
Coolah 45 31 48S 149 41 E
Coolamon 45 34 46S 147 8 E
Coolangatta 45 28 11S 153 29 E
Coolgardie 47 30 55S 121 8 E
Coolibah 46 15 33S 130 56 E
Coolidge 73 33 1N 111 35W
Coolidge Dam 73 33 10N 110 30W
Cooma 45 36 12S 149 8 E
Coonabarabran 45 31 14S 149 18 E
Coonamble 45 30 56S 148 27 E
Coonana 47 31 0S 123 0 E
Coondapoor 32 13 42N 74 40 E
Coongie 45 27 9S 140 8 E
Coongoola 45 27 43S 145 51 E
Cooninie, L. 45 26 4S 139 59 E
Cooper 71 33 20N 95 40W
Cooper → 69 33 0N 79 55W
Coopers Cr. → 45 28 29S 137 46 E
Cooperstown, N. Dak., U.S.A. 70 47 30N 98 6W
Cooperstown, N.Y., U.S.A. 68 42 42N 74 57W
Coorabie 47 31 54S 132 18 E
Coorabulka 44 23 41S 140 20 E
Coorong, The 45 35 50S 139 20 E
Coorow 47 29 53S 116 2 E
Cooroy 45 26 22S 152 54 E
Coos Bay 72 43 26N 124 7W
Cootamundra 45 34 36S 148 1 E
Cootehill 9 54 5N 7 5W
Cooyar 45 26 59S 151 51 E
Cooyeana 44 24 29S 138 45 E
Copainalá 74 17 8N 93 11W
Cope 70 39 44N 102 50W
Copenhagen = København 21 55 41N 12 34 E
Copiapó 80 27 30S 70 20W
Copiapó → 80 27 19S 70 56W
Copley 45 30 36S 138 26 E
Copp L. 64 60 14N 114 40W
Copper Center 60 62 10N 145 25W
Copper Cliff 62 46 28N 81 4W
Copper Harbor 68 47 31N 87 55W
Coppermine 60 67 50N 115 5W
Coppermine → 60 67 49N 116 4W
Coquet → 6 55 18N 1 45W
Coquilhatville = Mbandaka 54 0 1N 18 18 E
Coquille 72 43 15N 124 12W
Coquimbo 80 30 0S 71 20W
Corabia 15 43 48N 24 30 E
Coracora 78 15 5S 73 45W
Coral Gables 69 25 45N 80 16W
Coral Harbour 61 64 8N 83 10W
Coral Sea 40 15 0S 150 0 E
Corato 18 41 12N 16 22 E
Corbin 68 37 0N 84 3W
Corby 7 52 49N 0 31W
Corcoran 73 36 6N 119 35W
Corcubión 13 42 56N 9 12W
Cordele 69 31 55N 83 49W
Cordell 71 35 18N 99 0W
Córdoba, Argentina 80 31 20S 64 10W
Córdoba, Mexico 74 18 50N 97 0W
Córdoba, Spain 13 37 50N 4 50W
Córdoba, Sierra de 80 31 10S 64 25W
Cordon 35 16 42N 121 32 E
Cordova, Ala., U.S.A. 69 33 45N 87 12W
Cordova, Alaska, U.S.A. 60 60 36N 145 45W
Corella → 44 19 34S 140 47 E
Corfield 44 21 40S 143 21 E
Corfu = Kérkira 19 39 38N 19 50 E
Corigliano Cálabro 18 39 36N 16 31 E
Coringa Is. 44 16 58S 149 58 E
Corinna 44 41 35S 145 10 E
Corinth = Kórinthos 19 37 56N 22 55 E
Corinth 69 34 54N 88 30W
Corinth, G. of = Korinthiakós Kólpos 19 38 16N 22 30 E
Corinto, Brazil 79 18 20S 44 30W
Corinto, Nic. 75 12 30N 87 10W
Cork 9 51 54N 8 30W
Cork □ 9 51 50N 8 50W
Cork Harbour 9 51 46N 8 16W
Çorlu 30 41 11N 27 49 E
Cormack L. 64 60 56N 121 37W
Cormorant 65 54 14N 100 35W
Cormorant L. 65 54 15N 100 50W
Corn Is. = Maiz, Is. del 75 12 15N 83 4W
Cornell 70 45 10N 91 8W
Corner Brook 63 48 57N 57 58W
Corning, Ark., U.S.A. 71 36 27N 90 34W
Corning, Calif., U.S.A. 72 39 56N 122 9W
Corning, Iowa, U.S.A. 70 40 57N 94 40W
Corning, N.Y., U.S.A. 68 42 10N 77 3W
Cornwall 62 45 2N 74 44W
Cornwall □ 7 50 26N 4 40W
Corny Pt. 45 34 55S 137 0 E
Coro 78 11 25N 69 41W
Coroatá 79 4 8S 44 0W
Corocoro 78 17 15S 68 28W
Coroico 78 16 0S 67 50W
Coromandel 43 36 45S 175 31 E
Coromandel Coast 32 12 30N 81 0 E
Corona, Australia 45 31 16S 141 24 E
Corona, Calif., U.S.A. 73 33 49N 117 36W
Corona, N. Mex., U.S.A. 73 34 15N 105 32W
Coronada 73 32 45N 117 9W
Coronado, B. de 75 9 0N 83 40W
Coronation 64 52 5N 111 27W
Coronation Gulf 60 68 25N 110 0W
Coronation I. 64 55 52N 134 20W
Coronation Is. 46 14 57S 124 55 E
Coronel 80 37 0S 73 10W
Coronel Dorrego 80 38 40S 61 10W
Coronel Pringles 80 38 0S 61 30W
Coronel Suárez 80 37 30S 61 52W
Corowa 45 35 58S 146 21 E
Corozal, Belize 74 18 23N 88 23W
Corozal, Panama 74 8 59N 79 34W
Corpus Christi 71 27 50N 97 28W
Corpus Christi, L. 71 28 5N 97 54W

Dankhar Gompa

Corque 78 18 20S 67 41W
Correntes, C. das 57 24 6S 35 34 E
Corrèze □ 12 45 20N 1 45 E
Corrib, L. 9 53 5N 9 10W
Corrientes 80 27 30S 58 45W
Corrientes → 78 3 43S 74 35W
Corrientes, C., Colombia 78 5 30N 77 34W
Corrientes, C., Cuba 75 21 43N 84 30W
Corrientes, C., Mexico 74 20 25N 105 42W
Corrigan 71 31 0N 94 48W
Corrigin 47 32 20S 117 53 E
Corry 68 41 55N 79 39W
Corse 12 42 0N 9 0 E
Corse, C. 18 43 1N 9 25 E
Corse-du-Sud □ 12 41 45N 9 0 E
Corsica = Corse 12 42 0N 9 0 E
Corsicana 71 32 5N 96 30W
Cortez 73 37 24N 108 35W
Cortland 68 42 35N 76 11W
Cortona 18 43 16N 12 0 E
Çorum 30 40 30N 34 57 E
Corumbá 78 19 0S 57 30W
Corumbá de Goiás 79 16 0S 48 50W
Coruña, La 13 43 20N 8 25W
Corunna = Coruña, La 13 43 20N 8 25W
Corvallis 72 44 36N 123 15W
Corvette, L. de la 62 53 25N 74 3W
Corydon 70 40 42N 93 22W
Cosalá 74 24 28N 106 40W
Cosamaloapan 74 18 23N 95 50W
Cosenza 18 39 17N 16 14 E
Coshocton 68 40 17N 81 51W
Cosmo Newberry 47 28 0S 122 54 E
Costa Blanca 13 38 25N 0 10W
Costa Brava 13 41 30N 3 0 E
Costa del Sol 13 36 30N 4 30W
Costa Dorada 13 40 45N 1 15 E
Costa Rica ■ 75 10 0N 84 0W
Costilla 73 37 0N 105 30W
Cotabato 35 7 14N 124 15 E
Cotagaita 78 20 45S 65 40W
Côte-d'Or □ 12 47 30N 4 50 E
Coteau des Prairies 70 44 30N 97 0W
Coteau du Missouri 70 47 0N 101 0W
Cotentin 12 49 15N 1 30W
Côtes-du-Nord □ 12 48 25N 2 40W
Cotonou 53 6 20N 2 25 E
Cotopaxi, Vol. 76 0 40S 78 30W
Cotswold Hills 7 51 42N 2 10W
Cottage Grove 72 43 48N 123 2W
Cottbus 14 51 44N 14 20 E
Cottonwood 73 34 48N 112 1W
Cotulla 71 28 26N 99 14W
Coudersport 68 41 45N 78 1W
Couedic, C. du 45 36 5S 136 40 E
Coulee City 72 47 36N 119 18W
Coulonge → 62 45 52N 76 46W
Council, Alaska, U.S.A. 60 64 55N 163 45W
Council, Idaho, U.S.A. 72 44 44N 116 26W
Council Bluffs 70 41 20N 95 50W
Council Grove 70 38 41N 96 30W
Courantyne → 78 5 55N 57 5W
Courtenay 64 49 45N 125 0W
Courtrai = Kortrijk 11 50 50N 3 17 E
Coushatta 71 32 0N 93 21W
Coutts 64 49 0N 111 57W
Coventry 7 52 25N 1 31W
Coventry L. 65 61 15N 106 15W
Covilhã 13 40 17N 7 31W
Covington, Ga., U.S.A. 69 33 36N 83 50W
Covington, Ky., U.S.A. 68 39 5N 84 30W
Covington, Okla., U.S.A. 71 36 21N 97 36W
Covington, Tenn., U.S.A. 71 35 34N 89 39W
Cowal, L. 45 33 40S 147 25 E
Cowan 65 52 5N 100 45W
Cowan, L. 47 31 45S 121 45 E
Cowan L. 65 54 0N 107 15W
Cowangie 45 35 12S 141 26 E
Cowarie 45 27 45S 138 15 E
Cowcowing Lakes 47 30 55S 117 20 E
Cowdenbeath 8 56 7N 3 20W
Cowell 45 33 39S 136 56 E
Cowes 7 50 45N 1 18W
Cowra 45 33 49S 148 42 E
Coxim 79 18 30S 54 55W
Cox's Bazar 33 21 26N 91 59 E
Cox's Cove 63 49 7N 58 5W
Coyuca de Benitez 74 17 1N 100 8W
Coyuca de Catalan 74 18 18N 100 41W
Cozad 70 40 55N 99 57W
Cozumel, I. de 74 20 30N 86 40W
Craboon 45 32 3S 149 30 E
Cracow = Kraków 15 50 4N 19 57 E
Cracow 45 25 17S 150 17 E
Cradock 56 32 8S 25 36 E
Craig, Alaska, U.S.A. 64 55 30N 133 5W
Craig, Colo., U.S.A. 72 40 32N 107 33W
Craiova 15 44 21N 23 48 E
Cramsie 44 23 20S 144 15 E
Cranberry Portage 65 54 35N 101 23W
Cranbrook, Tas., Australia 44 42 0S 148 5 E
Cranbrook, W. Austral., Australia 47 34 18S 117 33 E
Cranbrook, Canada 64 49 30N 115 46W
Crandon 70 45 32N 88 52W
Crane, Oreg., U.S.A. 72 43 21N 118 39W
Crane, Tex., U.S.A. 71 31 26N 102 27W
Crater, L. 72 42 55N 122 3W
Crateús 79 5 10S 40 39W
Crato 79 7 10S 39 25W
Crawford 70 42 40N 103 25W
Crawfordsville 68 40 2N 86 51W
Crawley 7 51 7N 0 10W
Crazy Mts. 72 46 14N 110 30W
Crean L. 65 54 5N 106 9W
Crécy-en-Ponthieu 12 50 15N 1 53 E
Credo 47 30 28S 120 45 E
Cree →, Canada 65 58 57N 105 47W
Cree →, U.K. 8 54 51N 4 24W
Cree L. 65 57 30N 106 30W
Creede 73 37 56N 106 59W
Creel 74 27 45N 107 38W
Creighton 70 42 30N 97 52W
Cremona 18 45 8N 10 2 E
Cres 18 44 58N 14 25 E
Cresbard 70 45 13N 98 57W
Crescent, Okla., U.S.A. 71 35 58N 97 36W
Crescent, Oreg., U.S.A. 72 43 30N 121 37W
Crescent City 72 41 45N 124 12W
Cressy 45 38 2S 143 40 E
Crested Butte 73 38 57N 107 0W
Creston, Canada 64 49 10N 116 31W
Creston, Iowa, U.S.A. 70 41 0N 94 20W
Creston, Wash., U.S.A. 72 47 47N 118 36W
Crestview 69 30 45N 86 35W
Crete = Kriti 19 35 15N 25 0 E
Crete 70 40 38N 96 58W
Crete, La 64 58 11N 116 24W
Creus, C. 13 42 20N 3 19 E
Creuse □ 12 46 10N 2 0 E
Creuse → 12 47 0N 0 34 E
Creusot, Le 12 46 48N 4 24 E
Crewe 6 53 6N 2 28W
Crib Point 45 38 22S 145 13 E
Criciúma 80 28 40S 49 23W
Crieff 8 56 22N 3 50W
Crimea = Krymskiy Poluostrov 23 45 0N 34 0 E
Crinan 8 56 6N 5 34W
Cristóbal 74 9 19N 79 54W
Crişu Alb → 15 46 42N 21 17 E
Crişu Negru → 15 46 42N 21 16 E
Crna Gora 19 42 10N 21 30 E
Crna Gora □ 19 42 40N 19 20 E
Crna Reka → 19 41 33N 21 59 E
Croaghpatrick 9 53 46N 9 40W
Crocker, Banjaran 34 5 40N 116 30 E
Crocker I. 47 11 12S 132 32 E
Crockett 71 31 20N 95 30W
Crocodile = Krokodil → 57 25 14S 32 18 E
Crocodile Is. 44 12 3S 134 58 E
Croix, La, L. 62 48 20N 92 15W
Croker, C. 46 10 58S 132 35 E
Cromarty, Canada 65 58 3N 94 9W
Cromarty, U.K. 8 57 40N 4 2W
Cromer 6 52 56N 1 18 E
Cromwell 43 45 3S 169 14 E
Cronulla 45 34 3S 151 8 E
Crooked →, Canada 64 54 50N 122 54W
Crooked →, U.S.A. 72 44 30N 121 16W
Crooked I. 75 22 50N 74 10W
Crookston, Minn., U.S.A. 70 47 50N 96 40W
Crookston, Nebr., U.S.A. 70 42 56N 100 45W
Crooksville 68 39 45N 82 8W
Crookwell 45 34 28S 149 24 E
Crosby, Minn., U.S.A. 70 46 28N 93 57W
Crosby, N. Dak., U.S.A. 65 48 55N 103 18W
Crosbyton 71 33 37N 101 12W
Cross City 69 29 35N 83 5W
Cross Fell 6 54 44N 2 29W
Cross L. 65 54 45N 97 30W
Cross Plains 71 32 8N 99 7W
Cross River □ 53 6 0N 8 0 E
Cross Sound 60 58 20N 136 30W
Crosse, La, Kans., U.S.A. 70 38 33N 99 20W
Crosse, La, Wis., U.S.A. 70 43 48N 91 13W
Crossett 71 33 10N 91 57W
Crossfield 64 51 25N 114 0W
Crosshaven 9 51 48N 8 19W
Crotone 18 39 5N 17 6 E
Crow → 64 59 41N 124 20W
Crow Agency 72 45 40N 107 30W
Crow Hd. 9 51 34N 10 9W
Crowell 71 33 59N 99 45W
Crowley 71 30 15N 92 20W
Crown Point 68 41 24N 87 23W
Crows Nest 45 27 16S 152 4 E
Crowsnest Pass 64 49 40N 114 40W
Croydon, Australia 44 18 13S 142 14 E
Croydon, U.K. 7 51 18N 0 5W
Crozet Is. 3 46 27S 52 0 E
Cruz, C. 75 19 50N 77 50W
Cruz, La 74 23 55N 106 54W
Cruz Alta 80 28 45S 53 40W
Cruz del Eje 80 30 45S 64 50W
Cruzeiro 79 22 33S 45 0W
Cruzeiro do Sul 78 7 35S 72 35W
Cry L. 64 58 45N 129 0W
Crystal Brook 45 33 21S 138 12 E
Crystal City, Mo., U.S.A. 70 38 15N 90 23W
Crystal City, Tex., U.S.A. 71 28 40N 99 50W
Crystal Falls 68 46 9N 88 11W
Crystal River 69 28 54N 82 35W
Crystal Springs 71 31 59N 90 25W
Csongrád 15 46 43N 20 12 E
Cuamato 56 17 2S 15 7 E
Cuamba 55 14 45S 36 22 E
Cuando → 55 17 30S 23 15 E
Cuando Cubango □ 56 16 25S 20 0 E
Cuangar 56 17 36S 18 39 E
Cuanza → 48 9 2S 13 30 E
Cuarto → 80 33 25S 63 2W
Cuauhtémoc 74 28 25N 106 52W
Cuba 73 36 0N 107 0W
Cuba ■ 75 22 0N 79 0W
Cuballing 47 32 50S 117 10 E
Cubango → 56 18 50S 22 25 E
Cuchi 55 14 37S 16 58 E
Cuchumatanes, Sierra de los 75 15 35N 91 25W
Cúcuta 78 7 54N 72 31W
Cudahy 68 42 54N 87 50W
Cuddalore 32 11 46N 79 45 E
Cuddapah 32 14 30N 78 47 E
Cuddapan, L. 44 25 45S 141 26 E
Cudgewa 45 36 10S 147 42 E
Cue 47 27 25S 117 54 E
Cuenca, Ecuador 78 2 50S 79 9W
Cuenca, Spain 13 40 5N 2 10W
Cuenca, Serranía de 13 39 55N 1 50W
Cuernavaca 74 18 50N 99 20W
Cuero 71 29 5N 97 17W
Cuervo 71 35 5N 104 25W
Cuevas del Almanzora 13 37 18N 1 58W
Cuevo 78 20 15S 63 30W
Cuiabá 79 15 30S 56 0W
Cuiabá → 79 17 5S 56 36W
Cuillin Hills 8 57 14N 6 15W
Cuillin Sd. 8 57 4N 6 20W
Cuiluan 38 47 51N 128 32 E
Cuima 55 13 25S 15 45 E
Cuito → 56 18 1S 20 48 E
Cuitzeo, L. de 74 19 55N 101 5W
Cukai 34 4 13N 103 25 E
Culbertson 70 48 9N 104 30W
Culcairn 45 35 41S 147 3 E
Culebra, Sierra de la 13 41 55N 6 20W
Culgoa → 45 29 56S 146 20 E
Culiacán 74 24 50N 107 23W
Culion 35 11 54N 120 1 E
Cullarin Range 45 34 30S 149 30 E
Cullen, Australia 46 13 58S 131 54 E
Cullen, U.K. 8 57 45N 2 50W
Cullen Pt. 44 11 57S 141 54 E
Cullera 13 39 9N 0 17W
Cullman 69 34 13N 86 50W
Culloden Moor 8 57 29N 4 7W
Culpeper 68 38 29N 77 59W
Culuene → 79 12 56S 52 51W
Culver, Pt. 47 32 54S 124 43 E
Culverden 43 42 47S 172 49 E
Cumaná 78 10 30N 64 5W
Cumberland, Canada 64 49 40N 125 0W
Cumberland, Md., U.S.A. 68 39 40N 78 43W
Cumberland, Wis., U.S.A. 70 45 32N 92 3W
Cumberland → 69 36 15N 87 0W
Cumberland I. 69 30 52N 81 30W
Cumberland Is. 44 20 35S 149 10 E
Cumberland L. 65 54 3N 102 18W
Cumberland Pen. 61 67 0N 64 0W
Cumberland Plateau 69 36 0N 84 30W
Cumberland Sd. 61 65 30N 66 0W
Cumborah 45 29 40S 147 45 E
Cumbria □ 6 54 35N 2 55W
Cumbrian Mts. 6 54 30N 3 0W
Cumbum 32 15 40N 79 10 E
Cummins 45 34 16S 135 43 E
Cumnock, Australia 45 32 59S 148 46 E
Cumnock, U.K. 8 55 27N 4 18W
Cundeelee 47 30 43S 123 26 E
Cunderdin 47 31 37S 117 12 E
Cunene → 56 17 20S 11 50 E
Cúneo 18 44 23N 7 31 E
Cunnamulla 45 28 2S 145 38 E
Cupar, Canada 65 50 57N 104 10W
Cupar, U.K. 8 56 20N 3 0W
Cupica, G. de 78 6 25N 77 30W
Curaçao 75 12 10N 69 0W
Curaray → 78 2 20S 74 5W
Curiapo 78 8 33N 61 5W
Curicó 80 34 55S 71 20W
Curitiba 80 25 20S 49 10W
Currabubula 45 31 16S 150 44 E
Currais Novos 79 6 13S 36 30W
Curralinho 79 1 45S 49 46W
Currant 72 38 51N 115 32W
Curraweena 45 30 47S 145 54 E
Currawilla 44 25 10S 141 20 E
Current → 71 37 15N 91 10W
Currie, Australia 44 39 56S 143 53 E
Currie, U.S.A. 72 40 16N 114 45W
Currie, Mt. 57 30 29S 29 21 E
Currituck Sd. 69 36 20N 75 50W
Curtis 70 40 41N 100 32W
Curtis Group 44 39 30S 146 37 E
Curtis I. 44 23 35S 151 10 E
Curuápanema → 79 2 25S 55 2W
Curuçá 79 0 43S 47 50W
Çürüksu Çayi → 23 37 27N 27 11 E
Curundu 74 8 59N 79 38W
Curup 34 4 26S 102 13 E
Cururupu 79 1 50S 44 50W
Curuzú Cuatiá 80 29 50S 58 5W
Cushing 71 35 59N 96 46W
Cushing, Mt. 64 57 35N 126 57W
Cusihuiriáchic 74 28 10N 106 50W
Custer 70 43 45N 103 38W
Cut Bank 72 48 40N 112 15W
Cuthbert 69 31 47N 84 47W
Cuttaburra → 45 29 43S 144 22 E
Cuttack 33 20 25N 85 57 E
Cuvier, C. 47 23 14S 113 22 E
Cuvier I. 43 36 27S 175 50 E
Cuxhaven 14 53 51N 8 41 E
Cuyahoga Falls 68 41 8N 81 30W
Cuyo 35 10 50N 121 5 E
Cuzco, Bolivia 78 20 0S 66 50W
Cuzco, Peru 78 13 32S 72 0W
Cwmbran 7 51 39N 3 0W
Cyclades = Kikládhes 19 37 20N 24 30 E
Cygnet 44 43 8S 147 1 E
Cynthiana 68 38 23N 84 10W
Cypress Hills 65 49 40N 109 30W
Cyprus ■ 30 35 0N 33 0 E
Cyrenaica 51 27 0N 23 0 E
Cyrene = Shaḥḥāt 51 32 48N 21 54 E
Czar 65 52 27N 110 50W
Czechoslovakia ■ 14 49 0N 17 0 E
Czeremcha 15 52 31N 23 21 E
Częstochowa 15 50 49N 19 7 E

D

Da Hinggan Ling 38 48 0N 121 0 E
Da Lat 34 11 56N 108 25 E
Da Nang 34 16 4N 108 13 E
Da Qaidam 37 37 50N 95 15 E
Da Yunhe → 39 34 25N 120 5 E
Da'an 38 45 30N 124 7 E
Daba Shan 39 32 0N 109 0 E
Dabakala 50 8 15N 4 20W
Dabbūrīya 28 32 42N 35 22 E
Dąbie 14 53 27N 14 45 E
Dabo 34 0 30S 104 33 E
Dabola 50 10 50N 11 5W
Daboya 53 9 30N 1 20W
Dabrowa Tarnówska 15 50 10N 20 59 E
Dacca = Dhaka 33 23 43N 90 26 E
Dacca □ = Dhaka □ 33 24 25N 90 25 E
Dadanawa 78 2 50N 59 30W
Dade City 69 28 20N 82 12W
Dadiya 53 9 35N 11 24 E
Dadra and Nagar Haveli □ 32 20 5N 73 0 E
Dadu 32 26 45N 67 45 E
Daet 35 14 2N 122 55 E
Dafang 39 27 9N 105 39 E
Dagana 50 16 30N 15 35W
Daghestan A.S.S.R. □ 23 42 30N 47 0 E
Dagö = Hiiumaa 22 58 50N 22 45 E
Dagupan 35 16 3N 120 20 E
Dahlak Kebir 29 15 50N 40 10 E
Dahlonega 69 34 35N 83 59W
Dahod 32 22 50N 74 15 E
Dahomey = Benin ■ 53 10 0N 2 0 E
Dahra 50 15 22N 15 30W
Dai Shan 39 30 25N 122 10 E
Dai Xian 38 39 4N 112 58 E
Daingean 9 53 18N 7 15W
Daintree 44 16 20S 145 20 E
Daiō-Misaki 36 34 15N 136 45 E
Dairût 51 27 34N 30 43 E
Daisetsu-Zan 36 43 30N 142 57 E
Dajarra 44 21 42S 139 30 E
Dakar 50 14 34N 17 29W
Dakhla 50 23 50N 15 53W
Dakhla, El Wâhât el- 51 25 30N 28 50 E
Dakhovskaya 23 44 13N 40 13 E
Dakingari 53 11 37N 4 1 E
Dakota City 70 42 27N 96 28W
Đakovica 19 42 22N 20 26 E
Dalachi 38 36 48N 105 0 E
Dalai Nur 38 43 20N 116 45 E
Dalälven 21 60 12N 16 43 E
Dalandzadgad 37 43 27N 104 30 E
Dalarö 21 59 8N 18 24 E
Dālbandīn 31 29 0N 64 23 E
Dalbeattie 8 54 55N 3 50W
Dalby 45 27 10S 151 17 E
Dalgaranger, Mt. 47 27 50S 117 5 E
Dalhart 71 36 10N 102 30W
Dalhousie 63 48 5N 66 26W
Dali, Shaanxi, China 39 34 48N 109 58 E
Dali, Yunnan, China 37 25 40N 100 10 E
Dalian 38 38 50N 121 40 E
Daliang Shan 37 28 0N 102 45 E
Dāliyat el Karmel 28 32 43N 35 2 E
Dalkeith 8 55 54N 3 5W
Dall I. 64 54 59N 133 25W
Dallarnil 45 25 19S 152 2 E
Dallas, Oreg., U.S.A. 72 45 0N 123 15W
Dallas, Tex., U.S.A. 71 32 50N 96 50W
Dalmacija □ 18 43 20N 17 0 E
Dalmatia = Dalmacija □ 18 43 20N 17 0 E
Dalmellington 8 55 20N 4 25W
Dalnegorsk 25 44 32N 135 33 E
Dalneretchensk 25 45 50N 133 40 E
Daloa 50 7 0N 6 30W
Dalton, Canada 62 48 11N 84 1W
Dalton, Ga., U.S.A. 69 34 47N 84 58W
Dalton, Nebr., U.S.A. 70 41 27N 103 0W
Dalvík 20 65 58N 18 32W
Daly → 46 13 35S 130 19 E
Daly L. 65 56 32N 105 39W
Daly Waters 44 16 15S 133 24 E
Daman 32 20 25N 72 57 E
Damanhûr 51 31 0N 30 30 E
Damar 35 7 7S 128 40 E
Damaraland 56 21 0S 17 0 E
Damascus = Dimashq 30 33 30N 36 18 E
Damaturu 53 11 45N 11 55 E
Damāvand 31 35 47N 52 0 E
Damāvand, Qolleh-ye 31 35 56N 52 10 E
Damba 54 6 44S 15 20 E
Dāmghān 31 36 10N 54 17 E
Damietta = Dumyât 51 31 24N 31 48 E
Daming 38 36 15N 115 6 E
Dāmīya 28 32 6N 35 34 E
Damoh 32 23 50N 79 28 E
Dampier 46 20 41S 116 42 E
Dampier, Selat 35 0 40S 131 0 E
Dampier Arch. 46 20 38S 116 32 E
Dan Xian 39 19 31N 109 33 E
Dana 35 11 0S 122 52 E
Dana, L. 62 50 53N 77 20W
Danbury 68 41 23N 73 29W
Danby L. 73 34 17N 115 0W
Dandaragan 47 30 40S 115 40 E
Dandeldhura 33 29 20N 80 35 E
Dandeli 32 15 5N 74 30 E
Dandenong 45 38 0S 145 15 E
Dandong 38 40 10N 124 20 E
Danforth 63 45 39N 67 57W
Danger Is. = Pukapuka 41 10 53S 165 49W
Danger Pt. 56 34 40S 19 17 E
Dangora 53 11 30N 8 7 E
Dangriga 74 17 0N 88 13W
Dangshan 39 34 27N 116 22 E
Dangtu 39 31 32N 118 25 E
Dangyang 39 30 52N 111 44 E
Daniel 72 42 56N 110 2W
Daniel's Harbour 63 50 13N 57 35W
Danielskuil 56 28 11S 23 33 E
Danilov 22 58 16N 40 13 E
Dankalwa 53 11 52N 12 12 E
Dankhar Gompa 32 32 10N 78 10 E

Danlí 75 14 4N 86 35W
Dannemora, Sweden 21 60 12N 17 51 E
Dannemora, U.S.A. 68 44 41N 73 44W
Dannevirke 43 40 12S 176 8 E
Dannhauser 57 28 0S 30 3 E
Danshui 39 25 12N 121 25 E
Dansville 68 42 32N 77 41W
Dante 29 10 25N 51 16 E
Danube → 15 45 20N 29 40 E
Danville, Ill., U.S.A. 68 40 10N 87 40W
Danville, Ky., U.S.A. 68 37 40N 84 45W
Danville, Va., U.S.A. 69 36 40N 79 20W
Danzhai 39 26 11N 107 48 E
Danzig = Gdańsk 15 54 22N 18 40 E
Dao 35 10 30N 121 57 E
Dao Xian 39 25 36N 111 31 E
Daoud = Aïn Beïda 50 35 50N 7 29 E
Daqing Shan 38 40 40N 111 0 E
Daqu Shan 39 30 25N 122 20 E
Dar-es-Salaam, Tanzania 52 6 50S 39 12 E
Dar es Salaam, Tanzania 54 6 50S 39 12 E
Dar'ā 28 32 36N 36 7 E
Dārāb 31 28 50N 54 30 E
Daraj 50 30 10N 10 28 E
Darband 32 34 20N 72 50 E
Darbhanga 33 26 15N 85 55 E
Darby 72 46 2N 114 7W
Dardanelle 71 35 12N 93 9W
Dardanelles = Çanakkale Boğazı 30 40 3N 26 12 E
Dârfûr 51 13 40N 24 0 E
Dargai 32 34 25N 71 55 E
Dargan Ata 24 40 29N 62 10 E
Dargaville 43 35 57S 173 52 E
Darhan Muminggan Lianheqi 38 41 40N 110 28 E
Darien 74 9 7N 79 46W
Darién, G. del 78 9 0N 77 0W
Darjeeling = Darjiling 33 27 3N 88 18 E
Darjiling 33 27 3N 88 18 E
Dark Cove 63 48 47N 54 13W
Darkan 47 33 20S 116 43 E
Darling → 45 34 4S 141 54 E
Darling Downs 45 27 30S 150 30 E
Darling Ra. 47 32 30S 116 0 E
Darlington, U.K. 6 54 33N 1 33W
Darlington, S.C., U.S.A. 69 34 18N 79 50W
Darlington, Wis., U.S.A. 70 42 43N 90 7W
Darlot, L. 47 27 48S 121 35 E
Darłowo 14 54 25N 16 25 E
Darmstadt 14 49 51N 8 40 E
Darnah 51 32 40N 22 35 E
Darnall 57 29 23S 31 18 E
Darnley B. 60 69 30N 123 30W
Darr 44 23 13S 144 7 E
Darr → 44 23 39S 143 50 E
Darrington 72 48 14N 121 37W
Darror → 29 10 30N 50 0 E
Dart → 7 50 24N 3 36W
Dartmoor 7 50 36N 4 0W
Dartmouth, Australia 44 23 31S 144 44 E
Dartmouth, Canada 63 44 40N 63 30W
Dartmouth, U.K. 7 50 21N 3 35W
Dartmouth, L. 45 26 4S 145 18 E
Darvaza 24 40 11N 58 24 E
Darvel, Teluk 35 4 50N 118 20 E
Darwha 32 20 15N 77 45 E
Darwin 46 12 25S 130 51 E
Darwin River 46 12 50S 130 58 E
Dās 31 25 20N 53 30 E
Dasht → 31 25 10N 61 40 E
Dasht-e Kavīr 31 34 30N 55 0 E
Dasht-e Lūt 31 31 30N 58 0 E
Dasht-e Mārgow 31 30 40N 62 30 E
Dasseneiland 56 33 25S 18 3 E
Datia 32 25 39N 78 27 E
Datian 39 25 40N 117 50 E
Datong, Anhui, China 39 30 48N 117 44 E
Datong, Shanxi, China 38 40 6N 113 18 E
Datu, Tanjung 34 2 5N 109 39 E
Datu Piang 35 7 2N 124 30 E
Daugava → 22 57 4N 24 3 E
Daugavpils 22 55 53N 26 32 E
Daulpur 32 26 45N 77 59 E
Dauphin 65 51 9N 100 5W
Dauphin I. 69 30 16N 88 10W
Dauphin L. 65 51 20N 99 45W
Dauphiné 12 45 15N 5 25 E
Daura 53 11 31N 11 24 E
Davangere 32 14 25N 75 55 E
Davao 35 7 0N 125 40 E
Davao, G. of 35 6 30N 125 48 E
Dāvar Panāh 31 27 25N 62 15 E
Davenport, Iowa, U.S.A. 70 41 30N 90 40W
Davenport, Wash., U.S.A. 72 47 40N 118 5W
Davenport Downs 44 24 8S 141 7 E
Davenport Ra. 44 20 28S 134 0 E
David 75 8 30N 82 30W
David City 70 41 18N 97 10W
Davidson 65 51 16N 105 59W
Davis 72 38 33N 121 44W
Davis Dam 73 35 11N 114 35W
Davis Inlet 63 55 50N 60 59W
Davis Mts. 71 30 42N 104 15W
Davis Str. 61 65 0N 58 0W
Davos 14 46 48N 9 49 E
Davy L. 65 58 53N 108 18W
Dawes Ra. 44 24 40S 150 40 E
Dawson, Canada 60 64 10N 139 30W
Dawson, Ga., U.S.A. 69 31 45N 84 28W
Dawson, N. Dak., U.S.A. 70 46 56N 99 45W
Dawson, I. 80 53 50S 70 50W
Dawson Creek 64 55 45N 120 15W
Dawson Inlet 65 61 50N 93 25W
Dawson Range 44 24 30S 149 48 E
Daxian 39 31 15N 107 23 E
Daxin 39 22 50N 107 11 E
Daxue Shan 37 30 30N 101 30 E
Daye 39 30 6N 114 58 E
Dayong 39 29 11N 110 30 E
Dayr Abū Sa'īd 28 32 30N 35 42 E
Dayr al-Ghuṣūn 28 32 21N 35 4 E
Dayr az Zawr 30 35 20N 40 5 E
Dayr Dirwān 28 31 55N 35 15 E
Daysland 64 52 50N 112 20W
Dayton, Ohio, U.S.A. 68 39 45N 84 10W
Dayton, Tenn., U.S.A. 69 35 30N 85 1W
Dayton, Wash., U.S.A. 72 46 20N 118 10W
Daytona Beach 69 29 14N 81 0W
Dayu 39 25 24N 114 22 E
Dayville 72 44 33N 119 37W
Dazhu 39 30 41N 107 15 E
Dazu 39 29 40N 105 42 E
De Aar 56 30 39S 24 0 E
De Funiak Springs 69 30 42N 86 10W
De Grey 46 20 12S 119 12 E
De Grey → 46 20 12S 119 13 E
De Kalb 70 41 55N 88 45W
De Land 69 29 1N 81 19W
De Leon 71 32 9N 98 35W
De Pere 68 44 28N 88 1W
De Queen 71 34 3N 94 24W
De Quincy 71 30 30N 93 27W
De Ridder 71 30 48N 93 15W
De Smet 70 44 25N 97 35W
De Soto 70 38 7N 90 33W
De Tour 68 45 59N 83 56W
De Witt 71 34 19N 91 20W
Dead Sea 28 31 30N 35 30 E
Deadwood 70 44 23N 103 44W
Deadwood L. 64 59 10N 128 30W
Deakin 47 30 46S 128 58 E
Deal 7 51 13N 1 25 E
Deal I. 44 39 30S 147 20 E
Dealesville 56 28 41S 25 44 E
Dean, Forest of 7 51 50N 2 35W
Deán Funes 80 30 20S 64 20W
Dearborn 62 42 18N 83 15W
Dease → 64 59 56N 128 32W
Dease L. 64 58 40N 130 5W
Dease Lake 64 58 25N 130 6W
Death Valley 73 36 19N 116 52W
Death Valley Junc. 73 36 21N 116 30W
Death Valley Nat. Monument 73 36 30N 117 0W
Deba Habe 53 10 14N 11 20 E
Debao 39 23 21N 106 46 E
Debar 19 41 31N 20 30 E
Debden 65 53 30N 106 50W
Debolt 64 55 12N 118 1W
Deborah East, L. 47 30 45S 119 0 E
Deborah West, L. 47 30 45S 118 50 E
Debre Markos 51 10 20N 37 40 E
Debre Tabor 51 11 50N 38 26 E
Debrecen 15 47 33N 21 42 E
Decatur, Ala., U.S.A. 69 34 35N 87 0W
Decatur, Ga., U.S.A. 69 33 47N 84 17W
Decatur, Ill., U.S.A. 70 39 50N 89 0W
Decatur, Ind., U.S.A. 68 40 50N 84 56W
Decatur, Tex., U.S.A. 71 33 15N 97 35W
Deccan 32 18 0N 79 0 E
Deception L. 65 56 33N 104 13W
Decorah 70 43 20N 91 50W
Dedéagach = Alexandroúpolis 19 40 50N 25 54 E
Dédougou 50 12 30N 3 25W
Dee →, Scotland, U.K. 8 57 4N 2 7W
Dee →, Wales, U.K. 6 53 15N 3 7W
Deep B. 64 61 15N 116 35W
Deep Well 44 24 20S 134 0 E
Deepwater 45 29 25S 151 51 E
Deer → 65 58 23N 94 13W
Deer Lake, Nfld., Canada 63 49 11N 57 27W
Deer Lake, Ont., Canada 65 52 36N 94 20W
Deer Lodge 72 46 25N 112 40W
Deer Park 72 47 55N 117 21W
Deer River 70 47 21N 93 44W
Deeral 44 17 14S 145 55 E
Deerdepoort 56 24 37S 26 27 E
Defiance 68 41 20N 84 20W
Deganya 28 32 43N 35 34 E
Degeh Bur 29 8 11N 43 31 E
Degema 53 4 50N 6 48 E
Deggendorf 14 48 49N 12 59 E
Deh Bīd 31 30 39N 53 11 E
Dehi Titan 32 33 45N 63 50 E
Dehibat 50 32 0N 10 47 E
Dehkareqan 30 37 43N 45 55 E
Dehra Dun 32 30 20N 78 4 E
Dehui 38 44 30N 125 40 E
Deinze 11 50 59N 3 32 E
Dej 15 47 10N 23 52 E
Dekese 54 3 24S 21 24 E
Del Norte 73 37 40N 106 27W
Del Rio 71 29 23N 100 50W
Delano 73 35 48N 119 13W
Delareyville 56 26 41S 25 26 E
Delavan 70 42 40N 88 39W
Delaware 68 40 20N 83 0W
Delaware □ 68 39 0N 75 40W
Delaware → 68 39 20N 75 25W
Delegate 45 37 4S 148 56 E
Delft 11 52 1N 4 22 E
Delfzijl 11 53 20N 6 55 E
Delgado, C. 54 10 45S 40 40 E
Delgo 51 20 6N 30 40 E
Delhi 32 28 38N 77 17 E
Delia 64 51 38N 112 23W
Delice → 30 39 45N 34 15 E
Delicias 74 28 10N 105 30W
Dell City 73 31 58N 105 19W
Dell Rapids 70 43 53N 96 44W
Delmiro Gouveia 79 9 24S 38 6W
Delong, Ostrova 25 76 40N 149 20 E
Deloraine, Australia 44 41 30S 146 40 E
Deloraine, Canada 65 49 15N 100 29W
Delphi 68 40 37N 86 40W
Delphos 68 40 51N 84 17W
Delportshoop 56 28 22S 24 20 E
Delray Beach 69 26 27N 80 4W
Delta, Colo., U.S.A. 73 38 44N 108 5W
Delta, Utah, U.S.A. 72 39 21N 112 29W
Delungra 45 29 39S 150 51 E
Demanda, Sierra de la 13 42 15N 3 0W
Demba 54 5 28S 22 15 E
Dembecha 51 10 32N 37 30 E
Dembidolo 51 8 34N 34 50 E
Demer → 11 50 57N 4 42 E
Deming 73 32 10N 107 50W
Demini → 78 0 46S 62 56W
Demopolis 69 32 30N 87 48W
Dempo, Mt. 34 4 2S 103 15 E
Den Burg 11 53 3N 4 47 E
Den Haag = 's-Gravenhage 11 52 7N 4 17 E
Den Helder 11 52 57N 4 45 E
Den Oever 11 52 56N 5 2 E
Denain 11 50 20N 3 22 E
Denau 24 38 16N 67 54 E
Denbigh 6 53 12N 3 26W
Dendang 34 3 7S 107 56 E
Dendermonde 11 51 2N 4 5 E
Deng Xian 39 32 34N 112 4 E
Dengi 53 9 25N 9 55 E
Denham 47 25 56S 113 31 E
Denham Ra. 44 21 55S 147 46 E
Denham Sd. 47 25 45S 113 15 E
Denia 13 38 49N 0 8 E
Denial B. 45 32 14S 133 32 E
Deniliquin 45 35 30S 144 58 E
Denison, Iowa, U.S.A. 70 42 0N 95 18W
Denison, Tex., U.S.A. 71 33 50N 96 40W
Denison Plains 46 18 35S 128 0 E
Denizli 30 37 42N 29 2 E
Denmark 47 34 59S 117 25 E
Denmark ■ 21 55 30N 9 0 E
Denmark Str. 2 66 0N 30 0W
Denpasar 34 8 45S 115 14 E
Denton, Mont., U.S.A. 72 47 25N 109 56W
Denton, Tex., U.S.A. 71 33 12N 97 10W
D'Entrecasteaux Pt. 47 34 50S 115 57 E
Denver 70 39 45N 105 0W
Denver City 71 32 58N 102 48W
Deoghar 33 24 30N 86 42 E
Deolali 32 19 58N 73 50 E
Deoria 33 26 31N 83 48 E
Deosai Mts. 32 35 40N 75 0 E
Deping 38 37 25N 116 58 E
Depot Springs 47 27 55S 120 3 E
Deputatskiy 25 69 18N 139 54 E
Dêqên 37 28 34N 98 51 E
Deqing 39 23 8N 111 42 E
Dera Ghazi Khan 32 30 5N 70 43 E
Dera Ismail Khan 32 31 50N 70 50 E
Derbent 23 42 5N 48 15 E
Derby, Australia 46 17 18S 123 38 E
Derby, U.K. 6 52 55N 1 28W
Derby □ 6 52 55N 1 28W
Derg → 9 54 42N 7 26W
Derg, L. 9 53 0N 8 20W
Dergaon 33 26 45N 94 0 E
Dernieres Isles 71 29 0N 90 45W
Derry = Londonderry 9 55 0N 7 20W
Derryveagh Mts. 9 55 0N 8 40W
Derudub 51 17 31N 36 7 E
Derwent 65 53 41N 110 58W
Derwent →, Derby, U.K. 6 52 53N 1 17W
Derwent →, N. Yorks., U.K. 6 53 45N 0 57W
Derwent Water, L. 6 54 35N 3 9W
Des Moines, Iowa, U.S.A. 70 41 35N 93 37W
Des Moines, N. Mex., U.S.A. 71 36 50N 103 51W
Des Moines → 70 40 23N 91 25W
Desaguadero → 78 18 24S 67 5W
Deschaillons 63 46 32N 72 7W
Descharme → 65 56 51N 109 13W
Deschutes → 72 45 30N 121 0W
Dese 29 11 5N 39 40 E
Desert Center 73 33 45N 115 27W
Deskenatlata L. 64 60 55N 112 3W
Desna → 22 50 33N 30 32 E
Desolación, I. 80 53 0S 74 0W
Despeñaperros, Paso 13 38 24N 3 30W
Dessau 14 51 49N 12 15 E
Dessye = Dese 29 11 5N 39 40 E
D'Estrees B. 45 35 55S 137 45 E
Detmold 14 51 55N 8 50 E
Detour Pt. 68 45 37N 86 35W
Detroit, Mich., U.S.A. 62 42 23N 83 5W
Detroit, Tex., U.S.A. 71 33 40N 95 10W
Detroit Lakes 70 46 50N 95 50W
Deurne, Belgium 11 51 12N 4 24 E
Deurne, Neth. 11 51 27N 5 49 E
Deutsche Bucht 14 54 0N 8 0 E
Deux-Sèvres □ 12 46 35N 0 20W
Deva 15 45 53N 22 55 E
Devakottai 32 9 55N 78 45 E
Deventer 11 52 15N 6 10 E
Deveron → 8 57 40N 2 31W
Devils Lake 70 48 5N 98 50W
Devils Paw 64 58 47N 134 0W
Devizes 7 51 21N 2 0W
Devon 64 53 24N 113 44W
Devon I. 58 75 10N 85 0W
Devonport, Australia 44 41 10S 146 22 E
Devonport, N.Z. 43 36 49S 174 49 E
Devonport, U.K. 7 50 23N 4 11W
Devonshire □ 7 50 50N 3 40W
Dewas 32 22 59N 76 3 E
Dewetsdorp 56 29 33S 26 39 E
Dewsbury 6 53 42N 1 38W
Dexter, Mo., U.S.A. 71 36 50N 90 0W
Dexter, N. Mex., U.S.A. 71 33 15N 104 25W
Dey-Dey, L. 47 29 12S 131 4 E
Deyhūk 31 33 15N 57 30 E
Deyyer 31 27 55N 51 55 E
Dezadeash L. 64 60 28N 136 58W
Dezfūl 30 32 20N 48 30 E
Dezhneva, Mys 25 66 5N 169 40W
Dezhou 38 37 26N 116 18 E
Dhafra 31 23 20N 54 0 E
Dhahira 31 23 40N 57 0 E
Dhahran = Aẓ Ẓahrān 30 26 10N 50 7 E
Dhaka 33 23 43N 90 26 E
Dhaka □ 33 24 25N 90 25 E
Dhamar 29 14 30N 44 20 E
Dhamtari 33 20 42N 81 35 E
Dhanbad 33 23 50N 86 30 E
Dhangarhi 33 28 55N 80 40 E
Dhankuta 33 26 55N 87 40 E
Dhar 32 22 35N 75 26 E
Dharmapuri 32 12 10N 78 10 E
Dharwad 32 15 22N 75 15 E
Dharwar 32 15 43N 75 1 E
Dhaulagiri 33 28 39N 83 28 E
Dhenkanal 33 20 45N 85 35 E
Dhidhimótikhon 19 41 22N 26 29 E
Dhikti 19 35 8N 25 22 E
Dhírfis 19 38 40N 23 54 E
Dhodhekánisos 19 36 35N 27 0 E
Dhrol 32 22 33N 70 25 E
Dhubaibah 31 23 25N 54 35 E
Dhuburi 33 26 2N 89 59 E
Dhule 32 20 58N 74 50 E
Diablo Heights 74 8 58N 79 34W
Diafarabé 50 14 9N 4 57W
Diamantina 79 18 17S 43 40W
Diamantina → 45 26 45S 139 10 E
Diamantino 79 14 30S 56 30W
Diamond Harbour 33 22 11N 88 14 E
Diamond Is. 44 17 25S 151 5 E
Diamond Mts. 72 40 0N 115 58W
Diamondville 72 41 51N 110 30W
Diancheng 39 21 30N 111 4 E
Diapaga 53 12 5N 1 46 E
Dībā 31 25 45N 56 16 E
Dibaya 54 6 30S 22 57 E
Dibaya-Lubue 54 4 12S 19 54 E
Dibbi 29 4 10N 41 52 E
Dibete 56 23 45S 26 32 E
Dibrugarh 33 27 29N 94 55 E
Dickinson 70 46 50N 102 48W
Dickson, U.S.A. 69 36 5N 87 22W
Dickson, U.S.S.R. 24 73 40N 80 5 E
Didiéni 50 13 53N 8 6W
Didsbury 64 51 35N 114 10W
Diébougou 50 11 0N 3 15W
Diefenbaker L. 65 51 0N 106 55W
Diego Garcia 3 7 50S 72 50 E
Diekirch 11 49 52N 6 10 E
Dieppe 12 49 54N 1 4 E
Dieren 11 52 3N 6 6 E
Dierks 71 34 9N 94 0W
Diest 11 50 58N 5 4 E
Differdange 11 49 31N 5 54 E
Digby 63 44 38N 65 50W
Digges 65 58 40N 94 0W
Digges Is. 61 62 40N 77 50W
Dighinala 33 23 15N 92 5 E
Dighton 70 38 30N 100 26W
Digne 12 44 5N 6 12 E
Digos 35 6 45N 125 20 E
Digranes 20 66 4N 14 44 E
Digul → 35 7 7S 138 42 E
Dihang → 33 27 48N 95 30 E
Dijlah, Nahr → 30 31 0N 47 25 E
Dijon 12 47 20N 5 0 E
Dikomu di Kai 56 24 58S 24 36 E
Diksmuide 11 51 2N 2 52 E
Dikson = Dickson 24 73 40N 80 5 E
Dikwa 53 12 4N 13 30 E
Dili 35 8 39S 125 34 E
Dilley 71 28 40N 99 12W
Dilling 51 12 3N 29 35 E
Dillon, Canada 65 55 56N 108 35W
Dillon, Mont., U.S.A. 72 45 9N 112 36W
Dillon, S.C., U.S.A. 69 34 26N 79 20W
Dillon → 65 55 56N 108 56W
Dilolo 54 10 28S 22 18 E
Dilston 44 41 22S 147 10 E
Dimashq 30 33 30N 36 18 E
Dimbaza 57 32 50S 27 14 E
Dimbokro 50 6 45N 4 46W
Dimboola 45 36 28S 142 7 E
Dîmboviţa → 15 44 5N 26 35 E
Dimbulah 44 17 8S 145 4 E
Dimitrovgrad, Bulgaria 19 42 5N 25 35 E
Dimitrovgrad, U.S.S.R. 22 54 14N 49 39 E
Dimmitt 71 34 36N 102 16W
Dimona 28 31 2N 35 1 E
Dinagat 35 10 10N 125 40 E
Dinajpur 33 25 33N 88 43 E
Dinan 12 48 28N 2 2W
Dinant 11 50 16N 4 55 E
Dinar 30 38 5N 30 15 E
Dinara Planina 18 44 0N 16 30 E
Dinard 12 48 38N 2 6W
Dinaric Alps = Dinara Planina 18 44 0N 16 30 E
Dindigul 32 10 25N 78 0 E
Ding Xian 38 38 30N 114 59 E
Dingbian 38 37 35N 107 32 E
Dinghai 39 30 1N 122 6 E
Dingle 9 52 9N 10 17W
Dingle B. 9 52 3N 10 20W
Dingnan 39 24 45N 115 0 E
Dingo 44 23 38S 149 19 E
Dingtao 39 35 5N 115 35 E
Dinguiraye 50 11 18N 10 49W
Dingwall 8 57 36N 4 26W
Dingxi 38 35 30N 104 33 E
Dingxiang 38 38 30N 112 58 E
Dinokwe 56 23 29S 26 37 E
Dinosaur National Monument 72 40 30N 108 58W
Dinuba 73 36 31N 119 22W
Diourbel 50 14 39N 16 12W
Dipolog 35 8 36N 123 20 E
Dir 31 35 8N 71 59 E
Diré 50 16 20N 3 25W
Dire Dawa 29 9 35N 41 45 E
Diriamba 75 11 51N 86 19W
Dirico 55 17 50S 20 42 E
Dirk Hartog I. 47 25 50S 113 5 E
Dirranbandi 45 28 33S 148 17 E

Eagle Pt.

Disa 32 24 18N 72 10 E
Disappointment, C. 72 46 20N 124 0W
Disappointment L. 46 23 20S 122 40 E
Disaster B. 45 37 15S 150 0 E
Discovery B. 45 38 10S 140 40 E
Disko 58 69 45N 53 30W
Disteghil Sar 32 36 20N 75 12 E
Distrito Federal □ 79 15 45S 47 45W
Diu 32 20 45N 70 58 E
Divide 72 45 48N 112 47W
Dividing Ra. 47 27 45S 116 0 E
Divinópolis 79 20 10S 44 54W
Divnoye 23 45 55N 43 21 E
Diwäl Kol 32 34 23N 67 52 E
Dixon, Ill., U.S.A. 70 41 50N 89 30W
Dixon, Mont., U.S.A. 72 47 19N 114 25W
Dixon, N. Mex., U.S.A. 73 36 15N 105 57W
Dixon Entrance 64 54 30N 132 0W
Dixonville 64 56 32N 117 40W
Diyarbakir 30 37 55N 40 18 E
Diz Chah 31 35 30N 55 30 E
Djado 51 21 4N 12 14 E
Djakarta = Jakarta 35 6 9S 106 49 E
Djamba 56 16 45S 13 58 E
Djambala 54 2 32S 14 30 E
Djanet 50 24 35N 9 32 E
Djawa = Jawa 35 7 0S 110 0 E
Djelfa 50 34 40N 3 15 E
Djema 54 6 3N 25 15 E
Djenné 50 14 0N 4 30W
Djerid, Chott 50 33 42N 8 30 E
Djibo 53 14 9N 1 35W
Djibouti 29 11 30N 43 5 E
Djibouti ■ 29 12 0N 43 0 E
Djolu 54 0 35N 22 5 E
Djougou 53 9 40N 1 45 E
Djoum 54 2 41N 12 35 E
Djourab 51 16 40N 18 50 E
Djugu 54 1 55N 30 35 E
Djúpivogur 20 64 39N 14 17W
Dmitriya Lapteva, Proliv 25 73 0N 140 0 E
Dnepr → 23 46 30N 32 18 E
Dneprodzerzhinsk 23 48 32N 34 37 E
Dnepropetrovsk 23 48 30N 35 0 E
Dnestr → 23 46 18N 30 17 E
Dnestrovski = Belgorod 23 50 35N 36 35 E
Dnieper = Dnepr → 23 46 30N 32 18 E
Dniester = Dnestr → 23 46 18N 30 17 E
Doba 51 8 40N 16 50 E
Dobbyn 44 19 44S 140 2 E
Doberai, Jazirah 35 1 25S 133 0 E
Doblas 80 37 5S 64 0W
Dobo 35 5 45S 134 15 E
Dobruja 15 44 30N 28 15 E
Dodecanese = Dhodhekánisos 19 36 35N 27 0 E
Dodge Center 70 44 1N 92 50W
Dodge City 71 37 42N 100 0W
Dodge L. 65 59 50N 105 36W
Dodgeville 70 42 55N 90 8W
Dodoma 54 6 8S 35 45 E
Dodsland 65 51 50N 108 45W
Dodson 72 48 23N 108 16W
Doetinchem 11 51 59N 6 18 E
Dog Creek 64 51 35N 122 14W
Dog L., Man., Canada 65 51 2N 98 31W
Dog L., Ont., Canada 62 48 48N 89 30W
Dogger Bank 4 54 50N 2 0 E
Dogi 32 32 20N 62 50 E
Dogondoutchi 53 13 38N 4 2 E
Dohazari 33 22 10N 92 5 E
Doi 35 2 14N 127 49 E
Doig → 64 56 25N 120 40W
Dois Irmãos, Sa. 79 9 0S 42 30W
Dokka 21 60 49N 10 7 E
Dokkum 11 53 20N 5 59 E
Doland 70 44 55N 98 5W
Dolbeau 63 48 53N 72 18W
Dole 12 47 7N 5 31 E
Dolgellau 6 52 44N 3 53W
Dolgelley = Dolgellau 6 52 44N 3 53W
Dollart 11 53 20N 7 10 E
Dolomites = Dolomiti 18 46 30N 11 40 E
Dolomiti 18 46 30N 11 40 E
Dolores, Argentina 80 36 20S 57 40W
Dolores, U.S.A. 73 37 30N 108 30W
Dolores → 73 38 49N 108 17W
Dolphin, C. 80 51 10S 59 0W
Dolphin and Union Str. 60 69 5N 114 45W
Dombarovskiy 24 50 46N 59 32 E
Dombås 21 62 4N 9 8 E
Dombes 12 46 0N 5 0 E
Domburg 11 51 34N 3 30 E
Dominica ■ 75 15 20N 61 20W
Dominican Rep. ■ 75 19 0N 70 30W
Domo 29 7 50N 47 10 E
Domodóssola 18 46 6N 8 19 E
Domville, Mt. 45 28 1S 151 15 E
Don →, England, U.K. 6 53 41N 0 51W
Don →, Scotland, U.K. 8 57 14N 2 5W
Don →, U.S.S.R. 23 47 4N 39 18 E
Don, C. 46 11 18S 131 46 E
Don Benito 13 38 53N 5 51W
Don Martín, Presa de 74 27 30N 100 50W
Donaghadee 9 54 38N 5 32W
Donald 45 36 23S 143 0 E
Donalda 64 52 35N 112 34W
Donaldsonville 71 30 2N 91 0W
Donalsonville 69 31 3N 84 52W
Donau → 14 48 10N 17 0 E
Donauwörth 14 48 42N 10 47 E
Doncaster 6 53 31N 1 9W
Dondo, Angola 54 9 45S 14 25 E
Dondo, Mozam. 55 19 33S 34 46 E
Dondo, Teluk 35 0 29N 120 30 E
Dondra Head 32 5 55N 80 40 E
Donegal 9 54 39N 8 8W
Donegal □ 9 54 53N 8 0W
Donegal B. 9 54 30N 8 35W
Donets → 23 47 33N 40 55 E
Donetsk 23 48 0N 37 45 E
Dongara 47 29 14S 114 57 E
Dongfang 39 18 50N 108 33 E
Donggala 35 0 30S 119 40 E
Donggou 38 39 52N 124 10 E
Dongguan 39 22 58N 113 44 E
Dongguang 38 37 50N 116 30 E
Dongjingcheng 38 44 0N 129 10 E
Donglan 39 24 30N 107 21 E
Dongliu 39 30 13N 116 55 E
Dongola 51 19 9N 30 22 E
Dongou 54 2 0N 18 5 E
Dongping 38 35 55N 116 20 E
Dongshan 39 23 43N 117 30 E
Dongsheng 38 39 50N 110 0 E
Dongtai 39 32 51N 120 21 E
Dongting Hu 37 29 18N 112 45 E
Dongxing 39 21 34N 108 0 E
Dongyang 39 29 13N 120 15 E
Donington, C. 45 34 45S 136 0 E
Doniphan 71 36 40N 90 50W
Dønna, Norway 20 66 6N 12 30 E
Donna, U.S.A. 71 26 12N 98 2W
Donnaconna 63 46 41N 71 41W
Donnelly's Crossing 43 35 42S 173 38 E
Donnybrook, Australia 47 33 34S 115 48 E
Donnybrook, S. Africa 57 29 59S 29 48 E
Donor's Hill 44 18 42S 140 33 E
Doon → 8 55 26N 4 41W
Dor 28 32 37N 34 55 E
Dora, L. 46 22 0S 123 0 E
Dora Báltea → 18 45 11N 8 5 E
Dorada, La 78 5 30N 74 40W
Doran L. 65 61 13N 108 6W
Dorchester 7 50 42N 2 28W
Dorchester, C. 61 65 27N 77 27W
Dordogne □ 12 45 5N 0 40 E
Dordogne → 12 45 2N 0 36W
Dordrecht, Neth. 11 51 48N 4 39 E
Dordrecht, S. Africa 56 31 20S 27 3 E
Dore, Mts. 12 45 32N 2 50 E
Doré L. 65 54 46N 107 17W
Doré Lake 65 54 38N 107 36W
Dori 53 14 3N 0 2W
Doring → 56 31 54S 18 39 E
Doringbos 56 31 59S 19 16 E
Dorion 62 45 23N 74 3W
Dornoch 8 57 52N 4 0W
Dornoch Firth 8 57 52N 4 0W
Dorohoi 15 47 56N 26 30 E
Döröö Nuur 37 48 0N 93 0 E
Dorre I. 47 25 13S 113 12 E
Dorrigo 45 30 20S 152 44 E
Dorris 72 41 59N 121 58W
Dorset □ 7 50 48N 2 25W
Dortmund 14 51 32N 7 28 E
Doruma 54 4 42N 27 33 E
Dos Bahías, C. 80 44 58S 65 32W
Dosso 53 13 0N 3 13 E
Dothan 69 31 10N 85 25W
Douai 12 50 21N 3 4 E
Douala 54 4 0N 9 45 E
Douarnenez 12 48 6N 4 21W
Double Island Pt. 45 25 56S 153 11 E
Doubs □ 12 47 10N 6 20 E
Doubs → 12 46 53N 5 1 E
Doubtful Sd. 43 45 20S 166 49 E
Doubtless B. 43 34 55S 173 26 E
Douentza 50 14 58N 2 48W
Douglas, S. Africa 56 29 4S 23 46 E
Douglas, U.K. 6 54 9N 4 29W
Douglas, Alaska, U.S.A. 64 58 23N 134 24W
Douglas, Ariz., U.S.A. 73 31 21N 109 30W
Douglas, Ga., U.S.A. 69 31 32N 82 52W
Douglas, Wyo., U.S.A. 70 42 45N 105 20W
Douglastown 63 48 46N 64 24W
Douglasville 69 33 46N 84 43W
Doumé 54 4 15N 13 25 E
Dounreay 8 58 34N 3 44W
Dourados 80 22 9S 54 50W
Douro → 13 41 8N 8 40W
Douro Litoral □ 13 41 10N 8 20W
Dove → 6 52 51N 1 36W
Dove Creek 73 37 46N 108 59W
Dover, Australia 44 43 18S 147 2 E
Dover, U.K. 7 51 7N 1 19 E
Dover, Del., U.S.A. 68 39 10N 75 31W
Dover, N.H., U.S.A. 68 43 12N 70 51W
Dover, Ohio, U.S.A. 68 40 32N 81 30W
Dover, Pt. 47 32 32S 125 32 E
Dover, Str. of 12 51 0N 1 30 E
Dover-Foxcroft 63 45 14N 69 14W
Dovey → 7 52 32N 4 0W
Dovrefjell 20 62 15N 9 33 E
Dowagiac 68 41 58N 86 8W
Dowlat Yār 31 34 30N 65 45 E
Dowlatābād 31 28 20N 56 40W
Down □ 9 54 20N 6 0W
Downey 72 42 29N 112 3W
Downham Market 7 52 36N 0 22 E
Downieville 72 39 34N 120 50W
Downpatrick 9 54 20N 5 43W
Downpatrick Hd. 9 54 20N 9 21W
Dowshī 31 35 35N 68 43 E
Draa, Oued → 50 28 40N 11 10W
Drachten 11 53 7N 6 5 E
Dragoman, Prokhod 19 43 0N 22 53 E
Draguignan 12 43 32N 6 27 E
Drain 72 43 45N 123 17W
Drake, Australia 45 28 55S 152 25 E
Drake, U.S.A. 70 47 56N 100 21W
Drakensberg 57 31 0S 28 0 E
Dráma 19 41 9N 24 10 E
Drammen 21 59 42N 10 12 E
Drangajökull 20 66 9N 22 15W
Drau = Drava → 19 45 33N 18 55 E
Drava → 19 45 33N 18 55 E
Drayton Valley 64 53 12N 114 58W
Drenthe □ 11 52 52N 6 40 E
Dresden 14 51 2N 13 45 E
Dreux 12 48 44N 1 23 E
Driffield 6 54 0N 0 25W
Driggs 72 43 50N 111 8W
Drina → 19 44 53N 19 21 E
Drøbak 21 59 39N 10 39 E
Drogheda 9 53 45N 6 20W
Drogobych 23 49 20N 23 30 E
Droichead Nua 9 53 11N 6 50W
Droitwich 7 52 16N 2 10W
Drôme □ 12 44 38N 5 15 E
Dromedary, C. 45 36 17S 150 10 E
Dronfield 44 21 12S 140 3 E
Drumheller 64 51 25N 112 40W
Drummond 72 46 40N 113 4W
Drummond I. 62 46 0N 83 40W
Drummond Pt. 45 34 9S 135 16 E
Drummond Ra. 44 23 45S 147 10 E
Drummondville 62 45 55N 72 25W
Drumright 71 35 59N 96 38W
Druzhina 25 68 14N 145 18 E
Dry Tortugas 75 24 38N 82 55W
Dryden, Canada 65 49 47N 92 50W
Dryden, U.S.A. 71 30 3N 102 3W
Drysdale → 46 13 59S 126 51 E
Drysdale I. 44 11 41S 136 0 E
Dschang 53 5 32N 10 3 E
Du Bois 68 41 8N 78 46W
Du Quoin 70 38 0N 89 10W
Duaringa 44 23 42S 149 42 E
Ḍubā 30 27 10N 35 40 E
Dubai = Dubayy 31 25 18N 55 20 E
Dubawnt → 65 64 33N 100 6W
Dubawnt, L. 65 63 4N 101 42W
Dubayy 31 25 18N 55 20 E
Dubbo 45 32 11S 148 35 E
Dublin, Ireland 9 53 20N 6 18W
Dublin, Ga., U.S.A. 69 32 30N 82 34W
Dublin, Tex., U.S.A. 71 32 0N 98 20W
Dublin □ 9 53 24N 6 20W
Dublin B. 9 53 18N 6 5W
Dubois 72 44 7N 112 9W
Dubovka 23 49 5N 44 50 E
Dubréka 50 9 46N 13 31W
Dubrovnik 19 42 39N 18 6 E
Dubrovskoye 25 58 55N 111 10 E
Dubuque 70 42 30N 90 41W
Duchang 39 29 18N 116 12 E
Duchesne 72 40 14N 110 22W
Duchess 44 21 20S 139 50 E
Ducie I. 41 24 40S 124 48W
Duck Cr. → 46 22 37S 116 53 E
Duck Lake 65 52 50N 106 16W
Duck Mt. Prov. Parks 65 51 45N 101 0W
Dudhi 33 24 15N 83 10 E
Dudinka 25 69 30N 86 13 E
Dudley 7 52 30N 2 5W
Duero → 13 41 8N 8 40W
Dufftown 8 57 26N 3 9W
Dugi Otok 18 44 0N 15 0 E
Duifken Pt. 44 12 33S 141 38 E
Duisburg 14 51 27N 6 42 E
Duiwelskloof 57 23 42S 30 10 E
Duke I. 64 54 50N 131 20W
Dukhān 31 25 25N 50 50 E
Duki 32 30 14N 68 25 E
Duku 53 10 43N 10 43 E
Dulce → 80 30 32S 62 33W
Dulce, G. 75 8 40N 83 20W
Dulit, Banjaran 34 3 15N 114 30 E
Dululu 44 23 48S 150 15 E
Duluth 70 46 48N 92 10W
Dum Duma 33 27 40N 95 40 E
Dum Hadjer 51 13 18N 19 41 E
Dumaguete 35 9 17N 123 15 E
Dumai 34 1 35N 101 28 E
Dumaran 35 10 33N 119 50 E
Dumas, Ark., U.S.A. 71 33 52N 91 30W
Dumas, Tex., U.S.A. 71 35 50N 101 58W
Dumbarton 8 55 58N 4 35W
Dumbleyung 47 33 17S 117 42 E
Dumfries 8 55 4N 3 37W
Dumfries & Galloway □ 8 55 0N 4 0W
Dumoine → 62 46 13N 77 51W
Dumoine L. 62 46 55N 77 55W
Dumyât 51 31 24N 31 48 E
Dun Laoghaire 9 53 17N 6 9W
Dunaföldvár 15 46 50N 18 57 E
Dunărea → 15 45 20N 29 40 E
Dunback 43 45 23S 170 36 E
Dunbar, Australia 44 16 0S 142 22 E
Dunbar, U.K. 8 56 0N 2 32W
Dunblane 8 56 10N 3 58W
Duncan, Canada 64 48 45N 123 40W
Duncan, Ariz., U.S.A. 73 32 46N 109 6W
Duncan, Okla., U.S.A. 71 34 25N 98 0W
Duncan, L. 62 53 29N 77 58W
Duncan L. 64 62 51N 113 58W
Duncan Town 75 22 15N 75 45W
Dundalk 9 54 1N 6 25W
Dundalk Bay 9 53 55N 6 15W
Dundas 62 43 17N 79 59W
Dundas, L. 47 32 35S 121 50 E
Dundas I. 64 54 30N 130 50W
Dundas Str. 46 11 15S 131 35 E
Dundee, S. Africa 57 28 11S 30 15 E
Dundee, U.K. 8 56 29N 3 0W
Dundoo 45 27 40S 144 37 E
Dundrum 9 54 17N 5 50W
Dundrum B. 9 54 12N 5 40W
Dunedin, N.Z. 43 45 50S 170 33 E
Dunedin, U.S.A. 69 28 1N 82 45W
Dunedin → 64 59 30N 124 5W
Dunfermline 8 56 5N 3 28W
Dungannon 9 54 30N 6 47W
Dungannon □ 9 54 30N 6 55W
Dungarvan 9 52 6N 7 40W
Dungarvan Bay 9 52 5N 7 35W
Dungeness 7 50 54N 0 59 E
Dungo, L. do 56 17 15S 19 0 E
Dungog 45 32 22S 151 46 E
Dungu 54 3 40N 28 32 E
Dunhua 38 43 20N 128 14 E
Dunhuang 37 40 8N 94 36 E
Dunk I. 44 17 59S 146 29 E
Dunkeld 8 56 34N 3 36W
Dunkerque 12 51 2N 2 20 E
Dunkery Beacon 7 51 15N 3 37W
Dunkirk = Dunkerque 12 51 2N 2 20 E
Dunkirk 68 42 30N 79 18W
Dunkwa 50 6 0N 1 47W
Dunlap 70 41 50N 95 36W
Dúnleary = Dun Laoghaire 9 53 17N 6 9W
Dunmanus B. 9 51 31N 9 50W
Dunmara 44 16 42S 133 25 E
Dunmore 68 41 27N 75 38W
Dunmore Hd. 9 52 10N 10 35W
Dunn 69 35 18N 78 36W
Dunnellon 69 29 4N 82 28W
Dunnet Hd. 8 58 38N 3 22W
Dunning 70 41 52N 100 4W
Dunolly 45 36 51S 143 44 E
Dunoon 8 55 57N 4 56W
Dunqul 51 23 26N 31 37 E
Duns 8 55 47N 2 20W
Dunseith 70 48 49N 100 2W
Dunsmuir 72 41 10N 122 18W
Dunstable 7 51 53N 0 31W
Dunstan Mts. 43 44 53S 169 35 E
Dunster 64 53 8N 119 50W
Dunvegan L. 65 60 8N 107 10W
Duolun 38 42 12N 116 28 E
Dupree 70 45 4N 101 35W
Dupuyer 72 48 11N 112 31W
Dūrā 28 31 31N 35 1 E
Durack → 46 15 33S 127 52 E
Durack Range 46 16 50S 127 40 E
Durance → 12 43 55N 4 45 E
Durand 68 42 54N 83 58W
Durango, Spain 13 43 13N 2 40W
Durango, U.S.A. 73 37 16N 107 50W
Durango □ 74 25 0N 105 0W
Duranillin 47 33 30S 116 45 E
Durant 71 34 0N 96 25W
Durazno 80 33 25S 56 31W
Durazzo = Durrësi 19 41 19N 19 28 E
Durban 57 29 49S 31 1 E
Durg 33 21 15N 81 22 E
Durgapur 33 23 30N 87 20 E
Durham, Canada 62 44 10N 80 49W
Durham, U.K. 6 54 47N 1 34W
Durham, U.S.A. 69 36 0N 78 55W
Durham □ 6 54 42N 1 45W
Durham Downs 45 26 6S 141 47 E
Durmitor 16 43 10N 19 0 E
Durness 8 58 34N 4 45W
Durrësi 19 41 19N 19 28 E
Durrie 44 25 40S 140 15 E
D'Urville, Tanjung 35 1 28S 137 54 E
D'Urville I. 43 40 50S 173 55 E
Dusa Mareb 29 5 30N 46 15 E
Dushak 24 37 13N 60 1 E
Dushan 39 25 48N 107 30 E
Dushanbe 24 38 33N 68 48 E
Dusky Sd. 43 45 47S 166 30 E
Dussejour, C. 46 14 45S 128 13 E
Düsseldorf 14 51 15N 6 46 E
Dutch Harbor 60 53 54N 166 35W
Dutlwe 56 23 58S 23 46 E
Dutton → 44 20 44S 143 10 E
Duwādimi 30 24 35N 44 15 E
Duyun 39 26 18N 107 29 E
Duzce 30 40 50N 31 10 E
Duzdab = Zāhedān 31 29 30N 60 50 E
Dvina, Sev. → 22 64 32N 40 30 E
Dvinsk = Daugavpils 22 55 53N 26 32 E
Dvinskaya Guba 22 65 0N 39 0 E
Dwarka 32 22 18N 69 8 E
Dwellingup 47 32 43S 116 4 E
Dwight 68 41 5N 88 25W
Dyer, C. 61 66 40N 61 0W
Dyersburg 71 36 2N 89 20W
Dyfed □ 7 52 0N 4 30W
Dynevor Downs 45 28 10S 144 20 E
Dysart 65 50 57N 104 2W
Dzamin Üüd 37 43 50N 111 58 E
Dzerzhinsk, Byelorussian S.S.R., U.S.S.R. 22 53 40N 27 1 E
Dzerzhinsk, R.S.F.S.R., U.S.S.R. 22 56 14N 43 30 E
Dzhalinda 25 53 26N 124 0 E
Dzhambul 24 42 54N 71 22 E
Dzhankoi 23 45 40N 34 20 E
Dzhardzhan 25 68 10N 124 10 E
Dzhelinde 25 70 0N 114 20 E
Dzhetygara 24 52 11N 61 12 E
Dzhezkazgan 24 47 44N 67 40 E
Dzhikimde 25 59 1N 121 47 E
Dzhizak 24 40 6N 67 50 E
Dzhugdzur, Khrebet 25 57 30N 138 0 E
Dzhungarskiye Vorota 24 45 0N 82 0 E
Dzungaria = Junggar Pendi 37 44 30N 86 0 E
Dzungarian Gate = Alataw Shankou 37 45 5N 81 57 E
Dzungarian Gates = Dzhungarskiye Vorota 24 45 0N 82 0 E
Dzuumod 37 47 45N 106 58 E

E

Eabamet, L. 62 51 30N 87 46W
Eads 70 38 30N 102 46W
Eagle, Alaska, U.S.A. 60 64 44N 141 7W
Eagle, Colo., U.S.A. 72 39 39N 106 55W
Eagle → 63 53 36N 57 26W
Eagle Butt 70 45 1N 101 12W
Eagle Grove 70 42 37N 93 53W
Eagle L., Calif., U.S.A. 72 40 35N 120 50W
Eagle L., Maine, U.S.A. 63 46 23N 69 22W
Eagle Lake 71 29 35N 96 21W
Eagle Nest 73 36 33N 105 13W
Eagle Pass 71 28 45N 100 35W
Eagle Pt. 46 16 11S 124 23 E

Eagle River

Eagle River 70 45 55N 89 17W
Ealing 7 51 30N 0 19W
Earaheedy 47 25 34S 121 29 E
Earl Grey 65 50 57N 104 43W
Earle 71 35 18N 90 26W
Earlimart 73 35 53N 119 16W
Earn —► 8 56 20N 3 19W
Earn, L. 8 56 23N 4 14W
Earnslaw, Mt. 43 44 32S 168 27 E
Earoo 47 29 34S 118 22 E
Earth 71 34 18N 102 30W
Easley 69 34 52N 82 35W
East Angus 63 45 30N 71 40W
East B. 71 29 2N 89 16W
East Bengal 33 24 0N 90 0 E
East Beskids = Vychodné Beskydy 15 49 30N 22 0 E
East C. 43 37 42S 178 35 E
East Chicago 68 41 40N 87 30W
East China Sea 37 30 5N 126 0 E
East Coulee 64 51 23N 112 27W
East Falkland 80 51 30S 58 30W
East Germany ■ 14 52 0N 12 0 E
East Grand Forks 70 47 55N 97 5W
East Helena 72 46 37N 111 58W
East Indies 34 0 0 120 0 E
East Jordan 68 45 10N 85 7W
East Kilbride 8 55 46N 4 10W
East Lansing 68 42 44N 84 29W
East Liverpool 68 40 39N 80 35W
East London 57 33 0S 27 55 E
East Main = Eastmain 62 52 10N 78 30W
East Orange 68 40 46N 74 13W
East Pacific Ridge 41 15 0S 110 0W
East Pakistan = Bangladesh ■ 33 24 0N 90 0 E
East Pine 64 55 48N 120 12W
East Pt. 63 46 27N 61 58W
East Point 69 33 40N 84 28W
East Retford 6 53 19N 0 55W
East St. Louis 70 38 37N 90 4W
East Schelde —► = Oosterschelde 11 51 33N 4 0 E
East Siberian Sea 25 73 0N 160 0 E
East Sussex □ 7 51 0N 0 20 E
East Tawas 68 44 17N 83 31W
East Toorale 45 30 27S 145 28 E
Eastbourne, N.Z. 43 41 19S 174 55 E
Eastbourne, U.K. 7 50 46N 0 18 E
Eastend 65 49 32N 108 50W
Easter Islands 41 27 0S 109 0W
Eastern Cr. —► 44 20 40S 141 35 E
Eastern Ghats 32 14 0N 78 50 E
Eastern Group = Lau 43 17 0S 178 30W
Eastern Group 47 33 30S 124 30 E
Easterville 65 53 8N 99 49W
Eastland 71 32 26N 98 45W
Eastleigh 7 50 58N 1 21W
Eastmain 62 52 10N 78 30W
Eastmain —► 62 52 27N 78 26W
Eastman 69 32 13N 83 20W
Easton, Md., U.S.A. 68 38 47N 76 7W
Easton, Pa., U.S.A. 68 40 41N 75 15W
Easton, Wash., U.S.A. 72 47 14N 121 8W
Eastport 63 44 57N 67 0W
Eaton 70 40 35N 104 42W
Eatonia 65 51 13N 109 25W
Eatonton 69 33 22N 83 24W
Eau Claire 70 44 46N 91 30W
Ebagoola 44 14 15S 143 12 E
Ebbw Vale 7 51 47N 3 12W
Ebeltoft 21 56 12N 10 41 E
Eberswalde 14 52 49N 13 50 E
Eboli 18 40 39N 15 2 E
Ebolowa 54 2 55N 11 10 E
Ebro —► 13 40 43N 0 54 E
Ech Cheliff 50 36 10N 1 20 E
Echo Bay, N.W.T., Canada 60 66 5N 117 55W
Echo Bay, Ont., Canada 62 46 29N 84 4W
Echoing —► 65 55 51N 92 5W
Echternach 11 49 49N 6 25 E
Echuca 45 36 10S 144 20 E
Ecija 13 37 30N 5 10W
Eclipse Is. 46 13 54S 126 19 E
Ecuador ■ 78 2 0S 78 0W
Ed Dâmer 51 17 27N 34 0 E
Ed Debba 51 18 0N 30 51 E
Ed Dueim 51 14 0N 32 10 E
Edah 47 28 16S 117 10 E
Edam, Canada 65 53 11N 108 46W
Edam, Neth. 11 52 31N 5 3 E
Eday 8 59 11N 2 47W
Edd 29 14 0N 41 38 E
Eddrachillis B. 8 58 16N 5 10W
Eddystone 7 50 11N 4 16W
Eddystone Pt. 44 40 59S 148 20 E
Ede, Neth. 11 52 4N 5 40 E
Ede, Nigeria 53 7 45N 4 29 E
Édea 54 3 51N 10 9 E
Edehon L. 65 60 25N 97 15W
Eden, Australia 45 37 3S 149 55 E
Eden, N.C., U.S.A. 69 36 29N 79 53W
Eden, Tex., U.S.A. 71 31 16N 99 50W
Eden, Wyo., U.S.A. 72 42 2N 109 27W
Eden —► 6 54 57N 3 2W
Eden L. 65 56 38N 100 15W
Edenburg 56 29 43S 25 58 E
Edendale 57 29 39S 30 18 E
Edenderry 9 53 21N 7 3W
Edenton 69 36 5N 76 36W
Edenville 57 27 37S 27 34 E
Edgar 70 40 25N 98 0W
Edge Hill 7 52 7N 1 28W
Edgefield 69 33 50N 81 59W
Edgeley 70 46 27N 98 41W
Edgemont 70 43 15N 103 53W
Edhessa 19 40 48N 22 5 E
Edievale 43 45 49S 169 22 E
Edina 70 40 6N 92 10W
Edinburg 71 26 22N 98 10W
Edinburgh 8 55 57N 3 12W
Edirne 30 41 40N 26 34 E
Edithburgh 45 35 5S 137 43 E
Edjudina 47 29 48S 122 23 E
Edmond 71 35 37N 97 30W
Edmonds 72 47 47N 122 22W
Edmonton, Australia 44 17 2S 145 46 E
Edmonton, Canada 64 53 30N 113 30W
Edmund L. 65 54 45N 93 17W
Edmundston 63 47 23N 68 20W
Edna 71 29 0N 96 40W
Edna Bay 64 55 55N 133 40W
Edremit 30 39 34N 27 0 E
Edson 64 53 35N 116 28W
Edward —► 45 35 0S 143 30 E
Edward, L. 54 0 25S 29 40 E
Edward I. 62 48 22N 88 37W
Edwards Plateau 71 30 30N 101 5W
Edzo 64 62 49N 116 4W
Eekloo 11 51 11N 3 33 E
Ef'e, Nahal 28 31 9N 35 13 E
Effingham 68 39 8N 88 30W
Égadi, Ísole 18 37 55N 12 16 E
Eganville 62 45 32N 77 5W
Egeland 70 48 42N 99 6W
Egenolf L. 65 59 3N 100 0W
Eger = Cheb 14 50 9N 12 28 E
Eger 15 47 53N 20 27 E
Egersund 21 58 26N 6 1 E
Egg L. 65 55 5N 105 30W
Eginbah 46 20 53S 119 47 E
Egmont, C. 43 39 16S 173 45 E
Egmont, Mt. 43 39 17S 174 5 E
Eğridir 30 37 52N 30 51 E
Eğridir Gölü 30 37 53N 30 50 E
Egume 53 7 30N 7 14 E
Egvekinot 25 66 19N 179 50W
Egypt ■ 51 28 0N 31 0 E
Eha Amufu 53 6 30N 7 46 E
Ehime □ 36 33 30N 132 40 E
Eidsvold 45 25 25S 151 12 E
Eidsvoll 21 60 19N 11 14 E
Eifel 14 50 10N 6 45 E
Eigg 8 56 54N 6 10W
Eighty Mile Beach 46 19 30S 120 40 E
Eil 29 8 0N 49 50 E
Eil, L. 8 56 50N 5 15W
Eildon, L. 45 37 10S 146 0 E
Eileen L. 65 62 16N 107 37W
Einasleigh 44 18 32S 144 5 E
Einasleigh —► 44 17 30S 142 17 E
Eindhoven 11 51 26N 5 30 E
Eire ■ 9 53 0N 8 0W
Eiríksjökull 20 64 46N 20 24W
Eirunepé 78 6 35S 69 53W
Eisenach 14 50 58N 10 18 E
Eisenerz 14 47 32N 14 54 E
Ekalaka 70 45 55N 104 30W
Eket 53 4 38N 7 56 E
Eketahuna 43 40 38S 175 43 E
Ekibastuz 24 51 50N 75 10 E
Ekimchan 25 53 0N 133 0W
Ekwan —► 62 53 12N 82 15W
Ekwan Pt. 62 53 16N 82 7W
El Aaiún 50 27 9N 13 12W
El Aat 28 32 50N 35 45 E
El Alamein 51 30 48N 28 58 E
El Aricha 50 34 13N 1 10W
El Arîhā 28 31 52N 35 27 E
El Arish, Australia 44 17 35S 146 1 E
El 'Arîsh, Egypt 51 31 8N 33 50 E
El Asnam = Ech Cheliff 50 36 10N 1 20 E
El Bawiti 51 28 25N 28 45 E
El Bayadh 50 33 40N 1 1 E
El Bluff 75 11 59N 83 40W
El Buheirat □ 51 7 0N 30 0 E
El Cajon 73 32 49N 117 0W
El Callao 78 7 18N 61 50W
El Campo 71 29 10N 96 20W
El Centro 73 32 50N 115 40W
El Cerro 78 17 30S 61 40W
El Cuy 80 39 55S 68 25W
El Cuyo 74 21 30N 87 40W
El Dere 29 3 50N 47 8 E
El Diviso 78 1 22N 78 14W
El Djouf 50 20 0N 9 0W
El Dorado, Ark., U.S.A. 71 33 10N 92 40W
El Dorado, Kans., U.S.A. 71 37 55N 96 56W
El Dorado, Venezuela 78 6 55N 61 37W
El Escorial 13 40 35N 4 7W
El Faiyûm 51 29 19N 30 50 E
El Fâsher 51 13 33N 25 26 E
El Ferrol 13 43 29N 8 15W
El Fuerte 74 26 30N 108 40W
El Gal 29 10 58N 50 20 E
El Geteina 51 14 50N 32 27 E
El Gezira □ 51 15 0N 33 0 E
El Gîza 51 30 0N 31 10 E
El Goléa 50 30 30N 2 50 E
El Harrach 50 36 45N 3 5 E
El Iskandarîya 51 31 0N 30 0 E
El Jadida 50 33 11N 8 17W
El Jebelein 51 12 40N 32 55 E
El Kab 51 19 27N 32 46 E
El Kala 50 36 50N 8 30 E
El Kamlin 51 15 3N 33 11 E
El Kef 50 36 12N 8 47 E
El Khandaq 51 18 30N 30 30 E
El Khârga 51 25 30N 30 33 E
El Khartûm 51 15 31N 32 35 E
El Khartûm Bahrî 51 15 40N 32 31 E
El Laqâwa 51 11 25N 29 1 E
El Mafâza 51 13 38N 34 30 E
El Mahalla el Kubra 51 31 0N 31 0 E
El Mansûra 30 31 0N 31 19 E
El Minyâ 51 28 7N 30 33 E
El Obeid 51 13 8N 30 10 E
El Odaiya 51 12 8N 28 12 E
El Oro 74 19 48N 100 8W
El Oued 50 33 20N 6 58 E
El Palmito, Presa 74 25 40N 105 30W
El Paso 73 31 50N 106 30W
El Portal 73 37 44N 119 49W
El Progreso 75 15 26N 87 51W
El Pueblito 74 29 3N 105 4W
El Qâhira 51 30 1N 31 14 E
El Qantara 51 30 51N 32 20 E
El Qasr 51 25 44N 28 42 E
El Reno 71 35 30N 98 0W
El Salvador ■ 75 13 50N 89 0W
El Sauce 75 13 0N 86 40W
El Shallal 51 24 0N 32 53 E
El Suweis 51 29 58N 32 31 E
El Tigre 78 8 44N 64 15W
El Tocuyo 78 9 47N 69 48W
El Turbio 80 51 45S 72 5W
El Uqsur 51 25 41N 32 38 E
El Venado 74 22 56N 101 10W
El Vigía 78 8 38N 71 39W
El Wak 54 2 49N 40 56 E
El Wuz 51 15 0N 30 7 E
Elandsvlei 56 32 19S 19 31 E
Elat 28 29 30N 34 56 E
Elâzığ 30 38 37N 39 14 E
Elba, Italy 18 42 48N 10 15 E
Elba, U.S.A. 69 31 27N 86 4W
Elbasani 19 41 9N 20 9 E
Elbe —► 14 53 50N 9 0 E
Elbert, Mt. 73 39 5N 106 27W
Elberta 68 44 35N 86 14W
Elberton 69 34 7N 82 51W
Elbeuf 12 49 17N 1 2 E
Elbidtan 30 38 13N 37 12 E
Elbing = Elbląg 15 54 10N 19 25 E
Elbląg 15 54 10N 19 25 E
Elbow 65 51 7N 106 35W
Elbrus 23 43 21N 42 30 E
Elburg 11 52 26N 5 50 E
Elburz Mts. = Alborz, Reshteh-ye Kūhhā-ye 31 36 0N 52 0 E
Elche 13 38 15N 0 42W
Elcho I. 44 11 55S 135 45 E
Eldon 70 38 20N 92 38W
Eldora 70 42 20N 93 5W
Eldorado, Canada 65 59 35N 108 30W
Eldorado, Mexico 74 24 20N 107 22W
Eldorado, Ill., U.S.A. 68 37 50N 88 25W
Eldorado, Tex., U.S.A. 71 30 52N 100 35W
Eldorado Springs 71 37 54N 93 59W
Eldoret 54 0 30N 35 17 E
Electra 71 34 0N 99 0W
Elefantes —► 57 24 10S 32 40 E
Elektrostal 22 55 41N 38 32 E
Elephant Butte Res. 73 33 45N 107 30W
Eleuthera 75 25 0N 76 20W
Elgin, Canada 63 45 48N 65 10W
Elgin, U.K. 8 57 39N 3 20W
Elgin, Ill., U.S.A. 68 42 0N 88 20W
Elgin, N. Dak., U.S.A. 70 46 24N 101 46W
Elgin, Nebr., U.S.A. 70 41 58N 98 3W
Elgin, Nev., U.S.A. 73 37 21N 114 20W
Elgin, Oreg., U.S.A. 72 45 37N 118 0W
Elgin, Tex., U.S.A. 71 30 21N 97 22W
Elgon, Mt. 54 1 10N 34 30 E
Eliase 35 8 21S 130 48 E
Elida 71 33 56N 103 41W
Elim 56 34 35S 19 45 E
Elisabethville = Lubumbashi 55 11 40S 27 28 E
Elista 23 46 16N 44 14 E
Elizabeth, Australia 45 34 42S 138 41 E
Elizabeth, U.S.A. 68 40 37N 74 12W
Elizabeth City 69 36 18N 76 16W
Elizabethton 69 36 20N 82 13W
Elizabethtown 68 37 40N 85 54W
Elk City 71 35 25N 99 25W
Elk Island Nat. Park 64 53 35N 112 59W
Elk Lake 62 47 40N 80 25W
Elk Point 65 53 54N 110 55W
Elk River, Idaho, U.S.A. 72 46 50N 116 8W
Elk River, Minn., U.S.A. 70 45 17N 93 34W
Elkedra 44 21 9S 135 33 E
Elkedra —► 44 21 8S 136 22 E
Elkhart, Ind., U.S.A. 68 41 42N 85 55W
Elkhart, Kans., U.S.A. 71 37 3N 101 54W
Elkhorn 65 49 59N 101 14W
Elkhorn —► 70 41 7N 98 15W
Elkhovo 19 42 10N 26 40 E
Elkin 69 36 17N 80 50W
Elkins 68 38 53N 79 53W
Elko, Canada 64 49 20N 115 10W
Elko, U.S.A. 72 40 50N 115 50W
Ell, L. 47 29 13S 127 46 E
Ellendale, Australia 46 17 56S 124 48 E
Ellendale, U.S.A. 70 46 3N 98 30W
Ellensburg 72 47 0N 120 30W
Ellenville 68 41 42N 74 23W
Ellery, Mt. 45 37 28S 148 47 E
Ellesmere I. 58 79 30N 80 0W
Ellice Is. = Tuvalu ■ 3 8 0S 178 0 E
Ellinwood 70 38 27N 98 37W
Elliot, Australia 44 17 33S 133 32 E
Elliot, S. Africa 57 31 22S 27 48 E
Elliot Lake 62 46 25N 82 35W
Elliotdale = Xhora 57 31 55S 28 38 E
Ellis 70 39 0N 99 39W
Ellisville 71 31 38N 89 12W
Ellon 8 57 21N 2 5W
Ellore = Eluru 33 16 48N 81 8 E
Ells —► 64 57 18N 111 40W
Ellsworth 70 38 47N 98 15W
Ellwood City 68 40 52N 80 19W
Elma, Canada 65 49 52N 95 55W
Elma, U.S.A. 72 47 0N 123 30W
Elmalı 30 36 44N 29 56 E
Elmenteita 52 0 32S 36 14 E
Elmhurst 68 41 52N 87 58W
Elmira 68 42 8N 76 49W
Elmore 45 36 30S 144 37 E
Eloy 73 32 46N 111 33W
Elrose 65 51 12N 108 0W
Elsas 62 48 32N 82 55W
Elsinore = Helsingør 21 56 2N 12 35 E
Elsinore 73 38 40N 112 2W
Eltham 43 39 26S 174 19 E
Eluru 33 16 48N 81 8 E
Elvas 13 38 50N 7 10W
Elverum 21 60 53N 11 34 E
Elvire —► 46 17 51S 128 11 E
Elwood, Ind., U.S.A. 68 40 20N 85 50W
Elwood, Nebr., U.S.A. 70 40 38N 99 51W
Ely, U.K. 7 52 24N 0 16 E
Ely, Minn., U.S.A. 70 47 54N 91 52W
Ely, Nev., U.S.A. 72 39 10N 114 50W
Elyashiv 28 32 23N 34 55 E
Elyria 68 41 22N 82 8W
Emāmrūd 31 36 30N 55 0 E
Emba 24 48 50N 58 8 E
Emba —► 23 46 38N 53 14 E
Embarcación 80 23 10S 64 0W
Embarras Portage 65 58 27N 111 28W
Embetsu 36 44 44N 141 47 E
Embrun 12 44 34N 6 30 E
Embu 54 0 32S 37 38 E
Emden 14 53 22N 7 12 E
'Emeq Yizre'el 28 32 35N 35 12 E
Emerald 44 23 32S 148 10 E
Emerson 65 49 0N 97 10W
Emery 73 38 59N 111 17W
Emilia-Romagna □ 18 44 33N 10 40 E
Emmeloord 11 52 44N 5 46 E
Emmen 11 52 48N 6 57 E
Emmet 44 24 45S 144 30 E
Emmetsburg 70 43 3N 94 40W
Emmett 72 43 51N 116 33W
Empalme 74 28 1N 110 49W
Empangeni 57 28 50S 31 52 E
Empedrado 80 28 0S 58 46W
Emperor Seamount Chain 40 40 0N 170 0 E
Emporia, Kans., U.S.A. 70 38 25N 96 10W
Emporia, Va., U.S.A. 69 36 41N 77 32W
Emporium 68 41 30N 78 17W
Empress 65 50 57N 110 0W
Ems —► 14 53 22N 7 15 E
Emu 38 43 40N 128 6 E
Emu Park 44 23 13S 150 50 E
En Gedi 28 31 28N 35 25 E
En Gev 28 32 47N 35 38 E
En Harod 28 32 33N 35 22 E
'En Kerem 28 31 47N 35 6 E
En Nahud 51 12 45N 28 25 E
Enana 56 17 30S 16 23 E
Enaratoli 35 3 55S 136 21 E
Enard B. 8 58 5N 5 20W
Encanto, C. 35 15 45N 121 38 E
Encarnación 80 27 15S 55 50W
Encarnación de Diaz 74 21 30N 102 13W
Encinal 71 28 3N 99 25W
Encino 73 34 38N 105 40W
Encounter B. 45 35 45S 138 45 E
Ende 35 8 45S 121 40 E
Endeavour 65 52 10N 102 39W
Endeavour Str. 44 10 45S 142 0 E
Enderbury I. 40 3 8S 171 5W
Enderby 64 50 35N 119 10W
Enderby I. 46 20 35S 116 30 E
Enderlin 70 46 37N 97 41W
Endicott, N.Y., U.S.A. 68 42 6N 76 2W
Endicott, Wash., U.S.A. 72 47 0N 117 45W
Endyalgout I. 46 11 40S 132 35 E
Enez 23 40 45N 26 5 E
Enfield 7 51 39N 0 4W
Engadin 14 46 45N 10 10 E
Engaño, C., Dom. Rep. 75 18 30N 68 20W
Engaño, C., Phil. 35 18 35N 122 23 E
Engcobo 57 31 37S 28 0 E
Engels 22 51 28N 46 6 E
Engemann L. 65 58 0N 106 55W
Enggano 34 5 20S 102 40 E
Enghien 11 50 37N 4 2 E
Engkilili 34 1 3N 111 42 E
England 71 34 30N 91 58W
England □ 5 53 0N 2 0W
Englee 63 50 45N 56 5W
Englehart 62 47 49N 79 52W
Engler L. 65 59 8N 106 52W
Englewood, Colo., U.S.A. 70 39 40N 105 0W
Englewood, Kans., U.S.A. 71 37 7N 99 59W
English —► 65 50 35N 93 30W
English Bazar = Ingraj Bazar 33 24 58N 88 10 E
English Channel 7 50 0N 2 0W
English River 62 49 14N 91 0W
Enid 71 36 26N 97 52W
Enkhuizen 11 52 42N 5 17 E
Enna 18 37 34N 14 15 E
Ennadai 65 61 8N 100 53W
Ennadai L. 65 61 0N 101 0W
Ennedi 51 17 15N 22 0 E
Enngonia 45 29 21S 145 50 E
Ennis, Ireland 9 52 51N 8 59W
Ennis, Mont., U.S.A. 72 45 20N 111 42W
Ennis, Tex., U.S.A. 71 32 15N 96 40W
Enniscorthy 9 52 30N 6 35W
Enniskillen 9 54 20N 7 40W
Ennistimon 9 52 56N 9 18W
Enns —► 14 48 14N 14 32 E
Enontekiö 20 68 23N 23 37 E
Enping 39 22 16N 112 21 E
Enriquillo, L. 75 18 20N 72 5W
Enschede 11 52 13N 6 53 E
Ensenada 74 31 50N 116 50W
Enshi 39 30 18N 109 29 E
Entebbe 54 0 4N 32 28 E
Enterprise, Canada 64 60 47N 115 45W
Enterprise, Oreg., U.S.A. 72 45 30N 117 18W
Enterprise, Utah, U.S.A. 73 37 37N 113 36W
Entrecasteaux, Pt. d' 43 34 50S 115 56 E
Enugu 53 6 20N 7 30 E
Enugu Ezike 53 7 0N 7 29 E
Enumclaw 72 47 12N 122 0W
Eólie, Is. 18 38 30N 14 50 E
Epe, Neth. 11 52 21N 5 59 E
Epe, Nigeria 53 6 36N 3 59 E
Épernay 12 49 3N 3 56 E
Ephesus 30 37 50N 27 33 E
Ephraim 72 39 21N 111 37W
Ephrata 72 47 20N 119 32W
Épinal 12 48 10N 6 27 E

Feuilles

Epping 7 51 42N 0 8 E
Epukiro 56 21 40S 19 9 E
Equatorial Guinea ■ 54 2 0N 8 0 E
Er Rahad 51 12 45N 30 32 E
Er Rif 50 35 1N 4 1W
Er Roseires 51 11 55N 34 30 E
Erāwadī Myit → = Irrawaddy → 33 15 50N 95 6 E
Ercha 25 69 45N 147 20 E
Erciyaş Dağı 30 38 30N 35 30 E
Erdao Jiang → 38 43 0N 127 0 E
Erechim 80 27 35S 52 15W
Ereğli, Konya, Turkey 30 37 31N 34 4 E
Ereğli, Zonguldak, Turkey 30 41 15N 31 30 E
Erenhot 38 43 48N 111 59 E
Eresma → 13 41 26N 40 45W
Erewadi Myitwanya 33 15 30N 95 0 E
Erfenisdam 56 28 30S 26 50 E
Erfurt 14 50 58N 11 2 E
Ergani 30 38 17N 39 49 E
Erğene → 19 41 1N 26 22 E
Ergeni Vozvyshennost 23 47 0N 44 0 E
Ergun Zuoqi 38 50 47N 121 31 E
Eriboll, L. 8 58 28N 4 41W
Érice 18 38 4N 12 34 E
Erie 68 42 10N 80 7W
Erie, L. 68 42 15N 81 0W
Erigavo 29 10 35N 47 20 E
Eriksdale 65 50 52N 98 7W
Erímanthos 19 37 57N 21 50 E
Erimo-misaki 36 41 50N 143 15 E
Eritrea □ 51 14 0N 38 30 E
Erlangen 14 49 35N 11 0 E
Erldunda 44 25 14S 133 12 E
Ermelo, Neth. 11 52 18N 5 35 E
Ermelo, S. Africa 57 26 31S 29 59 E
Ermenak 30 36 38N 33 0 E
Ermoúpolis = Siros 19 37 28N 24 57 E
Ernakulam = Cochin 32 9 59N 76 22 E
Erne → 9 54 30N 8 16W
Erne, Lough 9 54 26N 7 46W
Ernest Giles Ra. 47 27 0S 123 45 E
Erode 32 11 24N 77 45 E
Eromanga 45 26 40S 143 11 E
Erongo 56 21 39S 15 58 E
Errabiddy 47 25 25S 117 5 E
Erramala Hills 32 15 30N 78 15 E
Errigal, Mt. 9 55 2N 8 8W
Erris Hd. 9 54 19N 10 0W
Erskine 70 47 37N 96 0W
Erwin 69 36 10N 82 28W
Erzgebirge 14 50 25N 13 0 E
Erzin 25 50 15N 95 10 E
Erzincan 30 39 46N 39 30 E
Erzurum 30 39 57N 41 15 E
Es Sahrâ' Esh Sharqîya 51 27 30N 32 30 E
Es Sînâ' 51 29 0N 34 0 E
Esan-Misaki 36 41 40N 141 10 E
Esbjerg 21 55 29N 8 29 E
Escalante 73 37 47N 111 37W
Escalante → 73 37 17N 110 53W
Escalón 74 26 46N 104 20W
Escambia → 69 30 32N 87 15W
Escanaba 68 45 44N 87 5W
Esch-sur-Alzette 11 49 32N 6 0 E
Escobal 74 9 6N 80 1W
Escondido 73 33 9N 117 4W
Escuinapa 74 22 50N 105 50W
Escuintla 75 14 20N 90 48W
Eşfahān 31 33 0N 51 30 E
Esh Sham = Dimashq 30 33 30N 36 18 E
Esh Shamâlîya □ 51 19 0N 29 0 E
Eshowe 57 28 50S 31 30 E
Eshta'ol 28 31 47N 35 0 E
Esk →, Dumf. & Gall., U.K. 8 54 58N 3 4W
Esk →, N. Yorks., U.K. 6 54 27N 0 36W
Eskifjörður 20 65 3N 13 55W
Eskilstuna 21 59 22N 16 32 E
Eskimo Pt. 65 61 10N 94 15W
Eskişehir 30 39 50N 30 35 E
Esla → 13 41 29N 6 3W
Eslāmābād-e Gharb 30 34 10N 46 30 E
Esmeraldas 78 1 0N 79 40W
Espanola 62 46 15N 81 46W
Esperance 47 33 45S 121 55 E
Esperance B. 47 33 48S 121 55 E
Esperanza 80 31 29S 61 3W
Espichel, C. 13 38 22N 9 16W
Espinal 78 4 9N 74 53W
Espinazo, Sierra del = Espinhaço, Serra do 79 17 30S 43 30W
Espinhaço, Serra do 79 17 30S 43 30W
Espírito Santo □ 79 20 0S 40 45W
Espíritu Santo, B. del 74 19 15N 87 0W
Espiritu Santo, I. 74 24 30N 110 23W
Espungabera 57 20 29S 32 45 E
Esquel 80 42 55S 71 20W
Esquina 80 30 0S 59 30W
Essaouira 50 31 32N 9 42W
Essen, Belgium 11 51 28N 4 28 E
Essen, W. Germany 14 51 28N 6 59 E
Essequibo → 78 6 50N 58 30W
Essex □ 7 51 48N 0 30 E
Esslingen 14 48 43N 9 19 E
Essonne □ 12 48 30N 2 20 E
Estados, I. de Los 80 54 40S 64 30W
Estância, Brazil 79 11 16S 37 26W
Estancia, U.S.A. 73 34 50N 106 1W
Estcourt 57 29 0S 29 53 E
Esteli 75 13 9N 86 22W
Estelline, S. Dak., U.S.A. 70 44 39N 96 52W
Estelline, Tex., U.S.A. 71 34 35N 100 27W
Esterhazy 65 50 37N 102 5W
Estevan 65 49 10N 102 59W
Estevan Group 64 53 3N 129 38W
Estherville 70 43 25N 94 50W
Eston 65 51 8N 108 40W
Estonian S.S.R. □ 22 58 30N 25 30 E
Estoril 13 38 42N 9 23W
Estrada, La 13 42 43N 8 27W
Estrêla, Serra da 13 40 10N 7 45W
Estremadura 13 39 0N 9 0W
Estrondo, Serra do 79 7 20S 48 0W
Esztergom 15 47 47N 18 44 E
Et Ţira 28 32 14N 34 56 E
Etadunna 45 28 43S 138 38 E
Etamamu 63 50 18N 59 59W
Etanga 56 17 55S 13 0 E
Etawah 32 26 48N 79 6 E
Etawah → 69 34 20N 84 15W
Etawney L. 65 57 50N 96 50W
Ete 53 7 2N 7 28 E
Ethel Creek 46 23 5S 120 11 E
Ethelbert 65 51 32N 100 25W
Ethiopia ■ 29 8 0N 40 0 E
Ethiopian Highlands 48 10 0N 37 0 E
Etive, L. 8 56 30N 5 12W
Etna 18 37 45N 15 0 E
Etolin I. 64 56 5N 132 20W
Etosha Pan 56 18 40S 16 30 E
Etowah 69 35 20N 84 30W
Étroits, Les 63 47 24N 68 54W
Ettrick Water 8 55 31N 2 55W
Etzatlán 74 20 48N 104 5W
Euboea = Évvoia 19 38 30N 24 0 E
Euclid 68 41 32N 81 31W
Eucumbene, L. 45 36 2S 148 40 E
Eudora 71 33 5N 91 17W
Eufaula, Ala., U.S.A. 69 31 55N 85 11W
Eufaula, Okla., U.S.A. 71 35 20N 95 33W
Eufaula, L. 71 35 15N 95 28W
Eugene 72 44 0N 123 8W
Eugowra 45 33 22S 148 24 E
Eulo 45 28 10S 145 3 E
Eunice, La., U.S.A. 71 30 35N 92 28W
Eunice, N. Mex., U.S.A. 71 32 30N 103 10W
Eupen 11 50 37N 6 3 E
Euphrates = Furāt, Nahr al → 30 31 0N 47 25 E
Eure □ 12 49 10N 1 0 E
Eure-et-Loir □ 12 48 22N 1 30 E
Eureka, Calif., U.S.A. 72 40 50N 124 0W
Eureka, Kans., U.S.A. 71 37 50N 96 20W
Eureka, Mont., U.S.A. 72 48 53N 115 6W
Eureka, Nev., U.S.A. 72 39 32N 116 2W
Eureka, S. Dak., U.S.A. 70 45 49N 99 38W
Eureka, Utah, U.S.A. 72 40 0N 112 9W
Eureka, Mt. 47 26 35S 121 35 E
Euroa 45 36 44S 145 35 E
Europa, I. 55 22 20S 40 22 E
Europa, Picos de 13 43 10N 4 49W
Europa, Pta. de 13 36 3N 5 21W
Europa Pt. = Europa, Pta. de 13 36 3N 5 21W
Europe 4 50 0N 20 0 E
Europoort 11 51 57N 4 10 E
Eustis 69 28 54N 81 36W
Eutsuk L. 64 53 20N 126 45W
Eva Downs 44 18 1S 134 52 E
Eval 28 32 15N 35 15 E
Evale 56 16 33S 15 44 E
Evans 70 40 25N 104 43W
Evans Head 45 29 7S 153 27 E
Evans L. 62 50 50N 77 0W
Evanston, Ill., U.S.A. 68 42 0N 87 40W
Evanston, Wyo., U.S.A. 72 41 10N 111 0W
Evansville, Ind., U.S.A. 68 38 0N 87 35W
Evansville, Wis., U.S.A. 70 42 47N 89 18W
Eveleth 70 47 29N 92 46W
Even Yahuda 28 32 16N 34 53 E
Evensk 25 62 12N 159 30 E
Everard, L. 45 31 30S 135 0 E
Everard Ras. 47 27 5S 132 28 E
Everest, Mt. 33 28 5N 86 58 E
Everett 72 48 0N 122 10W
Everglades 69 26 0N 80 30W
Everglades City 69 25 52N 81 23W
Everglades Nat. Park 69 25 27N 80 53W
Evergreen 69 31 28N 86 55W
Everson 72 48 57N 122 22W
Evesham 7 52 6N 1 57W
Evinayong 54 1 26N 10 35 E
Évora 13 38 33N 7 57W
Évreux 12 49 0N 1 8 E
Évvoia 19 38 30N 24 0 E
Ewe, L. 8 57 49N 5 38W
Ewing 70 42 18N 98 22W
Ewo 54 0 48S 14 45 E
Exaltación 78 13 10S 65 20W
Excelsior Springs 70 39 20N 94 10W
Exe → 7 50 38N 3 27W
Exeter, U.K. 7 50 43N 3 31W
Exeter, Calif., U.S.A. 73 36 17N 119 9W
Exeter, Nebr., U.S.A. 70 40 43N 97 30W
Exmoor 7 51 10N 3 59W
Exmouth, Australia 46 21 54S 114 10 E
Exmouth, U.K. 7 50 37N 3 26W
Exmouth G. 46 22 15S 114 15 E
Expedition Range 44 24 30S 149 12 E
Extremadura □ 13 39 30N 6 5W
Exuma Sound 75 24 30N 76 20W
Eyasi, L. 54 3 30S 35 0 E
Eyeberry L. 65 63 8N 104 43W
Eyemouth 8 55 53N 2 5W
Eyjafjörður 20 66 15N 18 30W
Eyrarbakki 20 63 52N 21 9W
Eyre 47 32 15S 126 18 E
Eyre (North), L. 45 28 30S 137 20 E
Eyre (South), L. 45 29 18S 137 25 E
Eyre Cr. → 45 26 40S 139 0 E
Eyre Mts. 43 45 25S 168 25 E
Eyre Pen. 45 33 30S 137 17 E

F

Fabens 73 31 30N 106 8W
Fabriano 18 43 20N 12 52 E
Facatativá 78 4 49N 74 22W
Fachi 50 18 6N 11 34 E
Fada 51 17 13N 21 34 E
Fada-n-Gourma 53 12 10N 0 30 E
Faddeyevskiy, Ostrov 25 76 0N 150 0 E
Fādiļī 30 26 55N 49 10 E
Faenza 18 44 17N 11 53 E
Fagam 53 11 1N 10 1 E
Făgăras 15 45 48N 24 58 E
Fagernes 21 60 59N 9 14 E
Fagersta 21 60 1N 15 46 E
Fagnano, L. 80 54 30S 68 0W
Fahraj 31 29 0N 59 0 E
Fahūd 31 22 18N 56 28 E
Fair Hd. 9 55 14N 6 10W
Fairbank 73 31 44N 110 12W
Fairbanks 60 64 50N 147 50W
Fairbury 70 40 5N 97 5W
Fairfax 71 36 37N 96 45W
Fairfield, Ala., U.S.A. 69 33 30N 87 0W
Fairfield, Calif., U.S.A. 72 38 14N 122 1W
Fairfield, Idaho, U.S.A. 72 43 21N 114 46W
Fairfield, Ill., U.S.A. 68 38 20N 88 20W
Fairfield, Iowa, U.S.A. 70 41 0N 91 58W
Fairfield, Mont., U.S.A. 72 47 40N 112 0W
Fairfield, Tex., U.S.A. 71 31 40N 96 0W
Fairford 65 51 37N 98 38W
Fairhope 69 30 35N 87 50W
Fairlie 43 44 5S 170 49 E
Fairmont, Minn., U.S.A. 70 43 37N 94 30W
Fairmont, W. Va., U.S.A. 68 39 29N 80 10W
Fairplay 73 39 9N 105 40W
Fairport 68 43 8N 77 29W
Fairview, Australia 44 15 31S 144 17 E
Fairview, Canada 64 56 5N 118 25W
Fairview, N. Dak., U.S.A. 70 47 49N 104 7W
Fairview, Okla., U.S.A. 71 36 19N 98 30W
Fairview, Utah, U.S.A. 72 39 50N 111 0W
Fairweather, Mt. 60 58 55N 137 45W
Faisalabad 32 31 30N 73 5 E
Faith 70 45 2N 102 4W
Faizabad 33 26 45N 82 10 E
Fajardo 75 18 20N 65 39W
Fakfak 35 3 0S 132 15 E
Faku 38 42 32N 123 21 E
Falaise 12 48 54N 0 12W
Falam 33 23 0N 93 45 E
Falcon Dam 71 26 50N 99 20W
Falfurrias 71 27 14N 98 8W
Falher 64 55 44N 117 15W
Falkenberg 21 56 54N 12 30 E
Falkirk 8 56 0N 3 47W
Falkland Is. 80 51 30S 59 0W
Falkland Sd. 80 52 0S 60 0W
Falköping 21 58 12N 13 33 E
Fall River 68 41 45N 71 5W
Fall River Mills 72 41 1N 121 30W
Fallbrook 73 33 25N 117 12W
Fallon, Mont., U.S.A. 70 46 52N 105 8W
Fallon, Nev., U.S.A. 72 39 31N 118 51W
Falls City, Nebr., U.S.A. 70 40 0N 95 40W
Falls City, Oreg., U.S.A. 72 44 54N 123 29W
Falmouth, Jamaica 75 18 30N 77 40W
Falmouth, U.K. 7 50 9N 5 5W
Falmouth, U.S.A. 68 38 40N 84 20W
False B. 56 34 15S 18 40 E
Falso, C. 75 15 12N 83 21W
Falster 21 54 45N 11 55 E
Falsterbo 21 55 23N 12 50 E
Falun 21 60 37N 15 37 E
Famagusta 30 35 8N 33 55 E
Family L. 65 51 54N 95 27W
Fan Xian 38 35 55N 115 38 E
Fandriana 57 20 14S 47 21 E
Fang Xian 39 32 3N 110 40 E
Fangchang 39 31 5N 118 4 E
Fangcheng 39 33 18N 112 59 E
Fangliao 39 22 22N 120 38 E
Fangzheng 38 49 50N 128 48 E
Fanjiatun 38 43 40N 125 0 E
Fannich, L. 8 57 40N 5 0W
Fanny Bay 64 49 37N 124 48W
Fano 18 43 50N 13 0 E
Fanshaw 64 57 11N 133 30W
Fao = Al Fāw 30 30 0N 48 30 E
Faradje 54 3 50N 29 45 E
Farafangana 57 22 49S 47 50 E
Farāh 31 32 20N 62 7 E
Farāh □ 31 32 25N 62 10 E
Farahalana 57 14 26S 50 10 E
Faranah 50 10 3N 10 45W
Farasān, Jazā'ir 29 16 45N 41 55 E
Faratsiho 57 19 24S 46 57 E
Fareham 7 50 52N 1 11W
Farewell, C. 43 40 29S 172 43 E
Farewell C. = Farvel, Kap 58 59 48N 43 55W
Fargo 70 46 52N 96 40W
Fari'a → 28 32 12N 35 27 E
Faribault 70 44 15N 93 19W
Farim 50 12 27N 15 9W
Farimān 31 35 40N 59 49 E
Farina 45 30 3S 138 15 E
Farmerville 71 32 48N 92 23W
Farmington, N. Mex., U.S.A. 73 36 45N 108 28W
Farmington, Utah, U.S.A. 72 41 0N 111 12W
Farmville 68 37 19N 78 22W
Farnborough 7 51 17N 0 46W
Farne Is. 6 55 38N 1 37W
Faro, Brazil 79 2 10S 56 39W
Faro, Portugal 13 37 2N 7 55W
Fårö, Sweden 21 57 55N 19 5 E
Faroe Is. = Føroyar 5 62 0N 7 0W
Farquhar, C. 47 23 50S 113 36 E
Farquhar Is. 3 11 0S 52 0 E
Farrar → 8 57 30N 4 30W
Farrars Cr. → 44 25 35S 140 43 E
Farrāshband 31 28 57N 52 5 E
Farrell 68 41 13N 80 29W
Farrell Flat 45 33 48S 138 48 E
Farrukhabad-cum-Fatehgarh 32 27 30N 79 32 E
Fārs □ 31 29 30N 55 0 E
Fársala 19 39 17N 22 23 E
Farsund 21 58 5N 6 55 E
Fartak, Râs 30 28 5N 34 34 E
Farvel, Kap 58 59 48N 43 55W
Farwell 71 34 25N 103 0W
Faryab 32 28 7N 57 14 E
Faryāb □ 31 36 0N 65 0 E
Fasā 31 29 0N 53 39 E
Fastnet Rock 9 51 22N 9 37W
Fatagar, Tanjung 35 2 46S 131 57 E
Fatehgarh 32 27 25N 79 35 E
Fatehpur, Raj., India 32 28 0N 74 40 E
Fatehpur, Ut. P., India 33 25 56N 81 13 E
Fatima 63 47 24N 61 53W
Faulkton 70 45 4N 99 8W
Faure I. 47 25 52S 113 50 E
Fauresmith 56 29 44S 25 17 E
Fauske 20 67 17N 15 25 E
Favara 18 37 19N 13 39 E
Favignana 18 37 56N 12 18 E
Favourable Lake 62 52 50N 93 39W
Fawn → 62 55 20N 87 35W
Faxaflói 20 64 29N 23 0W
Faya-Largeau 51 17 58N 19 6 E
Fayd 30 27 1N 42 52 E
Fayette, Ala., U.S.A. 69 33 40N 87 50W
Fayette, Mo., U.S.A. 70 39 10N 92 40W
Fayetteville, Ark., U.S.A. 71 36 0N 94 5W
Fayetteville, N.C., U.S.A. 69 35 0N 78 58W
Fayetteville, Tenn., U.S.A. 69 35 8N 86 30W
Fazilka 32 30 27N 74 2 E
Fdérik 50 22 40N 12 45W
Feale → 9 52 26N 9 40W
Fear, C. 69 33 51N 78 0W
Feather → 72 38 47N 121 36W
Featherston 43 41 6S 175 20 E
Fécamp 12 49 45N 0 22 E
Fehmarn 14 54 26N 11 10 E
Fehmarn Bælt 14 54 35N 11 20 E
Fei Xian 39 35 18N 117 59 E
Feilding 43 40 13S 175 35 E
Feira de Santana 79 12 15S 38 57W
Feldkirch 14 47 15N 9 37 E
Felipe Carrillo Puerto 74 19 38N 88 3W
Felixstowe 7 51 58N 1 22 E
Femunden 20 62 10N 11 53 E
Fen He → 38 35 36N 110 42 E
Feng Xian, Jiangsu, China 39 34 43N 116 35 E
Feng Xian, Shaanxi, China 39 33 54N 106 40 E
Fengcheng, Jiangxi, China 39 28 12N 115 48 E
Fengcheng, Liaoning, China 38 40 28N 124 5 E
Fengdu 39 29 55N 107 41 E
Fengfeng 38 36 28N 114 8 E
Fenghua 39 29 40N 121 25 E
Fenghuang 39 27 57N 109 29 E
Fengjie 39 31 5N 109 36 E
Fengkai 39 23 24N 111 30 E
Fengle 39 31 29N 112 29 E
Fengning 38 41 10N 116 33 E
Fengtai 38 39 50N 116 18 E
Fengxian 39 30 55N 121 26 E
Fengxiang 39 34 29N 107 25 E
Fengxin 39 28 41N 115 18 E
Fengyang 39 32 51N 117 29 E
Fengzhen 38 40 25N 113 2 E
Fenit 9 52 17N 9 51W
Fennimore 70 42 58N 90 41W
Fenoarivo Afovoany 57 18 26S 46 34 E
Fenoarivo Atsinanana 57 17 22S 49 25 E
Fens, The 6 52 45N 0 2 E
Fenton 68 42 47N 83 44W
Fenyang 38 37 18N 111 48 E
Feodosiya 23 45 2N 35 28 E
Ferdows 31 33 58N 58 2 E
Ferfer 29 5 4N 45 9 E
Fergana 24 40 23N 71 19 E
Fergus 62 43 43N 80 24W
Fergus Falls 70 46 18N 96 7W
Ferland 62 50 19N 88 27W
Fermanagh □ 9 54 21N 7 40W
Fermoy 9 52 4N 8 18W
Fernandina Beach 69 30 40N 81 30W
Fernando de Noronha 79 4 0S 33 10W
Fernando Póo = Bioko 53 3 30N 8 40 E
Ferndale, Calif., U.S.A. 72 40 37N 124 12W
Ferndale, Wash., U.S.A. 72 48 51N 122 41W
Fernie 64 49 30N 115 5W
Fernlees 44 23 51S 148 7 E
Fernley 72 39 36N 119 14W
Ferozepore = Firozpur 32 30 55N 74 40 E
Ferrara 18 44 50N 11 36 E
Ferreñafe 78 6 42S 79 50W
Ferriday 71 31 35N 91 33W
Ferron 73 39 3N 111 3W
Ferryland 63 47 2N 52 53W
Fertile 70 47 31N 96 18W
Fès 50 34 0N 5 0W
Feshi 54 6 8S 18 10 E
Fessenden 70 47 42N 99 38W
Fethiye 30 36 36N 29 10 E
Fetlar 8 60 36N 0 52W
Feuilles → 61 58 47N 70 4W

Gypsumville

Grande, B. **80** 50 30S 68 20W
Grande, La **72** 45 15N 118 0W
Grande Baie **63** 48 19N 70 52W
Grande Baleine, R. de la → **62** 55 16N 77 47W
Grande Cache **64** 53 53N 119 8W
Grande de Santiago → **74** 21 20N 105 50W
Grande-Entrée **63** 47 30N 61 40W
Grande Prairie **64** 55 10N 118 50W
Grande-Rivière **63** 48 26N 64 30W
Grande-Vallée **63** 49 14N 65 8W
Grandes-Bergeronnes **63** 48 16N 69 35W
Grandfalls **71** 31 21N 102 51W
Grandoe Mines **64** 56 29N 129 54W
Grandview **72** 46 13N 119 58W
Grange, La, Ga., U.S.A. **69** 33 4N 85 0W
Grange, La, Ky., U.S.A. **68** 38 20N 85 20W
Grange, La, Tex., U.S.A. **71** 29 54N 96 52W
Grangemouth **8** 56 1N 3 43W
Granger, Wash., U.S.A. **72** 46 25N 120 5W
Granger, Wyo., U.S.A. **72** 41 35N 109 58W
Grangeville **72** 45 57N 116 4W
Granite City **70** 38 45N 90 3W
Granite Falls **70** 44 45N 95 35W
Granite Peak **47** 25 40S 121 20 E
Granite Pk. **72** 45 8N 109 52W
Granity **43** 41 39S 171 51 E
Granja **79** 3 7S 40 50W
Granja de Torrehermosa **13** 38 19N 5 35W
Granollers **13** 41 39N 2 18 E
Grant **70** 40 53N 101 42W
Grant, I. **46** 11 10S 132 52 E
Grant, Mt. **72** 38 34N 118 48W
Grant City **70** 40 30N 94 25W
Grant Range Mts. **73** 38 30N 115 30W
Grantham **6** 52 55N 0 39W
Grantown-on-Spey **8** 57 19N 3 36W
Grants **73** 35 14N 107 51W
Grants Pass **72** 42 30N 123 22W
Grantsburg **70** 45 46N 92 44W
Grantsville **72** 40 35N 112 32W
Granville, France **12** 48 50N 1 35W
Granville, N. Dak., U.S.A. **70** 48 18N 100 48W
Granville, N.Y., U.S.A. **68** 43 24N 73 16W
Granville L. **65** 56 18N 100 30W
Grapeland **71** 31 30N 95 31W
Gras, L. de **60** 64 30N 110 30W
Graskop **57** 24 56S 30 49 E
Grass → **65** 56 3N 96 33W
Grass Range **72** 47 0N 109 0W
Grass River Prov. Park **65** 54 40N 100 50W
Grass Valley, Calif., U.S.A. **72** 39 18N 121 0W
Grass Valley, Oreg., U.S.A. **72** 45 22N 120 48W
Grasse **12** 43 38N 6 56 E
Grassmere **45** 31 24S 142 38 E
Gravelbourg **65** 49 50N 106 35W
's-Gravenhage **11** 52 7N 4 17 E
Gravesend, Australia **45** 29 35S 150 20 E
Gravesend, U.K. **7** 51 25N 0 22 E
Gravois, Pointe-à- **75** 16 15N 73 56W
Grayling **68** 44 40N 84 42W
Grayling → **64** 59 21N 125 0W
Grays Harbor **72** 46 55N 124 8W
Grays L. **72** 43 8N 111 30W
Grayson **65** 50 45N 102 40W
Graz **14** 47 4N 15 27 E
Greasy L. **64** 62 55N 122 12W
Great Abaco I. **75** 26 25N 77 10W
Great Australia Basin **44** 26 0S 140 0 E
Great Australian Bight **47** 33 30S 130 0 E
Great Bahama Bank **75** 23 15N 78 0W
Great Barrier I. **43** 36 11S 175 25 E
Great Barrier Reef **44** 18 0S 146 50 E
Great Basin **72** 40 0N 116 30W
Great Bear → **60** 65 0N 124 0W
Great Bear L. **60** 65 30N 120 0W
Great Bend **70** 38 25N 98 55W
Great Blasket I. **9** 52 5N 10 30W
Great Britain **4** 54 0N 2 15W
Great Central **64** 49 20N 125 10W
Great Dividing Ra. **44** 23 0S 146 0 E
Great Exuma I. **75** 23 30N 75 50W
Great Falls, Canada **65** 50 27N 96 1W
Great Falls, U.S.A. **72** 47 27N 111 12W
Great Fish → = Groot Vis → **56** 33 28S 27 5 E
Great Guana Cay **75** 24 0N 76 20W
Great Harbour Deep **63** 50 25N 56 32W
Great Inagua I. **75** 21 0N 73 20W
Great Indian Desert = Thar Desert **32** 28 0N 72 0 E
Great I. **65** 58 53N 96 35W
Great Karoo **56** 31 55S 21 0 E
Great Lake **44** 41 50S 146 40 E
Great Orme's Head **6** 53 20N 3 52W
Great Ouse → **6** 52 47N 0 22 E
Great Palm I. **44** 18 45S 146 40 E
Great Plains **58** 47 0N 105 0W
Great Ruaha → **54** 7 56S 37 52 E
Great Saint Bernard P. = Grand St-Bernard, Col du **14** 45 50N 7 10 E
Great Salt Lake **72** 41 0N 112 30W
Great Salt Lake Desert **72** 40 20N 113 50W
Great Salt Plains Res. **71** 36 40N 98 15W
Great Sandy Desert **46** 21 0S 124 0 E
Great Slave L. **64** 61 23N 115 38W
Great Smoky Mts. Nat. Park **69** 35 39N 83 30W
Great Stour = Stour → **7** 51 15N 1 20 E
Great Victoria Desert **47** 29 30S 126 30 E
Great Wall **38** 38 30N 109 30 E
Great Whernside **6** 54 9N 1 59W
Great Yarmouth **6** 52 40N 1 45 E
Greater Antilles **75** 17 40N 74 0W
Greater London □ **7** 51 30N 0 5W
Greater Manchester □ **6** 53 30N 2 15W
Greater Sunda Is. **34** 7 0S 112 0 E
Gredos, Sierra de **13** 40 20N 5 0W
Greece ■ **19** 40 0N 23 0 E
Greeley, Colo., U.S.A. **70** 40 30N 104 40W
Greeley, Nebr., U.S.A. **70** 41 36N 98 32W
Green →, Ky., U.S.A. **68** 37 54N 87 30W
Green →, Utah, U.S.A. **73** 38 11N 109 53W
Green B. **68** 45 0N 87 30W
Green Bay **68** 44 30N 88 0W
Green C. **45** 37 13S 150 1 E
Green Cove Springs **69** 29 59N 81 40W
Green Hd. **47** 30 5S 114 56 E
Green Island **43** 45 55S 170 26 E
Green River **73** 38 59N 110 10W
Greenbush **70** 48 46N 96 10W
Greencastle **68** 39 40N 86 48W
Greenfield, Ind., U.S.A. **68** 39 47N 85 51W
Greenfield, Iowa, U.S.A. **70** 41 18N 94 28W
Greenfield, Mass., U.S.A. **68** 42 38N 72 38W
Greenfield, Miss., U.S.A. **71** 37 28N 93 50W
Greenland ■ **2** 66 0N 45 0W
Greenock **8** 55 57N 4 46W
Greenore **9** 54 2N 6 8W
Greenore Pt. **9** 52 15N 6 20W
Greenough → **47** 28 51S 114 38 E
Greensboro, Ga., U.S.A. **69** 33 34N 83 12W
Greensboro, N.C., U.S.A. **69** 36 7N 79 46W
Greensburg, Ind., U.S.A. **68** 39 20N 85 30W
Greensburg, Kans., U.S.A. **71** 37 38N 99 20W
Greensburg, Pa., U.S.A. **68** 40 18N 79 31W
Greenville, Liberia **50** 5 1N 9 6W
Greenville, Ala., U.S.A. **69** 31 50N 86 37W
Greenville, Calif., U.S.A. **72** 40 8N 120 57W
Greenville, Ill., U.S.A. **70** 38 53N 89 22W
Greenville, Maine, U.S.A. **63** 45 30N 69 32W
Greenville, Mich., U.S.A. **68** 43 12N 85 14W
Greenville, Miss., U.S.A. **71** 33 25N 91 0W
Greenville, N.C., U.S.A. **69** 35 37N 77 26W
Greenville, Ohio, U.S.A. **68** 40 5N 84 38W
Greenville, Pa., U.S.A. **68** 41 23N 80 22W
Greenville, S.C., U.S.A. **69** 34 54N 82 24W
Greenville, Tenn., U.S.A. **69** 36 13N 82 51W
Greenville, Tex., U.S.A. **71** 33 5N 96 5W
Greenwater Lake Prov. Park **65** 52 32N 103 30W
Greenwich **7** 51 28N 0 0 E
Greenwood, Canada **64** 49 10N 118 40W
Greenwood, Miss., U.S.A. **71** 33 30N 90 4W
Greenwood, S.C., U.S.A. **69** 34 13N 82 13W
Greenwood, Mt. **46** 13 48S 130 4 E
Gregory **70** 43 14N 99 20W
Gregory → **44** 17 53S 139 17 E
Gregory, L., S. Austral., Australia **45** 28 55S 139 0 E
Gregory, L., W. Austral., Australia **47** 25 38S 119 58 E
Gregory Downs **44** 18 35S 138 45 E
Gregory Ra., Queens., Australia **44** 19 30S 143 40 E
Gregory Ra., W. Austral., Australia **46** 21 20S 121 12 E
Greifswald **14** 54 6N 13 23 E
Gremikha **22** 67 50N 39 40 E
Grenada **71** 33 45N 89 50W
Grenada ■ **75** 12 10N 61 40W
Grenadines **75** 12 40N 61 20W
Grenen **21** 57 44N 10 40 E
Grenfell, Australia **45** 33 52S 148 8 E
Grenfell, Canada **65** 50 30N 102 56W
Grenoble **12** 45 12N 5 42 E
Grenora **70** 48 38N 103 54W
Grenville, C. **44** 12 0S 143 13 E
Grenville Chan. **64** 53 40N 129 46W
Gresham **72** 45 30N 122 25W
Gresik **35** 7 13S 112 38 E
Gretna Green **8** 55 0N 3 3W
Grevenmacher **11** 49 41N 6 26 E
Grey → **43** 42 27S 171 12 E
Grey, C. **44** 13 0S 136 35 E
Grey Range **45** 27 0S 143 30 E
Grey Res. **63** 48 20N 56 30W
Greybull **72** 44 30N 108 3W
Greymouth **43** 42 29S 171 13 E
Greytown, N.Z. **43** 41 5S 175 29 E
Greytown, S. Africa **57** 29 1S 30 36 E
Gribbell I. **64** 53 23N 129 0W
Gridley **72** 39 27N 121 47W
Griekwastad **56** 28 49S 23 15 E
Griffin **69** 33 17N 84 14W
Griffith **45** 34 18S 146 2 E
Grimari **51** 5 43N 20 6 E
Grimsby **6** 53 35N 0 5W
Grimsey **20** 66 33N 18 0W
Grimshaw **64** 56 10N 117 40W
Grimstad **21** 58 22N 8 35 E
Grinnell **70** 41 45N 92 43W
Gris-Nez, C. **12** 50 52N 1 35 E
Groais I. **63** 50 55N 55 35W
Groblersdal **57** 25 15S 29 25 E
Grodno **22** 53 42N 23 52 E
Grodzisk Wielkopolski **14** 52 15N 16 22 E
Groesbeck **71** 31 32N 96 34W
Grójec **15** 51 50N 20 58 E
Grong **20** 64 25N 12 8 E
Groningen **11** 53 15N 6 35 E
Groningen □ **11** 53 16N 6 40 E
Groom **71** 35 12N 100 59W
Groot → **56** 33 45S 24 36 E
Groot Berg → **56** 32 47S 18 8 E
Groot-Brakrivier **56** 34 2S 22 18 E
Groot-Kei → **57** 32 41S 28 22 E
Groot Vis → **56** 33 28S 27 5 E
Groote Eylandt **44** 14 0S 136 40 E
Grootfontein **56** 19 31S 18 6 E
Grootlaagte → **56** 20 55S 21 27 E
Grootvloer **56** 30 0S 20 40 E
Gros C. **64** 61 59N 113 32W
Gross Glockner **14** 47 5N 12 40 E
Grossenhain **14** 51 17N 13 32 E
Grosseto **18** 42 45N 11 7 E
Groswater B. **63** 54 20N 57 40W
Groton **70** 45 27N 98 6W
Grouard Mission **64** 55 33N 116 9W
Groundhog → **62** 48 45N 82 58W
Grouse Creek **72** 41 44N 113 57W
Groveton, N.H., U.S.A. **68** 44 34N 71 30W
Groveton, Tex., U.S.A. **71** 31 5N 95 4W
Groznyy **23** 43 20N 45 45 E
Grudziądz **15** 53 30N 18 47 E
Grundy Center **70** 42 22N 92 45W
Gruver **71** 36 19N 101 20W
Gryazi **22** 52 30N 39 58 E
Gua **33** 22 18N 85 20 E
Guacanayabo, G. de **75** 20 40N 77 20W
Guadalajara, Mexico **74** 20 40N 103 20W
Guadalajara, Spain **13** 40 37N 3 12W
Guadalcanal **40** 9 32S 160 12 E
Guadalete → **13** 36 35N 6 13W
Guadalhorce → **13** 36 41N 4 27W
Guadalquivir → **13** 36 47N 6 22W
Guadalupe = Guadeloupe ■ **75** 16 20N 61 40W
Guadalupe **73** 34 59N 120 33W
Guadalupe → **71** 28 30N 96 53W
Guadalupe, Sierra de **13** 39 28N 5 30W
Guadalupe Bravos **74** 31 20N 106 10W
Guadalupe I. **41** 29 0N 118 50W
Guadalupe Pk. **73** 31 50N 105 30W
Guadarrama, Sierra de **13** 41 0N 4 0W
Guadeloupe ■ **75** 16 20N 61 40W
Guadeloupe Passage **75** 16 50N 62 15W
Guadiana → **13** 37 14N 7 22W
Guadix **13** 37 18N 3 11W
Guafo, Boca del **80** 43 35S 74 0W
Guaira **80** 24 5S 54 10W
Guaira, La **78** 10 36N 66 56W
Guaitecas, Is. **80** 44 0S 74 30W
Guajará-Mirim **78** 10 50S 65 20W
Guajira, Pen. de la **78** 12 0N 72 0W
Gualeguay **80** 33 10S 59 14W
Gualeguaychú **80** 33 3S 59 31W
Guam **3** 13 27N 144 45 E
Guamúchil **74** 25 25N 108 3W
Guan Xian **37** 31 2N 103 38 E
Guanabacoa **75** 23 8N 82 18W
Guanacaste, Cordillera del **75** 10 40N 85 4W
Guanaceví **74** 25 40N 106 0W
Guanahani = San Salvador **75** 24 0N 74 40W
Guanajay **75** 22 56N 82 42W
Guanajuato **74** 21 0N 101 20W
Guanajuato □ **74** 20 40N 101 20W
Guandacol **80** 29 30S 68 40W
Guane **75** 22 10N 84 7W
Guang'an **39** 30 28N 106 35 E
Guangde **39** 30 54N 119 25 E
Guangdong □ **39** 23 0N 113 0 E
Guanghua **39** 32 22N 111 38 E
Guangshun **39** 26 8N 106 21 E
Guangxi Zhuangzu Zizhiqu □ **39** 24 0N 109 0 E
Guangyuan **39** 32 26N 105 51 E
Guangze **39** 27 30N 117 12 E
Guangzhou **39** 23 5N 113 10 E
Guanipa → **78** 9 56N 62 26W
Guantánamo **75** 20 10N 75 14W
Guantao **38** 36 42N 115 25 E
Guanyun **39** 34 20N 119 18 E
Guápiles **75** 10 10N 83 46W
Guaporé → **78** 11 55S 65 4W
Guaqui **78** 16 41S 68 54W
Guarapuava **80** 25 20S 51 30W
Guarda **13** 40 32N 7 20W
Guardafui, C. = Asir, Ras **29** 11 55N 51 10 E
Guasdualito **78** 7 15N 70 44W
Guasipati **78** 7 28N 61 54W
Guatemala **75** 14 40N 90 22W
Guatemala ■ **75** 15 40N 90 30W
Guatire **78** 10 28N 66 32W
Guaviare → **78** 4 3N 67 44W
Guaxupé **79** 21 10S 47 5W
Guayama **75** 17 59N 66 7W
Guayaquil **78** 2 15S 79 52W
Guayaquil, G. de **78** 3 10S 81 0W
Guaymas **74** 27 59N 110 54W
Guazhou **39** 32 17N 119 21 E
Gudbrandsdalen **21** 61 33N 10 0 E
Guddu Barrage **32** 28 30N 69 50 E
Gudivada **33** 16 30N 81 3 E
Gudur **32** 14 12N 79 55 E
Guecho **13** 43 21N 2 59W
Guékédou **50** 8 40N 10 5W
Guelma **50** 36 25N 7 29 E
Guelph **62** 43 35N 80 20W
Güera, La **50** 20 51N 17 0W
Guéréda **51** 14 31N 22 5 E
Guéret **12** 46 11N 1 51 E
Guernica **13** 43 19N 2 40W
Guernsey, U.K. **7** 49 30N 2 35W
Guernsey, U.S.A. **70** 42 19N 104 45W
Guerrero □ **74** 17 30N 100 0W
Gueydan **71** 30 3N 92 30W
Gui Jiang → **39** 23 30N 111 15 E
Gui Xian **39** 23 8N 109 35 E
Guichi **39** 30 39N 117 27 E
Guidong **39** 26 7N 113 57 E
Guiglo **50** 6 45N 7 30W
Guijá **57** 24 27S 33 0 E
Guildford **7** 51 14N 0 34W
Guilford **63** 45 12N 69 25W
Guilin **39** 25 18N 110 15 E
Guilvinec **12** 47 48N 4 17W
Guimarães **79** 2 9S 44 42W
Guimaras **35** 10 35N 122 37 E
Guinea ■ **50** 10 20N 11 30W
Guinea, Gulf of **3** 3 0N 2 30 E
Guinea-Bissau ■ **50** 12 0N 15 0W
Güines **75** 22 50N 82 0W
Guingamp **12** 48 34N 3 10W
Guiping **39** 23 21N 110 2 E
Güiria **78** 10 32N 62 18W
Guiuan **35** 11 5N 125 55 E
Guixi **39** 28 16N 117 15 E
Guiyang, Guizhou, China **39** 26 32N 106 40 E
Guiyang, Hunan, China **39** 25 46N 112 42 E
Guizhou □ **39** 27 0N 107 0 E
Gujarat □ **32** 23 20N 71 0 E
Gujranwala **32** 32 10N 74 12 E
Gujrat **32** 32 40N 74 2 E
Gulbarga **32** 17 20N 76 50 E
Gulf, The **31** 27 0N 50 0 E
Gulfport **71** 30 21N 89 3W
Gulgong **45** 32 20S 149 49 E
Gull Lake **65** 50 10N 108 29W
Gulshad **24** 46 45N 74 25 E
Gulu **54** 2 48N 32 17 E
Gum Lake **45** 32 42S 143 9 E
Gumlu **44** 19 53S 147 41 E
Gumma □ **36** 36 30N 138 20 E
Gummi **53** 12 4N 5 9 E
Gümüsane **30** 40 30N 39 30 E
Gumzai **35** 5 28S 134 42 E
Guna **32** 24 40N 77 19 E
Gundagai **45** 35 3S 148 6 E
Gundih **35** 7 10S 110 56 E
Gungu **54** 5 43S 19 20 E
Gunisao → **65** 53 56N 97 53W
Gunisao L. **65** 53 33N 96 15W
Gunnbjørn Fjeld **58** 68 45N 31 0W
Gunnedah **45** 30 59S 150 15 E
Gunningbar Cr. → **45** 31 14S 147 6 E
Gunnison, Colo., U.S.A. **73** 38 32N 106 56W
Gunnison, Utah, U.S.A. **72** 39 11N 111 48W
Gunnison → **73** 39 3N 108 30W
Guntakal **32** 15 11N 77 27 E
Guntersville **69** 34 18N 86 16W
Guntur **33** 16 23N 80 30 E
Gunungapi **35** 6 45S 126 30 E
Gunungsitoli **34** 1 15N 97 30 E
Gunza **54** 10 50S 13 50 E
Guo He → **39** 32 59N 117 10 E
Guoyang **39** 33 32N 116 12 E
Gupis **32** 36 15N 73 20 E
Gürchañ **30** 34 55N 49 25 E
Gurdaspur **32** 32 5N 75 31 E
Gurdon **71** 33 55N 93 10W
Gurgaon **32** 28 27N 77 1 E
Gurkha **33** 28 5N 84 40 E
Gurley **45** 29 45S 149 48 E
Gurupá **79** 1 25S 51 35W
Gurupá, I. Grande de **79** 1 25S 51 45W
Gurupi → **79** 1 13S 46 6W
Guryev **23** 47 5N 52 0 E
Gusau **53** 12 12N 6 40 E
Gushan **38** 39 50N 123 35 E
Gushi **39** 32 11N 115 41 E
Gustine **73** 37 14N 121 0W
Güstrow **14** 53 47N 12 12 E
Gutha **47** 28 58S 115 55 E
Guthalongra **44** 19 52S 147 50 E
Guthrie **71** 35 55N 97 30W
Guttenberg **70** 42 46N 91 10W
Guyana ■ **78** 5 0N 59 0W
Guyang **38** 41 0N 110 5 E
Guyenne **12** 44 30N 0 40 E
Guymon **71** 36 45N 101 30W
Guyra **45** 30 15S 151 40 E
Guyuan **38** 36 0N 106 20 E
Guzhen **39** 33 22N 117 18 E
Guzinozersk **25** 51 20N 106 35 E
Guzmán, L. de **74** 31 25N 107 25W
Gwa **33** 17 36N 94 34 E
Gwaai **55** 19 15S 27 45 E
Gwabegar **45** 30 31S 149 0 E
Gwadabawa **53** 13 28N 5 15 E
Gwādar **31** 25 10N 62 18 E
Gwalia **47** 28 54S 121 20 E
Gwalior **32** 26 12N 78 10 E
Gwanda **55** 20 55S 29 0 E
Gwaram **53** 10 15N 10 25 E
Gwarzo **53** 12 20N 8 55 E
Gweebarra B. **9** 54 52N 8 21W
Gweedore **9** 55 4N 8 15W
Gwent □ **7** 51 45N 2 55W
Gweru **55** 19 28S 29 45 E
Gwinn **68** 46 15N 87 29W
Gwoza **53** 11 5N 13 40 E
Gwydir → **45** 29 27S 149 48 E
Gwynedd □ **6** 53 0N 4 0W
Gyaring Hu **37** 34 50N 97 40 E
Gydanskiy P-ov. **24** 70 0N 78 0 E
Gympie **45** 26 11S 152 38 E
Gyoda **36** 36 10N 139 30 E
Gyöngyös **15** 47 48N 19 56 E
Györ **15** 47 41N 17 40 E
Gypsum Pt. **64** 61 53N 114 35W
Gypsumville **65** 51 45N 98 40W

Ha 'Arava

H

Ha 'Arava → 28 30 50N 35 20 E
Haapamäki 20 62 18N 24 28 E
Haarlem 11 52 23N 4 39 E
Haast → 43 43 50S 169 2 E
Hab Nadi Chauki 32 25 0N 66 50 E
Habana, La 75 23 8N 82 22W
Habaswein 54 1 2N 39 30 E
Habay 64 58 50N 118 44W
Hachijō-Jima 36 33 5N 139 45 E
Hachinohe 36 40 30N 141 29 E
Hachiōji 36 35 40N 139 20 E
Hadarba, Ras 51 22 4N 36 51 E
Hadd, Ras al 31 22 35N 59 50 E
Haddington 8 55 57N 2 48W
Hadejia 53 12 30N 10 5 E
Haden 45 27 13S 151 54 E
Ḥadera 28 32 27N 34 55 E
Ḥadera, N. → 28 32 28N 34 52 E
Hadhramaut = Haḍramawt 29 15 30N 49 30 E
Hadramawt 29 15 30N 49 30 E
Hadrians Wall 6 55 0N 2 30W
Haeju 38 38 3N 125 45 E
Haerhpin = Harbin 38 45 48N 126 40 E
Hafar al Bāṭin 30 28 25N 46 0 E
Hafizabad 32 32 5N 73 40 E
Haflong 33 25 10N 93 5 E
Hafnarfjörour 20 64 4N 21 57W
Haft-Gel 30 31 30N 49 32 E
Hafun, Ras 31 10 29N 51 20 E
Hagalil 28 32 53N 35 18 E
Hagen 14 51 21N 7 29 E
Hagerman 71 33 5N 104 22W
Hagerstown 68 39 39N 77 46W
Hagfors 21 60 3N 13 45 E
Hagi, Iceland 20 65 28N 23 25W
Hagi, Japan 36 34 30N 131 22 E
Hagolan 28 33 0N 35 45 E
Hagondange-Briey 12 49 16N 6 11 E
Hags Hd. 9 52 57N 9 30W
Hague, C. de la 12 49 44N 1 56W
Hague, The = 's-Gravenhage 11 52 7N 4 17 E
Haguenau 12 48 49N 7 47 E
Haicheng 38 40 50N 122 45 E
Haifa = Ḥefa 28 32 46N 35 0 E
Haifeng 39 22 58N 115 10 E
Haig 47 30 55S 126 10 E
Haikang 39 20 52N 110 8 E
Haikou 39 20 1N 110 16 E
Ḥā'il 30 27 28N 41 45 E
Hailar 38 49 10N 119 38 E
Hailar He → 38 49 30N 117 50 E
Hailey 72 43 30N 114 15W
Haileybury 62 47 30N 79 38W
Hailin 38 44 37N 129 30 E
Hailing Dao 39 21 35N 111 47 E
Hailong 38 42 32N 125 40 E
Hailun 38 47 28N 126 50 E
Hailuoto 20 65 3N 24 45 E
Haimen 39 31 52N 121 10 E
Hainan Dao 39 19 0N 109 30 E
Hainaut □ 11 50 30N 4 0 E
Haines 72 44 51N 117 59W
Haines City 69 28 6N 81 35W
Haines Junction 64 60 45N 137 30W
Haining 39 30 28N 120 40 E
Haiphong 39 20 47N 106 41 E
Haiti ■ 75 19 0N 72 30W
Haiya Junction 51 18 20N 36 21 E
Haiyan 39 30 28N 120 58 E
Haiyang 38 36 47N 121 9 E
Haiyuan 38 36 35N 105 52 E
Haja 35 3 19S 129 37 E
Hajar Bangar 51 10 40N 22 45 E
Hajdúböszörmény 15 47 40N 21 30 E
Hajówka 15 52 47N 23 35 E
Hajr 31 24 0N 56 34 E
Hakken-Zan 36 34 10N 135 54 E
Hakodate 36 41 45N 140 44 E
Hala 32 25 43N 68 20 E
Ḥalab 30 36 10N 37 15 E
Ḥalabjah 30 35 10N 45 58 E
Halaib 51 22 12N 36 30 E
Halberstadt 14 51 53N 11 2 E
Halcombe 43 40 8S 175 30 E
Halcon, Mt. 35 13 0N 121 30 E
Halden 21 59 9N 11 23 E
Haldia 33 22 5N 88 3 E
Haldwani 32 29 31N 79 30 E
Hale → 44 24 56S 135 53 E
Haleakala Crater 66 20 43N 156 12W
Haleyville 69 34 15N 87 40W
Halfway → 64 56 12N 121 32W
Ḥalḥul 28 31 35N 35 7 E
Haliburton 62 45 3N 78 30W
Halifax, Australia 44 18 32S 146 22 E
Halifax, Canada 63 44 38N 63 35W
Halifax, U.K. 6 53 43N 1 51W
Halifax B. 44 18 50S 147 0 E
Halifax I. 56 26 38S 15 4 E
Halīl → 31 27 40N 58 30 E
Hall Beach 61 68 46N 81 12W
Hall Pt. 46 15 40S 124 23 E
Hallands län □ 21 56 50N 12 50 E
Halle, Belgium 11 50 44N 4 13 E
Halle, Germany 14 51 29N 12 0 E
Hällefors 21 59 47N 14 31 E
Hallett 45 33 25S 138 55 E
Hallettsville 71 29 28N 96 57W
Halliday 70 47 20N 102 25W
Halliday L. 65 61 21N 108 56W
Hallingdal → 21 60 34N 9 12 E
Hällnäs 20 64 19N 19 36 E
Hallock 65 48 47N 97 0W
Halls Creek 46 18 16S 127 38 E
Halmahera 35 0 40N 128 0 E
Halmstad 21 56 41N 12 52 E
Halq el Oued 51 36 53N 10 18 E
Hals 21 56 59N 10 18 E
Hälsingborg = Helsingborg 21 56 3N 12 42 E
Halstad 70 47 21N 96 50W
Halul 31 25 40N 52 40 E
Hamab 56 28 7S 19 16 E
Hamada 36 34 56N 132 4 E
Hamadān 30 34 52N 48 32 E
Hamadān □ 30 35 0N 49 0 E
Hamāh 30 35 5N 36 40 E
Hamamatsu 36 34 45N 137 45 E
Hamar 21 60 48N 11 7 E
Hamarøy 20 68 5N 15 38 E
Hambantota 32 6 10N 81 10 E
Hamber Prov. Park 64 52 20N 118 0W
Hamburg, Germany 14 53 32N 9 59 E
Hamburg, Ark., U.S.A. 71 33 15N 91 47W
Hamburg, Iowa, U.S.A. 70 40 37N 95 38W
Hame 21 61 30N 24 0 E
Hämeenlinna 20 61 0N 24 28 E
Hamelin Pool 47 26 22S 114 20 E
Hamelin Pool Bay 47 26 10S 114 5 E
Hameln 14 52 7N 9 24 E
Hamersley Ra. 46 22 0S 117 45 E
Hamhung 38 39 54N 127 30 E
Hami 37 42 55N 93 25 E
Hamilton, Australia 45 37 45S 142 2 E
Hamilton, Canada 62 43 15N 79 50W
Hamilton, N.Z. 43 37 47S 175 19 E
Hamilton, U.K. 8 55 47N 4 2W
Hamilton, Mo., U.S.A. 70 39 45N 93 59W
Hamilton, Mont., U.S.A. 72 46 20N 114 6W
Hamilton, N.Y., U.S.A. 68 42 49N 75 31W
Hamilton, Ohio, U.S.A. 68 39 20N 84 35W
Hamilton, Tex., U.S.A. 71 31 40N 98 5W
Hamilton → 44 23 30S 139 47 E
Hamilton Hotel 44 22 45S 140 40 E
Hamilton Inlet 63 54 0N 57 30W
Hamiota 65 50 11N 100 38W
Hamlet 69 34 56N 79 40W
Hamley Bridge 45 34 17S 138 35 E
Hamlin 71 32 58N 100 8W
Hamm 14 51 40N 7 49 E
Hammerfest 20 70 39N 23 41 E
Hammond, Ind., U.S.A. 68 41 40N 87 30W
Hammond, La., U.S.A. 71 30 32N 90 30W
Hammonton 68 39 40N 74 47W
Hampden 43 45 18S 170 50 E
Hampshire □ 7 51 3N 1 20W
Hampshire Downs 7 51 10N 1 10W
Hampton, Ark., U.S.A. 71 33 35N 92 29W
Hampton, Iowa, U.S.A. 70 42 42N 93 12W
Hampton, S.C., U.S.A. 69 32 52N 81 2W
Hampton, Va., U.S.A. 68 37 4N 76 18W
Hampton Tableland 47 32 0S 127 0 E
Hamrat esh Sheykh 51 14 38N 27 55 E
Han Jiang → 39 23 25N 116 40 E
Han Shui → 39 30 35N 114 18 E
Ḥana 66 20 45N 155 59W
Hanamaki 36 39 23N 141 7 E
Hanau 14 50 8N 8 56 E
Hancheng 38 35 31N 110 25 E
Hancock, Mich., U.S.A. 70 47 10N 88 40W
Hancock, Minn., U.S.A. 70 45 26N 95 46W
Handa, Japan 36 34 53N 137 0 E
Handa, Somalia 29 10 37N 51 2 E
Handan 38 36 35N 114 28 E
Handeni 54 5 25S 38 2 E
Hanegev 28 30 50N 35 0 E
Haney 64 49 12N 122 40W
Hanford 73 36 23N 119 39W
Hangang → 38 37 50N 126 30 E
Hangayn Nuruu 37 47 30N 100 0 E
Hangchou = Hangzhou 39 30 18N 120 11 E
Hanggin Houqi 38 40 58N 107 4 E
Hangklip, K. 56 34 26S 18 48 E
Hangö 21 59 50N 22 57 E
Hangu 38 39 18N 117 53 E
Hangzhou 39 30 18N 120 11 E
Hangzhou Wan 39 30 15N 120 45 E
Ḥanīsh 29 13 45N 42 46 E
Hanita 28 33 5N 35 10 E
Hankinson 70 46 9N 96 58W
Hanko 21 59 59N 22 57 E
Hankou 39 30 35N 114 30 E
Hanksville 73 38 19N 110 45W
Hanle 32 32 42N 79 4 E
Hanmer Springs 43 42 32S 172 50 E
Hann → 46 17 26S 126 17 E
Hann, Mt. 46 15 45S 126 0 E
Hanna 64 51 40N 111 54W
Hannaford 70 47 23N 98 11W
Hannah 70 48 58N 98 42W
Hannah B. 62 51 40N 80 0W
Hannibal 70 39 42N 91 22W
Hannover 14 52 23N 9 43 E
Hanoi 39 21 5N 105 55 E
Hanover = Hannover 14 52 23N 9 43 E
Hanover, S. Africa 56 31 4S 24 29 E
Hanover, N.H., U.S.A. 68 43 43N 72 17W
Hanover, Pa., U.S.A. 68 39 46N 76 59W
Hanover, I. 80 51 0S 74 50W
Hansi 32 29 10N 75 57 E
Hanson, L. 45 31 0S 136 15 E
Hanyang 39 30 35N 114 2 E
Hanyin 39 32 54N 108 28 E
Hanzhong 39 33 10N 107 1 E
Hanzhuang 39 34 33N 117 23 E
Haora 33 22 37N 88 20 E
Haparanda 20 65 52N 24 8 E
Happy 71 34 47N 101 50W
Happy Camp 72 41 52N 123 22W
Happy Valley-Goose Bay 63 53 15N 60 20W
Hapur 32 28 45N 77 45 E
Ḥaql 30 29 10N 35 0 E
Har 35 5 16S 133 14 E
Har Hu 37 38 20N 97 38 E
Har Us Nuur 37 48 0N 92 0 E
Har Yehuda 28 31 35N 34 57 E
Ḥaraḍ 30 24 22N 49 0 E
Haraisan Plateau 30 23 0N 47 40 E
Harardera 29 4 33N 47 38 E
Harare 55 17 43S 31 2 E
Harazé 51 14 20N 19 12 E
Harbin 38 45 48N 126 40 E
Harbor Beach 68 43 50N 82 38W
Harbor Springs 68 45 28N 85 0W
Harbour Breton 63 47 29N 55 50W
Harbour Grace 63 47 40N 53 22W
Harburg 14 53 27N 9 58 E
Hardangerfjorden 21 60 15N 6 0 E
Hardap Dam 56 24 32S 17 50 E
Hardenberg 11 52 34N 6 37 E
Harderwijk 11 52 21N 5 38 E
Hardey → 46 22 45S 116 8 E
Hardin 72 45 44N 107 35W
Harding 57 30 35S 29 55 E
Harding Ra. 46 16 17S 124 55 E
Hardisty 64 52 40N 111 18W
Hardman 72 45 12N 119 40W
Hardoi 32 27 26N 80 6 E
Hardwar = Haridwar 32 29 58N 78 9 E
Hardy 71 36 20N 91 30W
Hardy, Pen. 80 55 30S 68 20W
Hare B. 63 51 15N 55 45W
Hare Gilboa 28 32 31N 35 25 E
Hare Meron 28 32 59N 35 24 E
Harer 29 9 20N 42 8 E
Hargeisa 29 9 30N 44 2 E
Hargshamn 21 60 12N 18 30 E
Hari → 34 1 16S 104 5 E
Haridwar 32 29 58N 78 9 E
Haringhata → 33 22 0N 89 58 E
Harīrūd 31 35 0N 61 0 E
Harīrūd → 31 34 20N 62 30 E
Harlan, Iowa, U.S.A. 70 41 37N 95 20W
Harlan, Tenn., U.S.A. 69 36 50N 83 20W
Harlech 6 52 52N 4 7W
Harlem 72 48 29N 108 47W
Harlingen, Neth. 11 53 11N 5 25 E
Harlingen, U.S.A. 71 26 20N 97 50W
Harlowton 72 46 30N 109 54W
Harney Basin 72 43 30N 119 0W
Harney L. 72 43 0N 119 0W
Harney Pk. 70 43 52N 103 33W
Härnösand 20 62 38N 18 0 E
Harp L. 63 55 5N 61 50W
Harpe, La 70 40 30N 91 0W
Ḥarrat al Kishb 30 22 30N 40 15 E
Harrat al 'Uwairidh 30 26 50N 38 0 E
Harriman 69 36 0N 84 35W
Harrington Harbour 63 50 31N 59 30W
Harris 8 57 50N 6 55W
Harris, Sd. of 8 57 44N 7 6W
Harris L. 45 31 10S 135 10 E
Harrisburg, Ill., U.S.A. 71 37 42N 88 30W
Harrisburg, Nebr., U.S.A. 70 41 36N 103 46W
Harrisburg, Oreg., U.S.A. 72 44 16N 123 10W
Harrisburg, Pa., U.S.A. 68 40 18N 76 52W
Harrismith 57 28 15S 29 8 E
Harrison, Ark., U.S.A. 71 36 10N 93 4W
Harrison, Idaho, U.S.A. 72 47 30N 116 51W
Harrison, Nebr., U.S.A. 70 42 42N 103 52W
Harrison, C. 63 54 55N 57 55W
Harrison B. 60 70 25N 151 30W
Harrison L. 64 49 33N 121 50W
Harrisonburg 68 38 28N 78 52W
Harrisonville 70 38 39N 94 21W
Harriston 62 43 57N 80 53W
Harrisville 68 44 40N 83 19W
Harrogate 6 53 59N 1 32W
Harrow 7 51 35N 0 15W
Harstad 20 68 48N 16 30 E
Hart 68 43 42N 86 21W
Hart, L. 45 31 10S 136 25 E
Hartbees → 56 28 45S 20 32 E
Hartford, Conn., U.S.A. 68 41 47N 72 41W
Hartford, Ky., U.S.A. 68 37 26N 86 50W
Hartford, S. Dak., U.S.A. 70 43 40N 96 58W
Hartford, Wis., U.S.A. 70 43 18N 88 25W
Hartford City 68 40 22N 85 20W
Hartland 63 46 20N 67 32W
Hartland Pt. 7 51 2N 4 32W
Hartlepool 6 54 42N 1 11W
Hartley Bay 64 53 25N 129 15W
Hartmannberge 56 17 0S 13 0 E
Hartney 65 49 30N 100 35W
Harts → 56 28 24S 24 17 E
Hartselle 69 34 25N 86 55W
Hartshorne 71 34 51N 95 30W
Hartsville 69 34 23N 80 2W
Hartwell 69 34 21N 82 52W
Harvey, Australia 47 33 5S 115 54 E
Harvey, Ill., U.S.A. 68 41 40N 87 40W
Harvey, N. Dak., U.S.A. 70 47 50N 99 58W
Harwich 7 51 56N 1 18 E
Haryana □ 32 29 0N 76 10 E
Harz 14 51 40N 10 40 E
Hasa 30 26 0N 49 0 E
Hasharon 28 32 12N 34 49 E
Hashefela 28 31 30N 34 43 E
Haskell, Okla., U.S.A. 71 35 51N 95 40W
Haskell, Tex., U.S.A. 71 33 10N 99 45W
Hasselt 11 50 56N 5 21 E
Hassi Inifel 50 29 50N 3 41 E
Hassi Messaoud 50 31 43N 6 8 E
Hastings, N.Z. 43 39 39S 176 52 E
Hastings, U.K. 7 50 51N 0 36 E
Hastings, Mich., U.S.A. 68 42 40N 85 20W
Hastings, Minn., U.S.A. 70 44 41N 92 51W
Hastings, Nebr., U.S.A. 70 40 34N 98 22W
Hastings Ra. 45 31 15S 152 14 E
Hatch 73 32 45N 107 8W
Hatches Creek 44 20 56S 135 12 E
Hatchet L. 65 58 36N 103 40W
Hatfield P.O. 45 33 54S 143 49 E
Hatgal 37 50 26N 100 9 E
Hathras 32 27 36N 78 6 E
Hatia 33 22 30N 91 5 E
Hattah 45 34 48S 142 17 E
Hatteras, C. 69 35 10N 75 30W
Hattiesburg 71 31 20N 89 20W
Hatvan 15 47 40N 19 45 E
Hau Bon = Cheo Reo 34 13 25N 108 28 E
Haugesund 21 59 23N 5 13 E
Haultain → 65 55 51N 106 46W
Hauraki Gulf 43 36 35S 175 5 E
Hauran 28 32 50N 36 15 E
Haut Atlas 50 32 30N 5 0W
Haut-Rhin □ 12 48 0N 7 15 E
Hautah, Wahāt al 30 23 40N 47 0 E
Haute-Corse □ 12 42 30N 9 30 E
Haute-Garonne □ 12 43 30N 1 30 E
Haute-Loire □ 12 45 5N 3 50 E
Haute-Marne □ 12 48 10N 5 20 E
Haute-Saône □ 12 47 45N 6 10 E
Haute-Savoie □ 12 46 0N 6 20 E
Haute-Vienne □ 12 45 50N 1 10 E
Hauterive 63 49 10N 68 16W
Hautes-Alpes □ 12 44 42N 6 20 E
Hautes-Pyrénées □ 12 43 0N 0 10 E
Hauts-de-Seine □ 12 48 52N 2 15 E
Hauts Plateaux 50 35 0N 1 0 E
Havana = Habana, La 75 23 8N 82 22W
Havana 70 40 19N 90 3W
Havant 7 50 51N 0 59W
Havasu, L. 73 34 18N 114 28W
Havel → 14 52 40N 12 1 E
Havelange 11 50 23N 5 15 E
Havelock, N.B., Canada 63 46 2N 65 24W
Havelock, Ont., Canada 62 44 26N 77 53W
Havelock, N.Z. 43 41 17S 173 48 E
Haverfordwest 7 51 48N 4 59W
Haverhill 68 42 50N 71 2W
Havering 7 51 33N 0 20 E
Havlíčkův Brod 14 49 36N 15 33 E
Havre 72 48 34N 109 40W
Havre, Le 12 49 30N 0 5 E
Havre-Aubert 63 47 12N 61 56W
Havre-St.-Pierre 63 50 18N 63 33W
Havza 30 41 0N 35 35 E
Haw → 69 35 36N 79 3W
Hawaii □ 66 20 30N 157 0W
Hawaii I. 66 20 0N 155 0W
Hawaiian Is. 66 20 30N 156 0W
Hawaiian Ridge 41 24 0N 165 0W
Hawarden, Canada 65 51 25N 106 36W
Hawarden, U.S.A. 70 43 2N 96 28W
Hawea Lake 43 44 28S 169 19 E
Hawera 43 39 35S 174 19 E
Hawick 8 55 25N 2 48W
Hawk Junction 62 48 5N 84 38W
Hawke B. 43 39 25S 177 20 E
Hawke's Bay □ 43 39 45S 176 35 E
Hawkesbury 62 45 37N 74 37W
Hawkesbury I. 64 53 37N 129 3W
Hawkesbury Pt. 44 11 55S 134 5 E
Hawkinsville 69 32 17N 83 30W
Hawkwood 45 25 45S 150 50 E
Hawley 70 46 58N 96 20W
Hawrān 28 32 45N 36 15 E
Hawthorne 72 38 31N 118 37W
Haxtun 70 40 40N 102 39W
Hay 45 34 30S 144 51 E
Hay →, Australia 44 24 50S 138 0 E
Hay →, Canada 64 60 50N 116 26W
Hay, C. 46 14 5S 129 29 E
Hay L. 64 58 50N 118 50W
Hay Lakes 64 53 12N 113 2W
Hay-on-Wye 7 52 4N 3 9W
Hay River 64 60 51N 115 44W
Hay Springs 70 42 40N 102 38W
Hayden, Ariz., U.S.A. 73 33 2N 110 48W
Hayden, Colo., U.S.A. 72 40 30N 107 22W
Haydon 44 18 0S 141 30 E
Hayes 70 44 22N 101 1W
Hayes → 65 57 3N 92 12W
Haynesville 71 33 0N 93 7W
Hays, Canada 64 50 6N 111 48W
Hays, U.S.A. 70 38 55N 99 25W
Hayward 70 46 2N 91 30W
Hayward's Heath 7 51 0N 0 5W
Hazard 68 37 18N 83 10W
Hazaribag 33 23 58N 85 26 E
Hazelton, Canada 64 55 20N 127 42W
Hazelton, U.S.A. 70 46 30N 100 15W
Hazen, N. Dak., U.S.A. 70 47 18N 101 38W
Hazen, Nev., U.S.A. 72 39 37N 119 2W
Hazlehurst, Ga., U.S.A. 69 31 50N 82 35W
Hazlehurst, Miss., U.S.A. 71 31 52N 90 24W
Hazleton 68 40 58N 76 0W
Hazlett, L. 46 21 30S 128 48 E
Ḥazor 28 33 2N 35 32 E
He Xian 39 24 27N 111 30 E
Head of Bight 47 31 30S 131 25 E
Healdsburg 72 38 33N 122 51W
Healdton 71 34 16N 97 31W
Healesville 45 37 35S 145 30 E
Heanor 6 53 1N 1 20W
Heard I. 3 53 0S 74 0 E
Hearne 71 30 54N 96 35W
Hearne B. 65 60 10N 99 10W
Hearne L. 64 62 20N 113 10W
Hearst 62 49 40N 83 41W
Heart → 70 46 40N 100 51W
Heart's Content 63 47 54N 53 27W
Heath Pt. 63 49 8N 61 40W
Heath Steele 63 47 17N 66 5W
Heavener 71 34 54N 94 36W
Hebbronville 71 27 20N 98 40W
Hebei □ 38 39 0N 116 0 E
Hebel 45 28 58S 147 47 E

Jenkins

İnegöl 30 40 5N 29 31 E
Infante, Kaap 56 34 27S 20 51 E
Infiernillo, Presa del 74 18 9N 102 0W
Ingende 54 0 12S 18 57 E
Ingham 44 18 43S 146 10 E
Ingleborough 6 54 11N 2 23W
Inglewood, Queens., Australia 45 28 25S 151 2 E
Inglewood, Vic., Australia 45 36 29S 143 53 E
Inglewood, N.Z. 43 39 9S 174 14 E
Inglewood, U.S.A. 73 33 58N 118 21W
Ingólfshöfði 20 63 48N 16 39W
Ingolstadt 14 48 45N 11 26 E
Ingomar 72 46 35N 107 21W
Ingonish 63 46 42N 60 18W
Ingraj Bazar 33 24 58N 88 10 E
Ingulec 23 47 42N 33 14 E
Ingwavuma 57 27 9S 31 59 E
Inhaca, I. 57 26 1S 32 57 E
Inhafenga 57 20 36S 33 53 E
Inhambane 57 23 54S 35 30 E
Inhambane □ 57 22 30S 34 20 E
Inhaminga 55 18 26S 35 0 E
Inharrime 57 24 30S 35 0 E
Inharrime → 57 24 30S 35 0 E
Ining = Yining 37 43 58N 81 10 E
Inírida → 78 3 55N 67 52W
Inishbofin 9 53 35N 10 12W
Inishmore 9 53 8N 9 45W
Inishowen 9 55 14N 7 15W
Injune 45 25 53S 148 32 E
Inklin 64 58 56N 133 5W
Inklin → 64 58 50N 133 10W
Inkom 72 42 51N 112 15W
Inle L. 33 20 30N 96 58 E
Inn → 14 48 35N 13 28 E
Innamincka 45 27 44S 140 46 E
Inner Hebrides 8 57 0N 6 30W
Inner Mongolia = Nei Monggol Zizhiqu □ 38 42 0N 112 0 E
Inner Sound 8 57 30N 5 55W
Innetalling I. 62 56 0N 79 0W
Innisfail, Australia 44 17 33S 146 5 E
Innisfail, Canada 64 52 0N 113 57W
Innsbruck 14 47 16N 11 23 E
Inny → 9 53 30N 7 50W
Inongo 54 1 55S 18 30 E
Inoucdjouac 61 58 25N 78 15W
Inowrocław 15 52 50N 18 12 E
Inquisivi 78 16 50S 67 10W
Inscription, C. 47 25 29S 112 59 E
Insein 33 16 50N 96 5 E
Inta 22 66 5N 60 8 E
Interior 70 43 46N 101 59W
International Falls 70 48 36N 93 25W
Intiyaco 80 28 43S 60 5W
Inútil, B. 80 53 30S 70 15W
Inuvik 60 68 16N 133 40W
Inveraray 8 56 13N 5 5W
Inverbervie 8 56 50N 2 17W
Invercargill 43 46 24S 168 24 E
Inverell 45 29 45S 151 8 E
Invergordon 8 57 41N 4 10W
Invermere 64 50 30N 116 2W
Inverness, Canada 63 46 15N 61 19W
Inverness, U.K. 8 57 29N 4 12W
Inverness, U.S.A. 69 28 50N 82 20W
Inverurie 8 57 15N 2 21W
Inverway 46 17 50S 129 38 E
Investigator Group 45 34 45S 134 20 E
Investigator Str. 45 35 30S 137 0 E
Inya 24 50 28N 86 37 E
Inyo Mts. 73 37 0N 118 0W
Inyokern 73 35 38N 117 48W
Inza 22 53 55N 46 25 E
Iola 71 38 0N 95 20W
Iona 8 56 20N 6 25W
Ione, Calif., U.S.A. 72 38 20N 120 56W
Ione, Wash., U.S.A. 72 48 44N 117 29W
Ionia 68 42 59N 85 7W
Ionian Is. = Iónioi Nísoi 19 38 40N 20 0 E
Ionian Sea 17 37 30N 17 30 E
Iónioi Nísoi 19 38 40N 20 0 E
Íos 19 36 41N 25 20 E
Iowa □ 70 42 18N 93 30W
Iowa City 70 41 40N 91 35W
Iowa Falls 70 42 30N 93 15W
Ipameri 79 17 44S 48 9W
Ipatinga 79 19 32S 42 30W
Ipiales 78 0 50N 77 37W
Ipin = Yibin 37 28 45N 104 32 E
Ípiros □ 19 39 30N 20 30 E
Ipixuna 78 7 0S 71 40W
Ipoh 34 4 35N 101 5 E
Ippy 51 6 5N 21 7 E
Ipswich, Australia 45 27 35S 152 40 E
Ipswich, U.K. 7 52 4N 1 9 E
Ipswich, U.S.A. 70 45 28N 99 1W
Ipu 79 4 23S 40 44W
Iquique 78 20 19S 70 5W
Iquitos 78 3 45S 73 10W
Iracoubo 79 5 30N 53 10W
Iráklion 19 35 20N 25 12 E
Iran ■ 31 33 0N 53 0 E
Iran, Gunung-Gunung 34 2 20N 114 50 E
Īrānshahr 31 27 15N 60 40 E
Irapuato 74 20 40N 101 30W
Iraq ■ 30 33 0N 44 0 E
Irbid 28 32 35N 35 48 E
Irebu 54 0 40S 17 46 E
Ireland ■ 9 53 0N 8 0W
Ireland's Eye 9 53 25N 6 4W
Irele 53 7 40N 5 40 E
Iret 25 60 3N 154 20 E
Iri 38 35 59N 127 0 E
Irian Jaya □ 35 4 0S 137 0 E
Iringa 54 7 48S 35 43 E
Iriri → 79 3 52S 52 37W
Irish Republic ■ 9 53 0N 8 0W
Irish Sea 6 54 0N 5 0W
Irkineyeva 25 58 30N 96 49 E
Irkutsk 25 52 18N 104 20 E
Irma 65 52 55N 111 14W
Iron Baron 45 32 58S 137 11 E
Iron Gate = Portile de Fier 15 44 42N 22 30 E
Iron Knob 45 32 46S 137 8 E
Iron Mountain 68 45 49N 88 4W
Iron River 70 46 6N 88 40W
Ironbridge 7 52 38N 2 29W
Ironstone Kopje 56 25 17S 24 5 E
Ironton, Mo., U.S.A. 71 37 40N 90 40W
Ironton, Ohio, U.S.A. 68 38 35N 82 40W
Ironwood 70 46 30N 90 10W
Iroquois Falls 62 48 46N 80 41W
Irrara Cr. → 45 29 35S 145 31 E
Irrawaddy □ 33 17 0N 95 0 E
Irrawaddy → 33 15 50N 95 6 E
Irtysh → 24 61 4N 68 52 E
Irumu 54 1 32N 29 53 E
Irún 13 43 20N 1 52W
Irvine, Canada 65 49 57N 110 16W
Irvine, U.K. 8 55 37N 4 40W
Irvine, U.S.A. 68 37 42N 83 58W
Irvinestown 9 54 28N 7 38W
Irwin → 47 29 15S 114 54 E
Irwin, Pt. 47 35 5S 116 55 E
Irymple 45 34 14S 142 8 E
Isa 53 13 14N 6 24 E
Isaac → 44 22 55S 149 20 E
Isabel 70 45 27N 101 22W
Isabela, I. 74 21 51N 105 55W
Isabella 35 6 40N 122 10 E
Isabella, Cord. 75 13 30N 85 25W
Isabella Ra. 46 21 0S 121 4 E
Ísafjarðardjúp 20 66 10N 23 0W
Ísafjörður 20 66 5N 23 9W
Isangi 54 0 52N 24 10 E
Isar → 14 48 49N 12 58 E
Íschia 18 40 45N 13 51 E
Isdell → 46 16 27S 124 51 E
Ise 36 34 25N 136 45 E
Ise-Wan 36 34 43N 136 43 E
Isère □ 12 45 15N 5 40 E
Isère → 12 44 59N 4 51 E
Iseyin 53 8 0N 3 36 E
Ishikari-Wan 36 43 25N 141 1 E
Ishikawa □ 36 36 30N 136 30 E
Ishim 24 56 10N 69 30 E
Ishim → 24 57 45N 71 10 E
Ishinomaki 36 38 32N 141 20 E
Ishkuman 32 36 30N 73 50 E
Ishpeming 68 46 30N 87 40W
Isil Kul 24 54 55N 71 16 E
Isiolo 54 0 24N 37 33 E
Isipingo Beach 57 30 0S 30 57 E
Isiro 54 2 53N 27 40 E
Isisford 44 24 15S 144 21 E
İskenderun 30 36 32N 36 10 E
İskenderun Körfezi 23 36 40N 35 50 E
Iskut → 64 56 45N 131 49W
Isla → 8 56 32N 3 20W
Islamabad 32 33 40N 73 10 E
Island → 64 60 25N 121 12W
Island Falls, Canada 62 49 35N 81 20W
Island Falls, U.S.A. 63 46 0N 68 16W
Island L. 65 53 47N 94 25W
Island Lagoon 45 31 30S 136 40 E
Island Pt. 47 30 20S 115 1 E
Island Pond 68 44 50N 71 50W
Islands, B. of 63 49 11N 58 15W
Islay 8 55 46N 6 10W
Isle aux Morts 63 47 35N 59 0W
Isle of Wight □ 7 50 40N 1 20W
Isle Royale 70 48 0N 88 50W
Isleta 73 34 58N 106 46W
Ismail 23 45 22N 28 46 E
Ismâ'ilîya 30 30 37N 32 18 E
Ismay 70 46 33N 104 44W
Isna 51 25 17N 32 30 E
Isoka 52 10 4S 32 42 E
Isparta 30 37 47N 30 30 E
Íspica 18 36 47N 14 53 E
Israel ■ 28 32 0N 34 50 E
Isseka 47 28 30S 114 35 E
Issyk-Kul, Ozero 24 42 25N 77 15 E
İstanbul 30 41 0N 29 0 E
Istokpoga, L. 69 27 22N 81 14W
Istra 18 45 10N 14 0 E
Istria = Istra 18 45 10N 14 0 E
Itabaiana 79 7 18S 35 19W
Itaberaba 79 12 32S 40 18W
Itabira 79 19 37S 43 13W
Itabuna 79 14 48S 39 16W
Itaipu Dam 80 25 30S 54 30W
Itaituba 79 4 10S 55 50W
Itajaí 80 27 50S 48 39W
Italy ■ 18 42 0N 13 0 E
Itampolo 57 24 41S 43 57 E
Itapecuru-Mirim 79 3 24S 44 20W
Itaperuna 79 21 10S 41 54W
Itapicuru →, Bahia, Brazil 79 11 47S 37 32W
Itapicuru →, Maranhão, Brazil 79 2 52S 44 12W
Itapipoca 79 3 30S 39 35W
Itaquatiara 78 2 58S 58 30W
Itaquí 80 29 8S 56 30W
Itatuba 78 5 46S 63 20W
Itchen → 7 50 57N 1 20W
Ithaca = Itháki 19 38 25N 20 40 E
Ithaca 68 42 25N 76 30W
Itháki 19 38 25N 20 40 E
Ito 36 34 58N 139 5 E
Itonamas → 78 12 28S 64 24W
Itu 53 5 10N 7 58 E
Ituaçu 79 13 50S 41 18W
Ituiutaba 79 19 0S 49 25W
Itumbiara 79 18 20S 49 10W
Ituna 65 51 10N 103 24W
Iturbe 80 23 0S 65 25W
Iturup, Ostrov 25 45 0N 148 0 E
Ivalo 20 68 38N 27 35 E
Ivalojoki → 20 68 40N 27 40 E
Ivanhoe, N.S.W., Australia 45 32 56S 144 20 E
Ivanhoe, N. Terr., Australia 46 15 41S 128 41 E
Ivanhoe L. 65 60 25N 106 30W
Ivano-Frankovsk 23 48 40N 24 40 E
Ivanovo 22 57 5N 41 0 E
Ivato 57 20 37S 47 10 E
Ivdel 22 60 42N 60 24 E
Iviza = Ibiza 13 38 54N 1 26 E
Ivohibe 57 22 31S 46 57 E
Ivory Coast ■ 50 7 30N 5 0W
Ivrea 18 45 30N 7 52 E
Ivugivik 61 62 24N 77 55W
Iwahig 34 8 36N 117 32 E
Iwaki 36 37 3N 140 55 E
Iwakuni 36 34 15N 132 8 E
Iwamizawa 36 43 12N 141 46 E
Iwanai 36 42 58N 140 30 E
Iwanuma 36 38 7N 140 51 E
Iwata 36 34 42N 137 51 E
Iwate □ 36 39 30N 141 30 E
Iwate-San 36 39 51N 141 0 E
Iwo 53 7 39N 4 9 E
Ixiamas 78 13 50S 68 5W
Ixopo 57 30 11S 30 5 E
Ixtepec 74 16 32N 95 10W
Ixtlán del Río 74 21 5N 104 21W
Izabel, L. de 75 15 30N 89 10W
Izamal 74 20 56N 89 1W
Izegem 11 50 55N 3 12 E
Izhevsk = Ustinov 22 56 51N 53 14 E
İzmir 23 38 25N 27 8 E
İzmit 30 40 45N 29 50 E
Izra 28 32 51N 36 15 E
Izumi-sano 36 34 23N 135 18 E
Izumo 36 35 20N 132 46 E

J

Jaba' 28 32 20N 35 13 E
Jabalpur 32 23 9N 79 58 E
Jabālyah 28 31 32N 34 27 E
Jablah 30 35 20N 36 0 E
Jablonec 14 50 43N 15 10 E
Jaboatão 79 8 7S 35 1W
Jaburu 78 5 30S 64 0W
Jaca 13 42 35N 0 33W
Jacareí 80 23 20S 46 0W
Jacarèzinho 80 23 5S 50 0W
Jackman 63 45 35N 70 17W
Jacksboro 71 33 14N 98 15W
Jackson, Australia 45 26 39S 149 39 E
Jackson, Ala., U.S.A. 69 31 32N 87 53W
Jackson, Calif., U.S.A. 72 38 19N 120 47W
Jackson, Ky., U.S.A. 68 37 35N 83 22W
Jackson, Mich., U.S.A. 68 42 18N 84 25W
Jackson, Minn., U.S.A. 70 43 35N 95 0W
Jackson, Miss., U.S.A. 71 32 20N 90 10W
Jackson, Mo., U.S.A. 71 37 25N 89 42W
Jackson, Ohio, U.S.A. 68 39 0N 82 40W
Jackson, Tenn., U.S.A. 69 35 40N 88 50W
Jackson, Wyo., U.S.A. 72 43 30N 110 49W
Jackson, L. 72 43 55N 110 40W
Jackson Bay 43 43 58S 168 42 E
Jacksons 43 42 46S 171 32 E
Jacksonville, Ala., U.S.A. 69 33 49N 85 45W
Jacksonville, Fla., U.S.A. 69 30 15N 81 38W
Jacksonville, Ill., U.S.A. 70 39 42N 90 15W
Jacksonville, N.C., U.S.A. 69 34 50N 77 29W
Jacksonville, Oreg., U.S.A. 72 42 19N 122 56W
Jacksonville, Tex., U.S.A. 71 31 58N 95 19W
Jacksonville Beach 69 30 19N 81 26W
Jacmel 75 18 14N 72 32W
Jacob Lake 73 36 45N 112 12W
Jacobabad 32 28 20N 68 29 E
Jacobina 79 11 11S 40 30W
Jacob's Well 28 32 13N 35 13 E
Jacques-Cartier, Mt. 63 48 57N 66 0W
Jacundá → 79 1 57S 50 26W
Jadotville = Likasi 54 10 55S 26 48 E
Jādū 51 32 0N 12 0 E
Jaén, Peru 78 5 25S 78 40W
Jaén, Spain 13 37 44N 3 43W
Jaffa = Tel Aviv-Yafo 28 32 4N 34 48 E
Jaffa, C. 45 36 58S 139 40 E
Jaffna 32 9 45N 80 2 E
Jagadhri 32 30 10N 77 20 E
Jagdalpur 33 19 3N 82 0 E
Jagersfontein 56 29 44S 25 27 E
Jagraon 32 30 50N 75 25 E
Jagtial 32 18 50N 79 0 E
Jaguariaíva 80 24 10S 49 50W
Jaguaribe → 79 4 25S 37 45W
Jagüey Grande 75 22 35N 81 7W
Jahrom 31 28 30N 53 31 E
Jailolo 35 1 5N 127 30 E
Jailolo, Selat 35 0 5N 129 5 E
Jaipur 32 27 0N 75 50 E
Jakarta 35 6 9S 106 49 E
Jakobstad 20 63 40N 22 43 E
Jal 71 32 8N 103 8W
Jalai Nur 38 49 27N 117 42 E
Jalalabad 31 34 30N 70 29 E
Jalapa 75 14 39N 89 59W
Jalapa Enríquez 74 19 32N 96 55W
Jalas, Jabal al 30 27 30N 36 30 E
Jalgaon, Maharashtra, India 32 21 2N 76 31 E
Jalgaon, Maharashtra, India 32 21 0N 75 42 E
Jalingo 53 8 55N 11 25 E
Jalisco □ 74 20 0N 104 0W
Jalna 32 19 48N 75 38 E
Jalón → 13 41 47N 1 4W
Jalpa 74 21 38N 102 58W
Jalpaiguri 33 26 32N 88 46 E
Jalq 31 27 35N 62 46 E
Jaluit I. 40 6 0N 169 30 E
Jamaari 53 11 44N 9 53 E
Jamaica ■ 75 18 10N 77 30W
Jamalpur, Bangla. 33 24 52N 89 56 E
Jamalpur, India 33 25 18N 86 28 E
Jamanxim → 79 4 43S 56 18W
Jambe 35 1 15S 132 10 E
Jambi 34 1 38S 103 30 E
Jambi □ 34 1 30S 102 30 E
James → 70 42 52N 97 18W
James B. 62 51 30N 80 0W
James Ranges 46 24 10S 132 30 E
Jamestown, Australia 45 33 10S 138 32 E
Jamestown, S. Africa 56 31 6S 26 45 E
Jamestown, Ky., U.S.A. 68 37 0N 85 5W
Jamestown, N. Dak., U.S.A. 70 46 54N 98 42W
Jamestown, N.Y., U.S.A. 68 42 5N 79 18W
Jamestown, Tenn., U.S.A. 69 36 25N 85 0W
Jamkhandi 32 16 30N 75 15 E
Jammā'īn 28 32 8N 35 12 E
Jammu 32 32 43N 74 54 E
Jammu & Kashmir □ 32 34 25N 77 0 E
Jamnagar 32 22 30N 70 6 E
Jamrud 32 33 59N 71 24 E
Jamshedpur 33 22 44N 86 12 E
Jämtlands län □ 20 62 40N 13 50 E
Jan Kempdorp 56 27 55S 24 51 E
Jan L. 65 54 56N 102 55W
Jand 32 33 30N 72 6 E
Jandaq 31 34 3N 54 22 E
Jandowae 45 26 45S 151 7 E
Janesville 70 42 39N 89 1W
Janīn 28 32 28N 35 18 E
Januária 79 15 25S 44 25W
Janub Dârfûr □ 51 11 0N 25 0 E
Janub Kordofân □ 51 12 0N 30 0 E
Jaora 32 23 40N 75 10 E
Japan ■ 36 36 0N 136 0 E
Japan, Sea of 36 40 0N 135 0 E
Japan Trench 40 32 0N 142 0 E
Japen = Yapen 35 1 50S 136 0 E
Japurá → 78 3 8S 64 46W
Jaque 78 7 27N 78 8W
Jara, La 73 37 16N 106 0W
Jarama → 13 40 2N 3 39W
Jarash 28 32 17N 35 54 E
Jardines de la Reina, Is. 75 20 50N 78 50W
Jargalant = Hovd 37 48 2N 91 37 E
Jargalant 37 48 2N 91 37 E
Jarosław 15 50 2N 22 42 E
Jarrahdale 47 32 24S 116 5 E
Jarso 51 5 15N 37 30 E
Jarvis I. 41 0 15S 159 55W
Jarwa 33 27 38N 82 30 E
Jäsk 31 25 38N 57 45 E
Jasło 15 49 45N 21 30 E
Jasper, Canada 64 52 55N 118 5W
Jasper, Ala., U.S.A. 69 33 48N 87 16W
Jasper, Fla., U.S.A. 69 30 31N 82 58W
Jasper, Minn., U.S.A. 70 43 52N 96 22W
Jasper, Tex., U.S.A. 71 30 59N 93 58W
Jasper Nat. Park 64 52 50N 118 8W
Jassy = Iaşi 17 47 10N 27 40 E
Jászberény 15 47 30N 19 55 E
Jataí 79 17 58S 51 48W
Jatibarang 35 6 28S 108 18 E
Jatinegara 35 6 13S 106 52 E
Játiva 13 39 0N 0 32W
Jatt 28 32 24N 35 2 E
Jaú 79 22 10S 48 30W
Jauja 78 11 45S 75 15W
Jaunpur 33 25 46N 82 44 E
Java = Jawa 35 7 0S 110 0 E
Java Sea 34 4 35S 107 15 E
Java Trench 40 10 0S 110 0W
Javhlant = Ulyasutay 37 47 56N 97 28 E
Jawa 35 7 0S 110 0 E
Jay 71 36 25N 94 46W
Jaya, Puncak 35 3 57S 137 17 E
Jayanti 33 26 45N 89 40 E
Jayapura 35 2 28S 140 38 E
Jayawijaya, Pegunungan 35 5 0S 139 0 E
Jaynagar 33 26 43N 86 9 E
Jayton 71 33 17N 100 35W
Jean 73 35 47N 115 20W
Jean Marie River 60 61 32N 120 38W
Jean Rabel 75 19 50N 73 5W
Jeanerette 71 29 52N 91 38W
Jeanette, Ostrov 25 76 43N 158 0 E
Jebba 53 9 9N 4 48 E
Jebel, Bahr el → 51 9 30N 30 25 E
Jedburgh 8 55 28N 2 33W
Jedda = Jiddah 29 21 29N 39 10 E
Jędrzejów 15 50 35N 20 15 E
Jedway 64 52 17N 131 14W
Jefferson, Iowa, U.S.A. 70 42 3N 94 25W
Jefferson, Tex., U.S.A. 71 32 45N 94 23W
Jefferson, Wis., U.S.A. 70 43 0N 88 49W
Jefferson, Mt., Nev., U.S.A. 72 38 51N 117 0W
Jefferson, Mt., Oreg., U.S.A. 72 44 45N 121 50W
Jefferson City, Mo., U.S.A. 70 38 34N 92 10W
Jefferson City, Tenn., U.S.A. 69 36 8N 83 30W
Jeffersonville 68 38 20N 85 42W
Jega 53 12 15N 4 23 E
Jelenia Góra 14 50 50N 15 45 E
Jelgava 22 56 41N 23 49 E
Jellicoe 62 49 40N 87 30W
Jemaja 34 3 5N 105 45 E
Jember 35 8 11S 113 41 E
Jembongan 34 6 45N 117 20 E
Jemeppe 11 50 37N 5 30 E
Jena, Germany 14 50 56N 11 33 E
Jena, U.S.A. 71 31 41N 92 7W
Jenkins 68 37 13N 82 41W

Jennings

Jennings **71** 30 10N 92 45W
Jennings → **64** 59 38N 132 5W
Jeparit **45** 36 8S 142 1 E
Jequié **79** 13 51S 40 5W
Jequitinhonha **79** 16 30S 41 0W
Jequitinhonha → **79** 15 51S 38 53W
Jerada **50** 34 17N 2 10W
Jerantut **34** 3 56N 102 22 E
Jérémie **75** 18 40N 74 10W
Jerez, Punta **74** 22 58N 97 40W
Jerez de García Salinas **74** 22 39N 103 0W
Jerez de la Frontera **13** 36 41N 6 7W
Jerez de los Caballeros **13** 38 20N 6 45W
Jericho = El Arīḥā **28** 31 52N 35 27 E
Jericho **44** 23 38S 146 6 E
Jerilderie **45** 35 20S 145 41 E
Jerome **73** 34 50N 112 0W
Jersey, I. **7** 49 13N 2 7W
Jersey City **68** 40 41N 74 8W
Jersey Shore **68** 41 17N 77 18W
Jerseyville **70** 39 5N 90 20W
Jerusalem **28** 31 47N 35 10 E
Jervis B. **45** 35 8S 150 46 E
Jesselton = Kota Kinabalu **34** 6 0N 116 4 E
Jessore **33** 23 10N 89 10 E
Jesup **69** 31 36N 81 54W
Jetmore **71** 38 10N 99 57W
Jewett **71** 31 20N 96 8W
Jeypore **33** 18 50N 82 38 E
Jhal Jhao **31** 26 20N 65 35 E
Jhalawar **32** 24 40N 76 10 E
Jhang Maghiana **32** 31 15N 72 22 E
Jhansi **32** 25 30N 78 36 E
Jharsaguda **33** 21 50N 84 5 E
Jhelum **32** 33 0N 73 45 E
Jhelum → **32** 31 20N 72 10 E
Jhunjhunu **32** 28 10N 75 30 E
Ji Xian **38** 36 7N 110 40 E
Jia Xian **38** 38 12N 110 28 E
Jiamusi **38** 46 40N 130 26 E
Ji'an **39** 27 6N 114 59 E
Jianchuan **37** 26 38N 99 55 E
Jiande **39** 29 23N 119 15 E
Jiangbei **39** 29 40N 106 34 E
Jiange **39** 32 4N 105 32 E
Jiangjin **39** 29 14N 106 14 E
Jiangling **39** 30 25N 112 12 E
Jiangmen **39** 22 32N 113 0 E
Jiangshan **39** 28 40N 118 37 E
Jiangsu □ **39** 33 0N 120 0 E
Jiangxi □ **39** 27 30N 116 0 E
Jiangyin **39** 31 54N 120 17 E
Jiangyong **39** 25 20N 111 22 E
Jiangyou **39** 31 44N 104 43 E
Jianning **39** 26 50N 116 50 E
Jian'ou **39** 27 3N 118 17 E
Jianshi **39** 30 37N 109 38 E
Jianshui **37** 23 36N 102 43 E
Jianyang **39** 27 20N 118 5 E
Jiao Xian **38** 36 18N 120 1 E
Jiaohe **38** 38 2N 116 20 E
Jiaozhou Wan **38** 36 5N 120 10 E
Jiaozuo **39** 35 16N 113 12 E
Jiawang **39** 34 28N 117 26 E
Jiaxing **39** 30 49N 120 45 E
Jiayi **39** 23 30N 120 24 E
Jibuti = Djibouti ■ **29** 12 0N 43 0 E
Jiddah **29** 21 29N 39 10 E
Jido **33** 29 2N 94 58 E
Jifnā **28** 31 58N 35 13 E
Jihlava **14** 49 28N 15 35 E
Jihlava → **14** 48 55N 16 36 E
Jijel **50** 36 52N 5 50 E
Jijiga **29** 9 20N 42 50 E
Jilin **38** 43 44N 126 30 E
Jilin □ **38** 44 0N 124 0 E
Jiloca → **13** 41 21N 1 39W
Jilong **39** 25 8N 121 42 E
Jima **51** 7 40N 36 47 E
Jiménez **74** 27 10N 104 54W
Jimo **38** 36 23N 120 30 E
Jin Xian **38** 38 55N 121 42 E
Jinan **38** 36 38N 117 1 E
Jincheng **38** 35 29N 112 50 E
Jindabyne **45** 36 25S 148 35 E
Jing He → **39** 34 27N 109 4 E
Jing Xian **39** 26 33N 109 40 E
Jingchuan **38** 35 20N 107 20 E
Jingdezhen **39** 29 20N 117 11 E
Jinggu **37** 23 35N 100 41 E
Jinghai **38** 38 55N 116 55 E
Jingle **38** 38 20N 111 55 E
Jingmen **39** 31 0N 112 10 E
Jingning **38** 35 30N 105 43 E
Jingshan **39** 31 1N 113 7 E
Jingtai **38** 37 10N 104 6 E
Jingxi **39** 23 8N 106 27 E
Jingyu **38** 42 25N 126 45 E
Jingyuan **38** 36 30N 104 40 E
Jingziguan **39** 33 15N 111 0 E
Jinhe **38** 51 18N 121 32 E
Jinhua **39** 29 8N 119 38 E
Jining, Nei Mongol Zizhiqu, China **38** 41 5N 113 0 E
Jining, Shandong, China **39** 35 22N 116 34 E
Jinja **54** 0 25N 33 12 E
Jinmen Dao **39** 24 25N 118 25 E
Jinnah Barrage **31** 32 58N 71 33 E
Jinotega **75** 13 6N 85 59W
Jinotepe **75** 11 50N 86 10W
Jinshi **39** 29 40N 111 50 E
Jinxiang **39** 35 5N 116 22 E
Jinzhou **38** 41 5N 121 3 E
Jiparaná → **78** 8 3S 62 52W
Jipijapa **78** 1 0S 80 40W
Jiquilpan **74** 19 57N 102 42W
Jishou **39** 28 21N 109 43 E
Jisr al Ḥusayn **28** 31 53N 35 33 E
Jisr ash Shughūr **30** 35 49N 36 18 E
Jitarning **47** 32 48S 117 57 E
Jiu → **15** 43 47N 23 48 E
Jiudengkou **38** 39 56N 106 40 E
Jiujiang **39** 29 42N 115 58 E
Jiuling Shan **39** 28 40N 114 40 E
Jiuquan **37** 39 50N 98 20 E
Jixi **38** 45 20N 130 50 E
Jīzān **29** 17 0N 42 20 E
Joaçaba **80** 27 5S 51 31W
João Pessoa **79** 7 10S 34 52W
Joaquín V. González **80** 25 10S 64 0W
Jodhpur **32** 26 23N 73 8 E
Joensuu **22** 62 37N 29 49 E
Jofane **57** 21 15S 34 18 E
Joggins **63** 45 42N 64 27W
Jogjakarta = Yogyakarta **35** 7 49S 110 22 E
Johannesburg **57** 26 10S 28 2 E
John Day **72** 44 25N 118 57W
John Day → **72** 45 44N 120 39W
John H. Kerr Res. **69** 36 20N 78 30W
John o' Groats **8** 58 39N 3 3W
Johnson **71** 37 35N 101 48W
Johnson City, N.Y., U.S.A. **68** 42 7N 75 57W
Johnson City, Tenn., U.S.A. **69** 36 18N 82 21W
Johnson City, Tex., U.S.A. **71** 30 15N 98 24W
Johnson's Crossing **64** 60 29N 133 18W
Johnston, L. **47** 32 25S 120 30 E
Johnston Falls = Mambilima Falls **54** 10 31S 28 45 E
Johnston I. **41** 17 10N 169 8W
Johnstone Str. **64** 50 28N 126 0W
Johnstown, N.Y., U.S.A. **68** 43 1N 74 20W
Johnstown, Pa., U.S.A. **68** 40 19N 78 53W
Johor Baharu **34** 1 28N 103 46 E
Joinvile **80** 26 15S 48 55W
Jokkmokk **20** 66 35N 19 50 E
Jökulsá á Dal → **20** 65 40N 14 16W
Jökulsá Fjöllum → **20** 66 10N 16 30W
Joliet **68** 41 30N 88 0W
Joliette **62** 46 3N 73 24W
Jolo **35** 6 0N 121 0 E
Jombang **35** 7 33S 112 14 E
Jome **35** 1 16S 127 30 E
Jonesboro, Ark., U.S.A. **71** 35 50N 90 45W
Jonesboro, Ill., U.S.A. **71** 37 26N 89 18W
Jonesboro, La., U.S.A. **71** 32 15N 92 41W
Jonesport **63** 44 32N 67 38W
Jonglei □ **51** 7 30N 32 30 E
Jönköping **21** 57 45N 14 10 E
Jönköpings län □ **21** 57 30N 14 30 E
Jonquière **63** 48 27N 71 14W
Joplin **71** 37 0N 94 31W
Jordan **72** 47 25N 106 58W
Jordan ■ **30** 31 0N 36 0 E
Jordan → **28** 31 48N 35 32 E
Jordan Valley **72** 43 0N 117 2W
Jorhat **33** 26 45N 94 12 E
Jorm **31** 36 50N 70 52 E
Jörn **20** 65 4N 20 1 E
Jorong **34** 3 58S 114 56 E
Jos **53** 9 53N 8 51 E
Joseph **72** 45 27N 117 13W
Joseph, L. **63** 52 45N 65 18W
Joseph Bonaparte G. **46** 14 35S 128 50 E
Joseph City **73** 35 0N 110 16W
Jostedal **21** 61 35N 7 15 E
Jotunheimen **21** 61 35N 8 25 E
Jourdanton **71** 28 54N 98 32W
Joussard **64** 55 22N 115 50W
Jovellanos **75** 22 40N 81 10W
Jowzjān □ **31** 36 10N 66 0 E
Ju Xian **39** 36 35N 118 20 E
Juan Aldama **74** 24 20N 103 23W
Juan de Fuca Str. **72** 48 15N 124 0W
Juan de Nova **57** 17 3S 43 45 E
Juan Fernández, Arch. de **76** 33 50S 80 0W
Juárez **80** 37 40S 59 43W
Juárez, Sierra de **74** 32 0N 116 0W
Juàzeiro **79** 9 30S 40 30W
Juàzeiro do Norte **79** 7 10S 39 18W
Jubbulpore = Jabalpur **32** 23 9N 79 58 E
Jubilee L. **47** 29 0S 126 50 E
Juby, C. **50** 28 0N 12 59W
Júcar → **13** 39 5N 0 10W
Juchitán **74** 16 27N 95 5W
Judaea = Har Yehuda **28** 31 35N 34 57 E
Judith → **72** 47 44N 109 38W
Judith Gap **72** 46 40N 109 46W
Jugoslavia = Yugoslavia ■ **19** 44 0N 20 0 E
Juigalpa **75** 12 6N 85 26W
Juiz de Fora **79** 21 43S 43 19W
Julesburg **70** 41 0N 102 20W
Juli **78** 16 10S 69 25W
Julia Cr. → **44** 20 0S 141 11 E
Julia Creek **44** 20 39S 141 44 E
Juliaca **78** 15 25S 70 10W
Julian **73** 33 4N 116 38W
Julianehåb **2** 60 43N 46 0W
Jullundur **32** 31 20N 75 40 E
Julu **38** 37 15N 115 2 E
Jumentos Cays **75** 23 0N 75 40 E
Jumet **11** 50 27N 4 25 E
Jumilla **13** 38 28N 1 19W
Jumla **33** 29 15N 82 13 E
Jumna = Yamuna → **33** 25 30N 81 53 E
Junagadh **32** 21 30N 70 30 E
Junction, Tex., U.S.A. **71** 30 29N 99 48W
Junction, Utah, U.S.A. **73** 38 10N 112 15W
Junction B. **44** 11 52S 133 55 E
Junction City, Kans., U.S.A. **70** 39 4N 96 55W
Junction City, Oreg., U.S.A. **72** 44 14N 123 12W
Junction Pt. **44** 11 45S 133 50 E
Jundah **44** 24 46S 143 2 E
Jundiaí **80** 24 30S 47 0W
Juneau **60** 58 20N 134 20W
Junee **45** 34 53S 147 35 E
Junggar Pendi **37** 44 30N 86 0 E
Junin **80** 34 33S 60 57W
Junín de los Andes **80** 39 45S 71 0W
Jūniyah **30** 33 59N 35 38 E
Junta, La **71** 38 0N 103 30W
Juntura **72** 43 44N 118 4W
Jupiter → **63** 49 29N 63 37W
Jur, Nahr el → **51** 8 45N 29 15 E
Jura **8** 56 0N 5 50W
Jura □ **12** 46 47N 5 45 E
Jura, Mts. **12** 46 40N 6 5 E
Jura, Sd. of **8** 55 57N 5 45W
Jurado **78** 7 7N 77 46W
Juruá → **78** 2 37S 65 44W
Juruena → **78** 7 20S 58 3W
Juruti **79** 2 9S 56 4W
Justo Daract **80** 33 52S 65 12W
Juticalpa **75** 14 40N 86 12W
Jutland = Jylland **21** 56 25N 9 30 E
Juventud, I. de la **75** 21 40N 82 40W
Juwain **31** 31 45N 61 30 E
Jylland **21** 56 25N 9 30 E
Jyväskylä **20** 62 14N 25 50 E

K

K2, Mt. **32** 35 58N 76 32 E
Kaap die Goeie Hoop **56** 34 24S 18 30 E
Kaap Plateau **56** 28 30S 24 0 E
Kaapkruis **56** 21 55S 13 57 E
Kaapstad = Cape Town **56** 33 55S 18 22 E
Kabaena **35** 5 15S 122 0 E
Kabala **50** 9 38N 11 37W
Kabale **54** 1 15S 30 0 E
Kabalo **54** 6 0S 27 0 E
Kabambare **54** 4 41S 27 39 E
Kabanjahe **34** 3 6N 98 30 E
Kabara **50** 16 40N 2 50W
Kabardino-Balkar-A.S.S.R. □ **23** 43 30N 43 30 E
Kabare **35** 0 4S 130 58 E
Kabarega Falls **54** 2 15N 31 30 E
Kabarnet **52** 0 31N 35 44 E
Kabasalan **35** 7 47N 122 44 E
Kabba **53** 7 50N 6 3 E
Kabinakagami L. **62** 48 54N 84 25W
Kabīr, Zab al → **30** 36 0N 43 0 E
Kabīr Kūh **30** 33 0N 47 30 E
Kabkabīyah **51** 13 50N 24 0 E
Kabompo → **55** 14 10S 23 11 E
Kabongo **54** 7 22S 25 33 E
Kabra **44** 23 25S 150 25 E
Kabūd Gonbad **31** 37 5N 59 45 E
Kābul **31** 34 28N 69 11 E
Kābul □ **31** 34 30N 69 0 E
Kabul → **32** 33 55N 72 14 E
Kaburuang **35** 3 50N 126 30 E
Kabwe **55** 14 30S 28 29 E
Kachchh, Gulf of **32** 22 50N 69 15 E
Kachchh, Rann of **32** 24 0N 70 0 E
Kachin □ **33** 26 0N 97 30 E
Kachiry **24** 53 10N 75 50 E
Kackar **30** 40 45N 41 10 E
Kadan Kyun **34** 12 30N 98 20 E
Kade **53** 6 7N 0 56W
Kadina **45** 34 0S 137 43 E
Kadirli **30** 37 23N 36 5 E
Kadiyevka = Stakhanov **23** 48 35N 38 40 E
Kadoka **70** 43 50N 101 31W
Kadoma **55** 18 20S 29 52 E
Kâdugli **51** 11 0N 29 45 E
Kaduna **53** 10 30N 7 21 E
Kaduna □ **53** 11 0N 7 30 E
Kaédi **50** 16 9N 13 28W
Kaelé **53** 10 7N 14 27 E
Kaesŏng **38** 37 58N 126 35 E
Kāf **30** 31 25N 37 29 E
Kafakumba **54** 9 38S 23 46 E
Kafan **23** 39 18N 46 15 E
Kafanchan **53** 9 40N 8 20 E
Kafareti **53** 10 25N 11 12 E
Kaffrine **50** 14 8N 15 36W
Kafia Kingi **51** 9 20N 24 25 E
Kafirévs, Ákra **19** 38 9N 24 38 E
Kafr 'Ayn **28** 32 3N 35 7 E
Kafr Kammā **28** 32 44N 35 26 E
Kafr Kannā **28** 32 45N 35 20 E
Kafr Mālik **28** 32 0N 35 18 E
Kafr Mandā **28** 32 49N 35 15 E
Kafr Quaddūm **28** 32 14N 35 7 E
Kafr Rā'ī **28** 32 23N 35 9 E
Kafr Şir **28** 33 19N 35 23 E
Kafr Yāsīf **28** 32 58N 35 10 E
Kafue → **55** 15 30S 29 0 E
Kafulwe **54** 9 0S 29 1 E
Kaga Bandoro **51** 7 0N 19 10 E
Kagade **52** 0 58N 30 48 E
Kagan **24** 39 43N 64 33 E
Kagawa □ **36** 34 15N 134 0 E
Kağizman **30** 40 5N 43 10 E
Kagoshima **36** 31 35N 130 33 E
Kagoshima □ **36** 31 30N 130 30 E
Kagoshima-Wan **36** 31 25N 130 40 E
Kahama **54** 4 8S 32 30 E
Kahayan → **34** 3 40S 114 0 E
Kahe **52** 3 30S 37 25 E
Kahemba **54** 7 18S 18 55 E
Kahniah → **64** 58 15N 120 55W
Kahnūj **31** 27 55N 57 40 E
Kahoka **70** 40 25N 91 42W
Kahoolawe **66** 20 33N 156 35W
Kahramanmaras **30** 37 37N 36 53 E
Kai, Kepulauan **35** 5 55S 132 45W
Kai Besar **35** 5 35S 133 0 E
Kai-Ketil **35** 5 45S 132 40 E
Kaiama **53** 9 36N 4 1 E
Kaiapoi **43** 42 24S 172 40 E
Kaieteur Falls **78** 5 1N 59 10W
Kaifeng **39** 34 48N 114 21 E
Kaihua **39** 29 12N 118 20 E
Kaiingveld **56** 30 0S 22 0 E
Kaikohe **43** 35 25S 173 49 E
Kaikoura **43** 42 25S 173 43 E
Kaikoura Pen. **43** 42 25S 173 43 E
Kaikoura Ra. **43** 41 59S 173 41 E
Kaili **39** 26 33N 107 59 E
Kailu **38** 43 38N 121 18 E
Kailua **66** 19 39N 156 0W
Kaimana **35** 3 39S 133 45 E
Kaimanawa Mts. **43** 39 15S 175 56 E
Kaingaroa Forest **43** 38 24S 176 30 E
Kainji Res. **53** 10 1N 4 40 E
Kaipara Harbour **43** 36 25S 174 14 E
Kaiping **39** 22 23N 112 42 E
Kaipokok B. **63** 54 54N 59 47W
Kaironi **35** 0 47S 133 40 E
Kairouan **50** 35 45N 10 5 E
Kaiserslautern **14** 49 30N 7 43 E
Kaitaia **43** 35 8S 173 17 E
Kaitangata **43** 46 17S 169 51 E
Kaiwi Channel **66** 21 13N 157 30W
Kaiyuan **38** 42 28N 124 1 E
Kajaani **20** 64 17N 27 46 E
Kajabbi **44** 20 0S 140 1 E
Kajana = Kajaani **20** 64 17N 27 46 E
Kajo Kaji **51** 3 58N 31 40 E
Kaka **51** 10 38N 32 10 E
Kakabeka Falls **62** 48 24N 89 37W
Kakamas **56** 28 45S 20 33 E
Kakamega **54** 0 20N 34 46 E
Kakanui Mts. **43** 45 10S 170 30 E
Kakegawa **36** 34 45N 138 1 E
Kakhovka **23** 46 40N 33 15 E
Kakhovskoye Vdkhr. **23** 47 5N 34 16 E
Kakinada **33** 16 57N 82 11 E
Kakisa → **64** 61 3N 118 10W
Kakisa L. **64** 60 56N 117 43W
Kakogawa **36** 34 46N 134 51 E
Kakwa → **64** 54 37N 118 28W
Kala **53** 12 2N 14 40 E
Kalabagh **32** 33 0N 71 28 E
Kalabahi **35** 8 13S 124 31 E
Kalabáka **19** 39 42N 21 39 E
Kalabo **55** 14 58S 22 40 E
Kalach **23** 50 22N 41 0 E
Kaladan → **33** 20 20N 93 5 E
Kalahari **56** 24 0S 21 30 E
Kalahari Gemsbok Nat. Park **56** 25 30S 20 30 E
Kalakamati **57** 20 40S 27 25 E
Kalakan **25** 55 15N 116 45 E
Kalama **72** 46 0N 122 55W
Kalamata **19** 37 3N 22 10 E
Kalamazoo **68** 42 20N 85 35W
Kalamazoo → **68** 42 40N 86 12W
Kalan **30** 39 7N 39 32 E
Kalannie **47** 30 22S 117 5 E
Kalao **35** 7 21S 121 0 E
Kalaotoa **35** 7 20S 121 50 E
Kalat **31** 29 8N 66 31 E
Kalbarri **47** 27 40S 114 10 E
Kalegauk Kyun **33** 15 33N 97 35 E
Kalemie **54** 5 55S 29 9 E
Kalewa **33** 23 10N 94 15 E
Kálfafellsstaður **20** 64 11N 15 53W
Kalgan = Zhangjiakou **38** 40 48N 114 55 E
Kalgoorlie-Boulder **47** 30 40S 121 22 E
Kaliakra, Nos **19** 43 21N 28 30 E
Kalianda **34** 5 50S 105 45 E
Kalibo **35** 11 43N 122 22 E
Kalima **54** 2 33S 26 32 E
Kalimantan **34** 0 0 114 0 E
Kalimantan Barat □ **34** 0 0 110 30 E
Kalimantan Selatan □ **34** 2 30S 115 30 E
Kalimantan Tengah □ **34** 2 0S 113 30 E
Kalimantan Timur □ **34** 1 30N 116 30 E
Kálimnos **19** 37 0N 27 0 E
Kalinin **22** 56 55N 35 55 E
Kaliningrad, R.S.F.S.R., U.S.S.R. **22** 55 58N 37 54 E
Kaliningrad, R.S.F.S.R., U.S.S.R. **22** 54 42N 20 32 E
Kalispell **72** 48 10N 114 22W
Kalisz **15** 51 45N 18 8 E
Kaliua **54** 5 5S 31 48 E
Kalix → **20** 65 50N 23 11 E
Kalkaska **68** 44 44N 85 11W
Kalkfeld **56** 20 57S 16 14 E
Kalkfontein **56** 22 4S 20 57 E
Kalkrand **56** 24 1S 17 35 E
Kallia **28** 31 46N 35 30 E
Kallsjön **20** 63 38N 13 0 E
Kalmalo **53** 13 40N 5 20 E
Kalmar **21** 56 40N 16 20 E
Kalmyk A.S.S.R. □ **23** 46 5N 46 1 E
Kalmykovo **23** 49 0N 51 47 E
Kalocsa **15** 46 32N 19 0 E
Kalomo **55** 17 0S 26 30 E
Kaluga **22** 54 35N 36 10 E
Kalundborg **21** 55 41N 11 5 E
Kalutara **32** 6 35N 80 0 E
Kalya **22** 60 15N 59 59 E
Kama → **22** 55 45N 52 0 E
Kamaishi **36** 39 20N 142 0 E
Kamandorskiye Ostrava **25** 55 0N 167 0 E
Kamaran **29** 15 21N 42 35 E
Kambalda **47** 31 10S 121 37 E
Kambarka **22** 56 15N 54 11 E
Kamchatka, P-ov. **25** 57 0N 160 0 E
Kamen **24** 53 50N 81 30 E
Kamenets-Podolskiy **23** 48 45N 26 10 E
Kamenjak, Rt. **18** 44 47N 13 55 E
Kamenka **22** 65 58N 44 0 E
Kamensk Uralskiy **24** 56 25N 62 2 E
Kamenskoye **25** 62 45N 165 30 E
Kamiah **72** 46 12N 116 2W
Kamieskroon **56** 30 9S 17 56 E
Kamilukuak, L. **65** 62 22N 101 40W
Kamina **54** 8 45S 25 0 E
Kaminak L. **65** 62 10N 95 0W
Kamloops **64** 50 40N 120 20W
Kampala **54** 0 20N 32 30 E
Kampar → **34** 0 30N 103 8 E
Kampen **11** 52 33N 5 53 E

Khalmer Yu

Kampot 34 10 36N 104 10 E
Kampuchea =
Cambodia ■ 34 12 15N 105 0 E
Kampung ➤ 35 5 44S 138 24 E
Kampungbaru =
Tolitoli 35 1 5N 120 50 E
Kamrau, Teluk 35 3 30S 133 36 E
Kamsack 65 51 34N 101 54W
Kamskoye Vdkhr. 22 58 0N 56 0 E
Kamuchawie L. 65 56 18N 101 59W
Kamui-Misaki 36 43 20N 140 21 E
Kamyshin 23 50 10N 45 24 E
Kanaaupscow 62 54 2N 76 30W
Kanab 73 37 3N 112 29W
Kanab Creek 73 37 0N 112 40W
Kanagawa □ 36 35 20N 139 20 E
Kanairiktok ➤ 63 55 2N 60 18W
Kananga 54 5 55S 22 18 E
Kanarraville 73 37 34N 113 12W
Kanash 22 55 30N 47 32 E
Kanawha ➤ 68 38 50N 82 8W
Kanazawa 36 36 30N 136 38 E
Kanchanaburi 34 14 2N 99 31 E
Kanchenjunga 33 27 50N 88 10 E
Kanchipuram 32 12 52N 79 45 E
Kanda Kanda 54 6 52S 23 48 E
Kandahar =
Qandahār 31 31 32N 65 30 E
Kandalaksha 22 67 9N 32 30 E
Kandalakshkiy Zaliv 22 66 0N 35 0 E
Kandalu 32 29 55N 63 20 E
Kandangan 34 2 50S 115 20 E
Kandi 53 11 7N 2 55 E
Kandla 32 23 0N 70 10 E
Kandos 45 32 45S 149 58 E
Kandy 32 7 18N 80 43 E
Kane 68 41 39N 78 53W
Kane Basin 58 79 1N 73 0W
Kangaroo I. 45 35 45S 137 0 E
Kangaroo Mts. 44 23 25S 142 0 E
Kangavar 30 34 40N 48 0 E
Kangean, Kepulauan 34 6 55S 115 23 E
Kanggye 38 41 0N 126 35 E
Kangnŭng 38 37 45N 128 54 E
Kango 54 0 11N 10 5 E
Kangto 33 27 50N 92 35 E
Kaniapiskau ➤ 63 56 40N 69 30W
Kaniapiskau L. 63 54 10N 69 55W
Kanin, P-ov. 22 68 0N 45 0 E
Kanin Nos, Mys 22 68 45N 43 20 E
Kaniva 45 36 22S 141 18 E
Kankakee 68 41 6N 87 50W
Kankakee ➤ 68 41 23N 88 16W
Kankan 50 10 23N 9 15W
Kanker 33 20 10N 81 40 E
Kankunskiy 25 57 37N 126 8 E
Kannapolis 69 35 32N 80 37W
Kannauj 32 27 3N 79 56 E
Kannod 32 22 45N 76 40 E
Kano 53 12 2N 8 30 E
Kano □ 53 11 45N 9 0 E
Kanowit 34 2 14N 112 20 E
Kanowna 47 30 32S 121 31 E
Kanoya 36 31 25N 130 50 E
Kanpetlet 33 21 10N 93 59 E
Kanpur 32 26 28N 80 20 E
Kansas □ 70 38 40N 98 0W
Kansas ➤ 70 39 7N 94 36W
Kansas City, Kans.,
U.S.A. 70 39 0N 94 40W
Kansas City, Mo.,
U.S.A. 70 39 3N 94 30W
Kansk 25 56 20N 95 37 E
Kansu = Gansu □ 38 36 0N 104 0 E
Kantang 34 7 25N 99 31 E
Kantché 53 13 31N 8 30 E
Kanturk 9 52 10N 8 55W
Kanuma 36 36 34N 139 42 E
Kanus 56 27 50S 18 39 E
Kanye 56 25 0S 25 28 E
Kaohsiung =
Gaoxiong 39 22 38N 120 18 E
Kaokoveld 56 19 15S 14 30 E
Kaolack 50 14 5N 16 8W
Kapanga 54 8 30S 22 40 E
Kapchagai 24 43 51N 77 14 E
Kapela 18 44 40N 15 40 E
Kapfenberg 14 47 26N 15 18 E
Kapiri Mposhi 55 13 59S 28 43 E
Kāpīsā □ 31 35 0N 69 20 E
Kapiskau ➤ 62 52 47N 81 55W
Kapit 34 2 0N 112 55 E
Kapiti I. 43 40 50S 174 56 E
Kapoeta 51 4 50N 33 35 E
Kaposvár 15 46 25N 17 47 E
Kapps 56 22 32S 17 18 E
Kapuas ➤ 34 0 25S 109 20 E
Kapuas Hulu,
Pegunungan 34 1 30N 113 30 E
Kapunda 45 34 20S 138 56 E
Kapuskasing 62 49 25N 82 30W
Kapuskasing ➤ 62 49 49N 82 0W
Kaputar, Mt. 45 30 15S 150 10 E
Kara 24 69 10N 65 0 E
Kara Bogaz Gol,
Zaliv 23 41 0N 53 30 E
Kara Kalpak
A.S.S.R. □ 24 43 0N 60 0 E
Kara Kum =
Karakum, Peski 24 39 30N 60 0 E
Kara Sea 24 75 0N 70 0 E
Karabük 30 41 12N 32 37 E
Karabutak 24 49 59N 60 14 E
Karachi 32 24 53N 67 0 E
Karad 32 17 15N 74 10 E
Karadeniz Boğazı 30 41 10N 29 10 E
Karaganda 24 49 50N 73 10 E
Karagayly 24 49 26N 76 0 E
Karaginskiy, Ostrov 25 58 45N 164 0 E
Karagiye Depression 23 43 27N 51 45 E
Karaikal 32 10 59N 79 50 E
Karaikkudi 32 10 0N 78 45 E
Karaj 31 35 48N 51 0 E
Karakas 24 48 20N 83 30 E
Karakitang 35 3 14N 125 28 E
Karakoram Pass 32 35 33N 77 50 E
Karakoram Ra. 32 35 30N 77 0 E
Karakum, Peski 24 39 30N 60 0 E
Karalon 25 57 5N 115 50 E
Karaman 30 37 14N 33 13 E
Karamay 37 45 30N 84 58 E
Karambu 34 3 53S 116 6 E
Karamea Bight 43 41 22S 171 40 E
Karanganyar 35 7 38S 109 37 E
Karasburg 56 28 0S 18 44 E
Karasino 24 66 50N 86 50 E
Karasjok 20 69 27N 25 30 E
Karasuk 24 53 44N 78 2 E
Karatau 24 43 10N 70 28 E
Karatau, Khrebet 24 43 30N 69 30 E
Karawanken 18 46 30N 14 40 E
Karazhal 24 48 2N 70 49 E
Karbalā 30 32 36N 44 3 E
Karcag 15 47 19N 20 57 E
Karda 25 55 0N 103 16 E
Kardhitsa 19 39 23N 21 54 E
Kareeberge 56 30 59S 21 50 E
Karelian A.S.S.R. □ 22 65 30N 32 30 E
Kargānrūd 30 37 55N 49 0 E
Kargasok 24 59 3N 80 53 E
Kargat 24 55 10N 80 15 E
Kargil 32 34 32N 76 12 E
Kargopol 22 61 30N 38 58 E
Kariba Dam 55 16 30S 28 35 E
Kariba Gorge 55 16 30S 28 50 E
Kariba L. 55 16 40S 28 25 E
Karibib 56 22 0S 15 56 E
Karimata, Kepulauan 34 1 25S 109 0 E
Karimata, Selat 34 2 0S 108 40 E
Karimnagar 32 18 26N 79 10 E
Karimunjawa,
Kepulauan 34 5 50S 110 30 E
Karin 29 10 50N 45 52 E
Kariya 36 34 58N 137 1 E
Karkaralinsk 24 49 26N 75 30 E
Karkinitskiy Zaliv 23 45 56N 33 0 E
Karkur 28 32 29N 34 57 E
Karl-Marx-Stadt 14 50 50N 12 55 E
Karlovac 18 45 31N 15 36 E
Karlovy Vary 14 50 13N 12 51 E
Karlsborg 21 58 33N 14 33 E
Karlshamn 21 56 10N 14 51 E
Karlskoga 21 59 22N 14 33 E
Karlskrona 21 56 10N 15 35 E
Karlsruhe 14 49 3N 8 23 E
Karlstad, Sweden 21 59 23N 13 30 E
Karlstad, U.S.A. 70 48 38N 96 30W
Karnal 32 29 42N 77 2 E
Karnali ➤ 33 29 0N 83 20 E
Karnaphuli Res. 33 22 40N 92 20 E
Karnataka □ 32 13 15N 77 0 E
Karnes City 71 28 53N 97 53W
Karnische Alpen 14 46 36N 13 0 E
Kärnten □ 14 46 52N 13 30 E
Karonga 54 9 57S 33 55 E
Karoonda 45 35 1S 139 59 E
Karora 51 17 44N 38 15 E
Kárpathos 19 35 37N 27 10 E
Karpinsk 22 59 45N 60 1 E
Karpogory 22 63 59N 44 27 E
Kars 30 40 40N 43 5 E
Karsakpay 24 47 55N 66 40 E
Karshi 24 38 53N 65 48 E
Karsun 22 54 14N 46 57 E
Kartaly 24 53 3N 60 40 E
Karufa 35 3 50S 133 20 E
Karumba 44 17 31S 140 50 E
Karungu 54 0 50S 34 10 E
Karwar 32 14 55N 74 13 E
Kasai ➤ 54 3 30S 16 10 E
Kasama 54 10 16S 31 9 E
Kasane 56 17 34S 24 50 E
Kasanga 54 8 30S 31 10 E
Kasangulu 54 4 33S 15 15 E
Kasaragod 32 12 30N 74 58 E
Kasba L. 65 60 20N 102 10W
Kasempa 55 13 30S 25 44 E
Kasenga 54 10 20S 28 45 E
Kashabowie 62 48 40N 90 26W
Kāshān 31 34 5N 51 30 E
Kashi 37 39 30N 76 2 E
Kashiwazaki 36 37 22N 138 33 E
Kashk-e Kohneh 31 34 55N 62 30 E
Kāshmar 31 35 16N 58 26 E
Kashmir 32 34 0N 76 0 E
Kashun Noerh =
Gaxun Nur 37 42 22N 100 30 E
Kasimov 22 54 55N 41 20 E
Kasiruta 35 0 25S 127 12 E
Kaskaskia ➤ 70 37 58N 89 57W
Kaskattama ➤ 65 57 3N 90 4W
Kaskinen 20 62 22N 21 15 E
Kaskö 20 62 22N 21 15 E
Kaslo 64 49 55N 116 55W
Kasmere L. 65 59 34N 101 10W
Kasongo 54 4 30S 26 33 E
Kasongo Lunda 54 6 35S 16 49 E
Kásos 19 35 20N 26 55 E
Kassala 51 15 30N 36 0 E
Kassalâ □ 51 15 20N 36 26 E
Kassel 14 51 19N 9 32 E
Kassue 35 6 58S 139 21 E
Kastamonu 30 41 25N 33 43 E
Kastellorizon =
Megiste 17 36 8N 29 34 E
Kastoria 19 40 30N 21 19 E
Kasulu 54 4 37S 30 5 E
Kasur 32 31 5N 74 25 E
Kata 25 58 46N 102 40 E
Katako Kombe 54 3 25S 24 20 E
Katamatite 45 36 6S 145 41 E
Katangi 32 21 56N 79 50 E
Katangli 25 51 42N 143 14 E
Katha 33 24 10N 96 30 E
Katherine 46 14 27S 132 20 E
Kathiawar 32 22 20N 71 0 E
Katihar 33 25 34N 87 36 E
Katima Mulilo 56 17 28S 24 13 E
Katingan =
Mendawai ➤ 34 3 30S 113 0 E
Katiola 50 8 10N 5 10W
Katkopberg 56 30 0S 20 0 E
Katmandu 33 27 45N 85 20 E
Katoomba 45 33 41S 150 19 E
Katowice 15 50 17N 19 5 E
Katrine, L. 8 56 15N 4 30W
Katrineholm 21 59 9N 16 12 E
Katsepe 57 15 45S 46 15 E
Katsina 53 13 0N 7 32 E
Katsuura 36 35 10N 140 20 E
Kattegatt 21 57 0N 11 20 E
Katwe 52 0 8S 29 52 E
Katwijk-aan-Zee 11 52 12N 4 24 E
Kauai 66 22 0N 159 30W
Kauai Chan. 66 21 45N 158 50W
Kaufman 71 32 35N 96 20W
Kaukauna 68 44 20N 88 13W
Kaukauveld 56 20 0S 20 15 E
Kaukonen 20 67 31N 24 53 E
Kauliranta 20 66 27N 23 41 E
Kaunas 22 54 54N 23 54 E
Kaura Namoda 53 12 37N 6 33 E
Kautokeino 20 69 0N 23 4 E
Kavacha 25 60 16N 169 51 E
Kavali 32 14 55N 80 1 E
Kavála 19 40 57N 24 28 E
Kavkaz, Bolshoi 23 42 50N 44 0 E
Kaw 79 4 30N 52 15W
Kawagoe 36 35 55N 139 29 E
Kawaguchi 36 35 52N 139 45 E
Kawaihae 66 20 3N 155 50W
Kawambwa 54 9 48S 29 3 E
Kawardha 33 22 0N 81 17 E
Kawasaki 36 35 35N 139 42 E
Kawene 62 48 45N 91 15W
Kawerau 43 38 7S 176 42 E
Kawhia Harbour 43 38 5S 174 51 E
Kawio, Kepulauan 35 4 30N 125 30 E
Kawnro 33 22 48N 99 8 E
Kawthoolei □ =
Kawthule □ 33 18 0N 97 30 E
Kawthule □ 33 18 0N 97 30 E
Kaya 53 13 4N 1 10W
Kayah □ 33 19 15N 97 15 E
Kayan ➤ 34 2 55N 117 35 E
Kaycee 72 43 45N 106 46W
Kayeli 35 3 20S 127 10 E
Kayenta 73 36 46N 110 15W
Kayes 50 14 25N 11 30W
Kayoa 35 0 1N 127 28 E
Kayrunnera 45 30 40S 142 30 E
Kayseri 30 38 45N 35 30 E
Kaysville 72 41 2N 111 58W
Kayuagung 34 3 24S 104 50 E
Kazachinskoye 25 56 16N 107 36 E
Kazachye 25 70 52N 135 58 E
Kazakh S.S.R. □ 23 50 0N 70 0 E
Kazan 22 55 48N 49 3 E
Kazanlúk 19 42 38N 25 20 E
Kāzerūn 31 29 38N 51 40 E
Kazumba 54 6 25S 22 5 E
Kazym ➤ 24 63 54N 65 50 E
Ké-Macina 50 13 58N 5 22W
Kéa 19 37 35N 24 22 E
Keams Canyon 73 35 53N 110 9W
Kearney 70 40 45N 99 3W
Keban 23 38 50N 38 50 E
Kebnekaise 20 67 53N 18 33 E
Kebri Dehar 29 6 45N 44 17 E
Kebumen 35 7 42S 109 40 E
Kechika ➤ 64 59 41N 127 12W
Kecskemét 15 46 57N 19 42 E
Kedgwick 63 47 40N 67 20W
Kedia Hill 56 21 28S 24 37 E
Kediri 35 7 51S 112 1 E
Kédougou 50 12 35N 12 10W
Keeley L. 65 54 54N 108 8W
Keeling Is. = Cocos
Is. 3 12 10S 96 55 E
Keene 68 42 57N 72 17W
Keeper Hill 9 52 46N 8 17W
Keer-Weer, C. 44 14 0S 141 32 E
Keetmanshoop 56 26 35S 18 8 E
Keewatin 70 47 23N 93 0W
Keewatin □ 65 63 20N 95 0W
Keewatin ➤ 65 56 29N 100 46W
Kefallinía 19 38 20N 20 30 E
Kefamenanu 35 9 28S 124 29 E
Kefar 'Eqron 28 31 52N 34 49 E
Kefar Ḥasīdim 28 32 47N 35 5 E
Kefar Naḥum 28 32 54N 35 34 E
Kefar Sava 28 32 11N 34 54 E
Kefar Szold 28 33 11N 35 39 E
Kefar Vitkin 28 32 22N 34 53 E
Kefar Yehezqel 28 32 34N 35 22 E
Kefar Yona 28 32 20N 34 54 E
Kefar Zekharya 28 31 43N 34 57 E
Kefar Zetim 28 32 48N 35 27 E
Keffi 53 8 55N 7 43 E
Keflavík 20 64 2N 22 35W
Keg River 64 57 54N 117 55W
Kegaska 63 50 9N 61 18W
Keighley 6 53 52N 1 54W
Keimoes 56 28 41S 20 59 E
Keith, Australia 45 36 6S 140 20 E
Keith, U.K. 8 57 33N 2 58W
Keith Arm 60 64 20N 122 15W
Kekri 32 26 0N 75 10 E
Kël 25 69 30N 124 10 E
Kelan 38 38 43N 111 31 E
Kelang 34 3 2N 101 26 E
Kelibia 51 36 50N 11 3 E
Kellé 54 0 8S 14 38 E
Keller 72 48 2N 118 44W
Kellerberrin 47 31 36S 117 38 E
Kellogg 72 47 30N 116 5W
Kelloselkä 20 66 56N 28 53 E
Kells = Ceanannus
Mor 9 53 42N 6 53W
Kélo 51 9 10N 15 45 E
Kelowna 64 49 50N 119 25W
Kelsey Bay 64 50 25N 126 0W
Kelso, N.Z. 43 45 54S 169 15 E
Kelso, U.K. 8 55 36N 2 27W
Kelso, U.S.A. 72 46 10N 122 57W
Keluang 34 2 3N 103 18 E
Kelvington 65 52 10N 103 30W
Kem 22 65 0N 34 38 E
Kem ➤ 22 64 57N 34 41 E
Kema 35 1 22N 125 8 E
Kemah 30 39 32N 39 5 E
Kemano 64 53 35N 128 0W
Kemerovo 24 55 20N 86 5 E
Kemi 20 65 44N 24 34 E
Kemi älv =
Kemijoki ➤ 20 65 47N 24 32 E
Kemijärvi 20 66 43N 27 22 E
Kemijoki ➤ 20 65 47N 24 32 E
Kemmerer 72 41 52N 110 30W
Kemmuna =
Comino 18 36 0N 14 20 E
Kemp L. 71 33 45N 99 15W
Kempsey 45 31 1S 152 50 E
Kempt, L. 62 47 25N 74 22W
Kempten 14 47 42N 10 18 E
Kemptville 62 45 0N 75 38W
Kendal, Indonesia 34 6 56S 110 14 E
Kendal, U.K. 6 54 19N 2 44W
Kendall 45 31 35S 152 44 E
Kendall ➤ 44 14 4S 141 35 E
Kendallville 68 41 25N 85 15W
Kendari 35 3 50S 122 30 E
Kendawangan 34 2 32S 110 17 E
Kende 53 11 30N 4 12 E
Kendenup 47 34 30S 117 38 E
Kendrapara 33 20 35N 86 30 E
Kendrew 56 32 32S 24 30 E
Kendrick 72 46 43N 116 41W
Kenedy 71 28 49N 97 51W
Kenema 50 7 50N 11 14W
Keng Tawng 33 20 45N 98 18 E
Keng Tung 33 21 0N 99 30 E
Kenge 54 4 50S 17 4 E
Kenhardt 56 29 19S 21 12 E
Kenitra 50 34 15N 6 40W
Kenmare, Ireland 9 51 52N 9 35W
Kenmare, U.S.A. 70 48 40N 102 4W
Kenmare ➤ 9 51 40N 10 0W
Kennebec 70 43 56N 99 54W
Kennedy Ra. 47 24 45S 115 10 E
Kennedy Taungdeik 33 23 15N 93 45 E
Kennet ➤ 7 51 24N 0 58W
Kenneth Ra. 47 23 50S 117 8 E
Kennett 71 36 7N 90 0W
Kennewick 72 46 11N 119 2W
Kénogami 63 48 25N 71 15W
Kenogami ➤ 62 51 6N 84 28W
Kenora 65 49 47N 94 29W
Kenosha 68 42 33N 87 48W
Kensington, Canada 63 46 28N 63 34W
Kensington, U.S.A. 70 39 48N 99 2W
Kensington Downs 44 22 31S 144 19 E
Kent, Ohio, U.S.A. 68 41 8N 81 20W
Kent, Oreg., U.S.A. 72 45 11N 120 45W
Kent, Tex., U.S.A. 71 31 5N 104 12W
Kent □ 7 51 12N 0 40 E
Kent Group 44 39 30S 147 20 E
Kent Pen. 60 68 30N 107 0W
Kentau 24 43 32N 68 36 E
Kentland 68 40 45N 87 25W
Kenton 68 40 40N 83 35W
Kentucky □ 68 37 20N 85 0W
Kentucky ➤ 68 38 41N 85 11W
Kentucky L. 69 36 25N 88 0W
Kentville 63 45 6N 64 29W
Kentwood 71 31 0N 90 30W
Kenya ■ 54 1 0N 38 0 E
Kenya, Mt. 54 0 10S 37 18 E
Keokuk 70 40 25N 91 24W
Kepi 35 6 32S 139 19 E
Kepsut 30 39 40N 28 9 E
Kerala □ 32 11 0N 76 15 E
Kerang 45 35 40S 143 55 E
Keraudren, C. 46 19 58S 119 45 E
Kerch 23 45 20N 36 20 E
Kerchoual 50 17 12N 0 20 E
Kerem Maharal 28 32 39N 34 59 E
Keren 51 15 45N 38 28 E
Kerguelen 3 49 15S 69 10 E
Kericho 54 0 22S 35 15 E
Kerinci 34 1 40S 101 15 E
Kerki 24 37 50N 65 12 E
Kérkira 19 39 38N 19 50 E
Kerkrade 11 50 53N 6 4 E
Kermadec Is. 40 30 0S 178 15W
Kermadec Trench 40 30 30S 176 0W
Kermān 31 30 15N 57 1 E
Kermān □ 31 30 0N 57 0 E
Kermānshāh =
Bākhtarān 30 34 23N 47 0 E
Kermit 71 31 56N 103 3W
Kern ➤ 73 35 16N 119 18W
Kerrobert 65 51 56N 109 8W
Kerrville 71 30 1N 99 8W
Kerry □ 9 52 7N 9 35W
Kerry Hd. 9 52 26N 9 56W
Kertosono 35 7 38S 112 9 E
Kerulen ➤ 37 48 48N 117 0 E
Kerzaz 50 29 29N 1 37W
Kesagami ➤ 62 51 40N 79 45W
Kesagami L. 62 50 23N 80 15W
Keski-Suomen
lääni □ 20 62 0N 25 30 E
Kestell 57 28 17S 28 42 E
Kestenga 22 66 0N 31 50 E
Keswick 6 54 35N 3 9W
Ket ➤ 24 58 55N 81 32 E
Keta 53 5 49N 1 0 E
Ketapang 34 1 55S 110 0 E
Ketchikan 60 55 25N 131 40W
Ketchum 72 43 41N 114 27W
Kettering 7 52 24N 0 44W
Kettle ➤ 65 56 40N 89 34W
Kettle Falls 72 48 41N 118 2W
Kevin 72 48 45N 111 58W
Kewanee 70 41 18N 89 55W
Kewaunee 68 44 27N 87 30W
Keweenaw B. 68 46 56N 88 23W
Keweenaw Pen. 68 47 30N 88 0W
Keweenaw Pt. 68 47 26N 87 40W
Key Harbour 62 45 50N 80 45W
Key West 75 24 33N 82 0W
Keyser 68 39 26N 79 0W
Keystone 70 43 54N 103 27W
Kezhma 25 58 59N 101 9 E
Khabarovo 24 69 30N 60 30 E
Khabarovsk 25 48 30N 135 5 E
Khābūr ➤ 30 35 0N 40 30 E
Khairpur 32 27 32N 68 49 E
Khakhea 56 24 48S 23 22 E
Khalkhāl 30 37 37N 48 32 E
Khalkis 19 38 27N 23 42 E
Khalmer-Sede =
Tazovskiy 24 67 30N 78 44 E
Khalmer Yu 22 67 58N 65 1 E

Khalturin

Khalturin 22 58 40N 48 50 E
Khamas Country 56 21 45S 26 30 E
Khambat, G. of 32 20 45N 72 30 E
Khambhat 32 22 23N 72 33 E
Khamir 29 16 0N 44 0 E
Khān Yūnis 28 31 21N 34 18 E
Khānābād 31 36 45N 69 5 E
Khānaqīn 30 34 23N 45 25 E
Khandwa 32 21 49N 76 22 E
Khandyga 25 62 42N 135 35 E
Khanewal 32 30 20N 71 55 E
Khaniá 19 35 30N 24 4 E
Khanion Kólpos 19 35 33N 23 55 E
Khanka, Ozero 25 45 0N 132 24 E
Khanty-Mansiysk 24 61 0N 69 0 E
Khapcheranga 25 49 42N 112 24 E
Kharagpur 33 22 20N 87 25 E
Kharan Kalat 31 28 34N 65 21 E
Kharānaq 31 32 20N 54 45 E
Kharda 32 18 40N 75 34 E
Khârga, El Wâhât el 51 25 10N 30 35 E
Khargon 32 21 45N 75 35 E
Khārk, Jazireh 30 29 15N 50 28 E
Kharkov 23 49 58N 36 20 E
Kharovsk 22 59 56N 40 13 E
Kharsānīya 30 27 10N 49 10 E
Khartoum = El Khartûm 51 15 31N 32 35 E
Khasab 31 26 14N 56 15 E
Khāsh 31 28 15N 61 15 E
Khashm el Girba 51 14 59N 35 58 E
Khaskovo 19 41 56N 25 30 E
Khatanga 25 72 0N 102 20 E
Khatanga → 25 72 55N 106 0 E
Khatyrka 25 62 3N 175 15 E
Khaybar, Harrat 30 25 45N 40 0 E
Khed Brahma 32 24 7N 73 5 E
Khemmarat 34 16 10N 105 15 E
Khenchela 50 35 28N 7 11 E
Khenifra 50 32 58N 5 46W
Kherson 23 46 35N 32 35 E
Kheta → 25 71 54N 102 6 E
Khilok 25 51 30N 110 45 E
Khíos 19 38 27N 26 9 E
Khiuma = Hiiumaa 22 58 50N 22 45 E
Khiva 24 41 30N 60 18 E
Khīyāv 30 38 30N 47 45 E
Khmelnitskiy 23 49 23N 27 0 E
Khmer Rep. = Cambodia ■ 34 12 15N 105 0 E
Khojak P. 31 30 55N 66 30 E
Kholm, Afghan. 31 36 45N 67 40 E
Kholm, U.S.S.R. 22 57 10N 31 15 E
Kholmsk 25 47 40N 142 5 E
Khomas Hochland 56 22 40S 16 0 E
Khomayn 30 33 40N 50 7 E
Khon Kaen 34 16 30N 102 47 E
Khonu 25 66 30N 143 12 E
Khoper → 22 49 30N 42 20 E
Khorāsān □ 31 34 0N 58 0 E
Khorat = Nakhon Ratchasima 34 14 59N 102 12 E
Khorixas 56 20 16S 14 59 E
Khorog 24 37 30N 71 36 E
Khorramābād 30 33 30N 48 25 E
Khorrāmshahr 30 30 29N 48 15 E
Khouribga 50 32 58N 6 57W
Khowai 33 24 5N 91 40 E
Khu Khan 34 14 42N 104 12 E
Khūgīānī 32 31 28N 65 14 E
Khulna 33 22 45N 89 34 E
Khulna □ 33 22 25N 89 35 E
Khumago 56 20 26S 24 32 E
Khūr 31 32 55N 58 18 E
Khurayş 30 24 55N 48 5 E
Khūrīyā Mūrīyā, Jazā 'ir 29 17 30N 55 58 E
Khush 32 32 55N 62 10 E
Khushab 32 32 20N 72 20 E
Khuzdar 32 27 52N 66 30 E
Khūzestān □ 30 31 0N 49 0 E
Khvor 31 33 45N 55 0 E
Khvormūj 31 28 40N 51 30 E
Khvoy 30 38 35N 45 0 E
Khyber Pass 32 34 10N 71 8 E
Kiama 45 34 40S 150 50 E
Kiamba 35 6 2N 124 46 E
Kiambu 52 1 8S 36 50 E
Kiangsi = Jiangxi □ 39 27 30N 116 0 E
Kiangsu = Jiangsu □ 39 33 0N 120 0 E
Kibangou 54 3 26S 12 22 E
Kibombo 54 3 57S 25 53 E
Kibondo 54 3 35S 30 45 E
Kibwesa 54 6 30S 29 58 E
Kibwezi 54 2 27S 37 57 E
Kichiga 25 59 50N 163 5 E
Kicking Horse Pass 64 51 28N 116 16W
Kidal 50 18 26N 1 22 E
Kidderminster 7 52 24N 2 13W
Kidnappers, C. 43 39 38S 177 5 E
Kidston 44 18 52S 144 8 E
Kiel 14 54 16N 10 8 E
Kiel Kanal = Nord-Ostsee Kanal 14 54 15N 9 40 E
Kielce 15 50 52N 20 42 E
Kieler Bucht 14 54 30N 10 30 E
Kiev = Kiyev 23 50 30N 30 28 E
Kifār 'Aşyūn 28 31 39N 35 7 E
Kiffa 50 16 37N 11 24W
Kifrī 30 34 45N 45 0 E
Kigali 54 1 59S 30 4 E
Kigoma-Ujiji 54 4 55S 29 36 E
Kihee 45 27 23S 142 37 E
Kii-Suidō 36 33 40N 135 0 E
Kikinda 19 45 50N 20 30 E
Kikládhes 19 37 20N 24 30 E
Kikwit 54 5 0S 18 45 E
Kilauea Crater 66 19 24N 155 17W
Kilcoy 45 26 59S 152 30 E
Kildare 9 53 10N 6 50W
Kildare □ 9 53 10N 6 50W
Kilgore 71 32 22N 94 55W
Kilifi 52 3 40S 39 48 E
Kilimanjaro 54 3 7S 37 20 E
Kilindini 54 4 4S 39 40 E
Kilis 30 36 50N 37 10 E
Kiljŭ 38 40 57N 129 25 E
Kilkee 9 52 41N 9 40W
Kilkenny 9 52 40N 7 17W
Kilkenny □ 9 52 35N 7 15W
Kilkieran B. 9 53 18N 9 45W
Killala 9 54 13N 9 12W
Killala B. 9 54 20N 9 12W
Killaloe 9 52 48N 8 28W
Killam 64 52 47N 111 51W
Killarney, Australia 45 28 20S 152 18 E
Killarney, Canada 62 45 55N 81 30W
Killarney, Ireland 9 52 2N 9 30W
Killarney, Lakes of 9 52 0N 9 30W
Killary Harbour 9 53 38N 9 52W
Killdeer, Canada 65 49 6N 106 22W
Killdeer, U.S.A. 70 47 26N 102 48W
Killeen 71 31 7N 97 45W
Killiecrankie, Pass of 8 56 44N 3 46W
Killin 8 56 28N 4 20W
Killíni 19 37 54N 22 25 E
Killybegs 9 54 38N 8 26W
Kilmarnock 8 55 36N 4 30W
Kilmore 45 37 25S 144 53 E
Kilosa 54 6 48S 37 0 E
Kilrush 9 52 39N 9 30W
Kilwa Kisiwani 52 8 58S 39 32 E
Kilwa Kivinje 54 8 45S 39 25 E
Kim 71 37 18N 103 20W
Kimaam 35 7 58S 138 53 E
Kimba 45 33 8S 136 23 E
Kimball, Nebr., U.S.A. 70 41 17N 103 40W
Kimball, S. Dak., U.S.A. 70 43 47N 98 57W
Kimberley, Canada 64 49 40N 115 59W
Kimberley, S. Africa 56 28 43S 24 46 E
Kimberley Downs 46 17 24S 124 22 E
Kimberly 72 42 33N 114 25W
Kimchaek 38 40 40N 129 10 E
Kimchŏn 38 36 11N 128 4 E
Kimry 22 56 55N 37 15 E
Kimsquit 64 52 45N 126 57W
Kinabalu 34 6 3N 116 14 E
Kinaskan L. 64 57 38N 130 8W
Kinbasket L. 64 52 0N 118 10W
Kincaid 65 49 40N 107 0W
Kincardine 62 44 10N 81 40W
Kindersley 65 51 30N 109 10W
Kindia 50 10 0N 12 52W
Kindu 54 2 55S 25 50 E
Kineshma 22 57 30N 42 5 E
King, L. 47 33 10S 119 35 E
King, Mt. 44 25 10S 147 30 E
King City 73 36 11N 121 8W
King Cr. → 44 24 35S 139 30 E
King Edward → 46 14 14S 126 35 E
King George B. 80 51 30S 60 30W
King George Is. 61 57 20N 80 30W
King I. = Kadan Kyun 34 12 30N 98 20 E
King I., Australia 44 39 50S 144 0 E
King I., Canada 64 52 10N 127 40W
King Leopold Ranges 46 17 30S 125 45 E
King Sd. 46 16 50S 123 20 E
King William I. 60 69 10N 97 25W
King William's Town 56 32 51S 27 22 E
Kingaroy 45 26 32S 151 51 E
Kingfisher 71 35 50N 97 55W
Kingman, Ariz., U.S.A. 73 35 12N 114 2W
Kingman, Kans., U.S.A. 71 37 41N 98 9W
Kings → 73 36 10N 119 50W
Kings Canyon National Park 73 37 0N 118 35W
King's Lynn 6 52 45N 0 25 E
Kings Mountain 69 35 13N 81 20W
King's Peak 72 40 46N 110 27W
Kingsbridge 7 50 17N 3 46W
Kingsburg 73 36 35N 119 36W
Kingscote 45 35 40S 137 38 E
Kingscourt 9 53 55N 6 48W
Kingsley 70 42 37N 95 58W
Kingsport 69 36 33N 82 36W
Kingston, Canada 62 44 14N 76 30W
Kingston, Jamaica 75 18 0N 76 50W
Kingston, N.Z. 43 45 20S 168 43 E
Kingston, N.Y., U.S.A. 68 41 55N 74 0W
Kingston, Pa., U.S.A. 68 41 19N 75 58W
Kingston South East 45 36 51S 139 55 E
Kingston-upon-Thames 7 51 23N 0 20W
Kingstown 75 13 10N 61 10W
Kingstree 69 33 40N 79 48W
Kingsville, Canada 62 42 2N 82 45W
Kingsville, U.S.A. 71 27 30N 97 53W
Kingussie 8 57 5N 4 2W
Kinistino 65 52 57N 105 2W
Kinkala 54 4 18S 14 49 E
Kinleith 43 38 20S 175 56 E
Kinnaird 64 49 17N 117 39W
Kinnairds Hd. 8 57 40N 2 0W
Kinneret 28 32 44N 35 34 E
Kinoje → 62 52 8N 81 25W
Kinross 8 56 13N 3 25W
Kinsale 9 51 42N 8 31W
Kinsale, Old Hd. of 9 51 37N 8 32W
Kinshasa 54 4 20S 15 15 E
Kinsley 71 37 57N 99 30W
Kinston 69 35 18N 77 35W
Kintampo 53 8 5N 1 41W
Kintap 34 3 51S 115 13 E
Kintore Ra. 46 23 15S 128 47 E
Kintyre 8 55 30N 5 35W
Kintyre, Mull of 8 55 17N 5 55W
Kinushseo → 62 55 15N 83 45W
Kinuso 64 55 20N 115 25W
Kiosk 62 46 6N 78 53W
Kiowa, Kans., U.S.A. 71 37 3N 98 30W
Kiowa, Okla., U.S.A. 71 34 45N 95 50W
Kipahigan L. 65 55 20N 101 55W
Kiparissia 19 37 15N 21 40 E
Kiparissiakós Kólpos 19 37 25N 21 25 E
Kipembawe 54 7 38S 33 27 E
Kipili 54 7 28S 30 32 E
Kipini 52 2 30S 40 32 E
Kipling 65 50 6N 102 38W
Kippure 9 53 11N 6 23W
Kipushi 55 11 48S 27 12 E
Kirensk 25 57 50N 107 55 E
Kirgella Rocks 47 30 5S 122 50 E
Kirgiz S.S.R. □ 24 42 0N 75 0 E
Kirgiziya Steppe 23 50 0N 55 0 E
Kiri 54 1 29S 19 0 E
Kiribati ■ 3 1 0N 176 0 E
Kırıkkale 30 39 51N 33 32 E
Kirillov 22 59 51N 38 14 E
Kirin = Jilin 38 43 44N 126 30 E
Kirin □ = Jilin □ 38 44 0N 124 0 E
Kiritimati 2 1 58N 157 27W
Kirkcaldy 8 56 7N 3 10W
Kirkcudbright 8 54 50N 4 3W
Kirkee 32 18 34N 73 56 E
Kirkenes 20 69 40N 30 5 E
Kirkintilloch 8 55 57N 4 10W
Kirkjubæjarklaustur 20 63 47N 18 4W
Kirkland 73 34 29N 112 46W
Kirkland Lake 62 48 9N 80 2W
Kırklareli 30 41 44N 27 15 E
Kirksville 70 40 8N 92 35W
Kirkūk 30 35 30N 44 21 E
Kirkwall 8 58 59N 2 59W
Kirkwood 56 33 22S 25 15 E
Kirov 24 58 35N 49 40 E
Kirovabad 23 40 45N 46 20 E
Kirovakan 23 40 48N 44 30 E
Kirovograd 23 48 35N 32 20 E
Kirovsk, R.S.F.S.R., U.S.S.R. 22 67 48N 33 50 E
Kirovsk, Turkmen S.S.R., U.S.S.R. 24 37 42N 60 23 E
Kirovskiy 25 54 27N 155 42 E
Kirriemuir 8 56 41N 3 0W
Kirsanov 22 52 35N 42 40 E
Kırşehir 30 39 14N 34 5 E
Kirstonia 56 25 30S 23 45 E
Kirteh 31 32 15N 63 0 E
Kirthar Range 32 27 0N 67 0 E
Kiruna 20 67 52N 20 15 E
Kirundu 54 0 50S 25 35 E
Kirup 47 33 40S 115 50 E
Kiryū 36 36 24N 139 20 E
Kisangani 54 0 35N 25 15 E
Kisar 35 8 5S 127 10 E
Kisaran 34 3 0N 99 37 E
Kisarazu 36 35 23N 139 55 E
Kiselevsk 24 54 5N 86 39 E
Kishanganj 33 26 3N 88 14 E
Kishangarh 32 27 50N 70 30 E
Kishinev 23 47 0N 28 50 E
Kishiwada 36 34 28N 135 22 E
Kishon 28 32 49N 35 2 E
Kishtwar 32 33 20N 75 48 E
Kisii 54 0 40S 34 45 E
Kisiju 54 7 23S 39 19 E
Kiska I. 60 52 0N 177 30 E
Kiskatinaw → 64 56 8N 120 10W
Kiskittogisu L. 65 54 13N 98 20W
Kiskörös 15 46 37N 19 20 E
Kiskunfélegyháza 15 46 42N 19 53 E
Kiskunhalas 15 46 28N 19 37 E
Kislovodsk 23 43 50N 42 45 E
Kiso-Sammyaku 36 35 45N 137 45 E
Kissidougou 50 9 5N 10 0W
Kissimmee 69 28 18N 81 20W
Kissimmee → 69 27 20N 80 55W
Kississing L. 65 55 10N 101 20W
Kisumu 54 0 3S 34 45 E
Kit Carson 70 38 48N 102 45W
Kita 50 13 5N 9 25W
Kitab 24 39 7N 66 52 E
Kitaibaraki 36 36 50N 140 45 E
Kitakami-Gawa → 36 38 25N 141 19 E
Kitakyūshū 36 33 50N 130 50 E
Kitale 54 1 0N 35 0 E
Kitami 36 43 48N 143 54 E
Kitchener, Australia 47 30 55S 124 8 E
Kitchener, Canada 62 43 27N 80 29W
Kitega = Gitega 54 3 26S 29 56 E
Kitgum 54 3 17N 32 52 E
Kíthira 19 36 9N 23 0 E
Kíthnos 19 37 26N 24 27 E
Kitikmeot □ 60 70 0N 110 0W
Kitimat 64 54 3N 128 38W
Kitinen → 20 67 34N 26 40 E
Kittakittaooloo, L. 45 28 3S 138 14 E
Kittanning 68 40 49N 79 30W
Kittery 68 43 7N 70 42W
Kitui 54 1 17S 38 0 E
Kitwe 55 12 54S 28 13 E
Kivalo 20 66 18N 26 0 E
Kivu, L. 54 1 48S 29 0 E
Kiyev 23 50 30N 30 28 E
Kiyevskoye Vdkhr. 23 51 0N 30 0 E
Kizel 22 59 3N 57 40 E
Kızıl Irmak → 23 39 15N 36 0 E
Kizlyar 23 43 51N 46 40 E
Kizyl-Arvat 24 38 58N 56 15 E
Kladno 14 50 10N 14 7 E
Klagenfurt 14 46 38N 14 20 E
Klaipeda 22 55 43N 21 10 E
Klamath → 72 41 40N 124 4W
Klamath Falls 72 42 20N 121 50W
Klamath Mts. 72 41 20N 123 0W
Klappan → 64 58 0N 129 43W
Klarälven → 21 59 23N 13 32 E
Klaten 35 7 43S 110 36 E
Klatovy 14 49 23N 13 18 E
Klawak 64 55 35N 133 0W
Klawer 56 31 44S 18 36 E
Kleena Kleene 64 52 0N 124 59W
Klein 72 46 26N 108 31W
Klein-Karas 56 27 33S 18 7 E
Klerksdorp 56 26 53S 26 38 E
Klickitat 72 45 50N 121 10W
Klinaklini → 64 51 21N 125 40W
Klipdale 56 34 19S 19 57 E
Klipplaat 56 33 1S 24 22 E
Kłodzko 14 50 28N 16 38 E
Klondike 60 64 0N 139 26W
Klouto 53 6 57N 0 44 E
Kluane L. 60 61 15N 138 40W
Klyuchevskaya, Guba 25 55 50N 160 30 E
Knaresborough 6 54 1N 1 29W
Knee L., Man., Canada 65 55 3N 94 45W
Knee L., Sask., Canada 65 55 51N 107 0W
Knight Inlet 64 50 45N 125 40W
Knighton 7 52 21N 3 2W
Knight's Landing 72 38 50N 121 43W
Knob, C. 47 34 32S 119 16 E
Knockmealdown Mts. 9 52 16N 8 0W
Knokke 11 51 20N 3 17 E
Knossos 19 35 16N 25 10 E
Knox 68 41 18N 86 36W
Knox, C. 64 54 11N 133 5W
Knox City 71 33 26N 99 49W
Knoxville, Iowa, U.S.A. 70 41 20N 92 55W
Knoxville, Tenn., U.S.A. 69 35 58N 83 57W
Knysna 56 34 2S 23 2 E
Koartac 61 60 55N 69 40W
Koba, Aru, Indonesia 35 6 37S 134 37 E
Koba, Bangka, Indonesia 34 2 26S 106 14 E
Kobarid 18 46 15N 13 30 E
Kobayashi 36 31 56N 130 59 E
Kobdo = Hovd 37 48 2N 91 37 E
Kobdo = Jargalant 37 48 2N 91 37 E
Kōbe 36 34 45N 135 10 E
København 21 55 41N 12 34 E
Koblenz 14 50 21N 7 36 E
Kobroor, Kepulauan 35 6 10S 134 30 E
Kočani 19 41 55N 22 25 E
Kočevje 18 45 39N 14 50 E
Koch Bihar 33 26 22N 89 29 E
Kocheya 25 52 32N 120 42 E
Kōchi 36 33 30N 133 35 E
Kōchi □ 36 33 40N 133 30 E
Kochiu = Gejiu 37 23 20N 103 10 E
Kodiak 60 57 30N 152 45W
Kodiak I. 60 57 30N 152 45W
Koes 56 26 0S 19 15 E
Koffiefontein 56 29 30S 25 0 E
Kofiau 35 1 11S 129 50 E
Koforidua 53 6 3N 0 17W
Kōfu 36 35 40N 138 30 E
Kogaluk → 63 56 12N 61 44W
Kogan 45 27 2S 150 40 E
Kogota 36 38 33N 141 3 E
Koh-i-Bābā 31 34 30N 67 0 E
Kohat 32 33 40N 71 29 E
Kohima 33 25 35N 94 10 E
Kohkīlūyeh va Būyer Aḩmadi □ 31 31 30N 50 30 E
Kojonup 47 33 48S 117 10 E
Kokand 24 40 30N 70 57 E
Kokanee Glacier Prov. Park 64 49 47N 117 10W
Kokas 35 2 42S 132 26 E
Kokchetav 24 53 20N 69 25 E
Kokemäenjoki 21 61 32N 21 44 E
Kokkola 20 63 50N 23 8 E
Koko Kyunzu 33 14 10N 93 25 E
Kokomo 68 40 30N 86 6W
Kokonau 35 4 43S 136 26 E
Koksoak → 61 58 30N 68 10W
Kokstad 57 30 32S 29 29 E
Kokuora 25 71 35N 144 50 E
Kola, Indonesia 35 5 35S 134 30 E
Kola, U.S.S.R. 22 68 45N 33 8 E
Kola Pen. = Kolskiy Poluostrov 22 67 30N 38 0 E
Kolaka 35 4 3S 121 46 E
Kolar 32 13 12N 78 15 E
Kolar Gold Fields 32 12 58N 78 16 E
Kolari 20 67 20N 23 48 E
Kolayat 32 27 50N 72 50 E
Kolda 50 12 55N 14 57W
Kolding 21 55 30N 9 29 E
Kole 54 3 16S 22 42 E
Kolepom = Yos Sudarso, Pulau 35 8 0S 138 30 E
Kolguyev, Ostrov 22 69 20N 48 30 E
Kolhapur 32 16 43N 74 15 E
Kolín 14 50 2N 15 9 E
Kolmanskop 56 26 45S 15 14 E
Köln 14 50 56N 6 58 E
Koło 15 52 14N 18 40 E
Kołobrzeg 14 54 10N 15 35 E
Kolokani 50 13 35N 7 45W
Kolomna 22 55 8N 38 45 E
Kolomyya 23 48 31N 25 2 E
Kolonodale 35 2 3S 121 25 E
Kolosib 33 24 15N 92 45 E
Kolpashevo 24 58 20N 83 5 E
Kolpino 22 59 44N 30 39 E
Kolskiy Poluostrov 22 67 30N 38 0 E
Kolskiy Zaliv 22 69 23N 34 0 E
Kolwezi 54 10 40S 25 25 E
Kolyma → 25 69 30N 161 0 E
Kolymskoye, Okhotsko 25 63 0N 157 0 E
Komárno 15 47 49N 18 5 E
Komatipoort 57 25 25S 31 55 E
Komatsu 36 36 25N 136 30 E
Komi A.S.S.R. □ 22 64 0N 55 0 E
Kommunarsk 23 48 30N 38 45 E
Kommunizma, Pik 31 39 0N 72 2 E
Komodo 35 8 37S 119 20 E
Komono 54 3 10S 13 20 E
Komoran, Pulau 35 8 18S 138 45 E
Komotini 19 41 9N 25 26 E
Kompasberg 56 31 45S 24 32 E
Kompong Cham 34 12 0N 105 30 E
Kompong Chhnang 34 12 20N 104 35 E
Kompong Som 34 10 38N 103 30 E
Komsberg 56 32 40S 20 45 E
Komsomolets, Ostrov 25 80 30N 95 0 E
Komsomolsk 25 50 30N 137 0 E
Konarhá □ 31 35 30N 71 3 E
Konawa 71 34 59N 96 46W
Konch 32 26 0N 79 10 E
Kondakovo 25 69 36N 152 0 E
Kondinin 47 32 34S 118 8 E
Kondoa 54 4 55S 35 50 E
Kondopaga 22 62 12N 34 17 E
Kondratyevo 25 57 22N 98 15 E
Konduga 53 11 35N 13 26 E
Konevo 22 62 8N 39 20 E

Lafia

Kong 50 8 54N 4 36W
Kong, Koh 34 11 20N 103 0 E
Kongju 38 36 30N 127 0 E
Konglu 33 27 13N 97 57 E
Kongolo 54 5 22S 27 0 E
Kongor 51 7 1N 31 27 E
Kongsberg 21 59 39N 9 39 E
Kongsvinger 21 60 12N 12 2 E
Königsberg =
Kaliningrad 22 54 42N 20 32 E
Konin 15 52 12N 18 15 E
Konjic 19 43 42N 17 58 E
Konkiep 56 26 49S 17 15 E
Konosha 22 61 0N 40 5 E
Konotop 23 51 12N 33 7 E
Konqi He → 37 40 45N 90 10 E
Końskie 15 51 15N 20 23 E
Konstanz 14 47 39N 9 10 E
Kontagora 53 10 23N 5 27 E
Kontum 34 14 24N 108 0 E
Konya 30 37 52N 32 35 E
Konya Ovasi 30 38 30N 33 0 E
Konza 54 1 45S 37 7 E
Kookynie 47 29 17S 121 22 E
Kooline 46 22 57S 116 20 E
Kooloonong 45 34 48S 143 10 E
Koolyanobbing 47 30 48S 119 36 E
Koondrook 45 35 33S 144 8 E
Koorawatha 45 34 2S 148 33 E
Koorda 47 30 48S 117 35 E
Kooskia 72 46 9N 115 59W
Kootenai → 72 49 15N 117 39W
Kootenay L. 64 49 45N 116 50W
Kootenay Nat. Park 64 51 0N 116 0W
Kootjieskolk 56 31 15S 20 21 E
Kopaonik Planina 19 43 10N 21 50 E
Kópavogur 20 64 6N 21 55W
Koper 18 45 31N 13 44 E
Kopervik 21 59 17N 5 17 E
Kopeysk 24 55 7N 61 37 E
Kopi 45 33 24S 135 40 E
Köping 21 59 31N 16 3 E
Kopparberg 21 59 52N 15 0 E
Kopparbergs län □ 21 61 20N 14 15 E
Koppeh Dāgh 31 38 0N 58 0 E
Koppies 57 27 20S 27 30 E
Korab 19 41 44N 20 40 E
Korça 19 40 37N 20 50 E
Korce = Korça 19 40 37N 20 50 E
Korčula 18 42 57N 17 8 E
Kordestan 30 35 30N 42 0 E
Kordestān □ 30 36 0N 47 0 E
Korea, North ■ 38 40 0N 127 0 E
Korea, South ■ 38 36 0N 128 0 E
Korea Bay 38 39 0N 124 0 E
Korea Strait 39 34 0N 129 30 E
Koreh Wells 52 0 3N 38 45 E
Korhogo 50 9 29N 5 28W
Korim 35 0 58S 136 10 E
Korinthiakós Kólpos 19 38 16N 22 30 E
Kórinthos 19 37 56N 22 55 E
Kōriyama 36 37 24N 140 23 E
Koro, Fiji 43 17 19S 179 23 E
Koro, Ivory C. 50 8 32N 7 30W
Koro, Mali 50 14 1N 2 58W
Koro Sea 43 17 30S 179 45W
Korogwe 54 5 5S 38 25 E
Koroit 45 38 18S 142 24 E
Körös → 15 46 43N 20 12 E
Korraraika, Helodranon' i 57 17 45S 43 57 E
Korsakov 25 46 36N 142 42 E
Korshunovo 25 58 37N 110 10 E
Korsör 21 55 20N 11 9 E
Korti 51 18 6N 31 33 E
Kortrijk 11 50 50N 3 17 E
Koryakskiy Khrebet 25 61 0N 171 0 E
Kos 19 36 50N 27 15 E
Koschagyl 23 46 40N 54 0 E
Kościan 14 52 5N 16 40 E
Kosciusko 71 33 3N 89 34W
Kosciusko, Mt. 45 36 27S 148 16 E
Kosciusko I. 64 56 0N 133 40W
Kosha 51 20 50N 30 30 E
K'oshih = Kashi 37 39 30N 76 2 E
Kosi-meer 57 27 0S 32 50 E
Košice 15 48 42N 21 15 E
Koslan 22 63 28N 48 52 E
Kosŏng 38 38 40N 128 22 E
Kosovska-Mitrovica 19 42 54N 20 52 E
Kostamuksa 22 62 34N 32 44 E
Koster 56 25 52S 26 54 E
Kôstî 51 13 8N 32 43 E
Kostroma 22 57 50N 40 58 E
Koszalin 14 54 11N 16 8 E
Kota 32 25 14N 75 49 E
Kota Baharu 34 6 7N 102 14 E
Kota Belud 34 6 21N 116 26 E
Kota Kinabalu 34 6 0N 116 4 E
Kota Tinggi 34 1 44N 103 53 E
Kotaagung 34 5 38S 104 29 E
Kotabaru 34 3 20S 116 20 E
Kotabumi 34 4 49S 104 54 E
Kotagede 35 7 54S 110 26 E
Kotamobagu 35 0 57N 124 31 E
Kotaneelee → 64 60 11N 123 42W
Kotawaringin 34 2 28S 111 27 E
Kotcho L. 64 59 7N 121 12W
Kotelnich 22 58 20N 48 10 E
Kotelnyy, Ostrov 25 75 10N 139 0 E
Kotka 21 60 28N 26 58 E
Kotlas 22 61 15N 47 0 E
Kotli 32 33 30N 73 55 E
Kotor 19 42 25N 18 47 E
Kotri 32 25 22N 68 22 E
Kottayam 32 9 35N 76 33 E
Kotturu 32 14 45N 76 10 E
Kotuy → 25 71 54N 102 6 E
Kotzebue 60 66 50N 162 40W
Kouango 54 5 0N 20 10 E
Koudougou 50 12 10N 2 20W
Kougaberge 56 33 48S 23 50 E
Kouilou → 54 4 10S 12 5 E
Kouki 54 7 22N 17 3 E
Koula Moutou 54 1 15S 12 25 E
Koulen 34 13 50N 104 40 E
Koulikoro 50 12 40N 7 50W
Koumala 44 21 38S 149 15 E
Koumra 51 8 50N 17 35 E
Kounradskiy 24 46 59N 75 0 E
Kountze 71 30 20N 94 22W
Kouroussa 50 10 45N 9 45W
Kousseri 51 12 0N 14 55 E
Koutiala 50 12 25N 5 23W
Kovdor 22 67 34N 30 24 E
Kovel 22 51 10N 24 20 E
Kovrov 22 56 25N 41 25 E
Kowkash 62 50 20N 87 12W
Kowloon 39 22 20N 114 15 E
Koyabuti 35 2 36S 140 37 E
Koyuk 60 64 55N 161 20W
Koyukuk → 60 64 56N 157 30W
Kozan 30 37 35N 35 50 E
Kozáni 19 40 19N 21 47 E
Kozhikode = Calicut 32 11 15N 75 43 E
Kozhva 22 65 10N 57 0 E
Kpalimé 53 6 57N 0 44 E
Kra, Isthmus of = Kra, Kho Khot 34 10 15N 99 30 E
Kra, Kho Khot 34 10 15N 99 30 E
Kragan 35 6 43S 111 38 E
Kragerø 21 58 52N 9 25 E
Kragujevac 19 44 2N 20 56 E
Krakatau = Rakata, Pulau 34 6 10S 105 20 E
Kraków 15 50 4N 19 57 E
Kraksaan 35 7 43S 113 23 E
Kraljevo 19 43 44N 20 41 E
Kramatorsk 23 48 50N 37 30 E
Kramfors 20 62 55N 17 48 E
Krankskop 57 28 0S 30 47 E
Krasavino 22 60 58N 46 29 E
Kraskino 25 42 44N 130 48 E
Kraśnik 15 50 55N 22 5 E
Krasnodar 23 45 5N 39 0 E
Krasnokamsk 22 58 4N 55 48 E
Krasnoselkupsk 24 65 20N 82 10 E
Krasnoturinsk 22 59 46N 60 12 E
Krasnoufimsk 22 56 57N 57 46 E
Krasnouralsk 22 58 21N 60 3 E
Krasnovishersk 22 60 23N 57 3 E
Krasnovodsk 23 40 0N 52 52 E
Krasnoyarsk 25 56 8N 93 0 E
Krasnyy Luch 23 48 13N 39 0 E
Krasnyy Yar 23 46 43N 48 23 E
Kratie 34 12 32N 106 10 E
Krau 35 3 19S 140 5 E
Krawang 35 6 19N 107 18 E
Krefeld 14 51 20N 6 32 E
Kremenchug 23 49 5N 33 25 E
Kremenchugskoye Vdkhr. 23 49 20N 32 30 E
Kremmling 72 40 10N 106 30W
Kremnica 15 48 45N 18 50 E
Kribi 54 2 57N 9 56 E
Krishna → 33 15 57N 80 59 E
Krishnanagar 33 23 24N 88 33 E
Kristiansand 21 58 9N 8 1 E
Kristianstad 21 56 2N 14 9 E
Kristianstads län □ 21 56 15N 14 0 E
Kristiansund 20 63 7N 7 45 E
Kristiinankaupunki 20 62 16N 21 21 E
Kristinehamn 21 59 18N 14 13 E
Kristinestad 20 62 16N 21 21 E
Kriti 19 35 15N 25 0 E
Krivoy Rog 23 47 51N 33 20 E
Krk 18 45 8N 14 40 E
Krokodil → 57 25 14S 32 18 E
Kronobergs län □ 21 56 45N 14 30 E
Kronshtadt 22 60 5N 29 45 E
Kroonstad 56 27 43S 27 19 E
Kropotkin, R.S.F.S.R., U.S.S.R. 23 45 28N 40 28 E
Kropotkin, R.S.F.S.R., U.S.S.R. 25 59 0N 115 30 E
Krosno 15 49 42N 21 46 E
Krotoszyn 15 51 42N 17 23 E
Kruger Nat. Park 57 23 30S 31 40 E
Krugersdorp 57 26 5S 27 46 E
Kruisfontein 56 33 59S 24 43 E
Krung Thep = Bangkok 34 13 45N 100 35 E
Kruševac 19 43 35N 21 28 E
Kruzof I. 64 57 10N 135 40W
Krymskiy Poluostrov 23 45 0N 34 0 E
Ksar el Boukhari 50 35 51N 2 52 E
Ksar el Kebir 50 35 0N 6 0W
Ksar es Souk = Ar Rachidiya 50 31 58N 4 20W
Kuala 34 2 55N 105 47 E
Kuala Kubu Baharu 34 3 34N 101 39 E
Kuala Lipis 34 4 10N 102 3 E
Kuala Lumpur 34 3 9N 101 41 E
Kuala Trengganu 34 5 20N 103 8 E
Kualajelai 34 2 58S 110 46 E
Kualakapuas 34 2 55S 114 20 E
Kualakurun 34 1 10S 113 50 E
Kualapembuang 34 3 14S 112 38 E
Kualasimpang 34 4 17N 98 3 E
Kuandang 35 0 56N 123 1 E
Kuandian 38 40 45N 124 45 E
Kuangchou = Guangzhou 39 23 5N 113 10 E
Kuantan 34 3 49N 103 20 E
Kuba 23 41 21N 48 32 E
Kubak 31 27 10N 63 10 E
Kuban → 23 45 20N 37 30 E
Kucing 34 1 33N 110 25 E
Kuda 32 23 10N 71 15 E
Kudat 34 6 55N 116 55 E
Kudus 35 6 48S 110 51 E
Kudymkar 24 59 1N 54 39 E
Kueiyang = Guiyang 39 26 32N 106 40 E
Kufrinjah 28 32 20N 35 41 E
Kufstein 14 47 35N 12 11 E
Kugong I. 62 56 18N 79 50W
Kūh-e 'Alijūq 31 31 30N 51 41 E
Kūh-e Dīnār 31 30 40N 51 0 E
Kūh-e-Hazārām 31 29 35N 57 20 E
Kūh-e-Jebāl Bārez 31 29 0N 58 0 E
Kūh-e Sorkh 31 35 30N 58 45 E
Kūh-e Taftān 31 28 40N 61 0 E
Kūhak 31 27 12N 63 10 E
Kūhhā-ye-Bashākerd 31 26 45N 59 0 E
Kūhhā-ye Sabalān 30 38 15N 47 45 E
Kūhpāyeh 31 32 44N 52 20 E
Kuile He → 38 49 32N 124 42 E
Kuito 55 12 22S 16 55 E
Kuji 36 40 11N 141 46 E
Kukawa 51 12 58N 13 27 E
Kukerin 47 33 13S 118 0 E
Kulasekarappattinam 32 8 20N 78 0 E
Kuldja = Yining 37 43 58N 81 10 E
Kulin 47 32 40S 118 2 E
Kulja 47 30 28S 117 18 E
Kulm 70 46 22N 98 58W
Kulsary 23 46 59N 54 1 E
Kulumbura 46 13 55S 126 35 E
Kulunda 24 52 35N 78 57 E
Kulwin 45 35 0S 142 42 E
Kulyab 24 37 55N 69 50 E
Kum Tekei 24 43 10N 79 30 E
Kuma → 23 44 55N 47 0 E
Kumaganum 53 13 8N 10 38 E
Kumagaya 36 36 9N 139 22 E
Kumai 34 2 44S 111 43 E
Kumamba, Kepulauan 35 1 36S 138 45 E
Kumamoto 36 32 45N 130 45 E
Kumamoto □ 36 32 55N 130 55 E
Kumanovo 19 42 9N 21 42 E
Kumara 43 42 37S 171 12 E
Kumarl 47 32 47S 121 33 E
Kumasi 50 6 41N 1 38W
Kumba 54 4 36N 9 24 E
Kumbarilla 45 27 15S 150 55 E
Kumertau 22 52 46N 55 47 E
Kumla 21 59 8N 15 10 E
Kumo 53 10 1N 11 12 E
Kumon Bum 33 26 30N 97 15 E
Kunama 45 35 35S 148 4 E
Kunashir, Ostrov 25 44 0N 146 0 E
Kundip 47 33 42S 120 10 E
Kungala 45 29 58S 153 7 E
Kunghit I. 64 52 6N 131 3W
Kungrad 24 43 6N 58 54 E
Kungsbacka 21 57 30N 12 5 E
Kungur 22 57 25N 56 57 E
Kungurri 44 21 3S 148 46 E
Kuningan 35 6 59S 108 29 E
Kunlong 33 23 20N 98 50 E
Kunlun Shan 33 36 0N 86 30 E
Kunming 37 25 1N 102 41 E
Kunsan 38 35 59N 126 45 E
Kunshan 39 31 22N 120 58 E
Kununurra 46 15 40S 128 50 E
Kunwarara 44 22 55S 150 9 E
Kunya-Urgench 24 42 19N 59 10 E
Kuopio 20 62 53N 27 35 E
Kuopion lääni □ 20 63 25N 27 10 E
Kupa → 18 45 28N 16 24 E
Kupang 35 10 19S 123 39 E
Kuqa 37 41 35N 82 30 E
Kura → 23 39 50N 49 20 E
Kuranda 44 16 48S 145 35 E
Kurashiki 36 34 40N 133 50 E
Kurayoshi 36 35 26N 133 50 E
Kure 36 34 14N 132 32 E
Kurgaldzhino 24 50 35N 70 20 E
Kurgan 24 55 26N 65 18 E
Kuria Maria Is. = Khūrīyā Mūrīyā, Jazā 'ir 29 17 30N 55 58 E
Kuridala 44 21 16S 140 29 E
Kurigram 33 25 49N 89 39 E
Kuril Is. = Kurilskiye Ostrova 25 45 0N 150 0 E
Kuril Trench 40 44 0N 153 0 E
Kurilsk 25 45 14N 147 53 E
Kurilskiye Ostrova 25 45 0N 150 0 E
Kurmuk 51 10 33N 34 21 E
Kurnool 32 15 45N 78 0 E
Kurow 43 44 44S 170 29 E
Kurrajong 45 33 33S 150 42 E
Kurri Kurri 45 32 50S 151 28 E
Kursk 22 51 42N 36 11 E
Kuršumlija 19 43 9N 21 19 E
Kuruktag 37 41 0N 89 0 E
Kuruman 56 27 28S 23 28 E
Kuruman → 56 26 56S 20 39 E
Kurume 36 33 15N 130 30 E
Kurunegala 32 7 30N 80 23 E
Kurya 25 61 15N 108 10 E
Kusawa L. 64 60 20N 136 13W
Kushiro 36 43 0N 144 25 E
Kushiro → 36 42 59N 144 23 E
Kushka 24 35 20N 62 18 E
Kushtia 33 23 55N 89 5 E
Kushva 22 58 18N 59 45 E
Kuskokwim → 60 60 17N 162 27W
Kuskokwim Bay 60 59 50N 162 56W
Kussharo-Ko 36 43 38N 144 21 E
Kustanay 24 53 10N 63 35 E
Kütahya 30 39 30N 30 2 E
Kutaisi 23 42 19N 42 40 E
Kutaraja = Banda Aceh 34 5 35N 95 20 E
Kutch, Gulf of = Kachchh, Gulf of 32 22 50N 69 15 E
Kutch, Rann of = Kachchh, Rann of 32 24 0N 70 0 E
Kutno 15 52 15N 19 23 E
Kuttabul 44 21 5S 148 48 E
Kutu 54 2 40S 18 11 E
Kutum 51 14 10N 24 40 E
Kuujjuaq 61 58 6N 68 15W
Kuwait = Al Kuwayt 30 29 30N 48 0 E
Kuwait ■ 30 29 30N 47 30 E
Kuwana 36 35 0N 136 43 E
Kuybyshev, R.S.F.S.R., U.S.S.R. 22 53 8N 50 6 E
Kuybyshev, R.S.F.S.R., U.S.S.R. 24 55 27N 78 19 E
Kuybyshevskoye Vdkhr. 22 55 2N 49 30 E
Küysanjaq 30 36 5N 44 38 E
Kuyto, Oz. 22 64 40N 31 0 E
Kuyumba 25 60 58N 96 59 E
Kuzey Anadolu Dağlari 30 41 30N 35 0 E
Kuznetsk 22 53 12N 46 40 E
Kuzomen 22 66 22N 36 50 E
Kvænangen 20 70 5N 21 15 E
Kvarner 18 44 50N 14 10 E
Kvarnerič 18 44 43N 14 37 E
Kwabhaca 57 30 51S 29 0 E
Kwadacha → 64 57 28N 125 38W
Kwakhanai 56 21 39S 21 16 E
Kwakoegron 79 5 12N 55 25W
KwaMashu 57 29 45S 30 58 E
Kwamouth 54 3 9S 16 12 E
Kwando → 56 18 27S 23 32 E
Kwangju 38 35 9N 126 54 E
Kwangsi-Chuang = Guangxi Zhuangzu Zizhiqu □ 39 24 0N 109 0 E
Kwangtung = Guangdong □ 39 23 0N 113 0 E
Kwara □ 53 8 0N 5 0 E
Kwataboahegan → 62 51 9N 80 50W
Kwatisore 35 3 18S 134 50 E
Kweichow = Guizhou □ 39 27 0N 107 0 E
Kwekwe 55 18 58S 29 48 E
Kwiguk 60 63 45N 164 35W
Kwinana New Town 47 32 15S 115 47 E
Kwoka 35 0 31S 132 27 E
Kyabé 51 9 30N 19 0 E
Kyabra Cr. → 45 25 36S 142 55 E
Kyabram 45 36 19S 145 4 E
Kyakhta 25 50 30N 106 25 E
Kyangin 33 18 20N 95 20 E
Kyaukpadaung 33 20 52N 95 8 E
Kyaukpyu 33 19 28N 93 30 E
Kyaukse 33 21 36N 96 10 E
Kyle Dam 55 20 15S 31 0 E
Kyle of Lochalsh 8 57 17N 5 43W
Kyneton 45 37 10S 144 29 E
Kynuna 44 21 37S 141 55 E
Kyō-ga-Saki 36 35 45N 135 15 E
Kyoga, L. 54 1 35N 33 0 E
Kyogle 45 28 40S 153 0 E
Kyongju 38 35 51N 129 14 E
Kyongpyaw 33 17 12N 95 10 E
Kyōto 36 35 0N 135 45 E
Kyōto □ 36 35 15N 135 45 E
Kyren 25 51 45N 101 45 E
Kyrenia 30 35 20N 33 20 E
Kystatyam 25 67 20N 123 10 E
Kytal Ktakh 25 65 30N 123 40 E
Kyulyunken 25 64 10N 137 5 E
Kyunhla 33 23 25N 95 15 E
Kyuquot 64 50 3N 127 25W
Kyūshū 36 33 0N 131 0 E
Kyūshū-Sanchi 36 32 35N 131 17 E
Kyustendil 19 42 16N 22 41 E
Kyusyur 25 70 39N 127 15 E
Kywong 45 34 58S 146 44 E
Kyzyl 25 51 50N 94 30 E
Kyzyl-Kiya 24 40 16N 72 8 E
Kyzylkum, Peski 24 42 30N 65 0 E
Kzyl-Orda 24 44 48N 65 28 E

L

Labak 35 6 32N 124 5 E
Labe = Elbe → 14 53 50N 9 0 E
Labé 50 11 24N 12 16W
Laberge, L. 64 61 11N 135 12W
Labis 34 2 22N 103 2 E
Laboulaye 80 34 10S 63 30W
Labrador, Coast of □ 63 53 20N 61 0W
Labrador City 63 52 57N 66 55W
Lábrea 78 7 15S 64 51W
Labuan, Pulau 34 5 21N 115 13 E
Labuha 35 0 30S 127 30 E
Labuhan 35 6 22S 105 50 E
Labuhanbajo 35 8 28S 120 1 E
Labuk, Telok 34 6 10N 117 50 E
Labytnangi 22 66 39N 66 21 E
Lac Allard 63 50 33N 63 24W
Lac Bouchette 63 48 16N 72 11W
Lac du Flambeau 70 46 1N 89 51W
Lac Édouard 62 47 40N 72 16W
Lac La Biche 64 54 45N 111 58W
Lac la Martre 60 63 8N 117 16W
Lac-Mégantic 63 45 35N 70 53W
Lac Seul, Res. 62 50 25N 92 30W
Lacantúm → 74 16 36N 90 40W
Laccadive Is. = Lakshadweep Is. 3 10 0N 72 30 E
Lacepede B. 45 36 40S 139 40 E
Lacepede Is. 46 16 55S 122 0 E
Lachine 62 45 30N 73 40W
Lachlan → 45 34 22S 143 55 E
Lachute 62 45 39N 74 21W
Lackawanna 68 42 49N 78 50W
Lacombe 64 52 30N 113 44W
Laconia 68 43 32N 71 30W
Lacrosse 72 46 51N 117 58W
Ladakh Ra. 32 34 0N 78 0 E
Ladismith 56 33 28S 21 15 E
Lādīz 31 28 55N 61 15 E
Ladoga, L. = Ladozhskoye Ozero 22 61 15N 30 30 E
Ladozhskoye Ozero 22 61 15N 30 30 E
Lady Grey 56 30 43S 27 13 E
Ladybrand 56 29 9S 27 29 E
Ladysmith, Canada 64 49 0N 123 49W
Ladysmith, S. Africa 57 28 32S 29 46 E
Ladysmith, U.S.A. 70 45 27N 91 4W
Lae 40 6 40S 147 2 E
Læsø 21 57 15N 10 53 E
Lafayette, Colo., U.S.A. 70 40 0N 105 2W
Lafayette, Ga., U.S.A. 69 34 44N 85 15W
Lafayette, Ind., U.S.A. 68 40 22N 86 52W
Lafayette, La., U.S.A. 71 30 18N 92 0W
Lafayette, Tenn., U.S.A. 69 36 35N 86 0W
Laferte → 64 61 53N 117 44W
Lafia 53 8 30N 8 34 E

Longxi

Lévis 63 46 48N 71 9W
Levis, L. 64 62 37N 117 58W
Levkás 19 38 40N 20 43 E
Levkôsia = Nicosia 30 35 10N 33 25 E
Lewellen 70 41 22N 102 5W
Lewes, U.K. 7 50 53N 0 2 E
Lewes, U.S.A. 68 38 45N 75 8W
Lewis 8 58 10N 6 40W
Lewis, Butt of 8 58 30N 6 12W
Lewis Ra., Australia 46 20 3S 128 50 E
Lewis Ra., U.S.A. 72 48 0N 113 15W
Lewisburg 69 35 29N 86 46W
Lewisporte 63 49 15N 55 3W
Lewiston 72 46 25N 117 0W
Lewistown, Mont., U.S.A. 72 47 0N 109 25W
Lewistown, Pa., U.S.A. 68 40 37N 77 33W
Lexington, Ill., U.S.A. 70 40 37N 88 47W
Lexington, Ky., U.S.A. 68 38 6N 84 30W
Lexington, Miss., U.S.A. 71 33 8N 90 2W
Lexington, Mo., U.S.A. 70 39 7N 93 55W
Lexington, N.C., U.S.A. 69 35 50N 80 13W
Lexington, Nebr., U.S.A. 70 40 48N 99 45W
Lexington, Oreg., U.S.A. 72 45 29N 119 46W
Lexington, Tenn., U.S.A. 69 35 38N 88 25W
Lexington Park 68 38 16N 76 27W
Leyte 35 11 0N 125 0 E
Lhasa 37 29 25N 90 58 E
Lhazê 37 29 5N 87 38 E
Lhokkruet 34 4 55N 95 24 E
Lhokseumawe 34 5 10N 97 10 E
Lhuntsi Dzong 33 27 39N 91 10 E
Li Shui → 39 29 24N 112 1 E
Li Xian, Gansu, China 39 34 10N 105 5 E
Li Xian, Hunan, China 39 29 36N 111 42 E
Lianga 35 8 38N 126 6 E
Liangdang 39 33 56N 106 18 E
Lianhua 39 27 3N 113 54 E
Lianjiang 39 26 12N 119 27 E
Lianping 39 24 26N 114 30 E
Lianshanguan 38 40 53N 123 43 E
Lianyungang 39 34 40N 119 11 E
Liao He → 38 41 0N 121 50 E
Liaocheng 38 36 28N 115 58 E
Liaodong Bandao 38 40 0N 122 30 E
Liaodong Wan 38 40 20N 121 10 E
Liaoning □ 38 42 0N 122 0 E
Liaoyang 38 41 15N 122 58 E
Liaoyuan 38 42 58N 125 2 E
Liaozhong 38 41 23N 122 50 E
Liard → 64 61 51N 121 18W
Libau = Liepaja 22 56 30N 21 0 E
Libby 72 48 20N 115 33W
Libenge 54 3 40N 18 55 E
Liberal, Kans., U.S.A. 71 37 4N 101 0W
Liberal, Mo., U.S.A. 71 37 35N 94 30W
Liberec 14 50 47N 15 7 E
Liberia 75 10 40N 85 30W
Liberia ■ 50 6 30N 9 30W
Libertad, La 74 29 55N 112 41W
Liberty, Mo., U.S.A. 70 39 15N 94 24W
Liberty, Tex., U.S.A. 71 30 5N 94 50W
Libo 39 25 22N 107 53 E
Libobo, Tanjung 35 0 54S 128 28 E
Libode 57 31 33S 29 2 E
Libonda 55 14 28S 23 12 E
Libourne 12 44 55N 0 14W
Libramont 11 49 55N 5 23 E
Libreville 54 0 25N 9 26 E
Libya ■ 51 27 0N 17 0 E
Libyan Desert 48 25 0N 25 0 E
Licantén 80 35 55S 72 0W
Licata 18 37 6N 13 55 E
Lichfield 6 52 40N 1 50W
Lichtenburg 56 26 8S 26 8 E
Lichuan 39 30 18N 108 57 E
Lida 73 37 30N 117 30W
Lidköping 21 58 31N 13 14 E
Liechtenstein ■ 14 47 8N 9 35 E
Liège 11 50 38N 5 35 E
Liège □ 11 50 32N 5 35 E
Liegnitz = Legnica 14 51 12N 16 10 E
Lienyünchiangshih = Lianyungang 39 34 40N 119 11 E
Lienz 14 46 50N 12 46 E
Liepaja 22 56 30N 21 0 E
Lier 11 51 7N 4 34 E
Lièvre → 62 45 31N 75 26W
Liffey → 9 53 21N 6 20W
Lifford 9 54 50N 7 30W
Lightning Ridge 45 29 22S 148 0 E
Liguria □ 18 44 30N 9 0 E
Ligurian Sea 18 43 20N 9 0 E
Lihou Reefs and Cays 44 17 25S 151 40 E
Lihue 66 21 59N 159 24W
Lijiang 37 26 55N 100 20 E
Likasi 54 10 55S 26 48 E
Likati 54 3 20N 24 0 E
Liling 39 27 42N 113 29 E
Lille 12 50 38N 3 3 E
Lille Bælt 21 55 20N 9 45 E
Lillehammer 21 61 8N 10 30 E
Lillesand 21 58 15N 8 23 E
Lilleshall 7 52 45N 2 22W
Lillestrøm 21 59 58N 11 5 E
Lillian Point, Mt. 47 27 40S 126 6 E
Lillooet → 64 49 15N 121 57W
Lilongwe 55 14 0S 33 48 E
Liloy 35 8 4N 122 39 E
Lima, Indonesia 35 3 37S 128 4 E
Lima, Peru 78 12 0S 77 0W
Lima, Mont., U.S.A. 72 44 41N 112 38W
Lima, Ohio, U.S.A. 68 40 42N 84 5W
Limassol 30 34 42N 33 1 E
Limavady 9 55 3N 6 58W
Limavady □ 9 55 0N 6 55W
Limay → 80 39 0S 68 0W
Limay Mahuida 80 37 10S 66 45W
Limbang 34 4 42N 115 6 E
Limbe 54 4 1N 9 10 E
Limbri 45 31 3S 151 5 E
Limbunya 46 17 14S 129 50 E
Limburg □, Belgium 11 51 2N 5 25 E
Limburg □, Neth. 11 51 20N 5 55 E
Limeira 80 22 35S 47 28W
Limerick 9 52 40N 8 38W
Limerick □ 9 52 30N 8 50W
Limestone → 65 56 31N 94 7W
Limfjorden 21 56 55N 9 0 E
Limia → 13 41 41N 8 50W
Limmen Bight 44 14 40S 135 35 E
Limmen Bight → 44 15 7S 135 44 E
Límnos 19 39 50N 25 5 E
Limoeiro do Norte 79 5 5S 38 0W
Limoges 12 45 50N 1 15 E
Limón, C. Rica 75 10 0N 83 2W
Limon, Panama 74 9 17N 79 45W
Limon, U.S.A. 70 39 18N 103 38W
Limon B. 74 9 22N 79 56W
Limousin 12 45 30N 1 30 E
Limpopo → 57 25 5S 33 30 E
Limuru 54 1 2S 36 35 E
Linares, Chile 80 35 50S 71 40W
Linares, Mexico 74 24 50N 99 40W
Linares, Spain 13 38 10N 3 40W
Lincheng 38 37 25N 114 30 E
Linchuan 39 27 57N 116 15 E
Lincoln, Argentina 80 34 55S 61 30W
Lincoln, N.Z. 43 43 38S 172 30 E
Lincoln, U.K. 6 53 14N 0 32W
Lincoln, Ill., U.S.A. 70 40 10N 89 20W
Lincoln, Kans., U.S.A. 70 39 6N 98 9W
Lincoln, Maine, U.S.A. 63 45 27N 68 29W
Lincoln, N. Mex., U.S.A. 73 33 30N 105 26W
Lincoln, Nebr., U.S.A. 70 40 50N 96 42W
Lincoln □ 6 53 14N 0 32W
Lincoln Wolds 6 53 20N 0 5W
Lincolnton 69 35 30N 81 15W
Lind 72 47 0N 118 33W
Linden, Guyana 78 6 0N 58 10W
Linden, U.S.A. 71 33 0N 94 20W
Lindi 54 9 58S 39 38 E
Lindian 38 47 11N 124 52 E
Lindsay, Canada 62 44 22N 78 43W
Lindsay, Calif., U.S.A. 73 36 14N 119 6W
Lindsay, Okla., U.S.A. 71 34 51N 97 37W
Lindsborg 70 38 35N 97 40W
Línea de la Concepción, La 13 36 15N 5 23W
Linfen 38 36 3N 111 30 E
Ling Xian 38 37 22N 116 30 E
Lingao 39 19 56N 109 42 E
Lingayen 35 16 1N 120 14 E
Lingayen G. 35 16 10N 120 15 E
Lingchuan 39 25 26N 110 21 E
Lingen 14 52 32N 7 21 E
Lingga 34 0 12S 104 37 E
Lingga, Kepulauan 34 0 10S 104 30 E
Lingle 70 42 10N 104 18W
Lingling 39 26 17N 111 37 E
Lingshan 39 22 25N 109 18 E
Lingshi 38 36 48N 111 48 E
Lingshui 39 18 27N 110 0 E
Lingtai 39 35 0N 107 40 E
Linguéré 50 15 25N 15 5W
Lingyuan 38 41 10N 119 15 E
Lingyun 39 25 2N 106 35 E
Linhai 39 28 50N 121 8 E
Linhares 79 19 25S 40 4W
Linhe 38 40 48N 107 20 E
Linjiang 38 41 50N 127 0 E
Linköping 21 58 28N 15 36 E
Linkou 38 45 15N 130 18 E
Linlithgow 8 55 58N 3 38W
Linnhe, L. 8 56 36N 5 25W
Linqing 38 36 50N 115 42 E
Lins 80 21 40S 49 44W
Lintao 38 35 18N 103 52 E
Lintlaw 65 52 4N 103 14W
Linton, Canada 63 47 15N 72 16W
Linton, Ind., U.S.A. 68 39 0N 87 10W
Linton, N. Dak., U.S.A. 70 46 21N 100 12W
Linville 45 26 50S 152 11 E
Linwu 39 25 19N 112 31 E
Linxi 38 43 36N 118 2 E
Linxia 37 35 36N 103 10 E
Linyanti → 56 17 50S 25 5 E
Linyi 39 35 5N 118 21 E
Linz 14 48 18N 14 18 E
Lion, G. du 12 43 0N 4 0 E
Lion's Head 62 44 58N 81 15W
Lipa 35 13 57N 121 10 E
Lípari, Is. 18 38 30N 14 50 E
Lipetsk 22 52 37N 39 35 E
Liping 39 26 15N 109 7 E
Lippe → 14 51 39N 6 38 E
Lipscomb 71 36 16N 100 16W
Liptrap C. 45 38 50S 145 55 E
Lira 54 2 17N 32 57 E
Liria 13 39 37N 0 35W
Lisala 54 2 12N 21 38 E
Lisboa 13 38 42N 9 10W
Lisbon = Lisboa 13 38 42N 9 10W
Lisbon 70 46 30N 97 46W
Lisburn 9 54 30N 6 9W
Lisburne, C. 60 68 50N 166 0W
Liscannor, B. 9 52 57N 9 24W
Lishi 38 37 31N 111 8 E
Lishui 39 28 28N 119 54 E
Lisianski I. 40 26 2N 174 0W
Lisichansk 23 48 55N 38 30 E
Lisieux 12 49 10N 0 12 E
Lismore, Australia 45 28 44S 153 21 E
Lismore, Ireland 9 52 8N 7 58W
Lisse 11 52 16N 4 33 E
Lista, Norway 21 58 7N 6 39 E
Lista, Sweden 21 59 19N 16 16 E
Liston 45 28 39S 152 6 E
Listowel, Canada 62 43 44N 80 58W
Listowel, Ireland 9 52 27N 9 30W
Litang, China 39 23 12N 109 8 E
Litang, Malaysia 35 5 27N 118 31 E
Litani →, Lebanon 28 33 20N 35 14 E
Litani →, Surinam 30 3 40N 54 0W
Litchfield, Ill., U.S.A. 70 39 10N 89 40W
Litchfield, Minn., U.S.A. 70 45 5N 94 31W
Lithgow 45 33 25S 150 8 E
Líthinon, Ákra 19 34 55N 24 44 E
Lithuanian S.S.R. □ 22 55 30N 24 0 E
Litoměřice 14 50 33N 14 10 E
Little Abaco I. 75 26 50N 77 30W
Little Barrier I. 43 36 12S 175 8 E
Little Belt Mts. 72 46 50N 111 0W
Little Blue → 70 39 41N 96 40W
Little Bushman Land 56 29 10S 18 10 E
Little Cadotte → 64 56 41N 117 6W
Little Churchill → 65 57 30N 95 22W
Little Colorado → 73 36 11N 111 48W
Little Current 62 45 55N 82 0W
Little Current → 62 50 57N 84 36W
Little Falls, Minn., U.S.A. 70 45 58N 94 19W
Little Falls, N.Y., U.S.A. 68 43 3N 74 50W
Little Fork → 70 48 31N 93 35W
Little Grand Rapids 65 52 0N 95 29W
Little Humboldt → 72 41 0N 117 43W
Little Inagua I. 75 21 40N 73 50W
Little Karoo 56 33 45S 21 0 E
Little Lake 73 35 58N 117 58W
Little Minch 8 57 35N 6 45W
Little Missouri → 70 47 30N 102 25W
Little Namaqualand 56 29 0S 17 9 E
Little Ouse → 7 52 25N 0 50 E
Little Red → 71 35 11N 91 27W
Little River 43 43 45S 172 49 E
Little Rock 71 34 41N 92 10W
Little Sable Pt. 68 43 40N 86 32W
Little Sioux → 70 41 49N 96 4W
Little Smoky → 64 54 44N 117 11W
Little Snake → 72 40 27N 108 26W
Little Wabash → 68 37 54N 88 5W
Littlefield 71 33 57N 102 17W
Littlefork 70 48 24N 93 35W
Littlehampton 7 50 48N 0 32W
Littleton 68 44 19N 71 47W
Liuba 39 33 38N 106 55 E
Liucheng 39 24 38N 109 14 E
Liukang Tenggaja 35 6 45S 118 50 E
Liuwa Plain 55 14 20S 22 30 E
Liuyang 39 28 10N 113 37 E
Liuzhou 39 24 22N 109 22 E
Live Oak 69 30 17N 83 0W
Liveringa 46 18 3S 124 10 E
Livermore, Mt. 71 30 45N 104 8W
Liverpool, Australia 45 33 54S 150 58 E
Liverpool, Canada 63 44 5N 64 41W
Liverpool, U.K. 6 53 25N 3 0W
Liverpool Plains 45 31 15S 150 15 E
Liverpool Ra. 45 31 50S 150 30 E
Livingston, Guat. 75 15 50N 88 50W
Livingston, Mont., U.S.A. 72 45 40N 110 40W
Livingston, Tex., U.S.A. 71 30 44N 94 54W
Livingstone 55 17 46S 25 52 E
Livingstone Mts. 52 9 40S 34 20 E
Livingstonia 54 10 38S 34 5 E
Livny 22 52 30N 37 30 E
Livonia 68 42 25N 83 23W
Livorno 18 43 32N 10 18 E
Livramento 80 30 55S 55 30W
Liwale 54 9 48S 37 58 E
Lizard I. 44 14 42S 145 30 E
Lizard Pt. 7 49 57N 5 11W
Ljubljana 18 46 4N 14 33 E
Ljungan → 20 62 18N 17 23 E
Ljungby 21 56 49N 13 55 E
Ljusdal 21 61 46N 16 3 E
Ljusnan → 21 61 12N 17 8 E
Ljusne 21 61 13N 17 7 E
Llancanelo, Salina 80 35 40S 69 8W
Llandeilo 7 51 53N 4 0W
Llandovery 7 51 59N 3 49W
Llandrindod Wells 7 52 15N 3 23W
Llandudno 6 53 19N 3 51W
Llanelli 7 51 41N 4 11W
Llanes 13 43 25N 4 50W
Llangollen 6 52 58N 3 10W
Llanidloes 7 52 28N 3 31W
Llano 71 30 45N 98 41W
Llano → 71 30 50N 98 25W
Llano Estacado 71 34 0N 103 0W
Llanos 78 5 0N 71 35W
Llera 74 23 19N 99 1W
Llobregat → 13 41 19N 2 9 E
Lloret de Mar 13 41 41N 2 53 E
Lloyd B. 44 12 45S 143 27 E
Lloyd L. 65 57 22N 108 57W
Lloydminster 65 53 17N 110 0W
Llullaillaco, Volcán 80 24 43S 68 30W
Loa 73 38 18N 111 40W
Loa → 80 21 26S 70 41W
Lobatse 56 25 12S 25 40 E
Lobería 80 38 10S 58 40W
Lobito 55 12 18S 13 35 E
Lobos, I. 74 27 15N 110 30W
Lobos, Is. 76 6 57S 80 45W
Locarno 14 46 10N 8 47 E
Lochaber 8 56 55N 5 0W
Lochcarron 8 57 25N 5 30W
Loche, La 65 56 29N 109 26W
Lochem 11 52 9N 6 26 E
Loches 12 47 7N 1 0 E
Lochgelly 8 56 7N 3 18W
Lochgilphead 8 56 2N 5 37W
Lochinver 8 58 9N 5 15W
Lochnagar, Australia 44 23 33S 145 38 E
Lochnagar, U.K. 8 56 57N 3 14W
Lochy → 8 56 52N 5 3W
Lock 45 33 34S 135 46 E
Lock Haven 68 41 7N 77 31W
Lockeport 63 43 47N 65 4W
Lockerbie 8 55 7N 3 21W
Lockhart 71 29 55N 97 40W
Lockhart, L. 47 33 15S 119 3 E
Lockney 71 34 7N 101 27W
Lockport 68 43 12N 78 42W
Lod 28 31 57N 34 54 E
Lodeinoye Pole 22 60 44N 33 33 E
Lodge Grass 72 45 21N 107 20W
Lodgepole 70 41 12N 102 40W
Lodgepole Cr. → 70 41 20N 104 30W
Lodhran 32 29 32N 71 30 E
Lodi 72 38 12N 121 16W
Lodja 54 3 30S 23 23 E
Lodwar 54 3 10N 35 40 E
Łódź 15 51 45N 19 27 E
Loeriesfontein 56 31 0S 19 26 E
Lofoten 20 68 30N 15 0 E
Logan, Kans., U.S.A. 70 39 40N 99 35W
Logan, Ohio, U.S.A. 68 39 25N 82 22W
Logan, Utah, U.S.A. 72 41 45N 111 50W
Logan, W. Va., U.S.A. 68 37 51N 81 59W
Logan, Mt. 60 60 31N 140 22W
Logan Pass 64 48 41N 113 44W
Logansport, Ind., U.S.A. 68 40 45N 86 21W
Logansport, La., U.S.A. 71 31 58N 93 58W
Logroño 13 42 28N 2 27W
Lohardaga 33 23 27N 84 45 E
Loi-kaw 33 19 40N 97 17 E
Loimaa 21 60 50N 23 5 E
Loir → 12 47 33N 0 32W
Loir-et-Cher □ 12 47 40N 1 20 E
Loire □ 12 45 40N 4 5 E
Loire → 12 47 16N 2 10W
Loire-Atlantique □ 12 47 25N 1 40W
Loiret □ 12 47 55N 2 30 E
Loja, Ecuador 78 3 59S 79 16W
Loja, Spain 13 37 10N 4 10W
Loji 35 1 38S 127 28 E
Lokandu 54 2 30S 25 45 E
Lokeren 11 51 6N 3 59 E
Lokichokio 52 4 19N 34 13 E
Lokitaung 54 4 12N 35 48 E
Lokka 20 67 55N 27 35 E
Løkken Verk 20 63 7N 9 43 E
Lokoja 53 7 47N 6 45 E
Lokolama 54 2 35S 19 50 E
Lokwei 39 19 5N 110 31 E
Loliondo 54 2 2S 35 39 E
Lolland 21 54 45N 11 30 E
Lolo 72 46 50N 114 8W
Lom 19 43 48N 23 12 E
Loma 72 47 59N 110 29W
Lomami → 54 0 46N 24 16 E
Lombadina 46 16 31S 122 54 E
Lombardia □ 18 45 35N 9 45 E
Lombardy = Lombardia □ 18 45 35N 9 45 E
Lomblen 35 8 30S 123 32 E
Lombok 34 8 45S 116 30 E
Lomé 53 6 9N 1 20 E
Lomela 54 2 19S 23 15 E
Lomela → 54 0 15S 20 40 E
Lometa 71 31 15N 98 25W
Lomié 54 3 13N 13 38 E
Lomond 64 50 24N 112 36W
Lomond, L. 8 56 8N 4 38W
Lompobatang 35 5 24S 119 56 E
Lompoc 73 34 41N 120 32W
Łomza 15 53 10N 22 2 E
Loncoche 80 39 20S 72 50W
Londa 32 15 30N 74 30 E
Londiani 52 0 10S 35 33 E
London, Canada 62 42 59N 81 15W
London, U.K. 7 51 30N 0 5W
London, Ky., U.S.A. 68 37 11N 84 5W
London, Ohio, U.S.A. 68 39 54N 83 28W
London, Greater □ 7 51 30N 0 5W
Londonderry 9 55 0N 7 20W
Londonderry □ 9 55 0N 7 20W
Londonderry, C. 46 13 45S 126 55 E
Londonderry, I. 80 55 0S 71 0W
Londrina 80 23 18S 51 10W
Lone Pine 73 36 35N 118 2W
Long Beach, Calif., U.S.A. 73 33 46N 118 12W
Long Beach, Wash., U.S.A. 72 46 20N 124 1W
Long Branch 68 40 19N 74 0W
Long Creek 72 44 43N 119 6W
Long Eaton 6 52 54N 1 16W
Long I., Australia 44 22 8S 149 53 E
Long I., Bahamas 75 23 20N 75 10W
Long I., U.S.A. 68 40 50N 73 20W
Long L. 62 49 30N 86 50W
Long Pine 70 42 33N 99 41W
Long Pt. 63 48 47N 58 46W
Long Range Mts. 63 49 30N 57 30W
Long Xian 39 34 55N 106 55 E
Long Xuyen 34 10 19N 105 28 E
Long'an 39 23 10N 107 40 E
Longchuan 39 24 5N 115 17 E
Longde 38 35 30N 106 20 E
Longford, Australia 44 41 32S 147 3 E
Longford, Ireland 9 53 43N 7 50W
Longford □ 9 53 42N 7 45W
Longhua 38 41 18N 117 45 E
Longiram 34 0 5S 115 45 E
Longjiang 38 47 20N 123 12 E
Longkou 38 37 40N 120 18 E
Longlac 62 49 45N 86 25W
Longlin 39 24 47N 105 20 E
Longmen 39 23 40N 114 18 E
Longmont 70 40 10N 105 4W
Longnan 39 24 55N 114 47 E
Longnawan 34 1 51N 114 55 E
Longone → 51 10 0N 15 40 E
Longquan 39 28 7N 119 10 E
Longreach 44 23 28S 144 14 E
Longshan 39 29 29N 109 25 E
Longsheng 39 25 48N 110 0 E
Longton 44 20 58S 145 55 E
Longtown 7 51 58N 2 59W
Longview, Canada 64 50 32N 114 10W
Longview, Tex., U.S.A. 71 32 30N 94 45W
Longview, Wash., U.S.A. 72 46 9N 122 58W
Longxi 38 34 53N 104 40 E

Longzhou

Longzhou 39 22 22N 106 50 E
Lonoke 71 34 48N 91 57W
Lons-le-Saunier 12 46 40N 5 31 E
Lookout, C., Canada 62 55 18N 83 56W
Lookout, C., U.S.A. 69 34 30N 76 30W
Loon →, Alta., Canada 64 57 8N 115 3W
Loon →, Man., Canada 65 55 53N 101 59W
Loon Lake 65 54 2N 109 10W
Loongana 47 30 52S 127 5 E
Loop Hd. 9 52 34N 9 55W
Lop Nor = Lop Nur 37 40 20N 90 10 E
Lop Nur 37 40 20N 90 10 E
Lopatina, G. 25 50 47N 143 10 E
Lopez, C. 54 0 47S 8 40 E
Lopphavet 44 70 27N 21 15 E
Lora → 31 32 0N 67 15 E
Lora, Hamun-i- 31 29 38N 64 58 E
Lora Cr. → 45 28 10S 135 22 E
Lorain 68 41 28N 82 55W
Loralai 32 30 20N 68 41 E
Lorca 13 37 41N 1 42W
Lord Howe I. 40 31 33S 159 6 E
Lord Howe Ridge 40 30 0S 162 30 E
Lordsburg 73 32 22N 108 45W
Loreto, Brazil 79 7 5S 45 10W
Loreto, Italy 18 43 26N 13 36 E
Lorient 12 47 45N 3 23W
Loristān □ 30 33 20N 47 0 E
Lorn 8 56 26N 5 10W
Lorn, Firth of 8 56 20N 5 40W
Lorne 45 38 33S 143 59 E
Lorraine 12 48 30N 6 0 E
Lorrainville 62 47 21N 79 23W
Los Alamos 73 35 57N 106 17W
Los Andes 80 32 50S 70 40W
Los Angeles, Chile 80 37 28S 72 23W
Los Angeles, U.S.A. 73 34 0N 118 10W
Los Angeles Aqueduct 73 35 25N 118 0W
Los Banos 73 37 8N 120 56W
Los Blancos 80 23 40S 62 30W
Los Hermanos 75 11 45N 84 25W
Los Lunas 73 34 48N 106 47W
Los Mochis 74 25 45N 109 5W
Los Olivos 73 34 40N 120 7W
Los Roques 78 11 50N 66 45W
Los Testigos 78 11 23N 63 6W
Los Vilos 80 32 10S 71 30W
Loshkalakh 25 62 45N 147 20 E
Lošinj 18 44 30N 14 30 E
Lossiemouth 8 57 43N 3 17W
Lot □ 12 44 39N 1 40 E
Lot → 12 44 18N 0 20 E
Lot-et-Garonne □ 12 44 22N 0 30 E
Lota 80 37 5S 73 10W
Lothair 57 26 22S 30 27 E
Lothian □ 8 55 50N 3 0W
Loubomo 54 4 9S 12 47 E
Loudon 69 35 35N 84 22W
Louga 50 15 45N 16 5W
Loughborough 6 52 46N 1 11W
Loughrea 9 53 11N 8 33W
Loughros More B. 9 54 48N 8 30W
Louis Trichardt 57 23 1S 29 43 E
Louis XIV, Pte. 62 54 37N 79 45W
Louisa 68 38 5N 82 40W
Louisbourg 63 45 55N 60 0W
Louise I. 64 52 55N 131 50W
Louiseville 62 46 20N 72 56W
Louisiade Arch. 40 11 10S 153 0 E
Louisiana 70 39 25N 91 0W
Louisiana □ 71 30 50N 92 0W
Louisville, Ky., U.S.A. 68 38 15N 85 45W
Louisville, Miss., U.S.A. 71 33 7N 89 3W
Loulé 13 37 9N 8 0W
Loup City 70 41 19N 98 57W
Lourdes 12 43 6N 0 3W
Lourdes-du-Blanc-Sablon 63 51 24N 57 12W
Lourenço-Marques = Maputo 57 25 58S 32 32 E
Louth, Australia 45 30 30S 145 8 E
Louth, Ireland 9 53 47N 6 33W
Louth, U.K. 6 53 23N 0 0 E
Louth □ 9 53 55N 6 30W
Louvain = Leuven 11 50 52N 4 42 E
Louvière, La 11 50 27N 4 10 E
Louwsburg 57 27 37S 31 7 E
Love 65 53 29N 104 10W
Loveland 70 40 27N 105 4W
Lovell 72 44 51N 108 20W
Lovelock 72 40 17N 118 25W
Loviisa = Lovisa 21 60 28N 26 12 E
Loving 71 32 17N 104 4W
Lovington 71 33 0N 103 20W
Lovisa 21 60 28N 26 12 E
Low Pt. 47 32 25S 127 25 E
Lowell 68 42 38N 71 19W
Lower Arrow L. 64 49 40N 118 5W
Lower California = Baja California 74 31 10N 115 12W
Lower Hutt 43 41 10S 174 55 E
Lower L. 72 41 17N 120 3W
Lower Lake 72 38 56N 122 36W
Lower Post 64 59 58N 128 30W
Lower Red L. 70 48 0N 94 50W
Lowestoft 7 52 29N 1 44 E
Łowicz 15 52 6N 19 55 E
Lowville 68 43 48N 75 30W
Lowyar □ 31 34 0N 69 0 E
Loxton, Australia 45 34 28S 140 31 E
Loxton, S. Africa 56 31 30S 22 22 E
Loyalty Is. = Loyauté, Is. 40 21 0S 167 30 E
Loyang = Luoyang 39 34 40N 112 26 E
Loyauté, Is. 40 21 0S 167 30 E
Lozère □ 12 44 35N 3 30 E
Luachimo 54 7 23S 20 48 E
Luacono 54 11 15S 21 37 E
Lualaba → 54 0 26N 25 20 E
Lu'an 39 31 45N 116 29 E
Luan Xian 38 39 40N 118 40 E
Luanda 54 8 50S 13 15 E
Luangwa 55 15 35S 30 16 E
Luangwa → 55 14 25S 30 25 E
Luanping 38 40 53N 117 23 E
Luanshya 55 13 3S 28 28 E
Luapula → 54 9 26S 28 33 E
Luarca 13 43 32N 6 32W
Luashi 54 10 50S 23 36 E
Luau 54 10 40S 22 10 E
Lubalo 54 9 10S 19 15 E
Lubang Is. 35 13 50N 120 12 E
Lubbock 71 33 40N 101 53W
Lübeck 14 53 52N 10 41 E
Lubefu 54 4 47S 24 27 E
Lubero = Luofu 54 0 10S 29 15 E
Lubicon L. 64 56 23N 115 56W
Lublin 15 51 12N 22 38 E
Lubran 30 34 0N 36 0 E
Lubuagan 35 17 21N 121 10 E
Lubuk Antu 34 1 3N 111 50 E
Lubuklinggau 34 3 15S 102 55 E
Lubuksikaping 34 0 10N 100 15 E
Lubumbashi 55 11 40S 27 28 E
Lubutu 54 0 45S 26 30 E
Lucca 18 43 50N 10 30 E
Luce Bay 8 54 45N 4 48W
Lucea 75 18 25N 78 10W
Lucedale 69 30 55N 88 34W
Lucena, Phil. 35 13 56N 121 37 E
Lucena, Spain 13 37 27N 4 31W
Lučenec 15 48 18N 19 42 E
Lucerne = Luzern 14 47 3N 8 18 E
Lucira 55 14 0S 12 35 E
Luckenwalde 14 52 5N 13 11 E
Lucknow 33 26 50N 81 0 E
Lüda = Dalian 38 38 50N 121 40 E
Lüderitz 56 26 41S 15 8 E
Ludhiana 32 30 57N 75 56 E
Ludington 68 43 58N 86 27W
Ludlow, U.K. 7 52 23N 2 42W
Ludlow, U.S.A. 73 34 43N 116 10W
Ludvika 21 60 8N 15 14 E
Ludwigsburg 14 48 53N 9 11 E
Ludwigshafen 14 49 27N 8 27 E
Luebo 54 5 21S 21 23 E
Lüeyang 39 33 22N 106 10 E
Lufeng 39 22 57N 115 38 E
Lufira → 54 9 30S 27 0 E
Lufkin 71 31 25N 94 40W
Luga 22 58 40N 29 55 E
Lugang 39 24 4N 120 23 E
Lugano 14 46 0N 8 57 E
Lugansk = Voroshilovgrad 23 48 38N 39 15 E
Lugazi 52 0 32N 32 57 E
Lugh Ganana 29 3 48N 42 34 E
Lugnaquilla 9 52 58N 6 28W
Lugo 13 43 2N 7 35W
Lugoj 15 45 42N 21 57 E
Lugovoye 24 42 55N 72 43 E
Luiana 56 17 25S 22 59 E
Luís Correia 79 3 0S 41 35W
Luiza 54 7 40S 22 30 E
Luján 80 34 45S 59 5W
Lukanga Swamp 55 14 30S 27 40 E
Lukenie → 54 3 0S 18 50 E
Lukolela 54 1 10S 17 12 E
Łuków 15 51 55N 22 23 E
Lule älv → 20 65 35N 22 10 E
Luleå 20 65 35N 22 10 E
Lüleburgaz 30 41 23N 27 22 E
Luling 71 29 45N 97 40W
Lulong 38 39 53N 118 51 E
Lulonga → 54 1 0N 18 10 E
Lulua → 54 4 30S 20 30 E
Luluabourg = Kananga 54 5 55S 22 18 E
Lumai 55 13 13S 21 25 E
Lumajang 35 8 8S 113 13 E
Lumbala N'guimbo 55 14 18S 21 18 E
Lumberton, Miss., U.S.A. 71 31 4N 89 28W
Lumberton, N.C., U.S.A. 69 34 37N 78 59W
Lumberton, N. Mex., U.S.A. 73 36 58N 106 57W
Lumbwa 52 0 12S 35 28 E
Lumsden 43 45 44S 168 27 E
Lumut, Tg. 34 3 50S 105 58 E
Lund 72 38 53N 115 0W
Lundazi 55 12 20S 33 7 E
Lundu 34 1 40N 109 50 E
Lundy 7 51 10N 4 41W
Lune → 6 54 0N 2 51W
Lüneburg 14 53 15N 10 23 E
Lüneburg Heath = Lüneburger Heide 14 53 0N 10 0 E
Lüneburger Heide 14 53 0N 10 0 E
Lunenburg 63 44 22N 64 18W
Lunéville 12 48 36N 6 30 E
Lunglei 33 22 55N 92 45 E
Luni 32 26 0N 73 6 E
Luni → 32 24 41N 71 14 E
Luning 72 38 30N 118 10W
Luo He → 39 34 35N 110 20 E
Luobei 38 47 35N 130 50 E
Luocheng 39 24 48N 108 53 E
Luochuan 38 35 45N 109 26 E
Luoding 39 22 45N 111 40 E
Luodong 39 24 41N 121 46 E
Luofu 54 0 10S 29 15 E
Luoning 39 34 35N 111 40 E
Luoyang 39 34 40N 112 26 E
Luoyuan 39 26 28N 119 30 E
Luozi 54 4 54S 14 0 E
Łupków 12 49 15N 22 4 E
Luqa 18 35 48N 14 27 E
Luray 68 38 39N 78 26W
Luremo 54 8 30S 17 50 E
Lurgan 9 54 28N 6 20W
Lusaka 55 15 28S 28 16 E
Lusambo 54 4 58S 23 28 E
Luseland 65 52 5N 109 24W
Lushan 39 33 45N 112 55 E
Lushih 39 34 3N 111 3 E
Lushoto 54 4 47S 38 20 E
Lüshun 38 38 45N 121 15 E
Lusk 70 42 47N 104 27W
Luta = Dalian 38 38 50N 121 40 E
Luton 7 51 53N 0 24W
Lutong 34 4 28N 114 0 E
Lutsk 22 50 50N 25 15 E
Lutzputs 56 28 3S 20 40 E
Luverne 70 43 35N 96 12W
Luvua → 48 6 50S 27 30 E
Luwuk 35 0 56S 122 47 E
Luxembourg 11 49 37N 6 9 E
Luxembourg □ 11 49 58N 5 30 E
Luxembourg ■ 11 50 0N 6 0 E
Luxi 39 28 20N 110 7 E
Luxor = El Uqsur 51 25 41N 32 38 E
Luza 22 60 39N 47 10 E
Luzern 14 47 3N 8 18 E
Luzhai 39 24 29N 109 42 E
Luzhou 39 28 52N 105 20 E
Luziânia 79 16 20S 48 0W
Luzon 35 16 0N 121 0 E
Lvov 23 49 50N 24 0 E
Lyakhovskiye, Ostrova 25 73 40N 141 0 E
Lyallpur = Faisalabad 32 31 30N 73 5 E
Lycksele 20 64 38N 18 40 E
Lydda = Lod 28 31 57N 34 54 E
Lydenburg 57 25 10S 30 29 E
Lyell 43 41 48S 172 4 E
Lyell I. 64 52 40N 131 35W
Lyell Range 43 41 38S 172 20 E
Lyman 72 41 24N 110 15W
Lyme Regis 7 50 44N 2 57W
Lymington 7 50 46N 1 32W
Łyna → 15 54 37N 21 14 E
Lynchburg 68 37 23N 79 10W
Lynd → 44 16 28S 143 18 E
Lynd Ra. 45 25 30S 149 20 E
Lynden 72 48 56N 122 32W
Lyndhurst 45 30 15S 138 18 E
Lyndon → 47 23 29S 114 6 E
Lynher Reef 46 15 27S 121 55 E
Lynn 68 42 28N 70 57W
Lynn Canal 64 58 50N 135 20W
Lynn Lake 65 56 51N 101 3W
Lynton 7 51 14N 3 50W
Lynx L. 65 62 25N 106 15W
Lyon 12 45 46N 4 50 E
Lyonnais 12 45 45N 4 15 E
Lyons = Lyon 12 45 46N 4 50 E
Lyons, Colo., U.S.A. 70 40 17N 105 15W
Lyons, Ga., U.S.A. 69 32 10N 82 15W
Lyons, Kans., U.S.A. 70 38 24N 98 13W
Lyons, N.Y., U.S.A. 68 43 3N 77 0W
Lysva 22 58 7N 57 49 E
Lytle 71 29 14N 98 46W
Lyttelton 43 43 35S 172 44 E
Lytton 64 50 13N 121 31W
Lyubertsy 22 55 39N 37 50 E

M

Mā'ad 28 32 37N 35 36 E
Ma'alah 30 26 31N 47 20 E
Maamba 56 17 17S 26 28 E
Ma'ān 30 30 12N 35 44 E
Ma'anshan 39 31 44N 118 29 E
Maarianhamina 21 60 5N 19 55 E
Ma'arrat un Nu'man 30 35 38N 36 40 E
Maas → 11 51 45N 4 32 E
Maaseik 11 51 6N 5 45 E
Maassluis 11 51 56N 4 16 E
Maastricht 11 50 50N 5 40 E
Maave 57 21 4S 34 47 E
Mabel L. 64 50 35N 118 43W
Mablethorpe 6 53 21N 0 14 E
Mabrouk 50 19 29N 1 15W
Mabton 72 46 15N 120 12W
Macaé 79 22 20S 41 43W
McAlester 71 34 57N 95 46W
McAllen 71 26 12N 98 15W
Macamic 62 48 45N 79 0W
Macao = Macau ■ 39 22 16N 113 35 E
Macapá 79 0 5N 51 4W
McArthur → 44 15 54S 136 40 E
McArthur River 44 16 27S 136 7 E
Macau 79 5 0S 36 40W
Macau ■ 39 22 16N 113 35 E
McBride 64 53 20N 120 19W
McCall 72 44 55N 116 6W
McCamey 71 31 8N 102 15W
McCammon 72 42 41N 112 11W
McCauley I. 64 53 40N 130 15W
Macclesfield 6 53 16N 2 9W
McClintock 65 57 50N 94 10W
McClintock Ra. 46 18 44S 127 38 E
McCloud 72 41 14N 122 5W
McClure Str. 2 75 0N 119 0W
McClusky 70 47 30N 100 31W
McComb 71 31 13N 90 30W
McConaughy, L. 70 41 20N 101 40W
McCook 70 40 15N 100 35W
McCusker → 65 55 32N 108 39W
McDame 64 59 44N 128 59W
McDermitt 72 42 0N 117 45W
McDonald Is. 3 53 0S 73 0 E
Macdonald L. 46 23 30S 129 0 E
Macdonnell Ranges 46 23 40S 133 0 E
McDouall Peak 45 29 51S 134 55 E
Macdougall L. 60 66 0N 98 27W
MacDowell L. 62 52 15N 92 45W
Macduff 8 57 40N 2 30W
Macedonia = Makedhonía □ 19 40 39N 22 0 E
Macedonia = Makedonija □ 19 41 53N 21 40 E
Maceió 79 9 40S 35 41W
Macenta 50 8 35N 9 32W
Macerata 18 43 19N 13 28 E
McFarlane → 65 59 12N 107 58W
Macfarlane, L. 45 32 0S 136 40 E
McGehee 71 33 40N 91 25W
McGill 72 39 27N 114 50W
Macgillycuddy's Reeks 9 52 2N 9 45W
MacGregor 65 49 57N 98 48W
McGregor 70 43 0N 91 15W
McGregor → 64 55 10N 122 0W
McGregor Ra. 45 27 0S 142 45 E
Mach 31 29 50N 67 20 E
Machado = Jiparaná → 78 8 3S 62 52W
Machakos 54 1 30S 37 15 E
Machala 78 3 20S 79 57W
Machanga 57 20 59S 35 0 E
Machattie, L. 44 24 50S 139 48 E
Machava 57 25 54S 32 28 E
Macheng 39 31 12N 115 2 E
Machevna 25 61 20N 172 20 E
Machias 63 44 40N 67 28W
Machichi → 65 57 3N 92 6W
Machilipatnam 33 16 12N 81 8 E
Machiques 78 10 4N 72 34W
Machupicchu 78 13 8S 72 30W
Machynlleth 7 52 36N 3 51W
McIlwraith Ra. 44 13 50S 143 20 E
McIntosh 70 45 57N 101 20W
McIntosh L. 65 55 45N 105 0W
Macintyre → 45 28 37S 150 47 E
Mackay, Australia 44 21 8S 149 11 E
Mackay, U.S.A. 72 43 58N 113 37W
MacKay → 64 57 10N 111 38W
Mackay, L. 46 22 30S 129 0 E
McKay Ra. 46 23 0S 122 30 E
McKeesport 68 40 21N 79 50W
Mackenzie 64 55 20N 123 5W
McKenzie 69 36 10N 88 31W
Mackenzie →, Australia 44 23 38S 149 46 E
Mackenzie →, Canada 60 69 10N 134 20W
McKenzie → 72 44 2N 123 6W
Mackenzie City = Linden 78 6 0N 58 10W
Mackenzie Highway 64 58 0N 117 15W
Mackenzie Mts. 60 64 0N 130 0W
Mackinaw City 68 45 47N 84 44W
McKinlay 44 21 16S 141 18 E
McKinlay → 44 20 50S 141 28 E
McKinley, Mt. 60 63 2N 151 0W
McKinney 71 33 10N 96 40W
Mackintosh Ra. 47 27 39S 125 32 E
Macksville 45 30 40S 152 56 E
McLaughlin 70 45 50N 100 50W
Maclean 45 29 26S 153 16 E
McLean 71 35 15N 100 35W
McLeansboro 70 38 5N 88 30W
Maclear 57 31 2S 28 23 E
Macleay → 45 30 56S 153 0 E
McLennan 64 55 42N 116 50W
MacLeod, B. 65 62 53N 110 0W
McLeod L. 47 24 9S 113 47 E
MacLeod Lake 64 54 58N 123 0W
M'Clintock Chan. 60 72 0N 102 0W
McLoughlin, Mt. 72 42 10N 122 19W
McLure 64 51 2N 120 13W
McMillan L. 71 32 40N 104 20W
McMinnville, Oreg., U.S.A. 72 45 16N 123 11W
McMinnville, Tenn., U.S.A. 69 35 43N 85 45W
McMorran 65 51 19N 108 42W
McMurray = Fort McMurray 64 56 44N 111 7W
McNary 73 34 4N 109 53W
MacNutt 65 51 5N 101 36W
Macodoene 57 23 32S 35 5 E
Macomb 70 40 25N 90 40W
Mâcon, France 12 46 19N 4 50 E
Macon, Ga., U.S.A. 69 32 50N 83 37W
Macon, Miss., U.S.A. 69 33 7N 88 31W
Macon, Mo., U.S.A. 70 39 40N 92 26W
Macondo 55 12 37S 23 46 E
Macoun L. 65 56 32N 103 40W
Macovane 57 21 30S 35 0 E
McPherson 70 38 25N 97 40W
Macpherson Ra. 45 28 15S 153 15 E
Macquarie Harbour 44 42 15S 145 23 E
Macquarie Is. 40 54 36S 158 55 E
Macroom 9 51 54N 8 57W
Macroy 46 20 53S 118 2 E
Macuspana 74 17 46N 92 36W
Macusse 56 17 48S 20 23 E
McVille 70 47 46N 98 11W
Madadeni 57 27 43S 30 3 E
Madagali 53 10 56N 13 33 E
Madagascar ■ 57 20 0S 47 0 E
Madā'in Sālih 30 26 46N 37 57 E
Madama 51 22 0N 13 40 E
Madame I. 63 45 30N 60 58W
Madang 40 5 12S 145 49 E
Madaoua 53 14 5N 6 27 E
Madaripur 33 23 19N 90 15 E
Madauk 33 17 56N 96 52 E
Madawaska → 62 45 27N 76 21W
Madaya 33 22 12N 96 10 E
Madden Dam 74 9 13N 79 37W
Madden Lake 74 9 20N 79 37W
Madeira 50 32 50N 17 0W
Madeira → 78 3 22S 58 45W
Madeleine, Is. de la 63 47 30N 61 40W
Madera 73 36 58N 120 1W
Madha 32 18 0N 75 30 E
Madhya Pradesh □ 32 21 50N 81 0 E
Madikeri 32 12 30N 75 45 E
Madill 71 34 5N 96 49W
Madimba 54 5 0S 15 0 E
Madīnat ash Sha'b 29 12 50N 45 0 E
Madingou 54 4 10S 13 33 E
Madirovalo 57 16 26S 46 32 E
Madison, Fla., U.S.A. 69 30 29N 83 39W
Madison, Ind., U.S.A. 68 38 42N 85 20W
Madison, Nebr., U.S.A. 70 41 53N 97 25W
Madison, S. Dak., U.S.A. 70 44 0N 97 8W
Madison, Wis., U.S.A. 70 43 5N 89 25W
Madison → 72 45 56N 111 30W
Madisonville, Ky., U.S.A. 68 37 20N 87 30W
Madisonville, Tex., U.S.A. 71 30 57N 95 55W
Madista 56 21 15S 25 6 E
Madiun 35 7 38S 111 32 E
Madley 7 52 3N 2 51W
Madras = Tamil Nadu □ 32 11 0N 77 0 E
Madras, India 32 13 8N 80 19 E
Madras, U.S.A. 72 44 40N 121 10W
Madre, L., Mexico 74 25 0N 97 30W
Madre, L., U.S.A. 71 26 0N 97 40W
Madre, Sierra, Mexico 74 16 0N 93 0W

Maracay

Madre, Sierra, Phil. 35 17 0N 122 0 E
Madre de Dios → 78 10 59S 66 8W
Madre de Dios, I. 80 50 20S 75 10W
Madre del Sur, Sierra 74 17 30N 100 0W
Madre Occidental, Sierra 74 27 0N 107 0W
Madre Oriental, Sierra 74 25 0N 100 0W
Madrid 13 40 25N 3 45W
Madura, Selat 35 7 30S 113 20 E
Madura Motel 47 31 55S 127 0 E
Madurai 32 9 55N 78 10 E
Madurantakam 32 12 30N 79 50 E
Mae Sot 34 16 43N 98 34 E
Maebashi 36 36 24N 139 4 E
Maesteg 7 51 36N 3 40W
Maestra, Sierra 75 20 15N 77 0W
Maestrazgo, Mts. del 13 40 30N 0 25W
Maevatanana 57 16 56S 46 49 E
Mafeking 65 52 40N 101 10W
Mafeteng 56 29 51S 27 15 E
Maffra 45 37 53S 146 58 E
Mafia I. 54 7 45S 39 50 E
Mafikeng 56 25 50S 25 38 E
Mafra, Brazil 80 26 10S 50 0W
Mafra, Portugal 13 38 55N 9 20W
Magadan 25 59 38N 150 50 E
Magadi 54 1 54S 36 19 E
Magaliesburg 57 26 0S 27 32 E
Magallanes, Estrecho de 80 52 30S 75 0W
Magangué 78 9 14N 74 45W
Magburaka 50 8 47N 12 0W
Magdalena, Argentina 80 35 5S 57 30W
Magdalena, Bolivia 78 13 13S 63 57W
Magdalena, Malaysia 34 4 25N 117 55 E
Magdalena, Mexico 74 30 50N 112 0W
Magdalena, U.S.A. 73 34 10N 107 20W
Magdalena →, Colombia 78 11 6N 74 51W
Magdalena →, Mexico 74 30 40N 112 25W
Magdalena, B. 74 24 30N 112 10W
Magdalena, Llano de la 74 25 0N 111 30W
Magdeburg 14 52 8N 11 36 E
Magdelaine Cays 44 16 33S 150 18 E
Magdi'el 28 32 10N 34 54 E
Magee 71 31 53N 89 44W
Magee, I. 9 54 48N 5 44W
Magelang 35 7 29S 110 13 E
Magellan's Str. = Magallanes, Estrecho de 80 52 30S 75 0W
Magenta, L. 47 33 30S 119 2 E
Maggiore, L. 18 46 0N 8 35 E
Maghâr 28 32 54N 35 24 E
Magherafelt 9 54 44N 6 37W
Magnitogorsk 22 53 27N 59 4 E
Magnolia, Ark., U.S.A. 71 33 18N 93 12W
Magnolia, Miss., U.S.A. 71 31 8N 90 28W
Magog 63 45 18N 72 9W
Magosa = Famagusta 30 35 8N 33 55 E
Magpie L. 63 51 0N 64 41W
Magrath 64 49 25N 112 50W
Maguarinho, C. 79 0 15S 48 30W
Maguse L. 65 61 40N 95 10W
Maguse Pt. 65 61 20N 93 50W
Magwe 33 20 10N 95 0 E
Mahābād 30 36 50N 45 45 E
Mahabo 57 20 23S 44 40 E
Mahagi 54 2 20N 31 0 E
Mahajamba → 57 15 33S 47 8 E
Mahajamba, Helodranon' i 57 15 24S 47 5 E
Mahajanga 57 15 40S 46 25 E
Mahajanga □ 57 17 0S 47 0 E
Mahajilo → 57 19 42S 45 22 E
Mahakam → 34 0 35S 117 17 E
Mahalapye 56 23 1S 26 51 E
Mahallāt 31 33 55N 50 30 E
Mahanadi → 33 20 20N 86 25 E
Mahanoro 57 19 54S 48 48 E
Maharashtra □ 32 20 30N 75 30 E
Mahari Mts. 52 6 20S 30 0 E
Mahasolo 57 19 7S 46 22 E
Mahbubnagar 32 16 45N 77 59 E
Mahdia 51 35 28N 11 0 E
Mahé 3 5 0S 55 30 E
Mahenge 54 8 45S 36 41 E
Maheno 43 45 10S 170 50 E
Mahesana 32 23 39N 72 26 E
Mahia Pen. 43 39 9S 177 55 E
Mahnomen 70 47 22N 95 57W
Mahón 13 39 53N 4 16 E
Mahone Bay 63 44 30N 64 20W
Mai-Ndombe, L. 54 2 0S 18 20 E
Maicurú → 79 2 14S 54 17W
Maidenhead 7 51 31N 0 42W
Maidstone, Canada 65 53 5N 109 20W
Maidstone, U.K. 7 51 16N 0 31 E
Maiduguri 53 12 0N 13 20 E
Maijdi 33 22 48N 91 10 E
Maikala Ra. 33 22 0N 81 0 E
Main →, Germany 14 50 0N 8 18 E
Main →, U.K. 9 54 49N 6 20W
Main Centre 65 50 35N 107 21W
Maine 12 48 0N 0 0 E
Maine □ 63 45 20N 69 0W
Maine → 9 52 10N 9 40W
Maine-et-Loire □ 12 47 31N 0 30W
Maingkwan 33 26 15N 96 37 E
Mainit, L. 35 9 31N 125 30 E
Mainland, Orkney, U.K. 8 59 0N 3 10W
Mainland, Shetland, U.K. 8 60 15N 1 22W
Maintirano 57 18 3S 44 1 E
Mainz 14 50 0N 8 17 E
Maipú 80 36 52S 57 50W
Maiquetía 78 10 36N 66 57W
Mairabari 33 26 30N 92 22 E
Maisi, Pta. de 75 20 10N 74 10W
Maitland, N.S.W., Australia 45 32 33S 151 36 E
Maitland, S. Austral., Australia 45 34 23S 137 40 E
Maiz, Is. del 75 12 15N 83 4W
Maizuru 36 35 25N 135 22 E
Majalengka 35 6 50S 108 13 E
Majd el Kurūm 28 32 56N 35 15 E
Majene 35 3 38S 118 57 E
Maji 51 6 12N 35 30 E
Major 65 51 52N 109 37W
Majorca, I. = Mallorca 13 39 30N 3 0 E
Maka 50 13 40N 14 10W
Makale 35 3 6S 119 51 E
Makari 54 12 35N 14 28 E
Makarikari = Makgadikgadi Salt Pans 56 20 40S 25 45 E
Makarovo 25 57 40N 107 45 E
Makasar = Ujung Pandang 35 5 10S 119 20 E
Makasar, Selat 35 1 0S 118 20 E
Makat 23 47 39N 53 19 E
Makedhonía □ 19 40 39N 22 0 E
Makedonija □ 19 41 53N 21 40 E
Makena 66 20 39N 156 27W
Makeni 50 8 55N 12 5W
Makeyevka 23 48 0N 38 0 E
Makgadikgadi Salt Pans 56 20 40S 25 45 E
Makhachkala 23 43 0N 47 30 E
Makian 35 0 20N 127 20 E
Makindu 54 2 18S 37 50 E
Makinsk 24 52 37N 70 26 E
Makkah 29 21 30N 39 54 E
Makkovik 63 55 10N 59 10W
Maklakovo 25 58 16N 92 29 E
Makó 15 46 14N 20 33 E
Makokou 54 0 40N 12 50 E
Makoua 54 0 5S 15 50 E
Makrai 32 22 2N 77 0 E
Makran 31 26 13N 61 30 E
Makran Coast Range 31 25 40N 64 0 E
Maksimkin Yar 24 58 42N 86 50 E
Mākū 30 39 15N 44 31 E
Makumbi 54 5 50S 20 43 E
Makunda 56 22 30S 20 7 E
Makurazaki 36 31 15N 130 20 E
Makurdi 53 7 43N 8 35 E
Makwassie 56 27 17S 26 0 E
Mal B. 9 52 50N 9 30W
Mala, Pta. 75 7 28N 80 2W
Malabang 35 7 36N 124 3 E
Malabar Coast 32 11 0N 75 0 E
Malacca, Str. of 34 3 0N 101 0 E
Malad City 72 42 10N 112 20 E
Málaga, Spain 13 36 43N 4 23W
Malaga, U.S.A. 71 32 12N 104 2W
Málaga □ 13 36 38N 4 58W
Malaimbandy 57 20 20S 45 36 E
Malakâl 51 9 33N 31 40 E
Malakand 32 34 40N 71 55 E
Malakoff 71 32 10N 95 55W
Malamyzh 25 50 0N 136 50 E
Malang 35 7 59S 112 45 E
Malange 54 9 36S 16 17 E
Mälaren 21 59 30N 17 10 E
Malargüe 80 35 32S 69 30W
Malartic 62 48 9N 78 9W
Malatya 30 38 25N 38 20 E
Malawi ■ 55 11 55S 34 0 E
Malawi, L. 55 12 30S 34 30 E
Malay Pen. 34 7 25N 100 0 E
Malaybalay 35 8 5N 125 7 E
Malāyer 30 34 19N 48 51 E
Malaysia ■ 34 5 0N 110 0 E
Malazgirt 30 39 10N 42 33 E
Malbaie, La 63 47 40N 70 10W
Malbon 44 21 5S 140 17 E
Malbooma 45 30 41S 134 11 E
Malbork 15 54 3N 19 1 E
Malcolm 47 28 51S 121 25 E
Malcolm, Pt. 47 33 48S 123 45 E
Maldegem 11 51 14N 3 26 E
Malden 71 36 35N 90 0W
Malden I. 41 4 3S 155 1W
Maldives ■ 3 5 0N 73 0 E
Maldonado 80 35 0S 55 0W
Maldonado, Punta 74 16 19N 98 35W
Malé Karpaty 14 48 30N 17 20 E
Maléa, Ákra 19 36 28N 23 7 E
Malegaon 32 20 30N 74 38 E
Malema 55 14 57S 37 20 E
Malgomaj 20 64 40N 16 30 E
Malha 51 15 8N 25 10 E
Malhão, Sa. do 13 37 25N 8 0W
Malheur → 72 44 3N 116 59W
Malheur L. 72 43 19N 118 42W
Mali ■ 50 17 0N 3 0W
Mali → 33 25 40N 97 40 E
Malih → 28 32 20N 35 34 E
Malik 35 0 39S 123 16 E
Malili 35 2 42S 121 6 E
Malindi 54 3 12S 40 5 E
Malines = Mechelen 11 51 2N 4 29 E
Maling 35 1 0N 121 0 E
Malita 35 6 19N 125 39 E
Mallacoota Inlet 45 37 34S 149 40 E
Mallaig 8 57 0N 5 50W
Mallawi 51 27 44N 30 44 E
Mallorca 13 39 30N 3 0 E
Mallow 9 52 8N 8 40W
Malmberget 20 67 11N 20 40 E
Malmédy 11 50 25N 6 2 E
Malmesbury 56 33 28S 18 41 E
Malmö 21 55 36N 12 59 E
Malmöhus län □ 21 55 45N 13 30 E
Malolos 35 14 50N 120 49 E
Malone 68 44 50N 74 19W
Malozemelskaya Tundra 22 67 0N 50 0 E
Malpelo 78 4 3N 81 35W
Malta, Idaho, U.S.A. 72 42 15N 113 30W
Malta, Mont., U.S.A. 72 48 20N 107 55W
Malta ■ 18 35 50N 14 30 E
Maltahöhe 56 24 55S 17 0 E
Malton 6 54 9N 0 48W
Maluku 35 1 0S 127 0 E
Maluku □ 35 3 0S 128 0 E
Malvan 32 16 2N 73 30 E
Malvern, U.K. 7 52 7N 2 19W
Malvern, U.S.A. 71 34 22N 92 50W
Malvern Hills 7 52 0N 2 19W
Malvinas, Is. = Falkland Is. 80 51 30S 59 0W
Malyy Lyakhovskiy, Ostrov 25 74 7N 140 36 E
Mama 25 58 18N 112 54 E
Mamahatun 30 39 50N 40 23 E
Mamaia 15 44 18N 28 37 E
Mamanguape 79 6 50S 35 4W
Mamasa 35 2 55S 119 20 E
Mambasa 52 1 22N 29 3 E
Mamberamo → 35 2 0S 137 50 E
Mambilima Falls 54 10 31S 28 45 E
Mamburao 35 13 13N 120 39 E
Mameigwess L. 62 52 35N 87 50W
Mamfe 53 5 50N 9 15 E
Mammoth 73 32 46N 110 43W
Mamoré → 78 10 23S 65 53W
Mamou 50 10 15N 12 0W
Mamuju 35 2 41S 118 50 E
Man 50 7 30N 7 40W
Man, I. of 6 54 15N 4 30W
Man Na 33 23 27N 97 19 E
Mana 79 5 45N 53 55W
Manaar, Gulf of = Mannar, G. of 32 8 30N 79 0 E
Manacapuru 78 3 16S 60 37W
Manacor 13 39 34N 3 13 E
Manado 35 1 29N 124 51 E
Managua 75 12 6N 86 20W
Managua, L. 75 12 20N 86 30W
Manakara 57 22 8S 48 1 E
Manambao → 57 17 35S 44 0 E
Manambato 57 13 43S 49 7 E
Manambolo → 57 19 18S 44 22 E
Manambolosy 57 16 2S 49 40 E
Mananara 57 16 10S 49 46 E
Mananara → 57 23 21S 47 42 E
Mananjary 57 21 13S 48 20 E
Manantenina 57 24 17S 47 19 E
Manaos = Manaus 78 3 0S 60 0W
Manapouri 43 45 34S 167 39 E
Manapouri, L. 43 45 32S 167 32 E
Manas 37 44 17N 85 56 E
Manas → 33 26 12N 90 40 E
Manasir 31 24 30N 51 10 E
Manassa 73 37 12N 105 58W
Manaung 33 18 45N 93 40 E
Manaus 78 3 0S 60 0W
Manawan L. 65 55 24N 103 14W
Manay 35 7 17N 126 33 E
Mancelona 68 44 54N 85 5W
Mancha, La 13 39 10N 2 54W
Manche □ 12 49 10N 1 20W
Manchegorsk 22 67 40N 32 40 E
Manchester, U.K. 6 53 30N 2 15W
Manchester, Conn., U.S.A. 68 41 47N 72 30W
Manchester, Ga., U.S.A. 69 32 53N 84 32W
Manchester, Iowa, U.S.A. 70 42 28N 91 27W
Manchester, Ky., U.S.A. 68 37 9N 83 45W
Manchester, N.H., U.S.A. 68 42 58N 71 29W
Manchester L. 65 61 28N 107 29W
Mand → 31 28 20N 52 30 E
Manda 54 10 30S 34 40 E
Mandabé 57 21 0S 44 55 E
Mandal 21 58 2N 7 25 E
Mandalay 33 22 0N 96 4 E
Mandale = Mandalay 33 22 0N 96 4 E
Mandalī 30 33 43N 45 28 E
Mandan 70 46 50N 101 0W
Mandar, Teluk 35 3 35S 119 15 E
Mandasor = Mandsaur 32 24 3N 75 8 E
Mandaue 35 10 20N 123 56 E
Mandi 32 31 39N 76 58 E
Mandimba 55 14 20S 35 40 E
Mandioli 35 0 40S 127 20 E
Mandla 33 22 39N 80 30 E
Mandoto 57 19 34S 46 17 E
Mandrare → 57 25 10S 46 30 E
Mandritsara 57 15 50S 48 49 E
Mandsaur 32 24 3N 75 8 E
Mandurah 47 32 36S 115 48 E
Mandvi 32 22 51N 69 22 E
Mandya 32 12 30N 77 0 E
Maneroo 44 23 22S 143 53 E
Maneroo Cr. → 44 23 21S 143 53 E
Manfalût 51 27 20N 30 52 E
Manfred 45 33 19S 143 45 E
Mangaia 43 21 55S 157 55W
Mangalia 15 43 50N 28 35 E
Mangalore 32 12 55N 74 47 E
Manggar 34 2 50S 108 10 E
Manggawitu 35 4 8S 133 32 E
Mangkalihat, Tanjung 35 1 2N 118 59 E
Mangla Dam 32 33 9N 73 44 E
Mangnai 37 37 52N 91 43 E
Mango 53 10 20N 0 30 E
Mangoche 55 14 25S 35 16 E
Mangoky → 57 21 29S 43 41 E
Mangole 35 1 50S 125 55 E
Mangonui 43 35 1S 173 32 E
Mangueigne 51 10 30N 21 15 E
Mangueira, L. da 80 33 0S 52 50W
Mangum 71 34 50N 99 30W
Manhattan 70 39 10N 96 40W
Manhiça 57 25 23S 32 49 E
Manhuaçu 79 20 15S 42 2W
Mania → 57 19 42S 45 22 E
Manica 57 18 58S 32 59 E
Manica e Sofala □ 57 19 10S 33 45 E
Manicoré 78 5 48S 61 16W
Manicouagan → 63 49 30N 68 30W
Manifah 30 27 44N 49 0 E
Manifold 44 22 41S 150 40 E
Manifold, C. 44 22 41S 150 50 E
Manigotagan 65 51 6N 96 18W
Manihiki 41 10 24S 161 1W
Manila, Phil. 35 14 40N 121 3 E
Manila, U.S.A. 72 41 0N 109 44W
Manila Bay 35 14 0N 120 0 E
Manilla 45 30 45S 150 43 E
Manipur □ 33 25 0N 94 0 E
Manipur → 33 23 45N 94 20 E
Manisa 30 38 38N 27 30 E
Manistee 68 44 15N 86 20W
Manistee → 68 44 15N 86 21W
Manistique 68 45 59N 86 18W
Manito L. 65 52 43N 109 43W
Manitoba □ 65 55 30N 97 0W
Manitoba, L. 65 51 0N 98 45W
Manitou 65 49 15N 98 32W
Manitou I. 62 47 22N 87 30W
Manitou Is. 68 45 8N 86 0W
Manitou L. 63 50 55N 65 17W
Manitou Springs 70 38 52N 104 55W
Manitoulin I. 62 45 40N 82 30W
Manitowaning 62 45 46N 81 49W
Manitowoc 68 44 8N 87 40W
Manizales 78 5 5N 75 32W
Manja 57 21 26S 44 20 E
Manjacaze 57 24 45S 34 0 E
Manjakandriana 57 18 55S 47 47 E
Manjhand 32 25 50N 68 10 E
Manjil 30 36 46N 49 30 E
Manjimup 47 34 15S 116 6 E
Manjra → 32 18 49N 77 52 E
Mankato, Kans., U.S.A. 70 39 49N 98 11W
Mankato, Minn., U.S.A. 70 44 8N 93 59W
Mankayane 57 26 40S 31 4 E
Mankono 50 8 1N 6 10W
Mankota 65 49 25N 107 5W
Manly 45 33 48S 151 17 E
Manmad 32 20 18N 74 28 E
Mann Ranges, Mts. 47 26 6S 130 5 E
Manna 34 4 25S 102 55 E
Mannahill 45 32 25S 140 0 E
Mannar 32 9 1N 79 54 E
Mannar, G. of 32 8 30N 79 0 E
Mannar I. 32 9 5N 79 45 E
Mannheim 14 49 28N 8 29 E
Manning, Canada 64 56 53N 117 39W
Manning, U.S.A. 69 33 40N 80 9W
Manning Prov. Park 64 49 5N 120 45W
Mannington 68 39 35N 80 25W
Mannum 45 34 50S 139 20 E
Mano 50 8 3N 12 2W
Manokwari 35 0 54S 134 0 E
Manombo 57 22 57S 43 28 E
Manono 54 7 15S 27 25 E
Manouane, L. 63 50 45N 70 45W
Manresa 13 41 48N 1 50 E
Mans, Le 12 48 0N 0 10 E
Mansa 54 11 13S 28 55 E
Mansel I. 61 62 0N 80 0W
Mansfield, Australia 45 37 4S 146 6 E
Mansfield, U.K. 6 53 8N 1 12W
Mansfield, La., U.S.A. 71 32 2N 93 40W
Mansfield, Ohio, U.S.A. 68 40 45N 82 30W
Mansfield, Wash., U.S.A. 72 47 51N 119 44W
Manson Creek 64 55 37N 124 32W
Manta 78 1 0S 80 40W
Mantalingajan, Mt. 34 8 55N 117 45 E
Manteca 73 37 50N 121 12W
Manteo 69 35 55N 75 41W
Mantes-la-Jolie 12 49 0N 1 41 E
Manthani 32 18 40N 79 35 E
Manti 72 39 23N 111 32W
Mantiqueira, Serra da 79 22 0S 44 0W
Manton 68 44 23N 85 25W
Mántova 18 45 20N 10 42 E
Mänttä 20 62 0N 24 40 E
Mantua = Mántova 18 45 20N 10 42 E
Manu 78 12 10S 70 51W
Manua Is. 43 14 13S 169 35W
Manuae 41 19 30S 159 0W
Manuel Alves → 79 11 19S 48 28W
Manui 35 3 35S 123 5 E
Manville 70 42 48N 104 36W
Many 71 31 36N 93 28W
Manyara, L. 54 3 40S 35 50 E
Manych-Gudilo, Oz. 23 46 24N 42 38 E
Manyoni 54 5 45S 34 55 E
Manzai 32 32 12N 70 15 E
Manzanares 13 39 0N 3 22W
Manzanillo, Cuba 75 20 20N 77 31W
Manzanillo, Mexico 74 19 0N 104 20W
Manzanillo, Pta. 75 9 30N 79 40W
Manzano Mts. 73 34 30N 106 45W
Manzhouli 38 49 35N 117 25 E
Manzini 57 26 30S 31 25 E
Mao 51 14 4N 15 19 E
Maoke, Pegunungan 35 3 40S 137 30 E
Maoming 39 21 50N 110 54 E
Mapam Yumco 33 30 45N 81 28 E
Mapia, Kepulauan 35 0 50N 134 20 E
Mapimí 74 25 50N 103 50W
Mapimí, Bolsón de 74 27 30N 104 15W
Mapinhane 57 22 20S 35 0 E
Maple Creek 65 49 55N 109 29W
Mapleton 72 44 4N 123 58W
Mapuera → 78 1 5S 57 2W
Maputo 57 25 58S 32 32 E
Maputo, B. de 57 25 50S 32 45 E
Maqnā 30 28 25N 34 50 E
Maquela do Zombo 54 6 0S 15 15 E
Maquinchao 80 41 15S 68 50W
Maquoketa 70 42 4N 90 40W
Mar, Serra do 80 25 30S 49 0W
Mar Chiquita, L. 80 30 40S 62 50W
Mar del Plata 80 38 0S 57 30W
Mara 52 1 30S 34 32 E
Maraā 78 1 52S 65 25W
Marabá 79 5 20S 49 5W
Maracá, I. de 79 2 10N 50 30W
Maracaibo 78 10 40N 71 37W
Maracaibo, L. de 78 9 40N 71 30W
Maracay 78 10 15N 67 28W

Marādah

Marādah 51 29 15N 19 15 E
Maradi 53 13 29N 7 20 E
Marāgheh 30 37 30N 46 12 E
Marāh 30 25 0N 45 35 E
Marajó, I. de 79 1 0S 49 30W
Maralal 54 1 0N 36 38 E
Maralinga 47 30 13S 131 32 E
Marama 45 35 10S 140 10 E
Marampa 50 8 45N 12 28W
Marana 73 32 30N 111 9W
Maranboy 46 14 40S 132 39 E
Marand 30 38 30N 45 45 E
Maranguape 79 3 55S 38 50W
Maranhão = São Luís 79 2 39S 44 15W
Maranhão □ 79 5 0S 46 0W
Maranoa → 45 27 50S 148 37 E
Marañón → 78 4 30S 73 35W
Marão 57 24 18S 34 2 E
Marathon, Australia 44 20 51S 143 32 E
Marathon, Canada 62 48 44N 86 23W
Marathón, Greece 19 38 11N 23 58 E
Marathon, U.S.A. 71 30 15N 103 15W
Maratua 35 2 10N 118 35 E
Marbella 13 36 30N 4 57W
Marble Bar 46 21 9S 119 44 E
Marble Falls 71 30 30N 98 15W
Marburg 14 50 49N 8 36 E
March 7 52 33N 0 5 E
Marche 12 46 5N 1 20 E
Marche □ 18 43 22N 13 10 E
Marche-en-Famenne 11 50 14N 5 19 E
Marches = Marche □ 18 43 22N 13 10 E
Marcus 40 24 0N 153 45 E
Marcus Necker Ridge 40 20 0N 175 0 E
Mardan 32 34 20N 72 0 E
Mardie 46 21 12S 115 59 E
Mardin 30 37 20N 40 43 E
Maree L. 8 57 40N 5 30W
Mareeba 44 16 59S 145 28 E
Marek = Stanke Dimitrov 19 42 17N 23 9 E
Marek 35 4 41S 120 24 E
Maremma 18 42 45N 11 15 E
Marengo 70 41 42N 92 5W
Marerano 57 21 23S 44 52 E
Marfa 71 30 15N 104 0W
Margaret Bay 64 51 20N 127 35W
Margaret L. 64 58 56N 115 25W
Margarita 74 9 20N 79 55W
Margarita, I. de 78 11 0N 64 0W
Margate, S. Africa 57 30 50S 30 20 E
Margate, U.K. 7 51 23N 1 24 E
Margelan 24 40 27N 71 42 E
Marguerite 64 52 30N 122 25W
Mari A.S.S.R. □ 22 56 30N 48 0 E
Maria I., N. Terr., Australia 44 14 52S 135 45 E
Maria I., Tas., Australia 44 42 35S 148 0 E
Maria van Diemen, C. 43 34 29S 172 40 E
Marian L. 64 63 0N 116 15W
Mariana Trench 40 13 0N 145 0 E
Marianao 75 23 8N 82 24W
Marianna, Ark., U.S.A. 71 34 48N 90 48W
Marianna, Fla., U.S.A. 69 30 45N 85 15W
Marias → 72 47 56N 110 30W
Mariato, Punta 75 7 12N 80 52W
Ma'rib 29 15 25N 45 21 E
Maribor 18 46 36N 15 40 E
Marico → 56 23 35S 26 57 E
Maricopa, Ariz., U.S.A. 73 33 5N 112 2W
Maricopa, Calif., U.S.A. 73 35 7N 119 27W
Marīdī 51 4 55N 29 25 E
Marie-Galante 75 15 56N 61 16W
Mariecourt 61 61 30N 72 0W
Mariehamn 21 60 5N 19 55 E
Marienberg 11 52 30N 6 35 E
Marienbourg 11 50 6N 4 31 E
Mariental 56 24 36S 18 0 E
Mariestad 21 58 43N 13 50 E
Marietta, Ga., U.S.A. 69 34 0N 84 30W
Marietta, Ohio, U.S.A. 68 39 27N 81 27W
Mariinsk 24 56 10N 87 20 E
Marília 79 22 13S 50 0W
Marillana 46 22 37S 119 16 E
Marín 13 42 23N 8 42W
Marina Plains 44 14 37S 143 57 E
Marinduque 35 13 25N 122 0 E
Marine City 68 42 45N 82 29W
Marinel, Le 54 10 25S 25 17 E
Marinette 68 45 4N 87 40W
Maringá 80 23 26S 52 2W
Marion, Ala., U.S.A. 69 32 33N 87 20W
Marion, Ill., U.S.A. 71 37 45N 88 55W
Marion, Ind., U.S.A. 68 40 35N 85 40W
Marion, Iowa, U.S.A. 70 42 2N 91 36W
Marion, Kans., U.S.A. 70 38 25N 97 2W
Marion, Mich., U.S.A. 68 44 7N 85 8W
Marion, N.C., U.S.A. 69 35 42N 82 0W
Marion, Ohio, U.S.A. 68 40 38N 83 8W
Marion, S.C., U.S.A. 69 34 11N 79 22W
Marion, Va., U.S.A. 69 36 51N 81 29W
Marion, L. 69 33 30N 80 15W
Marion I. 3 47 0S 38 0 E
Mariposa 73 37 31N 119 59W
Mariscal Estigarribia 78 22 3S 60 40W
Maritsa → 19 41 40N 26 34 E
Marīvān 30 35 30N 46 25 E
Markazī □ 31 35 0N 49 30 E
Marked Tree 71 35 35N 90 24W
Marken 11 52 26N 5 12 E
Market Drayton 6 52 55N 2 30W
Market Harborough 7 52 29N 0 55W
Markham L. 65 62 30N 102 35W
Markovo 25 64 40N 169 40 E
Marks 22 51 45N 46 50 E
Marksville 71 31 10N 92 2W
Marla 45 27 19S 133 33 E
Marlborough 44 22 46S 149 52 E
Marlborough □ 43 41 45S 173 33 E
Marlborough Downs 7 51 25N 1 55W
Marlin 71 31 25N 96 50W
Marlow 71 34 40N 97 58W
Marmagao 32 15 25N 73 56 E
Marmara 30 40 35N 27 38 E
Marmara, Sea of = Marmara Denizi 30 40 45N 28 15 E
Marmara Denizi 30 40 45N 28 15 E
Marmaris 30 36 50N 28 14 E
Marmarth 70 46 21N 103 52W
Marmion L. 62 48 55N 91 20W
Marmion Mt. 47 29 16S 119 50 E
Marmolada, Mte. 18 46 25N 11 55 E
Marmora 62 44 28N 77 41W
Marne □ 12 48 50N 4 10 E
Marne → 12 48 48N 2 24 E
Maroala 57 15 23S 47 59 E
Maroantsetra 57 15 26S 49 44 E
Maromandia 57 14 13S 48 5 E
Marondera 55 18 5S 31 42 E
Maroni → 79 5 30N 54 0W
Maroochydore 45 26 29S 153 5 E
Maroona 45 37 27S 142 54 E
Marosakoa 57 15 26S 46 38 E
Maroua 53 10 40N 14 20 E
Marovoay 57 16 6S 46 39 E
Marquard 56 28 40S 27 28 E
Marquesas Is. 41 9 30S 140 0W
Marquette 68 46 30N 87 21W
Marracuene 57 25 45S 32 35 E
Marrakech 50 31 9N 8 0W
Marrawah 44 40 55S 144 42 E
Marree 45 29 39S 138 1 E
Marrilla 46 22 31S 114 25 E
Marrimane 57 22 58S 33 34 E
Marromeu 57 18 15S 36 25 E
Marrowie Creek 45 33 23S 145 40 E
Marrupa 55 13 8S 37 30 E
Mars, Le 70 43 0N 96 0W
Marsá Matrûh 51 31 19N 27 9 E
Marsá Susah 51 32 52N 21 59 E
Marsabit 54 2 18N 38 0 E
Marsala 18 37 48N 12 25 E
Marsaxlokk 18 35 47N 14 32 E
Marsden 45 33 47S 147 32 E
Marseille 12 43 18N 5 23 E
Marseilles = Marseille 12 43 18N 5 23 E
Marsh I. 71 29 35N 91 50W
Marsh L. 70 45 5N 96 0W
Marshall, Liberia 50 6 8N 10 22W
Marshall, Ark., U.S.A. 71 35 58N 92 40W
Marshall, Mich., U.S.A. 68 42 17N 84 59W
Marshall, Minn., U.S.A. 70 44 25N 95 45W
Marshall, Mo., U.S.A. 70 39 8N 93 15W
Marshall, Tex., U.S.A. 71 32 29N 94 20W
Marshall → 44 22 59S 136 59 E
Marshall Is. 40 9 0N 171 0 E
Marshalltown 70 42 5N 92 56W
Marshfield, Mo., U.S.A. 71 37 20N 92 58W
Marshfield, Wis., U.S.A. 70 44 42N 90 10W
Marstrand 21 57 53N 11 35 E
Mart 71 31 34N 96 51W
Martaban 33 16 30N 97 35 E
Martaban, G. of 33 16 5N 96 30 E
Martapura, Kalimantan, Indonesia 34 3 22S 114 47 E
Martapura, Sumatera, Indonesia 34 4 19S 104 22 E
Marte 53 12 23N 13 46 E
Martelange 11 49 49N 5 43 E
Martha's Vineyard 68 41 25N 70 35W
Martin, S. Dak., U.S.A. 70 43 11N 101 45W
Martin, Tenn., U.S.A. 71 36 23N 88 51W
Martin, L. 69 32 45N 85 50W
Martinborough 43 41 14S 175 29 E
Martinique 75 14 40N 61 0W
Martinique Passage 75 15 15N 61 0W
Martinsburg 68 39 30N 77 57W
Martinsville, Ind., U.S.A. 68 39 29N 86 23W
Martinsville, Va., U.S.A. 69 36 41N 79 52W
Marton 43 40 4S 175 23 E
Martos 13 37 44N 3 58W
Marudi 34 4 11N 114 19 E
Ma'ruf 31 31 30N 67 6 E
Marugame 36 34 15N 133 40 E
Marulan 45 34 43S 150 3 E
Marunga 56 17 28S 20 2 E
Marwar 32 25 43N 73 45 E
Mary 24 37 40N 61 50 E
Mary Frances L. 65 63 19N 106 13W
Mary Kathleen 44 20 44S 139 48 E
Maryborough = Port Laoise 9 53 2N 7 20W
Maryborough, Queens., Australia 45 25 31S 152 37 E
Maryborough, Vic., Australia 45 37 0S 143 44 E
Maryfield 65 49 50N 101 35W
Maryland □ 68 39 10N 76 40W
Maryport 6 54 43N 3 30W
Mary's Harbour 63 52 18N 55 51W
Marystown 63 47 10N 55 10W
Marysvale 73 38 25N 112 17W
Marysville, Canada 64 49 35N 116 0W
Marysville, Calif., U.S.A. 72 39 14N 121 40W
Marysville, Kans., U.S.A. 70 39 50N 96 49W
Marysville, Ohio, U.S.A. 68 40 15N 83 20W
Maryvale 45 28 4S 152 12 E
Maryville 69 35 50N 84 0W
Marzūq 51 25 53N 13 57 E
Masada = Mesada 28 31 20N 35 19 E
Masai Steppe 52 4 30S 36 30 E
Masaka 54 0 21S 31 45 E
Masalembo, Kepulauan 34 5 35S 114 30 E
Masalima, Kepulauan 34 5 4S 117 5 E
Masamba 35 2 30S 120 15 E
Masan 38 35 11N 128 32 E
Masandam, Ras 31 26 30N 56 30 E
Masasi 54 10 45S 38 52 E
Masaya 75 12 0N 86 7W
Masbate 35 12 21N 123 36 E
Mascara 50 35 26N 0 6 E
Mascarene Is. 3 22 0S 55 0 E
Mascota 74 20 30N 104 50W
Masela 35 8 9S 129 51 E
Maseru 56 29 18S 27 30 E
Mashābih 30 25 35N 36 30 E
Mashan 39 23 40N 108 11 E
Mashhad 31 36 20N 59 35 E
Mashike 36 43 31N 141 30 E
Mashkel, Hamun-i- 31 28 30N 63 0 E
Mashki Chāh 31 29 5N 62 30 E
Mashonaland Central □ 57 17 30S 31 0 E
Mashonaland East □ 57 18 0S 32 0 E
Mashonaland West □ 57 17 30S 29 30 E
Masi 20 69 26N 23 40 E
Masi Manimba 54 4 40S 17 54 E
Masindi 54 1 40N 31 43 E
Masisea 78 8 35S 74 22W
Masisi 52 1 23S 28 49 E
Masjed Soleyman 30 31 55N 49 18 E
Mask, L. 9 53 36N 9 24W
Masoala, Tanjon' i 57 15 59S 50 13 E
Masoarivo 57 19 3S 44 19 E
Masohi 35 3 20S 128 55 E
Masomeloka 57 20 17S 48 37 E
Mason 71 30 45N 99 15W
Mason City 70 43 9N 93 12W
Masqat 31 23 37N 58 36 E
Massa 18 44 2N 10 7 E
Massachusetts □ 68 42 25N 72 0W
Massada 28 33 41N 35 36 E
Massaguet 51 12 28N 15 26 E
Massakory 51 13 0N 15 49 E
Massangena 57 21 34S 33 0 E
Massawa = Mitsiwa 51 15 35N 39 25 E
Massena 68 44 52N 74 55W
Massénya 51 11 21N 16 9 E
Masset 64 54 2N 132 10W
Massif Central 12 45 30N 3 0 E
Massillon 68 40 47N 81 30W
Massinga 57 23 15S 35 22 E
Masterton 43 40 56S 175 39 E
Mastuj 32 36 20N 72 36 E
Mastung 31 29 50N 66 56 E
Masuda 36 34 40N 131 51 E
Masvingo 55 20 8S 30 49 E
Mataboor 35 1 41S 138 3 E
Matachewan 62 47 56N 80 39W
Matad 37 47 11N 115 27 E
Matadi 54 5 52S 13 31 E
Matagalpa 75 13 0N 85 58W
Matagami 62 49 45N 77 34W
Matagami, L. 62 49 50N 77 40W
Matagorda 71 28 43N 96 0W
Matagorda B. 71 28 30N 96 15W
Matagorda I. 71 28 10N 96 40W
Matak, P. 34 3 18N 106 16 E
Matakana 45 32 59S 145 54 E
Matam 50 15 34N 13 17W
Matamoros, Coahuila, Mexico 74 25 33N 103 15W
Matamoros, Puebla, Mexico 74 18 2N 98 17W
Matamoros, Tamaulipas, Mexico 74 25 50N 97 30W
Ma'ṭan as Sarra 51 21 45N 22 0 E
Matane 63 48 50N 67 33W
Matanuska 60 61 39N 149 19W
Matanzas 75 23 0N 81 40W
Matapan, C. = Taínaron, Ákra 19 36 22N 22 27 E
Matapédia 63 48 0N 66 59W
Matara 32 5 58N 80 30 E
Mataram 34 8 41S 116 10 E
Matarani 78 77 0S 72 10W
Mataranka 46 14 55S 133 4 E
Matatiele 57 30 20S 28 49 E
Mataura 43 46 11S 168 51 E
Matehuala 74 23 40N 100 40W
Matera 18 40 40N 16 37 E
Matheson Island 65 51 45N 96 56W
Mathis 71 28 4N 97 48W
Mathura 32 27 30N 77 40 E
Mati 35 6 55N 126 15 E
Matias Romero 74 16 53N 95 2W
Matima 56 20 15S 24 26 E
Matlock 6 53 8N 1 32W
Matmata 50 33 37N 9 59 E
Mato Grosso □ 79 14 0S 55 0W
Mato Grosso, Planalto do 79 15 0S 55 0W
Matochkin Shar 24 73 10N 56 40 E
Matosinhos 13 41 11N 8 42W
Matrah 31 23 37N 58 30 E
Matsena 53 13 5N 10 5 E
Matsue 36 35 25N 133 10 E
Matsumae 36 41 26N 140 7 E
Matsumoto 36 36 15N 138 0 E
Matsusaka 36 34 34N 136 32 E
Matsutō 36 36 31N 136 34 E
Matsuyama 36 33 45N 132 45 E
Mattagami → 62 50 43N 81 29W
Mattancheri 32 9 50N 76 15 E
Mattawa 62 46 20N 78 45W
Mattawamkeag 63 45 30N 68 21W
Matterhorn 14 45 58N 7 39 E
Matthew Town 75 20 57N 73 40W
Matthew's Ridge 78 7 37N 60 10W
Mattice 62 49 40N 83 20W
Matuba 57 24 28S 32 49 E
Matucana 78 11 55S 76 25W
Matun 32 33 22N 69 58 E
Maturín 78 9 45N 63 11W
Mau Ranipur 32 25 16N 79 8 E
Maud, Pt. 46 23 6S 113 45 E
Maude 45 34 29S 144 18 E
Maudin Sun 33 16 0N 94 30 E
Maués 78 3 20S 57 45W
Mauganj 33 24 50N 81 55 E
Maui 66 20 45N 156 20 E
Mauke 43 20 9S 157 20W
Maulamyaing 33 16 30N 97 40 E
Maumee 68 41 35N 83 40W
Maumee → 68 41 42N 83 28W
Maumere 35 8 38S 122 13 E
Maun 56 20 0S 23 26 E
Mauna Kea 66 19 50N 155 28W
Mauna Loa 66 21 8N 157 10W
Maungmagan Kyunzu 33 14 0N 97 48 E
Maupin 72 45 12N 121 9W
Maurepas L. 71 30 18N 90 35W
Maures 12 43 15N 6 15 E
Maurice L. 47 29 30S 131 0 E
Mauritania ■ 50 20 50N 10 0W
Mauritius ■ 3 20 0S 57 0 E
Mauston 70 43 48N 90 5W
Mavinga 55 15 50S 20 21 E
Mavqi'im 28 31 38N 34 32 E
Mawk Mai 33 20 14N 97 37 E
Mawlaik 33 23 40N 94 26 E
Max 70 47 50N 101 20W
Maxcanú 74 20 40N 92 0W
Maxesibeni 57 30 49S 29 23 E
Maxhamish L. 64 59 50N 123 17W
Maxixe 57 23 54S 35 17 E
Maxwelton 44 20 43S 142 41 E
May Downs 44 22 38S 148 55 E
May Pen 75 17 58N 77 15W
Maya → 25 54 31N 134 41 E
Maya Mts. 74 16 30N 89 0W
Mayaguana 75 22 30N 72 44W
Mayagüez 75 18 12N 67 9W
Mayarí 75 20 40N 75 41W
Maybell 72 40 30N 108 4W
Maydena 44 42 45S 146 30 E
Mayenne 12 48 20N 0 38W
Mayenne □ 12 48 10N 0 40W
Mayer 73 34 28N 112 17W
Mayerthorpe 64 53 57N 115 8W
Mayfield 69 36 45N 88 40W
Mayhill 73 32 58N 105 30W
Maykop 23 44 35N 40 25 E
Maynard Hills 47 28 28S 119 49 E
Mayne → 44 23 40S 141 55 E
Maynooth 9 53 22N 6 38W
Mayo 60 63 38N 135 57W
Mayo □ 9 53 47N 9 7W
Mayo L. 60 63 45N 135 0W
Mayon Volcano 35 13 15N 123 41 E
Mayor I. 43 37 16S 176 17 E
Mayson L. 65 57 55N 107 10W
Maysville 68 38 39N 83 46W
Maythalūn 28 32 21N 35 16 E
Mayu 35 1 30N 126 30 E
Mayville 70 47 30N 97 23W
Mayya 25 61 44N 130 18 E
Mazabuka 55 15 52S 27 44 E
Mazagán = El Jadida 50 33 11N 8 17W
Mazagão 79 0 7S 51 16W
Mazán 78 3 30S 73 0W
Māzandarān □ 31 36 30N 52 0 E
Mazar-e Sharīf 31 36 41N 67 0 E
Mazarredo 80 47 10S 66 50W
Mazarrón 13 37 38N 1 19W
Mazaruni → 78 6 25N 58 35W
Mazatenango 75 14 35N 91 30W
Mazatlán 74 23 10N 106 30W
Māzhān 31 32 30N 59 0 E
Mazīnān 31 36 19N 56 56 E
Mazoe → 55 16 20S 33 30 E
Mazu Dao 39 26 10N 119 55 E
Mazurian Lakes = Mazurski, Pojezierze 15 53 50N 21 0 E
Mazurski, Pojezierze 15 53 50N 21 0 E
Mbabane 57 26 18S 31 6 E
Mbaïki 54 3 53N 18 1 E
Mbala 54 8 46S 31 24 E
Mbale 54 1 8N 34 12 E
Mbalmayo 54 3 33N 11 33 E
Mbamba Bay 54 11 13S 34 49 E
Mbandaka 54 0 1N 18 18 E
Mbanza Congo 54 6 18S 14 16 E
Mbanza Ngungu 54 5 12S 14 53 E
Mbarara 54 0 35S 30 40 E
Mbashe → 57 32 15S 28 54 E
Mbeya 54 8 54S 33 29 E
Mbini □ 54 1 30N 10 0 E
Mbour 50 14 22N 16 54W
Mbout 50 16 1N 12 38W
Mbuji-Mayi 54 6 9S 23 40 E
Mbulu 54 3 45S 35 30 E
Mchinji 55 13 47S 32 58 E
Mdina 18 35 51N 14 25 E
Mead, L. 73 36 1N 114 44W
Meade 71 37 18N 100 25W
Meadow 47 26 35S 114 40 E
Meadow Lake 65 54 10N 108 26W
Meadow Lake Prov. Park 65 54 27N 109 0W
Meadow Valley Wash → 73 36 39N 114 35W
Meadville 68 41 39N 80 9W
Meaford 62 44 36N 80 35W
Mealy Mts. 63 53 10N 58 0W
Meander River 64 59 2N 117 42W
Meares, C. 72 45 37N 124 0W
Mearim → 79 3 4S 44 35W
Meath □ 9 53 32N 6 40W
Meath Park 65 53 27N 105 22W
Meaux 12 48 58N 2 50 E
Mecca = Makkah 29 21 30N 39 54 E
Mecca 73 33 37N 116 3W
Mechelen 11 51 2N 4 29 E
Mecheria 50 33 35N 0 18W
Mecklenburger Bucht 14 54 20N 11 40 E
Meconta 55 14 59S 39 50 E
Meda 46 17 22S 123 59 E

Miranda

Medan 34 3 40N 98 38 E
Medanosa, Pta. 80 48 8S 66 0W
Medéa 50 36 12N 2 50 E
Medellín 78 6 15N 75 35W
Medemblik 11 52 46N 5 8 E
Mederdra 50 17 0N 15 38W
Medford, Oreg., U.S.A. 72 42 20N 122 52W
Medford, Wis., U.S.A. 70 45 9N 90 21W
Mediaş 15 46 9N 24 22 E
Medical Lake 72 47 35N 117 42W
Medicine Bow 72 41 56N 106 11W
Medicine Bow Pk. 72 41 21N 106 19W
Medicine Bow Ra. 72 41 10N 106 25W
Medicine Hat 65 50 0N 110 45W
Medicine Lake 70 48 30N 104 30W
Medicine Lodge 71 37 20N 98 37W
Medina = Al Madīnah 29 24 35N 39 52 E
Medina, N. Dak., U.S.A. 70 46 57N 99 20W
Medina, N.Y., U.S.A. 68 43 15N 78 27W
Medina, Ohio, U.S.A. 68 41 9N 81 50W
Medina —► 71 29 10N 98 20W
Medina del Campo 13 41 18N 4 55W
Medina L. 71 29 35N 98 58W
Medina-Sidonia 13 36 28N 5 57W
Medinipur 33 22 25N 87 21 E
Mediterranean Sea 16 35 0N 15 0 E
Medley 65 54 25N 110 16W
Médoc 12 45 10N 0 50W
Medport = Marsaxlokk 18 35 47N 14 32 E
Medstead 65 53 19N 108 5W
Medveditsa —► 23 49 35N 42 41 E
Medvezhi, Ostrava 25 71 0N 161 0 E
Medvezhyegorsk 22 63 0N 34 25 E
Medway —► 7 51 28N 0 45 E
Meeberrie 47 26 57S 115 51 E
Meekatharra 47 26 32S 118 29 E
Meeker 72 40 1N 107 58W
Meerut 32 29 1N 77 42 E
Meeteetse 72 44 10N 108 56W
Mega 51 3 57N 38 19 E
Mégara 19 37 58N 23 22 E
Meghalaya □ 33 25 50N 91 0 E
Megiddo 28 32 36N 35 11 E
Mégiscane, L. 62 48 35N 75 55W
Megiste 17 36 8N 29 34 E
Mehadia 15 44 56N 22 23 E
Mei Jiang —► 39 24 25N 116 35 E
Mei Xian 39 24 16N 116 6 E
Meiganga 54 6 30N 14 25 E
Meiktila 33 20 53N 95 54 E
Me'ir Shefeya 28 32 35N 34 58 E
Meissen 14 51 10N 13 29 E
Meitan 39 27 45N 107 29 E
Mejillones 80 23 10S 70 30W
Meka 47 27 25S 116 48 E
Mékambo 54 1 2N 13 50 E
Mekdela 51 11 24N 39 10 E
Mekhtar 32 30 30N 69 15 E
Meknès 50 33 57N 5 33W
Mekong —► 34 9 30N 106 15 E
Mekongga 35 3 39S 121 15 E
Melagiri Hills 32 12 20N 77 30 E
Melaka 34 2 15N 102 15 E
Melalap 34 5 10N 116 5 E
Melanesia 40 4 0S 155 0 E
Melbourne, Australia 45 37 50S 145 0 E
Melbourne, U.S.A. 69 28 4N 80 35W
Melchor Múzquiz 74 27 50N 101 30W
Melchor Ocampo 74 24 52N 101 40W
Mélèzes —► 61 57 30N 71 0W
Melfi 51 11 0N 17 59 E
Melfort 65 52 50N 104 37W
Melilla 50 35 21N 2 57W
Melilot 28 31 22N 34 37 E
Melita 65 49 15N 101 0W
Melitopol 23 46 50N 35 22 E
Melk 14 48 13N 15 20 E
Mellansel 20 63 25N 18 17 E
Mellen 70 46 19N 90 36W
Mellerud 21 58 41N 12 28 E
Mellette 70 45 11N 98 29W
Melo 80 32 20S 54 10W
Melolo 35 9 53S 120 40 E
Melrose, N.S.W., Australia 45 32 42S 146 57 E
Melrose, W. Austral., Australia 47 27 50S 121 15 E
Melrose, U.K. 8 53 35N 2 44W
Melrose, U.S.A. 71 34 27N 103 33W
Melstone 72 46 36N 107 50W
Melton Mowbray 6 52 46N 0 52W
Melun 12 48 32N 2 39 E
Melut 51 10 30N 32 13 E
Melville 65 50 55N 102 50W
Melville, C. 44 14 11S 144 30 E
Melville, L. 63 53 30N 60 0W
Melville B. 44 12 0S 136 45 E
Melville I., Australia 46 11 30S 131 0 E
Melville I., Canada 58 75 30N 112 0W
Melville Pen. 61 68 0N 84 0W
Melvin —► 64 59 11N 117 31W
Memba 55 14 11S 40 30 E
Memboro 35 9 30S 119 30 E
Memel = Klaipeda 22 55 43N 21 10 E
Memel 57 27 38S 29 36 E
Memmingen 14 47 59N 10 12 E
Mempawah 34 0 30N 109 5 E
Memphis, Tenn., U.S.A. 71 35 7N 90 0W
Memphis, Tex., U.S.A. 71 34 45N 100 30W
Mena 71 34 40N 94 15W
Menai Strait 6 53 14N 4 10W
Ménaka 53 15 59N 2 18 E
Menan = Chao Phraya —► 34 13 32N 100 36 E
Menarandra —► 57 25 17S 44 30 E
Menard 71 30 57N 99 48W
Menasha 68 44 13N 88 27W
Menate 34 0 12S 113 3 E
Mendawai —► 34 3 30S 113 0 E
Mende 12 44 31N 3 30 E
Menderes —► 30 37 25N 28 45 E
Mendip Hills 7 51 17N 2 40W
Mendocino 72 39 26N 123 50W
Mendocino, C. 72 40 26N 124 25W
Mendocino Seascarp 41 41 0N 140 0W
Mendota, Calif., U.S.A. 73 36 46N 120 24W
Mendota, Ill., U.S.A. 70 41 35N 89 5W
Mendoza 80 32 50S 68 52W
Mene Grande 78 9 49N 70 56W
Menemen 30 38 34N 27 3 E
Menen 11 50 47N 3 7 E
Menfi 18 37 36N 12 57 E
Mengcheng 39 33 18N 116 31 E
Menggala 34 4 30S 105 15 E
Mengshan 39 24 14N 110 55 E
Mengzi 37 23 20N 103 22 E
Menihek L. 63 54 0N 67 0W
Menin = Menen 11 50 47N 3 7 E
Menindee 45 32 20S 142 25 E
Menindee, L. 45 32 20S 142 25 E
Meningie 45 35 35S 139 0 E
Menominee 68 45 9N 87 39W
Menominee —► 68 45 5N 87 36W
Menomonie 70 44 50N 91 54W
Menongue 55 14 48S 17 52 E
Menorca 13 40 0N 4 0 E
Mentawai, Kepulauan 34 2 0S 99 0 E
Menton 12 43 50N 7 29 E
Mentz Dam 56 33 10S 25 9 E
Menzelinsk 22 55 53N 53 1 E
Menzies 47 29 40S 120 58 E
Me'ona 28 33 1N 35 15 E
Meppel 68 52 42N 6 12 E
Mer Rouge 71 32 47N 91 48W
Merabéllou, Kólpos 19 35 10N 25 50 E
Meramangye, L. 47 28 25S 132 13 E
Meran = Merano 18 46 40N 11 10 E
Merano 18 46 40N 11 10 E
Merauke 35 8 29S 140 24 E
Merbabu 35 7 30S 110 40 E
Merbein 45 34 10S 142 2 E
Merca 29 1 48N 44 50 E
Merced 73 37 18N 120 30W
Mercedes, Buenos Aires, Argentina 80 34 40S 59 30W
Mercedes, Corrientes, Argentina 80 29 10S 58 5W
Mercedes, San Luis, Argentina 80 33 40S 65 21W
Mercedes, Uruguay 80 33 12S 58 0W
Merceditas 80 28 20S 70 35W
Mercer 43 37 16S 175 5 E
Mercy C. 61 65 0N 63 30W
Meredith, C. 80 52 15S 60 40W
Meredith, L. 71 35 30N 101 35W
Merga = Nukheila 51 19 1N 26 21 E
Mergui Arch. = Myeik Kyunzu 34 11 30N 97 30 E
Mérida, Mexico 74 20 9N 89 40W
Mérida, Spain 13 38 55N 6 25W
Mérida, Venezuela 78 8 24N 71 8W
Mérida, Cord. de 76 9 0N 71 0W
Meriden 68 41 33N 72 47W
Meridian, Idaho, U.S.A. 72 43 41N 116 25W
Meridian, Miss., U.S.A. 69 32 20N 88 42W
Meridian, Tex., U.S.A. 71 31 55N 97 37W
Meriruma 79 1 15N 54 50W
Merkel 71 32 30N 100 0W
Merksem 11 51 16N 4 25 E
Mermaid Reef 46 17 6S 119 36 E
Merowe 51 18 29N 31 46 E
Merredin 47 31 28S 118 18 E
Merrick 8 55 8N 4 30W
Merrill, Oreg., U.S.A. 72 42 2N 121 37W
Merrill, Wis., U.S.A. 70 45 11N 89 41W
Merriman 70 42 55N 101 42W
Merritt 64 50 10N 120 45W
Merriwa 45 32 6S 150 22 E
Merriwagga 45 33 47S 145 43 E
Merry I. 62 55 29N 77 31W
Merrygoen 45 31 51S 149 12 E
Merryville 71 30 47N 93 31W
Mersa Fatma 29 14 57N 40 17 E
Mersch 11 49 44N 6 7 E
Merseburg 14 51 20N 12 0 E
Mersey —► 6 53 20N 2 56W
Merseyside □ 6 53 25N 2 55W
Mersin 30 36 51N 34 36 E
Mersing 34 2 25N 103 50 E
Merthyr Tydfil 7 51 45N 3 23W
Mértola 13 37 40N 7 40 E
Mertzon 71 31 17N 100 48W
Meru 54 0 3N 37 40 E
Mesa 73 33 20N 111 56W
Mesa, La, Calif., U.S.A. 73 32 48N 117 5W
Mesa, La, N. Mex., U.S.A. 73 32 6N 106 48W
Mesada 28 31 20N 35 19 E
Mesgouez, L. 62 51 20N 75 0W
Meshed = Mashhad 31 36 20N 59 35 E
Meshra er Req 51 8 25N 29 18 E
Mesick 68 44 24N 85 42W
Mesilinka —► 64 56 6N 124 30W
Mesilla 73 32 20N 106 50W
Mesolóngion 19 38 21N 21 28 E
Mesopotamia = Al Jazirah 30 33 30N 44 0 E
Mesquite 73 36 47N 114 6W
Mess Cr. —► 64 57 55N 131 14W
Messina, Italy 18 38 10N 15 32 E
Messina, S. Africa 57 22 20S 30 0 E
Messina, Str. di 18 38 5N 15 35 E
Messíni 19 37 4N 22 1 E
Messiniakós, Kólpos 19 36 45N 22 5 E
Mesta —► 19 41 30N 24 0 E
Meta —► 78 6 12N 67 28W
Metairie 71 29 59N 90 9W
Metaline Falls 72 48 52N 117 22W
Metán 80 25 30S 65 0W
Metangula 55 12 40S 34 50 E
Metema 51 12 56N 36 13 E
Methven 43 43 38S 171 40 E
Methy L. 65 56 28N 109 30W
Metil 55 16 24S 39 0 E
Metlakatla 64 55 10N 131 33W
Metropolis 71 37 10N 88 47W
Mettur Dam 32 11 45N 77 45 E
Metulla 28 33 17N 35 34 E
Metz 12 49 8N 6 10 E
Meulaboh 34 4 11N 96 3 E
Meureudu 34 5 19N 96 10 E
Meurthe-et-Moselle □ 12 48 52N 6 0 E
Meuse □ 12 49 8N 5 25 E
Meuse —► 11 50 45N 5 41 E
Mexborough 6 53 29N 1 18W
Mexia 71 31 38N 96 32W
Mexiana, I. 79 0 0 49 30W
Mexicali 74 32 40N 115 30W
México, Mexico 74 19 20N 99 10W
Mexico, U.S.A. 70 39 10N 91 55W
México □ 74 19 20N 99 10W
Mexico ■ 74 25 0N 105 0W
Mexico, G. of 74 25 0N 90 0W
Meymaneh 31 35 53N 64 38 E
Mezen 22 65 50N 44 20 E
Mezen —► 22 66 11N 43 59 E
Mezőkövesd 15 47 49N 20 35 E
Mezőtúr 15 47 0N 20 41 E
Mezquital 74 23 29N 104 23W
Mhow 32 22 33N 75 50 E
Miahuatlán 74 16 21N 96 36W
Miallo 44 16 28S 145 22 E
Miami, Ariz., U.S.A. 73 33 25N 110 54W
Miami, Fla., U.S.A. 69 25 45N 80 15W
Miami, Tex., U.S.A. 71 35 44N 100 38W
Miami —► 68 39 20N 84 40W
Miami Beach 69 25 49N 80 6W
Miamisburg 68 39 40N 84 11W
Mian Xian 39 33 10N 106 32 E
Mianchi 39 34 48N 111 48 E
Mīāndowāb 30 37 0N 46 5 E
Miandrivazo 57 19 31S 45 29 E
Mīāneh 30 37 30N 47 40 E
Mianwali 32 32 38N 71 28 E
Mianyang, Hubei, China 39 30 25N 113 25 E
Mianyang, Sichuan, China 39 31 22N 104 47 E
Miaoli 39 24 37N 120 49 E
Miarinarivo 57 18 57S 46 55 E
Miass 22 54 59N 60 6 E
Michigan □ 67 44 40N 85 40W
Michigan, L. 68 44 0N 87 0W
Michigan City 68 41 42N 86 56W
Michikamau L. 63 54 20N 63 10W
Michipicoten 62 47 55N 84 55W
Michipicoten I. 62 47 40N 85 40W
Michoacan □ 74 19 0N 102 0W
Michurinsk 22 52 58N 40 27 E
Miclere 44 22 34S 147 32 E
Mico, Pta. 75 12 0N 83 30W
Micronesia 40 11 0N 160 0 E
Mid Glamorgan □ 7 51 40N 3 25W
Mid-Indian Ridge 40 40 0S 75 0 E
Mid-Oceanic Ridge 40 42 0S 90 0 E
Midai, P. 34 3 0N 107 47 E
Midale 65 49 25N 103 20W
Middelburg, Neth. 11 51 30N 3 36 E
Middelburg, C. Prov., S. Africa 56 31 30S 25 0 E
Middelburg, Trans., S. Africa 57 25 49S 29 28 E
Middelwit 56 24 51S 27 3 E
Middle Alkali L. 72 41 30N 120 3W
Middle Loup —► 70 41 17N 98 23W
Middleport 68 39 0N 82 5W
Middlesboro 69 36 36N 83 43W
Middlesbrough 6 54 35N 1 14W
Middleton, Australia 44 22 22S 141 32 E
Middleton, Canada 63 44 57N 65 4W
Middletown, Conn., U.S.A. 68 41 37N 72 40W
Middletown, N.Y., U.S.A. 68 41 28N 74 28W
Middletown, Ohio, U.S.A. 68 39 29N 84 25W
Midi, Canal du —► 12 43 45N 1 21 E
Midland, Australia 45 31 54S 115 59 E
Midland, Canada 62 44 45N 79 50W
Midland, Mich., U.S.A. 68 43 37N 84 17W
Midland, Tex., U.S.A. 71 32 0N 102 3W
Midleton 9 51 52N 8 12W
Midlothian 71 32 30N 97 0W
Midongy, Tangorombohitr' i 57 23 30S 47 0 E
Midongy Atsimo 57 23 35S 47 1 E
Midway Is. 2 28 13N 177 22W
Midwest 72 43 27N 106 19W
Midyat 30 37 25N 41 23 E
Mie □ 36 34 30N 136 10 E
Międzychód 14 52 35N 15 53 E
Międzyrzec Podlaski 15 51 58N 22 45 E
Mienga 56 17 12S 19 48 E
Miercurea Ciuc 15 46 21N 25 48 E
Mieres 13 43 18N 5 48W
Migdāl 28 32 51N 35 30 E
Migdal Afeq 28 32 5N 34 58 E
Miguel Alemán, Presa 74 18 15N 96 40W
Miguel Alves 79 4 11S 42 55W
Mihara 36 34 24N 133 5 E
Mikinai 19 37 43N 22 46 E
Mikkeli 21 61 43N 27 15 E
Mikkeli □ 20 62 0N 28 0 E
Mikkwa —► 64 58 25N 114 46W
Míkonos 19 37 30N 25 25 E
Mikun 22 62 20N 50 0 E
Mikura-Jima 36 33 52N 139 36 E
Milaca 70 45 45N 93 40W
Milagro 78 2 11S 79 36W
Milan = Milano 18 45 28N 9 10 E
Milan, Mo., U.S.A. 70 40 10N 93 5W
Milan, Tenn., U.S.A. 69 35 55N 88 45W
Milang 45 32 2S 139 10 E
Milano 18 45 28N 9 10 E
Milâs 30 37 20N 27 50 E
Milazzo 18 38 13N 15 13 E
Milbank 70 45 17N 96 38W
Milden 65 51 29N 107 32W
Mildura 45 34 13S 142 9 E
Miles, Australia 45 26 40S 150 9 E
Miles, U.S.A. 71 31 39N 100 11W
Miles City 70 46 24N 105 50W
Milestone 65 49 59N 104 31W
Mileura 47 26 22S 117 20 E
Milford, Del., U.S.A. 68 38 52N 75 27W
Milford, Utah, U.S.A. 73 38 20N 113 0W
Milford Haven 7 51 43N 5 2W
Milford Sd. 43 44 41S 167 47 E
Milgun 47 25 6S 118 18 E
Milh, Bahr al 30 32 40N 43 35 E
Milh, Ras al 51 31 54N 25 6 E
Miliana 50 27 20N 2 32 E
Miling 47 30 30S 116 17 E
Milk —► 72 48 5N 106 15W
Milk River 64 49 10N 112 5W
Mill City 72 44 45N 122 28W
Mille 69 33 7N 83 15W
Mille Lacs, L. 70 46 10N 93 30W
Mille Lacs, L. des 62 48 45N 90 35W
Millen 69 32 50N 81 57W
Miller 70 44 35N 98 59W
Millicent 45 37 34S 140 21 E
Millinocket 63 45 45N 68 45W
Millmerran 45 27 53S 151 16 E
Mills L. 64 61 30N 118 20W
Milltown Malbay 9 52 51N 9 25W
Millville 68 39 22N 75 0W
Millwood Res. 71 33 45N 94 0W
Milne —► 44 21 10S 137 33 E
Milne Inlet 61 72 30N 80 0W
Milnor 70 46 19N 97 29W
Milo 64 50 34N 112 53W
Mílos 19 36 44N 24 25 E
Milparinka 45 29 46S 141 57 E
Milton, N.Z. 43 46 7S 169 59 E
Milton, U.K. 8 57 18N 4 32W
Milton, Fla., U.S.A. 69 30 38N 87 0W
Milton, Pa., U.S.A. 68 41 0N 76 53W
Milton-Freewater 72 45 57N 118 24W
Milton Keynes 7 52 3N 0 42W
Miltou 51 10 14N 17 26 E
Milwaukee 68 43 9N 87 58W
Milwaukie 72 45 27N 122 39W
Min Jiang —►, Fujian, China 39 26 0N 119 35 E
Min Jiang —►, Sichuan, China 37 28 45N 104 40 E
Min Xian 39 34 25N 104 0 E
Mina 73 38 21N 118 9W
Mina Pirquitas 80 22 40S 66 30W
Minā Su'ud 30 28 45N 48 28 E
Minā'al Ahmadī 30 29 5N 48 10 E
Mīnāb 31 27 10N 57 1 E
Minago —► 65 54 33N 98 59W
Minaki 65 49 59N 94 40W
Minamata 36 32 10N 130 30 E
Minas 80 34 20S 55 10W
Minas, Sierra de las 75 15 9N 89 31W
Minas Basin 63 45 20N 64 12W
Minas de Rio Tinto 13 37 42N 6 35W
Minas Gerais □ 79 18 50S 46 0W
Minatitlán 74 17 58N 94 35W
Minbu 33 20 10N 94 52 E
Mindanao 35 8 0N 125 0 E
Mindanao Sea = Bohol Sea 35 9 0N 124 0 E
Mindanao Trench 35 8 0N 128 0 E
Minden, Germany 14 52 18N 8 45 E
Minden, U.S.A. 71 32 40N 93 20W
Mindiptana 35 5 55S 140 22 E
Mindoro 35 13 0N 121 0 E
Mindoro Strait 35 12 30N 120 30 E
Mindouli 54 4 12S 14 28 E
Minehead 7 51 12N 3 29W
Mineola 71 32 40N 95 30W
Mineral Wells 71 32 50N 98 5W
Minersville 73 38 14N 112 58W
Mingan 63 50 20N 64 0W
Mingechaurskoye Vdkhr. 23 40 56N 47 20 E
Mingela 44 19 52S 146 38 E
Mingenew 47 29 12S 115 21 E
Mingera Cr. —► 44 20 38S 137 45 E
Minggang 39 32 24N 114 3 E
Mingin 33 22 50N 94 30 E
Mingxi 39 26 18N 117 12 E
Minho □ 13 41 25N 8 20W
Minho —► 13 41 58N 8 40W
Minidoka 72 42 47N 113 34W
Minigwal L. 47 29 31S 123 14 E
Minilya 47 23 55S 114 0 E
Minilya —► 47 23 45S 114 0 E
Minipi, L. 63 52 25N 60 45W
Mink L. 64 61 54N 117 40W
Minna 53 9 37N 6 30 E
Minneapolis, Kans., U.S.A. 70 39 11N 97 40W
Minneapolis, Minn., U.S.A. 70 44 58N 93 20W
Minnedosa 65 50 14N 99 50W
Minnesota □ 70 46 40N 94 0W
Minnie Creek 47 24 3S 115 42 E
Minnitaki L. 62 49 57N 92 10W
Miño —► 13 41 52N 8 40W
Minorca = Menorca 13 40 0N 4 0 E
Minore 45 32 14S 148 27 E
Minot 70 48 10N 101 15W
Minqing 39 26 15N 118 50 E
Minsk 22 53 52N 27 30 E
Mińsk Mazowiecki 15 52 10N 21 33 E
Mintaka Pass 32 37 0N 74 58 E
Minto 60 64 55N 149 20W
Minton 65 49 10N 104 35W
Minturn 72 39 35N 106 25W
Minusinsk 25 53 50N 91 20 E
Minutang 33 28 15N 96 30 E
Minvoul 54 2 9N 12 8 E
Mir 51 14 5N 11 59 E
Miraflores Locks 74 8 59N 79 36W
Miraj 32 16 50N 74 45 E
Miram 44 21 15S 148 55 E
Miram Shah 32 33 0N 70 2 E
Miramar 57 23 50S 35 35 E
Miramichi B. 63 47 15N 65 0W
Miranda 79 20 10S 56 15W

Miranda de Ebro

Miranda de Ebro 13 42 41N 2 57W
Mirando City 71 27 28N 98 59W
Mirbāṭ 29 17 0N 54 45 E
Miri 34 4 23N 113 59 E
Miriam Vale 44 24 20S 151 33 E
Mirim, L. 80 32 45S 52 50W
Mirnyy 25 62 33N 113 53 E
Mirond L. 65 55 6N 102 47W
Mirpur Khas 32 25 30N 69 0 E
Mirror 64 52 30N 113 7W
Miryang 38 35 31N 128 44 E
Mirzapur 33 25 10N 82 34 E
Mirzapur-cum-Vindhyachal = Mirzapur 33 25 10N 82 34 E
Miscou I. 63 47 57N 64 31W
Mish'āb, Ra'as al 30 28 15N 48 43 E
Mishan 38 45 37N 131 48 E
Mishawaka 68 41 40N 86 8W
Mishima 36 35 10N 138 52 E
Mishmar Ayyalon 28 31 52N 34 57 E
Mishmar Ha' Emeq 28 32 37N 35 7 E
Mishmar Ha Negev 28 31 22N 34 48 E
Mishmar Ha Yarden 28 33 0N 35 36 E
Miskīn 31 23 44N 56 52 E
Miskitos, Cayos 75 14 26N 82 50W
Miskolc 15 48 7N 20 50 E
Misool 35 1 52S 130 10 E
Misrātah 51 32 24N 15 3 E
Misriç 30 37 55N 41 40 E
Missanabie 62 48 20N 84 6W
Missinaibi → 62 50 43N 81 29W
Missinaibi L. 62 48 23N 83 40W
Mission, S. Dak., U.S.A. 70 43 21N 100 36W
Mission, Tex., U.S.A. 71 26 15N 98 20W
Mission City 64 49 10N 122 15W
Missisa L. 62 52 20N 85 7W
Mississagi → 62 46 15N 83 9W
Mississippi → 71 29 0N 89 15W
Mississippi, Delta of the 71 29 15N 90 30W
Mississippi Sd. 71 30 25N 89 0W
Missoula 72 46 52N 114 0W
Missouri □ 70 38 25N 92 30W
Missouri → 70 38 50N 90 8W
Missouri Valley 70 41 33N 95 53W
Mistake B. 65 62 8N 93 0W
Mistassini → 63 48 42N 72 20W
Mistassini L. 62 51 0N 73 30W
Mistastin L. 63 55 57N 63 20W
Mistatim 65 52 52N 103 22W
Mistretta 13 37 56N 14 20 E
Misty L. 65 58 53N 101 40W
Mitchell, Australia 45 26 29S 147 58 E
Mitchell, Ind., U.S.A. 68 38 42N 86 25W
Mitchell, Nebr., U.S.A. 70 41 58N 103 45W
Mitchell, Oreg., U.S.A. 72 44 31N 120 8W
Mitchell, S. Dak., U.S.A. 70 43 40N 98 0W
Mitchell → 44 15 12S 141 35 E
Mitchell, Mt. 69 35 40N 82 20W
Mitchelstown 9 52 16N 8 18W
Mitiaro, I. 43 19 49S 157 43W
Mito 36 36 20N 140 30 E
Mitsinjo 57 16 1S 45 52 E
Mitsiwa 51 15 35N 39 25 E
Mittagong 45 34 28S 150 29 E
Mitú 78 1 8N 70 3W
Mitumba, Chaîne des 54 7 0S 27 30 E
Mitwaba 54 8 2S 27 17 E
Mitzic 54 0 45N 11 40 E
Mixteco → 74 18 11N 98 30W
Miyagi □ 36 38 15N 140 45 E
Miyake-Jima 36 34 0N 139 30 E
Miyako 36 39 40N 141 59 E
Miyakonojō 36 31 40N 131 5 E
Miyazaki 36 31 56N 131 30 E
Miyazaki □ 36 32 30N 131 30 E
Miyazu 36 35 35N 135 10 E
Miyet, Bahr el = Dead Sea 28 31 30N 35 30 E
Miyun 38 40 28N 116 50 E
Mizal 30 23 59N 45 11 E
Mizamis = Ozamis 35 8 15N 123 50 E
Mizdah 51 31 30N 13 0 E
Mizen Hd., Cork, Ireland 9 51 27N 9 50W
Mizen Hd., Wicklow, Ireland 9 52 52N 6 4W
Mizhi 38 37 47N 110 12 E
Mizoram □ 33 23 30N 92 40 E
Mizpe Ramon 28 30 34N 34 49 E
Mjanji 52 0 16N 34 0 E
Mjölby 21 58 20N 15 10 E
Mjøsa 21 60 48N 11 0 E
Mkomazi → 57 30 12S 30 50 E
Mkuze 57 27 10S 32 0 E
Mkuze → 57 27 45S 32 30 E
Mladá Boleslav 14 50 27N 14 53 E
Mława 15 53 9N 20 25 E
Mmabatho 56 25 49S 25 30 E
Mme 53 6 18N 10 14 E
Mo i Rana 20 66 15N 14 7 E
Moa 35 8 0S 128 0 E
Moab 73 38 40N 109 35W
Moabi 54 2 24S 10 59 E
Moala 43 18 36S 179 53 E
Moalie Park 45 29 42S 143 3 E
Moba 54 7 0S 29 48 E
Mobaye 54 4 25N 21 5 E
Mobayi 54 4 15N 21 8 E
Moberly 70 39 25N 92 25W
Moberly → 64 56 12N 120 55W
Mobile 69 30 41N 88 3W
Mobile B. 69 30 30N 88 0W
Mobridge 70 45 31N 100 28W
Mobutu Sese Seko, L. 54 1 30N 31 0 E
Moçambique 55 15 3S 40 42 E
Moçâmedes = Namibe 55 15 7S 12 11 E
Mochudi 56 24 27S 26 7 E
Mocimboa da Praia 54 11 25S 40 20 E
Moclips 72 47 14N 124 10W
Mocoa 78 1 7N 76 35W
Mocorito 74 25 30N 107 53W
Moctezuma 74 29 50N 109 0W
Moctezuma → 74 21 59N 98 34W
Mocuba 55 16 54S 36 57 E
Mocúzari, Presa 74 27 10N 109 10W
Modane 12 45 12N 6 40 E
Modder → 56 29 2S 24 37 E
Modderrivier 56 29 2S 24 38 E
Módena, Italy 18 44 39N 10 55 E
Modena, U.S.A. 73 37 55N 113 56W
Modesto 73 37 43N 121 0W
Módica 18 36 52N 14 45 E
Moe 45 38 12S 146 19 E
Moengo 79 5 45N 54 20W
Moffat 8 55 20N 3 27W
Mogadishu = Muqdisho 29 2 2N 45 25 E
Mogador = Essaouira 50 31 32N 9 42W
Mogalakwena → 57 22 38S 28 40 E
Mogami → 36 38 45N 140 0 E
Mogaung 33 25 20N 97 0 E
Mogi das Cruzes 80 23 31S 46 11W
Mogi-Mirim 80 22 29S 47 0W
Mogilev 22 53 55N 30 18 E
Mogilev-Podolskiy 23 48 20N 27 40 E
Mogocha 25 53 40N 119 50 E
Mogoi 35 1 55S 133 10 E
Mogok 33 23 0N 96 40 E
Mogumber 47 31 2S 116 3 E
Mohács 15 45 58N 18 41 E
Mohales Hoek 56 30 7S 27 26 E
Mohall 70 48 46N 101 30W
Moḥammadābād 31 37 52N 59 5 E
Mohe 38 53 28N 122 17 E
Mohoro 54 8 6S 39 8 E
Moidart, L. 8 56 47N 5 40W
Mointy 24 47 10N 73 18 E
Moisie 63 50 12N 66 1W
Moisie → 63 50 14N 66 5W
Moïssala 51 8 21N 17 46 E
Mojave 73 35 8N 118 8W
Mojave Desert 73 35 0N 116 30W
Mojokerto 35 7 28S 112 26 E
Mokai 43 38 32S 175 56 E
Mokhotlong 57 29 22S 29 2 E
Mokokchung 33 26 15N 94 30 E
Mol 11 51 11N 5 5 E
Molchanovo 24 57 40N 83 50 E
Mold 6 53 10N 3 10W
Moldavian S.S.R. □ 23 47 0N 28 0 E
Molde 20 62 45N 7 9 E
Molepolole 56 24 28S 25 28 E
Molfetta 18 41 12N 16 35 E
Moline 70 41 30N 90 30W
Moliro 54 8 12S 30 30 E
Molise □ 18 41 45N 14 30 E
Mollendo 78 17 0S 72 0W
Mollerin, L. 47 30 30S 117 35 E
Mölndal 21 57 40N 12 3 E
Molokai 66 21 8N 157 0W
Molong 45 33 5S 148 54 E
Molopo → 56 27 30S 20 13 E
Molotov = Perm 22 58 0N 57 10 E
Moloundou 54 2 8N 15 15 E
Molson L. 65 54 22N 96 40W
Molteno 56 31 22S 26 22 E
Molu 35 6 45S 131 40 E
Molucca Sea 35 4 0S 124 0 E
Moluccas = Maluku 35 1 0S 127 0 E
Moma 55 16 47S 39 4 E
Mombasa 54 4 2S 39 43 E
Mombetsu 36 42 27N 142 4 E
Mompós 78 9 14N 74 26W
Møn 21 54 57N 12 15 E
Mon → 33 20 25N 94 30 E
Mona, Canal de la 75 18 30N 67 45W
Mona, I. 75 18 5N 67 54W
Mona, Pta. 75 9 37N 82 36W
Monach Is. 8 57 32N 7 40W
Monaco ■ 12 43 46N 7 23 E
Monadhliath Mts. 8 57 10N 4 4W
Monaghan 9 54 15N 6 58W
Monaghan □ 9 54 10N 7 0W
Monahans 71 31 35N 102 50W
Monarch Mt. 64 51 55N 125 57W
Monastir = Bitola 19 41 5N 21 10 E
Monastir 51 35 50N 10 49 E
Monbetsu 36 44 21N 143 22 E
Moncayo, Sierra del 13 41 48N 1 50W
Mönchengladbach 14 51 12N 6 23 E
Monchique 13 37 19N 8 38W
Monchique, Sa. de 13 37 18N 8 39W
Monclova 74 26 50N 101 30W
Moncton 63 46 7N 64 51W
Mondego → 13 40 9N 8 52W
Mondeodo 35 3 34S 122 9 E
Mondovi, Italy 18 44 23N 7 49 E
Mondovi, U.S.A. 70 44 37N 91 40W
Mondrain I. 47 34 9S 122 14 E
Monessen 68 40 9N 79 50W
Monett 71 36 55N 93 56W
Monforte 13 39 6N 7 25W
Mong Hsu 33 21 54N 98 30 E
Mong Kung 33 21 35N 97 35 E
Mong Nai 33 20 32N 97 46 E
Mong Pawk 33 22 4N 99 16 E
Mong Ton 33 20 17N 98 45 E
Mong Wa 33 21 26N 100 27 E
Mong Yai 33 22 21N 98 3 E
Mongalla 51 5 8N 31 42 E
Mongers, L. 47 29 25S 117 5 E
Monghyr = Munger 33 25 23N 86 30 E
Mongo 51 12 14N 18 43 E
Mongolia ■ 37 47 0N 103 0 E
Mongororo 51 12 3N 22 26 E
Mongu 55 15 16S 23 12 E
Mõngua 56 16 43S 15 20 E
Monkira 44 24 46S 140 30 E
Monkoto 54 1 38S 20 35 E
Monmouth, U.K. 7 51 48N 2 43W
Monmouth, U.S.A. 70 40 50N 90 40W
Mono, L. 73 38 0N 119 9W
Monópoli 18 40 57N 17 18 E
Monqoumba 54 3 33N 18 40 E
Monroe, Ga., U.S.A. 69 33 47N 83 43W
Monroe, La., U.S.A. 71 32 32N 92 4W
Monroe, Mich., U.S.A. 68 41 55N 83 26W
Monroe, N.C., U.S.A. 69 35 2N 80 37W
Monroe, Utah, U.S.A. 73 38 45N 112 5W
Monroe, Wis., U.S.A. 70 42 38N 89 40W
Monroe City 70 39 40N 91 40W
Monroeville 69 31 33N 87 15W
Monrovia, Liberia 50 6 18N 10 47W
Monrovia, U.S.A. 73 34 7N 118 1W
Mons 11 50 27N 3 58 E
Monse 35 4 0S 123 10 E
Mont-de-Marsan 12 43 54N 0 31W
Mont-Joli 63 48 37N 68 10W
Mont-Laurier 62 46 35N 75 30W
Mont-St.-Michel, Le 12 48 40N 1 30W
Mont Tremblant Prov. Park 62 46 30N 74 30W
Montagu 56 33 45S 20 8 E
Montague, Canada 63 46 10N 62 39W
Montague, U.S.A. 72 41 47N 122 30W
Montague, I. 74 31 40N 114 56W
Montague I. 60 60 0N 147 0W
Montague Ra. 47 27 15S 119 30 E
Montague Sd. 46 14 28S 125 20 E
Montalbán 13 40 50N 0 45W
Montaña 78 6 0S 73 0W
Montana □ 66 47 0N 110 0W
Montargis 12 47 59N 2 43 E
Montauban 12 44 0N 1 21 E
Montauk 68 41 3N 71 57W
Montbéliard 12 47 31N 6 48 E
Monte Alegre 79 2 0S 54 0W
Monte Azul 79 15 9S 42 53W
Monte Bello Is. 46 20 30S 115 45 E
Monte-Carlo 12 43 46N 7 23 E
Monte Caseros 80 30 10S 57 50W
Monte Comán 80 34 40S 67 53W
Monte Sant' Ángelo 18 41 42N 15 59 E
Monte Santu, C. di 18 40 5N 9 42 E
Monte Vista 73 37 40N 106 8W
Montebello 62 45 40N 74 55W
Montecristi 78 1 0S 80 40W
Montego Bay 75 18 30N 78 0W
Montejinnie 46 16 40S 131 38 E
Montélimar 12 44 33N 4 45 E
Montello 70 43 49N 89 21W
Montemorelos 74 25 11N 99 42W
Montenegro = Crna Gora □ 19 42 40N 19 20 E
Montepuez 55 13 8S 38 59 E
Monterey 73 36 35N 121 57W
Montería 78 8 46N 75 53W
Monterrey 74 25 40N 100 30W
Montes Claros 79 16 30S 43 50W
Montesano 72 46 58N 123 39W
Montevideo, Uruguay 80 34 50S 56 11W
Montevideo, U.S.A. 70 44 55N 95 40W
Montezuma 70 41 32N 92 35W
Montgomery = Sahiwal 32 30 45N 73 8 E
Montgomery, U.K. 7 52 34N 3 9W
Montgomery, Ala., U.S.A. 69 32 20N 86 20W
Montgomery, W. Va., U.S.A. 68 38 9N 81 21W
Monticello, Ark., U.S.A. 71 33 40N 91 48W
Monticello, Fla., U.S.A. 69 30 35N 83 50W
Monticello, Ind., U.S.A. 68 40 40N 86 45W
Monticello, Iowa, U.S.A. 70 42 18N 91 12W
Monticello, Ky., U.S.A. 69 36 52N 84 50W
Monticello, Minn., U.S.A. 70 45 17N 93 52W
Monticello, Miss., U.S.A. 71 31 35N 90 8W
Monticello, Utah, U.S.A. 73 37 55N 109 27W
Montijo 13 38 52N 6 39W
Montilla 13 37 36N 4 40W
Montluçon 12 46 22N 2 36 E
Montmagny 63 46 58N 70 34W
Montmartre 65 50 14N 103 27W
Montmorency 63 46 53N 71 11W
Monto 44 24 52S 151 6 E
Montoro 13 38 1N 4 27W
Montpelier, Idaho, U.S.A. 72 42 15N 111 20W
Montpelier, Ohio, U.S.A. 68 41 34N 84 40W
Montpelier, Vt., U.S.A. 68 44 15N 72 38W
Montpellier 12 43 37N 3 52 E
Montréal 62 45 31N 73 34W
Montreal L. 65 54 20N 105 45W
Montreal Lake 65 54 3N 105 46W
Montreuil 12 50 27N 1 45 E
Montreux 14 46 26N 6 55 E
Montrose, U.K. 8 56 43N 2 28W
Montrose, U.S.A. 73 38 30N 107 52W
Monts, Pte. des 63 49 20N 67 12W
Montserrat 75 16 40N 62 10W
Monveda 54 2 52N 21 30 E
Monywa 33 22 7N 95 11 E
Monza 18 45 35N 9 15 E
Monze 55 16 17S 27 29 E
Monze, C. 32 24 47N 66 37 E
Monzón 13 41 52N 0 10 E
Mooi River 57 29 13S 29 50 E
Moolawatana 45 29 55S 139 45 E
Mooliabeenee 47 31 20S 116 2 E
Mooloogool 47 26 2S 119 5 E
Moomin, Cr. → 45 29 44S 149 20 E
Moonah → 44 22 3S 138 33 E
Moonbeam 62 49 20N 82 10W
Moonie 45 27 46S 150 20 E
Moonie → 45 29 19S 148 43 E
Moonta 45 34 6S 137 32 E
Moora 47 30 37S 115 58 E
Mooraberree 44 25 13S 140 54 E
Moorarie 47 25 56S 117 35 E
Moorcroft 70 44 17N 104 58W
Moore → 47 31 22S 115 30 E
Moore, L. 47 29 50S 117 35 E
Moore Reefs 44 16 0S 149 5 E
Moorefield 68 39 5N 78 59W
Mooresville 69 35 36N 80 45W
Moorfoot Hills 8 55 44N 3 8W
Moorhead 70 46 51N 96 44W
Mooroopna 45 36 25S 145 22 E
Moorreesburg 56 33 6S 18 38 E
Moose → 62 51 20N 80 25W
Moose Factory 62 51 16N 80 32W
Moose I. 65 51 42N 97 10W
Moose Jaw 65 50 24N 105 30W
Moose Jaw → 65 50 34N 105 18W
Moose Lake, Canada 65 53 43N 100 20W
Moose Lake, U.S.A. 70 46 27N 92 48W
Moose Mountain Cr. → 65 49 13N 102 12W
Moose Mountain Prov. Park 65 49 48N 102 25W
Moose River 62 50 48N 81 17W
Moosehead L. 63 45 34N 69 40W
Moosomin 65 50 9N 101 40W
Moosonee 62 51 17N 80 39W
Mopeia Velha 55 17 30S 35 40 E
Mopipi 56 21 6S 24 55 E
Mopti 50 14 30N 4 0W
Moquegua 78 17 15S 70 46W
Mora, Sweden 21 61 2N 14 38 E
Mora, Minn., U.S.A. 70 45 52N 93 19W
Mora, N. Mex., U.S.A. 73 35 58N 105 21W
Moradabad 32 28 50N 78 50 E
Morafenobe 57 17 50S 44 53 E
Moramanga 57 18 56S 48 12 E
Moran, Kans., U.S.A. 71 37 53N 94 35W
Moran, Wyo., U.S.A. 72 43 53N 110 37W
Moranbah 44 22 1S 148 6 E
Morant Cays 75 17 22N 76 0W
Morant Pt. 75 17 55N 76 12W
Morar L. 8 56 57N 5 40W
Moratuwa 32 6 45N 79 55 E
Morava → 14 48 10N 16 59 E
Moravia 70 40 50N 92 50W
Moravian Hts. = Ceskomoravská Vrchovina 14 49 30N 15 40 E
Morawa 47 29 13S 116 0 E
Morawhanna 78 8 30N 59 40W
Moray Firth 8 57 50N 3 30W
Morbihan □ 12 47 55N 2 50W
Morden 65 49 15N 98 10W
Mordovian A.S.S.R. □ 22 54 20N 44 30 E
Møre og Romsdal fylke □ 20 62 30N 8 0 E
Morea, Australia 45 36 45S 141 18 E
Morea, Greece 4 37 45N 22 10 E
Moreau → 70 45 15N 100 43W
Morecambe 6 54 5N 2 52W
Morecambe B. 6 54 7N 3 0W
Moree 45 29 28S 149 54 E
Morehead 68 38 12N 83 22W
Morehead City 69 34 46N 76 44W
Morelia 74 19 40N 101 11W
Morella, Australia 44 23 0S 143 52 E
Morella, Spain 13 40 35N 0 5W
Morelos □ 74 18 40N 99 10W
Morena, Sierra 13 38 20N 4 0W
Morenci 73 33 7N 109 20W
Moresby I. 64 52 30N 131 40W
Moreton 44 12 22S 142 30 E
Moreton I. 45 27 10S 153 25 E
Morgan, Australia 45 34 0S 139 35 E
Morgan, U.S.A. 72 41 3N 111 44W
Morgan City 71 29 40N 91 15W
Morganfield 68 37 40N 87 55W
Morganton 69 35 46N 81 48W
Morgantown 68 39 39N 79 58W
Morgenzon 57 26 45S 29 36 E
Morice L. 64 53 50N 127 40W
Moriki 53 12 52N 6 30 E
Morinville 64 53 49N 113 41W
Morioka 36 39 45N 141 8 E
Morlaix 12 48 36N 3 52W
Mornington, Vic., Australia 45 38 15S 145 5 E
Mornington, W. Austral., Australia 46 17 31S 126 6 E
Mornington, I. 80 49 50S 75 30W
Mornington I. 44 16 30S 139 30 E
Moro G. 35 6 30N 123 0 E
Morocco ■ 50 32 0N 5 50W
Morococha 78 11 40S 76 5W
Morogoro 54 6 50S 37 40 E
Moroleón 74 20 8N 101 32W
Morombe 57 21 45S 43 22 E
Morón 75 22 8N 78 39W
Mörön → 37 47 14N 110 37 E
Morón de la Frontera 13 37 6N 5 28W
Morondava 57 20 17S 44 17 E
Morotai 35 2 10N 128 30 E
Moroto 54 2 28N 34 42 E
Morpeth 6 55 11N 1 41W
Morphou 30 35 12N 32 59 E
Morrilton 71 35 10N 92 45W
Morrinhos 79 17 45S 49 10W
Morrinsville 43 37 40S 175 32 E
Morris, Canada 65 49 25N 97 22W
Morris, Ill., U.S.A. 68 41 20N 88 20W
Morris, Minn., U.S.A. 70 45 33N 95 56W
Morris, Mt. 47 26 9S 131 4 E
Morrisburg 62 44 55N 75 7W
Morrison 70 41 47N 90 0W
Morristown, Ariz., U.S.A. 73 33 54N 112 35W
Morristown, S. Dak., U.S.A. 70 45 57N 101 44W
Morristown, Tenn., U.S.A. 69 36 18N 83 20W
Morro Bay 73 35 27N 120 54W
Morrosquillo, G. de 75 9 35N 75 40W
Morrumbene 57 23 31S 35 16 E
Morshansk 22 53 28N 41 50 E
Morteros 80 30 50S 62 0W
Mortes, R. das → 79 11 45S 50 44W
Mortlake 45 38 5S 142 50 E
Morton, Tex., U.S.A. 71 33 39N 102 49W

Nairn

Morton, Wash., U.S.A. 72 46 33N 122 17W
Morundah 45 34 57S 146 19 E
Moruya 45 35 58S 150 3 E
Morvan 12 47 5N 4 0 E
Morven 45 26 22S 147 5 E
Morvern 8 56 38N 5 44W
Morwell 45 38 10S 146 22 E
Morzhovets, Ostrov 22 66 44N 42 35 E
Moscos Is. 34 14 0N 97 30 E
Moscow = Moskva 22 55 45N 37 35 E
Moscow 72 46 45N 116 59W
Mosel → 11 50 22N 7 36 E
Moselle = Mosel → 11 50 22N 7 36 E
Moselle □ 12 48 59N 6 33 E
Moses Lake 72 47 9N 119 17W
Mosgiel 43 45 53S 170 21 E
Moshi 54 3 22S 37 18 E
Moshupa 56 24 46S 25 29 E
Mosjøen 20 65 51N 13 12 E
Moskenesøya 20 67 58N 13 0 E
Moskenstraumen 20 67 47N 12 45 E
Moskva 22 55 45N 37 35 E
Moskva → 22 55 5N 38 51 E
Mosomane 56 24 2S 26 19 E
Mosquera 78 2 35N 78 24W
Mosquero 71 35 48N 103 57W
Mosquitos, G. de los 75 9 15N 81 10W
Moss 21 59 27N 10 40 E
Moss Vale 45 34 32S 150 25 E
Mossaka 54 1 15S 16 45 E
Mossbank 65 49 56N 105 56W
Mossburn 43 45 41S 168 15 E
Mosselbaai 56 34 11S 22 8 E
Mossendjo 54 2 55S 12 42 E
Mossgiel 45 33 15S 144 5 E
Mossman 44 16 21S 145 15 E
Mossoró 79 5 10S 37 15W
Mossuril 55 14 58S 40 42 E
Mossy → 65 54 5N 102 58W
Most 14 50 31N 13 38 E
Mosta 18 35 54N 14 24 E
Mostaganem 50 35 54N 0 5 E
Mostar 19 43 22N 17 50 E
Mostardas 80 31 2S 50 51W
Mosul = Al Mawşil 30 36 15N 43 5 E
Motagua → 75 15 44N 88 14W
Motala 21 58 32N 15 1 E
Motherwell 8 55 48N 4 0W
Motihari 33 26 30N 84 55 E
Motozintla de Mendoza 74 15 21N 92 14W
Mott 70 46 25N 102 29W
Motueka 43 41 7S 173 1 E
Motul 74 21 0N 89 20W
Mouanda 54 1 28S 13 7 E
Mouchalagane → 63 50 56N 68 41W
Moúdhros 19 39 50N 25 18 E
Moudjeria 50 17 50N 12 28W
Mouila 54 1 50S 11 0 E
Moulamein 45 35 3S 144 1 E
Moule 75 16 20N 61 22W
Moulins 12 46 35N 3 19 E
Moulmein 33 16 30N 97 40 E
Moulton 71 29 35N 97 8W
Moultrie 69 31 11N 83 47W
Moultrie, L. 69 33 25N 80 10W
Mound City, Mo., U.S.A. 70 40 2N 95 25W
Mound City, S. Dak., U.S.A. 70 45 46N 100 3W
Moundou 51 8 40N 16 10 E
Moundsville 68 39 53N 80 43W
Mount Airy 69 36 31N 80 37W
Mount Amherst 46 18 24S 126 58 E
Mount Angel 72 45 4N 122 46W
Mount Augustus 47 24 20S 116 56 E
Mount Barker, S. Austral., Australia 45 35 5S 138 52 E
Mount Barker, W. Austral., Australia 47 34 38S 117 40 E
Mount Carmel 68 38 20N 87 48W
Mount Clemens 62 42 35N 82 50W
Mount Coolon 44 21 25S 147 25 E
Mount Darwin 55 16 47S 31 38 E
Mount Desert I. 63 44 15N 68 25W
Mount Dora 69 28 49N 81 32W
Mount Douglas 44 21 35S 146 50 E
Mount Edgecumbe 64 57 8N 135 22W
Mount Elizabeth 46 16 0S 125 50 E
Mount Fletcher 57 30 40S 28 30 E
Mount Forest 62 43 59N 80 43W
Mount Gambier 45 37 50S 140 46 E
Mount Garnet 44 17 37S 145 6 E
Mount Hope, N.S.W., Australia 45 32 51S 145 51 E
Mount Hope, S. Austral., Australia 45 34 7S 135 23 E
Mount Hope, U.S.A. 68 37 52N 81 9W
Mount Horeb 70 43 0N 89 42W
Mount Howitt 45 26 31S 142 16 E
Mount Isa 44 20 42S 139 26 E
Mount Keith 47 27 15S 120 30 E
Mount Larcom 44 23 48S 150 59 E
Mount Lofty Ra. 45 34 35S 139 5 E
Mount McKinley Nat. Park 60 64 0N 150 0W
Mount Magnet 47 28 2S 117 47 E
Mount Margaret 45 26 54S 143 21 E
Mount Maunganui 43 37 40S 176 14 E
Mount Molloy 44 16 42S 145 20 E
Mount Monger 47 31 0S 122 0 E
Mount Morgan 44 23 40S 150 25 E
Mount Morris 68 42 43N 77 50W
Mount Mulligan 44 16 45S 144 47 E
Mount Narryer 47 26 30S 115 55 E
Mount Oxide Mine 44 19 30S 139 29 E
Mount Pearl 63 47 31N 52 47W
Mount Perry 45 25 13S 151 42 E
Mount Phillips 47 24 25S 116 15 E
Mount Pleasant, Iowa, U.S.A. 70 40 58N 91 35W
Mount Pleasant, Mich., U.S.A. 68 43 35N 84 47W
Mount Pleasant, S.C., U.S.A. 69 32 45N 79 48W
Mount Pleasant, Tenn., U.S.A. 69 35 31N 87 11W
Mount Pleasant, Tex., U.S.A. 71 33 5N 95 0W
Mount Pleasant, Utah, U.S.A. 72 39 40N 111 29W
Mount Rainier Nat. Park 72 46 50N 121 43W
Mount Revelstoke Nat. Park 64 51 5N 118 30W
Mount Robson Prov. Park 64 53 0N 119 0W
Mount Sandiman 47 24 25S 115 30 E
Mount Shasta 72 41 20N 122 18W
Mount Sterling, Ill., U.S.A. 70 39 59N 90 40W
Mount Sterling, Ky., U.S.A. 68 38 3N 83 57W
Mount Surprise 44 18 10S 144 17 E
Mount Vernon, Australia 47 24 9S 118 2 E
Mount Vernon, Ind., U.S.A. 70 38 17N 88 57W
Mount Vernon, N.Y., U.S.A. 68 40 57N 73 49W
Mount Vernon, Ohio, U.S.A. 68 40 20N 82 30W
Mount Vernon, Wash., U.S.A. 72 48 25N 122 20W
Mountain City, Nev., U.S.A. 72 41 54N 116 0W
Mountain City, Tenn., U.S.A. 69 36 30N 81 50W
Mountain Grove 71 37 5N 92 20W
Mountain Home, Ark., U.S.A. 71 36 20N 92 25W
Mountain Home, Idaho, U.S.A. 72 43 11N 115 45W
Mountain Iron 70 47 30N 92 37W
Mountain Park 64 52 50N 117 15W
Mountain View, Ark., U.S.A. 71 35 52N 92 10W
Mountain View, Calif., U.S.A. 73 37 26N 122 5W
Mountainair 73 34 35N 106 15W
Mountmellick 9 53 7N 7 20W
Moura, Australia 44 24 35S 149 58 E
Moura, Brazil 78 1 32S 61 38W
Mourdi, Dépression du 51 18 10N 23 0 E
Mourdiah 50 14 35N 7 25W
Moure, La 70 46 27N 98 17W
Mourilyan 44 17 35S 146 3 E
Mourne → 9 54 45N 7 39W
Mourne Mts. 9 54 10N 6 0W
Mouscron 11 50 45N 3 12 E
Moussoro 51 13 41N 16 35 E
Moutong 35 0 28N 121 13 E
Moville 9 55 11N 7 3W
Moy → 9 54 5N 8 50W
Moyale, Ethiopia 29 3 34N 39 4 E
Moyale, Kenya 54 3 30N 39 0 E
Moyamba 50 8 4N 12 30W
Moyen Atlas 50 33 0N 5 0W
Moyle □ 9 55 10N 6 15W
Moyo 34 8 10S 117 40 E
Moyobamba 78 6 0S 77 0W
Moyyero → 25 68 44N 103 42 E
Mozambique = Moçambique 55 15 3S 40 42 E
Mozambique ■ 55 19 0S 35 0 E
Mozambique Chan. 57 17 30S 42 30 E
Mozdok 23 43 45N 44 48 E
Mozyr 22 52 0N 29 15 E
Mpanda 54 6 23S 31 1 E
Mpika 55 11 51S 31 25 E
Mporokoso 52 9 25S 30 5 E
Mpumalanga 57 29 50S 30 33 E
Mpwapwa 54 6 23S 36 30 E
Msaken 51 35 49N 10 33 E
Msoro 55 13 35S 31 50 E
Mtubatuba 57 28 30S 32 8 E
Mtwara-Mikindani 52 10 20S 40 20 E
Mu Us Shamo 38 39 0N 109 0 E
Muaná 79 1 25S 49 15W
Muar 34 2 3N 102 34 E
Muarabungo 34 1 28S 102 52 E
Muaraenim 34 3 40S 103 50 E
Muarajuloi 34 0 12S 114 3 E
Muarakaman 34 0 2S 116 45 E
Muaratebo 34 1 30S 102 26 E
Muaratembesi 34 1 42S 103 8 E
Muaratewe 34 0 58S 114 52 E
Mubende 54 0 33N 31 22 E
Mubi 53 10 18N 13 16 E
Muck 8 56 50N 6 15W
Muckadilla 45 26 35S 148 23 E
Muconda 54 10 31S 21 15 E
Mucuri 79 18 0S 39 36W
Mucusso 56 18 1S 21 25 E
Mudanjiang 38 44 38N 129 30 E
Muddy → 73 38 0N 110 22W
Mudgee 45 32 32S 149 31 E
Mudjatik → 65 56 1N 107 36W
Muêda 52 11 36S 39 28 E
Mueller Ra. 46 18 18S 126 46 E
Muerto, Mar 74 16 10N 94 10W
Mufulira 55 12 32S 28 15 E
Muğla 30 37 15N 28 22 E
Mugu 33 29 45N 82 30 E
Muhammad Qol 51 20 53N 37 9 E
Muharraqa = Sa'ad 28 31 28N 34 33 E
Muikamachi 36 37 15N 138 50 E
Muine Bheag 9 52 42N 6 57W
Muir, L. 47 34 30S 116 40 E
Mukah 34 2 55N 112 5 E
Mukden = Shenyang 38 41 48N 123 27 E
Mukhtuya = Lensk 25 60 48N 114 55 E
Mukinbudin 47 30 55S 118 5 E
Mukomuko 34 2 30S 101 10 E
Muktsar 32 30 30N 74 30 E
Mukur 32 32 50N 67 42 E
Mukutawa → 65 53 10N 97 24W
Mulchén 80 37 45S 72 20W
Mulde → 14 51 50N 12 15 E
Mule Creek 70 43 19N 104 8W
Muleba 52 1 50S 31 37 E
Muleshoe 71 34 17N 102 42W
Mulgathing 45 30 15S 134 8 E
Mulgrave 63 45 38N 61 31W
Mulhacén 13 37 4N 3 20W
Mülheim 14 51 26N 6 53 E
Mulhouse 14 47 40N 7 20 E
Muling He → 38 45 53N 133 30 E
Mull 8 56 27N 6 0W
Mullaittvu 32 9 15N 80 49 E
Mullen 70 42 5N 101 0W
Mullengudgery 45 31 43S 147 23 E
Mullens 68 37 34N 81 22W
Muller, Pegunungan 34 0 30N 113 30 E
Mullet Pen. 9 54 10N 10 2W
Mullewa 47 28 29S 115 30 E
Mulligan → 45 26 40S 139 0 E
Mullin 71 31 33N 98 38W
Mullingar 9 53 31N 7 20W
Mullins 69 34 12N 79 15W
Mullumbimby 45 28 30S 153 30 E
Multan 32 30 15N 71 36 E
Mulvane 71 37 30N 97 15W
Mumbwa 55 15 0S 27 0 E
Muna 35 5 0S 122 30 E
München 14 48 8N 11 33 E
München-Gladbach = Mönchengladbach 14 51 12N 6 23 E
Muncho Lake 64 59 0N 125 50W
Muncie 68 40 10N 85 20W
Mundala 35 4 30S 141 0 E
Mundare 64 53 35N 112 20W
Munday 71 33 26N 99 39W
Münden 14 51 25N 9 42 E
Mundiwindi 46 23 47S 120 9 E
Mundo Novo 79 11 50S 40 29W
Mundrabilla 47 31 52S 127 51 E
Mungallala 45 26 28S 147 34 E
Mungallala Cr. → 45 28 53S 147 5 E
Mungana 44 17 8S 144 27 E
Mungbere 54 2 36N 28 28 E
Munger 33 25 23N 86 30 E
Mungindi 45 28 58S 149 1 E
Munhango 55 12 10S 18 38 E
Munich = München 14 48 8N 11 33 E
Munising 68 46 25N 86 39W
Munku-Sardyk 25 51 45N 100 20 E
Muñoz Gamero, Pen. 80 52 30S 73 5 E
Munroe L. 65 59 13N 98 35W
Münster 14 51 58N 7 37 E
Munster □ 9 52 20N 8 40W
Muntadgin 47 31 45S 118 33 E
Muntok 34 2 5S 105 10 E
Munyak 24 43 30N 59 15 E
Muonio 20 67 57N 23 40 E
Mupa 55 16 5S 15 50 E
Muping 38 37 22N 121 36 E
Muqdisho 29 2 2N 45 25 E
Mur → 14 46 35N 16 3 E
Murallón, Cuerro 80 49 48S 73 30W
Murang'a 54 0 45S 37 9 E
Murashi 22 59 30N 49 0 E
Murchison → 47 27 45S 114 0 E
Murchison Falls = Kabarega Falls 54 2 15N 31 30 E
Murchison House 47 27 39S 114 14 E
Murchison Ra. 44 20 0S 134 10 E
Murcia 13 38 20N 1 10W
Murcia □ 13 37 50N 1 30W
Murdo 70 43 56N 100 43W
Murdoch Pt. 44 14 37S 144 55 E
Mureş → 15 46 15N 20 13 E
Mureşul = Mureş → 15 46 15N 20 13 E
Murfreesboro 69 35 50N 86 21W
Murgab 24 38 10N 74 2 E
Murgon 45 26 15S 151 54 E
Murgoo 47 27 24S 116 28 E
Muria 35 6 36S 110 53 E
Müritz See 14 53 25N 12 40 E
Murmansk 22 68 57N 33 10 E
Murom 22 55 35N 42 3 E
Muroran 36 42 25N 141 0 E
Muroto-Misaki 36 33 15N 134 10 E
Murphy 72 43 11N 116 33W
Murphysboro 71 37 50N 89 20W
Murray, Ky., U.S.A. 69 36 40N 88 20W
Murray, Utah, U.S.A. 72 40 41N 111 58W
Murray →, Australia 45 35 20S 139 22 E
Murray →, Canada 64 56 11N 120 45W
Murray, L. 69 34 8N 81 30W
Murray Bridge 45 35 6S 139 14 E
Murray Downs 44 21 4S 134 40 E
Murray Harbour 63 46 0N 62 28W
Murray Seascarp 41 30 0N 135 0W
Murraysburg 56 31 58S 23 47 E
Murree 32 33 56N 73 28 E
Murrin Murrin 47 28 58S 121 33 E
Murrumbidgee → 45 34 43S 143 12 E
Murrumburrah 45 34 32S 148 22 E
Murrurundi 45 31 42S 150 51 E
Mursala 34 1 41N 98 28 E
Murtle L. 64 52 8N 119 38W
Murtoa 45 36 35S 142 28 E
Murwara 33 23 46N 80 28 E
Murwillumbah 45 28 18S 153 27 E
Mürzzuschlag 14 47 36N 15 41 E
Muş 30 38 45N 41 30 E
Mûsa, G. 30 28 33N 33 59 E
Musa Khel 32 30 59N 69 52 E
Mūsá Qal'eh 31 32 20N 64 50 E
Musaffargarh 32 30 10N 71 10 E
Musala 19 42 13N 23 37 E
Musan 38 42 12N 129 12 E
Musay'īd 31 25 0N 51 33 E
Muscat = Masqat 31 23 37N 58 36 E
Muscat & Oman = Oman ■ 29 23 0N 58 0 E
Muscatine 70 41 25N 91 5W
Musgrave Ras. 47 26 0S 132 0 E
Mushie 54 2 56S 16 55 E
Mushin 53 6 32N 3 21 E
Musi → 34 2 20S 104 56 E
Muskeg → 64 60 20N 123 20W
Muskegon 68 43 15N 86 17W
Muskegon → 68 43 25N 86 0W
Muskegon Hts. 68 43 12N 86 17W
Muskogee 71 35 50N 95 25W
Muskwa → 64 58 47N 122 48W
Musmar 51 18 13N 35 40 E
Musoma 54 1 30S 33 48 E
Musquaro, L. 63 50 38N 61 5W
Musquodoboit Harbour 63 44 50N 63 9W
Musselburgh 8 55 57N 3 3W
Musselshell → 72 47 21N 107 58W
Mussoorie 32 30 27N 78 6 E
Mussuco 56 17 2S 19 3 E
Mustang 33 29 10N 83 55 E
Musters, L. 80 45 20S 69 25W
Muswellbrook 45 32 16S 150 56 E
Mût, Egypt 51 25 28N 28 58 E
Mut, Turkey 30 36 40N 33 28 E
Mutanda 57 21 0S 33 34 E
Mutaray 25 60 56N 101 0 E
Mutare 55 18 58S 32 38 E
Muting 35 7 23S 140 20 E
Mutsu-Wan 36 41 5N 140 55 E
Muttaburra 44 22 38S 144 29 E
Muxima 54 9 33S 13 58 E
Muya 25 56 27N 115 50 E
Muzaffarabad 32 34 25N 73 30 E
Muzaffarnagar 32 29 26N 77 40 E
Muzaffarpur 33 26 7N 85 23 E
Muzhi 24 65 25N 64 40 E
Muzon C. 64 54 40N 132 40W
Muztag 37 36 20N 87 28 E
Mvuma 55 19 16S 30 30 E
Mwanza, Tanzania 54 2 30S 32 58 E
Mwanza, Zaïre 54 7 55S 26 43 E
Mweelrea 9 53 37N 9 48W
Mweka 54 4 50S 21 34 E
Mwenezi 55 21 15S 30 48 E
Mwenga 54 3 1S 28 28 E
Mweru, L. 54 9 0S 28 40 E
Mwinilunga 55 11 43S 24 25 E
Mwirasandu 52 0 56S 30 22 E
My Tho 34 10 29N 106 23 E
Myanaung 33 18 18N 95 22 E
Myaungmya 33 16 30N 94 40 E
Mycenae = Mikinai 19 37 43N 22 46 E
Myeik Kyunzu 34 11 30N 97 30 E
Myingyan 33 21 30N 95 20 E
Myitkyina 33 25 24N 97 26 E
Mymensingh 33 24 45N 90 24 E
Mynydd Du 7 51 45N 3 45W
Mýrdalsjökull 20 63 40N 19 6W
Myrtle Beach 69 33 43N 78 50W
Myrtle Creek 72 43 0N 123 9W
Myrtle Point 72 43 0N 124 4W
Mysore 32 12 17N 76 41 E
Mysore □ = Karnataka □ 32 13 15N 77 0 E
Myton 72 40 10N 110 2W
Mývatn 20 65 36N 17 0W
Mzimkulu → 57 30 44S 30 28 E
Mzimvubu → 57 31 38S 29 33 E

N

Naab → 14 49 1N 12 2 E
Na'an 28 31 53N 34 52 E
Naantali 21 60 29N 22 2 E
Naas 9 53 12N 6 40W
Nababiep 56 29 36S 17 46 E
Nabawa 47 28 30S 114 48 E
Nabberu, L. 47 25 50S 120 30 E
Nabeul 51 36 30N 10 44 E
Nabire 35 3 15S 135 26 E
Nabisipi → 63 50 14N 62 13W
Nablus = Nābulus 28 32 14N 35 15 E
Naboomspruit 57 24 32S 28 40 E
Nābulus 28 32 14N 35 15 E
Naches 72 46 48N 120 42W
Nachingwea 54 10 23S 38 49 E
Nackara 45 32 48S 139 12 E
Naco 73 31 24N 109 58W
Nacogdoches 71 31 33N 94 39W
Nacozari 74 30 24N 109 39W
Nadiad 32 22 41N 72 56 E
Nadūshan 31 32 2N 53 35 E
Nadvoitsy 22 63 52N 34 14 E
Nadym 24 65 35N 72 42 E
Nadym → 24 66 12N 72 0 E
Nafada 53 11 8N 11 20 E
Naftshahr 30 34 0N 45 30 E
Nafūd ad Dahy 30 22 0N 45 0 E
Naga 35 13 38N 123 15 E
Naga Hills 33 26 0N 94 30 E
Nagagami → 62 49 40N 84 40W
Nagaland □ 33 26 0N 94 30 E
Nagano 36 36 40N 138 10 E
Nagano □ 36 36 15N 138 0 E
Nagaoka 36 37 27N 138 51 E
Nagappattinam 32 10 46N 79 51 E
Nagar Parkar 32 24 30N 70 35 E
Nagasaki 36 32 47N 129 50 E
Nagasaki □ 36 32 50N 129 40 E
Nagaur 32 27 15N 73 45 E
Nagercoil 32 8 12N 77 26 E
Nagīneh 31 34 20N 57 15 E
Nagoorin 44 24 17S 151 15 E
Nagornyy 25 55 58N 124 57 E
Nagoya 36 35 10N 136 50 E
Nagpur 32 21 8N 79 10 E
Nagykanizsa 14 46 28N 17 0 E
Nagykörös 15 47 5N 19 48 E
Naha 39 26 13N 127 42 E
Nahalal 28 32 41N 35 12 E
Nahanni Butte 64 61 2N 123 31W
Nahanni Nat. Park 64 61 15N 125 0W
Nahariyya 28 33 1N 35 5 E
Nahāvand 30 34 10N 48 22 E
Nahf 28 32 56N 35 18 E
Nahlin 64 58 55N 131 38W
Naicam 65 52 30N 104 30W
Nā'ifah 29 19 59N 50 46 E
Nain, Canada 63 56 34N 61 40W
Nā'īn, Iran 31 32 54N 53 0 E
Nainpur 32 22 30N 80 10 E
Naira 35 4 28S 130 0 E
Nairn 8 57 35N 3 54W

Nairobi

Nairobi 54 1 17S 36 48 E
Naivasha 54 0 40S 36 30 E
Najafābād 31 32 40N 51 15 E
Najd 30 26 30N 42 0 E
Najibabad 32 29 40N 78 20 E
Najin 38 42 12N 130 15 E
Nakadōri-Shima 36 32 57N 129 4 E
Nakamura 36 33 0N 133 0 E
Nakfa 51 16 40N 38 32 E
Nakhichevan A.S.S.R. □ 23 39 14N 45 30 E
Nakhodka 25 42 53N 132 54 E
Nakhon Phanom 34 17 23N 104 43 E
Nakhon Ratchasima 34 14 59N 102 12 E
Nakhon Sawan 34 15 35N 100 10 E
Nakhon Si Thammarat 34 8 29N 100 0 E
Nakina, B.C., Canada 64 59 12N 132 52W
Nakina, Ont., Canada 62 50 10N 86 40W
Nakskov 21 54 50N 11 8 E
Naktong → 38 35 7N 128 57 E
Nakuru 54 0 15S 36 4 E
Nakusp 64 50 20N 117 45W
Nal → 32 25 20N 65 30 E
Nalchik 23 43 30N 43 33 E
Nalgonda 32 17 6N 79 15 E
Nallamalai Hills 32 15 30N 78 50 E
Nalón → 13 43 32N 6 4W
Nālūt 51 31 54N 11 0 E
Nam Co 37 30 30N 90 45 E
Nam-Phan 34 10 30N 106 0 E
Namacunde 56 17 18S 15 50 E
Namacurra 57 17 30S 36 50 E
Namak, Daryācheh-ye 31 34 30N 52 0 E
Namak, Kavir-e 31 34 30N 57 30 E
Namaland 56 24 30S 17 0 E
Namangan 24 41 0N 71 40 E
Namapa 55 13 43S 39 50 E
Namaqualand 56 30 0S 17 25 E
Namasagali 52 1 2N 33 0 E
Namber 35 1 2S 134 49 E
Nambour 45 26 32S 152 58 E
Nambucca Heads 45 30 37S 153 0 E
Nameh 34 2 34N 116 21 E
Namew L. 65 54 14N 101 56W
Namib Desert = Namibwoestyn 56 22 30S 15 0 E
Namibe 55 15 7S 12 11 E
Namibe □ 56 16 35S 12 30 E
Namibia ■ 56 22 0S 18 9 E
Namibwoestyn 56 22 30S 15 0 E
Namlea 35 3 18S 127 5 E
Namoi → 45 30 12S 149 30 E
Nampa 72 43 34N 116 34W
Nampula 55 15 6S 39 15 E
Namrole 35 3 46S 126 46 E
Namse Shankou 33 30 0N 82 25 E
Namsen → 20 64 27N 11 42 E
Namsos 20 64 29N 11 30 E
Namtay 25 62 43N 129 37 E
Namtu 33 23 5N 97 28 E
Namu 64 51 52N 127 50W
Namur 11 50 27N 4 52 E
Namur □ 11 50 17N 5 0 E
Namutoni 56 18 49S 16 55 E
Namwala 55 15 44S 26 30 E
Nanaimo 64 49 10N 124 0W
Nanam 38 41 44N 129 40 E
Nanan 39 24 59N 118 21 E
Nanango 45 26 40S 152 0 E
Nan'ao, China 39 23 28N 117 5 E
Nanao, Japan 36 37 0N 137 0 E
Nanbu 39 31 18N 106 3 E
Nanchang 39 28 42N 115 55 E
Nancheng 39 27 33N 116 35 E
Nanching = Nanjing 39 32 2N 118 47 E
Nanchong 39 30 43N 106 2 E
Nanchuan 39 29 9N 107 6 E
Nancy 12 48 42N 6 12 E
Nanda Devi 32 30 23N 79 59 E
Nandan 39 24 58N 107 29 E
Nanded 32 19 10N 77 20 E
Nandewar Ra. 45 30 15S 150 35 E
Nandi 43 17 42S 177 20 E
Nandurbar 32 21 20N 74 15 E
Nandyal 32 15 30N 78 30 E
Nanga 47 26 7S 113 45 E
Nanga-Eboko 54 4 41N 12 22 E
Nanga Parbat 32 35 10N 74 35 E
Nangapinoh 34 0 20S 111 44 E
Nangarhár □ 31 34 20N 70 0 E
Nangatayap 34 1 32S 110 34 E
Nanjiang 39 32 28N 106 51 E
Nanjing 39 32 2N 118 47 E
Nankang 39 25 40N 114 45 E
Nanking = Nanjing 39 32 2N 118 47 E
Nanning 39 22 48N 108 20 E
Nannup 47 33 59S 115 48 E
Nanpi 38 38 2N 116 45 E
Nanping 39 26 38N 118 10 E
Nansei-Shotō 37 26 0N 128 0 E
Nantes 12 47 12N 1 33W
Nanticoke 68 41 12N 76 1W
Nanton 64 50 21N 113 46W
Nantong 39 32 1N 120 52 E
Nantucket I. 58 41 16N 70 3W
Nanuque 79 17 50S 40 21W
Nanutarra 46 22 32S 115 30 E
Nanxiong 39 25 6N 114 15 E
Nanyang 39 33 11N 112 30 E
Nanyuan 38 39 44N 116 22 E
Nanyuki 54 0 2N 37 4 E
Nanzhang 39 31 45N 111 50 E
Náo, C. de la 13 38 44N 0 14 E
Naococane L. 63 52 50N 70 45W
Naoetsu 36 37 12N 138 10 E
Naoli He → 38 47 18N 134 9 E
Napa 72 38 18N 122 17W
Napanee 62 44 15N 77 0W
Napier 43 39 30S 176 56 E
Napier Broome B. 46 14 2S 126 37 E
Napier Downs 46 17 11S 124 36 E
Napier Pen. 44 12 4S 135 43 E
Naples = Nápoli 18 40 50N 14 17 E
Naples 69 26 10N 81 45W
Napo → 78 3 20S 72 40W
Napoleon, N. Dak., U.S.A. 70 46 32N 99 49W
Napoleon, Ohio, U.S.A. 68 41 24N 84 7W
Nápoli 18 40 50N 14 17 E
Nappa Merrie 45 27 36S 141 7 E
Nara, Japan 36 34 40N 135 49 E
Nara, Mali 50 15 10N 7 20W
Nara □ 36 34 30N 136 0 E
Nara Visa 71 35 39N 103 10W
Naracoorte 45 36 58S 140 45 E
Naradhan 45 33 34S 146 17 E
Narasapur 33 16 26N 81 40 E
Narathiwat 34 6 30N 101 48 E
Narayanganj 33 23 40N 90 33 E
Narayanpet 32 16 45N 77 30 E
Narbonne 12 43 11N 3 0 E
Nardò 19 40 10N 18 0 E
Narembeen 47 32 7S 118 24 E
Nares Stræde 58 80 0N 70 0W
Naretha 47 31 0S 124 45 E
Narin 32 36 5N 69 0 E
Narindra, Helodranon' i 57 14 55S 47 30 E
Narmada → 32 21 38N 72 36 E
Narodnaya 22 65 5N 60 0 E
Narok 52 1 55S 35 52 E
Narooma 45 36 14S 150 4 E
Narrabri 45 30 19S 149 46 E
Narran → 45 28 37S 148 12 E
Narrandera 45 34 42S 146 31 E
Narraway → 64 55 44N 119 55W
Narrogin 47 32 58S 117 14 E
Narromine 45 32 12S 148 12 E
Narsimhapur 32 22 54N 79 14 E
Narva 22 59 23N 28 12 E
Narvik 20 68 28N 17 26 E
Naryan-Mar 22 68 0N 53 0 E
Naryilco 45 28 37S 141 53 E
Narym 24 59 0N 81 30 E
Narymskoye 24 49 10N 84 15 E
Naryn 24 41 26N 75 58 E
Nasa 20 66 29N 15 23 E
Nasarawa 53 8 32N 7 41 E
Naseby 43 45 1S 170 10 E
Naser, Buheirat en 51 23 0N 32 30 E
Nashua, Iowa, U.S.A. 70 42 55N 92 34W
Nashua, Mont., U.S.A. 72 48 10N 106 25W
Nashua, N.H., U.S.A. 68 42 50N 71 25W
Nashville, Ark., U.S.A. 71 33 56N 93 50W
Nashville, Ga., U.S.A. 69 31 3N 83 15W
Nashville, Tenn., U.S.A. 69 36 12N 86 46W
Nasik 32 19 58N 73 50 E
Nasirabad 32 26 15N 74 45 E
Naskaupi → 63 53 47N 60 51W
Nass → 64 55 0N 129 40W
Nassau 75 25 0N 77 20W
Nassau, B. 80 55 20S 68 0W
Nasser, L. = Naser, Buheirat en 51 23 0N 32 30 E
Nässjö 21 57 39N 14 42 E
Nat Kyizin 33 14 57N 97 59 E
Nata 56 20 12S 26 12 E
Natagaima 78 3 37N 75 6W
Natal, Brazil 79 5 47S 35 13W
Natal, Canada 64 49 43N 114 51W
Natal, Indonesia 34 0 35N 99 7 E
Natal □ 57 28 30S 30 30 E
Naṭanz 31 33 30N 51 55 E
Natashquan 63 50 14N 61 46W
Natashquan → 63 50 7N 61 50W
Natchez 71 31 35N 91 25W
Natchitoches 71 31 47N 93 4W
Nathalia 45 36 1S 145 13 E
Nathdwara 32 24 55N 73 50 E
Natimuk 45 36 42S 142 0 E
Nation → 64 55 30N 123 32W
National City 73 32 39N 117 7W
Natitingou 53 10 20N 1 26 E
Natividad, I. 74 27 50N 115 10W
Natoma 70 39 14N 99 0W
Natron, L. 54 2 20S 36 0 E
Natuna Besar, Kepulauan 34 4 0N 108 15 E
Natuna Selatan, Kepulauan 34 2 45N 109 0 E
Naturaliste C. 44 40 50S 148 15 E
Naubinway 62 46 7N 85 27W
Naumburg 14 51 10N 11 48 E
Nauru ■ 3 1 0S 166 0 E
Naushahra = Nowshera 32 34 0N 72 0 E
Nauta 78 4 31S 73 35W
Nautanwa 33 27 20N 83 25 E
Nautla 74 20 20N 96 50W
Navajo Res. 73 36 55N 107 30W
Navalcarnero 13 40 17N 4 5W
Navan = An Uaimh 9 53 39N 6 40W
Navarino, I. 80 55 0S 67 40W
Navarra □ 13 42 40N 1 40W
Navasota 71 30 20N 96 5W
Navassa 75 18 30N 75 0W
Naver → 8 58 34N 4 15W
Navoi 24 40 9N 65 22 E
Navojoa 74 27 0N 109 30W
Navolok 22 62 33N 39 57 E
Návpaktos 19 38 23N 21 50 E
Návplion 19 37 33N 22 50 E
Navsari 32 20 57N 72 59 E
Nawabshah 32 26 15N 68 25 E
Nawakot 33 27 55N 85 10 E
Nawalgarh 32 27 50N 75 15 E
Nawāsif, Harrat 30 21 20N 42 10 E
Náxos 19 37 8N 25 25 E
Nāy Band 31 27 20N 52 40 E
Nayakhan 25 61 56N 159 0 E
Nayarit □ 74 22 0N 105 0W
Nazareth = Naẓerat 28 32 42N 35 17 E
Nazas 74 25 10N 104 6W
Nazas → 74 25 35N 103 25W
Naze, The 7 51 53N 1 19 E
Naẓerat 28 32 42N 35 17 E
Nazir Hat 33 22 35N 91 49 E
Nazko 64 53 1N 123 37W
Nazko → 64 53 7N 123 34W
Ncheu 55 14 50S 34 47 E
Ndala 52 4 45S 33 15 E
Ndalatando 54 9 12S 14 48 E
Ndélé 51 8 25N 20 36 E
Ndendé 54 2 22S 11 23 E
Ndjamena 51 12 10N 14 59 E
Ndjolé 54 0 10S 10 45 E
Ndola 55 13 0S 28 34 E
Neagh, Lough 9 54 35N 6 25W
Neah Bay 72 48 25N 124 40W
Neale L. 46 24 15S 130 0 E
Near Is. 60 53 0N 172 0 E
Neath 7 51 39N 3 49W
Nebine Cr. → 45 29 27S 146 56 E
Nebit Dag 23 39 30N 54 22 E
Nebo 44 59 12N 32 25 E
Nebraska □ 70 41 30N 100 0W
Nebraska City 70 40 40N 95 52W
Nébrodi, Monti 18 37 55N 14 50 E
Necedah 70 44 2N 90 7W
Nechako → 64 53 30N 122 44W
Neches → 71 29 55N 93 52W
Neckar → 14 49 31N 8 26 E
Necochea 80 38 30S 58 50W
Needles 73 34 50N 114 35W
Needles, The 7 50 39N 1 35W
Neemuch = Nimach 32 24 30N 74 56 E
Neenah 68 44 10N 88 30W
Neepawa 65 50 15N 99 30W
Neft-chala = imeni 26 Bakinskikh Komissarov 23 39 19N 49 12 E
Nefta 50 33 53N 7 50 E
Neftyannyye Kamni 23 40 20N 50 55 E
Negapatam = Nagappattinam 32 10 46N 79 51 E
Negaunee 68 46 30N 87 36W
Negba 28 31 40N 34 41 E
Negele 29 5 20N 39 36 E
Negev Desert = Hanegev 28 30 50N 35 0 E
Negoiul, Vf. 15 45 38N 24 35 E
Negombo 32 7 12N 79 50 E
Negotin 19 44 16N 22 37 E
Negra Pt. 35 18 40N 120 50 E
Negro →, Argentina 80 41 2S 62 47W
Negro →, Brazil 78 3 0S 60 0W
Negro →, Uruguay 80 33 24S 58 22W
Negros 35 9 30N 122 40 E
Nehbandān 31 31 35N 60 5 E
Nei Monggol Zizhiqu □ 38 42 0N 112 0 E
Neidpath 65 50 12N 107 20W
Neihart 72 47 0N 110 44W
Neijiang 39 29 35N 104 55 E
Neilton 72 47 24N 123 52W
Neisse → 14 52 4N 14 46 E
Neiva 78 2 56N 75 18W
Neixiang 39 33 10N 111 52 E
Nejanilini L. 65 59 33N 97 48W
Nekemte 51 9 4N 36 30 E
Neksø 21 55 4N 15 8 E
Nelia 44 20 39S 142 12 E
Neligh 70 42 11N 98 2W
Nelkan 25 57 40N 136 4 E
Nellore 32 14 27N 79 59 E
Nelma 25 47 39N 139 0 E
Nelson, Canada 64 49 30N 117 20W
Nelson, N.Z. 43 41 18S 173 16 E
Nelson, U.K. 6 53 50N 2 14W
Nelson, U.S.A. 73 35 35N 113 16W
Nelson □ 43 42 11S 172 15 E
Nelson → 65 54 33N 98 2W
Nelson, C. 45 38 26S 141 32 E
Nelson, Estrecho 80 51 30S 75 0W
Nelson Forks 64 59 30N 124 0W
Nelson House 65 55 47N 98 51W
Nelson L. 65 55 48N 100 7W
Nelspoort 56 32 7S 23 0 E
Nelspruit 57 25 29S 30 59 E
Néma 50 16 40N 7 15W
Neman → 22 55 25N 21 10 E
Nemeiben L. 65 55 20N 105 20W
Nemunas = Neman → 22 55 25N 21 10 E
Nemuro 36 43 20N 145 35 E
Nemuro-Kaikyō 36 43 30N 145 30 E
Nemuy 25 55 40N 136 9 E
Nen Jiang → 38 45 28N 124 30 E
Nenagh 9 52 52N 8 11W
Nenana 60 64 30N 149 20W
Nene → 6 52 38N 0 13 E
Nenjiang 38 49 10N 125 10 E
Nenusa, Kepulauan 35 4 45N 127 1 E
Neodesha 71 37 30N 95 37W
Neosho 71 36 56N 94 28W
Neosho → 71 35 59N 95 10W
Nepal ■ 33 28 0N 84 30 E
Nepalganj 33 28 5N 81 40 E
Nephi 72 39 43N 111 52W
Nephin 9 54 1N 9 21W
Nerchinsk 25 52 0N 116 39 E
Nerchinskiy Zavod 25 51 20N 119 40 E
Néret L. 63 54 45N 70 44W
Neretva → 19 43 1N 17 27 E
Nerva 13 37 42N 6 30W
Nes 20 65 53N 17 24W
Nes Ziyyona 28 31 56N 34 48W
Neskaupstaður 20 65 9N 13 42W
Ness, Loch 8 57 15N 4 30W
Nesttun 21 60 19N 5 21 E
Netanya 28 32 20N 34 51 E
Nète → 11 51 7N 4 14 E
Nether Stowey 7 51 0N 3 10W
Netherbury 7 50 46N 2 45W
Netherdale 44 21 10S 148 33 E
Netherlands ■ 11 52 0N 5 30 E
Netherlands Antilles ■ 78 12 15N 69 0W
Netherlands Guiana = Surinam ■ 79 4 0N 56 0W
Nettilling L. 61 66 30N 71 0W
Netzahualcoyotl, Presa 74 17 10N 93 30W
Neubrandenburg 14 53 33N 13 17 E
Neuchâtel 14 47 0N 6 55 E
Neuchâtel, Lac de 14 46 53N 6 50 E
Neufchâteau 11 49 50N 5 25 E
Neumünster 14 54 4N 9 58 E
Neunkirchen 14 49 23N 7 12 E
Neuquén 80 38 55S 68 0W
Neuruppin 14 52 56N 12 48 E
Neuse → 69 35 5N 76 30W
Neusiedler See 14 47 50N 16 47 E
Neuss 11 51 12N 6 39 E
Neustrelitz 14 53 22N 13 4 E
Neva → 22 59 50N 30 30 E
Nevada 71 37 51N 94 22W
Nevada □ 72 39 20N 117 0W
Nevada, Sierra, Spain 13 37 3N 3 15W
Nevada, Sierra, U.S.A. 72 39 0N 120 30W
Nevada City 72 39 20N 121 0W
Nevada de Sta. Marta, Sa. 78 10 55N 73 50W
Nevanka 25 56 31N 98 55 E
Nevers 12 47 0N 3 9 E
Nevertire 45 31 50S 147 44 E
Neville 65 49 58N 107 39W
Nevinnomyssk 23 44 40N 42 0 E
Nevis 75 17 0N 62 30W
Nevşehir 30 38 33N 34 40 E
Nevyansk 22 57 30N 60 13 E
New Albany, Ind., U.S.A. 68 38 20N 85 50W
New Albany, Miss., U.S.A. 71 34 30N 89 0W
New Amsterdam 78 6 15N 57 36W
New Angledool 45 29 5S 147 55 E
New Bedford 68 41 40N 70 52W
New Bern 69 35 8N 77 3W
New Boston 71 33 27N 94 21W
New Braunfels 71 29 43N 98 9W
New Brighton 43 43 29S 172 43 E
New Britain, Papua N. G. 40 5 50S 150 20 E
New Britain, U.S.A. 68 41 41N 72 47W
New Brunswick 68 40 30N 74 28W
New Brunswick □ 63 46 50N 66 30W
New Bussa 53 9 53N 4 31 E
New Caledonia 40 21 0S 165 0 E
New Castile = Castilla La Nueva 13 39 45N 3 20W
New Castle, Ind., U.S.A. 68 39 55N 85 23W
New Castle, Pa., U.S.A. 68 41 0N 80 20W
New Cristóbal 74 9 22N 79 40W
New Delhi 32 28 37N 77 13 E
New Denver 64 50 0N 117 25W
New England 70 46 36N 102 47W
New England Ra. 45 30 20S 151 45 E
New Forest 7 50 53N 1 40W
New Glasgow 63 45 35N 62 36W
New Guinea 40 4 0S 136 0 E
New Hampshire □ 68 43 40N 71 40W
New Hampton 70 43 2N 92 20W
New Hanover 57 29 22S 30 31 E
New Haven 68 41 20N 72 54W
New Hazelton 64 55 20N 127 30W
New Hebrides = Vanuatu ■ 3 15 0S 168 0 E
New Iberia 71 30 2N 91 54W
New Ireland 40 3 20S 151 50 E
New Jersey □ 68 40 30N 74 10W
New Kensington 68 40 36N 79 43W
New Lexington 68 39 40N 82 15W
New Liskeard 62 47 31N 79 41W
New London, Conn., U.S.A. 68 41 23N 72 8W
New London, Minn., U.S.A. 70 45 17N 94 55W
New London, Wis., U.S.A. 70 44 23N 88 43W
New Madrid 71 36 40N 89 30W
New Meadows 72 45 0N 116 32W
New Mexico □ 66 34 30N 106 0W
New Norcia 47 30 57S 116 13 E
New Norfolk 44 42 46S 147 2 E
New Orleans 71 30 0N 90 5W
New Philadelphia 68 40 29N 81 25W
New Plymouth, N.Z. 43 39 4S 174 5 E
New Plymouth, U.S.A. 72 43 58N 116 49W
New Providence 75 25 25N 78 35W
New Radnor 7 52 15N 3 10W
New Richmond 70 45 6N 92 34W
New Roads 71 30 43N 91 30W
New Rockford 70 47 44N 99 7W
New Ross 9 52 24N 6 58W
New Salem 70 46 51N 101 25W
New Siberian Is. = Novosibirskiye Ostrava 25 75 0N 142 0 E
New Smyrna Beach 69 29 0N 80 50W
New South Wales □ 45 33 0S 146 0 E
New Springs 47 25 49S 120 1 E
New Town 70 48 0N 102 30W
New Ulm 70 44 15N 94 30W
New Waterford 63 46 13N 60 4W
New Westminster 64 49 13N 122 55W
New York □ 68 42 40N 76 0W
New York City 68 40 45N 74 0W
New Zealand ■ 43 40 0S 176 0 E
Newala 54 10 58S 39 18 E
Newark, Del., U.S.A. 68 39 42N 75 45W
Newark, N.J., U.S.A. 68 40 41N 74 12W
Newark, N.Y., U.S.A. 68 43 2N 77 10W
Newark, Ohio, U.S.A. 68 40 5N 82 24W
Newark-on-Trent 6 53 6N 0 48W
Newaygo 68 43 25N 85 48W
Newberg 72 45 22N 123 0W
Newberry, Mich., U.S.A. 68 46 20N 85 32W
Newberry, S.C., U.S.A. 69 34 17N 81 37W
Newbrook 64 54 24N 112 57W
Newburgh 68 41 30N 74 1W
Newbury 7 51 24N 1 19W
Newburyport 68 42 48N 70 50W
Newcastle, Australia 45 33 0S 151 46 E
Newcastle, Canada 63 47 1N 65 38W
Newcastle, S. Africa 57 27 45S 29 58 E
Newcastle, U.K. 9 54 13N 5 54W

Novaya Ladoga

Newcastle, U.S.A. 70 43 50N 104 12W
Newcastle Emlyn 7 52 2N 4 29W
Newcastle Ra. 46 15 45S 130 15 E
Newcastle-under-Lyme 6 53 2N 2 15W
Newcastle-upon-Tyne 6 54 59N 1 37W
Newcastle Waters 44 17 30S 133 28 E
Newdegate 47 33 6S 119 0 E
Newe Etan 28 32 30N 35 32 E
Newe Sha'anan 28 32 47N 34 59 E
Newe Zohar 28 31 9N 35 21 E
Newell 70 44 48N 103 25W
Newenham, C. 60 58 40N 162 15W
Newfoundland □ 61 53 0N 58 0W
Newhalem 64 48 41N 121 16W
Newham 7 51 31N 0 2 E
Newhaven 7 50 47N 0 4 E
Newkirk 71 36 52N 97 3W
Newman 46 23 18S 119 45 E
Newmarket, Ireland 9 52 13N 9 0W
Newmarket, U.K. 7 52 15N 0 23 E
Newnan 69 33 22N 84 48W
Newport, Gwent, U.K. 7 51 35N 3 0W
Newport, I. of W., U.K. 7 50 42N 1 18W
Newport, Salop, U.K. 7 52 47N 2 22W
Newport, Ark., U.S.A. 71 35 38N 91 15W
Newport, Ky., U.S.A. 68 39 5N 84 23W
Newport, N.H., U.S.A. 68 43 23N 72 8W
Newport, Oreg., U.S.A. 72 44 41N 124 2W
Newport, R.I., U.S.A. 68 41 13N 71 19W
Newport, Tenn., U.S.A. 69 35 59N 83 12W
Newport, Vt., U.S.A. 68 44 57N 72 17W
Newport, Wash., U.S.A. 72 48 11N 117 2W
Newport Beach 73 33 40N 117 58W
Newport News 68 37 2N 76 30W
Newquay 7 50 24N 5 6W
Newry 9 54 10N 6 20W
Newry & Mourne □ 9 54 10N 6 15W
Newton, Iowa, U.S.A. 70 41 40N 93 3W
Newton, Mass., U.S.A. 68 42 21N 71 10W
Newton, Miss., U.S.A. 71 32 19N 89 10W
Newton, N.C., U.S.A. 69 35 42N 81 10W
Newton, N.J., U.S.A. 68 41 3N 74 46W
Newton, Tex., U.S.A. 71 30 54N 93 42W
Newton Abbot 7 50 32N 3 37W
Newton Boyd 45 29 45S 152 16 E
Newton Stewart 8 54 57N 4 30W
Newtonmore 8 57 4N 4 7W
Newtown 7 52 31N 3 19W
Newtownabbey 9 54 40N 5 55W
Newtownabbey □ 9 54 45N 6 0W
Newtownards 9 54 37N 5 40W
Neya 22 58 21N 43 49 E
Neyrīz 31 29 15N 54 19 E
Neyshābūr 31 36 10N 58 50 E
Nezhin 23 51 5N 31 55 E
Nezperce 72 46 13N 116 15W
Ngabang 34 0 23N 109 55 E
Ngabordamlu, Tanjung 35 6 56S 134 11 E
Ngami Depression 56 20 30S 22 46 E
Nganglong Kangri 33 33 0N 81 0 E
Nganjuk 35 7 32S 111 55 E
Ngaoundéré 54 7 15N 13 35 E
Ngapara 43 44 57S 170 46 E
Ngawi 35 7 24S 111 26 E
Ngoring Hu 37 34 55N 97 5 E
Ngorongoro 52 3 11S 35 32 E
Ngozi 52 2 54S 29 50 E
Ngudu 54 2 58S 33 25 E
Nguigmi 51 14 20N 13 20 E
Ngukurr 44 14 44S 134 44 E
Nguru 53 12 56N 10 29 E
Nha Trang 34 12 16N 109 10 E
Nhacoongo 57 24 18S 35 14 E
Nhangutazi, L. 57 24 0S 34 30 E
Nhill 45 36 18S 141 40 E
Nhulunbuy 44 12 10S 137 20 E
Niafounké 50 16 0N 4 5W
Niagara 68 45 45N 88 0W
Niagara Falls, Canada 62 43 7N 79 5W
Niagara Falls, U.S.A. 68 43 5N 79 0W
Niah 34 3 58N 113 46 E
Niamey 53 13 27N 2 6 E
Niangara 54 3 42N 27 50 E
Nianzishan 38 47 31N 122 53 E
Nias 34 1 0N 97 30 E
Nicaragua ■ 75 11 40N 85 30W
Nicaragua, L. de 75 12 0N 85 30W
Nicastro 18 39 0N 16 18 E
Nice 12 43 42N 7 14 E
Niceville 69 30 30N 86 30W
Nichinan 36 31 38N 131 23 E
Nicholás, Canal 75 23 30N 80 5W
Nicholasville 68 37 54N 84 31W
Nicholson 46 18 2S 128 54 E
Nicholson —► 44 17 31S 139 36 E
Nicholson Ra. 47 27 15S 116 45 E
Nicobar Is. 3 9 0N 93 0 E
Nicola 64 50 12N 120 40W
Nicolet 62 46 17N 72 35W
Nicolls Town 75 25 8N 78 0W
Nicosia 30 35 10N 33 25 E
Nicoya, G. de 75 10 0N 85 0W
Nicoya, Pen. de 75 9 45N 85 40W
Nidd —► 6 54 1N 1 32W
Niekerkshoop 56 29 19S 22 51 E
Nienburg 14 52 38N 9 15 E
Nieu Bethesda 56 31 51S 24 34 E
Nieuw Amsterdam 79 5 53N 55 5W
Nieuw Nickerie 79 6 0N 56 59W
Nieuwoudtville 56 31 23S 19 7 E
Nieuwpoort 11 51 8N 2 45 E
Nièvre □ 12 47 10N 3 40 E
Niğde 30 38 0N 34 40 E
Nigel 57 26 27S 28 25 E
Niger □ 53 10 0N 5 0 E
Niger ■ 50 17 30N 10 0 E
Niger —► 53 5 33N 6 33 E
Nigeria ■ 53 8 30N 8 0 E
Nightcaps 43 45 57S 168 2 E
Nii-Jima 36 34 20N 139 15 E
Niigata 36 37 58N 139 0 E
Niigata □ 36 37 15N 138 45 E
Niihama 36 33 55N 133 16 E
Niihau 66 21 55N 160 10W
Nijkerk 11 52 13N 5 30 E
Nijmegen 11 51 50N 5 52 E
Nijverdal 11 52 22N 6 28 E
Nike 53 6 26N 7 29 E
Nikel 20 69 24N 30 12 E
Nikiniki 35 9 49S 124 30 E
Nikki 53 9 58N 3 12 E
Nikkō 36 36 45N 139 35 E
Nikolayev 23 46 58N 32 0 E
Nikolayevsk 23 50 0N 45 35 E
Nikolayevsk-na-Amur 25 53 8N 140 44 E
Nikolskoye 25 55 12N 166 0 E
Nikopol 23 47 35N 34 25 E
Nīkshahr 31 26 15N 60 10 E
Nîl, Nahr en —► 51 30 10N 31 6 E
Nîl el Abyad —► 51 15 38N 32 31 E
Nîl el Azraq —► 51 15 38N 32 31 E
Niland 73 33 16N 115 30W
Nile = Nîl, Nahr en —► 51 30 10N 31 6 E
Niles 68 41 8N 80 40W
Nimach 32 24 30N 74 56 E
Nîmes 12 43 50N 4 23 E
Nimmitabel 45 36 29S 149 15 E
Nimneryskiy 25 57 50N 125 10 E
Nimrūz □ 31 30 0N 62 0 E
Nimule 54 3 32N 32 3 E
Nīnawá 30 36 25N 43 10 E
Nindigully 45 28 21S 148 50 E
Ninemile 64 56 0N 130 7W
Nineveh = Nīnawá 30 36 25N 43 10 E
Ningaloo 46 22 41S 113 41 E
Ning'an 38 44 22N 129 20 E
Ningbo 39 29 51N 121 28 E
Ningde 39 26 38N 119 23 E
Ningdu 39 26 25N 115 59 E
Ningjin 38 37 35N 114 57 E
Ningming 39 22 8N 107 4 E
Ningpo = Ningbo 39 29 51N 121 28 E
Ningqiang 39 32 47N 106 15 E
Ningshan 39 33 21N 108 21 E
Ningsia Hui A.R. = Ningxia Huizu Zizhiqu □ 38 38 0N 106 0 E
Ningwu 38 39 0N 112 18 E
Ningxia Huizu Zizhiqu □ 38 38 0N 106 0 E
Ningxiang 39 28 15N 112 30 E
Ningyuan 39 25 37N 111 57 E
Ninove 11 50 51N 4 2 E
Niobrara 70 42 48N 97 59W
Niobrara —► 70 42 45N 98 0W
Nioro du Sahel 50 15 15N 9 30W
Niort 12 46 19N 0 29W
Nipawin 65 53 20N 104 0W
Nipawin Prov. Park 65 54 0N 104 37W
Nipigon 62 49 0N 88 17W
Nipigon, L. 62 49 50N 88 30W
Nipin —► 65 55 46N 108 35W
Nipishish L. 63 54 12N 60 45W
Nipissing L. 62 46 20N 80 0W
Nipomo 73 35 4N 120 29W
Niquelândia 79 14 33S 48 23W
Nirmal 32 19 3N 78 20 E
Nirmali 33 26 20N 86 35 E
Niš 19 43 19N 21 58 E
Nişāb 29 14 25N 46 29 E
Nishinomiya 36 34 45N 135 20 E
Niskibi —► 62 56 29N 88 9W
Nisutlin —► 64 60 14N 132 34W
Nitā' 30 27 15N 48 35 E
Nitchequon 63 53 10N 70 58W
Niterói 79 22 52S 43 0W
Nith —► 8 55 20N 3 5W
Nitra 15 48 19N 18 4 E
Nitra —► 15 47 46N 18 10 E
Niuafo'ou 43 15 30S 175 58W
Niue I. 2 19 2S 169 54W
Niut 34 0 55N 110 6 E
Nivelles 11 50 35N 4 20 E
Nivernais 12 47 0N 3 20 E
Nixon 71 29 17N 97 45W
Nizamabad 32 18 45N 78 7 E
Nizamghat 33 28 20N 95 45 E
Nizhne Kolymsk 25 68 34N 160 55 E
Nizhneangarsk 25 55 47N 109 30 E
Nizhnekamsk 22 55 38N 51 49 E
Nizhneudinsk 25 54 54N 99 3 E
Nizhnevartovsk 24 60 56N 76 38 E
Nizhneyansk 25 71 26N 136 4 E
Nizhniy Novgorod = Gorkiy 22 56 20N 44 0 E
Nizhniy Tagil 22 57 55N 59 57 E
Nizhnyaya Tunguska —► 25 64 20N 93 0 E
Nizip 30 37 5N 37 50 E
Nizké Tatry 15 48 55N 20 0 E
Njombe 54 9 20S 34 50 E
Nkambe 53 6 35N 10 40 E
Nkawkaw 53 6 36N 0 49W
Nkhata Bay 54 11 33S 34 16 E
Nkhota Kota 55 12 56S 34 15 E
Nkongsamba 54 4 55N 9 55 E
Nkurenkuru 56 17 42S 18 32 E
Nmai —► 33 25 30N 97 25 E
Noakhali = Maijdi 33 22 48N 91 10 E
Noatak 60 67 32N 162 59W
Nobeoka 36 32 36N 131 41 E
Noblesville 68 40 1N 85 59W
Nocera Inferiore 18 40 45N 14 37 E
Nockatunga 45 27 42S 142 42 E
Nocona 71 33 48N 97 45W
Noel 71 36 36N 94 29W
Nogales, Mexico 74 31 20N 110 56W
Nogales, U.S.A. 73 31 33N 110 56W
Nōgata 36 33 48N 130 44 E
Noggerup 47 33 32S 116 5 E
Noginsk 25 64 30N 90 50 E
Nogoa —► 44 23 40S 147 55 E
Noirmoutier, I. de 12 46 58N 2 10W
Nojane 56 23 15S 20 14 E
Nok Kundi 31 28 50N 62 45 E
Nokaneng 56 19 40S 22 17 E
Nokhtuysk 25 60 0N 117 45 E
Nokomis 65 51 35N 105 0W
Nokomis L. 65 57 0N 103 0W
Nola 54 3 35N 16 4 E
Noma Omuramba —► 56 18 52S 20 53 E
Noman L. 65 62 15N 108 55W
Nome 60 64 30N 165 24W
Nonacho L. 65 61 42N 109 40W
Nonda 44 20 40S 142 28 E
Nong Khai 34 17 50N 102 46 E
Nong'an 38 44 25N 125 5 E
Nongoma 57 27 58S 31 35 E
Nonoava 74 27 28N 106 44W
Noonamah 46 12 40S 131 4 E
Noonan 70 48 51N 102 59W
Noondoo 45 28 35S 148 30 E
Noonkanbah 46 18 30S 124 50 E
Noord Brabant □ 11 51 40N 5 0 E
Noord Holland □ 11 52 30N 4 45 E
Noordbeveland 11 51 35N 3 50 E
Noordoostpolder 11 52 45N 5 45 E
Noordwijk aan Zee 11 52 14N 4 26 E
Nootka 64 49 38N 126 38W
Nootka I. 64 49 32N 126 42W
Nóqui 54 5 55S 13 30 E
Noranda 62 48 20N 79 0W
Nord □ 12 50 15N 3 30 E
Nord-Ostsee Kanal 14 54 15N 9 40 E
Nord-Trøndelag fylke □ 20 64 20N 12 0 E
Nordegg 64 52 29N 116 5W
Nordhausen 14 51 29N 10 47 E
Nordkapp 20 71 10N 25 44 E
Nordkinn 4 71 8N 27 40 E
Nordland fylke □ 20 65 40N 13 0 E
Nordrhein-Westfalen □ 14 51 45N 7 30 E
Nordvik 25 74 2N 111 32 E
Nore —► 9 52 40N 7 20W
Norembega 62 48 59N 80 43W
Norfolk, Nebr., U.S.A. 70 42 3N 97 25W
Norfolk, Va., U.S.A. 68 36 40N 76 15W
Norfolk □ 6 52 39N 1 0 E
Norfolk Broads 6 52 30N 1 15 E
Norfolk I. 3 28 58S 168 3 E
Norfork Res. 71 36 13N 92 15W
Norilsk 25 69 20N 88 6 E
Norley 45 27 45S 143 48 E
Norma, Mt. 44 20 55S 140 42 E
Normal 70 40 30N 89 0W
Norman 71 35 12N 97 30W
Norman —► 44 17 28S 140 49 E
Norman Wells 60 65 17N 126 51W
Normanby —► 44 14 23S 144 10 E
Normandie 12 48 45N 0 10 E
Normandin 62 48 49N 72 31W
Normandy = Normandie 12 48 45N 0 10 E
Normanhurst, Mt. 47 25 4S 122 30 E
Normanton 44 17 40S 141 10 E
Norquay 65 51 53N 102 5W
Norquinco 80 41 51S 70 55W
Norrbotten □ 20 66 30N 22 30 E
Norrby 20 64 55N 18 15 E
Nørresundby 21 57 5N 9 52 E
Norris 72 45 40N 111 40W
Norristown 68 40 9N 75 21W
Norrköping 21 58 37N 16 11 E
Norrland □ 20 66 50N 18 0 E
Norrtälje 21 59 46N 18 42 E
Norseman 47 32 8S 121 43 E
Norsk 25 52 30N 130 0 E
North Adams 68 42 42N 73 6W
North America 58 40 0N 100 0W
North Battleford 65 52 50N 108 17W
North Bay 62 46 20N 79 30W
North Belcher Is. 62 56 50N 79 50W
North Bend, Canada 64 49 50N 121 27W
North Bend, U.S.A. 72 43 28N 124 14W
North Berwick 8 56 4N 2 44W
North Canadian —► 71 35 17N 95 31W
North C., Canada 63 47 2N 60 20W
North C., N.Z. 43 34 23S 173 4 E
North Caribou L. 62 52 50N 90 40W
North Carolina □ 69 35 30N 80 0W
North Channel, Br. Is. 8 55 0N 5 30W
North Channel, Canada 62 46 0N 83 0W
North Chicago 68 42 19N 87 50W
North Dakota □ 70 47 30N 100 0W
North Dandalup 47 32 30S 115 57 E
North Down □ 9 54 40N 5 45W
North Downs 7 51 17N 0 30 E
North East Frontier Agency = Arunachal Pradesh □ 33 28 0N 95 0 E
North East Providence Chan. 75 26 0N 76 0W
North Esk —► 8 56 44N 2 25W
North European Plain 4 55 0N 20 0 E
North Foreland 7 51 22N 1 28 E
North Henik L. 65 61 45N 97 40W
North I. 43 38 0S 175 0 E
North Knife —► 65 58 53N 94 45W
North Korea ■ 38 40 0N 127 0 E
North Lakhimpur 33 27 14N 94 7 E
North Las Vegas 73 36 15N 115 6W
North Loup —► 70 41 17N 98 23W
North Minch 8 58 5N 5 55W
North Nahanni —► 64 62 15N 123 20W
North Ossetian A.S.S.R. □ 23 43 30N 44 30 E
North Palisade 73 37 6N 118 32W
North Platte 70 41 10N 100 50W
North Platte —► 70 41 15N 100 45W
North Pt. 63 47 5N 64 0W
North Portal 65 49 0N 102 33W
North Powder 72 45 2N 117 59W
North Ronaldsay 8 59 20N 2 30W
North Saskatchewan —► 65 53 15N 105 5W
North Sea 4 56 0N 4 0 E
North Sporades = Voriai Sporádhes 19 39 15N 23 30 E
North Sydney 63 46 12N 60 15W
North Thompson —► 64 50 40N 120 20W
North Tonawanda 68 43 5N 78 50W
North Truchas Pk. 73 36 0N 105 30W
North Twin I. 62 53 20N 80 0W
North Tyne —► 6 54 59N 2 7W
North Uist 8 57 40N 7 15W
North Vancouver 64 49 25N 123 3W
North Vernon 68 39 0N 85 35W
North Wabasca L. 64 56 0N 113 55W
North Walsham 6 52 49N 1 22 E
North West C. 46 21 45S 114 9 E
North West Christmas I. Ridge 41 6 30N 165 0W
North West Frontier □ 32 34 0N 71 0 E
North West Highlands 8 57 35N 5 2W
North West Providence Channel 75 26 0N 78 0W
North West River 63 53 30N 60 10W
North West Territories □ 60 67 0N 110 0W
North York Moors 6 54 25N 0 50W
North Yorkshire □ 6 54 15N 1 25W
Northallerton 6 54 20N 1 26W
Northam 56 24 56S 27 18 E
Northampton, Australia 47 28 27S 114 33 E
Northampton, U.K. 7 52 14N 0 54W
Northampton, U.S.A. 68 42 22N 72 31W
Northampton □ 7 52 16N 0 55W
Northampton Downs 44 24 35S 145 48 E
Northcliffe 47 34 39S 116 7 E
Northern Circars 33 17 30N 82 30 E
Northern Group 43 10 0S 160 0W
Northern Indian L. 65 57 20N 97 20W
Northern Ireland □ 9 54 45N 7 0W
Northern Light, L. 62 48 15N 90 39W
Northern Marianas 40 17 0N 145 0 E
Northern Territory □ 46 16 0S 133 0 E
Northfield 70 44 30N 93 10W
Northland □ 43 35 30S 173 30 E
Northome 70 47 53N 94 15W
Northport, Ala., U.S.A. 69 33 15N 87 35W
Northport, Mich., U.S.A. 68 45 8N 85 39W
Northport, Wash., U.S.A. 72 48 55N 117 48W
Northumberland □ 6 55 12N 2 0W
Northumberland, C. 45 38 5S 140 40 E
Northumberland Is. 44 21 30S 149 50 E
Northumberland Str. 63 46 20N 64 0W
Northwich 6 53 16N 2 30W
Northwood, Iowa, U.S.A. 70 43 27N 93 0W
Northwood, N. Dak., U.S.A. 70 47 44N 97 30W
Norton 70 39 50N 99 53W
Norton Sd. 60 64 0N 164 0W
Norwalk, Conn., U.S.A. 68 41 9N 73 25W
Norwalk, Ohio, U.S.A. 68 41 13N 82 38W
Norway 68 45 46N 87 57W
Norway ■ 21 63 0N 11 0 E
Norway House 65 53 59N 97 50W
Norwegian Sea 21 66 0N 1 0 E
Norwich, U.K. 6 52 38N 1 17 E
Norwich, U.S.A. 68 42 32N 75 30W
Noshiro 36 40 12N 140 0 E
Nosok 24 70 10N 82 20 E
Noşratābād 31 29 55N 60 0 E
Noss Hd. 8 58 29N 3 4W
Nossob —► 56 26 55S 20 45 E
Nosy Bé 55 13 25S 48 15 E
Nosy Boraha 57 16 50S 49 55 E
Nosy Mitsio 55 12 54S 48 36 E
Nosy Varika 57 20 35S 48 32 E
Notigi Dam 65 56 40N 99 10W
Notikewin —► 64 57 2N 117 38W
Noto 18 36 52N 15 4 E
Noto-Hanto 36 37 0N 137 0 E
Notre-Dame 63 46 18N 64 46W
Notre Dame B. 63 49 45N 55 30W
Notre Dame de Koartac = Koartac 61 60 55N 69 40W
Notre Dame d'Ivugivic = Ivugivik 61 62 24N 77 55W
Nottaway —► 62 51 22N 78 55W
Nottingham 6 52 57N 1 10W
Nottingham □ 6 53 10N 1 0W
Nottoway —► 68 36 33N 76 55W
Notwane —► 56 23 35S 26 58 E
Nouâdhibou 50 20 54N 17 0W
Nouâdhibou, Ras 50 20 50N 17 0W
Nouakchott 50 18 9N 15 58W
Nouméa 40 22 17S 166 30 E
Noupoort 56 31 10S 24 57 E
Nouveau Comptoir 62 53 0N 78 49W
Nouvelle Calédonie = New Caledonia 40 21 0S 165 0 E
Nova Casa Nova 79 9 25S 41 5W
Nova Cruz 79 6 28S 35 25W
Nova Friburgo 79 22 16S 42 30W
Nova Gaia 54 10 10S 17 35 E
Nova Iguaçu 79 22 45S 43 28W
Nova Iorque 79 7 0S 44 5W
Nova Lima 79 19 59S 43 51W
Nova Lisboa = Huambo 55 12 42S 15 54 E
Nova Mambone 57 21 0S 35 3 E
Nova Scotia □ 63 45 10N 63 0W
Nova Sofala 57 20 7S 34 42 E
Nova Venécia 79 18 45S 40 24W
Noval Iorque 79 6 48S 44 0W
Novara 18 45 27N 8 36 E
Novaya Ladoga 22 60 7N 32 16 E

Novaya Lyalya

Novaya Lyalya 24 59 10N 60 35 E
Novaya Sibir, Ostrov 25 75 10N 150 0 E
Novaya Zemlya 24 75 0N 56 0 E
Nové Zámky 15 48 2N 18 8 E
Novgorod 22 58 30N 31 25 E
Novgorod-Severskiy 22 52 2N 33 10 E
Novi Sad 19 45 18N 19 52 E
Novo Remanso 79 9 41S 42 4W
Novoaltaysk 24 53 30N 84 0 E
Novocherkassk 23 47 27N 40 5 E
Novokazalinsk 24 45 48N 62 6 E
Novokuybyshevsk 22 53 7N 49 58 E
Novokuznetsk 24 53 45N 87 10 E
Novomoskovsk 22 54 5N 38 15 E
Novorossiysk 23 44 43N 37 46 E
Novorybnoye 25 72 50N 105 50 E
Novoshakhtinsk 23 47 46N 39 58 E
Novosibirsk 24 55 0N 83 5 E
Novosibirskiye Ostrava 25 75 0N 142 0 E
Novotroitsk 22 51 10N 58 15 E
Novouzensk 23 50 32N 48 17 E
Novska 18 45 19N 17 0 E
Novvy Port 24 67 40N 72 30 E
Now Shahr 31 36 40N 51 30 E
Nowgong 33 26 20N 92 50 E
Nowra 45 34 53S 150 35 E
Nowshera 32 34 0N 72 0 E
Nowy Sącz 15 49 40N 20 41 E
Nowy Tomyśl 14 52 19N 16 10 E
Noxon 72 48 0N 115 43W
Noyes I. 64 55 30N 133 40W
Nsanje 55 16 55S 35 12 E
Nsawam 53 5 50N 0 24W
Nsukka 53 6 51N 7 29 E
Nûbîya, Es Sahrâ En 51 21 30N 33 30 E
Nuboai 35 2 10S 136 30 E
Nueces → 71 27 50N 97 30W
Nueima → 28 31 54N 35 25 E
Nueltin L. 65 60 30N 99 30W
Nueva Gerona 75 21 53N 82 49W
Nueva Imperial 80 38 45S 72 58W
Nueva Rosita 74 28 0N 101 11W
Nueva San Salvador 75 13 40N 89 18W
Nuéve de Julio 80 35 30S 61 0W
Nuevitas 75 21 30N 77 20W
Nuevo, G. 80 43 0S 64 30W
Nuevo Laredo 74 27 30N 99 30W
Nuevo León □ 74 25 0N 100 0W
Nugget Pt. 43 46 27S 169 50 E
Nuhaka 43 39 3S 177 45 E
Nukey Bluff, Mt. 45 32 26S 135 29 E
Nukheila 51 19 1N 26 21 E
Nuku'alofa 43 21 10S 174 0W
Nukus 24 42 20N 59 7 E
Nulato 60 64 40N 158 10W
Nullagine → 46 21 20S 120 20 E
Nullarbor 47 31 28S 130 55 E
Nullarbor Plain 47 31 10S 129 0 E
Numalla, L. 45 28 43S 144 20 E
Numan 53 9 29N 12 3 E
Numata 36 36 45N 139 4 E
Numazu 36 35 7N 138 51 E
Numbulwar 44 14 15S 135 45 E
Numfoor 35 1 0S 134 50 E
Numurkah 45 36 5S 145 26 E
Nunaksaluk I. 63 55 49N 60 20W
Nuneaton 7 52 32N 1 29W
Nunivak 60 60 0N 166 0W
Nunkun 32 33 57N 76 2 E
Nunspeet 11 52 21N 5 45 E
Nuomin He → 38 46 45N 126 55 E
Nuremburg = Nürnberg 14 49 26N 11 5 E
Nurina 47 30 56S 126 33 E
Nuriootpa 45 34 27S 139 0 E
Nürnberg 14 49 26N 11 5 E
Nurran, L. = Terewah, L. 45 29 52S 147 35 E
Nurrari Lakes 47 29 1S 130 5 E
Nusa Barung 35 8 10S 113 30 E
Nusa Kambangan 35 7 40S 108 10 E
Nusa Tenggara Barat □ 34 8 50S 117 30 E
Nusa Tenggara Timur □ 35 9 30S 122 0 E
Nusaybin 23 37 3N 41 10 E
Nushki 32 29 35N 66 0 E
Nutak 61 57 28N 61 59W
Nutwood Downs 44 15 49S 134 10 E
Nuwakot 33 28 10N 83 55 E
Nuweveldberge 56 32 10S 21 45 E
Nuyts, C. 47 32 2S 132 21 E
Nuyts Arch. 45 32 35S 133 20 E
Nxau-Nxau 56 18 57S 21 4 E
Nyah West 45 35 16S 143 21 E
Nyahanga 54 2 20S 33 37 E
Nyahururu 54 0 2N 36 27 E
Nyainqentanglha Shan 37 30 0N 90 0 E
Nyakanazi 52 3 2S 31 10 E
Nyakanyasi 52 1 10S 31 13 E
Nyâlâ 51 12 2N 24 58 E
Nyandoma 22 61 40N 40 12 E
Nyangana 56 18 0S 20 40 E
Nyanza 52 4 21S 29 36 E
Nyarling → 64 60 41N 113 23W
Nyasa, L. = Malawi, L. 55 12 30S 34 30 E
Nyazepetrovsk 22 56 3N 59 36 E
Nybro 21 56 44N 15 55 E
Nyda 24 66 40N 72 58 E
Nyeri 54 0 23S 36 56 E
Nyíregyháza 15 47 58N 21 47 E
Nykarleby 20 63 22N 22 31 E
Nykøbing 21 54 56N 11 52 E
Nyköping 21 58 45N 17 0 E
Nylstroom 57 24 42S 28 22 E
Nymagee 45 32 7S 146 20 E
Nynäshamn 21 58 54N 17 57 E
Nyngan 45 31 30S 147 8 E
Nysa 15 50 30N 17 22 E
Nysa → 14 52 4N 14 46 E
Nyssa 72 43 56N 117 2W
Nyurba 25 63 17N 118 28 E
Nzega 54 4 10S 33 12 E
N'Zérékoré 50 7 49N 8 48W
Nzeto 54 7 10S 12 52 E
Nzubuka 52 4 45S 32 50 E

O

Ō-Shima 36 34 44N 139 24 E
Oacoma 70 43 50N 99 26W
Oahe Dam 70 44 28N 100 25W
Oahe L. 70 45 30N 100 25W
Oahu 66 21 30N 158 0W
Oak Creek 72 40 15N 106 59W
Oak Harb. 72 48 20N 122 38W
Oak Hill 68 38 0N 81 7W
Oak Park 68 41 55N 87 45W
Oak Ridge 69 36 1N 84 12W
Oakbank 45 33 4S 140 33 E
Oakdale, Calif., U.S.A. 73 37 45N 120 55W
Oakdale, La., U.S.A. 71 30 50N 92 38W
Oakengates 6 52 42N 2 29W
Oakes 70 46 14N 98 4W
Oakesdale 72 47 11N 117 15W
Oakey 45 27 25S 151 43 E
Oakham 6 52 40N 0 43W
Oakland, Calif., U.S.A. 73 37 50N 122 18W
Oakland, Oreg., U.S.A. 72 43 23N 123 18W
Oakland City 68 38 20N 87 20W
Oakley, Idaho, U.S.A. 72 42 14N 113 55W
Oakley, Kans., U.S.A. 70 39 8N 100 51W
Oakover → 46 21 0S 120 40 E
Oakridge 72 43 47N 122 31W
Oamaru 43 45 5S 170 59 E
Oatman 73 35 1N 114 19W
Oaxaca 74 17 2N 96 40W
Oaxaca □ 74 17 0N 97 0W
Ob → 24 66 45N 69 30 E
Oba 62 49 4N 84 7W
Oban 8 56 25N 5 30W
Obbia 29 5 25N 48 30 E
Obed 64 53 30N 117 10W
Oberhausen 14 51 28N 6 50 E
Oberlin, Kans., U.S.A. 70 39 52N 100 31W
Oberlin, La., U.S.A. 71 30 42N 92 42W
Oberon 45 33 45S 149 52 E
Obi, Kepulauan 35 1 23S 127 45 E
Óbidos 79 1 50S 55 30W
Obihiro 36 42 56N 143 12 E
Obilatu 35 1 25S 127 20 E
Obluchye 25 49 1N 131 4 E
Obo 54 5 20N 26 32 E
Observatory Inlet 64 55 10N 129 54W
Obshchi Syrt 4 52 0N 53 0 E
Obskaya Guba 24 69 0N 73 0 E
Obuasi 53 6 17N 1 40W
Ocala 69 29 11N 82 5W
Ocampo 74 28 9N 108 24W
Ocaña 13 39 55N 3 30W
Ocanomowoc 70 43 7N 88 30W
Ocate 71 36 12N 104 59W
Occidental, Cordillera 78 5 0N 76 0W
Ocean, I. = Banaba 40 0 45S 169 50 E
Ocean City 68 39 18N 74 34W
Ocean Park 72 46 30N 124 2W
Oceanside 73 33 13N 117 26W
Ochil Hills 8 56 14N 3 40W
Ochre River 65 51 4N 99 47W
Ocilla 69 31 35N 83 12W
Ocmulgee → 69 31 58N 82 32W
Oconee → 69 31 58N 82 32W
Oconto 68 44 52N 87 53W
Oconto Falls 68 44 52N 88 10W
Ocotal 75 13 41N 86 31W
Ocotlán 74 20 21N 102 42W
Octave 73 34 10N 112 43W
Ocumare del Tuy 78 10 7N 66 46W
Oda 53 5 50N 0 51W
Ódáðahraun 20 65 5N 17 0W
Odate 36 40 16N 140 34 E
Odawara 36 35 20N 139 6 E
Odda 21 60 3N 6 35 E
Oddur 29 4 11N 43 52 E
Odei → 65 56 6N 96 54W
Ödemiş 30 38 15N 28 0 E
Odendaalsrus 56 27 48S 26 45 E
Odense 21 55 22N 10 23 E
Oder → 14 53 33N 14 38 E
Odessa, Tex., U.S.A. 71 31 51N 102 23W
Odessa, Wash., U.S.A. 72 47 19N 118 35W
Odessa, U.S.S.R. 23 46 30N 30 45 E
Odiakwe 56 20 12S 25 17 E
Odienné 50 9 30N 7 34W
Odintsovo 22 55 39N 37 15 E
O'Donnell 71 33 0N 101 48W
Odorheiu Secuiesc 15 46 21N 25 21 E
Odra → 14 53 33N 14 38 E
Odžak 19 45 3N 18 18 E
Odzi 57 19 0S 32 20 E
Oeiras 79 7 0S 42 8W
Oelrichs 70 43 11N 103 14W
Oelwein 70 42 41N 91 55W
Oenpelli 46 12 20S 133 4 E
Ofanto → 18 41 22N 16 13 E
Offa 53 8 13N 4 42 E
Offaly □ 9 53 15N 7 30W
Offenbach 14 50 6N 8 46 E
Ofotfjorden 20 68 27N 16 40 E
Oga-Hantō 36 39 58N 139 47 E
Ogahalla 62 50 6N 85 51W
Ōgaki 36 35 21N 136 37 E
Ogallala 70 41 12N 101 40W
Ogbomosho 53 8 1N 4 11 E
Ogden, Iowa, U.S.A. 70 42 3N 94 0W
Ogden, Utah, U.S.A. 72 41 13N 112 1W
Ogdensburg 68 44 40N 75 27W
Ogeechee → 69 31 51N 81 6W
Oglio → 18 45 2N 10 39 E
Ogmore 44 22 37S 149 35 E
Ogoja 53 6 38N 8 39 E
Ogoki → 62 51 38N 85 57W
Ogoki L. 62 50 50N 87 10W
Ogoki Res. 62 50 45N 88 15W
Ogooué → 54 1 0S 9 0 E
Ogowe = Ogooué → 54 1 0S 9 0 E
Oguta 53 5 44N 6 44 E
Ogwashi-Uku 53 6 15N 6 30 E
Ohai 43 44 55S 168 0 E
Ohakune 43 39 24S 175 24 E
Ohanet 50 28 44N 8 46 E
Ohau, L. 43 44 15S 169 53 E
Ohey 11 50 26N 5 8 E
Ohio □ 68 40 20N 84 10W
Ohio → 68 38 0N 86 0W
Ohre → 14 50 30N 14 10 E
Ohridsko, Jezero 19 41 8N 20 52 E
Ohrigstad 57 24 39S 30 36 E
Oil City 68 41 26N 79 40W
Oise □ 12 49 28N 2 30 E
Ōita 36 33 14N 131 36 E
Ōita □ 36 33 15N 131 30 E
Oiticica 79 5 3S 41 5W
Ojai 73 34 28N 119 16W
Ojinaga 74 29 34N 104 25W
Ojos del Salado, Cerro 80 27 0S 68 40W
Okaba 35 8 6S 139 42 E
Okahandja 56 22 0S 16 59 E
Okahukura 40 38 48S 175 14 E
Okanagan L. 64 50 0N 119 30W
Okandja 54 0 35S 13 45 E
Okanogan 72 48 6N 119 43W
Okanogan → 72 48 6N 119 43W
Okaputa 56 20 5S 17 0 E
Okara 32 30 50N 73 31 E
Okarito 43 43 15S 170 9 E
Okaukuejo 56 19 10S 16 0 E
Okavango Swamps 56 18 45S 22 45 E
Okaya 36 36 0N 138 10 E
Okayama 36 34 40N 133 54 E
Okayama □ 36 35 0N 133 50 E
Okazaki 36 34 57N 137 10 E
Oke-Iho 53 8 1N 3 18 E
Okeechobee 69 27 16N 80 46W
Okeechobee, L. 69 27 0N 80 50W
Okefenokee Swamp 69 30 50N 82 15W
Okehampton 7 50 44N 4 1W
Okene 53 7 32N 6 11 E
Okha 25 53 40N 143 0 E
Okhotsk 25 59 20N 143 10 E
Okhotsk, Sea of 25 55 0N 145 0 E
Okhotskiy Perevoz 25 61 52N 135 35 E
Okhotsko Kolymskoye 25 63 0N 157 0 E
Oki-Shotō 36 36 5N 133 15 E
Okiep 56 29 39S 17 53 E
Okigwi 53 5 52N 7 20 E
Okija 53 5 54N 6 55 E
Okitipupa 53 6 31N 4 50 E
Oklahoma □ 71 35 20N 97 30W
Oklahoma City 71 35 25N 97 30W
Okmulgee 71 35 38N 96 0W
Okolona 71 34 0N 88 45W
Okrika 53 4 40N 7 10 E
Oktabrsk 23 49 28N 57 25 E
Oktyabrskiy 22 54 28N 53 28 E
Oktyabrskoy Revolyutsii, Os. 25 79 30N 97 0 E
Oktyabrskoye 24 62 28N 66 3 E
Okuru 43 43 55S 168 55 E
Okushiri-Tō 36 42 15N 139 30 E
Okuta 53 9 14N 3 12 E
Okwa → 56 22 30S 23 0 E
Ola 71 35 2N 93 10W
Ólafsfjörður 20 66 4N 18 39W
Ólafsvík 20 64 53N 23 43W
Olancha 73 36 15N 118 1W
Olanchito 75 15 30N 86 30W
Öland 21 56 45N 16 38 E
Olary 45 32 18S 140 19 E
Olathe 70 38 50N 94 50W
Olavarría 80 36 55S 60 20W
Ólbia 18 40 55N 9 30 E
Old Bahama Chan. = Bahama, Canal Viejo de 75 22 10N 77 30W
Old Castile = Castilla La Vieja 13 41 55N 4 0W
Old Castle 9 53 46N 7 10W
Old Cork 44 22 57S 141 52 E
Old Crow 60 67 30N 140 5 E
Old Fort → 65 58 36N 110 24W
Old Town 63 45 0N 68 41W
Old Wives L. 65 50 5N 106 0W
Oldbury 7 51 38N 2 30W
Oldenburg 14 53 10N 8 10 E
Oldenzaal 11 52 19N 6 53 E
Oldham 6 53 33N 2 8W
Oldman → 64 49 57N 111 42W
Olds 64 51 50N 114 10W
Olean 68 42 8N 78 25W
Olekma → 25 60 22N 120 42 E
Olekminsk 25 60 25N 120 30 E
Olenegorsk 22 68 9N 33 18 E
Olenek 25 68 28N 112 18 E
Olenek → 25 73 0N 120 10 E
Oléron, I. d' 12 45 55N 1 15W
Oleśnica 15 51 13N 17 22 E
Olga 25 43 50N 135 14 E
Olga, L. 62 49 47N 77 15W
Olga, Mt. 47 25 20S 130 50 E
Olifants → 57 23 57S 31 58 E
Olifantshoek 56 27 57S 22 42 E
Ólimbos, Óros 19 40 6N 22 23 E
Olinda 79 8 1S 34 51W
Oliveira 79 20 39S 44 50W
Olivenza 13 38 41N 7 9W
Oliver 64 49 13N 119 37W
Oliver L. 65 56 56N 103 22W
Ollagüe 78 21 15S 68 10W
Olney, Ill., U.S.A. 68 38 40N 88 0W
Olney, Tex., U.S.A. 71 33 25N 98 45W
Olomane → 63 50 14N 60 37W
Olomouc 14 49 38N 17 12 E
Olonets 22 61 10N 33 0 E
Olongapo 35 14 50N 120 18 E
Olovo 19 44 0N 19 0 E
Olovyannaya 25 50 58N 115 35 E
Oloy → 25 66 29N 159 29 E
Olsztyn 15 53 48N 20 29 E
Olt → 15 43 43N 24 51 E
Olteniţa 15 44 7N 26 42 E
Olton 71 34 16N 102 7W
Oltu 30 40 35N 41 58 E
Olympia, Greece 19 37 39N 21 39 E
Olympia, U.S.A. 72 47 0N 122 58W
Olympic Mts. 72 47 50N 123 45W
Olympic Nat. Park 72 47 48N 123 30W
Olympus, Mt. = Ólimbos, Óros 19 40 6N 22 23 E
Olympus, Mt. 72 47 52N 123 40W
Om → 24 54 59N 73 22 E
Ōmachi 36 36 30N 137 50 E
Omagh 9 54 36N 7 20W
Omagh □ 9 54 35N 7 15W
Omaha 70 41 15N 96 0W
Omak 72 48 24N 119 31W
Oman ■ 29 23 0N 58 0 E
Oman, G. of 31 24 30N 58 30 E
Omaruru 56 21 26S 16 0 E
Omaruru → 56 22 7S 14 15 E
Omate 78 16 45S 71 0W
Ombai, Selat 35 8 30S 124 50 E
Omboué 54 1 35S 9 15 E
Ombrone → 18 42 39N 11 0 E
Omdurmân 51 15 40N 32 28 E
Ometepe, I. de 75 11 32N 85 35W
Ometepec 74 16 39N 98 23W
Omez 28 32 22N 35 0 E
Omineca → 64 56 3N 124 16W
Omitara 56 22 16S 18 2 E
Ōmiya 36 35 54N 139 38 E
Ommen 11 52 31N 6 26 E
Omo → 51 6 25N 36 10 E
Omolon → 25 68 42N 158 36 E
Omono-Gawa → 36 39 46N 140 3 E
Omsk 24 55 0N 73 12 E
Omsukchan 25 62 32N 155 48 E
Omul, Vf. 15 45 27N 25 29 E
Ōmura 36 32 56N 130 0 E
Omuramba Omatako → 55 17 45S 20 25 E
Ōmuta 36 33 0N 130 26 E
Onaga 70 39 32N 96 12W
Onalaska 70 43 53N 91 14W
Onamia 70 46 4N 93 38W
Onancock 68 37 42N 75 49W
Onang 35 3 2S 118 49 E
Onaping L. 62 47 3N 81 30W
Onarhā 31 35 30N 71 0 E
Onavas 74 28 28N 109 30W
Onawa 70 42 2N 96 2W
Onaway 68 45 21N 84 11W
Oncócua 56 16 30S 13 25 E
Onda 13 39 55N 0 17W
Ondangua 56 17 57S 16 4 E
Ondjiva 56 16 48S 15 50 E
Ondo 53 7 4N 4 47 E
Ondo □ 53 7 0N 5 0 E
Öndörhaan 37 47 19N 110 39 E
Öndverðarnes 20 64 52N 24 0W
Onega 22 64 0N 38 10 E
Onega → 22 63 58N 37 55 E
Onega, G. of = Onezhskaya Guba 22 64 30N 37 0 E
Onega, L. = Onezhskoye Ozero 22 62 0N 35 30 E
Onehunga 43 36 55S 174 48 E
Oneida 68 43 5N 75 40W
Oneida L. 68 43 12N 76 0W
O'Neill 70 42 30N 98 38W
Onekotan, Ostrov 25 49 25N 154 45 E
Oneonta, Ala., U.S.A. 69 33 58N 86 29W
Oneonta, N.Y., U.S.A. 68 42 26N 75 5W
Onezhskaya Guba 22 64 30N 37 0 E
Onezhskoye Ozero 22 62 0N 35 30 E
Ongarue 43 38 42S 175 19 E
Ongerup 47 33 58S 118 28 E
Ongniud Qi 38 43 0N 118 38 E
Ongole 32 15 33N 80 2 E
Onguren 25 53 38N 107 36 E
Onida 70 44 42N 100 5W
Onilahy → 57 23 34S 43 45 E
Onitsha 53 6 6N 6 42 E
Onoda 36 34 2N 131 25 E
Onslow 46 21 40S 115 12 E
Onslow B. 69 34 20N 77 20W
Onstwedde 11 53 2N 7 4 E
Ontake-San 36 35 53N 137 29 E
Ontario, Calif., U.S.A. 73 34 2N 117 40W
Ontario, Oreg., U.S.A. 72 44 1N 117 1W
Ontario □ 62 52 0N 88 10W
Ontario, L. 62 43 40N 78 0W
Ontonagon 70 46 52N 89 19W
Oodnadatta 45 27 33S 135 30 E
Ooldea 47 30 27S 131 50 E
Oombulgurri 46 15 15S 127 45 E
Oona River 64 53 57N 130 16W
Oorindi 44 20 40S 141 1 E
Oost-Vlaanderen □ 11 51 5N 3 50 E
Oostende 11 51 15N 2 54 E
Oosterhout 11 51 39N 4 47 E
Oosterschelde 11 51 33N 4 0 E
Ootacamund 32 11 30N 76 44 E
Ootsa L. 64 53 50N 126 2W
Opala, U.S.S.R. 25 51 58N 156 30 E
Opala, Zaïre 54 0 40S 24 20 E
Opanake 32 6 35N 80 40 E
Opasatika 62 49 30N 82 50W
Opasquia 65 53 16N 93 34W
Opava 15 49 57N 17 58 E
Opelousas 71 30 35N 92 7W
Opémisca, L. 62 49 56N 74 52W
Opheim 72 48 52N 106 30W
Ophir 60 63 10N 156 40W
Ophthalmia Ra. 46 23 15S 119 30 E
Opi 53 6 36N 7 28 E
Opinaca → 62 52 15N 78 2W
Opinaca L. 62 52 39N 76 20W
Opiskotish, L. 63 53 10N 67 50W
Opobo 53 4 35N 7 34 E
Opole 15 50 42N 17 58 E
Oporto = Porto 13 41 8N 8 40W

Port Alice

Peru, Ill., U.S.A. 70 41 18N 89 12W
Peru, Ind., U.S.A. 68 40 42N 86 0W
Peru ■ 78 8 0S 75 0W
Peru-Chile Trench 41 20 0S 72 0W
Perúgia 18 43 6N 12 24 E
Pervomaysk 23 48 10N 30 46 E
Pervouralsk 22 56 55N 60 0 E
Pésaro 18 43 55N 12 53 E
Pescara 18 42 28N 14 13 E
Peshawar 32 34 2N 71 37 E
Peshtigo 68 45 4N 87 46W
Pesqueira 79 8 20S 36 42W
Petah Tiqwa 28 32 6N 34 53 E
Petaluma 72 38 13N 122 39W
Petange 11 49 33N 5 55 E
Petatlán 74 17 31N 101 16W
Petauke 55 14 14S 31 20 E
Petawawa 62 45 54N 77 17W
Petén Itzá, L. 75 16 58N 89 50W
Peter Pond L. 65 55 55N 108 44W
Peterbell 62 48 36N 83 21W
Peterborough, Australia 45 32 58S 138 51 E
Peterborough, U.K. 7 52 35N 0 14W
Peterhead 8 57 30N 1 49W
Petersburg, Alaska, U.S.A. 60 56 50N 133 0W
Petersburg, Ind., U.S.A. 68 38 30N 87 15W
Petersburg, Va., U.S.A. 68 37 17N 77 26W
Petersburg, W. Va., U.S.A. 68 38 59N 79 10W
Petford 44 17 20S 144 58 E
Petit Bois I. 69 30 16N 88 25W
Petit-Cap 63 49 3N 64 30W
Petit Goâve 75 18 27N 72 51W
Petit Lac Manicouagan 63 51 25N 67 40W
Petitcodiac 63 45 57N 65 11W
Petite Baleine → 62 56 0N 76 45W
Petite Saguenay 63 48 15N 70 4W
Petitsikapau, L. 63 54 37N 66 25W
Petlad 32 22 30N 72 45 E
Peto 74 20 10N 88 53W
Petone 43 41 13S 174 53 E
Petoskey 68 45 22N 84 57W
Petra 28 30 20N 35 22 E
Petrich 19 41 24N 23 13 E
Petrolândia 79 9 5S 38 20W
Petrolia 62 42 54N 82 9W
Petrolina 79 9 24S 40 30W
Petropavlovsk 24 54 53N 69 13 E
Petropavlovsk-Kamchatskiy 25 53 3N 158 43 E
Petrópolis 79 22 33S 43 9W
Petroşeni 15 45 28N 23 20 E
Petroskey 68 45 22N 84 57W
Petrovaradin 19 45 16N 19 55 E
Petrovsk 22 52 22N 45 19 E
Petrovsk-Zabaykalskiy 25 51 20N 108 55 E
Petrozavodsk 22 61 41N 34 20 E
Petrus Steyn 57 27 38S 28 8 E
Petrusburg 56 29 4S 25 26 E
Peureulak 34 4 48N 97 45 E
Pevek 25 69 41N 171 19 E
Pforzheim 14 48 53N 8 43 E
Phagwara 32 31 10N 75 40 E
Phala 56 23 45S 26 50 E
Phalodi 32 27 12N 72 24 E
Phan Rang 34 11 34N 109 0 E
Phangan, Ko 34 9 45N 100 0 E
Phangnga 34 8 28N 98 30 E
Phanh Bho Ho Chi Minh 34 10 58N 106 40 E
Phatthalung 34 7 39N 100 6 E
Phelps 70 46 2N 89 2W
Phelps L. 65 59 15N 103 15W
Phenix City 69 32 30N 85 0W
Phetchabun 34 16 25N 101 8 E
Philadelphia, Miss., U.S.A. 71 32 47N 89 5W
Philadelphia, Pa., U.S.A. 68 40 0N 75 10W
Philip 70 44 4N 101 42W
Philippeville 11 50 12N 4 33 E
Philippi L. 44 24 20S 138 55 E
Philippines ■ 35 12 0N 123 0 E
Philippolis 56 30 15S 25 16 E
Philippopolis = Plovdiv 19 42 8N 24 44 E
Philipsburg 72 46 20N 113 21W
Philipstown 56 30 28S 24 30 E
Phillip, I. 45 38 30S 145 12 E
Phillips, Tex., U.S.A. 71 35 48N 101 17W
Phillips, Wis., U.S.A. 70 45 41N 90 22W
Phillipsburg 70 39 48N 99 20W
Phillott 45 27 53S 145 50 E
Philomath 72 44 28N 123 21W
Phitsanulok 34 16 50N 100 12 E
Phnom Dangrek 34 14 20N 104 0 E
Phnom Penh 34 11 33N 104 55 E
Phoenix 73 33 30N 112 10W
Phoenix Is. 40 3 30S 172 0W
Phra Nakhon Si Ayutthaya 34 14 25N 100 30 E
Phuket 34 7 52N 98 22 E
Piacenza 18 45 2N 9 42 E
Pialba 45 25 20S 152 45 E
Pian Cr. → 45 30 2S 148 12 E
Piapot 65 49 59N 109 8W
Piatra Neamţ 15 46 56N 26 21 E
Piauí □ 79 7 0S 43 0W
Piave → 18 45 32N 12 44 E
Piazza Ármerina 18 37 21N 14 20 E
Pibor Post 51 6 47N 33 3 E
Pica 78 20 35S 69 25W
Picardie 12 49 50N 3 0 E
Picardy = Picardie 12 49 50N 3 0 E
Picayune 71 30 31N 89 40W
Pichilemu 80 34 22S 72 0W
Pickerel L. 62 48 40N 91 25W
Pickle Lake 62 51 30N 90 12W
Pico Truncado 80 46 40S 68 0W
Picton, Australia 45 34 12S 150 34 E
Picton, Canada 62 44 1N 77 9W
Picton, N.Z. 43 41 18S 174 3 E
Pictou 63 45 41N 62 42W
Picture Butte 64 49 55N 112 45W
Picún Leufú 80 39 30S 69 5W
Pidurutalagala 32 7 10N 80 50 E
Piedad, La 74 20 20N 102 1W
Piedmont = Piemonte □ 18 45 0N 7 30 E
Piedmont 69 33 55N 85 39W
Piedmont Plateau 69 34 0N 81 30W
Piedras, R. de las → 78 12 30S 69 15W
Piedras Negras 74 28 35N 100 35W
Piemonte □ 18 45 0N 7 30 E
Pierce 72 46 29N 115 53W
Pierre 70 44 23N 100 20W
Piet Retief 57 27 1S 30 50 E
Pietarsaari = Jakobstad 20 63 40N 22 43 E
Pietermaritzburg 57 29 35S 30 25 E
Pietersburg 57 23 54S 29 25 E
Pietrosul 15 47 35N 24 43 E
Pigeon 68 43 50N 83 17W
Piggott 71 36 20N 90 10W
Pigüe 80 37 36S 62 25W
Pikes Peak 70 38 50N 105 10W
Piketberg 56 32 55S 18 40 E
Pikeville 68 37 30N 82 30W
Pikwitonei 65 55 35N 97 9W
Pilar, Brazil 79 9 36S 35 56W
Pilar, Paraguay 80 26 50S 58 20W
Pilas Group 35 6 45N 121 35 E
Pilbara 46 21 15S 118 16 E
Pilcomayo → 80 25 21S 57 42W
Pilibhit 32 28 40N 79 50 E
Pilica → 15 51 52N 21 17 E
Pílos 19 36 55N 21 42 E
Pilot Mound 65 49 15N 98 54W
Pilot Point 71 33 26N 97 0W
Pilot Rock 72 45 30N 118 50W
Pilsen = Plzeň 14 49 45N 13 22 E
Pima 73 32 54N 109 50W
Pimba 45 31 18S 136 46 E
Pimenta Bueno 78 11 35S 61 10W
Pimentel 78 6 45S 79 55W
Pinang 34 5 25N 100 15 E
Pinar del Río 75 22 26N 83 40W
Pincher Creek 64 49 30N 113 57W
Pinchi L. 64 54 38N 124 30W
Pinckneyville 70 38 5N 89 20W
Pińczów 15 50 32N 20 32 E
Pindar 47 28 30S 115 47 E
Pindiga 53 9 58N 10 53 E
Pindos Óros 19 40 0N 21 0 E
Pindus Mts. = Pindos Óros 19 40 0N 21 0 E
Pine 73 34 27N 111 30W
Pine → 65 58 50N 105 38W
Pine, C. 63 46 37N 53 32W
Pine, La 72 43 40N 121 30W
Pine Bluff 71 34 10N 92 0W
Pine City 70 45 46N 93 0W
Pine Falls 65 50 34N 96 11W
Pine Pass 64 55 25N 122 42W
Pine Point 64 60 50N 114 28W
Pine Ridge 70 43 0N 102 35W
Pine River, Canada 65 51 45N 100 30W
Pine River, U.S.A. 70 46 43N 94 24W
Pinega → 22 64 8N 46 54 E
Pinehill 44 23 38S 146 57 E
Pinerolo 18 44 47N 7 21 E
Pinetop 73 34 10N 109 57W
Pinetown 57 29 48S 30 54 E
Pinetree 72 43 42N 105 52W
Pineville, Ky., U.S.A. 69 36 42N 83 42W
Pineville, La., U.S.A. 71 31 22N 92 30W
Ping → 34 15 42N 100 9 E
Pingaring 47 32 40S 118 32 E
Pingding 38 37 47N 113 38 E
Pingdingshan 39 33 43N 113 27 E
Pingdong 39 22 39N 120 30 E
Pingdu 38 36 42N 119 59 E
Pingelly 47 32 32S 117 5 E
Pingguo 39 23 19N 107 36 E
Pinghe 39 24 17N 117 21 E
Pingjiang 39 28 45N 113 36 E
Pingle 39 24 40N 110 40 E
Pingliang 38 35 35N 106 31 E
Pingluo 38 38 52N 106 30 E
Pingnan 39 23 33N 110 22 E
Pingrup 47 33 32S 118 29 E
Pingtan Dao 39 25 29N 119 47 E
Pingwu 39 32 25N 104 30 E
Pingxiang, Guangxi Zhuangzu, China 39 22 6N 106 46 E
Pingxiang, Jiangxi, China 39 27 43N 113 48 E
Pingyao 38 37 12N 112 10 E
Pinhel 13 40 50N 7 1W
Pini 34 0 10N 98 40 E
Piniós → 19 39 55N 22 10 E
Pinjarra 47 32 37S 115 52 E
Pink → 65 56 50N 103 50W
Pinnacles 47 28 12S 120 26 E
Pinnaroo 45 35 17S 140 53 E
Pinos 74 22 20N 101 40W
Pinos Pt. 73 36 38N 121 57W
Pinrang 35 3 46S 119 41 E
Pinsk 22 52 10N 26 1 E
Pintados 78 20 35S 69 40W
Pintumba 47 31 30S 132 12 E
Pinyang 39 27 42N 120 31 E
Pinyug 22 60 5N 48 0 E
Pioche 73 38 0N 114 35W
Piombino 18 42 54N 10 30 E
Pioner, Os. 25 79 50N 92 0 E
Piorini, L. 78 3 15S 62 35W
Piotrków Trybunalski 15 51 23N 19 43 E
Pīp 31 26 45N 60 10 E
Pipestone 70 44 0N 96 20W
Pipestone → 62 52 53N 89 23W
Pipestone Cr. → 65 49 38N 100 15W
Pipmuacan, Rés. 63 49 45N 70 30W
Pippingarra 46 20 27S 118 42 E
Piqua 68 40 10N 84 10W
Piquiri → 80 24 3S 54 14W
Piracicaba 80 22 45S 47 40W
Piracuruca 79 3 50S 41 50W
Piræus = Piraiévs 19 37 57N 23 42 E
Piraiévs 19 37 57N 23 42 E
Pirané 80 25 42S 59 6W
Pirapora 79 17 20S 44 56W
Pírgos 19 37 40N 21 27 E
Pirin Planina 19 41 40N 23 30 E
Pírineos 13 42 40N 1 0 E
Piripiri 79 4 15S 41 46W
Pirot 19 43 9N 22 39 E
Piru 35 3 4S 128 12 E
Pisa 18 43 43N 10 23 E
Pisagua 78 19 40S 70 15W
Pisco 78 13 50S 76 12W
Písek 14 49 19N 14 10 E
Pishan 37 37 30N 78 33 E
Pising 35 5 8S 121 53 E
Pistóia 18 43 57N 10 53 E
Pistol B. 65 62 25N 92 37W
Pisuerga → 13 41 33N 4 52W
Pitarpunga, L. 45 34 24S 143 30 E
Pitcairn I. 2 25 5S 130 5W
Pite älv → 20 65 20N 21 25 E
Piteå 20 65 20N 21 25 E
Piteşti 15 44 52N 24 54 E
Pithapuram 33 17 10N 82 15 E
Pithara 47 30 20S 116 35 E
Pitlochry 8 56 43N 3 43W
Pitt I. 64 53 30N 129 50W
Pittsburg, Kans., U.S.A. 71 37 21N 94 43W
Pittsburg, Tex., U.S.A. 71 32 59N 94 58W
Pittsburgh 68 40 25N 79 55W
Pittsfield, Ill., U.S.A. 70 39 35N 90 46W
Pittsfield, Mass., U.S.A. 68 42 28N 73 17W
Pittston 68 41 19N 75 50W
Pittsworth 45 27 41S 151 37 E
Pituri → 44 22 35S 138 30 E
Piura 78 5 15S 80 38W
Pizzo 18 38 44N 16 10 E
Placentia 63 47 20N 54 0W
Placentia B. 63 47 0N 54 40W
Placerville 72 38 47N 120 51W
Placetas 75 22 15N 79 44W
Plain Dealing 71 32 56N 93 41W
Plainfield 68 40 37N 74 28W
Plains, Kans., U.S.A. 71 37 20N 100 35W
Plains, Mont., U.S.A. 72 47 27N 114 57W
Plains, Tex., U.S.A. 71 33 11N 102 50W
Plainview, Nebr., U.S.A. 70 42 25N 97 48W
Plainview, Tex., U.S.A. 71 34 10N 101 40W
Plainville 70 39 18N 99 19W
Plainwell 68 42 28N 85 40W
Plakhino 24 67 45N 86 5 E
Plankinton 70 43 45N 98 27W
Plano 71 33 0N 96 45W
Plant, La 70 45 11N 100 40W
Plant City 69 28 0N 82 8W
Plaquemine 71 30 20N 91 15W
Plasencia 13 40 3N 6 8W
Plaster Rock 63 46 53N 67 22W
Plata, La 80 35 0S 57 55W
Plata, Río de la 80 34 45S 57 30W
Platani → 18 37 23N 13 16 E
Plateau □ 53 8 0N 8 30 E
Plateau du Coteau du Missouri 70 47 9N 101 5W
Platí, Ákra 19 40 27N 24 0 E
Plato 78 9 47N 74 47W
Platte 70 43 28N 98 50W
Platte → 70 39 16N 94 50W
Platteville 70 40 18N 104 47W
Plattsburg 68 44 41N 73 30W
Plattsmouth 70 41 0N 95 50W
Plauen 14 50 29N 12 9 E
Playgreen L. 65 54 0N 98 15W
Pleasant Bay 63 46 51N 60 48W
Pleasant Hill 70 38 48N 94 14W
Pleasanton 71 29 0N 98 30W
Pleasantville 68 39 25N 74 30W
Pleiku 34 13 57N 108 0 E
Plenty → 44 23 25S 136 31 E
Plenty, Bay of 43 37 45S 177 0 E
Plentywood 70 48 45N 104 35W
Plesetsk 22 62 40N 40 10 E
Plessisville 63 46 14N 71 47W
Pletipi L. 63 51 44N 70 6W
Pleven 19 43 26N 24 37 E
Plevlja 19 43 21N 19 21 E
Płock 15 52 32N 19 40 E
Ploieşti 15 44 57N 26 5 E
Plonge, Lac la 65 55 8N 107 20W
Plovdiv 19 42 8N 24 44 E
Plummer 72 47 21N 116 59W
Plumtree 55 20 27S 27 55 E
Plymouth, U.K. 7 50 23N 4 9W
Plymouth, Ind., U.S.A. 68 41 20N 86 19W
Plymouth, N.C., U.S.A. 69 35 54N 76 46W
Plymouth, Wis., U.S.A. 68 43 42N 87 58W
Plymouth Sd. 7 50 20N 4 10W
Plynlimon = Pumlumon Fawr 7 52 29N 3 47W
Plzeň 14 49 45N 13 22 E
Po → 18 44 57N 12 4 E
Po Hai = Bo Hai 38 39 0N 120 0 E
Pobé 53 7 0N 2 56 E
Pobeda 25 65 12N 146 12 E
Pobedino 25 49 51N 142 49 E
Pobedy Pik 24 40 45N 79 58 E
Pocahontas, Ark., U.S.A. 71 36 18N 91 0W
Pocahontas, Iowa, U.S.A. 70 42 41N 94 42W
Pocatello 72 42 50N 112 25W
Pochutla 74 15 50N 96 31W
Pocomoke City 68 38 4N 75 32W
Poços de Caldas 79 21 50S 46 33W
Podgorica = Titograd 19 42 30N 19 19 E
Podkamennaya Tunguska → 25 61 50N 90 13 E
Podolsk 22 55 25N 37 30 E
Podor 50 16 40N 15 2W
Podporozhy 22 60 55N 34 2 E
Pofadder 56 29 10S 19 22 E
Pogamasing 62 46 55N 81 50W
Poh 35 0 46S 122 51 E
Pohang 38 36 1N 129 23 E
Point Edward 62 43 0N 82 30W
Point Pedro 32 9 50N 80 15 E
Point Pleasant 68 38 50N 82 7W
Pointe-à-la Hache 71 29 35N 89 55W
Pointe-à-Pitre 75 16 10N 61 30W
Pointe Noire 54 4 48S 11 53 E
Poisonbush Ra. 46 22 30S 121 30 E
Poitiers 12 46 35N 0 20 E
Pojoaque Valley 73 35 55N 106 0W
Pokaran 32 27 0N 71 50 E
Pokataroo 45 29 30S 148 36 E
Pokrovsk 25 61 29N 126 12 E
Polacca 73 35 52N 110 25W
Polan 31 25 30N 61 10 E
Poland ■ 15 52 0N 20 0 E
Polcura 80 37 17S 71 43W
Polden Hills 7 51 7N 2 50W
Polesye 22 52 0N 28 10 E
Polevskoy 22 56 26N 60 11 E
Polewali 35 3 21S 119 23 E
Poli 54 8 34N 13 15 E
Polillo Is. 35 14 56N 122 0 E
Políyiros 19 40 23N 23 25 E
Pollachi 32 10 35N 77 0 E
Pollock 70 45 58N 100 18W
Polnovat 24 63 50N 65 54 E
Polo 70 41 59N 89 38W
Polotsk 22 55 30N 28 50 E
Polson 72 47 45N 114 12W
Poltava 23 49 35N 34 35 E
Polunochnoye 22 60 52N 60 25 E
Polyarny 22 69 8N 33 20 E
Polynesia 41 10 0S 162 0W
Pombal, Brazil 79 6 45S 37 50W
Pombal, Portugal 13 39 55N 8 40W
Pomeroy, Ohio, U.S.A. 68 39 0N 82 0W
Pomeroy, Wash., U.S.A. 72 46 30N 117 33W
Pomona 73 34 2N 117 49W
Pompano Beach 69 26 12N 80 6W
Pompeys Pillar 72 46 0N 108 0W
Ponape 40 6 55N 158 10 E
Ponask, L. 62 54 0N 92 41W
Ponass L. 65 52 16N 103 58W
Ponca 70 42 38N 96 41W
Ponca City 71 36 40N 97 5W
Ponce 75 18 1N 66 37W
Ponchatoula 71 30 27N 90 25W
Poncheville, L. 62 50 10N 76 55W
Pond Inlet 61 72 40N 77 0W
Pondicherry 32 11 59N 79 50 E
Ponds, I. of 63 53 27N 55 52W
Ponferrada 13 42 32N 6 35W
Ponnani 32 10 45N 75 59 E
Ponnyadaung 33 22 0N 94 10 E
Ponoi 22 67 0N 41 0 E
Ponoi → 22 66 59N 41 17 E
Ponoka 64 52 42N 113 40W
Ponorogo 35 7 52S 111 27 E
Ponta Grossa 80 25 7S 50 10W
Ponta Pora 80 22 20S 55 35W
Pontarlier 12 46 54N 6 20 E
Pontchartrain, L. 71 30 12N 90 0W
Ponte Macassar 35 9 30S 123 58 E
Ponte Nova 79 20 25S 42 54W
Pontedera 18 43 40N 10 37 E
Pontefract 6 53 42N 1 19W
Ponteix 65 49 46N 107 29W
Pontevedra 13 42 26N 8 40W
Pontiac, Ill., U.S.A. 70 40 50N 88 40W
Pontiac, Mich., U.S.A. 68 42 40N 83 20W
Pontianak 34 0 3S 109 15 E
Pontine Is. = Ponziane, Isole 18 40 55N 13 0 E
Pontine Mts. = Kuzey Anadolu Dağlari 30 41 30N 35 0 E
Ponton → 64 58 27N 116 11W
Pontypool 7 51 42N 3 1W
Pontypridd 7 51 36N 3 21W
Ponziane, Isole 18 40 55N 13 0 E
Poochera 45 32 43S 134 51 E
Poole 7 50 42N 1 58W
Pooley I. 64 52 45N 128 15W
Poona = Pune 32 18 29N 73 57 E
Pooncarie 45 33 22S 142 31 E
Poopelloe, L. 45 31 40S 144 0 E
Poopó, L. de 78 18 30S 67 35W
Popanyinning 47 32 40S 117 2 E
Popayán 78 2 27N 76 36W
Poperinge 11 50 51N 2 42 E
Popigay 25 72 1N 110 39 E
Popilta, L. 45 33 10S 141 42 E
Popio, L. 45 33 10S 141 52 E
Poplar 70 48 3N 105 9W
Poplar →, Man., Canada 65 53 0N 97 19W
Poplar →, N.W.T., Canada 64 61 22N 121 52W
Poplar Bluff 71 36 45N 90 22W
Poplarville 71 30 55N 89 30W
Popocatepetl 74 19 10N 98 40W
Popokabaka 54 5 41S 16 40 E
Porbandar 32 21 44N 69 43 E
Porcher I. 64 53 50N 130 30W
Porcupine →, Canada 65 59 11N 104 46W
Porcupine →, U.S.A. 60 66 35N 145 15W
Pori 21 61 29N 21 48 E
Porjus 20 66 57N 19 50 E
Porkkala 21 59 59N 24 26 E
Porlamar 78 10 57N 63 51W
Poronaysk 25 49 13N 143 0 E
Poroshiri-Dake 36 42 41N 142 52 E
Porretta, Passo di 18 44 2N 10 56 E
Porsangen 20 70 40N 25 40 E
Port Adelaide 45 34 46S 138 30 E
Port Alberni 64 49 14N 124 50W
Port Alfred, Canada 63 48 18N 70 53W
Port Alfred, S. Africa 56 33 36S 26 55 E
Port Alice 64 50 20N 127 25W

Port Allegany

Port Allegany **68** 41 49N 78 17W
Port Allen **71** 30 30N 91 15W
Port Alma **44** 23 38S 150 53 E
Port Angeles **72** 48 7N 123 30W
Port Antonio **75** 18 10N 76 30W
Port Aransas **71** 27 49N 97 4W
Port Arthur = Lüshun **38** 38 45N 121 15 E
Port Arthur, Australia **44** 43 7S 147 50 E
Port Arthur, U.S.A. **71** 30 0N 94 0W
Port au Port B. **63** 48 40N 58 50W
Port-au-Prince **75** 18 40N 72 20W
Port Augusta **45** 32 30S 137 50 E
Port Augusta West **45** 32 29S 137 29 E
Port Austin **68** 44 3N 82 59W
Port Bergé Vaovao **57** 15 33S 47 40 E
Port Blandford **63** 48 20N 54 10W
Port Bradshaw **44** 12 30S 137 20 E
Port Broughton **45** 33 37S 137 56 E
Port Burwell **62** 42 40N 80 48W
Port-Cartier **63** 50 2N 66 50W
Port Chalmers **43** 45 49S 170 30 E
Port Chester **68** 41 0N 73 41W
Port Clements **64** 53 40N 132 10W
Port Clinton **68** 41 30N 82 58W
Port Colborne **62** 42 50N 79 10W
Port Coquitlam **64** 49 15N 122 45W
Port Curtis **44** 23 57S 151 20 E
Port Darwin, Australia **46** 12 24S 130 45 E
Port Darwin, Falk. Is. **80** 51 50S 59 0W
Port Davey **44** 43 16S 145 55 E
Port-de-Paix **75** 19 50N 72 50W
Port Dickson **34** 2 30N 101 49 E
Port Douglas **44** 16 30S 145 30 E
Port Edward **64** 54 12N 130 10W
Port Elgin **62** 44 25N 81 25W
Port Elizabeth **56** 33 58S 25 40 E
Port Ellen **8** 55 38N 6 10W
Port-en-Bessin **12** 49 21N 0 45W
Port Erin **6** 54 5N 4 45W
Port Essington **46** 11 15S 132 10 E
Port Etienne = Nouâdhibou **50** 20 54N 17 0W
Port Fairy **45** 38 22S 142 12 E
Port-Gentil **54** 0 40S 8 50 E
Port Gibson **71** 31 57N 91 0W
Port Glasgow **8** 55 57N 4 40W
Port Harcourt **53** 4 40N 7 10 E
Port Hardy **64** 50 41N 127 30W
Port Harrison = Inoucdjouac **61** 58 25N 78 15W
Port Hawkesbury **63** 45 36N 61 22W
Port Hedland **46** 20 25S 118 35 E
Port Henry **68** 44 0N 73 30W
Port Hood **63** 46 0N 61 32W
Port Hope **62** 43 56N 78 20W
Port Huron **68** 43 0N 82 28W
Port Isabel **71** 26 4N 97 9W
Port Jefferson **68** 40 58N 73 5W
Port Kembla **45** 34 52S 150 49 E
Port-la-Nouvelle **12** 43 1N 3 3 E
Port Laoise **9** 53 2N 7 20W
Port Lavaca **71** 28 38N 96 38W
Port Lincoln **45** 34 42S 135 52 E
Port Loko **50** 8 48N 12 46W
Port Louis **3** 20 10S 57 30 E
Port Lyautey = Kenitra **50** 34 15N 6 40W
Port Macdonnell **45** 38 0S 140 48 E
Port Macquarie **45** 31 25S 152 25 E
Port Maria **75** 18 25N 77 5W
Port Mellon **64** 49 32N 123 31W
Port-Menier **63** 49 51N 64 15W
Port Moresby **40** 9 24S 147 8 E
Port Mouton **63** 43 58N 64 50W
Port Musgrave **44** 11 55S 141 50 E
Port Nelson **65** 57 3N 92 36W
Port Nolloth **56** 29 17S 16 52 E
Port Nouveau-Québec **61** 58 30N 65 59W
Port O'Connor **71** 28 26N 96 24W
Port of Spain **75** 10 40N 61 31W
Port Orchard **72** 47 31N 122 38W
Port Orford **72** 42 45N 124 28W
Port Pegasus **43** 47 12S 167 41 E
Port Perry **62** 44 6N 78 56W
Port Phillip B. **45** 38 10S 144 50 E
Port Pirie **45** 33 10S 138 1 E
Port Radium = Echo Bay **60** 66 5N 117 55W
Port Renfrew **64** 48 30N 124 20W
Port Roper **44** 14 45S 135 25 E
Port Rowan **62** 42 40N 80 30W
Port Safaga = Bûr Safâga **51** 26 43N 33 57 E
Port Said = Bûr Sa'îd **51** 31 16N 32 18 E
Port St. Joe **69** 29 49N 85 20W
Port St. Johns **57** 31 38S 29 33 E
Port-St.-Louis-du-Rhône **12** 43 23N 4 49 E
Port Sanilac **62** 43 26N 82 33W
Port Saunders **63** 50 40N 57 18W
Port Shepstone **57** 30 44S 30 28 E
Port Simpson **64** 54 30N 130 20W
Port Stanley **62** 42 40N 81 10W
Port Sudan = Bûr Sûdân **51** 19 32N 37 9 E
Port Talbot **7** 51 35N 3 48W
Port Townsend **72** 48 7N 122 50W
Port-Vendres **12** 42 32N 3 8 E
Port Vladimir **22** 69 25N 33 6 E
Port Wakefield **45** 34 12S 138 10 E
Port Washington **68** 43 25N 87 52W
Port Weld **34** 4 50N 100 38 E
Portachuelo **78** 17 10S 63 20W
Portadown **9** 54 27N 6 26W
Portage **70** 43 31N 89 25W
Portage La Prairie **65** 49 58N 98 18W
Portageville **71** 36 25N 89 40W
Portalegre **13** 39 19N 7 25W
Portalegre □ **13** 39 20N 7 40W
Portales **71** 34 12N 103 25W
Portarlington **9** 53 10N 7 10W
Porte, La **68** 41 36N 86 43W
Porter L., N.W.T., Canada **65** 61 41N 108 5W
Porter L., Sask., Canada **65** 56 20N 107 20W
Porterville, S. Africa **56** 33 0S 19 0 E
Porterville, U.S.A. **73** 36 5N 119 0W
Porthcawl **7** 51 28N 3 42W
Porthill **72** 49 0N 116 30W
Portile de Fier **15** 44 42N 22 30 E
Portimão **13** 37 8N 8 32W
Portland, N.S.W., Australia **45** 33 20S 150 0 E
Portland, Vic., Australia **45** 38 20S 141 35 E
Portland, Maine, U.S.A. **63** 43 40N 70 15W
Portland, Mich., U.S.A. **68** 42 52N 84 58W
Portland, Oreg., U.S.A. **72** 45 35N 122 40W
Portland, Bill of **7** 50 31N 2 27W
Portland, I. of **7** 50 32N 2 25W
Portland B. **45** 38 15S 141 45 E
Portland Prom. **61** 58 40N 78 33W
Portneuf **63** 46 43N 71 55W
Porto **13** 41 8N 8 40W
Pôrto Alegre **80** 30 5S 51 10W
Porto Amboim = Gunza **54** 10 50S 13 50 E
Pôrto de Móz **79** 1 41S 52 13W
Porto Empédocle **18** 37 18N 13 30 E
Pôrto Esperança **78** 19 37S 57 29W
Pôrto Franco **79** 6 20S 47 24W
Pôrto Mendes **80** 24 30S 54 15W
Pôrto Murtinho **78** 21 45S 57 55W
Pôrto Nacional **79** 10 40S 48 30W
Porto Novo **53** 6 23N 2 42 E
Porto Santo **50** 33 45N 16 25W
Pôrto Seguro **79** 16 26S 39 5W
Porto Tórres **18** 40 50N 8 23 E
Pôrto União **80** 26 10S 51 10W
Pôrto Válter **78** 8 15S 72 40W
Porto-Vecchio **12** 41 35N 9 16 E
Pôrto Velho **78** 8 46S 63 54W
Portoferráio **18** 42 50N 10 20 E
Portola **72** 39 49N 120 28W
Portoscuso **18** 39 12N 8 22 E
Portoviejo **78** 1 7S 80 28W
Portpatrick **8** 54 50N 5 7W
Portree **8** 57 25N 6 11W
Portrush **9** 55 13N 6 40W
Portsmouth, Domin. **75** 15 34N 61 27W
Portsmouth, U.K. **7** 50 48N 1 6W
Portsmouth, N.H., U.S.A. **68** 43 5N 70 45W
Portsmouth, Ohio, U.S.A. **68** 38 45N 83 0W
Portsmouth, Va., U.S.A. **68** 36 50N 76 20W
Portsoy **8** 57 41N 2 41W
Porttipahta **20** 68 5N 26 40 E
Portugal ■ **13** 40 0N 7 0W
Portuguese-Guinea = Guinea-Bissau ■ **50** 12 0N 15 0W
Portuguese Timor ■ = Timor **35** 9 0S 125 0 E
Portumna **9** 53 5N 8 12W
Porvenir **80** 53 10S 70 16W
Porvoo **21** 60 24N 25 40 E
Posadas **80** 27 30S 55 50W
Poshan = Boshan **38** 36 28N 117 49 E
Poso **35** 1 20S 120 55 E
Posse **79** 14 4S 46 18W
Possel **54** 5 5N 19 10 E
Post **71** 33 13N 101 21W
Post Falls **72** 47 46N 116 59W
Poste Maurice Cortier **50** 22 14N 1 2 E
Postmasburg **56** 28 18S 23 5 E
Postojna **19** 45 46N 14 12 E
Potchefstroom **56** 26 41S 27 7 E
Poteau **71** 35 5N 94 37W
Poteet **71** 29 4N 98 35W
Potenza **18** 40 40N 15 50 E
Poteriteri, L. **43** 46 5S 167 10 E
Potgietersrus **57** 24 10S 28 55 E
Poti **23** 42 10N 41 38 E
Potiskum **53** 11 39N 11 2 E
Potomac –► **68** 38 0N 76 23W
Potosí **78** 19 38S 65 50W
Pototan **35** 10 54N 122 38 E
Potrerillos **80** 26 30S 69 30W
Potsdam, Germany **14** 52 23N 13 4 E
Potsdam, U.S.A. **68** 44 40N 74 59W
Potter **70** 41 15N 103 20W
Pottstown **68** 40 17N 75 40W
Pottsville **68** 40 39N 76 12W
Pottuvil **32** 6 55N 81 50 E
Pouce Coupé **64** 55 40N 120 10W
Poughkeepsie **68** 41 40N 73 57W
Poulaphouca Res. **9** 53 8N 6 30W
Poulsbo **72** 47 45N 122 39W
Pouso Alegre **79** 11 46S 57 16W
Povenets **22** 62 50N 34 50 E
Poverty Bay **43** 38 43S 178 2 E
Póvoa de Varzim **13** 41 25N 8 46W
Powassan **62** 46 5N 79 25W
Powder –► **70** 46 47N 105 12W
Powder River **72** 43 5N 107 0W
Powell **72** 44 45N 108 45W
Powell, L. **73** 37 25N 110 45W
Powell River **64** 49 50N 124 35W
Powers, Mich., U.S.A. **68** 45 40N 87 32W
Powers, Oreg., U.S.A. **72** 42 53N 124 2W
Powers Lake **70** 48 37N 102 38W
Powys □ **7** 52 20N 3 20W
Poyang Hu **39** 29 5N 116 20 E
Poyarkovo **25** 49 36N 128 41 E
Poza Rica **74** 20 33N 97 27W
Požarevac **19** 44 35N 21 18 E
Poznań **14** 52 25N 16 55 E
Pozo Almonte **78** 20 10S 69 50W
Pozoblanco **13** 38 23N 4 51W
Prachuap Khiri Khan **34** 11 49N 99 48 E
Prado **79** 17 20S 39 13W
Prague = Praha **14** 50 5N 14 22 E
Praha **14** 50 5N 14 22 E
Praid **15** 46 32N 25 10 E
Prainha, Amazonas, Brazil **78** 7 10S 60 30W
Prainha, Pará, Brazil **79** 1 45S 53 30W
Prairie **44** 20 50S 144 35 E
Prairie –► **71** 34 30N 99 23W
Prairie City **72** 44 27N 118 44W
Prairie du Chien **70** 43 1N 91 9W
Prapat **34** 2 41N 98 58 E
Prata **79** 19 25S 48 54W
Prato **18** 43 53N 11 5 E
Pratt **71** 37 40N 98 45W
Prattville **69** 32 30N 86 28W
Pravia **13** 43 30N 6 12W
Praya **34** 8 39S 116 17 E
Preeceville **65** 51 57N 102 40W
Prelate **65** 50 51N 109 24W
Premier **64** 56 4N 129 56W
Premont **71** 27 19N 98 8W
Prentice **70** 45 31N 90 19W
Prenzlau **14** 53 19N 13 51 E
Prepansko Jezero **19** 40 55N 21 0 E
Preparis North Channel **33** 15 12N 93 40 E
Preparis South Channel **33** 14 36N 93 40 E
Přerov **15** 49 28N 17 27 E
Prescott, Canada **62** 44 45N 75 30W
Prescott, Ariz., U.S.A. **73** 34 35N 112 30W
Prescott, Ark., U.S.A. **71** 33 49N 93 22W
Preservation Inlet **43** 46 8S 166 35 E
Presho **70** 43 56N 100 4W
Presidencia Roque Saenz Peña **80** 26 45S 60 30W
Presidente Epitácio **79** 21 56S 52 6W
Presidente Hermes **78** 11 17S 61 55W
Presidente Prudente **79** 22 5S 51 25W
Presidio **71** 29 30N 104 20W
Prespa, L. = Prepansko Jezero **19** 40 55N 21 0 E
Presque Isle **63** 46 40N 68 0W
Prestbury **7** 51 54N 2 2W
Presteigne **7** 52 17N 3 0W
Preston, U.K. **6** 53 46N 2 42W
Preston, Idaho, U.S.A. **72** 42 10N 111 55W
Preston, Minn., U.S.A. **70** 43 39N 92 3W
Preston, Nev., U.S.A. **72** 38 59N 115 2W
Preston, C. **46** 20 51S 116 12 E
Prestonpans **8** 55 58N 3 0W
Prestwick **8** 55 30N 4 38W
Pretoria **57** 25 44S 28 12 E
Préveza **19** 38 57N 20 47 E
Příbram **14** 49 41N 14 2 E
Price **72** 39 40N 110 48W
Price I. **64** 52 23N 128 41W
Prichard **69** 30 47N 88 5W
Prieska **56** 29 40S 22 42 E
Priest L. **72** 48 30N 116 55W
Priest River **72** 48 11N 116 55W
Priestly **64** 54 8N 125 20W
Prikaspiyskaya Nizmennost **23** 47 0N 48 0 E
Prilep **19** 41 21N 21 37 E
Priluki **23** 50 30N 32 24 E
Prime Seal I. **44** 40 3S 147 43 E
Primrose L. **65** 54 55N 109 45W
Prince Albert, Canada **65** 53 15N 105 50W
Prince Albert, S. Africa **56** 33 12S 22 2 E
Prince Albert Nat. Park **65** 54 0N 106 25W
Prince Albert Pen. **60** 72 30N 116 0W
Prince Albert Sd. **60** 70 25N 115 0W
Prince Charles I. **61** 67 47N 76 12W
Prince Edward I. □ **63** 46 20N 63 20W
Prince Edward Is. **3** 46 35S 38 0 E
Prince George **64** 53 55N 122 50W
Prince of Wales I., Canada **60** 73 0N 99 0W
Prince of Wales I., U.S.A. **60** 55 30N 133 0W
Prince of Wales Is. **44** 10 40S 142 10 E
Prince Rupert **64** 54 20N 130 20W
Princess Charlotte B. **44** 14 25S 144 0 E
Princess May Ranges **46** 15 30S 125 30 E
Princess Royal I. **64** 53 0N 128 40W
Princeton, Canada **64** 49 27N 120 30W
Princeton, Ill., U.S.A. **70** 41 25N 89 25W
Princeton, Ind., U.S.A. **68** 38 20N 87 35W
Princeton, Ky., U.S.A. **68** 37 6N 87 55W
Princeton, Mo., U.S.A. **70** 40 23N 93 35W
Princeton, N.J., U.S.A. **68** 40 18N 74 40W
Princeton, W. Va., U.S.A. **68** 37 21N 81 8W
Principe, I. de **48** 1 37N 7 27 E
Principe Chan. **64** 53 28N 130 0W
Principe da Beira **78** 12 20S 64 30W
Prineville **72** 44 17N 120 50W
Priozersk **22** 61 2N 30 7 E
Pripet = Pripyat –► **22** 51 20N 30 9 E
Pripet Marshes = Polesye **22** 52 0N 28 10 E
Pripyat –► **22** 51 20N 30 9 E
Pripyat Marshes = Polesye **22** 52 0N 28 10 E
Priština **19** 42 40N 21 13 E
Privas **12** 44 45N 4 37 E
Privolzhskaya Vozvyshennost **23** 51 0N 46 0 E
Prizren **19** 42 13N 20 45 E
Probolinggo **35** 7 46S 113 13 E
Proddatur **32** 14 45N 78 30 E
Progreso **74** 21 20N 89 40W
Prokopyevsk **24** 54 0N 86 45 E
Prome = Pyè **33** 18 49N 95 13 E
Prophet –► **64** 58 48N 122 40W
Propriá **79** 10 13S 36 51W
Proserpine **44** 20 21S 148 36 E
Prosser **72** 46 11N 119 52W
Prostějov **14** 49 30N 17 9 E
Proston **45** 26 8S 151 32 E
Protection **71** 37 16N 99 30W
Provence **12** 43 40N 5 46 E
Providence, Ky., U.S.A. **68** 37 25N 87 46W
Providence, R.I., U.S.A. **68** 41 50N 71 28W
Providence Bay **62** 45 41N 82 15W
Providence Mts. **73** 35 0N 115 30W
Providencia, I. de **75** 13 25N 81 26W
Provideniya **25** 64 23N 173 18W
Provins **12** 48 33N 3 15 E
Provo **72** 40 16N 111 37W
Provost **65** 52 25N 110 20W
Prud'homme **65** 52 20N 105 54W
Pruszków **15** 52 9N 20 49 E
Prut –► **15** 45 28N 28 10 E
Pryor **71** 36 17N 95 20W
Przemysl **15** 49 50N 22 45 E
Przeworsk **15** 50 6N 22 32 E
Przhevalsk **24** 42 30N 78 20 E
Pskov **22** 57 50N 28 25 E
Puán **80** 37 30S 62 45W
Pucallpa **78** 8 25S 74 30W
Pucheng **39** 27 59N 118 31 E
Pudozh **22** 61 48N 36 32 E
Pudukkottai **32** 10 28N 78 47 E
Puebla **74** 19 0N 98 10W
Puebla □ **74** 18 30N 98 0W
Pueblo **70** 38 20N 104 40W
Pueblo Hundido **80** 26 20S 70 5W
Puelches **80** 38 5S 65 51W
Puente Alto **80** 33 32S 70 35W
Puente-Genil **13** 37 22N 4 47W
Puerco –► **73** 34 22N 107 50W
Puerto Aisén **80** 45 27S 73 0W
Puerto Armuelles **75** 8 20N 82 51W
Puerto Ayacucho **78** 5 40N 67 35W
Puerto Barrios **75** 15 40N 88 32W
Puerto Bermejo **80** 26 55S 58 34W
Puerto Bermúdez **78** 10 20S 75 0W
Puerto Bolívar **78** 3 19S 79 55W
Puerto Cabello **78** 10 28N 68 1W
Puerto Cabezas **75** 14 0N 83 30W
Puerto Carreño **78** 6 12N 67 22W
Puerto Castilla **75** 16 0N 86 0W
Puerto Chicama **78** 7 45S 79 20W
Puerto Coig **80** 50 54S 69 15W
Puerto Cortes, C. Rica **75** 8 55N 84 0W
Puerto Cortés, Hond. **75** 15 51N 88 0W
Puerto Cumarebo **78** 11 29N 69 30W
Puerto de Santa María **13** 36 36N 6 13W
Puerto del Rosario **50** 28 30N 13 52W
Puerto Deseado **80** 47 55S 66 0W
Puerto Heath **78** 12 34S 68 39W
Puerto Juárez **74** 21 11N 86 49W
Puerto La Cruz **78** 10 13N 64 38W
Puerto Leguízamo **78** 0 12S 74 46W
Puerto Lobos **80** 42 0S 65 3W
Puerto Madryn **80** 42 48S 65 4W
Puerto Maldonado **78** 12 30S 69 10W
Puerto Montt **80** 41 28S 73 0W
Puerto Morelos **74** 20 49N 86 52W
Puerto Natales **80** 51 45S 72 15W
Puerto Padre **75** 21 13N 76 35W
Puerto Páez **78** 6 13N 67 28W
Puerto Peñasco **74** 31 20N 113 33W
Puerto Pinasco **80** 22 36S 57 50W
Puerto Pirámides **80** 42 35S 64 20W
Puerto Plata **75** 19 48N 70 45W
Puerto Princesa **35** 9 46N 118 45 E
Puerto Quellón **80** 43 7S 73 37W
Puerto Quepos **75** 9 29N 84 6W
Puerto Rico ■ **75** 18 15N 66 45W
Puerto Sastre **78** 22 2S 57 55W
Puerto Suárez **78** 18 58S 57 52W
Puerto Vallarta **74** 20 36N 105 15W
Puerto Wilches **78** 7 21N 73 54W
Puertollano **13** 38 43N 4 7W
Pueyrredón, L. **80** 47 20S 72 0W
Pugachev **22** 52 0N 48 49 E
Puget Sd. **72** 47 15N 122 30W
Púglia □ **18** 41 0N 16 30 E
Puigcerdá **13** 42 24N 1 50 E
Pukaki L. **43** 44 4S 170 1 E
Pukapuka **41** 10 53S 165 49W
Pukatawagan **65** 55 45N 101 20W
Pukekohe **43** 37 12S 174 55 E
Pukou **39** 32 7N 118 38 E
Pulaski, N.Y., U.S.A. **68** 43 32N 76 9W
Pulaski, Tenn., U.S.A. **69** 35 10N 87 0W
Pulaski, Va., U.S.A. **68** 37 4N 80 49W
Pulicat, L. **32** 13 40N 80 15 E
Pullman **72** 46 49N 117 10W
Pulog, Mt. **35** 16 40N 120 50 E
Pumlumon Fawr **7** 52 29N 3 47W
Puna **78** 19 45S 65 28W
Puná, I. **78** 2 55S 80 5W
Punakha **33** 27 42N 89 52 E
Punata **78** 17 32S 65 50W
Punch **32** 33 48N 74 4 E
Pune **32** 18 29N 73 57 E
Puning **39** 23 20N 116 12 E
Punjab □, India **32** 31 0N 76 0 E
Punjab □, Pakistan **32** 31 0N 72 0 E
Puno **78** 15 55S 70 3W
Punta Alta **80** 38 53S 62 4W
Punta Arenas **80** 53 10S 71 0W
Punta de Díaz **80** 28 0S 70 45W
Punta Gorda, Belize **74** 16 10N 88 45W
Punta Gorda, U.S.A. **69** 26 55N 82 0W
Puntabie **45** 32 12S 134 13 E
Puntarenas **75** 10 0N 84 50W
Punto Fijo **78** 11 50N 70 13W
Punxsutawney **68** 40 56N 79 0W
Puqi **39** 29 40N 113 50 E
Puquio **78** 14 45S 74 10W
Pur –► **24** 67 31N 77 55 E
Purace, Vol. **78** 2 21N 76 23W
Purbeck, Isle of **7** 50 40N 2 5W
Purcell **71** 35 0N 97 25W
Puri **33** 19 50N 85 58 E
Purmerend **11** 52 30N 4 58 E

Purnia **33** 25 45N 87 31 E
Purukcahu **34** 0 35S 114 35 E
Puruliya **33** 23 17N 86 24 E
Purus → **78** 3 42S 61 28W
Purwakarta **35** 6 35S 107 29 E
Purwodadi, Jawa, Indonesia **35** 7 7S 110 55 E
Purwodadi, Jawa, Indonesia **35** 7 51S 110 0 E
Purwokerto **35** 7 25S 109 14 E
Purworejo **35** 7 43S 110 2 E
Pusan **38** 35 5N 129 0 E
Push, La **72** 47 55N 124 38W
Pushchino **25** 54 10N 158 0 E
Pushkino **23** 51 16N 47 0 E
Putahow L. **65** 59 54N 100 40W
Putao **33** 27 28N 97 30 E
Putaruru **43** 38 2S 175 50 E
Puthein Myit → **33** 15 56N 94 18 E
Putian **39** 25 23N 119 0 E
Putignano **18** 40 50N 17 5 E
Puting, Tanjung **34** 3 31S 111 46 E
Putorana, Gory **25** 69 0N 95 0 E
Puttalam **32** 8 1N 79 55 E
Putten **11** 52 16N 5 36 E
Puttgarden **14** 54 28N 11 15 E
Putumayo → **78** 3 7S 67 58W
Putussibau **34** 0 50N 112 56 E
Puy, Le **12** 45 3N 3 52 E
Puy-de-Dôme **12** 45 46N 2 57 E
Puy-de-Dôme □ **12** 45 40N 3 5 E
Puyallup **72** 47 10N 122 22W
Puyang **38** 35 40N 115 1 E
Pweto **54** 8 25S 28 51 E
Pwllheli **6** 52 54N 4 26W
Pya-ozero **22** 66 5N 30 58 E
Pyapon **33** 16 20N 95 40 E
Pyasina → **25** 73 30N 87 0 E
Pyatigorsk **23** 44 2N 43 6 E
Pyè **33** 18 49N 95 13 E
Pyinmana **33** 19 45N 96 12 E
Pyŏngyang **38** 39 0N 125 30 E
Pyote **71** 31 34N 103 5W
Pyramid L. **72** 40 0N 119 30W
Pyrénées **12** 42 45N 0 18 E
Pyrénées-Atlantiques □ **12** 43 10N 0 50W
Pyrénées-Orientales □ **12** 42 35N 2 26 E
Pyu **33** 18 30N 96 28 E

Q

Qabalān **28** 32 8N 35 17 E
Qabātiyah **28** 32 25N 35 16 E
Qachasnek **57** 30 6S 28 42 E
Qādib **29** 12 37N 53 57 E
Qā'emshahr **31** 36 30N 52 55 E
Qahremānshahr = Bākhtarān **30** 34 23N 47 0 E
Qaidam Pendi **37** 37 0N 95 0 E
Qalāt **31** 32 15N 66 58 E
Qal'at al Akhḑar **30** 28 0N 37 10 E
Qal'eh Shaharak **32** 34 10N 64 20 E
Qal'eh-ye Now **31** 35 0N 63 5 E
Qalqīlya **28** 32 12N 34 58 E
Qam **28** 32 36N 35 43 E
Qamar, Ghubbat al **29** 16 20N 52 30 E
Qamruddin Karez **32** 31 45N 68 20 E
Qāna **28** 33 12N 35 17 E
Qandahār **31** 31 32N 65 30 E
Qandahār □ **32** 31 0N 65 0 E
Qâra **51** 29 38N 26 30 E
Qarachuk **30** 37 0N 42 2 E
Qārah **30** 29 55N 40 3 E
Qarqan **37** 38 5N 85 20 E
Qarqan He → **37** 39 30N 88 30 E
Qāsim **28** 32 59N 36 2 E
Qaṣr-e Qand **31** 26 15N 60 45 E
Qasr Farâfra **51** 27 0N 28 1 E
Qatar ■ **31** 25 30N 51 15 E
Qattâra, Munkhafed el **51** 29 30N 27 30 E
Qattâra Depression = Qattâra, Munkhafed el **51** 29 30N 27 30 E
Qāyen **31** 33 40N 59 10 E
Qazvin **30** 36 15N 50 0 E
Qena **51** 26 10N 32 43 E
Qeshm **31** 26 55N 56 10 E
Qezi'ot **28** 30 52N 34 26 E
Qian Xian **39** 34 31N 108 15 E
Qianshan **39** 30 37N 116 35 E
Qianxi **39** 27 3N 106 3 E
Qianyang **39** 27 18N 110 10 E
Qijiang **39** 28 57N 106 35 E
Qila Safed **31** 29 0N 61 30 E
Qila Saifullāh **32** 30 45N 68 17 E
Qilian Shan **37** 38 30N 96 0 E
Qin Ling = Qinling Shandi **39** 33 50N 108 10 E
Qin'an **39** 34 48N 105 40 E
Qingdao **38** 36 5N 120 20 E
Qinghai □ **37** 36 0N 98 0 E
Qinghai Hu **37** 36 40N 100 10 E
Qingjiang, Jiangsu, China **39** 33 30N 119 2 E
Qingjiang, Jiangxi, China **39** 28 4N 115 29 E
Qingliu **39** 26 11N 116 48 E
Qingshuihe **38** 39 55N 111 35 E
Qingyang **38** 36 2N 107 55 E
Qingyuan **39** 23 40N 112 59 E
Qinhuangdao **38** 39 56N 119 30 E
Qinling Shandi **39** 33 50N 108 10 E
Qinyang **39** 35 7N 112 57 E
Qinyuan **38** 36 29N 112 20 E
Qinzhou **39** 21 58N 108 38 E
Qiongshan **39** 19 51N 110 26 E
Qiongzhou Haixia **39** 20 10N 110 15 E
Qiqihar **38** 47 26N 124 0 E
Qiryat 'Anavim **28** 31 49N 35 7 E
Qiryat Ata **28** 32 47N 35 6 E
Qiryat Bialik **28** 32 50N 35 5 E
Qiryat Gat **28** 31 32N 34 46 E
Qiryat Ḩayyim **28** 32 49N 35 4 E
Qiryat Mal'akhi **28** 31 44N 34 44 E
Qiryat Shemona **28** 33 13N 35 35 E
Qiryat Yam **28** 32 51N 35 4 E
Qishan **39** 22 52N 120 25 E
Qishon → **28** 32 49N 35 2 E
Qitai **37** 44 2N 89 35 E
Qiyahe **38** 53 0N 120 35 E
Qiyang **39** 26 35N 111 50 E
Qom **31** 34 40N 51 0 E
Qomsheh **31** 32 0N 51 55 E
Qondūz **31** 36 50N 68 50 E
Qondūz □ **31** 36 50N 68 50 E
Qu Jiang → **39** 30 1N 106 24 E
Qu Xian, Sichuan, China **39** 30 48N 106 58 E
Qu Xian, Zhejiang, China **39** 28 57N 118 54 E
Quairading **47** 32 0S 117 21 E
Qualeup **47** 33 48S 116 48 E
Quambatook **45** 35 49S 143 34 E
Quambone **45** 30 57S 147 53 E
Quan Long **34** 9 7N 105 8 E
Quanan **71** 34 20N 99 45W
Quandialla **45** 34 1S 147 47 E
Quang Ngai **34** 15 13N 108 58 E
Quantock Hills **7** 51 8N 3 10W
Quanzhou, Fujian, China **39** 24 55N 118 34 E
Quanzhou, Guangxi Zhuangzu, China **39** 25 57N 111 5 E
Quaraí **80** 30 15S 56 20W
Quartzsite **73** 33 44N 114 16W
Quatsino **64** 50 30N 127 40W
Quatsino Sd. **64** 50 25N 127 58W
Qubab = Mishmar Ayyalon **28** 31 52N 34 57 E
Qūchān **31** 37 10N 58 27 E
Queanbeyan **45** 35 17S 149 14 E
Québec **63** 46 52N 71 13W
Québec □ **63** 50 0N 70 0W
Queen Charlotte **64** 53 15N 132 2W
Queen Charlotte Is. **64** 53 20N 132 10W
Queen Charlotte Sd. **43** 41 10S 174 15 E
Queen Charlotte Str. **64** 51 0N 128 0W
Queen Elizabeth Is. **2** 76 0N 95 0W
Queen Maud G. **60** 68 15N 102 30W
Queens Chan. **46** 15 0S 129 30 E
Queenscliff **45** 38 16S 144 39 E
Queensland □ **44** 22 0S 142 0 E
Queenstown, Australia **44** 42 4S 145 35 E
Queenstown, N.Z. **43** 45 1S 168 40 E
Queenstown, S. Africa **56** 31 52S 26 52 E
Queimadas **79** 11 0S 39 38W
Quela **54** 9 10S 16 56 E
Quelimane **55** 17 53S 36 58 E
Quelpart = Cheju Do **39** 33 29N 126 34 E
Quemado, N. Mex., U.S.A. **73** 34 17N 108 28W
Quemado, Tex., U.S.A. **71** 28 58N 100 35W
Quequén **80** 38 30S 58 30W
Querétaro **74** 20 40N 100 23W
Querétaro □ **74** 20 30N 100 0W
Queshan **39** 32 55N 114 2 E
Quesnel **64** 53 0N 122 30W
Quesnel → **64** 52 58N 122 29W
Quesnel L. **64** 52 30N 121 20W
Questa **73** 36 45N 105 35W
Quetico Prov. Park **62** 48 30N 91 45W
Quetta **31** 30 15N 66 55 E
Quezaltenango **75** 14 50N 91 30W
Quezon City **35** 14 38N 121 0 E
Qui Nhon **34** 13 40N 109 13 E
Quiaca, La **80** 22 5S 65 35W
Quibaxe **54** 8 24S 14 27 E
Quibdo **78** 5 42N 76 40W
Quiberon **12** 47 29N 3 9W
Quick **64** 54 36N 126 54W
Quiet L. **64** 61 5N 133 5W
Quilán, C. **80** 43 15S 74 30W
Quilengues **55** 14 12S 14 12 E
Quillabamba **78** 12 50S 72 50W
Quillagua **78** 21 40S 69 40W
Quillota **80** 32 54S 71 16W
Quilon **32** 8 50N 76 38 E
Quilpie **45** 26 35S 144 11 E
Quimilí **80** 27 40S 62 30W
Quimper **12** 48 0N 4 9W
Quimperlé **12** 47 53N 3 33W
Quincy, Calif., U.S.A. **72** 39 56N 120 56W
Quincy, Fla., U.S.A. **69** 30 34N 84 34W
Quincy, Ill., U.S.A. **70** 39 55N 91 20W
Quincy, Mass., U.S.A. **68** 42 14N 71 0W
Quincy, Wash., U.S.A. **72** 47 22N 119 56W
Quines **80** 32 13S 65 48W
Quinga **55** 15 49S 40 15 E
Quintana Roo □ **74** 19 0N 88 0W
Quintanar de la Orden **13** 39 36N 3 5W
Quintanar de la Sierra **13** 41 57N 2 55W
Quintero **80** 32 45S 71 30W
Quinyambie **45** 30 15S 141 0 E
Quipungo **55** 14 37S 14 40 E
Quirindi **45** 31 28S 150 40 E
Quissanga **55** 12 24S 40 28 E
Quitilipi **80** 26 50S 60 13W
Quitman, Ga., U.S.A. **69** 30 49N 83 35W
Quitman, Miss., U.S.A. **69** 32 2N 88 42W
Quitman, Tex., U.S.A. **71** 32 48N 95 25W
Quito **78** 0 15S 78 35W
Quixadá **79** 4 55S 39 0W
Qumbu **57** 31 10S 28 48 E
Qumrān **28** 31 43N 35 27 E
Quneitra **28** 33 7N 35 48 E
Quoin I. **46** 14 54S 129 32 E
Quoin Pt. **56** 34 46S 19 37 E
Quondong **45** 33 6S 140 18 E
Quorn **45** 32 25S 138 0 E
Qûs **51** 25 55N 32 50 E
Quseir **51** 26 7N 34 16 E
Qusrah **28** 32 5N 35 20 E
Quthing **57** 30 25S 27 36 E

R

Raahe **20** 64 40N 24 28 E
Ra'ananna **28** 32 12N 34 52 E
Raasay **8** 57 25N 6 4W
Raasay, Sd. of **8** 57 30N 6 8W
Raba **35** 8 36S 118 55 E
Rabat, Malta **18** 35 53N 14 25 E
Rabat, Morocco **50** 34 2N 6 48W
Rabaul **40** 4 24S 152 18 E
Rabbit → **64** 59 41N 127 12W
Rabbit Lake **65** 53 8N 107 46W
Rabbitskin → **64** 61 47N 120 42W
Rābigh **30** 22 50N 39 5 E
Race, C. **63** 46 40N 53 5W
Rach Gia **34** 10 5N 105 5 E
Racine **68** 42 41N 87 51W
Radama, Nosy **57** 14 0S 47 47 E
Radama, Saikanosy **57** 14 16S 47 53 E
Rădăuţi **15** 47 50N 25 59 E
Radford **68** 37 8N 80 32W
Radhwa, Jabal **30** 24 34N 38 18 E
Radisson **65** 52 30N 107 20W
Radium Hot Springs **64** 50 35N 116 2W
Radnor Forest **7** 52 17N 3 10W
Radom **15** 51 23N 21 12 E
Radomir **19** 42 37N 23 4 E
Radomsko **15** 51 5N 19 28 E
Radstock **7** 51 17N 2 25W
Radstock, C. **45** 33 12S 134 20 E
Radville **65** 49 30N 104 15W
Rae **64** 62 50N 116 3W
Rae Bareli **33** 26 18N 81 20 E
Rae Isthmus **61** 66 40N 87 30W
Raeren **11** 50 41N 6 7 E
Raeside, L. **47** 29 20S 122 0 E
Raetihi **43** 39 25S 175 17 E
Rafaela **80** 31 10S 61 30W
Rafai **54** 4 59N 23 58 E
Rafḩā **30** 29 35N 43 35 E
Rafsanjān **31** 30 30N 56 5 E
Raft Pt. **46** 16 4S 124 26 E
Ragama **32** 7 0N 79 50 E
Ragged Mt. **47** 33 27S 123 25 E
Raglan, Australia **44** 23 42S 150 49 E
Raglan, N.Z. **43** 37 55S 174 55 E
Ragusa **18** 36 56N 14 42 E
Raha **35** 4 55S 123 0 E
Rahad al Bardī **51** 11 20N 23 40 E
Rahaeng = Tak **34** 16 52N 99 8 E
Rahimyar Khan **32** 28 30N 70 25 E
Raichur **32** 16 10N 77 20 E
Raigarh **33** 21 56N 83 25 E
Raijua **35** 10 37S 121 36 E
Railton **44** 41 25S 146 28 E
Rainbow Lake **64** 58 30N 119 23W
Rainier **72** 46 4N 122 58W
Rainier, Mt. **72** 46 50N 121 50W
Rainy L. **65** 48 42N 93 10W
Rainy River **65** 48 43N 94 29W
Raipur **33** 21 17N 81 45 E
Ra'is **30** 23 33N 38 43 E
Raj Nandgaon **33** 21 0N 81 0 E
Raja, Ujung **34** 3 40N 96 25 E
Raja Ampat, Kepulauan **35** 0 30S 130 0 E
Rajahmundry **33** 17 1N 81 48 E
Rajang → **34** 2 30N 112 0 E
Rajapalaiyam **32** 9 25N 77 35 E
Rajasthan □ **32** 26 45N 73 30 E
Rajasthan Canal **32** 28 0N 72 0 E
Rajgarh **32** 24 2N 76 45 E
Rajkot **32** 22 15N 70 56 E
Rajojooseppi **20** 68 25N 28 30 E
Rajpipla **32** 21 50N 73 30 E
Rajshahi **33** 24 22N 88 39 E
Rajshahi □ **33** 25 0N 89 0 E
Rakaia **43** 43 45S 172 1 E
Rakaia → **43** 43 36S 172 15 E
Rakan, Ra's **31** 26 10N 51 20 E
Rakaposhi **32** 36 10N 74 25 E
Rakata, Pulau **34** 6 10S 105 20 E
Rakops **56** 21 1S 24 28 E
Raleigh **69** 35 47N 78 39W
Raleigh B. **69** 34 50N 76 15W
Ralls **71** 33 40N 101 20W
Ram → **64** 62 1N 123 41W
Râm Allâh **28** 31 55N 35 10 E
Ram Hd. **45** 37 47S 149 30 E
Rama **28** 32 56N 35 21 E
Ramanathapuram **32** 9 25N 78 55 E
Ramanetaka, B. de **57** 14 13S 47 52 E
Ramat Gan **28** 32 4N 34 48 E
Ramat HaSharon **28** 32 7N 34 50 E
Ramatlhabama **56** 25 37S 25 33 E
Rambipuji **35** 8 12S 113 37 E
Ramea **63** 47 31N 57 23W
Ramechhap **33** 27 25N 86 10 E
Ramelau **35** 8 55S 126 22 E
Ramgarh, Bihar, India **33** 23 40N 85 35 E
Ramgarh, Raj., India **32** 27 30N 70 36 E
Rāmhormoz **30** 31 15N 49 35 E
Ramla **28** 31 55N 34 52 E
Rammūn **28** 31 55N 35 17 E
Ramnad = Ramanathapuram **32** 9 25N 78 55 E
Ramon, Har **28** 30 30N 34 38 E
Ramona **73** 33 1N 116 56W
Ramore **62** 48 30N 80 25W
Ramotswa **56** 24 50S 25 52 E
Rampart **60** 65 0N 150 15W
Rampur **32** 28 50N 79 5 E
Rampur Hat **33** 24 10N 87 50 E
Ramree Kyun **33** 19 0N 94 0 E
Ramsey, Canada **62** 47 25N 82 20W
Ramsey, U.K. **6** 54 20N 4 21W
Ramsgate **7** 51 20N 1 25 E
Ramtek **32** 21 20N 79 15 E
Ranaghat **33** 23 15N 88 35 E
Ranau **34** 6 2N 116 40 E
Rancagua **80** 34 10S 70 50W
Rancheria → **64** 60 13N 129 7W
Ranchester **72** 44 57N 107 12W
Ranchi **33** 23 19N 85 27 E
Randers **21** 56 29N 10 1 E
Randfontein **57** 26 8S 27 45 E
Randolph **72** 41 43N 111 10W
Råne älv → **20** 65 50N 22 20 E
Rangaunu B. **43** 34 51S 173 15 E
Rangeley **68** 44 58N 70 33W
Rangely **72** 40 3N 108 53W
Ranger **71** 32 30N 98 42W
Rangia **33** 26 28N 91 38 E
Rangiora **43** 43 19S 172 36 E
Rangitaiki → **43** 37 54S 176 49 E
Rangitata → **43** 43 45S 171 15 E
Rangkasbitung **35** 6 21S 106 15 E
Rangon → **33** 16 28N 96 40 E
Rangoon **33** 16 45N 96 20 E
Rangpur **33** 25 42N 89 22 E
Rangwe **52** 0 38S 34 35 E
Ranibennur **32** 14 35N 75 30 E
Raniganj **33** 23 40N 87 5 E
Raniwara **32** 24 50N 72 10 E
Ranken → **44** 20 31S 137 36 E
Rankin **71** 31 16N 101 56W
Rankin Inlet **60** 62 30N 93 0W
Rankins Springs **45** 33 49S 146 14 E
Rannoch, L. **8** 56 41N 4 20W
Rannoch Moor **8** 56 38N 4 48W
Ranobe, Helodranon' i **57** 23 3S 43 33 E
Ranohira **57** 22 29S 45 24 E
Ranomafana, Toamasina, Madag. **57** 18 57S 48 50 E
Ranomafana, Toliara, Madag. **57** 24 34S 47 0 E
Ranong **34** 9 56N 98 40 E
Ransiki **35** 1 30S 134 10 E
Rantau **34** 2 56S 115 9 E
Rantauprapat **34** 2 15N 99 50 E
Rantekombola **35** 3 15S 119 57 E
Rantis **28** 32 4N 35 3 E
Rantoul **68** 40 18N 88 10W
Raohe **38** 46 47N 134 0 E
Rapa Iti **41** 27 35S 144 20W
Rāpch **31** 25 40N 59 15 E
Rapid → **64** 59 15N 129 5W
Rapid City **70** 44 0N 103 0W
Rapid River **68** 45 55N 87 0W
Rapides des Joachims **62** 46 13N 77 43W
Rarotonga **41** 21 30S 160 0W
Ra's al Khaymah **31** 25 50N 56 5 E
Ra's al-Unuf **51** 30 25N 18 15 E
Ras Bânâs **51** 23 57N 35 59 E
Ras Dashen **54** 13 8N 38 26 E
Râs Timirist **50** 19 21N 16 30W
Rasa, Punta **80** 40 50S 62 15W
Rashad **51** 11 55N 31 0 E
Rashîd **51** 31 21N 30 22 E
Rasht **30** 37 20N 49 40 E
Rason, L. **47** 28 45S 124 25 E
Rat Is. **60** 51 50N 178 15 E
Rat River **64** 61 7N 112 36W
Ratangarh **32** 28 5N 74 35 E
Rath Luirc **9** 52 21N 8 40W
Rathdrum **9** 52 57N 6 13W
Rathenow **14** 52 38N 12 23 E
Rathkeale **9** 52 32N 8 57W
Rathlin I. **9** 55 18N 6 14W
Rathlin O'Birne I. **9** 54 40N 8 50W
Ratlam **32** 23 20N 75 0 E
Ratnagiri **32** 16 57N 73 18 E
Raton **71** 37 0N 104 30W
Rattray Hd. **8** 57 38N 1 50W
Ratz, Mt. **64** 57 23N 132 12W
Raufarhöfn **20** 66 27N 15 57W
Raukumara Ra. **43** 38 5S 177 55 E
Rauma **21** 61 10N 21 30 E
Raurkela **33** 22 14N 84 50 E
Rāvar **31** 31 20N 56 51 E
Ravenna, Italy **18** 44 28N 12 15 E
Ravenna, U.S.A. **70** 41 3N 98 58W
Ravensburg **14** 47 48N 9 38 E
Ravenshoe **44** 17 37S 145 29 E
Ravensthorpe **47** 33 35S 120 2 E
Ravenswood, Australia **44** 20 6S 146 54 E
Ravenswood, U.S.A. **68** 38 58N 81 47W
Ravi → **32** 30 35N 71 49 E
Rawalpindi **32** 33 38N 73 8 E
Rawāndūz **30** 36 40N 44 30 E
Rawdon **62** 46 3N 73 40W
Rawene **43** 35 25S 173 32 E
Rawlinna **47** 30 58S 125 28 E
Rawlins **72** 41 50N 107 20W
Rawlinson Range **47** 24 40S 128 30 E
Rawson **80** 43 15S 65 0W
Ray **70** 48 21N 103 6W
Ray, C. **63** 47 33N 59 15W
Rayadurg **32** 14 40N 76 50 E
Rayagada **33** 19 15N 83 20 E
Raychikhinsk **25** 49 46N 129 25 E
Raymond, Canada **64** 49 30N 112 35W
Raymond, U.S.A. **72** 46 45N 123 48W
Raymondville **71** 26 30N 97 50W
Raymore **65** 51 25N 104 31W
Rayne **71** 30 16N 92 16W
Rayville **71** 32 30N 91 45W
Raz, Pte. du **12** 48 2N 4 47W
Razgrad **19** 43 33N 26 34 E
Ré, I. de **12** 46 12N 1 30W
Reading, U.K. **7** 51 27N 0 57W
Reading, U.S.A. **68** 40 20N 75 53W
Realicó **80** 35 0S 64 15W
Rebecca L. **47** 30 0S 122 15 E
Rebi **35** 6 23S 134 7 E
Rebiana **51** 24 12N 22 10 E
Rebun-Tō **36** 45 23N 141 2 E
Recherche, Arch. of the **47** 34 15S 122 50 E
Recife **79** 8 0S 35 0W
Recklinghausen **11** 51 36N 7 10 E
Reconquista **80** 29 10S 59 45W
Recreo **80** 29 25S 65 10W
Red → = Hong → **26** 20 17N 106 34 E

Red →, Canada . 65 50 24N 96 48W
Red →, Minn., U.S.A. 70 48 10N 97 0W
Red →, Tex., U.S.A. 71 31 0N 91 40W
Red Bay 63 51 44N 56 25W
Red Bluff 72 40 11N 122 11W
Red Bluff L. 71 31 59N 103 58W
Red Cliffs 45 34 19S 142 11 E
Red Cloud 70 40 8N 98 33W
Red Deer 64 52 20N 113 50W
Red Deer →, Alta., Canada 65 50 58N 110 0W
Red Deer →, Man., Canada 65 52 53N 101 1W
Red Deer L. 65 52 55N 101 20W
Red Indian L. 63 48 35N 57 0W
Red Lake 65 51 3N 93 49W
Red Lake Falls 70 47 54N 96 15W
Red Lodge 72 45 10N 109 10W
Red Oak 70 41 0N 95 10W
Red Rock 62 48 55N 88 15W
Red Rock, L. 70 41 30N 93 15W
Red Rock's Pt. 47 32 13S 127 32 E
Red Sea 29 25 0N 36 0 E
Red Sucker L. 65 54 9N 93 40W
Red Tower Pass = Turnu Rosu Pasul 15 45 33N 24 17 E
Red Wing 70 44 32N 92 35W
Redbridge 7 51 35N 0 7 E
Redcar 6 54 37N 1 4W
Redcliff 65 50 10N 110 50W
Redcliffe 45 27 12S 153 0 E
Redcliffe, Mt. 47 28 30S 121 30 E
Reddersburg 56 29 41S 26 10 E
Redding 72 40 30N 122 25W
Redditch 7 52 18N 1 57W
Redfield 70 45 0N 98 30W
Redknife → 64 61 14N 119 22W
Redlands 73 34 0N 117 11W
Redmond, Australia 47 34 55S 117 40 E
Redmond, U.S.A. 72 44 19N 121 11W
Redonda 75 16 58N 62 19W
Redondela 13 42 15N 8 38W
Redondo 13 38 39N 7 37W
Redrock Pt. 64 62 11N 115 2W
Redruth 7 50 14N 5 14W
Redvers 65 49 35N 101 40W
Redwater 64 53 55N 113 6W
Redwood City 73 37 30N 122 15W
Redwood Falls 70 44 30N 95 2W
Ree, L. 9 53 35N 8 0W
Reed, L. 65 54 38N 100 30W
Reed City 68 43 52N 85 30W
Reeder 70 46 7N 102 52W
Reedley 73 36 36N 119 27W
Reedsburg 70 43 34N 90 5W
Reedsport 72 43 45N 124 4W
Reefton 43 42 6S 171 51 E
Refugio 71 28 18N 97 17W
Regavim 28 32 32N 35 2 E
Regensburg 14 49 1N 12 7 E
Réggio di Calábria 18 38 7N 15 38 E
Réggio nell' Emilia 18 44 42N 10 38 E
Regina 65 50 27N 104 35W
Rehoboth 56 23 15S 17 4 E
Rehovot 28 31 54N 34 48 E
Rei-Bouba 51 8 40N 14 15 E
Reichenbach 14 50 36N 12 19 E
Reid 47 30 49S 128 26 E
Reid River 44 19 40S 146 48 E
Reidsville 69 36 21N 79 40W
Reigate 7 51 14N 0 11W
Reims 12 49 15N 4 1 E
Reina 28 32 43N 35 18 E
Reina Adelaida, Arch. 80 52 20S 74 0W
Reinbeck 70 42 18N 92 40W
Reindeer → 65 55 36N 103 11W
Reindeer I. 65 52 30N 98 0W
Reindeer L. 65 57 15N 102 15W
Reine, La 62 48 50N 79 30W
Reinga, C. 43 34 25S 172 43 E
Reitz 57 27 48S 28 29 E
Reivilo 56 27 36S 24 8 E
Rekinniki 25 60 51N 163 40 E
Reliance 65 63 0N 109 20W
Remarkable, Mt. 45 32 48S 138 10 E
Rembang 35 6 42S 111 21 E
Remeshk 31 26 55N 58 50 E
Remich 11 49 32N 6 22 E
Remscheid 14 51 11N 7 12 E
Rendsburg 14 54 18N 9 41 E
Rene 25 66 2N 179 25W
Renfrew, Canada 62 45 30N 76 40W
Renfrew, U.K. 8 55 52N 4 24W
Rengat 34 0 30S 102 45 E
Renhuai 39 27 48N 106 24 E
Renk 51 11 50N 32 50 E
Renkum 11 51 58N 5 43 E
Renmark 45 34 11S 140 43 E
Rennell Sd. 64 53 23N 132 35W
Renner Springs T.O. 44 18 20S 133 47 E
Rennes 12 48 7N 1 41W
Reno 72 39 30N 119 50W
Reno → 18 44 37N 12 17 E
Renovo 68 41 20N 77 47W
Rensselaer 68 40 57N 87 10W
Renton 72 47 30N 122 9W
Republic, Mich., U.S.A. 68 46 25N 87 59W
Republic, Wash., U.S.A. 72 48 38N 118 42W
Republican → 70 39 3N 96 48W
Republican City 70 40 9N 99 20W
Repulse Bay 61 66 30N 86 30W
Requena, Peru 78 5 5S 73 52W
Requena, Spain 13 39 30N 1 4W
Reserve, Canada 65 52 28N 102 39W
Reserve, U.S.A. 73 33 50N 108 54W
Resht = Rasht 30 37 20N 49 40 E
Resistencia 80 27 30S 59 0W
Reşiţa 15 45 18N 21 53 E
Resolution I., Canada 61 61 30N 65 0W
Resolution I., N.Z. 43 45 40S 166 40 E
Ressano Garcia 57 25 25S 32 0 E
Reston 65 49 33N 101 6W
Retalhuleu 75 14 33N 91 46W
Réthímnon 19 35 18N 24 30 E
Réunion 3 21 0S 56 0 E
Reutlingen 14 48 28N 9 13 E
Reval = Tallinn 22 59 22N 24 48 E
Revda 22 56 48N 59 57 E
Revelstoke 64 51 0N 118 10W
Revilla Gigedo, Is. 41 18 40N 112 0W
Revillagigedo I. 64 55 50N 131 20W
Rewa 33 24 33N 81 25 E
Rewari 32 28 15N 76 40 E
Rexburg 72 43 55N 111 50W
Rey Malabo 54 3 45N 8 50 E
Reykjahlið 20 65 40N 16 55W
Reykjanes 20 63 48N 22 40W
Reykjavík 20 64 10N 21 57 E
Reynolds 65 49 40N 95 55W
Reynolds Ra. 46 22 30S 133 0 E
Reynosa 74 26 5N 98 18W
Rhayader 7 52 19N 3 30W
Rheden 11 52 0N 6 3 E
Rhein 65 51 25N 102 15W
Rhein → 11 51 52N 6 2 E
Rheine 14 52 17N 7 25 E
Rheinland-Pfalz □ 14 50 0N 7 0 E
Rhin = Rhein → 11 51 52N 6 2 E
Rhine = Rhein → 11 51 52N 6 2 E
Rhineland-Palatinate □ = Rheinland-Pfalz □ 14 50 0N 7 0 E
Rhinelander 70 45 38N 89 29W
Rhode Island □ 68 41 38N 71 37W
Rhodes = Ródhos 19 36 15N 28 10 E
Rhodesia = Zimbabwe ■ 55 19 0S 30 0 E
Rhodope Mts. = Rhodopi Planina 19 41 40N 24 20 E
Rhodopi Planina 19 41 40N 24 20 E
Rhondda 7 51 39N 3 30W
Rhône □ 12 45 54N 4 35 E
Rhône → 14 43 28N 4 42 E
Rhum 8 57 0N 6 20W
Rhyl 6 53 19N 3 29W
Rhymney 7 51 32N 3 7W
Riachão 79 7 20S 46 37W
Riasi 32 33 10N 74 50 E
Riau □ 34 0 0 102 35 E
Riau, Kepulauan 34 0 30N 104 20 E
Ribadeo 13 43 35N 7 5W
Ribatejo □ 13 39 15N 8 30W
Ribble → 6 54 13N 2 20W
Ribe 21 55 19N 8 44 E
Ribeirão Prêto 79 21 10S 47 50W
Riberalta 78 11 0S 66 0W
Riccarton 43 43 32S 172 37 E
Rice Lake 70 45 30N 91 42W
Rich Hill 71 38 5N 94 22W
Richards Bay 57 28 48S 32 6 E
Richards L. 65 59 10N 107 10W
Richardson → 65 58 25N 111 14W
Richardton 70 46 56N 102 22W
Riche, C. 47 34 36S 118 47 E
Richey 70 47 42N 105 5W
Richfield, Idaho, U.S.A. 72 43 2N 114 5W
Richfield, Utah, U.S.A. 73 38 50N 112 0W
Richibucto 63 46 42N 64 54W
Richland, Ga., U.S.A. 69 32 7N 84 40W
Richland, Oreg., U.S.A. 72 44 49N 117 9W
Richland, Wash., U.S.A. 72 46 15N 119 15W
Richland Center 70 43 21N 90 22W
Richlands 68 37 7N 81 49W
Richmond, N.S.W., Australia 45 33 35S 150 42 E
Richmond, Queens., Australia 44 20 43S 143 8 E
Richmond, N.Z. 43 41 20S 173 12 E
Richmond, S. Africa 57 29 51S 30 18 E
Richmond, N. Yorks., U.K. 6 54 24N 1 43W
Richmond, Surrey, U.K. 7 51 28N 0 18W
Richmond, Calif., U.S.A. 72 37 58N 122 21W
Richmond, Ind., U.S.A. 68 39 50N 84 50W
Richmond, Ky., U.S.A. 68 37 40N 84 20W
Richmond, Mo., U.S.A. 70 39 15N 93 58W
Richmond, Tex., U.S.A. 71 29 32N 95 42W
Richmond, Utah, U.S.A. 72 41 55N 111 48W
Richmond, Va., U.S.A. 68 37 33N 77 27W
Richmond Ra., Australia 45 29 0S 152 45 E
Richmond Ra., N.Z. 43 41 32S 173 22 E
Richton 69 31 23N 88 58W
Richwood 68 38 17N 80 32W
Ridgedale 65 53 0N 104 10W
Ridgeland 69 32 30N 80 58W
Ridgelands 44 23 16S 150 17 E
Ridgetown 62 42 26N 81 52W
Ridgway 68 41 25N 78 43W
Riding Mt. Nat. Park 65 50 50N 100 0W
Ridley Mt. 47 33 12S 122 7 E
Ried 14 48 14N 13 30 E
Riet → 56 29 0S 23 54 E
Rieti 18 42 23N 12 50 E
Rifle 72 39 40N 107 50W
Rifstangi 20 66 32N 16 12W
Rig Rig 51 14 13N 14 25 E
Riga 22 56 53N 24 8 E
Riga, G. of = Rīgas Jūras Līcis 22 57 40N 23 45 E
Rīgas Jūras Līcis 22 57 40N 23 45 E
Rigby 72 43 41N 111 58W
Rīgestān □ 31 30 15N 65 0 E
Riggins 72 45 29N 116 26W
Rigolet 63 54 10N 58 23W
Riihimäki 21 60 45N 24 48 E
Rijeka 18 45 20N 14 21 E
Rijn → 11 52 12N 4 21 E
Rijssen 11 52 19N 6 30 E
Rijswijk 11 52 4N 4 22 E
Riley 72 43 35N 119 33W
Rima → 53 13 4N 5 10 E
Rimah, Wadi ar → 30 26 5N 41 30 E
Rimbey 64 52 35N 114 15W
Rímini 18 44 3N 12 33 E
Rîmnicu Sărat 15 45 26N 27 3 E
Rîmnicu Vîlcea 15 45 9N 24 21 E
Rimouski 63 48 27N 68 30W
Rinca 35 8 45S 119 35 E
Rinconada 80 22 26S 66 10W
Rineanna 9 52 42N 85 7W
Ringkøbing 21 56 5N 8 15 E
Ringling 72 46 16N 110 56W
Ringvassøy 20 69 56N 19 15 E
Rinía 19 37 23N 25 13 E
Rinjani 34 8 24S 116 28 E
Rio Branco, Brazil 78 9 58S 67 49W
Río Branco, Uruguay 80 32 40S 53 40W
Río Claro 75 10 20N 61 25W
Río Colorado 80 39 0S 64 0W
Río Cuarto 80 33 10S 64 25W
Rio das Pedras 57 23 8S 35 28 E
Rio de Janeiro 79 23 0S 43 12W
Rio de Janeiro □ 79 22 50S 43 0W
Rio do Sul 80 27 13S 49 37W
Río Gallegos 80 51 35S 69 15W
Río Grande, Argentina 80 53 50S 67 45W
Rio Grande, Brazil 80 32 0S 52 20W
Rio Grande → 71 25 57N 97 9W
Rio Grande City 71 26 23N 98 49W
Río Grande del Norte → 66 26 0N 97 0W
Rio Grande do Norte □ 79 5 40S 36 0W
Rio Grande do Sul □ 80 30 0S 53 0W
Rio Largo 79 9 28S 35 50W
Río Mulatos 78 19 40S 66 50W
Río Muni = Mbini □ 54 1 30N 10 0 E
Rio Negro 80 26 0S 50 0W
Rio Verde, Brazil 79 17 50S 51 0W
Río Verde, Mexico 74 21 56N 99 59W
Rio Vista 72 38 11N 121 44W
Ríobamba 78 1 50S 78 45W
Ríohacha 78 11 33N 72 55W
Rioja, La 80 29 20S 67 0W
Rioja, La □ 13 42 20N 2 20W
Riosucio, Caldas, Colombia 78 5 30N 75 40W
Ríosucio, Choco, Colombia 78 7 27N 77 7W
Riou L. 65 59 7N 106 25W
Ripley 71 35 43N 89 34W
Ripon, U.K. 6 54 8N 1 31W
Ripon, U.S.A. 68 43 51N 88 50W
Rishiri-Tō 36 45 11N 141 15 E
Rishon le Ziyyon 28 31 58N 34 48 E
Rishpon 28 32 12N 34 49 E
Rison 71 33 57N 92 11W
Risør 21 58 43N 9 13 E
Ritzville 72 47 10N 118 21W
Rivadavia 80 29 57S 70 35W
Rivas 75 11 30N 85 50W
Rivera 80 31 0S 55 50W
Riverdsale 56 34 7S 21 15 E
Riverhead 68 40 53N 72 40W
Riverhurst 65 50 55N 106 50W
Riverina 47 29 45S 120 40 E
Rivers 65 50 2N 100 14W
Rivers □ 53 5 0N 6 30 E
Rivers, L. of the 65 49 49N 105 44W
Rivers Inlet 64 51 42N 127 15W
Riverside, Calif., U.S.A. 73 34 0N 117 22W
Riverside, Wyo., U.S.A. 72 41 12N 106 57W
Riversleigh 44 19 5S 138 40 E
Riverton, Australia 45 34 10S 138 46 E
Riverton, Canada 65 51 1N 97 0W
Riverton, N.Z. 43 46 21S 168 0 E
Riverton, U.S.A. 72 43 1N 108 27W
Riviera 14 44 0N 8 30 E
Rivière-à-Pierre 63 46 59N 72 11W
Rivière-au-Renard 63 48 59N 64 23W
Rivière-du-Loup 63 47 50N 69 30W
Rivière-Pentecôte 63 49 57N 67 1W
Rivoli B. 45 37 32S 140 3 E
Riyadh = Ar Riyāḍ 29 24 41N 46 42 E
Rize 30 41 0N 40 30 E
Rizhao 39 35 25N 119 30 E
Rizzuto, C. 18 38 54N 17 5 E
Rjukan 21 59 54N 8 33 E
Roag, L. 8 58 10N 6 55W
Roanne 12 46 3N 4 4 E
Roanoke, Ala., U.S.A. 69 33 9N 85 23W
Roanoke, Va., U.S.A. 68 37 19N 79 55W
Roanoke → 69 35 56N 76 43W
Roanoke I. 69 35 55N 75 40W
Roanoke Rapids 69 36 28N 77 42W
Roatán 75 16 18N 86 35W
Robbins I. 44 40 42S 145 0 E
Robe →, Australia 46 21 42S 116 15 E
Robe →, Ireland 9 53 38N 9 10W
Robert Lee 71 31 55N 100 26W
Roberts 72 43 44N 112 8W
Robertson 56 33 46S 19 50 E
Robertson Ra. 46 23 15S 121 0 E
Robertsport 50 6 45N 11 26W
Robertstown 45 33 58S 139 5 E
Roberval 63 48 32N 72 15W
Robinson → 44 16 3S 137 16 E
Robinson Crusoe I. 41 33 38S 78 52W
Robinson Ranges 47 25 40S 119 0 E
Robinson River 44 16 45S 136 58 E
Robinvale 45 34 40S 142 45 E
Robla, La 13 42 50N 5 41W
Roblin 65 51 14N 101 21W
Roboré 78 18 10S 59 45W
Robson, Mt. 64 53 10N 119 10W
Robstown 71 27 47N 97 40W
Roca, C. da 13 38 40N 9 31W
Rocas, I. 79 4 0S 34 1W
Rocha 80 34 30S 54 25W
Rochdale 6 53 36N 2 10W
Rochefort, Belgium 11 50 9N 5 12 E
Rochefort, France 12 45 56N 0 57W
Rochelle 70 41 55N 89 5W
Rochelle, La 12 46 10N 1 9W
Rocher River 64 61 23N 112 44W
Rochester, Canada 64 54 22N 113 27W
Rochester, U.K. 7 51 22N 0 30 E
Rochester, Ind., U.S.A. 68 41 5N 86 15W
Rochester, Minn., U.S.A. 70 44 1N 92 28W
Rochester, N.H., U.S.A. 68 43 19N 70 57W
Rochester, N.Y., U.S.A. 68 43 10N 77 40W
Rock → 64 60 7N 127 7W
Rock Hill 69 34 55N 81 2W
Rock Island 70 41 30N 90 35W
Rock Port 70 40 26N 95 30W
Rock Rapids 70 43 25N 96 10W
Rock River 72 41 49N 106 0W
Rock Sound 75 24 54N 76 12W
Rock Sprs., Mont., U.S.A. 72 46 55N 106 11W
Rock Sprs., Wyo., U.S.A. 72 41 40N 109 10W
Rock Valley 70 43 10N 96 17W
Rockall 4 57 37N 13 42W
Rockdale 71 30 40N 97 0W
Rockford 70 42 20N 89 0W
Rockglen 65 49 11N 105 57W
Rockhampton 44 23 22S 150 32 E
Rockhampton Downs 44 18 57S 135 10 E
Rockingham 47 32 15S 115 38 E
Rockingham B. 44 18 5S 146 10 E
Rockingham Forest 7 52 28N 0 42W
Rocklake 70 48 50N 99 13W
Rockland, Idaho, U.S.A. 72 42 37N 112 57W
Rockland, Maine, U.S.A. 63 44 6N 69 6W
Rockland, Mich., U.S.A. 70 46 40N 89 10W
Rockmart 69 34 1N 85 2W
Rockport 71 28 2N 97 3W
Rocksprings 71 30 2N 100 11W
Rockville 68 39 7N 77 10W
Rockwall 71 32 55N 96 30W
Rockwell City 70 42 20N 94 35W
Rockwood 69 35 52N 84 40W
Rocky Ford 70 38 7N 103 45W
Rocky Gully 47 34 30S 116 57 E
Rocky Lane 64 58 31N 116 22W
Rocky Mount 69 35 55N 77 48W
Rocky Mountain House 64 52 22N 114 55W
Rocky Mts. 60 55 0N 121 0W
Rockyford 64 51 14N 113 10W
Rod 31 28 10N 63 5 E
Roda, La 13 39 13N 2 15W
Rødbyhavn 21 54 39N 11 22 E
Roddickton 63 50 51N 56 8W
Roderick I. 64 52 38N 128 22W
Rodez 12 44 21N 2 33 E
Ródhos 19 36 15N 28 10 E
Rodney, C. 43 36 17S 174 50 E
Rodriguez 3 19 45S 63 20 E
Roe → 9 55 10N 6 59W
Roebourne 46 20 44S 117 9 E
Roebuck B. 46 18 5S 122 20 E
Roebuck Plains 46 17 56S 122 28 E
Roermond 11 51 12N 6 0 E
Roes Welcome Sd. 61 65 0N 87 0W
Roeselare 11 50 57N 3 7 E
Rogagua, L. 78 13 43S 66 50W
Rogaland fylke □ 21 59 12N 6 20 E
Rogers 71 36 20N 94 5W
Rogers City 68 45 25N 83 49W
Rogerson 72 42 10N 114 40W
Rogersville 69 36 27N 83 1W
Roggan River 62 54 25N 79 32W
Roggeveldberge 56 32 10S 20 10 E
Rogoaguado, L. 78 13 0S 65 30W
Rogue → 72 42 30N 124 0W
Rohri 32 27 45N 68 51 E
Rohtak 32 28 55N 76 43 E
Roi Et 34 16 4N 103 40 E
Rojas 80 34 10S 60 45W
Rojo, C. 74 21 33N 97 20W
Rokan → 34 2 0N 100 50 E
Rokeby 44 13 39S 142 40 E
Rolândia 80 23 18S 51 23W
Rolette 70 48 42N 99 50W
Rolla, Kans., U.S.A. 71 37 10N 101 40W
Rolla, Mo., U.S.A. 71 37 56N 91 42W
Rolla, N. Dak., U.S.A. 70 48 50N 99 36W
Rolleston 44 24 28S 148 35 E
Rollingstone 44 19 2S 146 24 E
Roma, Australia 45 26 32S 148 49 E
Roma, Italy 18 41 54N 12 30 E
Roma, Sweden 21 57 32N 18 26 E
Roman, Romania 15 46 57N 26 55 E
Roman, U.S.S.R. 25 66 4N 112 14 E
Romana, La 75 18 27N 68 57W
Romang 35 7 30S 127 20 E
Romania ■ 15 46 0N 25 0 E
Romano, Cayo 75 22 0N 77 30W
Romblon 35 12 33N 122 17 E
Rome = Roma 18 41 54N 12 30 E
Rome, Ga., U.S.A. 69 34 20N 85 0W
Rome, N.Y., U.S.A. 68 43 14N 75 29W
Romney 68 39 21N 78 45W
Romney Marsh 7 51 0N 1 0 E
Romorantin-Lanthenay 12 47 21N 1 45 E
Romsdalen 20 62 25N 8 0 E
Rona 8 57 33N 6 0W
Ronan 72 47 30N 114 6W
Roncador, Cayos 75 13 32N 80 4W
Roncador, Serra do 79 12 30S 52 30W
Ronceverte 68 37 45N 80 28W
Ronda 13 36 46N 5 12W
Rondane 21 61 57N 9 50 E
Rondônia □ 78 11 0S 63 0W
Rondonópolis 79 16 28S 54 38W
Rong Xian 39 29 23N 104 22 E
Rong'an 39 25 14N 109 22 E
Ronge, L. la 65 55 6N 105 17W

St. Lawrence

Ronge, La 65 55 5N 105 20W
Rongshui 39 25 5N 109 12 E
Ronsard, C. 47 24 46S 113 10 E
Ronse 11 50 45N 3 35 E
Roodepoort 57 26 11S 27 54 E
Roof Butte 73 36 29N 109 5W
Roorkee 32 29 52N 77 59 E
Roosendaal 11 51 32N 4 29 E
Roosevelt, Minn., U.S.A. 70 48 51N 95 2W
Roosevelt, Utah, U.S.A. 72 40 19N 110 1W
Roosevelt, Mt. 64 58 26N 125 20W
Roosevelt Res. 73 33 46N 111 0W
Roper → 44 14 43S 135 27 E
Ropesville 71 33 25N 102 10W
Roraima □ 78 2 0N 61 30W
Roraima, Mt. 78 5 10N 60 40W
Rorketon 65 51 24N 99 35W
Røros 20 62 35N 11 23 E
Rosa 54 9 33S 31 15 E
Rosa, Monte 14 45 57N 7 53 E
Rosalia 72 47 14N 117 25W
Rosario, Argentina 80 33 0S 60 40W
Rosário, Brazil 79 3 0S 44 15W
Rosario, Baja Calif. N., Mexico 74 30 0N 115 50W
Rosario, Sinaloa, Mexico 74 23 0N 105 52W
Rosario, Paraguay 80 24 30S 57 35W
Rosario de la Frontera 80 25 50S 65 0W
Rosário do Sul 80 30 15S 54 55W
Rosas 13 42 19N 3 10 E
Rosas, G. de 13 42 10N 3 15 E
Roscoe 70 45 27N 99 20W
Roscommon, Ireland 9 53 38N 8 11W
Roscommon, U.S.A. 68 44 27N 84 35W
Roscommon □ 9 53 40N 8 15W
Roscrea 9 52 58N 7 50W
Rose → 44 14 16S 135 45 E
Rose Blanche 63 47 38N 58 45W
Rose Harbour 64 52 15N 131 10W
Rose Pt. 64 54 11N 131 39W
Rose Valley 65 52 19N 103 49W
Roseau, Domin. 75 15 20N 61 24W
Roseau, U.S.A. 70 48 51N 95 46W
Rosebery 44 41 46S 145 33 E
Rosebud 71 31 5N 97 0W
Roseburg 72 43 10N 123 20W
Rosedale, Australia 44 24 38S 151 53 E
Rosedale, U.S.A. 71 33 51N 91 0W
Rosemary 64 50 46N 112 5W
Rosenberg 71 29 30N 95 48W
Rosenheim 14 47 51N 12 9 E
Rosetown 65 51 35N 107 59W
Rosetta = Rashîd 51 31 21N 30 22 E
Roseville 72 38 46N 121 17W
Rosewood, N. Terr., Australia 46 16 28S 128 58 E
Rosewood, Queens., Australia 45 27 38S 152 36 E
Rosh Haniqra, Kefar 28 33 5N 35 5 E
Rosh Pinna 28 32 58N 35 32 E
Rosignol 78 6 15N 57 30W
Roskilde 21 55 38N 12 3 E
Roslavl 22 53 57N 32 55 E
Roslyn 45 34 29S 149 37 E
Rosmead 56 31 29S 25 8 E
Ross, Australia 44 42 2S 147 30 E
Ross, N.Z. 43 42 53S 170 49 E
Ross L. 72 48 50N 121 5W
Ross on Wye 7 51 55N 2 34W
Rossan Pt. 9 54 42N 8 47W
Rossburn 65 50 40N 100 49W
Rossignol, L. 62 52 43N 73 40W
Rossignol Res. 63 44 12N 65 10W
Rossland 64 49 6N 117 50W
Rosslare 9 52 17N 6 23W
Rosso 50 16 40N 15 45W
Rossosh 23 50 15N 39 28 E
Rossport 62 48 50N 87 30W
Røssvatnet 20 65 45N 14 5 E
Rossville 44 15 48S 145 15 E
Rosthern 65 52 40N 106 20W
Rostock 14 54 4N 12 9 E
Rostov, Don, U.S.S.R. 23 47 15N 39 45 E
Rostov, Moskva, U.S.S.R. 22 57 14N 39 25 E
Roswell 71 33 26N 104 32W
Rosyth 8 56 2N 3 26W
Rotan 71 32 52N 100 30W
Rothaargebirge 14 51 0N 8 20 E
Rother → 7 50 59N 0 40 E
Rotherham 6 53 26N 1 21W
Rothes 8 57 31N 3 12W
Rothesay, Canada 63 45 23N 66 0W
Rothesay, U.K. 8 55 50N 5 3W
Roti 35 10 50S 123 0 E
Roto 45 33 0S 145 30 E
Rotoroa, L. 43 41 55S 172 39 E
Rotorua 43 38 9S 176 16 E
Rotorua, L. 43 38 5S 176 18 E
Rotterdam 11 51 55N 4 30 E
Rottnest I. 47 32 0S 115 27 E
Rottumeroog 11 53 33N 6 34 E
Rottweil 14 48 9N 8 38 E
Rotuma 40 12 25S 177 5 E
Roubaix 12 50 40N 3 10 E
Rouen 12 49 27N 1 4 E
Rouleau 65 50 10N 104 56W
Round Mt. 45 30 26S 152 16 E
Round Mountain 72 38 46N 117 3W
Roundup 72 46 25N 108 35W
Rousay 8 59 10N 3 2W
Roussillon 12 42 30N 2 35 E
Rouxville 56 30 25S 26 50 E
Rouyn 62 48 20N 79 0W
Rovaniemi 20 66 29N 25 41 E
Rovereto 18 45 53N 11 3 E
Rovigo 18 45 4N 11 48 E
Rovinj 18 45 5N 13 40 E
Rovno 23 50 40N 26 10 E
Rovuma → 54 10 29S 40 28 E
Rowena 45 29 48S 148 55 E
Rowley Shoals 46 17 30S 119 0 E
Roxas 35 11 36N 122 49 E
Roxboro 69 36 24N 78 59W
Roxborough Downs 44 22 30S 138 45 E
Roxburgh 43 45 33S 169 19 E
Roy, Mont., U.S.A. 72 47 17N 109 0W
Roy, N. Mex., U.S.A. 71 35 57N 104 8W
Roy, Le 71 38 8N 95 35W
Roy Hill 46 22 37S 119 58 E
Royan 12 45 37N 1 2W
Rtishchevo 22 55 16N 43 50 E
Ruacaná 56 17 20S 14 12 E
Ruahine Ra. 43 39 55S 176 2 E
Ruapehu 43 39 17S 175 35 E
Ruapuke I. 43 46 46S 168 31 E
Rub' al Khali 29 18 0N 48 0 E
Rubh a' Mhail 8 55 55N 6 10W
Rubha Hunish 8 57 42N 6 20W
Rubicone → 18 44 8N 12 28 E
Rubio 78 7 43N 72 22W
Rubtsovsk 24 51 30N 81 10 E
Ruby 60 64 40N 155 35W
Ruby L. 72 40 10N 115 28W
Ruby Mts. 72 40 30N 115 30W
Rudall 45 33 43S 136 17 E
Rudnichnyy 22 59 38N 52 26 E
Rudnogorsk 25 57 15N 103 42 E
Rudnyy 24 52 57N 63 7 E
Rudolf, Ostrov 24 81 45N 58 30 E
Rudyard 68 46 14N 84 35W
Rufa'a 51 14 44N 33 22 E
Rufiji → 54 7 50S 39 15 E
Rufino 80 34 20S 62 50W
Rufisque 50 14 40N 17 15W
Rugao 39 32 23N 120 31 E
Rugby, U.K. 7 52 23N 1 16W
Rugby, U.S.A. 70 48 21N 100 0W
Rügen 14 54 22N 13 25 E
Ruhama 28 31 31N 34 43 E
Ruhr → 14 51 25N 6 44 E
Rui'an 39 27 47N 120 40 E
Ruidosa 71 29 59N 104 39W
Ruidoso 73 33 19N 105 39W
Rukwa L. 54 8 0S 32 20 E
Rulhieres, C. 46 13 56S 127 22 E
Rum Cay 75 23 40N 74 58W
Rum Jungle 46 13 0S 130 59 E
Rumāḥ 30 25 29N 47 10 E
Rumania = Romania ■ 15 46 0N 25 0 E
Rumbalara 44 25 20S 134 29 E
Rumbêk 51 6 54N 29 37 E
Rumford 68 44 30N 70 30W
Rumoi 36 43 56N 141 39W
Rumsey 64 51 51N 112 48W
Rumula 44 16 35S 145 20 E
Rumuruti 52 0 17N 36 32 E
Runan 39 33 0N 114 30 E
Runanga 43 42 25S 171 15 E
Runcorn 6 53 20N 2 44W
Rungwa 54 6 55S 33 32 E
Runka 53 12 28N 7 20 E
Ruoqiang 37 38 55N 88 10 E
Rupa 33 27 15N 92 21 E
Rupat 34 1 45N 101 40 E
Rupert → 62 51 29N 78 45W
Rupert House = Fort Rupert 62 51 30N 78 40W
Rurrenabaque 78 14 30S 67 32W
Rusape 55 18 35S 32 8 E
Ruschuk = Ruse 19 43 48N 25 59 E
Ruse 19 43 48N 25 59 E
Rushden 7 52 17N 0 37W
Rushford 70 43 48N 91 46W
Rushville, Ill., U.S.A. 70 40 6N 90 35W
Rushville, Ind., U.S.A. 68 39 38N 85 22W
Rushville, Nebr., U.S.A. 70 42 43N 102 28W
Russas 79 4 55S 37 50W
Russell, Canada 65 50 50N 101 20W
Russell, N.Z. 43 35 16S 174 10 E
Russell, U.S.A. 70 38 56N 98 55W
Russell L., Man., Canada 65 56 15N 101 30W
Russell L., N.W.T., Canada 64 63 5N 115 44W
Russellkonda 33 19 57N 84 42 E
Russellville, Ala., U.S.A. 69 34 30N 87 44W
Russellville, Ark., U.S.A. 71 35 15N 93 8W
Russellville, Ky., U.S.A. 69 36 50N 86 50W
Russian S.F.S.R. □ 25 62 0N 105 0 E
Russkaya Polyana 24 53 47N 73 53 E
Rustavi 23 41 30N 45 0 E
Rustenburg 56 25 41S 27 14 E
Ruston 71 32 30N 92 58W
Ruteng 35 8 35S 120 30 E
Ruth 72 39 15N 115 1W
Rutherglen 8 55 50N 4 11W
Rutland Plains 44 15 38S 141 43 E
Rutledge → 65 61 4N 112 0W
Rutledge L. 65 61 33N 110 47W
Rutshuru 54 1 13S 29 25 E
Ruurlo 11 52 5N 6 24 E
Ruwenzori 54 0 30N 29 55 E
Ružomberok 15 49 3N 19 17 E
Rwanda ■ 54 2 0S 30 0 E
Ryan, L. 8 55 0N 5 2W
Ryazan 22 54 40N 39 40 E
Ryazhsk 22 53 45N 40 3 E
Rybache 24 46 40N 81 20 E
Rybachiy Poluostrov 22 69 43N 32 0 E
Rybinsk = Andropov 22 58 5N 38 50 E
Rybinskoye Vdkhr. 22 58 30N 38 25 E
Ryde 7 50 44N 1 9W
Rye 7 50 57N 0 46 E
Rye → 6 54 12N 0 53W
Rye Patch Res. 72 40 38N 118 20W
Ryegate 72 46 21N 109 15W
Rylstone 45 32 46S 149 58 E
Rypin 15 53 3N 19 25 E
Ryūkyū Is. = Nansei-Shotō 37 26 0N 128 0 E
Rzeszów 15 50 5N 21 58 E
Rzhev 22 56 20N 34 20 E

S

Sa Dec 34 10 20N 105 46 E
Sa'ad 28 31 28N 34 33 E
Sa'ādatābād 31 30 10N 53 5 E
Saale → 14 51 57N 11 56 E
Saar → 14 49 41N 6 32 E
Saarbrücken 14 49 15N 6 58 E
Saaremaa 22 58 30N 22 30 E
Saariselkä 20 68 16N 28 15 E
Saba 75 17 42N 63 26W
Sabadell 13 41 28N 2 7 E
Sabah □ 34 6 0N 117 0 E
Şabāḩ, Wadi → 30 23 50N 48 30 E
Sábana de la Mar 75 19 7N 69 24W
Sábanalarga 78 10 38N 74 55W
Sabang 34 5 50N 95 15 E
Sabará 79 19 55S 43 46W
Sabarania 35 2 5S 138 18 E
Sabasṭiyah 28 32 17N 35 12 E
Sabáudia 18 41 17N 13 2 E
Sabhah 51 27 9N 14 29 E
Sabie 57 25 10S 30 48 E
Sabinal, Mexico 74 30 58N 107 25W
Sabinal, U.S.A. 71 29 20N 99 27W
Sabinas 74 27 50N 101 10W
Sabinas Hidalgo 74 26 33N 100 10W
Sabine → 71 30 0N 93 35W
Sabine L. 71 29 50N 93 50W
Sabine Pass 71 29 42N 93 54W
Sablayan 35 12 50N 120 50 E
Sable, C., Canada 63 43 29N 65 38W
Sable, C., U.S.A. 75 25 13N 81 0W
Sable I. 63 44 0N 60 0W
Sables-d'Olonne, Les 12 46 30N 1 45W
Sabolev 25 54 20N 155 30 E
Sabulubek 34 1 36S 98 40 E
Sabzevār 31 36 15N 57 40 E
Sabzvārān 31 28 45N 57 50 E
Sac City 70 42 26N 95 0W
Sachigo → 62 55 6N 88 58W
Sachigo, L. 62 53 50N 92 12W
Saco, Maine, U.S.A. 69 43 30N 70 27W
Saco, Mont., U.S.A. 72 48 28N 107 19W
Sacramento 72 38 33N 121 30W
Sacramento → 72 38 3N 121 56W
Sacramento Mts. 73 32 30N 105 30W
Sádaba 13 42 19N 1 12W
Sadani 54 5 58S 38 35 E
Sadd el Aali 51 23 54N 32 54 E
Sado 36 38 0N 138 25 E
Sado, Shima 36 38 15N 138 30 E
Sadon 33 25 28N 98 0 E
Säffle 21 59 8N 12 55 E
Safford 73 32 50N 109 43W
Saffron Walden 7 52 2N 0 15 E
Safi 50 32 18N 9 20W
Safīd Kūh 31 34 45N 63 0 E
Saga, Indonesia 35 2 40S 132 55 E
Saga, Japan 36 33 15N 130 16 E
Saga □ 36 33 15N 130 20 E
Sagaing □ 33 23 55N 95 56 E
Sagala 50 14 9N 6 38W
Sagar 32 14 14N 75 6 E
Sagil 37 50 15N 91 15 E
Saginaw 68 43 26N 83 55W
Saginaw B. 68 43 50N 83 40W
Sagīr, Zab as → 30 35 10N 43 20 E
Saglouc 61 62 14N 75 38W
Sagra, La 13 37 57N 2 35W
Sagres 13 37 0N 8 58W
Sagua la Grande 75 22 50N 80 10W
Saguache 73 38 10N 106 10W
Saguenay → 63 48 22N 71 0W
Sagunto 13 39 42N 0 18W
Sahagún 13 42 18N 5 2W
Saham 28 32 42N 35 46 E
Saḥam al Jawlān 28 32 45N 35 55 E
Sahand, Kūh-e 30 37 44N 46 27 E
Sahara 50 23 0N 5 0 E
Saharan Atlas 48 34 9N 3 29 E
Saharanpur 32 29 58N 77 33 E
Saharien, Atlas 50 33 30N 1 0 E
Sahasinaka 57 21 49S 47 49 E
Sahiwal 32 30 45N 73 8 E
Sahtaneh → 64 59 2N 122 28W
Sahuaripa 74 29 0N 109 13W
Sahuarita 73 31 58N 110 59W
Sahuayo 74 20 4N 102 43W
Sa'id Bundas 51 8 24N 24 48 E
Saïda 50 34 50N 0 11 E
Saīdābād 31 29 30N 55 45 E
Sa'idiyeh 30 36 20N 48 55 E
Saidpur 33 25 48N 89 0 E
Saidu 32 34 43N 72 24 E
Saigon = Phanh Bho Ho Chi Minh 34 10 58N 106 40 E
Saih-al-Malih 31 23 37N 58 31 E
Saijō 36 33 55N 133 11 E
Saikhoa Ghat 33 27 50N 95 40 E
Saiki 36 32 58N 131 51 E
Sailolof 35 1 7S 130 46 E
St. Abb's Head 8 55 55N 2 10W
St. Alban's, Canada 63 47 51N 55 50W
St. Albans, U.K. 7 51 44N 0 19W
St. Albans, Vt., U.S.A. 68 44 49N 73 7W
St. Albans, W. Va., U.S.A. 68 38 21N 81 50W
St. Alban's Head 7 50 34N 2 3W
St. Albert 64 53 37N 113 32W
St. Andrew's, Canada 63 47 45N 59 15W
St. Andrews, U.K. 8 56 20N 2 48W
St. Ann B. 63 46 22N 60 25W
St. Anthony, Canada 63 51 22N 55 35W
St. Anthony, U.S.A. 72 44 0N 111 40W
St. Arnaud 45 36 40S 143 16 E
St. Arnaud Ra. 43 42 1S 172 53 E
St. Arthur 63 47 33N 67 46W
St. Asaph 6 53 15N 3 27W
St-Augustin-Saguenay 63 51 13N 58 38W
St. Augustine 69 29 52N 81 20W
St. Austell 7 50 20N 4 48W
St.-Barthélemy, I. 75 17 50N 62 50W
St. Bee's Hd. 6 54 30N 3 38 E
St. Boniface 65 49 53N 97 5W
St. Bride's 63 46 56N 54 10W
St. Brides B. 7 51 48N 5 15W
St.-Brieuc 12 48 30N 2 46W
St. Catharines 62 43 10N 79 15W
St. Catherines I. 69 31 35N 81 10W
St. Catherine's Pt. 7 50 34N 1 18W
St. Charles, Ill., U.S.A. 68 41 55N 88 21W
St. Charles, Mo., U.S.A. 70 38 46N 90 30W
St. Christopher 75 17 20N 62 40W
St. Christopher-Nevis ■ 75 17 20N 62 40W
St. Clair, L. 62 42 30N 82 45W
St. Claude 65 49 40N 98 20W
St. Cloud, Fla., U.S.A. 69 28 15N 81 15W
St. Cloud, Minn., U.S.A. 70 45 30N 94 11W
St-Coeur de Marie 63 48 39N 71 43W
St. Cricq, C. 47 25 17S 113 6 E
St. Croix 75 17 45N 64 45W
St. Croix → 70 44 45N 92 50W
St. Croix Falls 70 45 18N 92 22W
St. David's, Canada 63 48 12N 58 52W
St. David's, U.K. 7 51 54N 5 16W
St. David's Head 7 51 55N 5 16W
St.-Denis, France 12 48 56N 2 22 E
St.-Denis, Réunion 3 20 52S 55 27 E
St. Elias, Mt. 60 60 14N 140 50W
St. Elias Mts. 64 60 33N 139 28W
St.-Étienne 12 45 27N 4 22 E
St. Eustatius 75 17 20N 63 0W
St-Félicien 62 48 40N 72 25W
St.-Flour 12 45 2N 3 6 E
St. Francis 70 39 48N 101 47W
St. Francis → 71 34 38N 90 36W
St. Francis, C. 56 34 14S 24 49 E
St. Francisville 71 30 48N 91 22W
St-Gabriel-de-Brandon 62 46 17N 73 24W
St. George, Australia 45 28 1S 148 30 E
St. George, Canada 63 45 11N 66 50W
St. George, S.C., U.S.A. 69 33 13N 80 37W
St. George, Utah, U.S.A. 73 37 10N 113 35W
St. George, C., Canada 63 48 30N 59 16W
St. George, C., U.S.A. 69 29 36N 85 2W
St. George Ra. 46 18 40S 125 0 E
St-Georges 11 50 37N 5 20 E
St. George's 63 48 26N 58 31W
St-Georges 63 46 8N 70 40W
St.-Georges, Fr. Gui. 79 4 0N 52 0W
St. George's, Grenada 75 12 5N 61 43W
St. George's B. 63 48 24N 58 53W
St. George's Channel 9 52 0N 6 0W
St. Georges Head 45 35 12S 150 42 E
St. Gotthard P. = San Gottardo, Paso del 14 46 33N 8 33 E
St. Helena, Atl. Oc. 2 15 55S 5 44W
St. Helena, U.S.A. 72 38 29N 122 30W
St. Helena B. 56 32 40S 18 10 E
St. Helens, Australia 44 41 20S 148 15 E
St. Helens, U.K. 6 53 28N 2 44W
St. Helens, U.S.A. 72 45 55N 122 50W
St. Helier 7 49 11N 2 6W
St-Hubert 11 50 2N 5 23 E
St-Hyacinthe 62 45 40N 72 58W
St. Ignace 68 45 53N 84 43W
St. Ignace I. 62 48 45N 88 0W
St. Ignatius 72 47 19N 114 8W
St. Ives, Cambs., U.K. 7 52 20N 0 5W
St. Ives, Cornwall, U.K. 7 50 13N 5 29W
St. James 70 43 57N 94 40W
St-Jean 62 45 20N 73 20W
St-Jean → 63 50 17N 64 20W
St-Jean, L. 63 48 40N 72 0W
St. Jean Baptiste 65 49 15N 97 20W
St-Jean-Port-Joli 63 47 15N 70 13W
St-Jérôme, Qué., Canada 62 45 47N 74 0W
St-Jérôme, Qué., Canada 63 48 26N 71 53W
St. John, Canada 63 45 20N 66 8W
St. John, Kans., U.S.A. 71 37 59N 98 45W
St. John, N. Dak., U.S.A. 70 48 58N 99 40W
St. John → 63 45 15N 66 4W
St. John, C. 63 50 0N 55 32W
St. John's, Antigua 75 17 6N 61 51W
St. John's, Canada 63 47 35N 52 40W
St. Johns, Ariz., U.S.A. 73 34 31N 109 26W
St. Johns, Mich., U.S.A. 68 43 0N 84 31W
St. John's → 69 30 20N 81 30W
St. Johnsbury 68 44 25N 72 1W
St. Joseph, La., U.S.A. 71 31 55N 91 15W
St. Joseph, Mich., U.S.A. 68 42 5N 86 30W
St. Joseph, Mo., U.S.A. 70 39 46N 94 50W
St. Joseph → 68 42 7N 86 30W
St. Joseph, I. 62 46 12N 83 58W
St. Joseph, L. 62 51 10N 90 35W
St-Jovite 62 46 8N 74 38W
St. Kilda 43 45 53S 170 31 E
St. Kitts = St. Christopher 75 17 20N 62 40W
St. Laurent, Canada 65 50 25N 97 58W
St.-Laurent, Fr. Gui. 79 5 29N 54 3W
St. Lawrence, Australia 44 22 16S 149 31 E
St. Lawrence, Canada 63 46 54N 55 23W
St. Lawrence → 63 49 30N 66 0W

Sebastián Vizcaíno, B.

San Ygnacio 71 27 6N 99 24W
Sana' 29 15 27N 44 12 E
Sana → 18 45 3N 16 23 E
Sanaga → 54 3 35N 9 38 E
Sanak I. 60 53 30N 162 30W
Sanana 35 2 5S 125 59 E
Sanandaj 30 35 18N 47 1 E
Sancha He → 39 26 48N 106 7 E
Sanco Pt. 35 8 15N 126 27 E
Sancti-Spíritus 75 21 52N 79 33W
Sand → 57 22 25S 30 5 E
Sand Springs 71 36 12N 96 5W
Sandakan 34 5 53N 118 4 E
Sanday 8 59 15N 2 30W
Sanders 73 35 12N 109 25W
Sanderson 71 30 5N 102 30W
Sandfly L. 65 55 43N 106 6W
Sandgate 45 27 18S 153 3 E
Sandía 78 14 10S 69 30W
Sandıklı 30 38 30N 30 20 E
Sandnes 21 58 50N 5 45 E
Sandness 8 60 18N 1 38W
Sandoa 54 9 41S 23 0 E
Sandomierz 15 50 40N 21 43 E
Sandover → 44 21 43S 136 32 E
Sandoway 33 18 20N 94 30 E
Sandpoint 72 48 20N 116 34W
Sandringham 6 52 50N 0 30 E
Sandspit 64 53 14N 131 49W
Sandstone 47 27 59S 119 16 E
Sandusky, Mich., U.S.A. 62 43 26N 82 50W
Sandusky, Ohio, U.S.A. 68 41 25N 82 40W
Sandviken 21 60 38N 16 46 E
Sandwich, C. 44 18 14S 146 18 E
Sandwich B., Canada 63 53 40N 57 15W
Sandwich B., Namibia 56 23 25S 14 20 E
Sandwip Chan. 33 22 35N 91 35 E
Sandy Bight 47 33 50S 123 20 E
Sandy C., Queens., Australia 45 24 42S 153 15 E
Sandy C., Tas., Australia 44 41 25S 144 45 E
Sandy Cr. → 72 41 15N 109 47W
Sandy L. 62 53 2N 93 0W
Sandy Lake 62 53 0N 93 15W
Sandy Narrows 65 55 5N 103 4W
Sanford, Fla., U.S.A. 69 28 45N 81 20W
Sanford, N.C., U.S.A. 69 35 30N 79 10W
Sanford → 47 27 22S 115 53 E
Sanford Mt. 60 62 30N 143 0W
Sanga → 54 1 5S 17 0 E
Sanga-Tolon 25 61 50N 149 40 E
Sangamner 32 19 37N 74 15 E
Sangar 25 64 2N 127 31 E
Sangasangadalam 34 0 36S 117 13 E
Sangeang 35 8 12S 119 6 E
Sanger 73 36 41N 119 35W
Sanggan He → 38 38 12N 117 15 E
Sanggau 34 0 5N 110 30 E
Sangihe, Kepulauan 35 3 0N 126 0 E
Sangihe, P. 35 3 45N 125 30 E
Sangkapura 34 5 52S 112 40 E
Sangli 32 16 55N 74 33 E
Sangmélina 54 2 57N 12 1 E
Sangonera → 13 37 59N 1 4W
Sangre de Cristo Mts. 71 37 0N 105 0W
Sangudo 64 53 50N 114 54W
Sangzhi 39 29 25N 110 12 E
Sanjiang 39 25 48N 109 37 E
Sankt Gallen 14 47 26N 9 22 E
Sankt Moritz 14 46 30N 9 50 E
Sankuru → 54 4 17S 20 25 E
Sanlúcar de Barrameda 13 36 46N 6 21W
Sanmenxia 39 34 47N 111 12 E
Sannaspos 56 29 6S 26 34 E
Sannicandro Gargánico 18 41 50N 15 34 E
Sannieshof 56 26 30S 25 47 E
Sanok 15 49 35N 22 10 E
Sanquhar 8 55 21N 3 56W
Sanshui 39 23 10N 112 56 E
Santa Ana, Bolivia 78 13 50S 65 40W
Santa Ana, Ecuador 78 1 16S 80 20W
Santa Ana, El Salv. 75 14 0N 89 31W
Santa Ana, Mexico 74 30 31N 111 8W
Santa Ana, U.S.A. 73 33 48N 117 55W
Santa Bárbara, Mexico 74 26 48N 105 50W
Santa Barbara, U.S.A. 73 34 25N 119 40W
Santa Catalina 74 25 40N 110 50W
Santa Catalina, G. of 73 33 0N 118 0W
Santa Catalina I. 73 33 20N 118 30W
Santa Catarina □ 80 27 25S 48 30W
Santa Clara, Cuba 75 22 20N 80 0W
Santa Clara, Calif., U.S.A. 73 37 21N 122 0W
Santa Clara, Utah, U.S.A. 73 37 10N 113 38W
Santa Clotilde 78 2 33S 73 45W
Santa Coloma de Gramanet 13 41 27N 2 13 E
Santa Cruz, Argentina 80 50 0S 68 32W
Santa Cruz, Bolivia 78 17 43S 63 10W
Santa Cruz, C. Rica 75 10 15N 85 35W
Santa Cruz, Phil. 35 14 20N 121 24 E
Santa Cruz, U.S.A. 73 36 55N 122 1W
Santa Cruz □ 78 17 43S 63 10W
Santa Cruz → 80 50 10S 68 20W
Santa Cruz, Is. 40 10 30S 166 0 E
Santa Cruz de Tenerife 50 28 28N 16 15W
Santa Cruz del Sur 75 20 44N 78 0W
Santa Cruz do Sul 80 29 42S 52 25W
Santa Cruz I. 73 34 0N 119 45W
Santa Domingo, Cay 75 21 25N 75 15W
Santa Elena 78 2 16S 80 52W
Santa Elena, C. 75 10 54N 85 56W
Santa Eugenia, Pta. 74 27 50N 115 5W
Santa Fe, Argentina 80 31 35S 60 41W
Santa Fe, U.S.A. 73 35 40N 106 0W
Santa Filomena 79 9 6S 45 50W
Santa Inés, I. 80 54 0S 73 0W
Santa Isabel = Rey Malabo 54 3 45N 8 50 E
Santa Isabel, Argentina 80 36 10S 66 54W
Santa Isabel, Brazil 79 11 45S 51 30W
Santa Lucia Range 73 36 0N 121 20W
Santa Magdalena, I. 74 24 40N 112 15W
Santa Margarita 74 24 30N 111 50W
Santa Maria, Brazil 80 29 40S 53 48W
Santa Maria, U.S.A. 73 34 58N 120 29W
Santa María → 74 31 0N 107 14W
Santa María, B. de 74 25 10N 108 40W
Santa Maria da Vitória 79 13 24S 44 12W
Santa Maria di Leuca, C. 19 39 48N 18 20 E
Santa Marta 78 11 15N 74 13W
Santa Marta, Sierra Nevada de 78 10 55N 73 50W
Santa Maura = Levkás 19 38 40N 20 43 E
Santa Monica 73 34 0N 118 30W
Santa Rita 73 32 50N 108 0W
Santa Rosa, La Pampa, Argentina 80 36 40S 64 17W
Santa Rosa, San Luis, Argentina 80 32 21S 65 10W
Santa Rosa, Bolivia 78 10 36S 67 20W
Santa Rosa, Brazil 80 27 52S 54 29W
Santa Rosa, Calif., U.S.A. 72 38 26N 122 43W
Santa Rosa, N. Mex., U.S.A. 71 34 58N 104 40W
Santa Rosa de Copán 75 14 47N 88 46W
Santa Rosa I., Calif., U.S.A. 73 34 0N 120 6W
Santa Rosa I., Fla., U.S.A. 69 30 23N 87 0W
Santa Rosa Ra. 72 41 45N 117 30W
Santa Rosalía 74 27 20N 112 20W
Santa Tecla = Nueva San Salvador 75 13 40N 89 18W
Santa Vitória do Palmar 80 33 32S 53 25W
Santai 39 31 5N 104 58 E
Santana, Coxilha de 80 30 50S 55 35W
Santana do Livramento 80 30 55S 55 30W
Santander 13 43 27N 3 51W
Santander Jiménez 74 24 11N 98 29W
Santaquin 72 40 0N 111 51W
Santarém, Brazil 79 2 25S 54 42W
Santarém, Portugal 13 39 12N 8 42W
Santaren Channel 75 24 0N 79 30W
Santiago, Brazil 80 29 11S 54 52W
Santiago, Chile 80 33 24S 70 40W
Santiago, Panama 75 8 0N 81 0W
Santiago → 78 4 27S 77 38W
Santiago de Compostela 13 42 52N 8 37W
Santiago de Cuba 75 20 0N 75 49W
Santiago de los Cabelleros 75 19 30N 70 40W
Santiago del Estero 80 27 50S 64 15W
Santiago Ixcuintla 74 21 50N 105 11W
Santiago Papasquiaro 74 25 0N 105 20W
Santiaguillo, L. de 74 24 50N 104 50W
Santo Amaro 79 12 30S 38 43W
Santo Ângelo 80 28 15S 54 15W
Santo Antonio 79 15 50S 56 0W
Santo Corazón 78 18 0S 58 45W
Santo Domingo, Dom. Rep. 75 18 30N 69 59W
Santo Domingo, Baja Calif. N., Mexico 74 30 43N 116 2W
Santo Domingo, Baja Calif. S., Mexico 74 25 32N 112 2W
Santo Domingo, Nic. 75 12 14N 84 59W
Santo Tomás 78 14 26S 72 8W
Santo Tomé 80 28 40S 56 5W
Santo Tomé de Guayana = Ciudad Guayana 78 8 0N 62 30W
Santoña 13 43 29N 3 27W
Santos 80 24 0S 46 20W
Santos Dumont 80 22 55S 43 10W
Sânūr 28 32 22N 35 15 E
Sanyuan 39 34 35N 108 58 E
Sanza Pombo 54 7 18S 15 56 E
São Anastácio 80 22 0S 51 40W
São Bernado de Campo 79 23 45S 46 34W
São Borja 80 28 39S 56 0W
São Carlos 80 22 0S 47 50W
São Cristóvão 79 11 1S 37 15W
São Domingos 79 13 25S 46 19W
São Francisco 79 16 0S 44 50W
São Francisco → 79 10 30S 36 24W
São Francisco do Sul 80 26 15S 48 36W
São Gabriel 80 30 20S 54 20W
São João del Rei 79 21 8S 44 15W
São João do Araguaia 79 5 23S 48 46W
São João do Piauí 79 8 21S 42 15W
São José do Rio Prêto 80 20 50S 49 20W
São Leopoldo 80 29 50S 51 10W
São Lourenço 79 22 7S 45 3W
São Lourenço → 79 17 53S 57 27W
São Luís 79 2 39S 44 15W
São Marcos → 79 18 15S 47 37W
São Marcos, B. de 79 2 0S 44 0W
São Mateus 79 18 44S 39 50W
São Paulo 80 23 32S 46 37W
São Paulo □ 80 22 0S 49 0W
Sao Paulo, I. 2 0 50N 31 40W
São Roque, C. de 79 5 30S 35 16W
São Sebastião, I. de 80 23 50S 45 18W
São Tomé & Principe ■ 3 0 12N 6 39 E
São Vicente, C. de 13 37 0N 9 0W
Saona, I. 75 18 10N 68 40W
Saône → 12 45 44N 4 50 E
Saône-et-Loire □ 12 46 30N 4 50 E
Saonek 35 0 22S 130 55 E
Saparua 35 3 33S 128 40 E
Sapele 53 5 50N 5 40 E
Sapelo I. 69 31 28N 81 15W
Saposoa 78 6 55S 76 45W
Sapporo 36 43 0N 141 21 E
Sapudi 35 7 6S 114 20 E
Sapulpa 71 36 0N 96 0W
Saqqez 30 36 15N 46 20 E
Sar-e Pol 31 36 10N 66 0 E
Sar Planina 19 42 10N 21 0 E
Sarāb 30 38 0N 47 30 E
Sarada → 33 27 21N 81 23 E
Saragossa = Zaragoza 13 41 39N 0 53W
Saraguro 78 3 35S 79 16W
Sarajevo 19 43 52N 18 26 E
Saran, G. 34 0 30S 111 25 E
Saranac Lake 68 44 20N 74 10W
Sarandí del Yi 80 33 18S 55 38W
Sarangani B. 35 6 0N 125 13 E
Sarangani Is. 35 5 25N 125 25 E
Sarangarh 33 21 30N 83 5 E
Saransk 22 54 10N 45 10 E
Sarapul 22 56 28N 53 48 E
Sarasota 69 27 20N 82 30W
Saratoga 72 41 30N 106 48W
Saratoga Springs 68 43 5N 73 47W
Saratov 22 51 30N 46 2 E
Saravane 34 15 43N 106 25 E
Sarawak □ 34 2 0N 113 0 E
Sarbāz 31 26 38N 61 19 E
Sarbīsheh 31 32 30N 59 40 E
Sardalas 50 25 50N 10 34 E
Sardarshahr 32 28 30N 74 29 E
Sardegna 18 39 57N 9 0 E
Sardinia = Sardegna 18 39 57N 9 0 E
Sargent 70 41 42N 99 24W
Sargodha 32 32 10N 72 40 E
Sarh 51 9 5N 18 23 E
Sārī 31 36 30N 53 4 E
Sarida → 28 32 4N 34 45 E
Sarikamiş 30 40 22N 42 35 E
Sarikei 34 2 8N 111 30 E
Sarina 44 21 22S 149 13 E
Sarita 71 27 14N 97 49W
Sark 7 49 25N 2 20W
Sarlat-la-Canéda 12 44 54N 1 13 E
Sarles 70 48 58N 99 0W
Sarmi 35 1 49S 138 44 E
Sarmiento 80 45 35S 69 5W
Sarnia 62 42 58N 82 23W
Sarny 22 51 17N 26 40 E
Sarolangun 34 2 19S 102 42 E
Saronikós Kólpos 19 37 45N 23 45 E
Saros Körfezi 19 40 30N 26 15 E
Sarpsborg 21 59 16N 11 12 E
Sarre = Saar → 14 49 41N 6 32 E
Sarre, La 62 48 45N 79 15W
Sarro 50 13 40N 5 15W
Sartène 18 41 38N 8 58 E
Sarthe □ 12 47 58N 0 10 E
Sarthe → 12 47 33N 0 31W
Sartynya 24 63 22N 63 11 E
Sarvestān 31 29 20N 53 10 E
Sary-Tash 24 39 44N 73 15 E
Saryshagan 24 46 12N 73 38 E
Sasa 28 33 2N 35 23 E
Sasabeneh 29 7 59N 44 43 E
Sasaram 33 24 57N 84 5 E
Sasebo 36 33 10N 129 43 E
Saser Mt. 32 34 50N 77 50 E
Saskatchewan □ 65 54 40N 106 0W
Saskatchewan → 65 53 37N 100 40W
Saskatoon 65 52 10N 106 38W
Saskylakh 25 71 55N 114 1 E
Sasolburg 57 26 46S 27 49 E
Sasovo 22 54 25N 41 55 E
Sassandra 50 5 0N 6 8W
Sassandra → 50 4 58N 6 5W
Sássari 18 40 44N 8 33 E
Sassnitz 14 54 29N 13 39 E
Sata-Misaki 36 30 59N 130 40 E
Satadougou 50 12 25N 11 25W
Satanta 71 37 30N 101 0W
Satara 32 17 44N 73 58 E
Satilla → 69 30 59N 81 28W
Satka 22 55 3N 59 1 E
Satmala Hills 32 20 15N 74 40 E
Satna 33 24 35N 80 50 E
Sátoraljaújhely 15 48 25N 21 41 E
Satpura Ra. 32 21 25N 76 10 E
Satu Mare 15 47 46N 22 55 E
Satui 34 3 50S 115 27 E
Saturnina → 78 12 15S 58 10W
Saucillo 74 28 1N 105 17W
Sauda 21 59 40N 6 20 E
Sauðarkrókur 20 65 45N 19 40W
Saudi Arabia ■ 29 26 0N 44 0 E
Saugerties 68 42 4N 73 58W
Sauk Centre 70 45 42N 94 56W
Sauk Rapids 70 45 35N 94 10W
Sault Ste. Marie, Canada 62 46 30N 84 20W
Sault Ste. Marie, U.S.A. 68 46 27N 84 22W
Saumlaki 35 7 55S 131 20 E
Saumur 12 47 15N 0 5W
Saunders C. 43 45 53S 170 45 E
Saunders Point, Mt. 47 27 52S 125 38 E
Saurbær, Borgarfjarðarsýsla, Iceland 20 64 24N 21 35W
Saurbær, Eyjafjarðarsýsla, Iceland 20 65 27N 18 13W
Sauri 53 11 42N 6 44 E
Saurimo 54 9 40S 20 12 E
Sava → 19 44 50N 20 26 E
Savage 70 47 27N 104 20W
Savage I. = Niue I. 2 19 2S 169 54W
Savai'i 43 13 28S 172 24W
Savalou 53 7 57N 1 58 E
Savanna 70 42 5N 90 10W
Savanna la Mar 75 18 10N 78 10W
Savannah, Ga., U.S.A. 69 32 4N 81 4W
Savannah, Mo., U.S.A. 70 39 55N 94 46W
Savannah, Tenn., U.S.A. 69 35 12N 88 18W
Savannah → 69 32 2N 80 53W
Savannakhet 34 16 30N 104 49 E
Savant L. 62 50 16N 90 44W
Savant Lake 62 50 14N 90 40W
Savanur 32 14 59N 75 21 E
Savé 53 8 2N 2 29 E
Save → 57 21 16S 34 0 E
Sāveh 30 35 2N 50 20 E
Savelugu 53 9 38N 0 54W
Savoie □ 12 45 26N 6 25 E
Savona 18 44 19N 8 29 E
Savonlinna 22 61 52N 28 53 E
Sawahlunto 34 0 40S 100 52 E
Sawai 35 3 0S 129 5 E
Sawai Madhopur 32 26 0N 76 25 E
Sawara 36 35 55N 140 30 E
Sawatch Mts. 73 38 30N 106 30W
Sawel, Mt. 9 54 48N 7 5W
Sawmills 55 19 30S 28 2 E
Sawu 35 10 35S 121 50 E
Sawu Sea 35 9 30S 121 50 E
Saxby → 44 18 25S 140 53 E
Say 53 13 8N 2 22 E
Sayabec 63 48 35N 67 41W
Sayán 78 11 8S 77 12W
Sayan, Vostochnyy 25 54 0N 96 0 E
Sayan, Zapadnyy 25 52 30N 94 0 E
Saydā 30 33 35N 35 25 E
Sayghān 31 35 10N 67 55 E
Sayḩūt 29 15 12N 51 10 E
Saynshand 37 44 55N 110 11 E
Sayre, Okla., U.S.A. 71 35 20N 99 40W
Sayre, Pa., U.S.A. 68 42 0N 76 30W
Sayula 74 19 50N 103 40W
Sazan 19 40 30N 19 20 E
Sázava → 14 49 53N 14 24 E
Sazin 32 35 35N 73 30 E
Scafell Pikes 6 54 26N 3 14W
Scalpay 8 57 51N 6 40W
Scandia 64 50 20N 112 0W
Scandinavia 20 64 0N 12 0 E
Scapa Flow 8 58 52N 3 6W
Scarborough, Trin. & Tob. 75 11 11N 60 42W
Scarborough, U.K. 6 54 17N 0 24W
Scenic 70 43 49N 102 32W
Schaffhausen 14 47 42N 8 39 E
Schagen 11 52 49N 4 48 E
Schefferville 63 54 48N 66 50W
Schelde → 11 51 15N 4 16 E
Schell Creek Ra. 72 39 15N 114 30W
Schenectady 68 42 50N 73 58W
Scheveningen 11 52 6N 4 16 E
Schiedam 11 51 55N 4 25 E
Schiermonnikoog 11 53 30N 6 15 E
Schio 18 45 42N 11 21 E
Schleswig 14 54 32N 9 34 E
Schleswig-Holstein □ 14 54 10N 9 40 E
Schofield 70 44 54N 89 39W
Schouten I. 44 42 20S 148 20 E
Schouwen 11 51 43N 3 45 E
Schreiber 62 48 45N 87 20W
Schuler 65 50 20N 110 6W
Schumacher 62 48 30N 81 16W
Schurz 72 38 57N 118 48W
Schuyler 70 41 30N 97 3W
Schwäbische Alb 14 48 30N 9 30 E
Schwaner, Pegunungan 34 1 0S 112 30 E
Schwarzwald 14 48 0N 8 0 E
Schweinfurt 14 50 3N 10 12 E
Schweizer-Reneke 56 27 11S 25 18 E
Schwerin 14 53 37N 11 22 E
Schwyz 14 47 2N 8 39 E
Sciacca 18 37 30N 13 3 E
Scie, La 63 49 57N 55 36W
Scilla 18 38 18N 15 44 E
Scilly, Isles of 7 49 55N 6 15W
Scioto → 68 38 44N 83 0W
Scobey 70 48 47N 105 30W
Scone, Australia 45 32 5S 150 52 E
Scone, U.K. 8 56 25N 3 26W
Scotia 72 40 36N 124 4W
Scotland 70 43 10N 97 45W
Scotland □ 8 57 0N 4 0W
Scotland Neck 69 36 6N 77 32W
Scott, C. 46 13 30S 129 49 E
Scott City 70 38 30N 100 52W
Scott Inlet 61 71 0N 71 0W
Scott Is. 64 50 48N 128 40W
Scott L. 65 59 55N 106 18W
Scott Reef 46 14 0S 121 50 E
Scottburgh 57 30 15S 30 47 E
Scottsbluff 70 41 55N 103 35W
Scottsboro 69 34 40N 86 0W
Scottsburg 68 38 40N 85 46W
Scottsdale 44 41 9S 147 31 E
Scottsville 69 36 48N 86 10W
Scottville 68 43 57N 86 18W
Scranton 68 41 22N 75 41W
Scunthorpe 6 53 35N 0 38W
Scusciuban 29 10 18N 50 12 E
Scutari = Üsküdar 30 41 0N 29 5 E
Seabrook, L. 47 30 55S 119 40 E
Seaford 68 38 37N 75 36W
Seaforth 62 43 35N 81 25W
Seagraves 71 32 56N 102 30W
Seal → 65 59 4N 94 48W
Seal Cove 63 49 57N 56 22W
Seal L. 63 54 20N 61 30W
Sealy 71 29 46N 96 9W
Searchlight 73 35 31N 114 55W
Searcy 71 35 15N 91 45W
Searles L. 73 35 47N 117 17W
Seaside 72 45 59N 123 55W
Seaspray 45 38 25S 147 15 E
Seattle 72 47 41N 122 15W
Seaview Ra. 44 18 40S 145 45 E
Sebastián Vizcaíno, B. 74 28 0N 114 30W

Tonantins

Tepalcatepec → 74 18 35N 101 59W
Tepic 74 21 30N 104 54W
Teplice 14 50 40N 13 48 E
Tepoca, C. 74 30 20N 112 25W
Tequila 74 20 54N 103 47W
Ter → 13 42 0N 3 12 E
Ter Apel 11 52 53N 7 5 E
Téra 53 14 0N 0 45 E
Teraina, I. 41 4 43N 160 25W
Téramo 18 42 40N 13 40 E
Terang 45 38 15S 142 55 E
Terek → 23 44 0N 47 30 E
Teresina 79 5 9S 42 45W
Terewah, L. 45 29 52S 147 35 E
Terhazza 50 23 38N 5 22W
Teridgerie Cr. → 45 30 25S 148 50 E
Termez 24 37 15N 67 15 E
Términos, L. de 74 18 35N 91 30W
Térmoli 18 42 0N 15 0 E
Ternate 35 0 45N 127 25 E
Terneuzen 11 51 20N 3 50 E
Terney 25 45 3N 136 37 E
Terni 18 42 34N 12 38 E
Ternopol 22 49 30N 25 40 E
Terowie 45 32 27S 147 52 E
Terrace 64 54 30N 128 35W
Terrace Bay 62 48 47N 87 5W
Terracina 18 41 17N 13 12 E
Terralba 18 39 42N 8 38 E
Terranova = Ólbia 18 40 55N 9 30 E
Terre Haute 68 39 28N 87 24W
Terrebonne B. 71 29 15N 90 28W
Terrell 71 32 44N 96 19W
Terrenceville 63 47 40N 54 44W
Terrick Terrick 44 24 44S 145 5 E
Territoire de Belfort □ 12 47 40N 6 55 E
Terry 70 46 47N 105 20W
Terschelling 11 53 25N 5 20 E
Teruel 13 40 22N 1 8W
Tervola 20 66 6N 24 49 E
Teryaweyna L. 45 32 18S 143 22 E
Tešanj 19 44 38N 17 59 E
Teshio 36 44 53N 141 44 E
Teshio-Gawa → 36 44 53N 141 45 E
Tesiyn Gol → 37 50 40N 93 20 E
Teslin 60 60 10N 132 43W
Teslin → 64 61 34N 134 35W
Teslin L. 64 60 15N 132 57W
Tessalit 50 20 12N 1 0 E
Tessaoua 53 13 47N 7 56 E
Test → 7 51 7N 1 30W
Tetachuck L. 64 53 18N 125 55W
Tetas, Pta. 80 23 31S 70 38W
Tete 55 16 13S 33 33 E
Teteven 19 42 58N 24 17 E
Tethul → 64 60 35N 112 12W
Teton → 72 47 58N 111 0W
Tétouan 50 35 35N 5 21W
Tetovo 19 42 1N 21 2 E
Tetuán = Tétouan 50 35 35N 5 21W
Teuco → 80 25 35S 60 11W
Teulon 65 50 23N 97 16W
Teun 35 6 59S 129 8 E
Teutoburger Wald 14 52 5N 8 20 E
Tevere → 18 41 44N 12 14 E
Teverya 28 32 47N 35 32 E
Teviot → 8 55 21N 2 51W
Tewantin 45 26 27S 153 3 E
Tewkesbury 7 51 59N 2 8W
Texada I. 64 49 40N 124 25W
Texarkana, Ark., U.S.A. 71 33 25N 94 0W
Texarkana, Tex., U.S.A. 71 33 25N 94 3W
Texas 45 28 49S 151 9 E
Texas □ 71 31 40N 98 30W
Texas City 71 29 20N 94 55W
Texel 11 53 5N 4 50 E
Texhoma 71 36 32N 101 47W
Texline 71 36 26N 103 0W
Texoma L. 71 34 0N 96 38W
Teyvareh 31 33 30N 64 24 E
Teziutlán 74 19 50N 97 22W
Tezpur 33 26 40N 92 45 E
Tezzeron L. 64 54 43N 124 30W
Tha-anne → 65 60 31N 94 37W
Thaba Nchu 56 29 17S 26 52 E
Thaba Putsoa 57 29 45S 28 0 E
Thabana Ntlenyana 57 29 30S 29 16 E
Thabazimbi 57 24 40S 27 21 E
Thailand ■ 34 16 0N 102 0 E
Thailand, G. of 34 11 30N 101 0 E
Thakhek 34 17 25N 104 45 E
Thal 32 33 28N 70 33 E
Thala La 33 28 25N 97 23 E
Thallon 45 28 39S 148 49 E
Thame → 7 51 35N 1 8W
Thames 43 37 7S 175 34 E
Thames →, Canada 62 42 20N 82 25W
Thames →, U.K. 7 51 30N 0 35 E
Thane 32 19 12N 72 59 E
Thanet, I. of 7 51 21N 1 20 E
Thangoo 46 18 10S 122 22 E
Thangool 44 24 38S 150 42 E
Thanh Pho Ho Chi Minh = Phanh Bho Ho Chi Minh 34 10 58N 106 40 E
Thanjavur 32 10 48N 79 12 E
Thanlwin Myit → 33 20 0N 98 0 E
Thar Desert 32 28 0N 72 0 E
Tharad 32 24 30N 71 44 E
Thargomindah 45 27 58S 143 46 E
Tharrawaddy 33 17 38N 95 48 E
Thásos 19 40 40N 24 40 E
Thatcher, Ariz., U.S.A. 73 32 54N 109 46W
Thatcher, Colo., U.S.A. 71 37 38N 104 6W
Thaton 33 16 55N 97 22 E
Thaungdut 33 24 30N 94 40 E
Thayer 71 36 34N 91 34W
Thayetmyo 33 19 20N 95 10 E
Thazi 33 21 0N 96 5 E
The Alberga → 45 27 6S 135 33 E
The Bight 75 24 19N 75 24W
The Dalles 72 45 40N 121 11W
The English Company's Is. 44 11 50S 136 32 E
The Frome → 45 29 8S 137 54 E
The Grenadines, Is. 75 12 40N 61 20W
The Hague = 's-Gravenhage 11 52 7N 4 17 E
The Hamilton → 45 26 40S 135 19 E
The Lynd 44 19 12S 144 20 E
The Macumba → 45 27 52S 137 12 E
The Neales → 45 28 8S 136 47 E
The Officer → 47 27 46S 132 30 E
The Pas 65 53 45N 101 15W
The Rock 45 35 15S 147 2 E
The Salt Lake 45 30 6S 142 8 E
The Stevenson → 45 27 6S 135 33 E
The Warburton → 45 28 4S 137 28 E
Thebes = Thívai 19 38 19N 23 19 E
Thedford 70 41 59N 100 31W
Theebine 45 25 57S 152 34 E
Thekulthili L. 65 61 3N 110 0W
Thelon → 65 62 35N 104 3W
Theodore 44 24 55S 150 3 E
Thermaïkos Kólpos 19 40 15N 22 45 E
Thermopolis 72 43 35N 108 10W
Thermopylae P. 19 38 48N 22 35 E
Thessalía □ 19 39 30N 22 0 E
Thessalon 62 46 20N 83 30W
Thessaloníki 19 40 38N 22 58 E
Thessaloniki, Gulf of = Thermaïkos Kólpos 19 40 15N 22 45 E
Thessaly = Thessalía □ 19 39 30N 22 0 E
Thetford 7 52 25N 0 44 E
Thetford Mines 63 46 8N 71 18W
Theunissen 56 28 26S 26 43 E
Thevenard 45 32 9S 133 38 E
Thibodaux 71 29 48N 90 49W
Thicket Portage 65 55 19N 97 42W
Thief River Falls 70 48 15N 96 48W
Thiérache 12 49 51N 3 45 E
Thies 50 14 50N 16 51W
Thika 54 1 1S 37 5 E
Thikombia 43 15 44S 179 55W
Thimphu 33 27 31N 89 45 E
þingvallavatn 20 64 11N 21 9W
Thionville 12 49 20N 6 10 E
Thíra 19 36 23N 25 27 E
Thirsk 6 54 15N 1 20W
Thisted 21 56 58N 8 40 E
Thistle I. 45 35 0S 136 8 E
Thívai 19 38 19N 23 19 E
þjórsá → 20 63 47N 20 48W
Thlewiaza →, Man., Canada 65 59 43N 100 5W
Thlewiaza →, N.W.T., Canada 65 60 29N 94 40W
Thoa → 65 60 31N 109 47W
Thomas, Okla., U.S.A. 71 35 48N 98 48W
Thomas, W. Va., U.S.A. 68 39 10N 79 30W
Thomas, L. 45 26 4S 137 58 E
Thomaston 69 32 54N 84 20W
Thomasville, Ala., U.S.A. 69 31 55N 87 42W
Thomasville, Ga., U.S.A. 69 30 50N 84 0W
Thomasville, N.C., U.S.A. 69 35 55N 80 4W
Thompson, Canada 65 55 45N 97 52W
Thompson, U.S.A. 73 39 0N 109 50W
Thompson →, Canada 64 50 15N 121 24W
Thompson →, U.S.A. 70 39 46N 93 37W
Thompson Falls 72 47 37N 115 20W
Thompson Landing 65 62 56N 110 40W
Thompson Pk. 72 41 0N 123 3W
Thomson → 44 25 11S 142 53 E
Thomson's Falls = Nyahururu 54 0 2N 36 27 E
þórisvatn 20 64 20N 18 55W
þorlákshöfn 20 63 51N 21 22W
Thornaby on Tees 6 54 36N 1 19W
þórshöfn 20 66 12N 15 20W
Thouin, C. 46 20 20S 118 10 E
Thrace = Thráki □ 19 41 9N 25 30 E
Thráki □ 19 41 9N 25 30 E
Three Forks 72 45 55N 111 32W
Three Hills 64 51 43N 113 15W
Three Hummock I. 44 40 25S 144 55 E
Three Lakes 70 45 48N 89 10W
Three Points, C. 50 4 42N 2 6W
Three Rivers, Australia 47 25 10S 119 5 E
Three Rivers, U.S.A. 71 28 30N 98 10W
Three Sisters, Mt. 72 44 10N 121 46W
Throssell, L. 47 27 33S 124 10 E
Throssell Ra. 46 22 3S 121 43 E
Thubun Lakes 65 61 30N 112 0W
Thuin 11 50 20N 4 17 E
Thun 14 46 45N 7 38 E
Thundelarra 47 28 53S 117 7 E
Thunder B. 68 45 0N 83 20W
Thunder Bay 62 48 20N 89 15W
Thung Song 34 8 10N 99 40 E
Thunkar 33 27 55N 91 0 E
Thüringer Wald 14 50 35N 11 0 E
Thurles 9 52 40N 7 53W
Thurloo Downs 45 29 15S 143 30 E
Thursday I. 44 10 30S 142 3 E
Thurso, Canada 62 45 36N 75 15W
Thurso, U.K. 8 58 34N 3 31W
Thutade L. 64 57 0N 126 55W
Thylungra 45 26 4S 143 28 E
Thysville = Mbanza Ngungu 54 5 12S 14 53 E
Tia 45 31 10S 150 34 E
Tian Shan 37 43 0N 84 0 E
Tiandu 39 18 18N 109 36 E
Tian'e 39 25 1N 107 9 E
Tianhe 39 24 48N 108 40 E
Tianjin 38 39 8N 117 10 E
Tianshui 39 34 32N 105 40 E
Tianyang 39 23 42N 106 53 E
Tianzhen 38 40 24N 114 5 E
Tiaret 50 35 20N 1 21 E
Tiassalé 50 5 58N 4 57W
Tibati 51 6 22N 12 30 E
Tiber = Tevere → 18 41 44N 12 14 E
Tiber Res. 72 48 20N 111 15W
Tiberias = Teverya 28 32 47N 35 32 E
Tiberias, L. = Yam Kinneret 28 32 45N 35 35 E
Tibesti 51 21 0N 17 30 E
Tibet = Xizang □ 37 32 0N 88 0 E
Tibnīn 28 33 12N 35 24 E
Tibooburra 45 29 26S 142 1 E
Tiburón 74 29 0N 112 30W
Tichīt 50 18 21N 9 29W
Ticino → 14 45 9N 9 14 E
Ticonderoga 68 43 50N 73 28W
Ticul 74 20 20N 89 31W
Tiddim 33 23 28N 93 45 E
Tidjikja 50 18 29N 11 35W
Tidore 35 0 40N 127 25 E
Tiel, Neth. 11 51 53N 5 26 E
Tiel, Senegal 50 14 55N 15 5W
Tieling 38 42 20N 123 55 E
Tielt 11 51 0N 3 20 E
Tien Shan 31 42 0N 80 0 E
Tien-tsin = Tianjin 38 39 8N 117 10 E
T'ienching = Tianjin 38 39 8N 117 10 E
Tienen 11 50 48N 4 57 E
Tientsin = Tianjin 38 39 8N 117 10 E
Tierra Amarilla 73 36 42N 106 33W
Tierra de Campos 13 42 10N 4 50W
Tierra del Fuego, I. Gr. de 80 54 0S 69 0W
Tiétar → 13 39 50N 6 1W
Tieyon 45 26 12S 133 52 E
Tiffin 68 41 8N 83 10W
Tiflis = Tbilisi 23 41 43N 44 50 E
Tifrah 28 31 19N 34 42 E
Tifton 69 31 28N 83 32W
Tifu 35 3 39S 126 24 E
Tigil 25 57 49N 158 40 E
Tignish 63 46 58N 64 2W
Tigre → 78 4 30S 74 10W
Tigris = Dijlah, Nahr → 30 31 0N 47 25 E
Tigyaing 33 23 45N 96 10 E
Tîh, Gebel el 51 29 32N 33 26 E
Tijuana 74 32 30N 117 10W
Tikal 75 17 13N 89 24W
Tikamgarh 32 24 44N 78 50 E
Tikhoretsk 23 45 56N 40 5 E
Tiko 53 4 4N 9 20 E
Tikrīt 30 34 35N 43 37 E
Tiksi 25 71 40N 128 45 E
Tilamuta 35 0 32N 122 23 E
Tilburg 11 51 31N 5 6 E
Tilbury, Canada 62 42 17N 82 23W
Tilbury, U.K. 7 51 27N 0 24 E
Tilden, Nebr., U.S.A. 70 42 3N 97 45W
Tilden, Tex., U.S.A. 71 28 28N 98 33W
Tilichiki 25 60 27N 166 5 E
Till → 6 55 35N 2 3W
Tillabéri 53 14 28N 1 28 E
Tillamook 72 45 29N 123 55W
Tillsonburg 62 42 53N 80 44W
Tílos 19 36 27N 27 27 E
Tilpa 45 30 57S 144 24 E
Tilsit = Sovetsk 22 55 6N 21 50 E
Tilt → 8 56 50N 3 50W
Timagami L. 62 47 0N 80 10W
Timanskiy Kryazh 22 65 58N 50 5 E
Timaru 43 44 23S 171 14 E
Timau 52 0 4N 37 15 E
Timbedgha 50 16 17N 8 16W
Timber Lake 70 45 29N 101 6W
Timboon 45 38 30S 142 58 E
Timbuktu = Tombouctou 50 16 50N 3 0W
Timimoun 50 29 14N 0 16 E
Timişoara 15 45 43N 21 15 E
Timmins 62 48 28N 81 25W
Timok → 19 44 10N 22 40 E
Timon 79 5 8S 42 52W
Timor 35 9 0S 125 0 E
Timor □ 35 9 0S 125 0 E
Timor Sea 46 10 0S 127 0 E
Tinaca Pt. 35 5 30N 125 25 E
Tindouf 50 27 42N 8 10W
Tingo Maria 78 9 10S 75 54W
Tinjoub 50 29 45N 5 40W
Tinkurrin 47 32 59S 117 46 E
Tinnevelly = Tirunelveli 32 8 45N 77 45 E
Tinnoset 21 59 55N 9 3 E
Tinogasta 80 28 5S 67 32W
Tínos 19 37 33N 25 8 E
Tintinara 45 35 48S 140 2 E
Tioman, Pulau 34 2 50N 104 10 E
Tipongpani 33 27 20N 95 55 E
Tipperary 9 52 28N 8 10W
Tipperary □ 9 52 37N 7 55W
Tipton, U.K. 7 52 32N 2 4W
Tipton, Calif., U.S.A. 73 36 3N 119 19W
Tipton, Ind., U.S.A. 68 40 17N 86 0W
Tipton, Iowa, U.S.A. 70 41 45N 91 12W
Tiptonville 71 36 22N 89 30W
Tīrān 31 32 45N 51 8 E
Tirana 19 41 18N 19 49 E
Tiranë = Tirana 19 41 18N 19 49 E
Tiraspol 23 46 55N 29 35 E
Tirat Karmel 28 32 46N 34 58 E
Tirat Yehuda 28 32 1N 34 56 E
Tirat Zevi 28 32 26N 35 31 E
Tire 30 38 5N 27 50 E
Tirebolu 30 40 58N 38 45 E
Tiree 8 56 31N 6 55W
Tirgovişte 15 44 55N 25 27 E
Tirgu-Jiu 15 45 5N 23 19 E
Tirgu Mureş 15 46 31N 24 38 E
Tirich Mir 31 36 15N 71 55 E
Tirodi 32 21 40N 79 44 E
Tirol □ 14 47 3N 10 43 E
Tirso → 18 39 52N 8 33 E
Tiruchchirappalli 32 10 45N 78 45 E
Tirunelveli 32 8 45N 77 45 E
Tirupati 32 13 39N 79 25 E
Tiruppur 32 11 5N 77 22 E
Tiruvannamalai 32 12 15N 79 5 E
Tisa → 15 45 15N 20 17 E
Tisdale 65 52 50N 104 0W
Tishomingo 71 34 14N 96 38W
Tisza → 15 46 8N 20 2 E
Tit-Ary 25 71 55N 127 2 E
Titicaca, L. 78 15 30S 69 30W
Titiwa 53 12 14N 12 53 E
Titograd 19 42 30N 19 19 E
Titov Veles 19 41 46N 21 47 E
Titovo Užice 19 43 55N 19 50 E
Titule 54 3 15N 25 31 E
Titusville, Fla., U.S.A. 69 28 37N 80 49W
Titusville, Pa., U.S.A. 68 41 35N 79 39W
Tivaouane 50 14 56N 16 45W
Tiverton 7 50 54N 3 30W
Tívoli 18 41 58N 12 45 E
Tiwī 31 22 45N 59 12 E
Tizi-Ouzou 50 36 42N 4 3 E
Tizimín 74 21 0N 88 1W
Tiznit 50 29 48N 9 45W
Tjeggelvas 20 66 37N 17 45 E
Tjirebon = Cirebon 35 6 45S 108 32 E
Tlahualilo 74 26 20N 103 30W
Tlaxcala 74 19 20N 98 14W
Tlaxcala □ 74 19 30N 98 20W
Tlaxiaco 74 17 18N 97 40W
Tlell 64 53 34N 131 56W
Tlemcen 50 34 52N 1 21W
Tmassah 51 26 19N 15 51 E
Toad → 64 59 25N 124 57W
Toamasina 57 18 10S 49 25 E
Toamasina □ 57 18 0S 49 0 E
Toay 80 36 43S 64 38W
Toba 36 34 30N 136 51 E
Toba Kakar 32 31 30N 69 0 E
Tobago 75 11 10N 60 30W
Tobelo 35 1 45N 127 56 E
Tobermorey 44 22 12S 138 0 E
Tobermory, Canada 62 45 12N 81 40W
Tobermory, U.K. 8 56 37N 6 4W
Tobin, L. 46 21 45S 125 49 E
Tobin L. 65 53 35N 103 30W
Toboali 34 3 0S 106 25 E
Tobol 24 52 40N 62 39 E
Tobol → 24 58 10N 68 12 E
Toboli 35 0 38S 120 5 E
Tobolsk 24 58 15N 68 10 E
Tobruk = Tubruq 51 32 7N 23 55 E
Tocantinópolis 79 6 20S 47 25W
Tocantins → 79 1 45S 49 10W
Toccoa 69 34 32N 83 17W
Tochigi 36 36 25N 139 45 E
Tochigi □ 36 36 45N 139 45 E
Tocopilla 80 22 5S 70 10W
Tocumwal 45 35 51S 145 31 E
Tocuyo → 78 11 3N 68 23W
Todd → 44 24 52S 135 48 E
Todeli 35 1 38S 124 34 E
Todenyang 54 4 35N 35 56 E
Todos los Santos, B. de 79 12 48S 38 38W
Todos Santos 74 23 27N 110 13W
Tofield 64 53 25N 112 40W
Tofino 64 49 11N 125 55W
Tofua 43 19 45S 175 5W
Togba 50 17 26N 10 12W
Togian, Kepulauan 35 0 20S 121 50 E
Togliatti 22 53 32N 49 24 E
Togo ■ 53 8 30N 1 35 E
Togtoh 38 40 15N 111 10 E
Toinya 51 6 17N 29 46 E
Tojo 35 1 20S 121 15 E
Tokachi-Gawa → 36 42 44N 143 42 E
Tokaj 15 48 8N 21 27 E
Tokala 35 1 30S 121 40 E
Tōkamachi 36 37 8N 138 43 E
Tokanui 43 46 34S 168 56 E
Tokar 51 18 27N 37 56 E
Tokara Kaikyō 36 30 0N 130 0 E
Tokarahi 43 44 56S 170 39 E
Tokat 30 40 22N 36 35 E
Tokelau Is. 2 9 0S 171 45W
Tokmak 24 42 49N 75 15 E
Toko Ra. 44 23 5S 138 20 E
Tokushima 36 34 4N 134 34 E
Tokushima □ 36 34 15N 134 0 E
Tokuyama 36 34 3N 131 50 E
Tōkyō 36 35 45N 139 45 E
Tōkyō □ 36 35 40N 139 30 E
Tolbukhin 19 43 37N 27 49 E
Toledo, Spain 13 39 50N 4 2W
Toledo, Ohio, U.S.A. 68 41 37N 83 33W
Toledo, Oreg., U.S.A. 72 44 40N 123 59W
Toledo, Wash., U.S.A. 72 46 29N 122 51W
Toledo, Montes de 13 39 33N 4 20W
Tolga 50 34 40N 5 22 E
Toliara 57 23 21S 43 40 E
Toliara □ 57 21 0S 45 0 E
Tolima, Vol. 78 4 40N 75 19W
Tolitoli 35 1 5N 120 50 E
Tolleson 73 33 29N 112 10W
Tolo 54 2 55S 18 34 E
Tolo, Teluk 35 2 20S 122 10 E
Tolosa 13 43 8N 2 5W
Toluca 74 19 20N 99 40W
Tom Burke 57 23 5S 28 0 E
Tom Price 46 22 40S 117 48 E
Tomah 70 43 59N 90 30W
Tomahawk 70 45 28N 89 40W
Tomakomai 36 42 38N 141 36 E
Tomar 13 39 36N 8 25W
Tomaszów Mazowiecki 15 51 30N 19 57 E
Tombé 51 5 53N 31 40 E
Tombigbee → 69 31 4N 87 58W
Tombouctou 50 16 50N 3 0W
Tombstone 73 31 40N 110 4W
Tombua 56 15 55S 11 55 E
Tomelloso 13 39 10N 3 2W
Tomingley 45 32 6S 148 16 E
Tomini 35 0 30N 120 30 E
Tomini, Teluk 35 0 10S 122 0 E
Tomkinson Ranges 47 26 11S 129 5 E
Tommot 25 59 4N 126 20 E
Tomnavoulin 8 57 19N 3 18W
Tomsk 24 56 30N 85 5 E
Tonalá 74 16 8N 93 41W
Tonalea 73 36 17N 110 58W
Tonantins 78 2 45S 67 45W

Tonasket

Tonasket 72 48 45N 119 30W
Tonawanda 68 43 0N 78 54W
Tonbridge 7 51 12N 0 18 E
Tondano 35 1 35N 124 54 E
Tonekābon 31 36 45N 51 12 E
Tong Xian 38 39 55N 116 35 E
Tonga ■ 43 19 50S 174 30W
Tonga Trench 40 18 0S 175 0W
Tongaat 57 29 33S 31 9 E
Tongareva 41 9 0S 158 0W
Tongatapu 43 21 10S 174 0W
Tongcheng 39 31 4N 116 56 E
Tongchuan 39 35 6N 109 3 E
Tongdao 39 26 10N 109 42 E
Tongeren 11 50 47N 5 28 E
Tongguan 39 34 40N 110 25 E
Tonghua 38 41 42N 125 58 E
Tongjiang, Heilongjiang, China 38 47 40N 132 27 E
Tongjiang, Sichuan, China 39 31 58N 107 11 E
Tongking, G. of = Tonkin, G. of 39 20 0N 108 0 E
Tongliao 38 43 38N 122 18 E
Tongling 39 30 55N 117 48 E
Tonglu 39 29 45N 119 37 E
Tongnan 39 30 9N 105 50 E
Tongobory 57 23 32S 44 20 E
Tongoy 80 30 16S 71 31W
Tongren 39 27 43N 109 11 E
Tongres = Tongeren 11 50 47N 5 28 E
Tongsa Dzong 33 27 31N 90 31 E
Tongue 8 58 29N 4 25W
Tongue → 70 46 24N 105 52W
Tongyu 38 44 45N 123 4 E
Tongzi 39 28 9N 106 49 E
Tonk 32 26 6N 75 54 E
Tonkawa 71 36 44N 97 22W
Tonkin, G. of 39 20 0N 108 0 E
Tonlé Sap 34 13 0N 104 0 E
Tonopah 73 38 4N 117 12W
Tønsberg 21 59 19N 10 25 E
Tooele 72 40 30N 112 20W
Toompine 45 27 15S 144 19 E
Toonpan 44 19 28S 146 48 E
Toora 45 38 39S 146 23 E
Toora-Khem 25 52 28N 96 17 E
Toowoomba 45 27 32S 151 56 E
Top-ozero 22 65 35N 32 0 E
Topeka 70 39 3N 95 40W
Topki 24 55 20N 85 35 E
Topley 64 54 49N 126 18W
Topock 73 34 46N 114 29W
Topolobampo 74 25 40N 109 4W
Toppenish 72 46 27N 120 16W
Toraka Vestale 57 16 20S 43 58 E
Torata 78 17 23S 70 1W
Torbat-e Heydārīyeh 31 35 15N 59 12 E
Torbat-e Jām 31 35 16N 60 35 E
Torbay, Canada 63 47 40N 52 42W
Torbay, U.K. 7 50 26N 3 31W
Tordesillas 13 41 30N 5 0W
Torey 25 50 33N 104 50 E
Torfajökull 20 63 54N 19 0W
Torgau 14 51 32N 13 0 E
Torhout 11 51 5N 3 7 E
Torin 74 27 33N 110 15W
Torino 18 45 4N 7 40 E
Torit 51 4 27N 32 31 E
Tormes → 13 41 18N 6 29W
Tornado Mt. 64 49 55N 114 40W
Torne älv → 20 65 50N 24 12 E
Torneå = Tornio 20 65 50N 24 12 E
Torneträsk 20 68 24N 19 15 E
Tornio 20 65 50N 24 12 E
Tornionjoki → 20 65 50N 24 12 E
Tornquist 80 38 8S 62 15W
Toro, Cerro del 80 29 10S 69 50W
Toro, Pta. 74 9 22N 79 57W
Toroníios Kólpos 19 40 5N 23 30 E
Toronto, Australia 45 33 0S 151 30 E
Toronto, Canada 62 43 39N 79 20W
Toronto, U.S.A. 68 40 27N 80 36W
Toropets 22 56 30N 31 40 E
Tororo 54 0 45N 34 12 E
Toros Dağlari 30 37 0N 35 0 E
Torowie 45 33 8S 138 55 E
Torquay, Canada 65 49 9N 103 30W
Torquay, U.K. 7 50 27N 3 31W
Tôrre de Moncorvo 13 41 12N 7 8W
Torre del Greco 18 40 47N 14 22 E
Torrelavega 13 43 20N 4 5W
Torremolinos 13 36 38N 4 30W
Torrens, L. 45 31 0S 137 50 E
Torrens Cr. → 44 22 23S 145 9 E
Torrens Creek 44 20 48S 145 3 E
Torréon 74 25 33N 103 25W
Torres 74 28 46N 110 47W
Torres Strait 40 9 50S 142 20 E
Torres Vedras 13 39 5N 9 15W
Torrevieja 13 37 59N 0 42W
Torrey 73 38 18N 111 25W
Torridge → 7 50 51N 4 10W
Torridon, L. 8 57 35N 5 50W
Torrington, Conn., U.S.A. 68 41 50N 73 9W
Torrington, Wyo., U.S.A. 70 42 5N 104 8W
Tortola 75 18 19N 65 0W
Tortosa 13 40 49N 0 31 E
Tortosa, C. 13 40 41N 0 52 E
Tortue, I. de la 75 20 5N 72 57W
Tortuga, La 75 11 0N 65 22W
Torūd 31 35 25N 55 5 E
Toruń 15 53 0N 18 39 E
Tory I. 9 55 17N 8 12W
Tosa-Wan 36 33 15N 133 30 E
Toscana 18 43 30N 11 5 E
Tostado 80 29 15S 61 50W
Tosya 30 41 1N 34 2 E
Toteng 56 20 22S 22 58 E
Totma 22 60 0N 42 40 E
Totnes 7 50 26N 3 41W
Totonicapán 75 14 58N 91 12W
Tottenham 45 32 14S 147 21 E
Tottori 36 35 30N 134 15 E
Tottori □ 36 35 30N 134 12 E
Touba 50 8 22N 7 40W
Toubkal, Djebel 50 31 0N 8 0W
Tougan 50 13 11N 2 58W
Touggourt 50 33 6N 6 4 E
Tougué 50 11 25N 11 50W
Toul 12 48 40N 5 53 E
Toulepleu 50 6 32N 8 24W
Toulon 12 43 10N 5 55 E
Toulouse 12 43 37N 1 27 E
Toummo 51 22 45N 14 8 E
Toungoo 33 19 0N 96 30 E
Touraine 12 47 20N 0 30 E
Tourane = Da Nang 34 16 4N 108 13 E
Tourcoing 12 50 42N 3 10 E
Tournai 11 50 35N 3 25 E
Tournon 12 45 4N 4 50 E
Tours 12 47 22N 0 40 E
Touwsrivier 56 33 20S 20 2 E
Towamba 45 37 6S 149 43 E
Towanda 68 41 46N 76 30W
Towang 33 27 37N 91 50 E
Tower 70 47 49N 92 17W
Towerhill Cr. → 44 22 28S 144 35 E
Towner 70 48 25N 100 26W
Townsend 72 46 25N 111 32W
Townshend I. 44 22 10S 150 31 E
Townsville 44 19 15S 146 45 E
Towson 68 39 26N 76 34W
Toyah 71 31 20N 103 48W
Toyahvale 71 30 58N 103 45W
Toyama 36 36 40N 137 15 E
Toyama □ 36 36 45N 137 30 E
Toyama-Wan 36 37 0N 137 30 E
Toyohashi 36 34 45N 137 25 E
Toyokawa 36 34 48N 137 27 E
Toyonaka 36 34 50N 135 28 E
Toyooka 36 35 35N 134 48 E
Toyota 36 35 3N 137 7 E
Tozeur 50 33 56N 8 8 E
Trabzon 30 41 0N 39 45 E
Tracadie 63 47 30N 64 55W
Tracy, Calif., U.S.A. 73 37 46N 121 27W
Tracy, Minn., U.S.A. 70 44 12N 95 38W
Trafalgar, C. 13 36 10N 6 2W
Trail 64 49 5N 117 40W
Trainor L. 64 60 24N 120 17W
Tralee 9 52 16N 9 42W
Tralee B. 9 52 17N 9 55W
Tramore 9 52 10N 7 10W
Tranås 21 58 3N 14 59 E
Trancas 80 26 11S 65 20W
Trang 34 7 33N 99 38 E
Trangahy 57 19 7S 44 31 E
Trangan 35 6 40S 134 20 E
Trangie 45 32 4S 148 0 E
Trani 18 41 17N 16 24 E
Tranoroa 57 24 42S 45 4 E
Transcaucasia = Zakavkazye 23 42 0N 44 0 E
Transcona 65 49 55N 97 0W
Transilvania 15 46 19N 25 0 E
Transkei □ 57 32 15S 28 15 E
Transvaal □ 56 25 0S 29 0 E
Transylvania = Transilvania 15 46 19N 25 0 E
Transylvanian Alps 4 45 30N 25 0 E
Trápani 18 38 1N 12 30 E
Trapper Peak 72 45 56N 114 29W
Traralgon 45 38 12S 146 34 E
Tras os Montes e Alto Douro □ 13 41 25N 7 20W
Trasimeno, L. 18 43 10N 12 5 E
Traveller's L. 45 33 20S 142 0 E
Travers, Mt. 43 42 1S 172 45 E
Traverse City 68 44 45N 85 39W
Travnik 19 44 17N 17 39 E
Trayning 47 31 7S 117 16 E
Trébbia → 18 45 4N 9 41 E
Trebinje 19 42 44N 18 22 E
Třeboň 14 48 59N 14 48 E
Tredegar 7 51 47N 3 16W
Tregaron 7 52 14N 3 56W
Tregrosse Is. 44 17 41S 150 43 E
Tréguier 12 48 47N 3 16W
Treherne 65 49 38N 98 42W
Treinta y Tres 80 33 16S 54 17W
Trekveld 56 30 35S 19 45 E
Trelew 80 43 10S 65 20W
Trelleborg 21 55 20N 13 10 E
Tremonton 72 41 45N 112 10W
Tremp 13 42 10N 0 52 E
Trenche → 62 47 46N 72 53W
Trenggalek 35 8 3S 111 43 E
Trenque Lauquen 80 36 5S 62 45W
Trent → 6 53 33N 0 44W
Trentino-Alto Adige □ 18 46 30N 11 0 E
Trento 18 46 5N 11 8 E
Trenton, Canada 62 44 10N 77 34W
Trenton, Mo., U.S.A. 70 40 5N 93 37W
Trenton, N.J., U.S.A. 68 40 15N 74 41W
Trenton, Nebr., U.S.A. 70 40 14N 101 4W
Trenton, Tenn., U.S.A. 71 35 58N 88 57W
Trepassey 63 46 43N 53 25W
Tréport, Le 12 50 3N 1 20 E
Tres Arroyos 80 38 26S 60 20W
Três Corações 79 21 44S 45 15W
Três Lagoas 79 20 50S 51 43W
Tres Marías 74 21 25N 106 28W
Tres Montes, C. 80 46 50S 75 30W
Tres Puentes 80 27 50S 70 15W
Tres Puntas, C. 80 47 0S 66 0W
Três Rios 79 22 6S 43 15W
Treungen 21 59 1N 8 31 E
Treviso 18 45 40N 12 15 E
Triabunna 44 42 30S 147 55 E
Tribulation, C. 44 16 5S 145 29 E
Tribune 70 38 30N 101 45W
Trichinopoly = Tiruchchirappalli 32 10 45N 78 45 E
Trichur 32 10 30N 76 18 E
Trida 45 33 1S 145 1 E
Trier 14 49 45N 6 37 E
Trieste 18 45 39N 13 45 E
Triglav 18 46 21N 13 50 E
Tríkkala 19 39 34N 21 47 E
Trikora, Puncak 35 4 15S 138 45 E
Trim 9 53 34N 6 48W
Trincomalee 32 8 38N 81 15 E
Trindade, I. 2 20 20S 29 50W
Trinidad, Bolivia 78 14 46S 64 50W
Trinidad, Colombia 78 5 25N 71 40W
Trinidad, Cuba 75 21 48N 80 0W
Trinidad, Uruguay 80 33 30S 56 50W
Trinidad, U.S.A. 71 37 15N 104 30W
Trinidad, W. Indies 75 10 30N 61 15W
Trinidad → 74 17 49N 95 9W
Trinidad, I. 80 39 10S 62 0W
Trinidad & Tobago ■ 75 10 30N 61 20W
Trinity, Canada 63 48 59N 53 55W
Trinity, U.S.A. 71 30 59N 95 25W
Trinity →, Calif., U.S.A. 72 41 11N 123 42W
Trinity →, Tex., U.S.A. 71 30 30N 95 0W
Trinity B. 63 48 20N 53 10W
Trinity Mts. 72 40 20N 118 50W
Trinkitat 51 18 45N 37 51 E
Trion 69 34 35N 85 18W
Tripoli = Tarābulus, Lebanon 30 34 31N 35 50 E
Tripoli = Tarābulus, Libya 51 32 49N 13 7 E
Tripolis 19 37 31N 22 25 E
Tripp 70 43 16N 97 58W
Tripura □ 33 24 0N 92 0 E
Tristan da Cunha 2 37 6S 12 20W
Trivandrum 32 8 41N 77 0 E
Trnava 15 48 23N 17 35 E
Trochu 64 51 50N 113 13W
Trodely I. 62 52 15N 79 26W
Troglav 18 43 56N 16 36 E
Troilus, L. 62 50 50N 74 35W
Trois-Pistoles 63 48 5N 69 10W
Trois-Rivières 62 46 25N 72 34W
Troitsk 24 54 10N 61 35 E
Troitsko Pechorsk 22 62 40N 56 10 E
Trölladyngja 20 64 54N 17 16W
Trollhättan 21 58 17N 12 20 E
Tromelin I. 3 15 52S 54 25 E
Troms fylke □ 20 68 56N 19 0 E
Tromsø 20 69 40N 18 56 E
Tronador 80 41 10S 71 50W
Trondheim 20 63 36N 10 25 E
Trondheimsfjorden 20 63 35N 10 30 E
Troon 8 55 33N 4 40W
Tropic 73 37 36N 112 4W
Trossachs, The 8 56 14N 4 24W
Trostan 9 55 4N 6 10W
Trotternish 8 57 32N 6 15W
Troup 71 32 10N 95 3W
Trout → 64 61 19N 119 51W
Trout L., N.W.T., Canada 64 60 40N 121 14W
Trout L., Ont., Canada 65 51 20N 93 15W
Trout Lake 62 46 10N 85 2W
Trout River 63 49 29N 58 8W
Trouville-sur-Mer 12 49 21N 0 5 E
Trowbridge 7 51 18N 2 12W
Troy, Turkey 30 39 57N 26 12 E
Troy, Ala., U.S.A. 69 31 50N 85 58W
Troy, Idaho, U.S.A. 72 46 44N 116 46W
Troy, Kans., U.S.A. 70 39 47N 95 2W
Troy, Mo., U.S.A. 70 38 56N 90 59W
Troy, Mont., U.S.A. 72 48 30N 115 58W
Troy, N.Y., U.S.A. 68 42 45N 73 39W
Troy, Ohio, U.S.A. 68 40 0N 84 10W
Troyes 12 48 19N 4 3 E
Trucial States = United Arab Emirates ■ 31 23 50N 54 0 E
Truckee 72 39 20N 120 11W
Trujillo, Hond. 75 16 0N 86 0W
Trujillo, Peru 78 8 6S 79 0W
Trujillo, Spain 13 39 28N 5 55W
Trujillo, U.S.A. 71 35 34N 104 44W
Trujillo, Venezuela 78 9 22N 70 38W
Trumann 71 35 42N 90 32W
Trumbull, Mt. 73 36 25N 113 8W
Trundle 45 32 53S 147 35 E
Trung-Phan 34 16 0N 108 0 E
Truro, Canada 63 45 21N 63 14W
Truro, U.K. 7 50 17N 5 2W
Truslove 47 33 20S 121 45 E
Truth or Consequences 73 33 9N 107 16W
Trutnov 14 50 37N 15 54 E
Tryon 69 35 15N 82 16W
Tsaratanana 57 16 47S 47 39 E
Tsaratanana, Mt. de 57 14 0S 49 0 E
Tsau 56 20 8S 22 22 E
Tselinograd 24 51 10N 71 30 E
Tsetserleg 37 47 36N 101 32 E
Tshabong 56 26 2S 22 29 E
Tshane 56 24 5S 21 54 E
Tshela 54 4 57S 13 4 E
Tshesebe 57 21 51S 27 32 E
Tshikapa 54 6 28S 20 48 E
Tshofa 54 5 13S 25 16 E
Tshwane 56 22 24S 22 1 E
Tsigara 56 20 22S 25 54 E
Tsihombe, Madag. 55 25 10S 45 41 E
Tsihombe, Madag. 57 25 18S 45 29 E
Tsimlyanskoye Vdkhr. 23 48 0N 43 0 E
Tsinan = Jinan 38 36 38N 117 1 E
Tsineng 56 27 5S 23 5 E
Tsinghai = Qinghai □ 37 36 0N 98 0 E
Tsingtao = Qingdao 38 36 5N 120 20 E
Tsinjomitondraka 57 15 40S 47 8 E
Tsiroanomandidy 57 18 46S 46 2 E
Tsivory 57 24 4S 46 5 E
Tskhinvali 23 42 14N 44 1 E
Tsna → 22 54 55N 41 58 E
Tsodilo Hill 56 18 49S 21 43 E
Tsolo 57 31 18S 28 37 E
Tsomo 57 32 0S 27 42 E
Tsu 36 34 45N 136 25 E
Tsu L. 64 60 40N 111 52W
Tsuchiura 36 36 5N 140 15 E
Tsugaru-Kaikyō 36 41 35N 141 0 E
Tsumeb 56 19 9S 17 44 E
Tsumis 56 23 39S 17 29 E
Tsuruga 36 35 45N 136 2 E
Tsuruoka 36 38 44N 139 50 E
Tsushima 36 34 20N 129 20 E
Tual 35 5 38S 132 44 E
Tuam 9 53 30N 8 50W
Tuamotu Arch. 41 17 0S 144 0W
Tuamotu Ridge 41 20 0S 138 0W
Tuao 35 17 55N 122 22 E
Tuapse 23 44 5N 39 10 E
Tuatapere 43 46 8S 167 41 E
Tuba City 73 36 8N 111 18W
Tuban 35 6 54S 112 3 E
Tubarão 80 28 30S 49 0W
Tūbās 28 32 20N 35 22 E
Tubau 34 3 10N 113 40 E
Tübingen 14 48 31N 9 4 E
Tubruq 51 32 7N 23 55 E
Tubuaeran I. 41 3 51N 159 22W
Tubuai Is. 41 25 0S 150 0W
Tucacas 78 10 48N 68 19W
Tuchodi → 64 58 17N 123 42W
Tucson 73 32 14N 110 59W
Tucumcari 71 35 12N 103 45W
Tucupita 78 9 2N 62 3W
Tucuruí 79 3 42S 49 44W
Tudela 13 42 4N 1 39W
Tudmur 30 34 36N 38 15 E
Tudor, L. 63 55 50N 65 25W
Tuen 45 28 33S 145 37 E
Tugela → 57 29 14S 31 30 E
Tuguegarao 35 17 35N 121 42 E
Tugur 25 53 44N 136 45 E
Tukangbesi, Kepulauan 35 6 0S 124 0 E
Tukarak I. 62 56 15N 78 45W
Tūkrah 51 32 30N 20 37 E
Tuktoyaktuk 60 69 27N 133 2W
Tukuyu 54 9 17S 33 35 E
Tula, Hidalgo, Mexico 74 20 0N 99 20W
Tula, Tamaulipas, Mexico 74 23 0N 99 40W
Tula, U.S.S.R. 22 54 13N 37 38 E
Tulak 31 33 55N 63 40 E
Tulancingo 74 20 5N 99 22W
Tulare 73 36 15N 119 26W
Tulare Lake Bed 73 36 0N 119 48W
Tularosa 73 33 4N 106 1W
Tulbagh 56 33 16S 19 6 E
Tulcán 78 0 48N 77 43W
Tulcea 15 45 13N 28 46 E
Tulemalu L. 65 62 58N 99 25W
Tuli, Indonesia 35 1 24S 122 26 E
Tuli, Zimbabwe 55 21 58S 29 13 E
Tulia 71 34 35N 101 44W
Ţulkarm 28 32 19N 35 2 E
Tullahoma 69 35 23N 86 12W
Tullamore, Australia 45 32 39S 147 36 E
Tullamore, Ireland 9 53 17N 7 30W
Tulle 12 45 16N 1 46 E
Tullibigeal 45 33 25S 146 44 E
Tullow 9 52 48N 6 45W
Tully 44 17 56S 145 55 E
Ţulmaythah 51 32 40N 20 55 E
Tulmur 44 22 40S 142 20 E
Tulsa 71 36 10N 96 0W
Tulsequah 64 58 39N 133 35W
Tulua 78 4 6N 76 11W
Tulun 25 54 32N 100 35 E
Tulungagung 34 8 5S 111 54 E
Tum 35 3 36S 130 21 E
Tuma → 75 13 6N 84 35W
Tumaco 78 1 50N 78 45W
Tumatumari 78 5 20N 58 55W
Tumba, L. 54 0 50S 18 0 E
Tumbarumba 45 35 44S 148 0 E
Túmbes 78 3 37S 80 27W
Tumby Bay 45 34 21S 136 8 E
Tumen 38 43 0N 129 50 E
Tumen Jiang → 38 42 20N 130 35 E
Tumeremo 78 7 18N 61 30W
Tumkur 32 13 18N 77 6 E
Tummel, L. 8 56 43N 3 55W
Tump 31 26 7N 62 16 E
Tumpat 34 6 11N 102 10 E
Tumu 50 10 56N 1 56W
Tumucumaque, Serra 79 2 0N 55 0W
Tumut 45 35 16S 148 13 E
Tumwater 72 47 0N 122 58W
Tunas de Zaza 75 21 39N 79 34W
Tunbridge Wells 7 51 7N 0 16 E
Tuncurry 45 32 17S 152 29 E
Tunduma 52 9 20S 32 48 E
Tunduru 54 11 8S 37 25 E
Tundzha → 19 41 40N 26 35 E
Tunga Pass 33 29 0N 94 14 E
Tungabhadra → 32 15 57N 78 15 E
Tungaru 51 10 9N 30 52 E
Tungla 75 13 24N 84 21W
Tungnafellsjökull 20 64 45N 17 55W
Tungsten 64 61 57N 128 16W
Tunguska, Nizhnyaya → 25 65 48N 88 4 E
Tunguska, Podkamennaya → 25 61 36N 90 18 E
Tunica 71 34 43N 90 23W
Tunis 50 36 50N 10 11 E
Tunisia ■ 50 33 30N 9 10 E
Tunja 78 5 33N 73 25W
Tunliu 38 36 13N 112 52 E
Tunnsjøen 20 64 45N 13 25 E
Tunungayualok I. 63 56 0N 61 0W
Tunuyán → 80 33 33S 67 30W
Tunxi 39 29 42N 118 25 E
Tuolumne 73 37 59N 120 16W
Tuoy-Khaya 25 62 32N 111 25 E
Tupelo 69 34 15N 88 42W
Tupik 25 54 26N 119 57 E
Tupinambaranas 78 3 0S 58 0W
Tupiza 80 21 30S 65 40W
Tupper 64 55 32N 120 1W
Tupper Lake 68 44 18N 74 30W
Tupungato, Cerro 80 33 15S 69 50W
Tuquan 38 45 18N 121 38 E
Tuque, La 62 47 30N 72 50W
Túquerres 78 1 5N 77 37W
Tura 25 64 20N 100 17 E

Valle Hermoso

Turabah 30 28 20N 43 15 E
Tūrān, Iran 31 35 39N 56 42 E
Turan, U.S.S.R. 25 51 55N 95 0 E
Turayf 30 31 41N 38 39 E
Turda 15 46 34N 23 47 E
Turek 15 52 3N 18 30 E
Turfan = Turpan 37 43 58N 89 10 E
Turfan Depression = Turpan Hami 37 42 40N 89 25 E
Turgutlu 30 38 30N 27 48 E
Turhal 30 40 24N 36 5 E
Turia → 13 39 27N 0 19W
Turiaçu 79 1 40S 45 19W
Turiaçu → 79 1 36S 45 19W
Turin = Torino 18 45 4N 7 40 E
Turin 64 49 58N 112 31W
Turkana, L. 54 3 30N 36 5 E
Turkestan 24 43 17N 68 16 E
Turkey ■ 30 39 0N 36 0 E
Turkey Creek 46 17 2S 128 12 E
Turkmen S.S.R. □ 24 39 0N 59 0 E
Turks Is. 75 21 20N 71 20W
Turks Island Passage 75 21 30N 71 30W
Turku 21 60 30N 22 19 E
Turlock 73 37 30N 120 55W
Turnagain → 64 59 12N 127 35W
Turnagain, C. 43 40 28S 176 38 E
Turneffe Is. 74 17 20N 87 50W
Turner, Australia 46 17 52S 128 16 E
Turner, U.S.A. 72 48 52N 108 25W
Turner Pt. 44 11 47S 133 32 E
Turner Valley 64 50 40N 114 17W
Turnhout 11 51 19N 4 57 E
Turnor L. 65 56 35N 108 35W
Tŭrnovo 19 43 5N 25 41 E
Turnu Măgurele 15 43 46N 24 56 E
Turnu Rosu Pasul 15 45 33N 24 17 E
Turnu-Severin 15 44 39N 22 41 E
Turon 71 37 48N 98 27W
Turpan 37 43 58N 89 10 E
Turpan Hami 37 42 40N 89 25 E
Turriff 8 57 32N 2 28W
Turtle Hd. I. 44 10 56S 142 37 E
Turtle L. 65 53 36N 108 38W
Turtle Lake, N. Dak., U.S.A. 70 47 30N 100 55W
Turtle Lake, Wis., U.S.A. 70 45 22N 92 10W
Turtleford 65 53 23N 108 57W
Turukhansk 25 65 21N 88 5 E
Turun ja Porin lääni □ 21 60 27N 22 15 E
Tuscaloosa 69 33 13N 87 31W
Tuscany = Toscana 18 43 30N 11 5 E
Tuscola, Ill., U.S.A. 68 39 48N 88 15W
Tuscola, Tex., U.S.A. 71 32 15N 99 48W
Tuscumbia 69 34 42N 87 42W
Tuskar Rock 9 52 12N 6 10W
Tuskegee 69 32 24N 85 39W
Tuticorin 32 8 50N 78 12 E
Tutóia 79 2 45S 42 20W
Tutong 34 4 47N 114 40 E
Tutrakan 19 44 2N 26 40 E
Tutshi L. 64 59 56N 134 30W
Tuttle 70 47 9N 100 0W
Tuttlingen 14 47 59N 8 50 E
Tutuala 35 8 25S 127 15 E
Tutuila 43 14 19S 170 50W
Tuva A.S.S.R. □ 25 51 30N 95 0 E
Tuvalu ■ 3 8 0S 178 0 E
Tuxpan 74 20 58N 97 23W
Tuxtla Gutiérrez 74 16 50N 93 10W
Tuy 13 42 3N 8 39W
Tuya L. 64 59 7N 130 35W
Tuz Gölü 30 38 45N 33 30 E
Ṭūz Khurmātū 30 34 56N 44 38 E
Tuzla 19 44 34N 18 41 E
Tweed → 8 55 42N 2 10W
Tweed Heads 45 28 10S 153 31 E
Tweedsmuir Prov. Park 64 53 0N 126 20W
Twentynine Palms 73 34 10N 116 4W
Twillingate 63 49 42N 54 45W
Twin Bridges 72 45 33N 112 23W
Twin Falls 72 42 30N 114 30W
Twin Valley 70 47 18N 96 15W
Twisp 72 48 21N 120 5W
Two Harbors 70 47 1N 91 40W
Two Hills 64 53 43N 111 52W
Two Rivers 68 44 10N 87 31W
Twofold B. 45 37 8S 149 59 E
Tychy 15 50 9N 18 59 E
Tyler, Minn., U.S.A. 70 44 18N 96 8W
Tyler, Tex., U.S.A. 71 32 18N 95 18W
Tynda 25 55 10N 124 43 E
Tyne → 6 54 58N 1 28W
Tyne & Wear □ 6 54 55N 1 35W
Tynemouth 6 55 1N 1 27W
Tyre = Sūr 28 33 19N 35 16 E
Tyrifjorden 21 60 2N 10 8 E
Tyrol = Tirol □ 14 47 3N 10 43 E
Tyrrell → 45 35 26S 142 51 E
Tyrrell, L. 45 35 20S 142 50 E
Tyrrell Arm 65 62 27N 97 30W
Tyrrell L. 65 63 7N 105 27W
Tyrrhenian Sea 16 40 0N 12 30 E
Tysfjorden 20 68 7N 16 25 E
Tyulgan 22 52 22N 56 12 E
Tyumen 24 57 11N 65 29 E
Tywi → 7 51 48N 4 20W
Tywyn 7 52 36N 4 5W
Tzaneen 57 23 47S 30 9 E
Tzukong = Zigong 39 29 15N 104 48 E

U

Uanda 44 21 37S 144 55 E
Uarsciek 29 2 28N 45 55 E
Uato-Udo 35 9 7S 125 36 E
Uatumã → 78 2 26S 57 37W
Uaupés 78 0 8S 67 5W
Uaupés → 78 0 2N 67 16W
Ubá 80 21 8S 43 0W
Ubaitaba 79 14 18S 39 20W
Ubangi = Oubangi → 54 0 30S 17 50 E
Ubauro 32 28 15N 69 45 E
Ube 36 33 56N 131 15 E
Ubeda 13 38 3N 3 23W
Uberaba 79 19 50S 47 55W
Uberlândia 79 19 0S 48 20W
Ubombo 57 27 31S 32 4 E
Ubon Ratchathani 34 15 15N 104 50 E
Ubundu 54 0 22S 25 30 E
Ucayali → 78 4 30S 73 30W
Uchi Lake 65 51 5N 92 35W
Uchiura-Wan 36 42 25N 140 40 E
Uchur → 25 58 48N 130 35 E
Ucluelet 64 48 57N 125 32W
Uda → 25 54 42N 135 14 E
Udaipur 32 24 36N 73 44 E
Udaipur Garhi 33 27 0N 86 35 E
Uddevalla 21 58 21N 11 55 E
Uddjaur 20 65 25N 21 15 E
Udgir 32 18 25N 77 5 E
Udhampur 32 33 0N 75 5 E
Udi 53 6 17N 7 21 E
Údine 18 46 5N 13 10 E
Udmurt A.S.S.R. □ 22 57 30N 52 30 E
Udon Thani 34 17 29N 102 46 E
Udupi 32 13 25N 74 42 E
Ueda 36 36 24N 138 16 E
Uele → 54 3 45N 24 45 E
Uelen 25 66 10N 170 0W
Uelzen 14 53 0N 10 33 E
Ufa 22 54 45N 55 55 E
Ufa → 22 54 40N 56 0 E
Ugab → 56 20 55S 13 30 E
Ugalla → 54 5 8S 30 42 E
Uganda ■ 54 2 0N 32 0 E
Ugie 57 31 10S 28 13 E
Uglegorsk 25 49 5N 142 2 E
Ugolyak 25 64 33N 120 30 E
Uhrichsville 68 40 23N 81 22W
Uíge 54 7 30S 14 40 E
Üiju 38 40 15N 124 35 E
Uinta Mts. 72 40 45N 110 30W
Uitenhage 56 33 40S 25 28 E
Uithuizen 11 53 24N 6 41 E
Ujjain 32 23 9N 75 43 E
Újpest 15 47 32N 19 6 E
Ujung Pandang 35 5 10S 119 20 E
Uka 25 57 50N 162 0 E
Ukerewe I. 54 2 0S 33 0 E
Ukhrul 33 25 10N 94 25 E
Ukhta 22 63 55N 54 0 E
Ukiah 72 39 10N 123 9W
Ukrainian S.S.R. □ 23 49 0N 32 0 E
Ukwi 56 23 29S 20 30 E
Ulaanbaatar 37 47 55N 106 53 E
Ulaangom 37 50 0N 92 10 E
Ulan Bator = Ulaanbaatar 37 47 55N 106 53 E
Ulan Ude 25 51 45N 107 40 E
Ulcinj 19 41 58N 19 10 E
Ulco 56 28 21S 24 15 E
Ulhasnagar 32 19 15N 73 10 E
Ulladulla 45 35 21S 150 29 E
Ullapool 8 57 54N 5 10W
Ullswater 6 54 35N 2 52W
Ullung-do 38 37 30N 130 30 E
Ulm 14 48 23N 10 0 E
Ulmarra 45 29 37S 153 4 E
Ulonguè 55 14 37S 34 19 E
Ulricehamn 21 57 46N 13 26 E
Ulster □ 9 54 35N 6 30W
Ulungur → 37 47 1N 87 24 E
Ulutau 24 48 39N 67 1 E
Ulverston 6 54 13N 3 7W
Ulverstone 44 41 11S 146 11 E
Ulya 25 59 10N 142 0 E
Ulyanovsk 22 54 20N 48 25 E
Ulyasutay 37 47 56N 97 28 E
Ulysses 71 37 39N 101 25W
Umala 78 17 25S 68 5W
Uman 23 48 40N 30 12 E
Umaria 33 23 35N 80 50 E
Umarkot 32 25 15N 69 40 E
Umatilla 72 45 58N 119 17W
Umba 22 66 50N 34 20 E
Umbrella Mts. 43 45 35S 169 5 E
Umbria □ 18 42 53N 12 30 E
Ume älv → 20 63 45N 20 20 E
Umeå 20 63 45N 20 20 E
Umera 35 0 12S 129 37 E
Umkomaas 57 30 13S 30 48 E
Umm al Qaywayn 31 25 30N 55 35 E
Umm Bel 51 13 35N 28 0 E
Umm el Fahm 28 32 31N 35 9 E
Umm Lajj 30 25 0N 37 23 E
Umm Qays 28 32 40N 35 41 E
Umm Ruwaba 51 12 50N 31 20 E
Umnak 60 53 20N 168 20W
Umniati → 55 16 49S 28 45 E
Umpqua → 72 43 42N 124 3W
Umtata 57 31 36S 28 49 E
Umuarama 79 23 45S 53 20W
Umzimvubu = Port St. Johns 57 31 38S 29 33 E
Umzinto 57 30 15S 30 45 E
Unac → 18 44 30N 16 9 E
Unalaska 60 53 40N 166 40W
Uncía 78 18 25S 66 40W
Uncompahgre Pk. 73 38 5N 107 32W
Underberg 57 29 50S 29 22 E
Underbool 45 35 10S 141 51 E
Ungarie 45 33 38S 146 56 E
Ungarra 45 34 12S 136 2 E
Ungava B. 61 59 30N 67 30W
Ungava Pen. 61 60 0N 74 0W
Unggi 38 42 16N 130 28 E
União da Vitória 80 26 13S 51 5W
Unimak 60 55 0N 164 0W
Unimak Pass. 60 53 30N 165 15W
Union, Miss., U.S.A. 71 32 34N 89 14W
Union, Mo., U.S.A. 70 38 25N 91 0W
Union, S.C., U.S.A. 69 34 43N 81 39W
Unión, La, Chile 80 40 10S 73 0W
Unión, La, El Salv. 75 13 20N 87 50W
Union, Mt. 73 34 34N 112 21W
Union City, Pa., U.S.A. 68 41 53N 79 50W
Union City, Tenn., U.S.A. 71 36 25N 89 0W
Union Gap 72 46 38N 120 29W
Union of Soviet Socialist Republics ■ 25 60 0N 100 0 E
Union Springs 69 32 9N 85 44W
Uniondale 56 33 39S 23 7 E
Uniontown 68 39 54N 79 45W
Unionville 70 40 29N 93 1W
United Arab Emirates ■ 31 23 50N 54 0 E
United Kingdom ■ 5 55 0N 3 0W
United States of America ■ 67 37 0N 96 0W
United States Trust Terr. of the Pacific Is. □ 40 10 0N 160 0 E
Unity 65 52 30N 109 5W
Unnao 33 26 35N 80 30 E
Unst 8 60 50N 0 55W
Unuk → 64 56 5N 131 3W
Ünye 30 41 5N 37 15 E
Upata 78 8 1N 62 24W
Upemba, L. 54 8 30S 26 20 E
Upington 56 28 25S 21 15 E
Upolu 43 13 58S 172 0W
Upper Alkali Lake 72 41 47N 120 8W
Upper Arrow L. 64 50 30N 117 50W
Upper Foster L. 65 56 47N 105 20W
Upper Hutt 43 41 8S 175 5 E
Upper Klamath L. 72 42 16N 121 55W
Upper L. Erne 9 54 14N 7 22W
Upper Lake 72 39 10N 122 55W
Upper Musquodoboit 63 45 10N 62 58W
Upper Red L. 70 48 0N 95 0W
Upper Sandusky 68 40 50N 83 17W
Upper Taimyr → 25 74 15N 99 48 E
Upper Volta = Burkina Faso ■ 50 12 0N 1 0W
Uppsala 21 59 53N 17 38 E
Uppsala län □ 21 60 0N 17 30 E
Upstart, C. 44 19 41S 147 45 E
Upton 70 44 8N 104 35W
Ur 30 30 55N 46 25 E
Uracara 78 2 20S 57 50W
Urad Qianqi 38 40 40N 108 30 E
Urakawa 36 42 9N 142 47 E
Ural → 23 47 0N 51 48 E
Ural, Mt. 45 33 21S 146 12 E
Ural Mts. = Uralskie Gory 22 60 0N 59 0 E
Ural Mts. 4 60 0N 59 0 E
Uralla 45 30 37S 151 29 E
Uralsk 22 51 20N 51 20 E
Uralskie Gory 22 60 0N 59 0 E
Urandangi 44 21 32S 138 14 E
Uranium City 65 59 34N 108 37W
Uranquinty 45 35 10S 147 12 E
Urawa 36 35 50N 139 40 E
Uray 24 60 5N 65 15 E
Urbana, Ill., U.S.A. 68 40 7N 88 12W
Urbana, Ohio, U.S.A. 68 40 9N 83 44W
Urbana, La 78 7 8N 66 56W
Urbino 18 43 43N 12 38 E
Urbión, Picos de 13 42 1N 2 52W
Urcos 78 13 40S 71 38W
Urda 23 48 52N 47 23 E
Urdzhar 24 47 5N 81 38 E
Ure → 6 54 20N 1 25W
Urengoy 24 65 58N 28 25 E
Ures 74 29 30N 110 30W
Urfa 30 37 12N 38 50 E
Urfahr 14 48 19N 14 17 E
Urgench 24 41 40N 60 41 E
Uribia 78 11 43N 72 16W
Urim 28 31 18N 34 32 E
Urique → 74 26 29N 107 58W
Urk 11 52 39N 5 36 E
Urla 30 38 20N 26 47 E
Urmia = Orūmīyeh 30 37 40N 45 0 E
Urmia, L. = Orūmīyeh, Daryācheh-ye 30 37 50N 45 30 E
Uruana 79 15 30S 49 41W
Uruapan 74 19 30N 102 0W
Urubamba 78 13 20S 72 10W
Urubamba → 78 10 43S 73 48W
Uruçuí 79 7 20S 44 28W
Uruguai → 80 26 0S 53 30W
Uruguaiana 80 29 50S 57 0W
Uruguay ■ 80 32 30S 56 30W
Uruguay → 80 34 12S 58 18W
Urumchi = Ürümqi 37 43 45N 87 45 E
Ürümqi 37 43 45N 87 45 E
Urup, Os. 25 46 0N 151 0 E
Uryung-Khaya 25 72 48N 113 23 E
Usa → 22 65 57N 56 55 E
Uşak 30 38 43N 29 28 E
Usakos 56 21 54S 15 31 E
Usedom 14 53 50N 13 55 E
Ush-Tobe 24 45 16N 78 0 E
Ushant = Ouessant, I. d' 12 48 28N 5 6W
Ushuaia 80 54 50S 68 23W
Ushumun 25 52 47N 126 32 E
Usk → 7 51 37N 2 56W
Üsküdar 30 41 0N 29 5 E
Usman 22 52 5N 39 48 E
Usoke 54 5 8S 32 24 E
Usolye Sibirskoye 25 52 48N 103 40 E
Usoro 53 5 33N 6 11 E
Uspallata, P. de 80 32 37S 69 22W
Uspenskiy 24 48 41N 72 43 E
Ussuriysk 25 43 48N 131 59 E
Ust-Aldan = Batamay 25 63 30N 129 15 E
Ust Amginskoye = Khandyga 25 62 42N 135 35 E
Ust-Bolsheretsk 25 52 50N 156 15 E
Ust chaun 25 68 47N 170 30 E
Ust'-Ilga 25 55 5N 104 55 E
Ust Ilimpeya = Yukti 25 63 26N 105 42 E
Ust-Ilimsk 25 58 3N 102 39 E
Ust Ishim 24 57 45N 71 10 E
Ust-Kamchatsk 25 56 10N 162 28 E
Ust-Kamenogorsk 24 50 0N 82 36 E
Ust-Karenga 25 54 25N 116 30 E
Ust Khayryuzova 25 57 15N 156 45 E
Ust-Kut 25 56 50N 105 42 E
Ust Kuyga 25 70 1N 135 43 E
Ust Maya 25 60 30N 134 28 E
Ust-Mil 25 59 40N 133 11 E
Ust-Nera 25 64 35N 143 15 E
Ust-Nyukzha 25 56 34N 121 37 E
Ust Olenek 25 73 0N 119 48 E
Ust-Omchug 25 61 9N 149 38 E
Ust Port 24 69 40N 84 26 E
Ust Tsilma 22 65 25N 52 0 E
Ust-Tungir 25 55 25N 120 36 E
Ust Urt = Ustyurt, Plato 24 44 0N 55 0 E
Ust Usa 22 66 0N 56 30 E
Ust Vorkuta 24 67 24N 64 0 E
Ústí nad Labem 14 50 41N 14 3 E
Ustica 18 38 42N 13 10 E
Ustinov 22 56 51N 53 14 E
Ustroń 12 49 43N 18 48 E
Ustye 25 57 46N 94 37 E
Ustyurt, Plato 24 44 0N 55 0 E
Usu 37 44 27N 84 40 E
Usuki 36 33 8N 131 49 E
Usulután 75 13 25N 88 28W
Usumacinta → 74 17 0N 91 0W
Usumbura = Bujumbura 54 3 16S 29 18 E
Uta 35 4 33S 136 0 E
Utah □ 72 39 30N 111 30W
Utah, L. 72 40 10N 111 58W
Ute Cr. → 71 35 21N 103 45W
Utete 54 8 0S 38 45 E
Utiariti 78 13 0S 58 10W
Utica 68 43 5N 75 18W
Utik L. 65 55 15N 96 0W
Utikuma L. 64 55 50N 115 30W
Utrecht, Neth. 11 52 5N 5 8 E
Utrecht, S. Africa 57 27 38S 30 20 E
Utrecht □ 11 52 6N 5 7 E
Utrera 13 37 12N 5 48W
Utsjoki 20 69 51N 26 59 E
Utsunomiya 36 36 30N 139 50 E
Uttar Pradesh □ 32 27 0N 80 0 E
Uttaradit 34 17 36N 100 5 E
Uttoxeter 6 52 53N 1 50W
Uudenmaan lääni □ 21 60 25N 25 0 E
Uusikaarlepyy 20 63 32N 22 31 E
Uusikaupunki 21 60 47N 21 25 E
Uva 22 56 59N 52 13 E
Uvalde 71 29 15N 99 48W
Uvat 24 59 5N 68 50 E
Uvinza 54 5 5S 30 24 E
Uvira 54 3 22S 29 3 E
Uvs Nuur 37 50 20N 92 30 E
Uwajima 36 33 10N 132 35 E
Uxin Qi 38 38 50N 109 5 E
Uxmal 74 20 22N 89 46W
Uyandi 25 69 19N 141 0 E
Uyo 53 5 1N 7 53 E
Uyuni 78 20 35S 66 47W
Uzbek S.S.R. □ 24 41 30N 65 0 E
Uzen 23 43 27N 53 10 E
Uzerche 12 45 25N 1 34 E
Uzhgorod 22 48 36N 22 18 E

V

Vaal → 56 29 4S 23 38 E
Vaal Dam 57 27 0S 28 14 E
Vaalwater 57 24 15S 28 8 E
Vaasa 20 63 6N 21 38 E
Vaasan lääni □ 20 63 2N 22 50 E
Vác 15 47 49N 19 10 E
Vacaville 72 38 21N 122 0W
Vach → 24 60 45N 76 45 E
Vache, I.-à- 75 18 2N 73 35W
Vadodara 32 22 20N 73 10 E
Vadsø 20 70 3N 29 50 E
Værøy 20 67 40N 12 40 E
Váh → 15 47 55N 18 0 E
Vaigach 24 70 10N 59 0 E
Val-de-Marne □ 12 48 45N 2 28 E
Val-d'Oise □ 12 49 5N 2 10 E
Val d'Or 62 48 7N 77 47W
Val Marie 65 49 15N 107 45W
Valahia 15 44 35N 25 0 E
Valcheta 80 40 40S 66 8W
Valdayskaya Vozvyshennost 22 57 0N 33 30 E
Valdepeñas 13 38 43N 3 25W
Valdés, Pen. 80 42 30S 63 45W
Valdez 60 61 14N 146 17W
Valdivia 80 39 50S 73 14W
Valdosta 69 30 50N 83 20W
Vale 72 44 0N 117 15W
Valença 79 13 20S 39 5W
Valença do Piauí 79 6 20S 41 45W
Valence 12 44 57N 4 54 E
Valencia, Spain 13 39 27N 0 23W
Valencia, Venezuela 78 10 11N 68 0W
Valencia □ 13 39 20N 0 40W
Valencia, Albufera de 13 39 20N 0 27W
Valencia, G. de 13 39 30N 0 20 E
Valencia de Alcántara 13 39 25N 7 14W
Valenciennes 12 50 20N 3 34 E
Valentia Harbour 9 51 56N 10 17W
Valentia I. 9 51 54N 10 22W
Valentim, Sa. do 79 6 0S 43 30W
Valentine, Nebr., U.S.A. 70 42 50N 100 35W
Valentine, Tex., U.S.A. 71 30 36N 104 28W
Valera 78 9 19N 70 37W
Valier 72 48 25N 112 9W
Valjevo 19 44 18N 19 53 E
Valkeakoski 21 61 16N 24 2 E
Valkenswaard 11 51 21N 5 29 E
Valladolid, Mexico 74 20 40N 88 11W
Valladolid, Spain 13 41 38N 4 43W
Valle d'Aosta □ 18 45 45N 7 22 E
Valle de la Pascua 78 9 13N 66 0W
Valle de Santiago 74 20 25N 101 15W
Valle Hermoso 74 25 35N 97 40W

Wendell

Vulcan, U.S.A. 68 45 46N 87 51W
Vulcano 18 38 25N 14 58 E
Vung Tau 34 10 21N 107 4 E
Vyatka → 22 56 30N 51 0 E
Vyatskiye Polyany 22 56 5N 51 0 E
Vyazemskiy 25 47 32N 134 45 E
Vyazma 22 55 10N 34 15 E
Vyborg 22 60 43N 28 47 E
Vychegda → 22 61 18N 46 36 E
Vychodné Beskydy 15 49 30N 22 0 E
Vyg-ozero 22 63 30N 34 0 E
Vyrnwy, L. 6 52 48N 3 30W
Vyshniy Volochek 22 57 30N 34 30 E
Vyshzha = imeni 26 Bakinskikh Komissarov 23 39 22N 54 10 E
Vytegra 22 61 0N 36 27 E

W

W.A.C. Bennett Dam 64 56 2N 122 6W
Wa 50 10 7N 2 25W
Waal → 11 51 59N 4 30 E
Wabakimi L. 62 50 38N 89 45W
Wabana 63 47 40N 53 0W
Wabasca 64 55 57N 113 56W
Wabash 68 40 48N 85 46W
Wabash → 68 37 46N 88 2W
Wabeno 68 45 25N 88 40W
Wabigoon L. 65 49 44N 92 44W
Wabowden 65 54 55N 98 38W
Wąbrzeźno 15 53 16N 18 57 E
Wabuk Pt. 62 55 20N 85 5W
Wabush 63 52 55N 66 52W
Wabuska 72 39 9N 119 13W
Waco 71 31 33N 97 5W
Waconichi, L. 62 50 8N 74 0W
Wad Banda 51 13 10N 27 56 E
Wad Hamid 51 16 30N 32 45 E
Wâd Medanî 51 14 28N 33 30 E
Waddeneilanden 11 53 25N 5 10 E
Waddenzee 11 53 6N 5 10 E
Wadderin Hill 47 32 0S 118 25 E
Waddington, Mt. 64 51 23N 125 15W
Waddy Pt. 45 24 58S 153 21 E
Wadena, Canada 65 51 57N 103 47W
Wadena, U.S.A. 70 46 25N 95 8W
Wadesboro 69 35 2N 80 2W
Wadhams 64 51 30N 127 30W
Wadi Halfa 51 21 53N 31 19 E
Wadsworth 72 39 38N 119 22W
Wafrah 30 28 33N 47 56 E
Wageningen 11 51 58N 5 40 E
Wager B. 61 65 26N 88 40W
Wager Bay 61 65 56N 90 49W
Wagga Wagga 45 35 7S 147 24 E
Waghete 35 4 10S 135 50 E
Wagin 47 33 17S 117 25 E
Wagon Mound 71 36 1N 104 44W
Wagoner 71 36 0N 95 20W
Wah 32 33 45N 72 40 E
Wahai 35 2 48S 129 35 E
Wahiawa 66 21 30N 158 2W
Wahoo 70 41 15N 96 35W
Wahpeton 70 46 20N 96 35W
Waiau → 43 42 47S 173 22 E
Waibeem 35 0 30S 132 59 E
Waigeo 35 0 20S 130 40 E
Waihi 43 37 23S 175 52 E
Waihou → 43 37 15S 175 40 E
Waikabubak 35 9 45S 119 25 E
Waikaremoana 43 38 42S 177 12 E
Waikari 43 42 58S 172 41 E
Waikato → 43 37 23S 174 43 E
Waikerie 45 34 9S 140 0 E
Waikokopu 43 39 3S 177 52 E
Waikouaiti 43 45 36S 170 41 E
Waimate 43 44 45S 171 3 E
Wainganga → 32 18 50N 79 55 E
Waingapu 35 9 35S 120 11 E
Wainwright, Canada 65 52 50N 110 50W
Wainwright, U.S.A. 60 70 39N 160 1W
Waiouru 43 39 28S 175 41 E
Waipara 43 43 3S 172 46 E
Waipawa 43 39 56S 176 38 E
Waipiro 43 38 2S 178 22 E
Waipu 43 35 59S 174 29 E
Waipukurau 43 40 1S 176 33 E
Wairakei 43 38 37S 176 6 E
Wairarapa, L. 43 41 14S 175 15 E
Wairoa 43 39 3S 177 25 E
Waitaki → 43 44 56S 171 7 E
Waitara 43 38 59S 174 15 E
Waitsburg 72 46 15N 118 0W
Waiuku 43 37 15S 174 45 E
Wajima 36 37 30N 137 0 E
Wajir 54 1 42N 40 5 E
Wakasa-Wan 36 35 40N 135 30 E
Wakatipu, L. 43 45 5S 168 33 E
Wakaw 65 52 39N 105 44W
Wakayama 36 34 15N 135 15 E
Wakayama-ken □ 36 33 50N 135 30 E
Wake Forest 69 35 58N 78 30W
Wake I. 3 19 18N 166 36 E
Wakefield, N.Z. 43 41 24S 173 5 E
Wakefield, U.K. 6 53 41N 1 31W
Wakefield, U.S.A. 70 46 28N 89 53W
Wakema 33 16 30N 95 11 E
Wakkanai 36 45 28N 141 35 E
Wakkerstroom 57 27 24S 30 10 E
Wakool 45 35 28S 144 23 E
Wakool → 45 35 5S 143 33 E
Wakre 35 0 19S 131 5 E
Wakuach L. 63 55 34N 67 32W
Wałbrzych 14 50 45N 16 18 E
Walbury Hill 7 51 22N 1 28W
Walcha 45 30 55S 151 31 E
Walcheren 11 51 30N 3 35 E
Walcott 72 41 50N 106 55W
Waldburg Ra. 47 24 40S 117 35 E
Walden 72 40 47N 106 20W
Waldport 72 44 30N 124 2W
Waldron 71 34 52N 94 4W
Wales □ 7 52 30N 3 30W
Walgett 45 30 0S 148 5 E
Walhalla, Australia 45 37 56S 146 29 E
Walhalla, U.S.A. 65 48 55N 97 55W
Walkaway 47 28 59S 114 48 E
Walker 70 47 4N 94 35W
Walker L., Man., Canada 65 54 42N 95 57W
Walker L., Qué., Canada 63 50 20N 67 11W
Walker L., U.S.A. 72 38 56N 118 46W
Walkerston 44 21 11S 149 8 E
Wall 70 44 0N 102 14W
Walla Walla 72 46 3N 118 25W
Wallabadah 44 17 57S 142 15 E
Wallace, Idaho, U.S.A. 72 47 30N 116 0W
Wallace, N.C., U.S.A. 69 34 44N 77 59W
Wallace, Nebr., U.S.A. 70 40 51N 101 12W
Wallaceburg 62 42 34N 82 23W
Wallachia = Valahia 15 44 35N 25 0 E
Wallal 45 26 32S 146 7 E
Wallal Downs 46 19 47S 120 40 E
Wallambin, L. 47 30 57S 117 35 E
Wallaroo 45 33 56S 137 39 E
Wallasey 6 53 26N 3 2W
Wallerawang 45 33 25S 150 4 E
Wallhallow 44 17 50S 135 50 E
Wallingford 6 51 40N 1 15W
Wallis & Futuna 40 13 18S 176 10W
Wallowa 72 45 40N 117 35W
Wallowa, Mts. 72 45 20N 117 30W
Wallsend, Australia 45 32 55S 151 40 E
Wallsend, U.K. 6 54 59N 1 30W
Wallula 72 46 3N 118 59W
Wallumbilla 45 26 33S 149 9 E
Walmsley, L. 65 63 25N 108 36W
Walney, Isle of 6 54 5N 3 15W
Walnut Ridge 71 36 7N 90 58W
Walsall 7 52 36N 1 59W
Walsenburg 71 37 42N 104 45W
Walsh 71 37 28N 102 15W
Walsh → 44 16 31S 143 42 E
Walsh P.O. 44 16 40S 144 0 E
Walterboro 69 32 53N 80 40W
Walters 71 34 25N 98 20W
Waltham Sta. 62 45 57N 76 57W
Waltman 72 43 8N 107 15W
Walvisbaai 56 23 0S 14 28 E
Wamba 54 2 10N 27 57 E
Wamego 70 39 14N 96 22W
Wamena 35 4 4S 138 57 E
Wamsasi 35 3 27S 126 7 E
Wana 32 32 20N 69 32 E
Wanaaring 45 29 38S 144 9 E
Wanaka L. 43 44 33S 169 7 E
Wan'an 39 26 26N 114 49 E
Wanapiri 35 4 30S 135 59 E
Wanapitei L. 62 46 45N 80 40W
Wanbi 45 34 46S 140 17 E
Wanda Shan 38 46 0N 132 0 E
Wandoan 45 26 5S 149 55 E
Wangal 35 6 8S 134 9 E
Wanganella 45 35 6S 144 49 E
Wanganui 43 39 56S 175 3 E
Wangaratta 45 36 21S 146 19 E
Wangdu 38 38 40N 115 7 E
Wangerooge 14 53 47N 7 52 E
Wangiwangi 35 5 22S 123 37 E
Wangjiang 39 30 10N 116 42 E
Wangqing 38 43 12N 129 42 E
Wanless 65 54 11N 101 21W
Wanning 39 18 48N 110 22 E
Wanquan 38 40 50N 114 40 E
Wanxian 39 30 42N 108 20 E
Wanyuan 39 32 4N 108 3 E
Wanzai 39 28 7N 114 30 E
Wapakoneta 68 40 35N 84 10W
Wapato 72 46 30N 120 25W
Wapawekka L. 65 54 55N 104 40W
Wapikopa L. 62 52 56N 87 53W
Wapsipinicon → 70 41 44N 90 19W
Warangal 32 17 58N 79 35 E
Waratah 44 41 30S 145 30 E
Waratah B. 45 38 54S 146 5 E
Warburton, Vic., Australia 45 37 47S 145 42 E
Warburton, W. Austral., Australia 47 26 8S 126 35 E
Warburton Ra. 47 25 55S 126 28 E
Ward 43 41 49S 174 11 E
Ward → 45 26 28S 146 6 E
Ward Cove 64 55 25N 132 43W
Warden 57 27 50S 29 0 E
Wardha 32 20 45N 78 39 E
Wardha → 32 19 57N 79 11 E
Wardlow 64 50 56N 111 31W
Ware 64 57 26N 125 41W
Warialda 45 29 29S 150 33 E
Wariap 35 1 30S 134 5 E
Warkopi 35 1 12S 134 9 E
Warley 7 52 30N 2 0W
Warm Springs 73 38 16N 116 32W
Warman 65 52 19N 106 30W
Warmbad, Namibia 56 28 25S 18 42 E
Warmbad, S. Africa 57 24 51S 28 19 E
Warnambool Downs 44 22 48S 142 52 E
Warnemünde 14 54 9N 12 5 E
Warner 64 49 17N 112 12W
Warner Mts. 72 41 30N 120 20W
Warner Robins 69 32 41N 83 36W
Waroona 47 32 50S 115 58 E
Warragul 45 38 10S 145 58 E
Warrawagine 46 20 51S 120 42 E
Warrego → 45 30 24S 145 21 E
Warrego Ra. 44 24 58S 146 0 E
Warren, Australia 45 31 42S 147 51 E
Warren, Ark., U.S.A. 71 33 35N 92 3W
Warren, Mich., U.S.A. 68 42 31N 83 2W
Warren, Minn., U.S.A. 70 48 12N 96 46W
Warren, Ohio, U.S.A. 68 41 18N 80 52W
Warren, Pa., U.S.A. 68 41 52N 79 10W
Warrenpoint 9 54 7N 6 15W
Warrensburg 70 38 45N 93 45W
Warrenton, S. Africa 56 28 9S 24 47 E
Warrenton, U.S.A. 72 46 11N 123 59W
Warrenville 45 25 48S 147 22 E
Warri 53 5 30N 5 41 E
Warrina 45 28 12S 135 50 E
Warrington, U.K. 6 53 25N 2 38W
Warrington, U.S.A. 69 30 22N 87 16W
Warrnambool 45 38 25S 142 30 E
Warroad 70 48 54N 95 19W
Warsa 35 0 47S 135 55 E
Warsaw = Warszawa 15 52 13N 21 0 E
Warsaw 68 41 14N 85 50W
Warszawa 15 52 13N 21 0 E
Warta → 14 52 35N 14 39 E
Warthe = Warta → 14 52 35N 14 39 E
Waru 35 3 30S 130 36 E
Warwick, Australia 45 28 10S 152 1 E
Warwick, U.K. 7 52 17N 1 36W
Warwick, U.S.A. 68 41 43N 71 25W
Warwick □ 7 52 20N 1 30W
Wasatch Ra. 72 40 30N 111 15W
Wasbank 57 28 15S 30 9 E
Wasco, Calif., U.S.A. 73 35 37N 119 16W
Wasco, Oreg., U.S.A. 72 45 36N 120 46W
Waseca 70 44 3N 93 31W
Wasekamio L. 65 56 45N 108 45W
Wash, The 6 52 58N 0 20 E
Washburn, N. Dak., U.S.A. 70 47 17N 101 0W
Washburn, Wis., U.S.A. 70 46 38N 90 55W
Washim 32 20 3N 77 0 E
Washington, D.C., U.S.A. 68 38 52N 77 0W
Washington, Ga., U.S.A. 69 33 45N 82 45W
Washington, Ind., U.S.A. 68 38 40N 87 8W
Washington, Iowa, U.S.A. 70 41 20N 91 45W
Washington, Mo., U.S.A. 70 38 35N 91 1W
Washington, N.C., U.S.A. 69 35 35N 77 1W
Washington, Pa., U.S.A. 68 40 10N 80 20W
Washington, Utah, U.S.A. 73 37 10N 113 30W
Washington □ 72 47 45N 120 30W
Washington, Mt. 68 44 15N 71 18W
Washington I. 68 45 24N 86 54W
Wasian 35 1 47S 133 19 E
Wasior 35 2 43S 134 30 E
Waskaiowaka, L. 65 56 33N 96 23W
Waskesiu Lake 65 53 55N 106 5W
Wassenaar 11 52 8N 4 24 E
Waswanipi 62 49 40N 76 29W
Waswanipi, L. 62 49 35N 76 40W
Watangpone 35 4 29S 120 25 E
Water Park Pt. 44 22 56S 150 47 E
Water Valley 71 34 9N 89 38W
Waterberge 57 24 10S 28 0 E
Waterbury 68 41 32N 73 0W
Waterbury L. 65 58 10N 104 22W
Waterford 9 52 16N 7 8W
Waterford □ 9 52 10N 7 40W
Waterford Harb. 9 52 10N 6 58W
Waterhen L., Man., Canada 65 52 10N 99 40W
Waterhen L., Sask., Canada 65 54 28N 108 25W
Waterloo, Belgium 11 50 43N 4 25 E
Waterloo, Canada 62 43 30N 80 32W
Waterloo, S. Leone 50 8 26N 13 8W
Waterloo, Ill., U.S.A. 70 38 22N 90 6W
Waterloo, Iowa, U.S.A. 70 42 27N 92 20W
Watersmeet 70 46 15N 89 12W
Waterton Glacier Int. Peace Park 72 48 35N 113 40W
Watertown, N.Y., U.S.A. 68 43 58N 75 57W
Watertown, S. Dak., U.S.A. 70 44 57N 97 5W
Watertown, Wis., U.S.A. 70 43 15N 88 45W
Waterval-Boven 57 25 40S 30 18 E
Waterville, Maine, U.S.A. 63 44 35N 69 40W
Waterville, Wash., U.S.A. 72 47 38N 120 1W
Watervliet 68 42 46N 73 43W
Wates 35 7 51S 110 10 E
Watford 7 51 38N 0 23W
Watford City 70 47 50N 103 23W
Wathaman → 65 57 16N 102 59W
Watheroo 47 30 15S 116 0W
Watkins Glen 68 42 25N 76 55W
Watling I. = San Salvador 75 24 0N 74 40W
Watonga 71 35 51N 98 24W
Watrous, Canada 65 51 40N 105 25W
Watrous, U.S.A. 71 35 50N 104 55W
Watsa 54 3 4N 29 30 E
Watseka 68 40 45N 87 45W
Watson, Australia 47 30 29S 131 31 E
Watson, Canada 65 52 10N 104 30W
Watson Lake 60 60 6N 128 49W
Watsonville 73 36 55N 121 49W
Wattiwarriganna Cr. → 45 28 57S 136 10 E
Watuata = Batuata 35 6 12S 122 42 E
Watubela, Kepulauan 35 4 28S 131 35 E
Waubay 70 45 22N 97 17W
Waubra 45 37 21S 143 39 E
Wauchope 45 31 28S 152 45 E
Wauchula 69 27 35N 81 50W
Waugh 65 49 40N 95 11W
Waukegan 68 42 22N 87 54W
Waukesha 68 43 0N 88 15W
Waukon 70 43 14N 91 33W
Wauneta 70 40 27N 101 25W
Waupaca 70 44 22N 89 8W
Waupun 70 43 38N 88 44W
Waurika 71 34 12N 98 0W
Wausau 70 44 57N 89 40W
Wautoma 70 44 3N 89 20W
Wauwatosa 68 43 6N 87 59W
Wave Hill 46 17 32S 131 0 E
Waveney → 7 52 24N 1 20 E
Waverley 43 39 46S 174 37 E
Waverly, Iowa, U.S.A. 70 42 40N 92 30W
Waverly, N.Y., U.S.A. 68 42 0N 76 33W
Wavre 11 50 43N 4 38 E
Wâw 51 7 45N 28 1 E
Wâw al Kabîr 51 25 20N 16 43 E
Wawa 62 47 59N 84 47W
Wawanesa 65 49 36N 99 40W
Waxahachie 71 32 22N 96 53W
Way, L. 47 26 45S 120 16 E
Wayabula Rau 35 2 29N 128 17 E
Wayatinah 44 42 19S 146 27 E
Waycross 69 31 12N 82 25W
Wayne, Nebr., U.S.A. 70 42 16N 97 0W
Wayne, W. Va., U.S.A. 68 38 15N 82 27W
Waynesboro, Ga., U.S.A. 69 33 6N 82 1W
Waynesboro, Miss., U.S.A. 69 31 40N 88 39W
Waynesboro, Pa., U.S.A. 68 39 46N 77 32W
Waynesboro, Va., U.S.A. 68 38 4N 78 57W
Waynesburg 68 39 54N 80 12W
Waynesville 69 35 31N 83 0W
Waynoka 71 36 38N 98 53W
Wazirabad 32 32 30N 74 8 E
We 34 5 51N 95 18 E
Weald, The 7 51 7N 0 9 E
Wear → 6 54 55N 1 22W
Weatherford, Okla., U.S.A. 71 35 30N 98 45W
Weatherford, Tex., U.S.A. 71 32 45N 97 48W
Weaverville 72 40 44N 122 56W
Webb City 71 37 9N 94 30W
Webster, S. Dak., U.S.A. 70 45 24N 97 33W
Webster, Wis., U.S.A. 70 45 53N 92 25W
Webster City 70 42 30N 93 50W
Webster Green 70 38 38N 90 20W
Webster Springs 68 38 30N 80 25W
Weda 35 0 21N 127 50 E
Weda, Teluk 35 0 30N 127 50 E
Weddell I. 80 51 50S 61 0W
Wedderburn 45 36 26S 143 33 E
Wedgeport 63 43 44N 65 59W
Wee Waa 45 30 11S 149 26 E
Weed 72 41 29N 122 22W
Weemelah 45 29 2S 149 15 E
Weenen 57 28 48S 30 7 E
Weert 11 51 15N 5 43 E
Wei He →, Hebei, China 38 36 10N 115 45 E
Wei He →, Shaanxi, China 39 34 38N 110 15 E
Weifang 38 36 44N 119 7 E
Weihai 38 37 30N 122 6 E
Weimar 14 51 0N 11 20 E
Weinan 39 34 31N 109 29 E
Weipa 44 12 40S 141 50 E
Weir →, Australia 45 28 20S 149 50 E
Weir →, Canada 65 56 54N 93 21W
Weir River 65 56 49N 94 6W
Weiser 72 44 10N 117 0W
Weishan 39 34 47N 117 5 E
Weiyuan 38 35 7N 104 10 E
Weizhou Dao 39 21 0N 109 5 E
Wejherowo 15 54 35N 18 12 E
Wekusko L. 65 54 40N 99 50W
Welbourn Hill 45 27 21S 134 6 E
Welch 68 37 29N 81 36W
Welkom 56 28 0S 26 46 E
Welland 62 43 0N 79 15W
Welland → 6 52 43N 0 10W
Wellesley Is. 44 16 42S 139 30 E
Wellin 11 50 5N 5 6 E
Wellingborough 7 52 18N 0 41W
Wellington, Australia 45 32 35S 148 59 E
Wellington, Canada 62 43 57N 77 20W
Wellington, N.Z. 43 41 19S 174 46 E
Wellington, S. Africa 56 33 38S 19 1 E
Wellington, Salop, U.K. 6 52 42N 2 31W
Wellington, Somerset, U.K. 7 50 58N 3 13W
Wellington, Colo., U.S.A. 70 40 43N 105 0W
Wellington, Kans., U.S.A. 71 37 15N 97 25W
Wellington, Nev., U.S.A. 72 38 47N 119 28W
Wellington, Tex., U.S.A. 71 34 55N 100 13W
Wellington □ 43 40 8S 175 36 E
Wellington, I. 80 49 30S 75 0W
Wellington, L. 45 38 6S 147 20 E
Wells, Norfolk, U.K. 6 52 57N 0 51 E
Wells, Somerset, U.K. 7 51 12N 2 39W
Wells, Minn., U.S.A. 70 43 44N 93 45W
Wells, Nev., U.S.A. 72 41 8N 115 0W
Wells Gray Prov. Park 64 52 30N 120 15W
Wells L. 47 26 44S 123 15 E
Wellsboro 68 41 45N 77 20W
Wellsville, Mo., U.S.A. 70 39 4N 91 30W
Wellsville, N.Y., U.S.A. 68 42 9N 77 53W
Wellsville, Ohio, U.S.A. 68 40 36N 80 40W
Wellsville, Utah, U.S.A. 72 41 35N 111 59W
Wellton 73 32 39N 114 6W
Wels 14 48 9N 14 1 E
Welshpool 7 52 40N 3 9W
Wem 6 52 52N 2 45W
Wen Xian 39 32 43N 104 36 E
Wenatchee 72 47 30N 120 17W
Wenchang 39 19 38N 110 42 E
Wenchi 50 7 46N 2 8W
Wenchow = Wenzhou 39 28 0N 120 38 E
Wendell 72 42 50N 114 42W

Yokote

Wood Is. 46 16 24S 123 19 E
Wood L. 65 55 17N 103 17W
Wood Lake 70 42 38N 100 14W
Woodah I. 44 13 27S 136 10 E
Woodanilling 47 33 31S 117 24 E
Woodburn 45 29 6S 153 23 E
Woodenbong 45 28 24S 152 39 E
Woodend 45 37 20S 144 33 E
Woodgreen 44 22 26S 134 12 E
Woodland 72 38 40N 121 50W
Woodlands 47 24 46S 118 8 E
Woodpecker 64 53 30N 122 40W
Woodridge 65 49 20N 96 9W
Woodroffe, Mt. 47 26 20S 131 45 E
Woodruff, Ariz., U.S.A. 73 34 51N 110 1W
Woodruff, Utah, U.S.A. 72 41 30N 111 4W
Woods, L., Australia 44 17 50S 133 30 E
Woods, L., Canada 63 54 30N 65 13W
Woods, L. of the 65 49 15N 94 45W
Woodside 45 38 31S 146 52 E
Woodstock, Queens., Australia 44 19 35S 146 50 E
Woodstock, W. Austral., Australia 46 21 41S 118 57 E
Woodstock, N.B., Canada 63 46 11N 67 37W
Woodstock, Ont., Canada 62 43 10N 80 45W
Woodstock, U.K. 7 51 51N 1 20W
Woodstock, U.S.A. 70 42 17N 88 30W
Woodsville 68 44 10N 72 0W
Woodville, N.Z. 43 40 20S 175 53 E
Woodville, U.S.A. 71 30 45N 94 25W
Woodward 71 36 24N 99 28W
Woolamai, C. 45 38 30S 145 23 E
Woolgoolga 45 30 6S 153 11 E
Woombye 45 26 40S 152 55 E
Woomera 45 31 30S 137 10 E
Woonsocket, R.I., U.S.A. 68 42 0N 71 30W
Woonsocket, S. Dak., U.S.A. 70 44 5N 98 15W
Wooramel 47 25 45S 114 17 E
Wooramel → 47 25 47S 114 10 E
Wooroloo 47 31 48S 116 18 E
Wooster 68 40 48N 81 55W
Worcester, S. Africa 56 33 39S 19 27 E
Worcester, U.K. 7 52 12N 2 12W
Worcester, U.S.A. 68 42 14N 71 49W
Workington 6 54 39N 3 34W
Worksop 6 53 19N 1 9W
Workum 11 52 59N 5 26 E
Worland 72 44 0N 107 59W
Worms 14 49 37N 8 21 E
Wortham 71 31 48N 96 27W
Worthing 7 50 49N 0 21W
Worthington 70 43 35N 95 36W
Wosi 35 0 15S 128 0 E
Wou-han = Wuhan 39 30 31N 114 18 E
Wour 51 21 14N 16 0 E
Wowoni 35 4 5S 123 5 E
Woy Woy 45 33 30S 151 19 E
Wrangel I. 26 71 0N 180 0 E
Wrangell 60 56 30N 132 25W
Wrangell, I. 64 56 20N 132 10W
Wrangell Mts. 60 61 40N 143 30W
Wrath, C. 8 58 38N 5 0W
Wray 70 40 8N 102 18W
Wrekin, The 6 52 41N 2 35W
Wrens 69 33 13N 82 23W
Wrexham 6 53 5N 3 0W
Wright, Canada 64 51 52N 121 40W
Wright, Phil. 35 11 42N 125 2 E
Wrightson, Mt. 73 31 43N 110 56W
Wrigley 60 63 16N 123 37W
Wrocław 14 51 5N 17 5 E
Września 15 52 21N 17 36 E
Wu Jiang → 39 29 40N 107 20 E
Wubin 47 30 6S 116 37 E
Wuchang 38 44 55N 127 5 E
Wuchuan 39 28 25N 108 3 E
Wuding He → 38 37 2N 110 23 E
Wugang 39 26 44N 110 35 E
Wugong Shan 39 27 30N 114 0 E
Wuhan 39 30 31N 114 18 E
Wuhsi = Wuxi 39 31 33N 120 18 E
Wuhu 39 31 22N 118 21 E
Wukari 53 7 51N 9 42 E
Wuliaru 35 7 27S 131 0 E
Wulumuchi = Ürümqi 37 43 45N 87 45 E
Wum 53 6 24N 10 2 E
Wuning 39 29 17N 115 5 E
Wunnummin L. 62 52 55N 89 10W
Wuntho 33 23 55N 95 45 E
Wuping 39 25 5N 116 5 E
Wuppertal, Germany 14 51 15N 7 8 E
Wuppertal, S. Africa 56 32 13S 19 12 E
Wuqing 38 39 23N 117 4 E
Wurung 44 19 13S 140 38 E
Würzburg 14 49 46N 9 55 E
Wushan 39 31 7N 109 54 E
Wuting = Huimin 38 37 27N 117 28 E
Wutongqiao 37 29 22N 103 50 E
Wuwei, Anhui, China 39 31 18N 117 54 E
Wuwei, Gansu, China 37 37 57N 102 34 E
Wuxi, Jiangsu, China 39 31 33N 120 18 E
Wuxi, Sichuan, China 39 31 23N 109 35 E
Wuxing 39 30 51N 120 8 E
Wuyi, Hebei, China 38 37 46N 115 56 E
Wuyi, Zhejiang, China 39 28 52N 119 50 E
Wuyi Shan 37 27 0N 117 0 E
Wuying 38 47 53N 129 56 E
Wuyuan 38 41 2N 108 20 E
Wuzhai 38 38 54N 111 48 E
Wuzhi Shan 39 18 45N 109 45 E
Wuzhong 38 38 2N 106 12 E
Wuzhou 39 23 30N 111 18 E
Wyaaba Cr. → 44 16 27S 141 35 E
Wyalkatchem 47 31 8S 117 22 E
Wyandotte 68 42 14N 83 13W
Wyandra 45 27 12S 145 56 E
Wyangala Res. 45 33 54S 149 0 E
Wyara, L. 45 28 42S 144 14 E
Wycheproof 45 36 0S 143 17 E
Wye → 7 51 36N 2 40W
Wyemandoo, Mt. 47 28 28S 118 29 E
Wymondham 7 52 45N 0 42W
Wymore 70 40 10N 96 40W
Wynbring 45 30 33S 133 32 E
Wyndham, Australia 46 15 33S 128 3 E
Wyndham, N.Z. 43 46 20S 168 51 E
Wyndmere 70 46 23N 97 7W
Wynne 71 35 15N 90 50W
Wynnum 45 27 27S 153 9 E
Wynyard, Australia 44 41 5S 145 44 E
Wynyard, Canada 65 51 45N 104 10W
Wyola, L. 47 29 8S 130 17 E
Wyoming □ 66 42 48N 109 0W
Wyong 45 33 14S 151 24 E
Wytheville 68 37 0N 81 3W

X

Xai-Xai 57 25 6S 33 31 E
Xainza 37 30 58N 88 35 E
Xangongo 56 16 45S 15 5 E
Xánthi 19 41 10N 24 58 E
Xapuri 78 10 35S 68 35W
Xau, L. 56 21 15S 24 44 E
Xenia 68 39 42N 83 57W
Xhora 57 31 55S 28 38 E
Xhumo 56 21 7S 24 35 E
Xi Jiang → 39 22 5N 113 20 E
Xi Xian 38 36 41N 110 58 E
Xiachengzi 38 44 40N 130 18 E
Xiachuan Dao 39 21 40N 112 40 E
Xiaguan 37 25 32N 100 16 E
Xiajiang 39 27 30N 115 10 E
Xiamen 38 24 25N 118 4 E
Xi'an 39 34 15N 109 0 E
Xianfeng 39 29 40N 109 8 E
Xiang Jiang → 39 28 55N 112 50 E
Xiangfan 39 32 2N 112 8 E
Xiangning 38 35 58N 110 50 E
Xiangtan 39 27 51N 112 54 E
Xiangxiang 39 27 43N 112 28 E
Xiangyang 39 32 1N 112 8 E
Xiangyin 39 28 38N 112 54 E
Xiangzhou 39 23 58N 109 40 E
Xianju 39 28 51N 120 44 E
Xianyang 39 34 20N 108 40 E
Xiao Hinggan Ling 38 49 0N 127 0 E
Xiaogan 39 30 52N 113 55 E
Xiapu 39 26 54N 119 59 E
Xichang 37 27 51N 102 19 E
Xichuan 39 33 0N 111 30 E
Xifeng 39 27 7N 106 42 E
Xigazê 37 29 5N 88 45 E
Xihe 39 34 2N 105 20 E
Xiliao He → 38 43 32N 123 35 E
Xilin 39 24 30N 105 6 E
Xin Xian 38 38 22N 112 46 E
Xinavane 57 25 2S 32 47 E
Xinbin 38 41 40N 125 2 E
Xincheng 39 24 5N 108 39 E
Xinfeng 39 25 27N 114 58 E
Xing'an, Guangxi Zhuangzu, China 39 25 38N 110 40 E
Xingan, Jiangxi, China 39 27 46N 115 20 E
Xingcheng 38 40 40N 120 45 E
Xingguo 39 26 21N 115 21 E
Xinghua 39 32 58N 119 48 E
Xinghua Wan 39 25 15N 119 20 E
Xingning 39 24 3N 115 42 E
Xingren 37 25 24N 105 11 E
Xingshan 39 31 15N 110 45 E
Xingtai 38 37 3N 114 32 E
Xingu → 79 1 30S 51 53W
Xingyang 39 34 45N 112 52 E
Xinhua 39 27 42N 111 13 E
Xining 37 36 34N 101 40 E
Xinjiang 38 35 34N 111 11 E
Xinjiang Uygur Zizhiqu □ 37 42 0N 86 0 E
Xinjin 38 39 25N 121 58 E
Xinle 38 38 25N 114 40 E
Xinmin 38 41 59N 122 50 E
Xinning 39 26 28N 110 50 E
Xinxiang 39 35 18N 113 50 E
Xinyang 39 32 6N 114 3 E
Xinzheng 39 34 20N 113 45 E
Xinzhou 39 19 43N 109 17 E
Xinzhu 39 24 49N 120 57 E
Xiongyuecheng 38 40 12N 122 5 E
Xiping 39 33 22N 114 0 E
Xique-Xique 79 10 50S 42 40W
Xiuyan 38 40 18N 123 11 E
Xixabangma Feng 33 28 20N 85 40 E
Xixiang 39 33 0N 107 44 E
Xizang □ 37 32 0N 88 0 E
Xuancheng 39 30 56N 118 43 E
Xuan'en 39 30 0N 109 30 E
Xuanhan 39 31 18N 107 38 E
Xuanhua 38 40 40N 115 2 E
Xuchang 39 34 2N 113 48 E
Xuguit Qi 38 49 17N 120 44 E
Xunke 38 49 35N 128 27 E
Xupu 39 27 53N 110 32 E
Xuwen 39 20 20N 110 10 E
Xuyong 39 28 10N 105 22 E
Xuzhou 39 34 18N 117 10 E

Y

Ya 'Bad 28 32 27N 35 10 E
Yaamba 44 23 8S 150 22 E
Ya'an 37 29 58N 103 5 E
Yaapeet 45 35 45S 142 3 E
Yabelo 51 4 50N 38 8 E
Yablonovy Khrebet 25 53 0N 114 0 E
Yablonovy Ra. = Yablonovy Khrebet 25 53 0N 114 0 E
Yacheng 39 18 22N 109 6 E
Yacuiba 80 22 0S 63 43W
Yadgir 32 16 45N 77 5 E
Yadkin → 69 35 23N 80 3W
Yagodnoye 25 62 33N 149 40 E
Yagoua 54 10 20N 15 13 E
Yagur 28 32 45N 35 4 E
Yahk 64 49 6N 116 10W
Yahuma 54 1 0N 23 10 E
Yakima 72 46 42N 120 30W
Yakima → 72 47 0N 120 30W
Yakut A.S.S.R. □ 25 62 0N 130 0 E
Yakutat 60 59 29N 139 44W
Yakutsk 25 62 5N 129 50 E
Yala 34 6 33N 101 18 E
Yalbalgo 47 25 10S 114 45 E
Yalboroo 44 20 50S 148 40 E
Yalgoo 47 28 16S 116 39 E
Yalinga 51 6 33N 23 10 E
Yalkubul, Punta 74 21 32N 88 37W
Yalleroi 44 24 3S 145 42 E
Yalobusha → 71 33 30N 90 12W
Yalong Jiang → 37 26 40N 101 55 E
Yalta 23 44 30N 34 10 E
Yalu He → 38 46 56N 123 30 E
Yalu Jiang → 38 40 0N 124 22 E
Yalutorovsk 24 56 41N 66 12 E
Yam Ha Melaḥ = Dead Sea 28 31 30N 35 30 E
Yam Kinneret 28 32 45N 35 35 E
Yamagata 36 38 15N 140 15 E
Yamagata □ 36 38 30N 140 0 E
Yamaguchi 36 34 10N 131 32 E
Yamaguchi □ 36 34 20N 131 40 E
Yamal, Poluostrov 24 71 0N 70 0 E
Yamanashi □ 36 35 40N 138 40 E
Yamantau 22 54 20N 57 40 E
Yamantau, Gora 22 54 15N 58 6 E
Yamba, N.S.W., Australia 45 29 26S 153 23 E
Yamba, S. Austral., Australia 45 34 10S 140 52 E
Yambah 44 23 10S 133 50 E
Yambarran Ra. 46 15 10S 130 25 E
Yâmbiô 51 4 35N 28 16 E
Yambol 19 42 30N 26 36 E
Yamdena 35 7 45S 131 20 E
Yamethin 33 20 29N 96 18 E
Yamma-Yamma, L. 45 26 16S 141 20 E
Yamoussoukro 50 6 49N 5 17W
Yampa → 72 40 37N 108 59W
Yampi Sd. 46 16 8S 123 38 E
Yamuna → 33 25 30N 81 53 E
Yamzho Yumco 37 28 48N 90 35 E
Yan 53 10 5N 12 11 E
Yana → 25 71 30N 136 0 E
Yanac 45 36 8S 141 25 E
Yanai 36 33 58N 132 7 E
Yan'an 38 36 35N 109 26 E
Yanaul 22 56 25N 55 0 E
Yanbu 'al Baḥr 30 24 0N 38 5 E
Yancannia 45 30 12S 142 35 E
Yanchang 38 36 43N 110 1 E
Yancheng, Henan, China 39 33 35N 114 0 E
Yancheng, Jiangsu, China 39 33 23N 120 8 E
Yanchi 38 37 48N 107 20 E
Yanchuan 38 36 51N 110 10 E
Yanco Cr. → 45 35 14S 145 35 E
Yandal 47 27 35S 121 10 E
Yandanooka 47 29 18S 115 29 E
Yandaran 44 24 43S 152 6 E
Yandoon 33 17 0N 95 40 E
Yangambi 54 0 47N 24 20 E
Yangch'ü = Taiyuan 38 37 52N 112 33 E
Yangchun 39 22 11N 111 48 E
Yanggao 38 40 21N 113 55 E
Yangi-Yer 24 40 17N 68 48 E
Yangjiang 39 21 50N 110 59 E
Yangquan 38 37 58N 113 31 E
Yangshan 39 24 30N 112 40 E
Yangshuo 39 24 48N 110 29 E
Yangtze Kiang = Chang Jiang → 39 31 48N 121 10 E
Yangxin 39 29 50N 115 12 E
Yangzhou 39 32 21N 119 26 E
Yanji 38 42 59N 129 30 E
Yankton 70 42 55N 97 25W
Yanna 45 26 58S 146 0 E
Yanqi 37 42 5N 86 35 E
Yanqing 38 40 30N 115 58 E
Yanshan 39 28 15N 117 41 E
Yantabulla 45 29 21S 145 0 E
Yantai 38 37 34N 121 22 E
Yanting 39 31 11N 105 24 E
Yanzhou 38 35 35N 116 49 E
Yao 51 12 56N 17 33 E
Yaoundé 54 3 50N 11 35 E
Yap Is. 40 9 30N 138 10 E
Yapen 35 1 50S 136 0 E
Yapen, Selat 35 1 20S 136 10 E
Yappar → 44 18 22S 141 16 E
Yaqui → 74 27 37N 110 39W
Yar-Sale 24 66 50N 70 50 E
Yaraka 44 24 53S 144 3 E
Yarangüme 30 37 35N 29 8 E
Yaransk 22 57 22N 47 49 E
Yardea P.O. 45 32 23S 135 32 E
Yare → 7 52 36N 1 28 E
Yarensk 22 61 10N 49 8 E
Yarí → 78 0 20S 72 20W
Yarkand = Shache 37 38 20N 77 10 E
Yarkhun → 32 36 17N 72 30 E
Yarmouth 63 43 50N 66 7W
Yarmūk → 28 32 42N 35 40 E
Yaroslavl 22 57 35N 39 55 E
Yarra Yarra Lakes 47 29 40S 115 45 E
Yarraden 44 14 17S 143 15 E
Yarraloola 46 21 33S 115 52 E
Yarram 45 38 29S 146 9 E
Yarraman 45 26 50S 152 0 E
Yarranvale 45 26 50S 145 20 E
Yarras 45 31 25S 152 20 E
Yarrowmere 44 21 27S 145 53 E
Yartsevo 25 60 20N 90 0 E
Yasawa Group 43 17 0S 177 23 E
Yasinski, L. 62 53 16N 77 35W
Yass 45 34 49S 148 54 E
Yas'ur 28 32 54N 35 10 E
Yates Center 71 37 53N 95 45W
Yathkyed L. 65 62 40N 98 0W
Yatsushiro 36 32 30N 130 40 E
Yaṭṭah 28 31 27N 35 6 E
Yauyos 78 12 19S 75 50W
Yavari → 78 4 21S 70 2W
Yavatmal 32 20 20N 78 15 E
Yavne 28 31 52N 34 45 E
Yawatahama 36 33 27N 132 24 E
Yazd 31 31 55N 54 27 E
Yazd □ 31 32 0N 55 0 E
Yazdān 31 33 30N 60 50 E
Yazoo → 71 32 35N 90 50W
Yazoo City 71 32 48N 90 28W
Yding Skovhøj 21 55 59N 9 46 E
Ye Xian 38 37 8N 119 57 E
Yealering 47 32 36S 117 36 E
Yebyu 33 14 15N 98 13 E
Yecla 13 38 35N 1 5W
Yeeda 46 17 31S 123 38 E
Yeelanna 45 34 9S 135 45 E
Yegros 80 26 20S 56 25W
Yehuda, Midbar 28 31 35N 35 15 E
Yei 51 4 9N 30 40 E
Yelanskoye 25 61 25N 128 0 E
Yelarbon 45 28 33S 150 38 E
Yelets 22 52 40N 38 30 E
Yell 8 60 35N 1 5W
Yell Sd. 8 60 33N 1 15W
Yellow Sea 38 35 0N 123 0 E
Yellowhead P. 64 52 53N 118 25W
Yellowknife 64 62 27N 114 29W
Yellowknife → 60 62 31N 114 19W
Yellowstone → 70 47 58N 103 59W
Yellowstone L. 72 44 30N 110 20W
Yellowstone National Park 72 44 35N 110 0W
Yellowtail Res. 72 45 6N 108 8W
Yelvertoft 44 20 13S 138 45 E
Yemen ■ 29 15 0N 44 0 E
Yenangyaung 33 20 30N 95 0 E
Yenda 45 34 13S 146 14 E
Yenisey → 24 71 50N 82 40 E
Yeniseysk 25 58 27N 92 13 E
Yeniseyskiy Zaliv 24 72 20N 81 0 E
Yenyuka 25 57 57N 121 15 E
Yeo, L. 47 28 0S 124 30 E
Yeola 32 20 0N 74 30 E
Yeovil 7 50 57N 2 38W
Yeppoon 44 23 5S 150 47 E
Yerbent 24 39 30N 58 50 E
Yerbogachen 25 61 16N 108 0 E
Yerevan 23 40 10N 44 31 E
Yerilla 47 29 24S 121 47 E
Yermak 24 52 2N 76 55 E
Yermakovo 25 52 25N 126 20 E
Yermo 73 34 58N 116 50W
Yerofey Pavlovich 25 54 0N 122 0 E
Yershov 23 51 22N 48 16 E
Yerushalayim 28 31 47N 35 10 E
Yes Tor 7 50 41N 3 59W
Yeso 71 34 29N 104 37W
Yessey 25 68 29N 102 10 E
Yeu, I. d' 12 46 42N 2 20W
Yevpatoriya 23 45 15N 33 20 E
Yeysk 23 46 40N 38 12 E
Yezd = Yazd 31 31 55N 54 27 E
Yi Xian 38 41 30N 121 22 E
Yiannitsa 19 40 46N 22 24 E
Yibin 37 28 45N 104 32 E
Yichang 39 30 40N 111 20 E
Yicheng 38 35 42N 111 40 E
Yichuan 38 36 2N 110 10 E
Yichun, Heilongjiang, China 38 47 44N 128 52 E
Yichun, Jiangxi, China 39 27 48N 114 22 E
Yidu 38 36 43N 118 28 E
Yihuang 39 27 30N 116 12 E
Yijun 38 35 28N 109 8 E
Yilan, China 38 46 19N 129 34 E
Yilan, Taiwan 39 24 51N 121 44 E
Yilehuli Shan 38 51 20N 124 20 E
Yimianpo 38 45 7N 128 2 E
Yinchuan 38 38 30N 106 15 E
Yindarlgooda, L. 47 30 40S 121 52 E
Ying He → 39 32 30N 116 30 E
Ying Xian 38 39 32N 113 10 E
Yingcheng 39 30 56N 113 35 E
Yingde 39 24 10N 113 25 E
Yingkou 38 40 37N 122 18 E
Yingshan 39 30 41N 115 32 E
Yingshang 39 32 38N 116 12 E
Yingtan 37 28 12N 117 0 E
Yining 37 43 58N 81 10 E
Yinjiang 39 28 1N 108 21 E
Yinmabin 33 22 10N 94 55 E
Yinnietharra 47 24 39S 116 12 E
Yipinglang 37 25 10N 101 52 E
Yirshi 38 47 18N 119 49 E
Yishan 39 24 28N 108 38 E
Yíthion 19 36 46N 22 34 E
Yitong 38 43 13N 125 20 E
Yitulihe 38 50 38N 121 34 E
Yixing 39 31 21N 119 48 E
Yiyang, Henan, China 39 34 27N 112 10 E
Yiyang, Hunan, China 39 28 35N 112 18 E
Yizhang 39 25 27N 112 57 E
Yizre'el 28 32 34N 35 19 E
Ylitornio 20 66 19N 23 39 E
Ylivieska 20 64 4N 24 28 E
Ynykchanskiy 25 60 15N 137 35 E
Yoakum 71 29 20N 97 20W
Yog Pt. 35 14 6N 124 12 E
Yogyakarta 35 7 49S 110 22 E
Yoho Nat. Park 64 51 25N 116 30W
Yojoa, L. de 75 14 53N 88 0W
Yokadouma 54 3 26N 14 55 E
Yokkaichi 36 35 0N 136 38 E
Yoko 51 5 32N 12 20 E
Yokohama 36 35 27N 139 28 E
Yokosuka 36 35 20N 139 40 E
Yokote 36 39 20N 140 30 E

Z

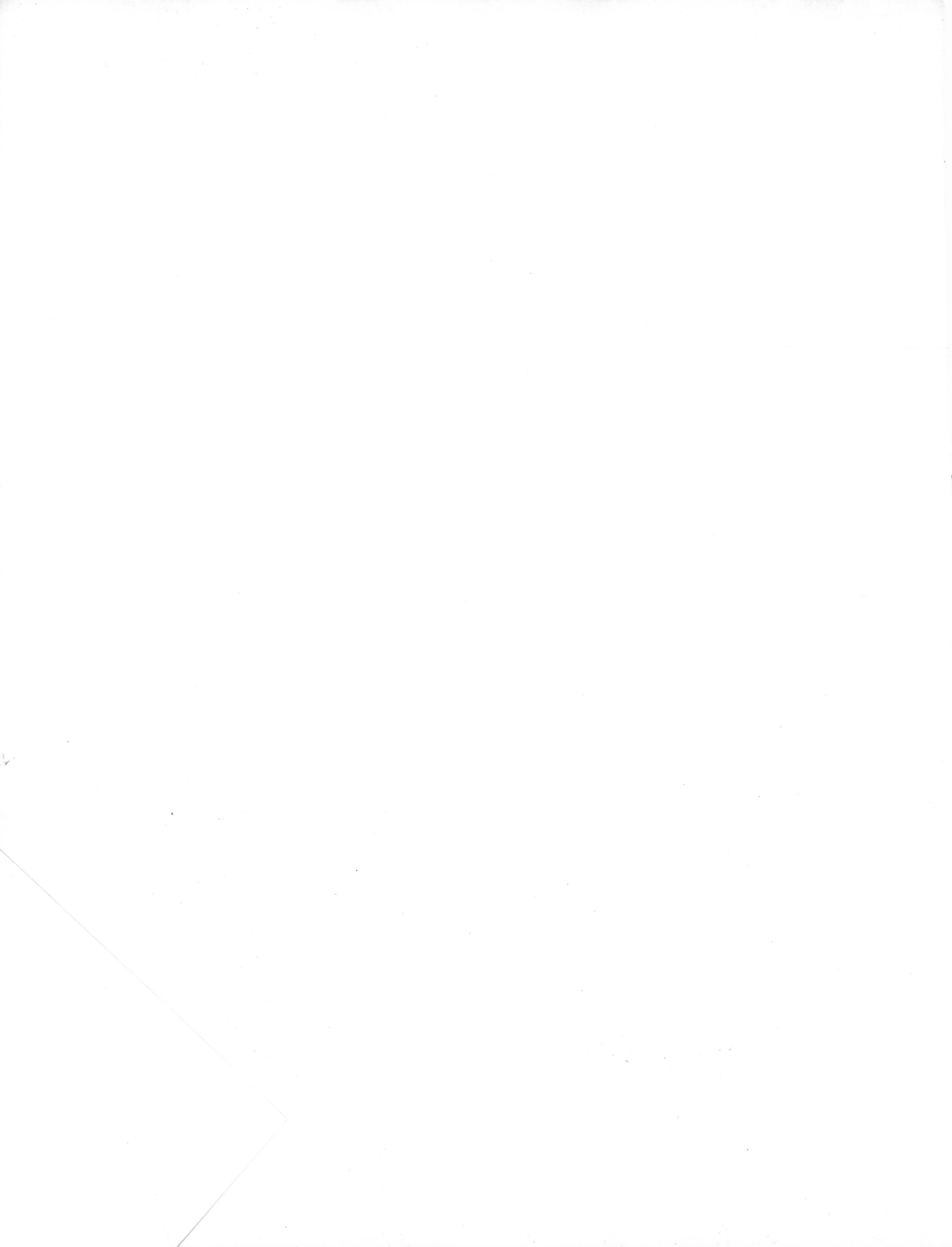